Contemporary Architecture

5
ARCHITECTURE SUSTAINABLE

Edited and Produced by
EDITORIAL PENCIL, S.L
Valencia 36, bajo derecha-46120 Alboraya (Valencia)
Contac Telephone: +34 96 133 81 68
Fax: +34 96 133 65 71
E-mail: international@editorialpencil.es

Publishers
Antonio Giménez
Conchi Monzonis

Publishing Coordinators
Antonio Giménez
Publisher's Technical Direction
Juan Regojo Zapata (Architect)

Works selection, texts and plans corrections
Environmental and Architectural Analysis
Claudio Pirillo (Dr. Architect)
César Reyes (Arquitecto)
Ethel Baraona Pohl (Architect)

Contents Control and Supervision
Pencil's Technical Department

Pre-Layout
Ethel Baraona Pohl (Architect)
Antonio Giménez

Design
Juan Nava diseño gráfico

Image setting
MP Estudio Diseño Global

Technical Advisor
Andrés Ros Campos (Architect)

English Language Translation
María José Riera (Architect)
Christos-Romanos Tsomos (Architect)
María Luz Navarro Eslava (Architect)
Mario García Cantero

Texts, Photograph and Architectural Projects
Mentioned Authors

Greetings
Editorial Pencil would like to thank all the authors and colaborators of the projects included in this edition, for their effort and patience in the verification of data and the compilation of information.

Special Acknowledgements
Gerardo Wadel (Architect)
Flavia Ceballos (Ingeniero)
Paola Ponciano (Architect)
Melissa Arce (Architect)
Rosario Talevi (Est. Architecture)
Juan Calduch (Architect)
Ramon Monfort (Architect)
Julio Gómez Perretta (Architect)Martín Valle (Architect)
Toni del Campo (Architect)
Ricardo Santonja (Profesor de la ETSAM-UPM)

Editorial Pencil would like to thank the effort and dedication of all the Pencil's members of the staff and collaborators on the production of this book.

gràfiques
LITOLEMA

Printed in Spain
ISBN-13: 978-84-935145-4-9
Legal Deposit: V-2204-2007

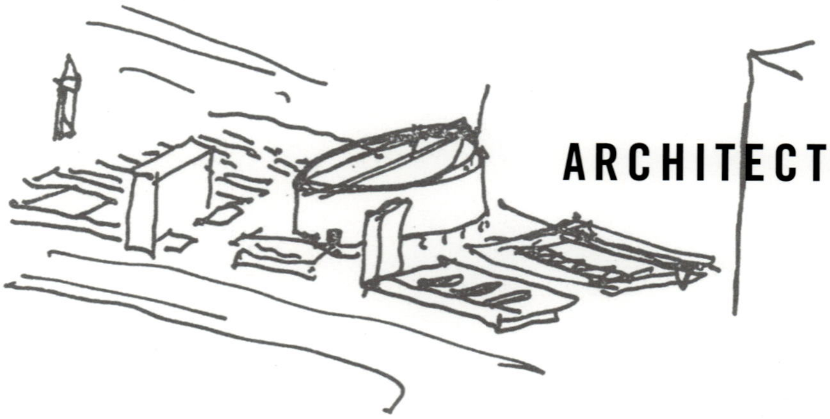

ARCHITECTURE SUSTAINABLE

César Reyes
Ethel Baraona Pohl
Claudio Pirillo

pencil

"Now then, the house is like the human body: its heart and its body are in the house, and have made the house. The interior and the exterior are not but one thing, and only if the circumstances are favorable. The inside and the outside, the surroundings are not but one whole. Take possession of the environment. And the environment is the intelligible space"
Le Corbusier, 1946

PROLOGUE

César Reyes
Ethel Baraona Pohl
Claudio Pirillo

How can architecture be made sustainable?

We have already got used to the word sustainability. We hear it in the daily news and we find it in magazines and market shelves. Everybody uses this word nowadays, but when trying to specify what it means for architecture it is difficult to materialize an answer with a specific application.

Sustainability is simply a paradigm and thus it does not have an absolute definition. As far as sustainable architecture is concerned, it could be simply said that we are on a journey towards sustainability.

Curitiba. Brasil

Nowadays, there is a widespread consensus that in order to achieve this it is necessary that our projects fulfill a series of requirements:

. Integration with environmental characteristics of the surroundings
. Study and use of energy sources (renewable and non-renewable) available on the site.
. Precise use of materials according to their features.
. Waste management in phases of construction and operation.
. Mobility and social characteristics of users.

In order to describe all selected examples, we have used innate tools in architectural composition such as balance, module and rhythm; and we have joined them to sustainable parameters with the purpose to guide professionals in the application of these new premises in their projects.

Fortunately, new efforts in the application of principles of sustainable development can be found nowadays in cities, towns and individual buildings.

Ecobulevar, Vallecas. Urban Ecosistem

At an urban scale, the experience of emblematic examples such as Curitiba in Brazil or Stuttgart in Germany are widely renowned; or at a neighborhood scale such as Reisefeld or Valuban in Friburg, also in Germany.

It has gotten to the point of admitting that besides a physical structure, the development of a social, economical and environmental fabric is necessary, which allows the inhabitants of the urban center to have at their disposal all of the basic conditions to be able to inhabit their cities in a sustainable way.

However, there are isolated interventions that, like urban acupuncture, look to generate environmental progress while sustainable urban solutions, more extended over time, start to become noticeable.

In Vallecas, Madrid a team of young architects using technology found in the food and agriculture industry of Southern Spain, have proposed the cultivation of artificial trees, which in addition to serving as air conditioning units, while the definitive trees grow, they generate public meeting spaces.

On the opposite end of the planet, and already cited in this book, a team of Chilean architects propose the renovation of a city block in the urban center, to house one hundred families who had occupied the site for 30 years, thus avoiding their social exclusion (Project 02 Elemental Iquique).

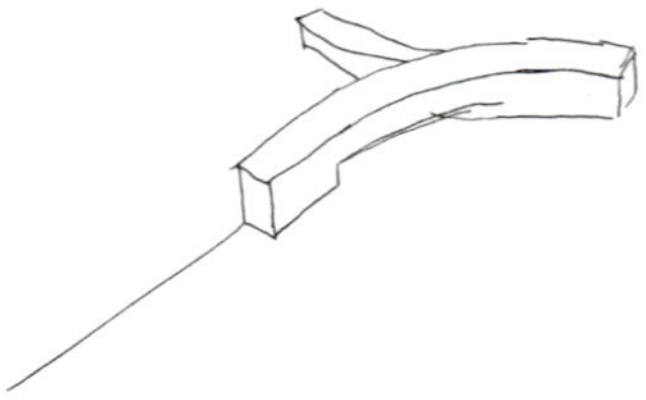

Ayora House, Fran Silvestre

At an institutional level, one can find examples in such different environmental conditions as the humid tropic in Costa Rica (Project 06 Holcim Building), the Mediterranean climate of Barcelona (Project 18 Biomedical Research Park of Barcelona), or the dry winter of British Columbia in Canada (Project 04 Nk´Mip Desert Center).

This publication also illustrates examples of service buildings such as the school in the extreme desert at the foot of the Himalayas in India (Project 03 Druk White Lotus School), or the old people's home in Zamora, Spain with continental weather favorable for agricultural activities (Project 10 Residential Home).

At a residential level, projects in barren and dry environments such as Cartagena, are reviewed (Project 13 House for Two Collectors), with continental weather (Project 14 House in Ayora) or wooded and humid ones in Asturias, Spain (Project 20 Steel and Wood House).

This book has been structured in a linear fashion, but it also allows for different readings of the selected projects: by geographical location, by project typology or by environmental strategies applied. At the beginning of the publication, a thematic index is proposed as a map to locate projects according to these classifications.

Once arrived at this point, it seems reasonable to question why these projects have been defined as sustainable. In this sense, presently there is no general consensus as to how a building's sustainability is determined.

Measurement systems have been developed in different countries that allow valuing the degree of sustainability of a building. In the United States and Canada, the LEED certification is utilized (Leadership in Energy and Environmental Design), in Europe there are efforts being made to implement the GBTool certification(Green Building Challenge), whereas at a local level every country develops its own evaluation system (VERDE in Spain, Breeam in the United Kingdom, MINERGIE in Switzerland, table DCBA in Holland, table Pimwag in Finland, Escale in France). These tools represent a valuable device for analysis, and their functioning can be summed up in the comparison of different parameters of a given building with the ideal environmental solution for the same location.

This publication is materialized without the intention of delving deeper into the analysis of these tools. However, common evaluation criteria are taken from them to describe the strategies used by the designers in the selected examples.

Without being exhaustive, and parting from a similar analytical scheme, it is intended to show that there are several parameters that should always be taken into account if one looks to integrate the building in the environment. This analysis is complemented with graphic information with the sufficient quality to illustrate that the highlighted environmental strategies can perfectly be integrated with the architectural language. In addition, a glossary has been included, with a series of terms that will help to comprehend the projects from a sustainable point of view.

Focusing on the construction; architecture generates a flow of systems and materials which can used to measure its environmental impact. As a synthesis, it can be said that in order to be sustainable there are several basic parameters that must always be taken into account, regardless of the buildings site: location, consumption of water, consumption of energy, and consumption of materials.

There are several basic criteria such as orientation, shape and materiality of a building which, in an obvious way, affect a project's comfort level, but from the architectural production point of view, exclusively aesthetic, are hardly taken into account. Finally, it is the user who lives and sometimes suffers a building's final result, autographed but sick; with poor orientation and ventilation. Or, that in order to function, a building needs lighting and artificial conditioning elements that make it energetically ostentatious.

With the examples compiled in this publication, it is demonstrated that 'a priori' there are neither bad materials nor poor technologies. What does exist is a correct or incorrect application of these, according to the particulars of a project. Steel or concrete are high energy cost materials, but might be advisable in places where resources like wood are scarce. On the other hand, use of materials like soil is totally compatible with institutional typologies and not only a mark of identity for rural or self-built projects.

We are in a learning stage, which must be taken on with humility and responsibility. The new Technical Building Code in Spain will obligate the designer to incorporate sustainable parameters in their projects. In that sense, we will all be, by law, more sustainable. However, it is difficult to incorporate the new requirements into an architectural language. We hope that the journey the reader will make below will help him understand that sustainability in architecture implies an additional effort to understand that our activity has consequences in environment. And, besides being a responsibility, it can become a richer compositional language through buildings that interact with their environment, while also standing out for their architectural quality.

To describe the examples selected in this publication we use tools like balance, module and rhythm, innate to architectural composition, combined with sustainable parameters, in order to guide professionals in the application of these new premises in their projects.

ARCHITECTURE SUSTAINABLE

Gerardo Wadel[1]

Sustainability, physical demands and a challenge for Architecture

It was in the decade of the 60's, with the first protests on the massive use of nuclear energy, when the environmental problem of the industrial society reached a world level and stirred up public opinion for the first time. The decade of the 70's, marked by the petroleum crisis and the shortage of its derived fuels, placed the whole world on alert about what could happen if there were a stop in the absolute and indiscriminate disposal of energy available until then. In 1972 the Club of Rome2 published the report The Limits of Growth and since, for many people of the entire world, it was no longer possible to think about economic development without keeping in mind the consequences on the natural resources.

Quite a bit later, toward 1987 and due to the appearance of Our Common Future, a United Nations report, the first world agreement on the contemporary conception of the environmental problem took place, with the incorporation of sustainability and sustainable development concepts through the ideas of many disciplines, among them also Architecture. The Earth Summit of Rio de Janeiro in 1992, although also that of Johannesburg 2002, diffused the agreement on a global scale thanks to the contribution of dozens of governments, hundreds of organizations, and thousands of people participating in different activities. The idea that being conscience of the seriousness of the world's environmental problem implied a before and after, had already become fact.

The concept of sustainability that is the basis for what we could refer to as sustainable architecture is based on sustainable development as defined by Our Common Future, resulting in something like the capacity to satisfy the necessities of the present generations without compromising the capacity of future generations to satisfy their own needs. From here, economic growth and its associated ecological deterioration were indissolubly bound. This matter can be easily exemplified in the use of fossil fuels. Our development based on the consumption and the contamination caused by the combustion of petroleum based fuels is not sustainable, since the exhaustion of the natural resource and the contamination that it supposes severely determine the possibilities of future generations, whom we force to face the consequences of our behavior.

Architecture is materialized through construction, that just like other industries is based on the productive dominant model, originated back in the industrial revolution about two hundred fifty years ago. Before then, society was organic and was characterized by the use of resources from the biosphere which neither surpassed the capacity of nature to produce them, nor the possibilities of absorption of the waste they generated. Thus, man did not have the capacity to produce environmental damage on a global scale.

The rupture began with the indiscriminate readiness of energy resources that allowed gaining access to mineral resources as never before, starting a spiral of limitless growth in the consumption of resources and in the consequential generation of waste. This acceleration, together with the increase of per capita income, demographic explosion and the extension of horizontal transport, has originated another form of cultural organization: the industrial society, where each extracted material from the lithosphere ends up degraded and poured onto the thin biosphere layer that covers the planet, contaminating it and putting in danger the conditions for the continuity of life.

This productive dominant model which, as aforementioned, also characterizes the production of Architecture, can be synthesized in the linear sequence extraction > production > waste. Except for a few industries that base their organization on what is called industrial ecology, a metabolism of production which imitates the conditions of the biosphere where the word waste does not exist, every product is designed to finally become waste. A carpet can last ten years, a window thirty and a building seventy, but all will end up transformed into waste because they respond to the same linear productive paradigm, ignoring that this transformation of resources into waste products implies a decrease, slow but relentless, of the only thing we have of true value: the stock of the planet's natural resources.

Opposite that and again resorting to the biosphere example, the great recycling machine,

Architecture could – and the good news is that it's already beginning to do so- begin to base itself on an alternative productive model, although it's as old as the Earth itself. It's about the end of material lifecycles, where all the open links of the production systems which create waste in the air, water, or on the earth begin to close by eliminating the word waste and replacing it with the concept resource. The resultant production model is no longer linear but cyclical and it is defined by the cycle recycling – manufacturing - recycling determining, in this way, a new challenge for architecture.

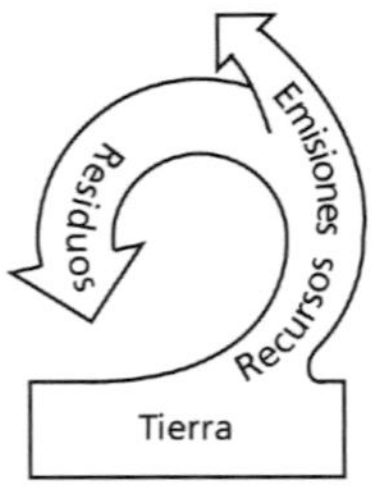

SXX: Ciclos materiales abiertos

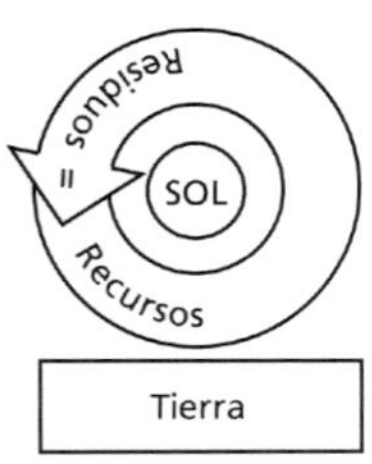

SXXI: Ciclos materiales cerrados

1 Gerardo Wadel is an architect specialized in sustainability. Member of Organic Society, an environmental consultancy in edification business. He is a specialist in technology and Production of Habitat. Practice lecturer of the La Salle school in University Ramon Llull. Advisor of green office of *Colegio de Arquitectos de Cataluña*. He has been director of *Constructiva* magazine (1999-2005).

Productive model demands everytime more raw materials

Resources that are not recycled become waste material. Photo: European Comission

The environmental impact of construction or the trace of buildings

The main causes of the environmental impact of architecture are found in the consumption of non-renewable resources and in the generation of polluting wastes, both in rapid increase. Their main effect is the destruction of the stock of natural resources by entropic degradation – an increase in the excesses and material dispersion caused by human activity - and that it is especially tangible when we observe its more visible effects.

Indeed, construction is directly or indirectly involved in the deforestation of the native forests, the depletion of fossil fuels, the decrease of fresh water reserves, solid wastes or the contamination of the atmosphere through the emissions of such gases as carbon dioxide CO2, nitrogen oxides NOx and sulphur oxides SOx which are translated into the greenhouse effect, acid rain, and the destruction of the ozone layer.

extraction of raw materials exhausts resources. Photo: www.basurama.org

Buildings represent an important part of the energy that is consumed by society, which is mostly used in the production of construction materials and in maintaining the habitability conditions demanded in buildings. The use of energy is one of the most widespread and accepted indicators of the environmental impact of construction as a unit of global measure, since it can express both the power and work used, as well as a consumption of non-renewable resources and a liberation of polluting emissions. Such energy consumption, originated mostly from burning fossil fuels, is responsible of an important part of the global emissions of CO2, the main gas cause of the greenhouse effect.

Eco- toxicity and human toxicity are two groups of impacts that summarize different environmental effects and provide a general reference about how nature is affected by the use of resources demanded by society. The solid, liquids and gaseous wastes of the production process of materials, as well as of the construction and demolishing of buildings, have a repercussion in these two toxicity groups through the combination of different effects. The liberation of sulphides, nitrogen oxides, ammonia and heavy metals, for example, provoke the increase of the acidity and the toxicity of the ground which affects the flora and the superficial and underground water supplies.

Other environmental effects generated in part by the construction industry are the acid rains caused by the emissions of sulphur dioxide and nitrogen oxides from the combustion of by-products of fuel oil, which modify the composition of the ground and the water supplies; the eutrophication caused by the dumping of industrial compounds rich in nitrogen and phosphorous, which cause the imbalance of certain nutrients in an ecosystem; and the smog composed by the emissions of carbon dioxide, the solid particles and the sulphur dioxide caused by the combustion of coal in electric power plants and boilers, which cause different health problems to living beings.

Buildings have an ecological footprint that has been growing, as the consumption of materials and the use of the energy has increased. Nevertheless, some impacts have been partially controlled thanks to the innovation in product design, construction solutions, buildings or housing developments. The course can still be corrected, and the large global agreements reached by society play a great role in this.

Some years ago the ozone layer, the stratum of the atmosphere that partially retains the ultraviolet solar radiation avoiding that its harmful effects reach the planet's surface, was being attacked by the CFC (chlorofluorocarbons) and HCFC (Hydro chlorofluorocarbons) gases that formed part of certain liquid coolants, fire extinguisher agents, and propellants used in certain thermal isolation materials and air conditioning facilities. The Montreal Protocol impelled the massive substitution of this type of gases, drastically reducing its liberation into the atmosphere.

Waste materials spread out and contaminate our environment

At this moment, the greatest environmental challenge that has been proposed in civilization, through the Kyoto Protocol, is the limitation of the emissions of CO2 and other greenhouse effect gases in order to try to slow down the climatic change that is occurring, parting from the global increase of temperature on the earth's surface. Although the problem is more complex because it affects the use of energy during the entire lifespan of the building, it is also expected that the scope of this great agreement radically modify the way in which buildings are conceived and produced.

Material flows: energy, materials, waste and water

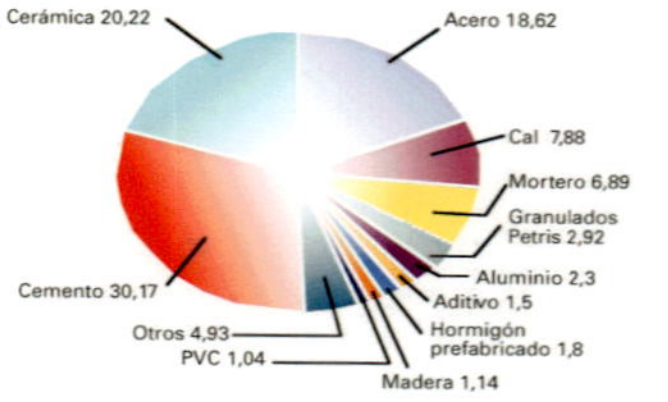

CO_2 emissions due to manufacturing of materials involved in the construction of a square meter of standard building and relative incidence of each one of them in total result

Emisiones de CO_2 en la vivienda

Repartición por usos	kg CO_2/ vivienda/año	%
Calefacción	992,9	32
Agua caliente	633,1	21
Cocina y horno	211	7
Aparatos domésticos	942,5	31
Iluminación	279,5	9
TOTAL	3059	100

CO_2 emissions due to utilization of a square metre of standard building and relative involvement in different uses in total.

Although, of course, there are more complex and complete systems, there is a certain general consent about the parameters that can be taken into account when evaluating, in a summarized way, the environmental impact of construction. The answer that architecture is looking for about the physical demands of sustainability pursues the long-term objective of closing the material lifecycle by means of recycling all resources. Within this guideline and as demonstrated in this book, the environmental analysis of a certain project can be synthesized in the consumption of energy, water, and materials as well as in the generation of waste to the air, to the water, and to the earth.

Building designers, we architects, are more prepared to understand the laws of generation and the performance of the stocks of resources we use to materialize our projects, than with the flows that they represent. The consideration of these flows, as well as the understanding of the new environmental units of measure of architecture, represents an effort of understanding. In this way, the analysis of the examples selected for this volume exemplifies the expansion experienced by the profession, due to the incorporation of the criteria of sustainability in architecture.

Using the available information in Spain[2], and although it may have supposed a certain cutback of the geographic scope of this book, following, the environmental impact of the construction of housing will try to be quantified through the measure of the flows of energy, water, materials and waste.

Energy. The manufacturing of materials to build a square meter of standard construction can suppose an equivalence in energy of 5.754MJ (Mega Joules) that are equal to about 150 liters of gasoline. The use of the same building under usual conditions, during a period of one year, and also expressed in square meters, can reach 473,5MJ, which represents about 12 liters of gasoline. Considering the energy for the use of the building during a 50 year-long lifespan and adding it to that of the production of the materials, a total value is reached of 29.429MJ/m2 or 755 liters of gasoline/m2. A simple form of representing the consumption of energy of a building would be to imagine almost 5 barrels of crude oil (Brent Crude) for each square meter of surface area.

Water. In a conventional house an average volume of 140 liters of drinking water is consumed by each person daily. Around 90% is only used to transport certain waste far from the house. Indeed, only 10% of the treated water we consume is used to drink or cook, although all of it ends up transformed into waste water and therefore is not suitable for any other use, and should be treated before being returned to the water cycle, from where it will be collected again. A simple way to represent this consumption is to think that, every day, each person consumes around twice their own weight in water.

Materials. The construction of an inhabitable square meter of a standard building, making an abstract of the consumption due to maintenance and renovation during the life-span of the buildings, means the use of 2.500kg of materials that enter directly to the construction site, with a great number of environmental impacts associated to it. If we also consider the ecological backpack - the quantity of waste that has been generated during the extraction of prime materials and the manufacturing of products - the original value should be multiplied at least by three, reaching a total figure of 7.500kg/m2. If we use concrete as a reference, with a density of 2.500 kg/m3, the weight of the materials plus the ecological backpack corresponding to a square meter of construction would represent three cubic meters of that material, quantity enough to fill all of the volume of the building.

Waste. Currently the construction, maintenance, and demolishing of buildings represent a quantity of waste equivalent to 3kg per person and day. Of this amount only 10% to 15% is recycled. Domestic waste, on the other hand, represents 1.7kg per person and day, with a recycling rate that oscillates around 20%. The energy consumed by the buildings, mentioned above, represents the generation of approximately 2kg of CO2 per person and day.

Let's suppose that each morning we should leave our house, taking with us our own waste, which adds up to about 6.7kg. It would be somewhat cumbersome, but we could do it, although since we have forgotten to consider water, in fact we should carry out about 150kg. It is obvious that we would not be able to go far, even with just our own waste.

2 Parameters of Sustainability, by Albert Cuchí, Daniel Castelló, Glòria Diez, Albert Sagrera and Fructuós Mañà, published by the Institute of Technology of the Construction of Catalonia in 2003, from the catalog of the exhibition Inhabit the World from Barcelona Forum 2004, whose chief directors were Ramón Folch, Salvador Rueda and Oriol Pibernat, of studies carried out by CIES, Center for Initiatives for Sustainable Construction of Catalonia, and also from self-elaborated criteria.

Situation scheme, strategies and objectives

Aaron Crun

As has been demonstrated, the environmental impact of architecture is not a minor problem for the whole of society, and much less for the construction sector itself. It is an activity with great incidence on the consumption of resources and in the generation of waste. This is confirmed by the figures of the indicators of energy, water, materials, and waste that have just been seen.

Among the many strategies that can be formulated for the environmental improvement of construction, the five following are especially interesting because they allow to order all the possible actions in coherent courses of action, and to undertake the multiple fronts that the topic supposes. In the first place is reduction of the demand [1] that represents the elimination of all unnecessary consumption. Subsequently we have efficient use [2] or the election of the systems that offer a certain service with the least consumption possible. After this, it makes sense to talk about the use of local resources [3] that represents the appropriate use of the resources offered by the immediate surroundings, so often ignored. Then we could mention recycling [4] that doesn't need more explanations, and finally we will mention the recovery of the generated impact [5] that means a compensation of the imbalance caused by the activity. These five strategies (numbered in order to identify them in the following examples), can be recognized in the analysis of the works included in this publication and they are of great help for the materialization of a truly sustainable architecture.

How much energy does a house spend?

A lot; it represents up to 15% of all of the energy consumed by our society. About 18,000 kW/ hour per year; this is just like having 22 bulbs of 100W always turned on. However, avoiding unnecessary consumption along with better insulation, using thermal inertia, and appropriate windows and framework [1]; improving the performance of mechanical air conditioning devices, lighting and appliances [2]; taking advantage of the conditions of the natural climate by means of natural ventilation and collection of solar energy [3]; choosing clean energy like biogas [4] and making rehabilitating buildings energy-wise [5], it is possible to save up to 40-60% of this energy.

How much water is consumed in a house?

A lot; up to 16% of all the water we use. About 50,000 liters per year per person, just like the volume of a pool of 8 x 4m with an average depth of 1.5m. However, avoiding the unnecessary consumption by means of efficient irrigation and low consumption sanitary devices [1]; using faucets and toilets with flow reduction discharges [2]; collecting and using rainwater [3]; recycling wastewater [4] and using natural treatment [5], it is possible to save up to 70% of this water.

Judy Gr

How many materials does a house spend?

A lot; if it is considered jointly with the rest of buildings, up to 25% of the total mineral extractions of the planet. However, adjusting the building elements strictly to the real necessities [1]; designing constructive solutions that require a smaller quantity of material [2], using natural materials and of local origin [3]; recycling construction and demolition waste [4] and buying materials that neutralize waste (for example CO_2 emissions) [5], it is possible to save significantly not only on the materials consumed, but also on their associated environmental impacts.

How much domestic waste does a house generate?

A lot; around 20% of all those generated by society. It is about 2,500kg per year for a family of four, twice as much than thirty years ago. However, buying strictly the amount used and selecting options with minimum packaging[1]; choosing high durability products which adapt to diverse necessities [2], taking advantage of the energy contained in the wastes [3]; recycling [4] and using recycled products [5] it is possible to reduce the quantity of waste drastically and to increase the recycling rate up to 80%.

Nevertheless, there is also good news. As confirmed by the examples shown in this book, architecture, in the search for new values which relate it with sustainability has begun to find certain paths that allow it to reduce its environmental impact significantly and to explore possible ways to stop generating waste or at least reduce them drastically.

Ovidio

Gerardo Wadel
www.societatorganica.com

Selva Morales

8
5
4
7
3
1
6
2
9

20
10
17
12
18
16
19
15
11
14
13
TEMATIC INDEX
TIPOLOGY
Urban
Institutional
Corporative
Housing
Cultural
ENVIROMENTAL PARAMETERS
Water
Social Service
Materials
Energy

01

Arup

DONGTAN ECOCITY

Shangai, China

	ARUP
	www.arup.com
ARCHITECTS	ARUP -Urban Design, planning, Engineering, Transport, Socioeconomic Research and sustainability
PROMOTERS	Shanghai Industrial Investment Corporation (SIIC)
	Mr. Wang Yibin, Marketing Manager of SIIC Dongtan Investment & Development (Holdings); China's President Hu Jintao; Mr Ma, Executive Director SIIC
	COLLABORATING COMPANIES
Energy	ALSOP
Digital Images	ARUP
	DATES
BEGINNING OF WORKS	November 2005
WORK COMPLETION	2010-2040 in stages

DESCRIPTIVE BRIEF

China, Shanghai and cities for the XXI century: sustainable infrastructures

According to Chinese government's official line, 300 million inhabitants should be accommodated in cities over the next 15 years. As it occurred 150 years ago in Europe, today China faces the challenge of a dramatic movement of population towards its cities, in a contemporary version of the migration field / city. The logic of the problem is known, but its scale and speed are not; even less, its consequences. Shanghai is - economically -the most dynamic city in the most dynamic country in the world. In the Yangtze River delta, 100 million inhabitants live, and the demand for urban space is not only nourished by migration, but also by a sustained growth of the CPI of 10% in the last 15 years. People want to live in the city, and also a significant proportion demand more space for living, working and leisure. Additionally, 4 million illegal immigrants work in Shanghai, generating problems but also allowing economy to carry on growing. Pressure for urban development in Shanghai is manifested in its plan for regional development that proposes the construction of nine satellite cities to absorb part of the demand. However, this measure is insufficient, even according to the most conservative estimations. Additionally, pressures not only affect the territory, but also social structures, environment and economy. Arup was called by a company of Shanghai government to develop a new satellite city in an 8,400 hectare site, equivalent to the whole island of Manhattan. Our interest to get involved in the project resided in the client's vision and his priority to develop a sustainable city. Challenges associated to this vision are evident: in a context where pressures for development are the most extreme in the planet, a city would be designed and built to prove that it is possible to generate more progress with less victims. Definitely, we are talking about a city in which life quality is associated to a sustainable appoach to economical, social and environmental development.

What is a sustainable city? How to build a sustainable city

This is a difficult definition, but it is not a utopian vision-although images of Brasilia and Chandighar came flooding in during the first visit to Chongming Island. The base of our project is simple: a sustainable city is where social, economic, physical and environmental aspects are integrated simultaneously in the process and implementation of the project; a city seen not only as a physical structure or for economic relationships. The consultant team proposed simple ideas to trigger the development process, and many of them are related to elements of physical infrastructure. But this leaves us at the plan of Brasilia. The sustainable city that we want to build favours innovation and increasing changes in the social, economic and environmental infrastructure. Main operations conceive these infrastructures as supports: social infrastructure, as a support for social mobility, inclusion and competitiveness; economic infrastructure, as a support for incentives that promote an economically sustainable base and competitiveness, and environmental infrastructure, as a support for life quality. Finally, physical infrastructure should be a flexible support and facilitator of other infrastructures.

In the context of a new city, physical infrastructure plays a fundamental role in guiding and proving how to be sustainable and how the other infrastructures will eventually be developed. Inversely, the other infrastructures will eventually generate pressure for change and evolution of the physical infrastructure. The capacity of the physical infrastructure to adapt itself to this evolutionary process is, from our point of view, the key to an appropriate urban strategy: the quality of the physical infrastructure is decisive in the direction that a new city can take. If financing a large scale physical infrastructure is not easy per se, common sense indicates that financing a sustainable and quality physical infrastructure is even more complex.

How to make it: financing of sustainability, new rules of the game[1]

The application of the Kyoto Protocol, since February of 2005 proposes new rules of the game for any type of sustainable project. Sustainability was synonymous of good intentions and bad businesses, and today is synonymous of good intentions and better businesses. Projects like Dongtan that propose decreases in energy consumption and in CO2 emissions, can be financed through the carbon market. Dongtan proposes a design of its physical infrastructure that, compared to a conventional project, is able to reduce CO2 emissions. After an evaluation process, a committee of UNFCCC (United Nations Framework Convention on Climate Change) grants several CERs (Certified Emmissions Reduction) to Dongtan for an amount equivalent to this reduction. CERs are equivalent to actions, and they can be traded in any currency exchange or financial market of the world; buyers are any projects or countries that cannot – or do not want to – comply with reductions of CO2 emissions agreed to in the Kyoto Protocol.

A city of 500,000 inhabitants like the one we are designing, can reduce the equivalent of 22 million US$ of CO2 emissions a year. This, in a period of 25 years, turns into approximately 500 million US$ - current value. These new resources will be used to finance the costs incurred in the city to obtain better standards in buildings, energy generating plants, plazas, parks, public transport infrastructure and roads. Sustainable physical infrastructure projects, which can act as support for other infrastructures, will be encouraged by this mechanism. Dongtan will be a laboratory where this mechanism is used for the first time at urban scale; from our perspective, sustainable physical infrastructures which take advantage of these new game rules will be the ones that will define our XXIst century cities.

Alejandro Gutiérrez, Arup, China

1 Ver http://www.pointcarbon.com

ENVIRONMENTAL ANALYSIS

1. Choosing the Site. Project and Development.

1.1. Location

Latitud: 31°30'52"N
Longitud: 121°56'10"E
Altitud: 0 m

The project is located in the Chongming Island, the greatest alluvial island in the world[1] and the third greatest island in China after Hainan and Taiwan. The site is at sea level in the delta of Yangtze River. It is featured by a northern subtropical marine monsoon climate (warm and humid), has four remarked seasons along the year, with extended sunshine and abundant rainfall. Spring and autumn are relatively short, compared to summer and winter.

Until recently, the island was only one of the neighboring rural areas near of Shanghai, and it was used as an agricultural field for the city. Now it is subject to an ambitious master plan that includes agricultural planning, the construction of a tunnel that crosses the Yangtze River, and the relocation of a considerable number of displaced people due to the construction of the Three Gorges Dam that will considerably increase the population of the island.

The city of Dongtan will be located in an area of 86 Km2, equivalent to three fourth parts of the island of Manhattan in the United States. In 2010 its population will reach 25.000 inhabitants, whereas after 2030 it will reach half a million. Its construction is planned as sustainable city with reduced ecological repercussion, in order to be used as a model of development for the 400 cities that the Chinese government plans to build in the next twenty years.

1.2 Urban Design and Site Improvement

The fragile nature of the Dongtan swamps and its importance in the migratory cycle of the birds and the rest of local fauna, have been one of the key factors for the design of the city.

It is planned to enhance the existent swamps, returning the ground previously dedicated to agriculture to its original state, in order to create a reserve area between the city and the swamps that will have four kilometers wide at its narrowest point.

Only 30% of Dongtan's area will be urbanized and constructed and thus preventing the contamination in adjacent zones to swamps.

1.3 Project

The city was raised from the beginning as a support for all the human activities, and not as a result of them. It is based on the principle that all the citizens can be in contact with green open spaces, lakes and channels. It's intended that their buildings are highly energy efficient, and that the energy provision comes from renewable sources like the wind and the sun or subproducts utilizations such as biomass.

It has been foreseen the development of the city to be carried out in several stages throughout the following thirty or forty years. Dongtan's first phase is conceived as a village formed by three pedestrian avenues with different urban character. Besides, several urban parks will be designed, of ecological and leisure reserve, foreseeing their construction before 2010, year of the Universal Exhibition in neighbour Shanghai.

Site Plan

Afterwards the city will grow like a succession of villages connected by bicycle routes and public transport corridors, promoting displacements on foot, cab, bus or bicycle.

2. Consumption of Energy and Resources

Ironically, the city will be raised in an island that emerged as a result of an environmental disparity in the delta of Yangtze River. In the last fifty years, the island of Chongming has doubled its size, due to the eroded soil accumulation produced by deforestation on the margins of the river. The island has grown from the 600 Km2 that it had in 1950 to 1290 Km2 at present time.

The first challenge faced by planners was the preservation of the swamp located at the south of the island, which represents one of the largest reserves of migratory birds existing in China. To achieve this goal, maintenance is enhanced with minimum affection to local vegetation. In that sense, the city is part of the ecosystem, and not an environmental obstacle.
The second challenge deals with energy. It is foreseen that the city generates all of the energy it will consume, while reducing the environmental load due to CO_2 emissions. This includes the energy necessary for transportation inside the city. The use of local materials will be favoured for the execution of the projects, with the aim to reduce transport and energy associated to construction. By means of the combination of sustainable local technologies and new development it is intended to reach a reduction of 70% of the current energy requirements for the operation of the buildings.
The third challenge is to deal with management of wastes generated by inhabitants and economic activities such as agriculture.

The fourth challenge is of economic nature, since the urban development pattern must be able to be execute and maintained by itself. This is why, a compact urban design based on the development of small villages is proposed, which will reduce infrastructures while generating friendly urban routes at human scale. Exchange of Certified Emissions Reduction (CER) granted by CMNUCC[2] is also contemplated to prove that actions of environmental nature can become economic benefits, which should be reflected in the maintenance of infrastructures of the city.

1 Chongmign, Changxing y Hengsha Islands emerged as a result of a water level change of Yangtze River.

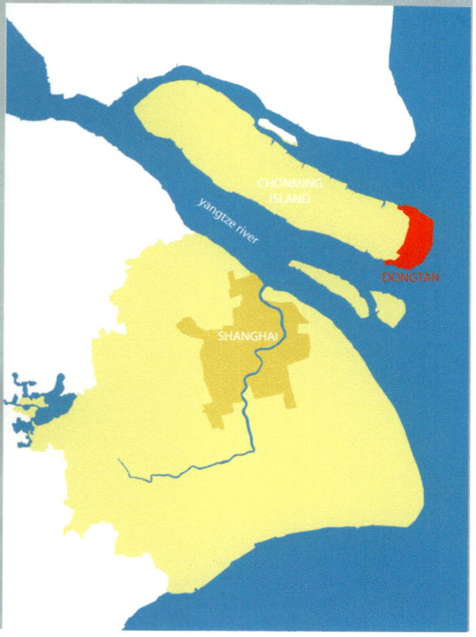

- Eco farming demostration
- Wind Turbines
- Bird Park / large scale visitor atraccion
- Main Nodes / Future Dogtan phases
- Secondary Nodes / Future Dogtan phases
- Other Nodes
- Zerp emissions road accesse
- Waterbus

Current Chongming island marsh, located on the Yangtse Delta

3. Transport Management

In 2020, China will have the unusual figure of 140 million cars. The promotion of public and less polluting transportation means, is one of the strategies that urban planners must use in order to minimize the environmental impact generated by car emissions.

Villages that will form the city of Dongtan will be connected by a system that combines bicycle rails, pedestrian routes and public transportation, including hydrogen buses and water taxis operated by solar energy. Channels, lakes, and projected ports will facilitate the transport among them, as well as generating a wide variety of public leisure spaces.

4. Energy Management

Energy sources will take advantage of the renewable energy potential of the site:

- Monsoon winds will be used as source to generate wind energy Extended periods of sunshine will facilitate capture of solar energy.
- Due to agricultural activities in the site, a series of by-products with enormous potential, such as raw material for biomass, will be generated.

An Energy Center will contain the energy supply for the entire city. It will also be a tourist attraction, as well as a park of leisure, scientific exhibitions and an educational center.

5. Water Management

The project looks to take advantage of the high rainfall index of the area, with an annual rainfall range of 1300mm[3]. This is why, the use of green roofs on buildings will be favoured, which will capture rainwater as well as maintain the permeable area of the city. This valuable resource will improve the insulation of the buildings, as it filters and stores rainwater which will later be used for irrigation or sanitary purposes.

6. Waste Management

Chinese cities are experiencing a fast industrialization process that is quickly leading the country to become one of the main consumers in the world, while the amount of wastes, contamination and gases that contribute to the global heating are increased exponentially.

A high percentage of wastes of this city will be recycled and organic wastes will be used as biomass for energy production. Landfills will not exist, and human wastes will be processed as manure for agricultural activity in the area, thus ensuring its long-term fertility.

7. Economic and Social Aspects

Parallel to the environmental conservation of the area, special care has been taken in conserving the current population and thier sustaining activities. For this reason, agricultural and fishing communities of the area will be supported to find new market opportunities. Due to the empowering of social infrastructure and to the maintenance of agricultural and fishing activities, local nutritional self-sufficiency will be favoured.

The originality of the proposal relies on the qualitative innovations of the infrastructural concept as the support of a city:

- Social Infrastructure, as support of social mobility, inclusion and competitiveness.
- Economical Infrastructure, as support of incentives that promote a sustainable economic base and the permanence of the original sustaining activities.
- Physical Infrastructure as flexible support an facilitator of other infrastructures.

Dongtan is a local project with a global perspective, designed with the certainty that China will play a key role in the development of environmental and economically sustainable settlements. It is evident that, if 1.3 trillions Chinese and 1.2 trillions Indian people adopt the extraction, consumption and contamination model which developed western countries are used to, the planet will be overloaded beyond its possibilities[4]. It is not fair to try that these people behave differently from the West people, as we maintain the current model. In that sense it seems necessary to define a new mechanism to be followed.

Dongtan will be a laboratory to use this mechanism on an urban scale for the first time. In this way, the physical sustainable infrastructures that take advantage of these new rules of the game will be those that define the cities of the XXI century.

8. The Architect's eye

The challenge of designing a city from scratch invites to reflect on experiences like those of Brasilia and Chandighar. Nevertheless, a series of issues always seem to appear when undertaking projects with a long temporal scale such as this one:

- Besides the environmental impact, is it possible to control the social impact of the proposal?

- How many generations of inhabitants will have to be born in Dongtan so that their citizens adopt the city's identity?

This challenge is inherent to all architects who project a space imagining its use. Imagining is a projection to the future. Living is a manifestation of the present. Herein lies one of the greatest challenges of Architecture.

2 http://unfccc.int/2860.php
3 In Spain the annual precipitation average index is about 684mm.
Source: System Espanola de Information sober el Ague. http://hispagua.cedex.es/
4 http://www.myfootprint.org/

Eyesight where the wild mills will be located

Part of the zone to be developed. North sideways

Part of the zone to be developed. South sideways

02

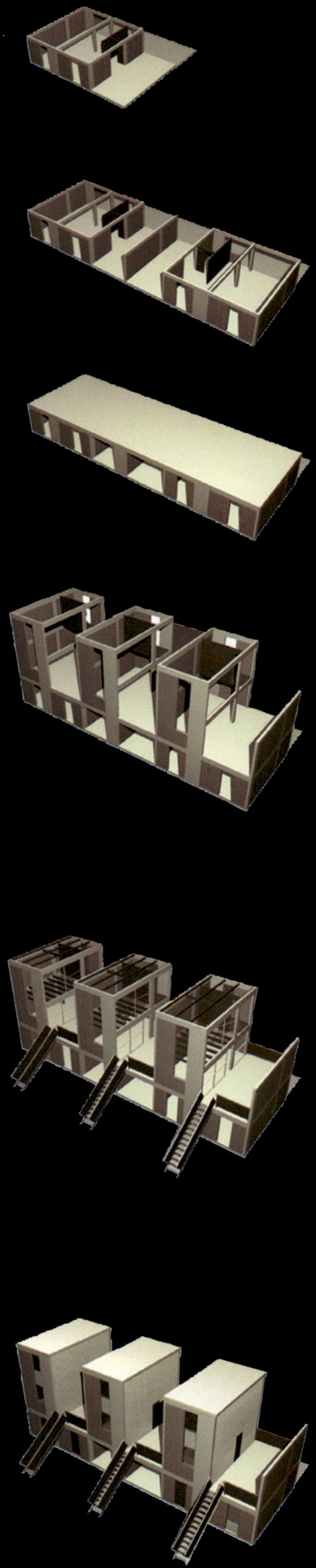

Alejandro Aravena

QUINTA MONROY PROJECT

IQUIQUE, Chile

ARCHITECTS	Alejandro Aravena, Alfonso Montero, Tomás Cortese, Emilio de la Cerda, Andrés Iacobelli
ENGINEERS	Juan Carlos de la Llera, Mario Alvarez Tomás Fischer, Alejandro Ampuero Carl Lüders, José Gajardo
PROMOTER	Gobierno regional de Tarapacá Programa Chile-Barrio del Gobierno de Chile
	COLLABORATING COMPANIES
Urbanization Works	Proingel, Abraham Guerra
Builder	Constructora Loga S.A.
Structural Mechanics	Juan Carlo de la Llera, Karl Lüders Mario Alvarez, José Gajardo
Photography	Alejandro Aravena
	DATES
BEGINNING OF WORKS	2003
WORK COMPLETION	2005

DESCRIPTIVE BRIEF

The Chilean Government asked us to resolve a difficult equation:
To situate 100 families, in the same 5.000 m2 site that they have illegally occupied for the last 30 years which is located in the very center of Iquique, a city in the Chilean desert.

And despite the site's price (3 times more than what social housing can normally afford), the aim was to avoid displacing the families to the periphery, and instead to settle them in the same site.

We had to work within the framework of the current Housing Policy (VSDSD) which is directed to the poorest of society, those that have no capacity for debt, using a US$ 7,500 subsidy which we had to pay for the land, the infrastructure and the architecture. Considering the current values in the Chilean building industry, in the best case scenario, this US$ 7.500 allows for just around 30 m2 of built space. This obligates the recipients to be themselves the ones who 'dynamically' transform, over time, the situation of mere housing into a home.

If to answer the question, one starts assuming 1 house = 1 lot, even when using the small lots of social housing, we were just able to host 30 families in the site. The problem with isolated houses, is that they are very inefficient in terms of land use; That is why social housing tends to look for land that costs as little as possible. That land, is normally on the periphery, far away from the network of opportunities, which cities offer.

If to try to make a more efficient use of the land, we reduce the width of the lot making it coincident with the width of the house, what we get then, instead of efficiency, is overcrowding.

If, in order to create density we build up in height, which is very efficient in terms of land use, the resultant typology blocks expansion. And here we needed that every house could at least double their initial built space.

So, what to do?
Our first task was to find a new way of looking at the problem:
Instead of designing the best possible unit for US$ 7500, to be multiplied 100 times, we asked ourselves what was the best possible building for US$750.000, capable of accommodating 100 families and their respective expansions.

But we saw that a building blocks expansions. That is true, except on the ground and the top floor. The ground floor could always grow horizontally over the adjacent ground, and the last could always grow vertically towards the sky. So, we worked on a building that had just the ground and top floor.

What is our point?
We propose that social housing be seen as a social investment and not as an expense. So we had to guarantee that the initial subsidy that the families received could be revalued over time. All of us, when buying a house expect it to increase in value. In fact, real estate is almost synonymous with a sure investment. But social housing, in an unacceptably high proportion, is more similar to buying a car than to buying a house; every day, its value decreases. It is very important to correct this, because at the country scale, Chile will spend 10 billion dollars in the next 20 years, (only if we project the current budget of the Ministry of Housing). But also at the scale of a poor family, it is key to understand that the housing subsidy received from the State will be, by far, the biggest aid ever; So, its that very subsidy which should be transformed into capital, and the house as a means to that end, which could allow the families to leave poverty and not merely protect themselves from the elements.

This project has identified a set of architectural design conditions by which a housing unit can increase its value over time.

In first place, we developed a typology that allowed us to achieve enough density to be able to pay for the site, which was very well located within the city, immersed in the network of opportunities that the city offered (work, education, transportation and health). The good location is key for the conservation of the economy of each family, and for the increase in value of each property.

Second, we decided to introduce In between the public space (of the streets and passages) and the private (of each house), the collective space: a common property with restricted access that allows for the creation of social networks, a key mechanism for the success of fragile environments. Clustering the 100 families in four groups of around 20 families, we achieved a small enough urban scale to allow the neighbors to relate, but not so small that we eliminated the existing social network.

Third, due to the fact that 50% of each unit's volume will eventually be self-built, the building had to be porous enough to allow each unit to expand within its structure. On the one hand we wanted to support, rather than constrain, spontaneous construction in order to avoid the deterioration of the urban environment over time, but also we were hoping to facilitate the expansion process for each family.

Finally, instead a designing a small house (in 30 m2 everything is small), we opted for designing a middle-income house, out of which could hand over, (given the available resources), only a small part. In that regard, the difficult parts of the house (kitchens, bathrooms, stairs, dividing walls) are designed for the final scenario (once extended), that is to say, for a house of more than 70m2.

In the end, when the given money is enough for just half of the house, the relevant question is which half to do. We chose to take charge of that half that a family, individually, will never be able to achieve on its own, no matter how much money, energy or time they spend. That is how we expect to contribute using architectural tools, to a non-architectural question: how to overcome poverty.

Violeta Parra Housing Ensemble in Iquique

Chile has a leading housing policy among Latin American countries, both because of its continuity and because of its efficiency of coverage, particularly because of its capacity to produce units that contribute to reducing the housing deficit.

However, in the last years, the volume of demand has obligated, as never before, to choose between quality and quantity of proposed solutions. Problems resulting from this dilemma have affected the quality of construction (structural uncertainty, accelerated degradation, poor living conditions); architectural typology of current housing (insufficient size, incapacity to grow and to constitute urban tissue, overcrowding, poor environmental quality, lack of privacy) and urban design (displacement to peripheral lands, far from services and equipments, unsafe environments).

Iquique Project is part of an action plan called ELEMENTAL whose objective is the design and implementation of urban projects with high social value and public impact.

1. Choosing the Site. Project and Development.

1.1 Location

Latitude:	20°13'33"S
Longitude:	70°08'00"O
Altitude:	37 m

For the Iquique project, the designers had to accommodate 100 families that during the last 30 years had illegally occupied a half hectare land called Quinta Monroy in the center of Iquique, a city in the Chilean desert. Despite the land's cost (three times more than what social housing can normally pay for the land), what it intended to avoid was the eradication of these families to outlying districts.

1.2 Urban Design and Site Improvement

In idealistic terms a social housing project should be located in well placed lands in the city, close to the opportunities net, forming neighborhoods around collective spaces, using architectural typologies that, strategically placed in the terrain, can sustain the future quality of the urban space. Such typologies should also allow easy and safe development of self-construction.

Iquique's proposal has resulted when defining the project inside a pre-existing urban fabric, where social meeting is fostered inside a square-shaped plaza space, where multiple paths are established to favor the maintenance of human relationships in the neighborhood.

1.3 Project

An import limitation was the State subsidy, which was given to designers for each housing unit. It consisted of 7500 US$ per family with which to finance the land's purchase, urbanization works and the architecture. This scarce amount, at best, only allowed building around 30 m2. This obligated beneficiaries to be themselves who "dynamically" transformed, over time, their own housing solution into a house.

In order to accommodate 100 families in the available room the following reasoning was followed:

Site Plan

- If an isolated housing typology had been chosen, only 30 families would have had room on the site. With this solution, the land's use is extremely inefficient, and they would have had to find a larger and cheaper piece of land on the outskirts to accommodate all of the families.

- If a lot's size was reduced making it equivalent to the size of a house, rather than efficiency, overcrowding would have been achieved.

- If in order to achieve density, they were built up in height, they would have limited possible future housing growth. In a building, just the ground floor can be extended in a horizontal direction and the last floor vertically.

- The adopted solution was to make buildings of only ground and last floors. This achieves a medium density and expandable solution, which allowed accommodating all 100 families in the available space.

This proposal consisted of dividing the land in 9x9 lots for each house; with a 6x6x2,5m initial construction volume containing a bathroom and a kitchen, under a reinforced concrete slab. Over this slab, 6x6x5m duplex apartments were arranged; with these apartments a 3x6x5m tower is provided with a double height space that also includes bathroom and kitchen. Both properties have direct access to the community space and their growth limit is of 72m2 in safe and good living conditions.

Private space is defined for a modern urban property, in its minimum expression of a sanitary core, with an additional un-programmed space where each user can expand as they wish.

Every housing unit is resolved by means of a ground floor, permeable towards a central space, a first floor of access to the house where daytime activities are located, and a second floor where night activities are placed.

2. Control of Environmental Impact

With a medium density level, the extension of water and electricity supply networks is reduced. The layout in four semi-public squares involves users in the maintenance of the public space. It constitutes, in addition, an acoustic insulation strategy, partially insulating homes from surrounding vehicular traffic.

3. Transport Management

Since inhabitants have not been moved away from city center, in addition to maintaining the social fabric, extensive journeys from the houses to work are avoided. A good location is the key to conserving each family's economy and to increasing each property in value.

The layout of four interior courtyards prioritizes pedestrian circulation in front of the houses. This space is used as a parking lot, but its communal character also allows it to be used as a children's playground.

4. Energy Management

Construction is one of the sectors that most consumes energy. This consumption is especially intense in the building stage. In social housing, structure represents 70% of the building whereas the finishes comprise the remaining 30%[1]. Designers focused on optimizing this 70% to guarantee the project's habitability. By rationalizing the process, unnecessary expenses were avoided and all available scarce resources were used to optimize the final result of the gross work.

[1] Salas, Julian. "Contra el hambre de vivienda. Soluciones tecnológicas latinoamericanas". Editorial Escala. Colombia. 1992

5. Water Management

One of the consequences of urbanization is the waterproofing of the ground. This fact prevents water filtration to the terrain, thus altering the pre-existing phreatic level. The finish of the plazas is permeable which facilitates rainwater filtration to the subsoil.

The medium density adopted permits reducing the water supply network according to the number of families served.

6. Waste Management

At least 50% of the built land was considered to be self-constructed. This involves little subsequent control and an increase of waste because of deficient execution. Expecting to control the way to make the extensions was certainly unreal, so these extensions were divided and framed.

Buildings were designed sufficiently 'porous' to make them work as supports for the improvised extensions. These pores are the spaces set aside for the extensions for each family.

They are supported on solid structures and are large enough to satisfy the standard of a good enclosure, but small enough to permit constructively simple and low technology extensions.

Since these 'pores' are separated by portions of building the eventual low quality of the extensions are framed and rationed.

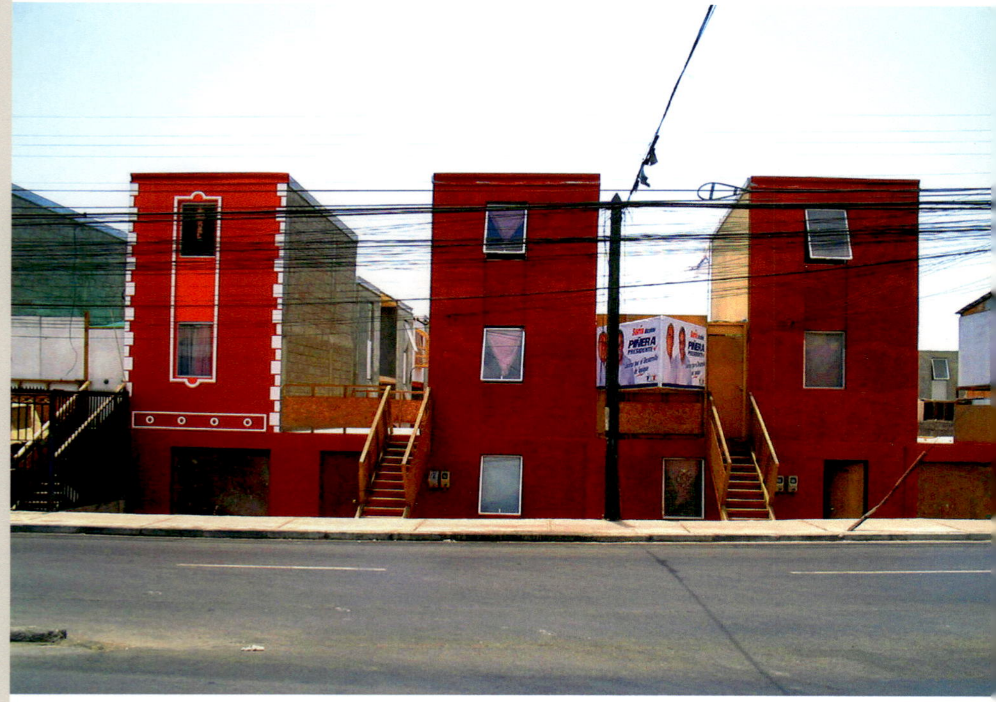

7. Social Aspects

Latin-American cities are characterized, among other things, by their fragmentation. In order to improve the quality of life in a city, exclusion must be reduced and the social balance between the different population groups that inhabit it must be favored. This project's largest contribution is the idea of not thinking of housing as an expense, but instead begin to see it as a social investment. Users were not separated from the social and urban network to which they had belonged for 30 years.

One more important social aspect is that during the design process, the families were the ones to choose among the alternatives presented by the design team. For their cost and efficiency in land use, it was nearly the same thing to make a single central space, several passageways or some courtyards. The families were the ones who preferred courtyards, because they better adapted to their method and scale of social organization.

Originally, 50 families had invaded the land; later they had built and illegally rented apartments over their houses. So the proposed typology was not alien to users. Families asked the designers to correctly carry out what they spontaneously had not been able to coordinate: dividing walls, safe structures, ventilated and lit rooms, community spaces.

8. The Architect's Eye

The technical resources of symmetry, rhythm and modulation successfully handled by the architect, takes us back to solutions explored by le Corbusier in the housing projects of Pessac in 1925. The difference lies in having achieved the essence of the practice of architecture. Allowing families to be themselves who finish configuring their own home; providing them with a real basic space and an imaginary one to expand their desires for progress, with the advantage of doing it a familiar urban environment, close to their work, study and leisure activities.

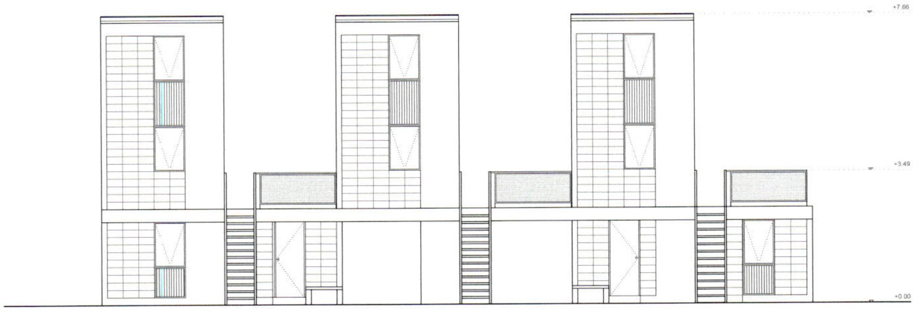

Front Elevation

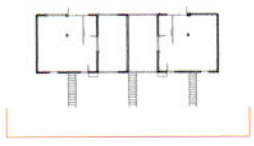

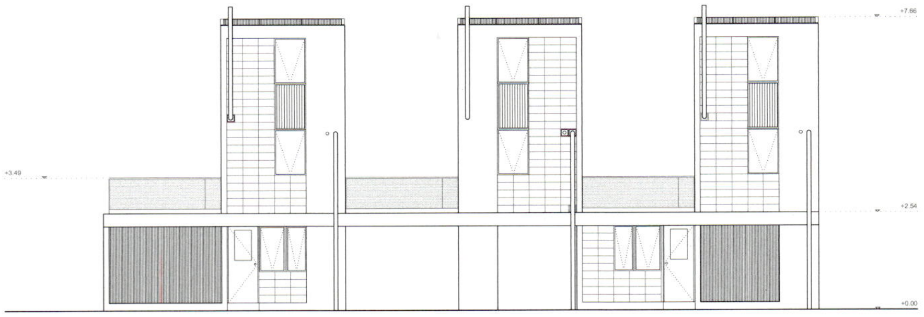

Back Elevation

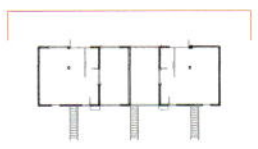

1:200

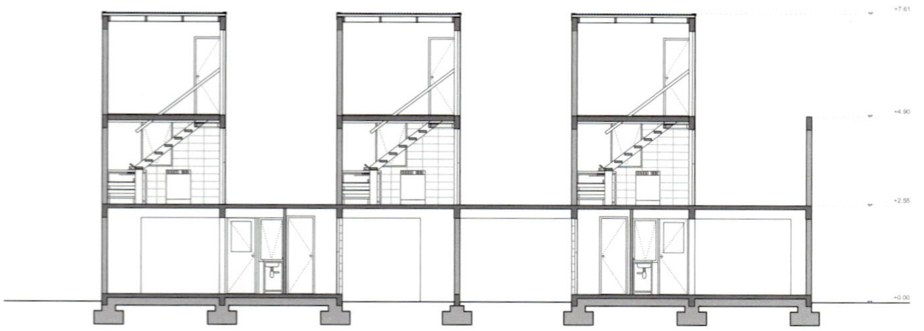

Section 1

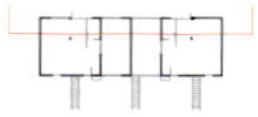

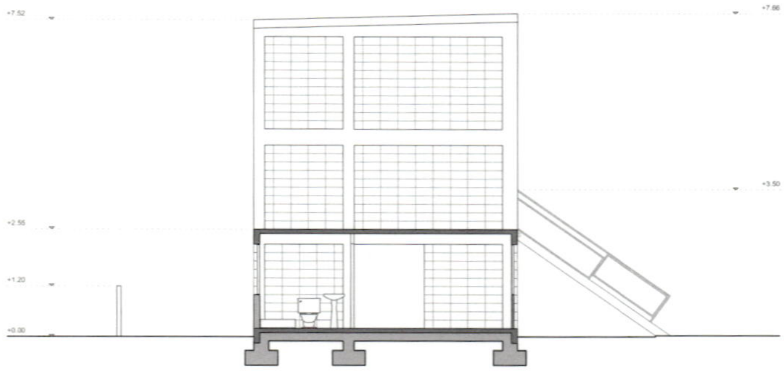

Section 3

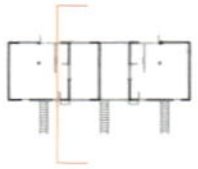

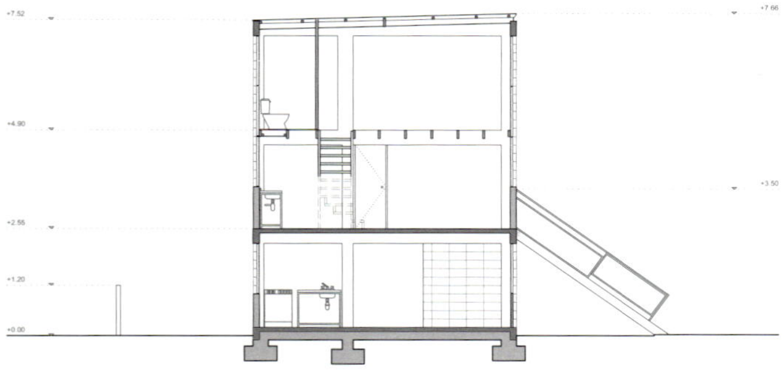

Section 4

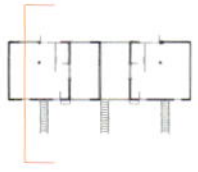

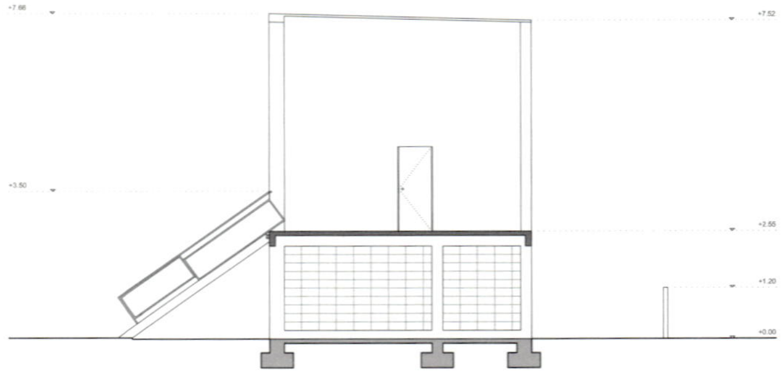

Section 2

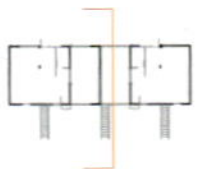

INITIAL CONSTRUCTION

1. Courtyard access to house
2. Dining Room
3. Living Room
4. Bathroom
5. Kitchen

EXTENSION

6. Bedroom 1
7. Bedroom 2
8. Bedroom 3
9. Access Terrace
10. Shop - Workshop
11. Void
12. Terrace

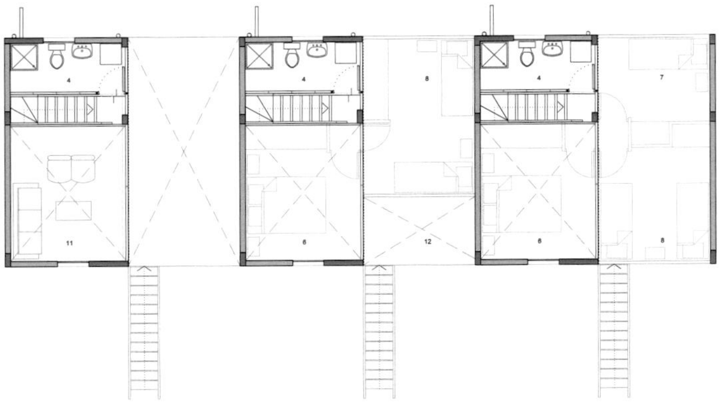

Second Floor. Type B

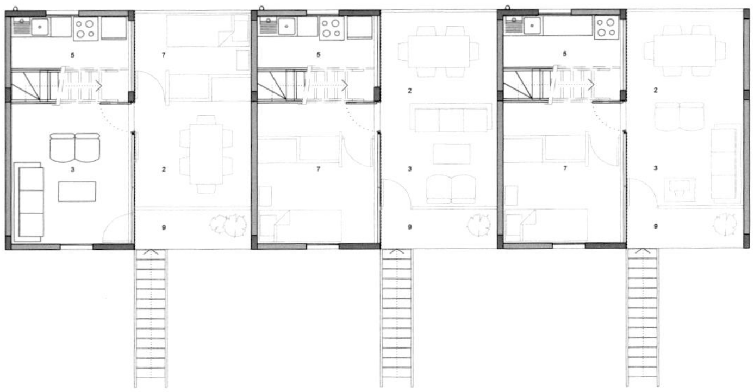

First Floor. Type B

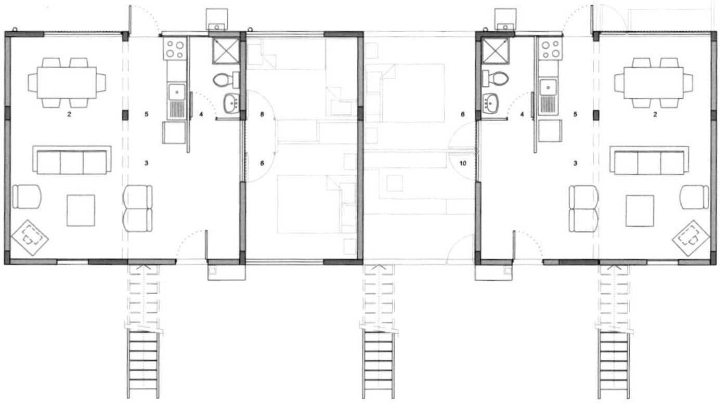

First Floor. Type A

PHILIPS

03

Arup Associates - Arup

DRUK WHITE LOTUS SCHOOL

LADAKH, India

ARUP ASSOCIATES & ARUP

www.arupassociates.com
www.arup.com

LANDLORD	His Holiness the 14th Dalai Lama
FOUNDER	His Holiness the 12th Gyalwang Drukpa
PROMOTERS	Drukpa Trust Druk Padma Karpo Education Society
BUILDER	Sonam Wangdus
PHOTOGRAPHY	Christian Ritchers Roland Reinardy Caroline Sohie

AWARDS Y PUBLICATIOS

AWARDS	2002 World Architecture Award: Best educative building Best asian building Best ecologic building
PUBLICATIONS	"Energy Efficient Architecture", Roberto Gonzalo, Karl J. Habermann, published May 2006 "Design Like You Give a Damn : Architectural Reponses to Humanitarian Crises", Cameron Sinclair May 2006

DATES

BEGINNING OF WORKS	1995
WORK COMPLETION	1st Phase 2001 2nd Phase 2006

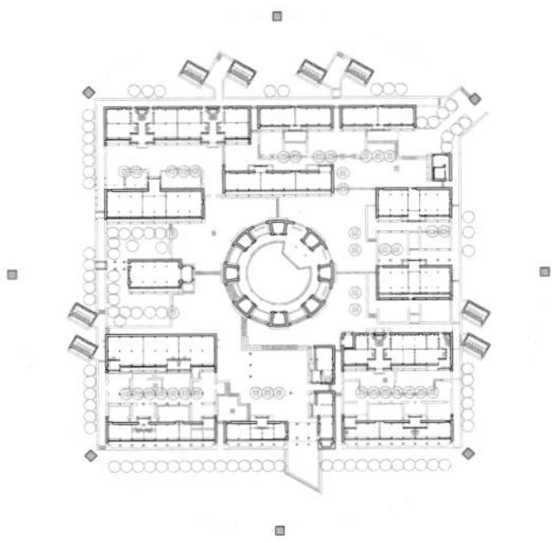

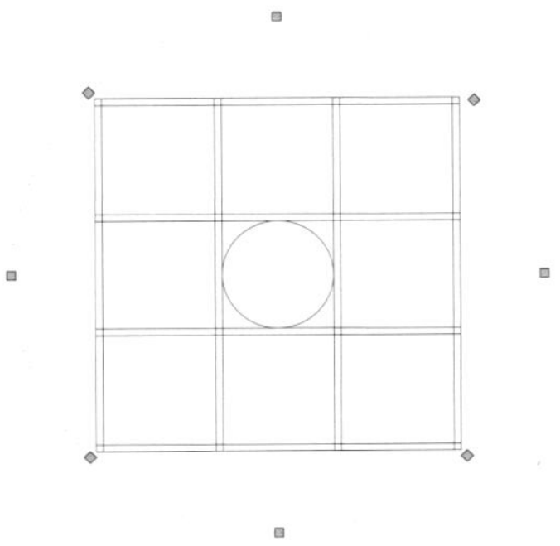

1:3000

DESCRIPTIVE BRIEF

The school is in a small village called Shey, about 16km away from the main city Leh, in the middle of the Ladakh Valley. Also known as "little Tibet", Ladakh is an ancient kingdom in the Indian Himalayas, close to Tibet's western border. This distant desert of high altitude (3500m above sea level) is covered in snow during approximately six months a year, facing winter temperatures of up to -30°C in some areas. Despite this, in the summer the sun heats and the thawing Indus River bring new life to the rich and fertile valleys of the area. The population is mainly Buddhist, with Christian and Muslim minorities; for centuries, the monasteries have been the learning centers and the focal point for the practice of the community's spiritual necessities.

Drukpa Trust, a UK social action association, registered under the sponsorship of the Dalai Lama's S.S. e, initiated the creation of the Druk school in 1999, which was built in phases.

In order to meet the educational necessities of approximately 750 persons, mixing the education of children and pupils of up to 18 years of age, the project is conceived as a model for sustainable modernization in Ladakh, creating a high quality teaching environment and a live community within the school. It offers an academic curricular plan combined with the education necessary for the development of the local community, in a culture which currently suffers a great pressure for change. Even though the project is a local initiative, its context is international, financed by charitable donations from the United Kingdom and Europe, along with the local community.

Masterplan and construction program

The ecological context is fragile, so environmental strategies need to guarantee an entirely self-regulated system considering water, energy and waste management. There are gardens and extensive plantations, and the infrastructure related to the use of water is generated from a well supplied by a pump, driven by solar energy.

The design of the buildings is based on taking maximum advantage of the local climate and the unique solar potential of this altitude (3700m above sea level). Surrounded by the rising peaks which surpass heights of 7000m, the school's building complex is organized in a square grid divided into 9 equal parts, and a circle surrounding it, according to the mandala, a symbolic figure of particular significance in Tibetan tradition (although this underlying symbolic geometry shall be less obvious from the ground).

There are four main areas, interconnected. The first being the entrance to the school, which gives access to pedestrians; the second, the daytime teaching classrooms, and the third, the spine which makes up the residential part that rises to the north. The fourth area, where the well and the energy generating infrastructure are located, is situated next to the service area towards the west.

Construction will continue for six more years. With these first phases complete and functioning, the teaching community's current development is being generated at an accelerated pace. The design team and the confidence of Drukpa Trust look forward to a process of continuous learning about the school's functioning and the results brought about by the lessons learned in the process of sustainable construction.

"We have not inherited the world from our forefathers, we have borrowed it from our children "

Kashmiri proverb

ENVIRONMENTAL ANALYSIS

1. Choosing the site. Project and Development

1.1. Location

Latitude: 37° 06' N
Longitude: 3° 57' 47.59"W

A school complex located in the village of Shey, it is found in the center of the Ladakh Valley. It is defined by the Indus River which crosses the valley at an altitude of 3500m above sealevel and is delimited by the Karakoram and the Himalaya. It is a scarcely settled place whose connection to the south plains is covered in snow during large periods of the year. The desert-like landscape is very hot during the summer and extremely cold in the winter. The location has a high exposure to direct sunlight all year long and minimal rainfall. The water used to irrigate the crops is mainly obtained from the thawed snow, even though there are aquiferous layers in the area.

1.2 Urban Design and Site Improvement

The ecological environment is fragile, so the project seeks to guarantee a closed self-regulated system that manages water, energy and waste. The project's biggest success is that it's inclusion in this particular environment attempts a minimum impact on the existing ecosystem. A multidisciplinary team formed by specialists in urbanism, environment and anti-seismic construction worked on the development of a Master Plan that undertook the definition, design and construction in phases, with the goal to implant itself in an organized manner into the natural environment.

The buildings planned on one level are orientated along a north-south axis and are open towards the south and the south-east in order to optimize the morning sun. Because of its placement, a solution was opted for which will foster vernacular construction techniques. These techniques applied in singular buildings, like the monasteries of the region, are rich in the use of local materials such as soil and wood.

Water is a limited resource in the region and its use is regulated in the communities, in a way the even the landscape is defined by the irrigation networks within the valley. In the very same way, the water distribution system of this project is clearly recognizable in the final design and forms an integral part of the school's educational program, which promotes the hygiene and care of this scarce resource.

1.3 Project

In the layout of the buildings one can find symbolic spiritual connotations, borrowed from the Buddhist culture, like the mandala and the path of life. The buildings are defined by two uses: school and residence. The composition of the school is based on the structure of a mandala. It is divided in nine equal squares: the central one is destined to a space of communal use and the eight perimeter squares contain the classrooms, conceived as autonomous units.

The school is delimited by a path which makes up the borders of the square. The latrines are separated like singular elements of the composition. Their rotation in relation to the rest of the

Site Image

ensemble is due to the southern orientation of the walls, which facilitates organic decomposition, thanks to solar radiation.

The buildings destined to residential use are placed in a linear axis from the school up to the existing temple on the summit. They are also planned as autonomous blocks. The blocks on the right side are positioned with the same alternation between full and empty. On the left side, the disposition of the units is neither constant, nor aligned between themselves. This variation on each side of the path breaks the monotony of the linear axis towards the temple.

Each autonomous unit is accessed through a tree-covered patio, from which you can reach the remaining spaces. Each building is made up of three opaque sides with small openings. The third [fourth] side is glazed because of an environmental determinant and relates the interior space with the patio.

2. Consumption of Energy and Resources

2.1 Consumption of Energy

The energy load attributable to the building's construction has been reduced through the increased use of local materials and intense manpower. Another success of the project was the maximized solar exposure already considered in the design phase, saving energy in the conditioning of interiors. It is important to note the use of passive control elements, such as the Trombe walls in the residences or the dry latrines in which, by way of a double chamber and a solar chimney, an air stream facilitates the waste decomposition, avoiding unpleasant odors and the presence of flies, and at the same time generates manure which can be used in the gardens of the complex.

2.2 Consumption of Water

This is a key element of the Environmental Master Plan. Completed in 2001, the water system was the first phase of the project to be completed. The water supply begins at a pump driven by solar energy which extracts subterranean water and introduces it through gravity into the complex. The domestic wastewater is absorbed and later piped, through a trickle irrigation system, in order to water the project's trees. The use of these latrines, which make no use of water as a waste conveying element, is an example of the careful study of the idiosyncrasy of the inhabitants of the area, who are not habituated to a running water network and stable electric energy supply.

2.3 Consumption of Materials

The use of local materials such as stone, adobe, wood and straw was encouraged; along with intense manpower. One can observe an interesting reinterpretation of vernacular construction techniques, adapted in order to obtain comfortable spaces with adequate seismic resistance. The granite stone applied on the walls is found onsite and the soil used in the mortar, blocks and roofs was excavated right next to the construction site. The poplar and willow wood used in the ceiling's bearing structures was acquired from local producers. The cement and glass employed was obtained from distributors of the Cachemira Region, in order to reduce its energy impact due to transport.

3. Environmental Loads

3.1 Emissions

Favoring local materials and reducing the environmental load due to transport, reduces the emissions attributable to the constructive process. The use of solar energy and temperature-controlling passive elements influences energy consumption in a positive way and consequently in the emissions due to the operation of the complex.

3.2 Solid Waste

As prime materials, the waste caused by construction [stone, soil, straw] return to their point of origin, closing a simple circle of use.

It is worth paying attention to the manner in which solid waste, generated by the operation of the building, is being treated. The use of dry latrines results in the reuse of the users' organic waste in form of fertilizer for the projects' gardens, instead of just being transported via water.

3.3 Water Management

In consideration of its scarce existence, and as a fundamental element of the project, its reused has been especially cared for. A system was designed which takes advantage the aquiferous layers of the site for the project. The cycle was completed through treatment and recycling of the used water, by way of irrigating the vegetation on site.

4. Interior Environmental Quality

4.1 Ventilation

The roofs bearing structure, made of wood frames, is structurally independent from the facades. These were positioned in a way which facilitates the natural ventilation of the spaces. The walls of bigger thermal inertia are complemented with Trombe walls in the residential area. These are oriented towards the south in order to facilitate heat gain and dispose of workable openings in the upper and lower parts. The north walls have fewer openings to avoid heat loss, but enough of them to be able to alternately control air-flows which, at different temperatures, guarantee the conditioning and air-renovation in the spaces.

4.2 Natural Lighting

The same structural concept enables the arrangement of windows primarily oriented to the south, guaranteeing natural lighting in the spaces. The wooden frames project out from the southern facade, filtering the light and avoiding direct solar exposure in the summer with wooden shading elements.

4.3 Acoustics

The general arrangement of area separations and the isolated buildings avoid causing any acoustic interference between the spaces of different use: daytime-school / nighttime-residential. Either way the projects' character favors interaction, not isolation, thus this aspect is not dominant in the complex's design and function.

5. Control of Construction System

5.1 Functionality and Efficiency

The adopted construction system has considered vernacular techniques, a fundamental fact when securing the collaboration of local craftsmen, reducing the influence of foreign techniques and materials. The waste generated by a construction activity with a low grade of industrialization is minimized through the use of native materials (soil, stone and straw), closing their cycle by simply returning them to their place of extraction.

The appropriate combination of vernacular techniques with passive control systems was achieved, like in the Trombe walls of the residences and dry latrines.

5.2 Control of Construction System

The users participate actively in the control of some of the applied conditioning devices. The apertures of the Trombe walls can be opened or closed in the residences, in order to permit air circulation at different temperatures. On the other hand simple systems, like wooden panes in addition to double glazing and dense interior curtains, reduce the heat loss during the night.

6. Long-term Performance

6.1 Flexibility and Adaptability

The vernacular techniques used within a simple structural system, with the load-bearing structure independent from the enclosure, have allowed open and flexible spaces, permitting the application of the same system for the project's two principal uses: education and residence.

6.2 Maintenance and Operative Performance

The use of local manpower during the construction process has taught the local craftsmen the compatibility of their techniques with passive environmental control systems. Good construction practice which makes use of elements of the natural environment allows the reproduction of the solution. For instance, the system employed in the classroom walls, in which the north, east and west facades are made up of an exterior wall of granite-stone joined with soil mortar and an interior adobe wall; This improves the elements' thermal behavior and guarantees its durability in comparison to adobe walls covered with soil commonly used in the region.

7. Economic and Social Aspects

7.1 Social Aspects

Another key element of the project was the careful study and integration of the idiosyncrasy of the inhabitants while defining the Master Plan. The architectural program was defined in parallel with the school's curricular program in which modern educational concepts (Montessori) were integrated with Buddhist practices and principles.

Involving the users in the definition and execution of the project, they develop a feeling of appropriation towards the constructed solution. The respect towards their idiosyncrasy is reflected in the plastic expression of the employed local materials and in the optimization of the systems, like the dry latrines, similar to the local customs.

7.2 Economic Aspects

The optimization of the construction systems, like the adobe, improved by the incorporation of an external stone wall, guarantees its durability and reduces maintenance costs. The use of local materials favors commercial exchange with local producers and facilitates the supply of stock materials. The improvement of vernacular constructive techniques implies an improvement in the local constructors' abilities, and favors the reproduction of the adopted technical solutions.

8. The Architect's Eye

It is discovered while observing the project, and the places and the designer's culture are interchanged.

From the Master Plan until the definition of each building's typology, native symbolic elements have been applied like the mandala structure, for instance, while designing the complex; not only as an anecdotal or decorative element.

The technological contribution is adapted to the place's idiosyncrasy, like in the latrine's case; in which a system, which successfully combines materials and orientation, allows the acceleration of a natural organic cycle.

1. Daycare and Pre-school Education
2. Professor's Residence
3. Work Area
4. Service Area
5. Kitchen + Dining Area
6. Solar Latrines
7. Primary School
8. Entrance to Primary School
9. Multi-purpose Space
10. Primary School Education

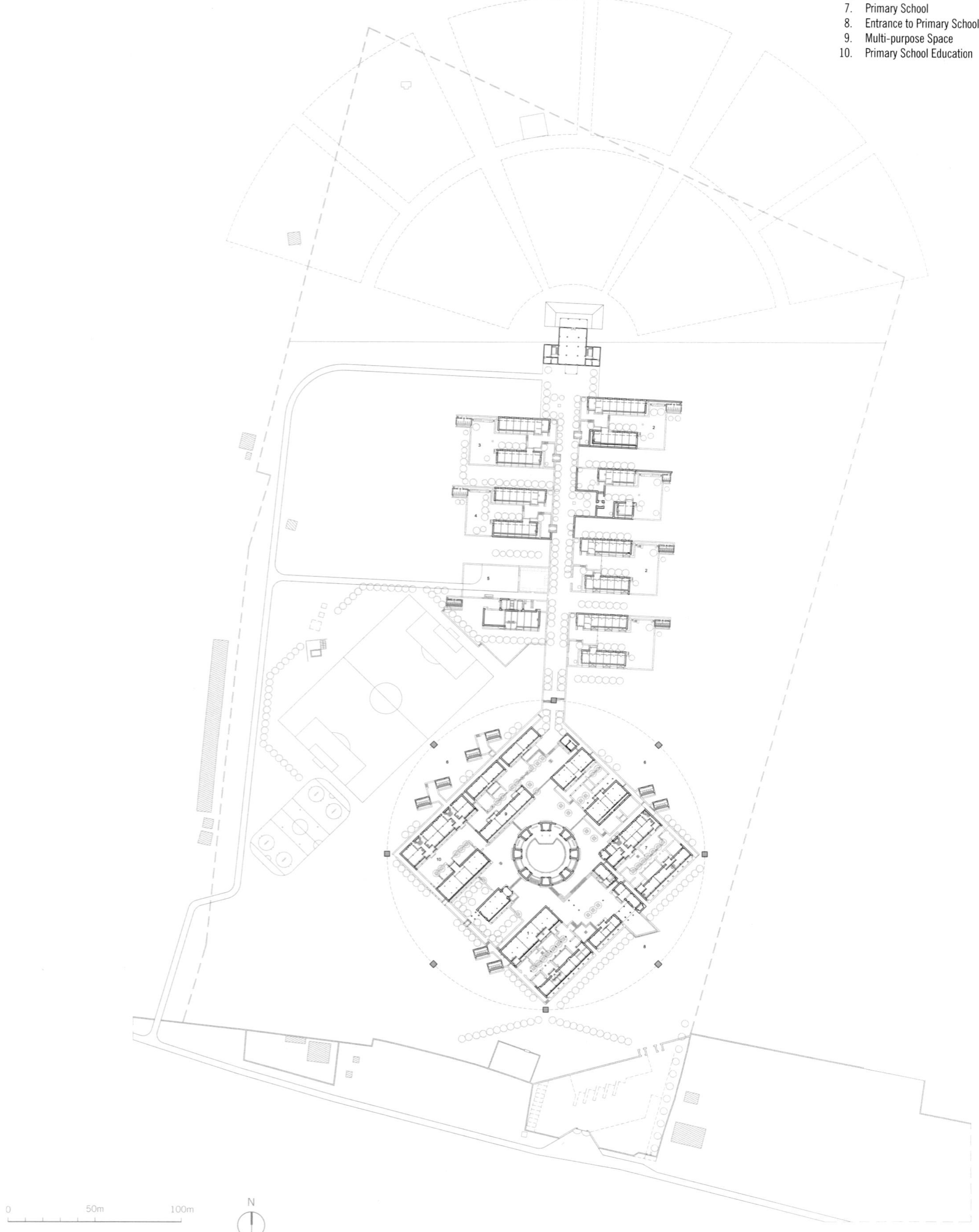

1:3000

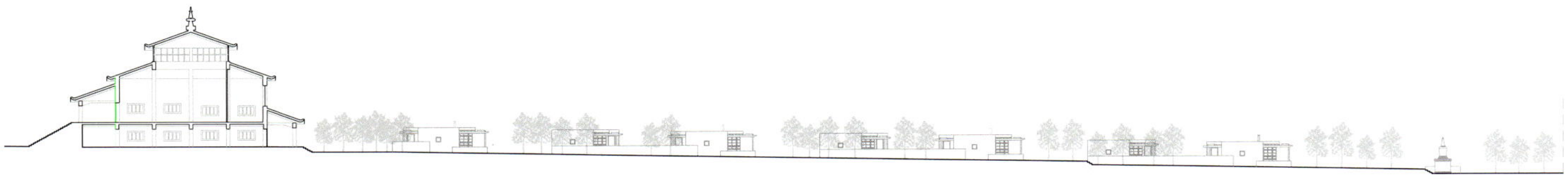

Section 1

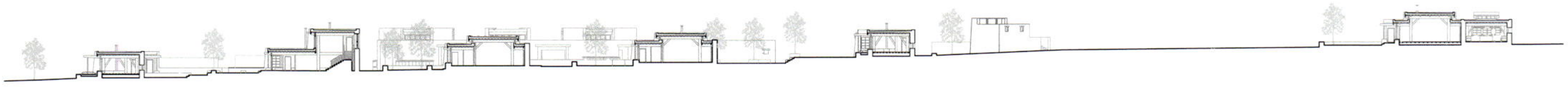

Section 2

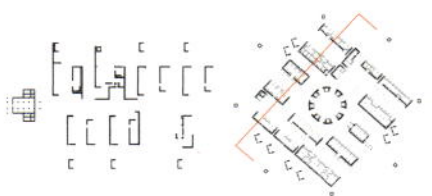

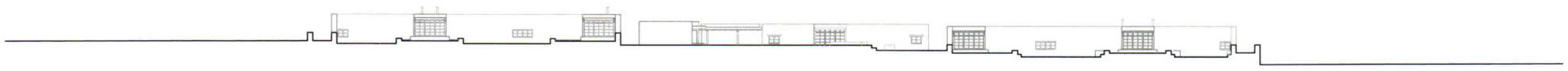

Section 4

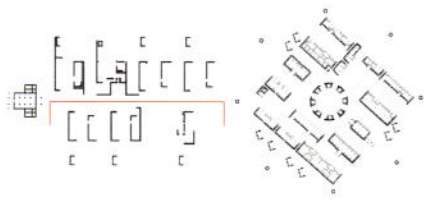

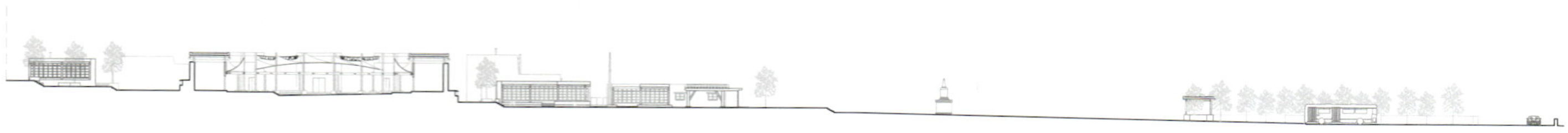

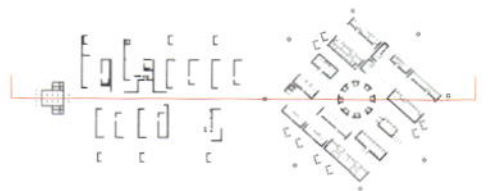

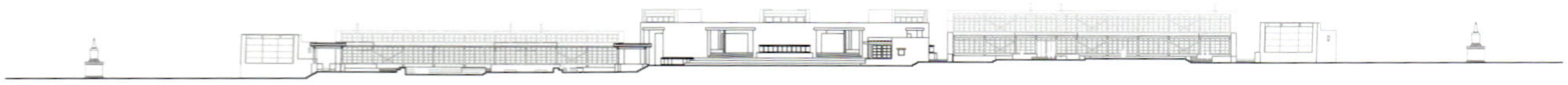

Section 3

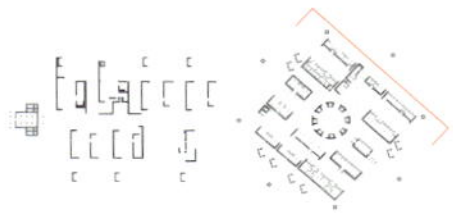

0 5 10m

1:500

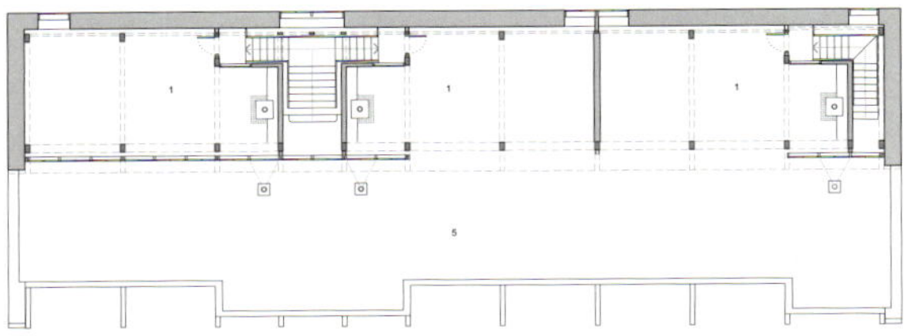

Upper Floor Level. Primary School Education

0 5 10m
1:500

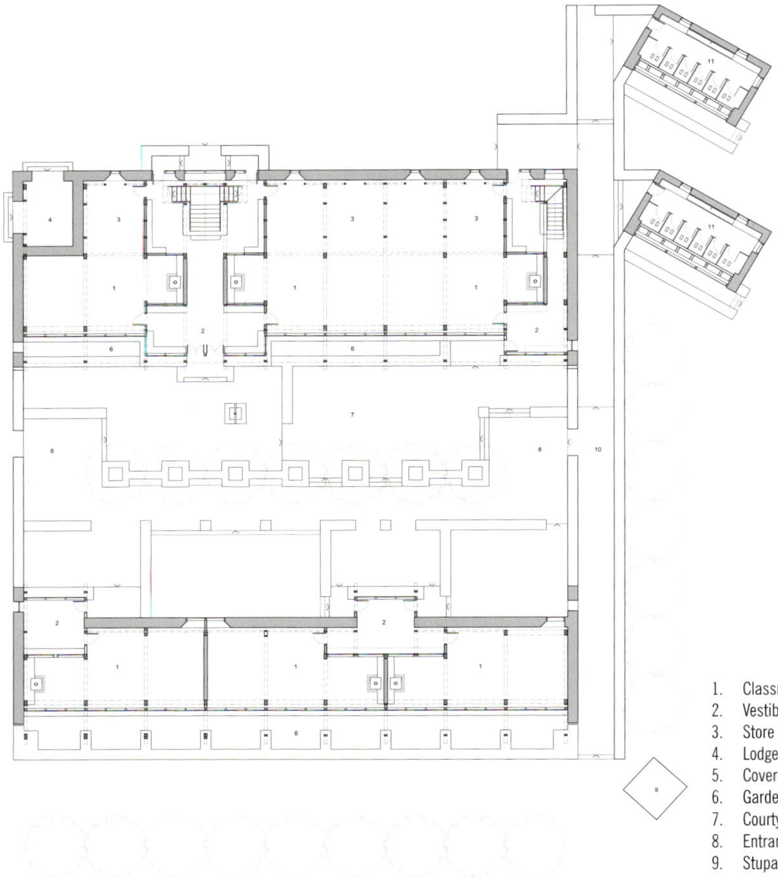

1. Classrooms
2. Vestibule
3. Store
4. Lodge
5. Covered Terrace
6. Garden Area
7. Courtyard
8. Entrance
9. Stupa
10. Hallway towards Service Area
11. Solar Latrines

Ground floor level. Primary School Education

Section B

0 5 10m
1:300

JUNIOR 3B

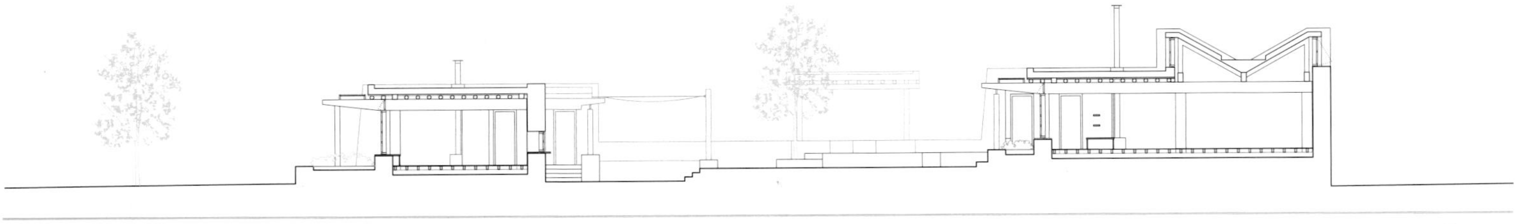

Section A

0 5 10m

1:300

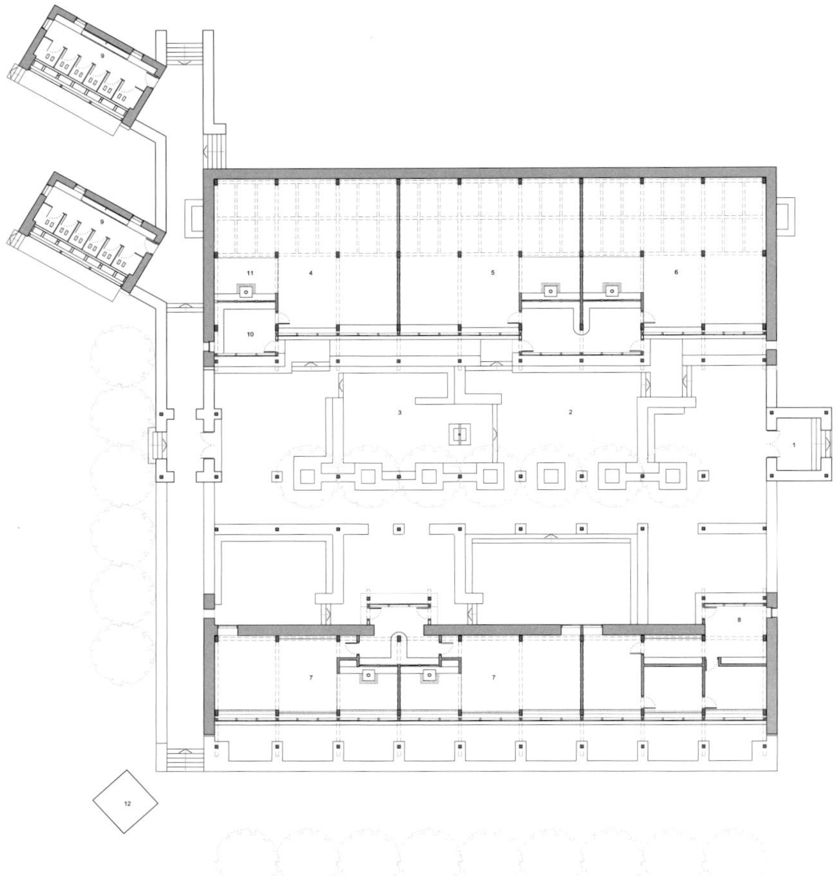

1. Courtyard Entrance
2. Outdoor Study Areas
3. Fountain and Play Area
4. Daycare
5. Classrooms 1
6. Classrooms 2
7. Children's Classroom 1st year
8. Professor Room
9. Solar Latrines
10. Lockers
11. Meditation Area
12. Stupa

Ground floor level. Daycare And Pre-School

0 5 10m

1:500

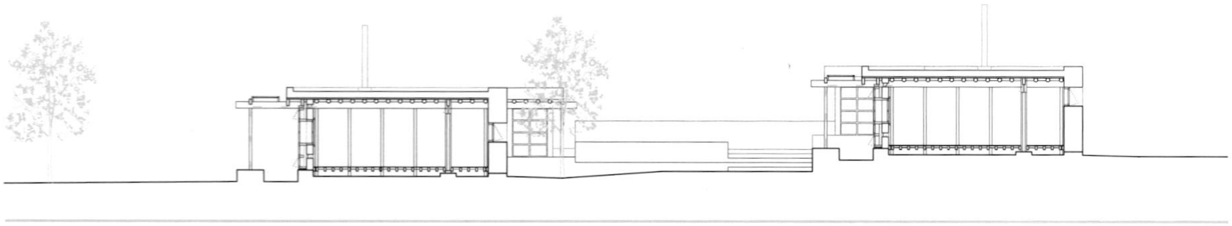

Section D

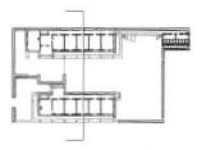

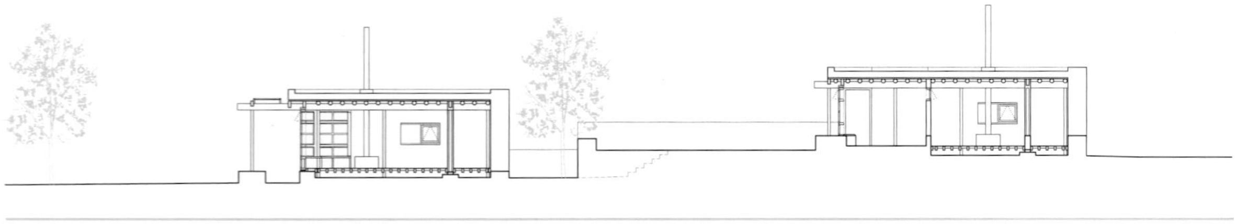

Section E

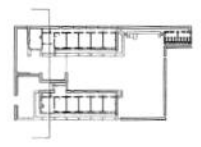

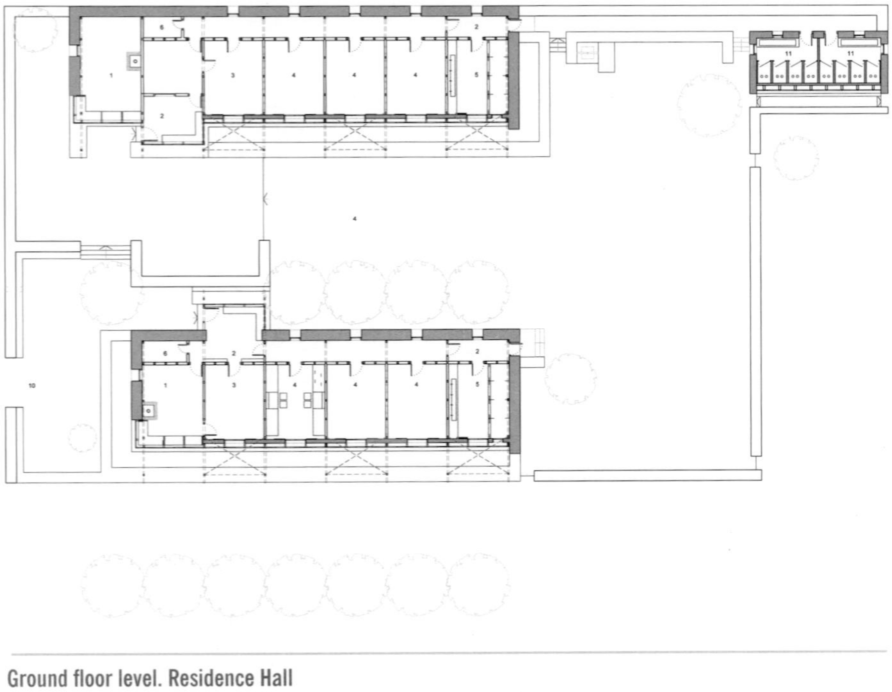

1. Living Room
2. Vestibule
3. Professor Dormitories
4. Student Dormitories
5. Wash Area
6. Store
7. Hallway
8. Bed of Flowers
9. Courtyard
10. Entrance Door
11. Solar Latrines

Ground floor level. Residence Hall

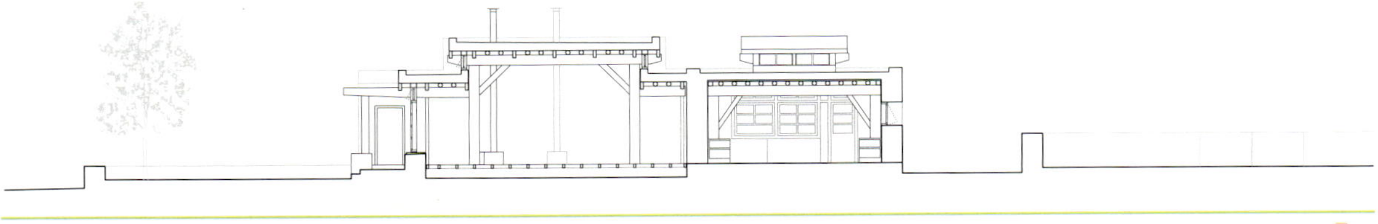

Sección C

0 5 10m
1:300

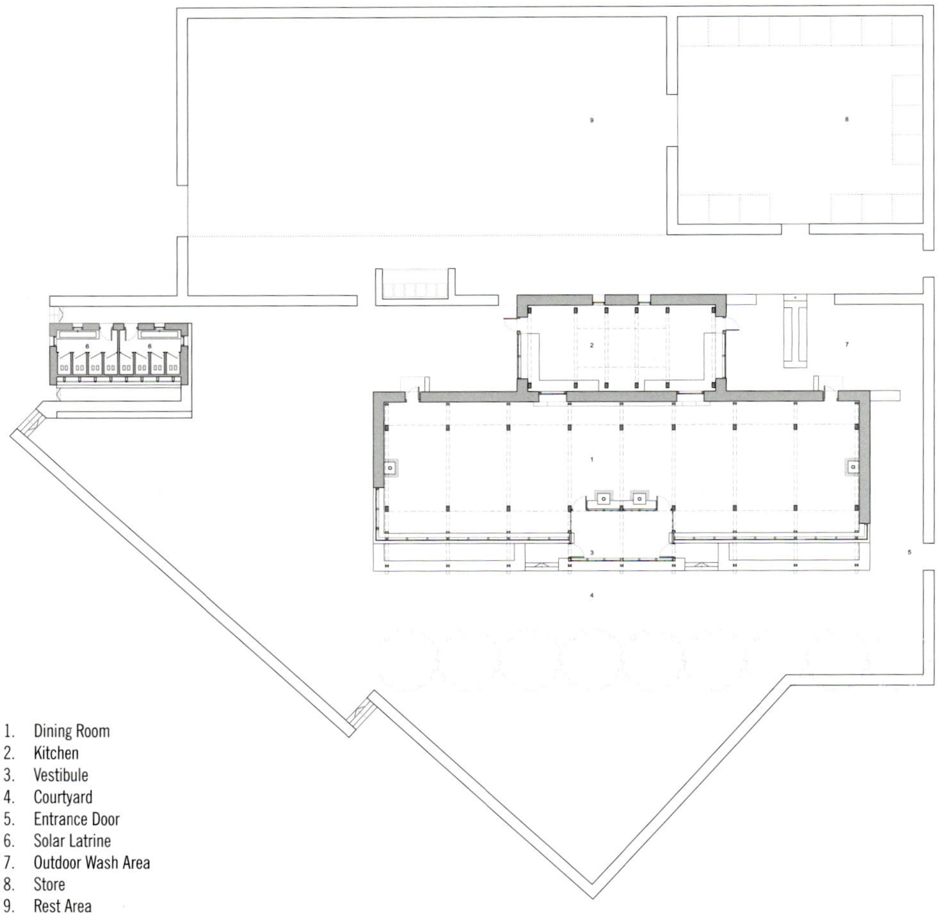

1. Dining Room
2. Kitchen
3. Vestibule
4. Courtyard
5. Entrance Door
6. Solar Latrine
7. Outdoor Wash Area
8. Store
9. Rest Area

Ground floor level. Dining Hall

0 5 10m
1:500

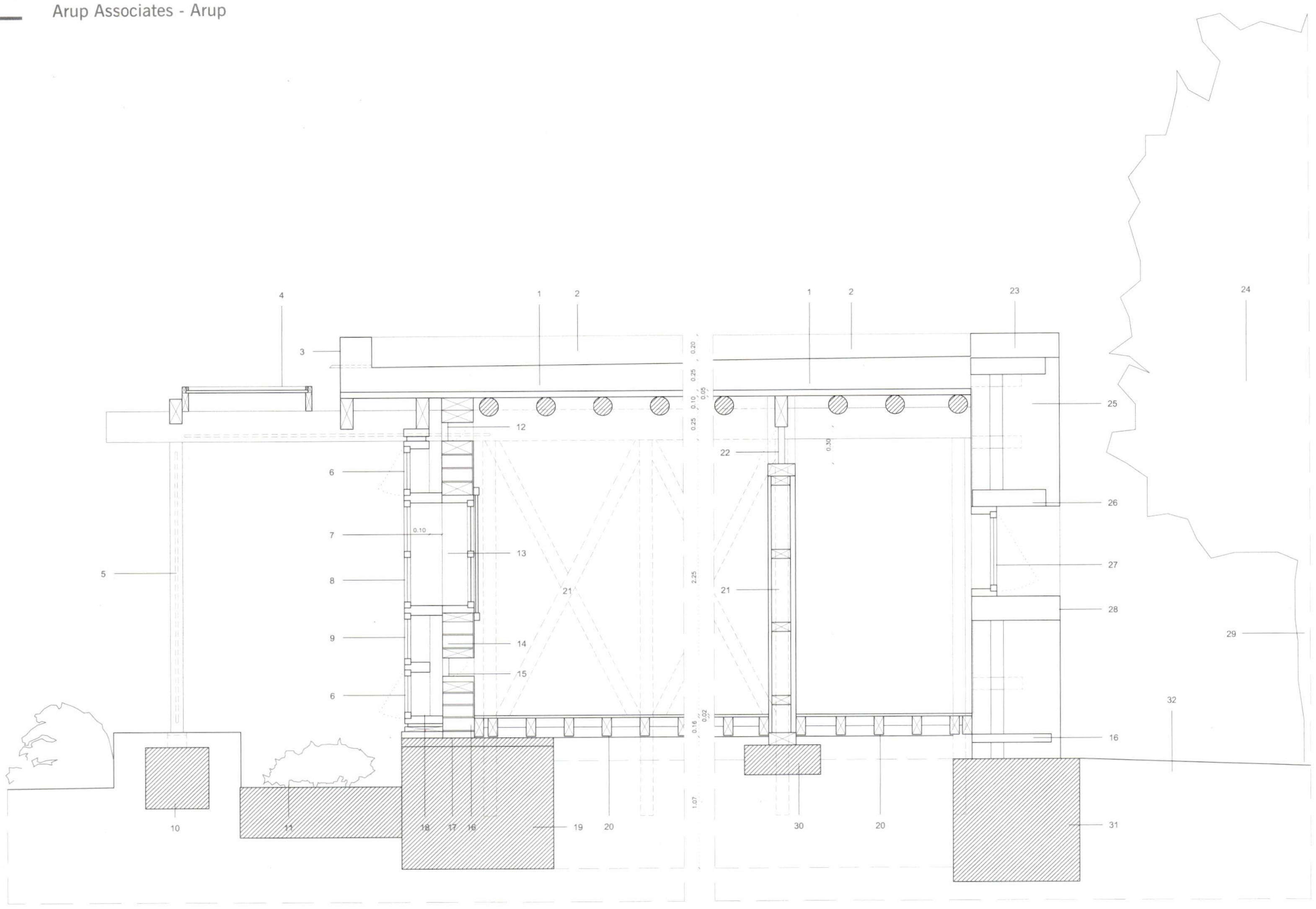

Section Detail 1

1:50

From the old times, adobe or stone thick walls have been used to capture sun heat during the daylight and to transmit it slowly and uniformly towards room interior in the night time. Some buildings use a storing and giving heat thermal system called Trombe wall, thus called by its French inventor Félix Trombe 50 years ago. The thick wall is externally coated with a dark coloured material to capture heat towards internal side by means of a glazing unit, well simple or double one, separated by 100-150mm to create an air chamber. Natural heat going through glass is absorbed by the dark surface, then stored in the chamber, and slowly driven inside through building work. Apertures in upper and lower part of the internal wall allow a heat transfer by means of convection and thus increasing the system's efficiency.

1. Roof: 150mm diameter joists, positioned between beams.
   Willow tree wood supports of 50mm, layer of adobe of 250mm of which 50mm are clay for waterproofing.
2. Parapet
3. Exposed surface with grainy finish, painted black for protection of wood.
   Traditional ladakhi detail
4. Seasonal panels (only summer) of Willow with detachable fabric for shading device
5. Steel support in cross form
6. Window with double glazing. Fixed central pane.
7. 100mm space between windows and Trombe wall for air circulation
8. Double enameled window. Air cavity for Trombe wall.
9. Fixed glazed window with double enamel.
10. Stone finish over concrete foundation. Between footings, placement of stone instead of concrete.
11. Plant bed for flowers
12. Internal control of ventilation. The steel ring is placed directly over the central panel
13. Double enameled glazing with seal in wood panels
14. Adobe wall reinforced with wood shavings of 200mm thickness. Finished with blue/black paint towards exterior, which functions as Trombe wall and painted with native decorative motifs. Painted adobe mortar as interior finish.
15. Manual ventilation device
16. Waterproofed footing
17. Baseboard
18. Wooden crossbeam
19. Footing for fastening wooden framework.
20. Floor: wooden planks of150mm x 75mm. Wooden joists over concrete dpc. 75mm x 150mm. Joists each 300mm on axis.
21. Wood column. Joint bolt between columns and fillet; finished in painted plaster; interior walls with acoustic insulation; wooden framework and structural connections.
22. Seal nº 2 in bedrooms
23. Stone piece; support for concrete beams
24. Access
25. Brick walls of 700mm thickness. Outside layer of 450mm, finished with layer of adobe of150mm. Interior adobe wall of 600mm; Air chamber of 100mm, finished on the interior of mud mortar painted white.
26. Concrete lintel
27. Double enameled glazed window
28. Stone block
29. Native trees
30. Granite base. Concrete foundation for support of columns
31. Walls of 700mm thickness, centered over footings of 1000mm with a depth equal to or greater than 1000mm
32. Compacted Adobe

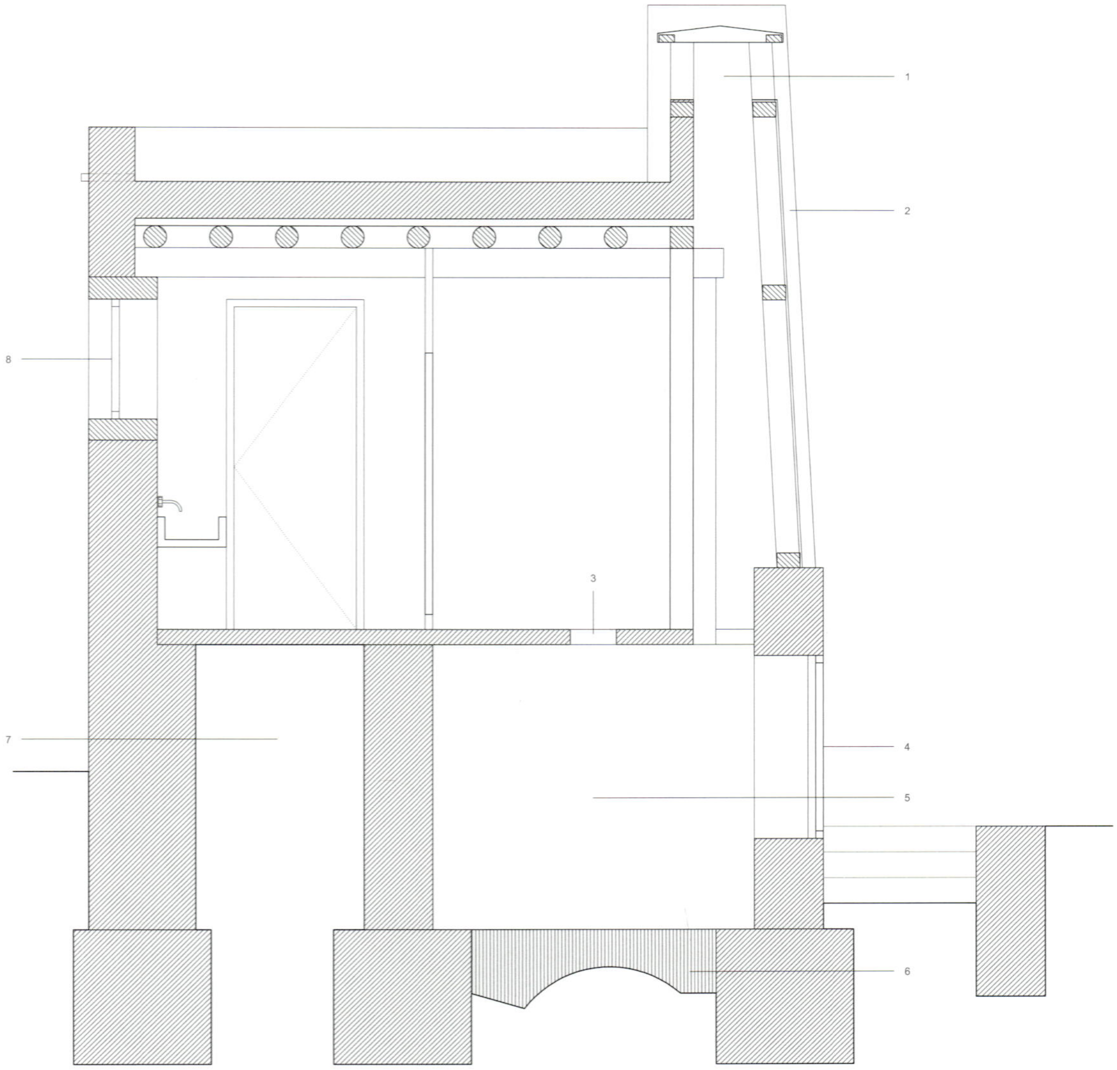

Section Detail of Solar Latrine

1. Hot air rises through the pipe, taking with it flies, odors, and humidity
2. Black metal finish heats the solar pipe
3. Cold air is sucked into the trench together with flies and odors
4. Access door to empty trench
5. Dry waste of plant manure in twin trenches
6. Filter towards the terrain of liquid waste
7. Drainage
8. Minimal entrance of natural light

04

Hotson Bakker Boniface Haden

NK'MIP DESERT CULTURAL CENTRE

BRITISH COLUMBIA, Canada

Hotson Bakker Boniface Haden
Architects + Urbanistes

http://www.hotsonbakker.com/

MAIN ARCHITECT	Bruce Haden
PROJECT MANAGER	Brady Dunlop
COLLABORATORS	Norm Hotson, Stephanie Forsythe, Tina Hubert, Julie Bogdanowicz
PROJECT MANAGEMENT	Tim Brown
PHOTOGRAPHY	Hotson Bakker Boniface Haden
	COLLABORATING COMPANIES
Contractor	Greyback Construction
Structuctural Analysis	Equilibrium Consulting Inc.
Mecanical Engineer	Cobalt Engineering
Electrical Engineer	MCL Engineering
Landscape	Phillips Farevaag Smallenberg
Acoustics	BKL Consulting
	PRIZES AND PUBLICATIONS
	New Institutional Architecture Award - RAIA Victorian Architecture Awards 2005
	DATES
IMPLEMENTATION PROJECT	2004
BEGINNING OF WORKS	2005
WORK COMPLETION	JUNIO 2006

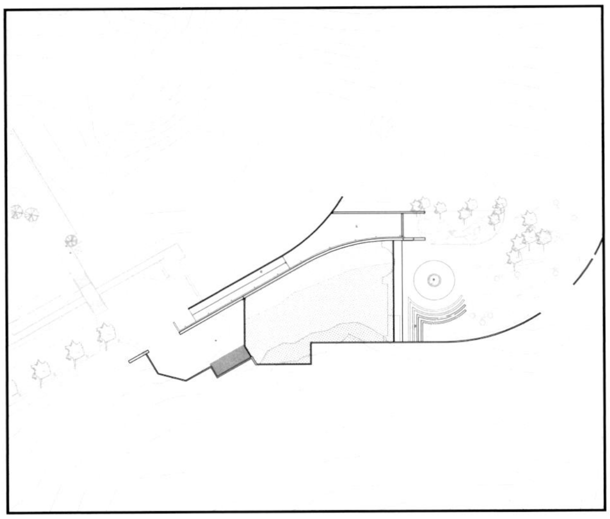

Site Plan

DESCRIPTIVE BRIEF

The Nk'Mip Desert Cultural Centre is designed to be a specific and sustainable response to the building's unique context—the unusual Canadian desert found south of the Okanagan Valley in Osoyoos, British Columbia. Sited adjacent to a remnant of the Great Basin Desert (approximately 1,600 acres are being preserved by the band as a conservation area), this interpretative centre is part of a larger 200-acre master plan that includes a winery, golf club, and a resort hotel.

Nk'Mip is the first of a number of new B.C. aboriginal centres, and part of a growing trend to explore the expressive potential of architecture to convey the rich past and the transforming future of aboriginal culture. The practical reasons behind this architectural exploration grow out of provincial leadership—a premier whose efforts to improve aboriginal relations have resulted in changes to the treaty process—as well as a shift in the regulatory environment governing the types of buildings permitted on reserve land.

The building features indoor and outdoor exhibits that celebrate the culture and the history of the band, and is designed to be an extension of the remarkable site, and reflects the band's role as stewards of the land. The desert landscape flows over the building's green roof, held back by a rammed earth wall. The partially submerged building is sited very specifically to focus the visitor's eye away from the encroaching development of Osoyoos to the west, with the height of the wall set to create a layered view of the desert rising up in the middle ground, receding to the riparian landscape adjacent, and the mountains in the distance.

The attenuated entry sequence from the parking area moves visitors through a series of nested concrete walls up to an entry plaza at the end of the rammed earth wall. The plaza—used for collecting large groups, and signage about events of the day—leads along a low concrete wall that separates the original desert landscape and the building. This route is further defined by channel of water that draws people towards the entry, past the cor-ten steel gate of the service court and administration access. Entry into the interpretive centre occurs at the midpoint of the gently arcing wall. Inside, a theatre and "black box" exhibition space present information about the band and its historical relationship with the land. The round volume of the "pit house" at the centre of the exhibition space invokes the experience of conversation around a fire. From here, visitors move through a glazed wall into exterior exhibit space featuring information on native planting, an outdoor performance area and amphitheatre, a tule mat teepee, a large figural sculpture, and a snake research area demonstration space. This area also serves as a trailhead for guided and unguided walks along 50 kilometres of paths through the desert. Small interpretive pavilions and a village of reconstructed pit houses and interpretive sculptures punctuate these trails.

"Architects are the moderators between the objective world of building and the poetic world of living".

Owen A. Rose

ENVIRONMENTAL ANALYSIS

1. Choosing the Site. Project and Development

1.1 Location

Latitude: 49º09'22"N
Longitude: 119º14'15"O
Altitude: 1822 m

Placed in a singular location, this project has been posed as a sustainable response to a unique context: The center of a 1,600 acre reserve in Great Basin Canadian desert located South of Okangan valley in Osoyoos, British Columbia. This region is home of the Osoyoos Indians, members of the Okanaga Nation that expands throughout the south of the United States and joins several tribes under a common language. This location is featured by its dry winters and summers, with average temperature oscillations between – 18ºC and 33ºC (40ºC in the summer).

1.2 Urban design and Site Improvement

This project represents an extension of the site on which sits, and this is its greatest success. The relationship with its environment has been simplified, establishing a relationship that joins the natural space with the inhabited space. A desert landscape flows over a green roof supported partly by a compacted earth wall that integrates the ensemble in the site. The incorporation of native plants on the roof makes the site permeable, minimizing the impact generated by construction in a natural reserve.

1.3 Project

The extreme dry and arid climate conditions of where this project is located made the bioclimatic design of the complex a true challenge. In order to solve it, the designers used two main strategies: the building's position and orientation.

. The first one was solved by partially burying the complex to take advantage of the land's thermal inertia, minimizing indoor temperature oscillations.

. With the second, solar passive performance is optimized reducing apertures to the west and favoring filtered solar light from the north and south.

The building's program necessities has been concentrated formally in a wall, shaped into a volume that allows it to relate with the landscape, both because of its dimensions and its materiality. A wall is a limit, on the one side the natural landscape, and on the other the building and its program of necessities.

Three levels of relationship between the building and environment can be detected. The first one is at the approach, marked by the horizontality of the earth wall. The second level is accessed through a ramp that takes visitors to the north side of the building where outdoor exhibitions take place. The round volume in the exhibitions' central space invokes the experience of conversation around a fire. Finally, one reaches the interior, third semi-buried level; closed to the east by the mountain and to the west by the isolating mud wall which, with its micro perforations, reminds us of the extreme outdoor conditions.

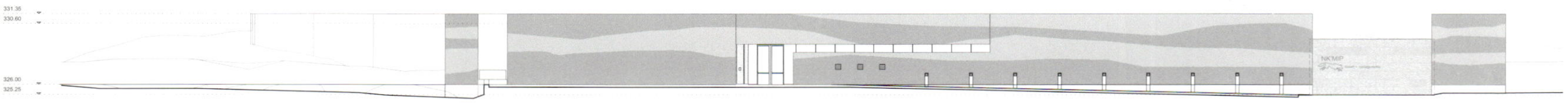

West Elevation

0 5 10m

1:500

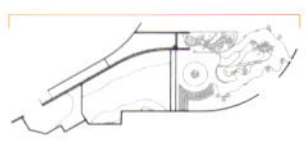

Welcome to the Nk'Mip Desert Cultural Centre

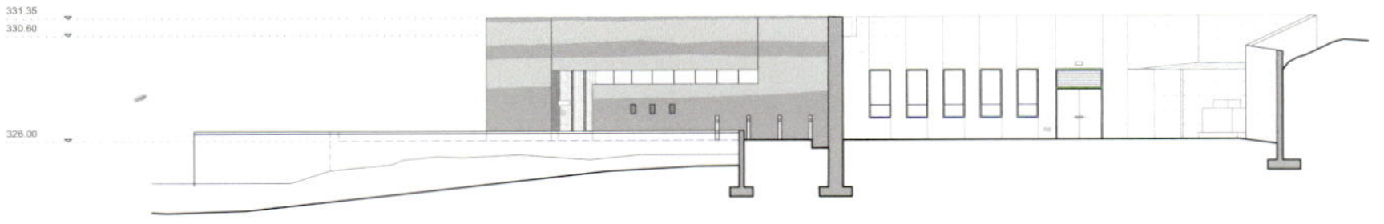

South Elevation

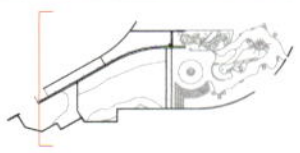

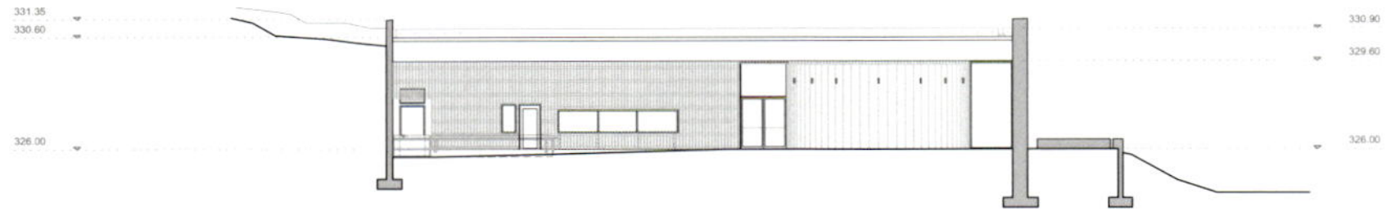

North Elevation

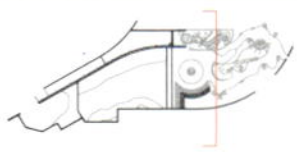

0 5 10m

1:500

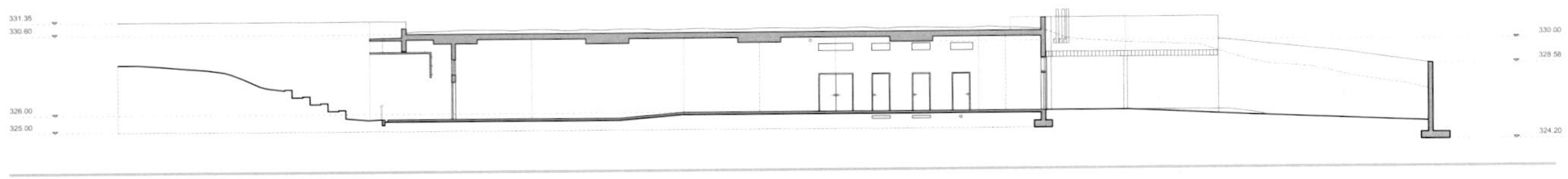

Section 1

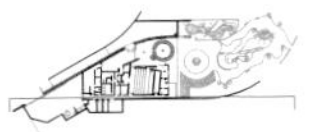

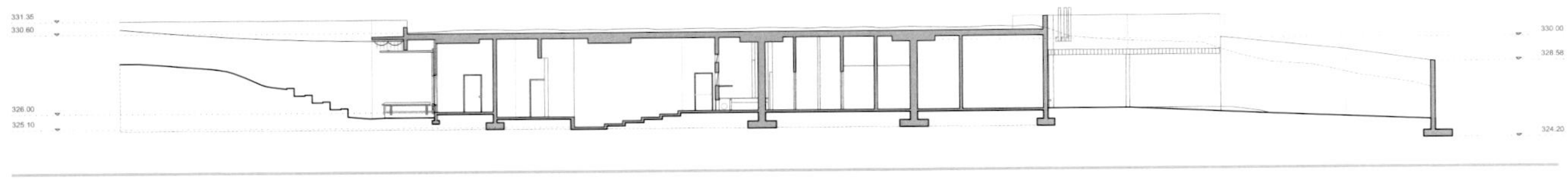

Section 2

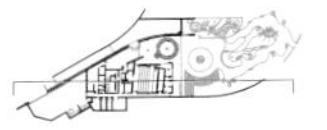

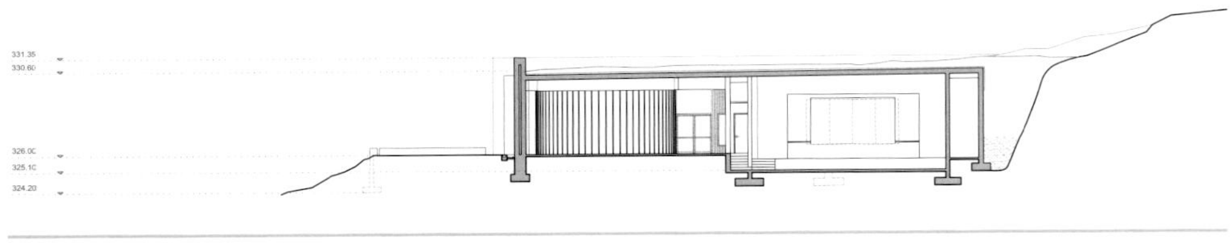

Section 3

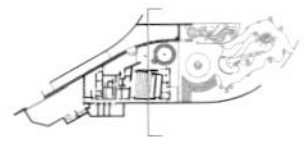

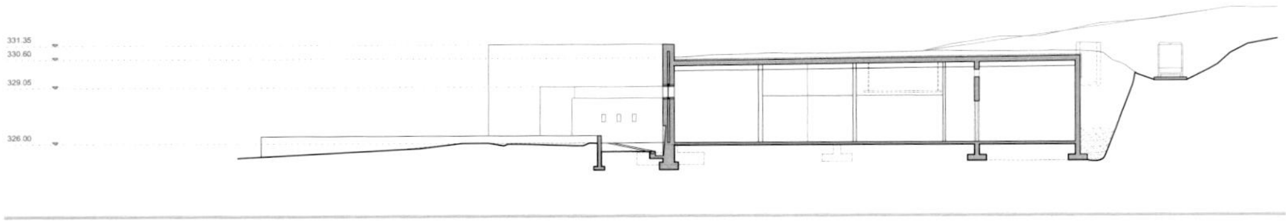

1:500

Section 4

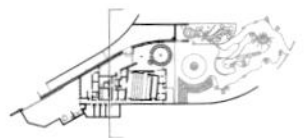

NK'MIP DESERT CULTURAL CENTRE

Hotson Bakker Boniface Haden

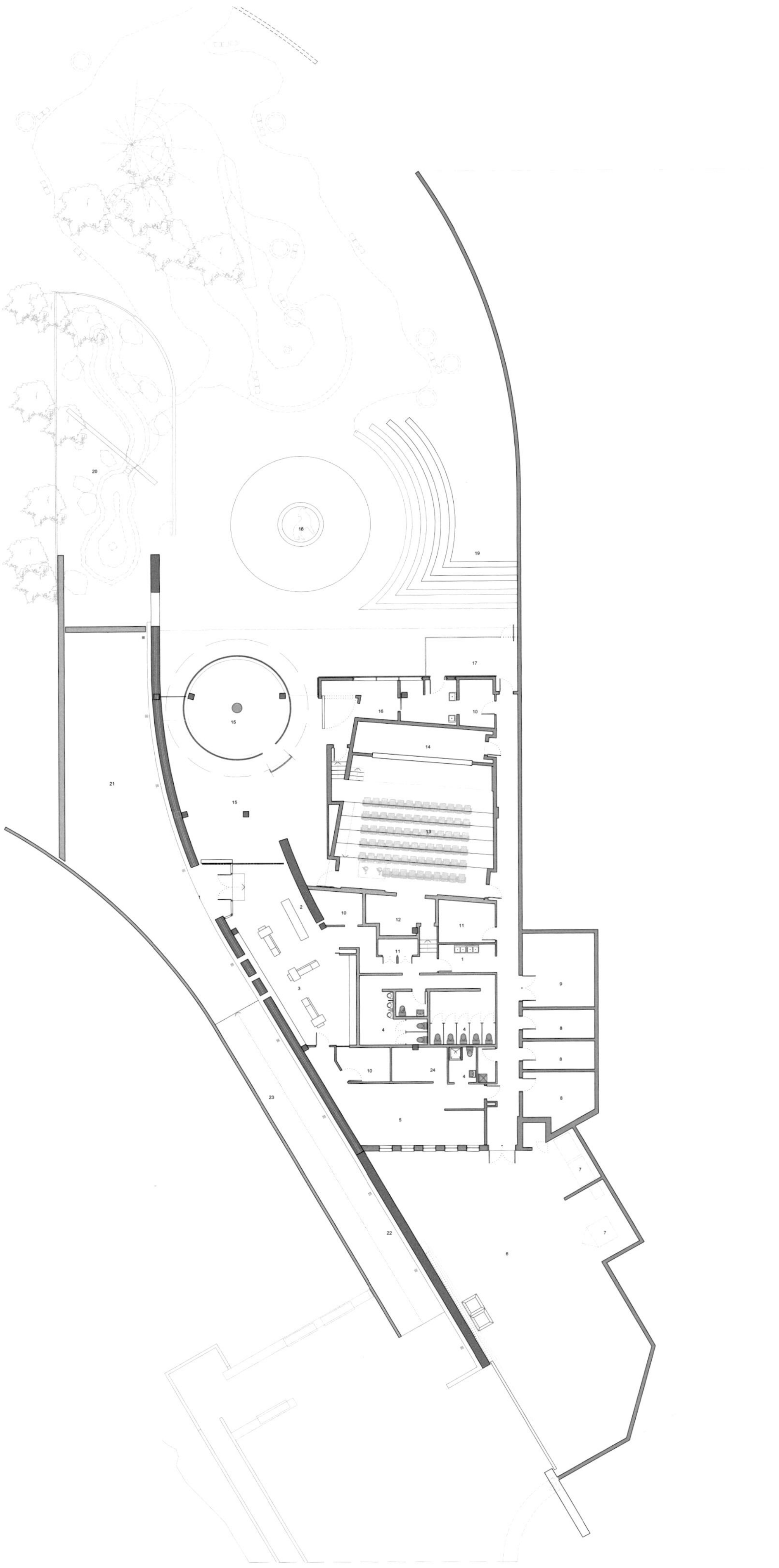

1. Access
2. Reception
3. Store
4. Bathroom
5. Administration
6. Service courtyard
7. Rubbish recycling
8. Service room
9. Workshop
10. Office
11. Storage
12. Audiovisual control room
13. Auditorium
14. Stage
15. Exhibition gallery
16. Animal habitat (serpents)
17. Demonstration area
18. Amphitheater
19. Exhibition area
20. Exterior reservoir
21. Terrace
22. Stream
23. Access staircase

Ground Foor Level

0 5 10m

1:400

NK'MIP
Desert Cultural Centre

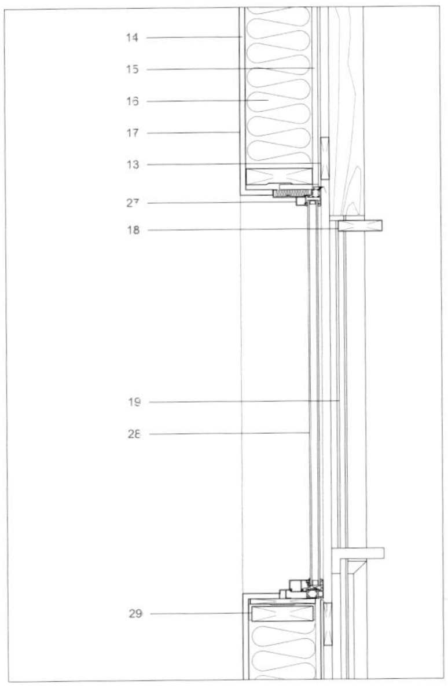

D. 1

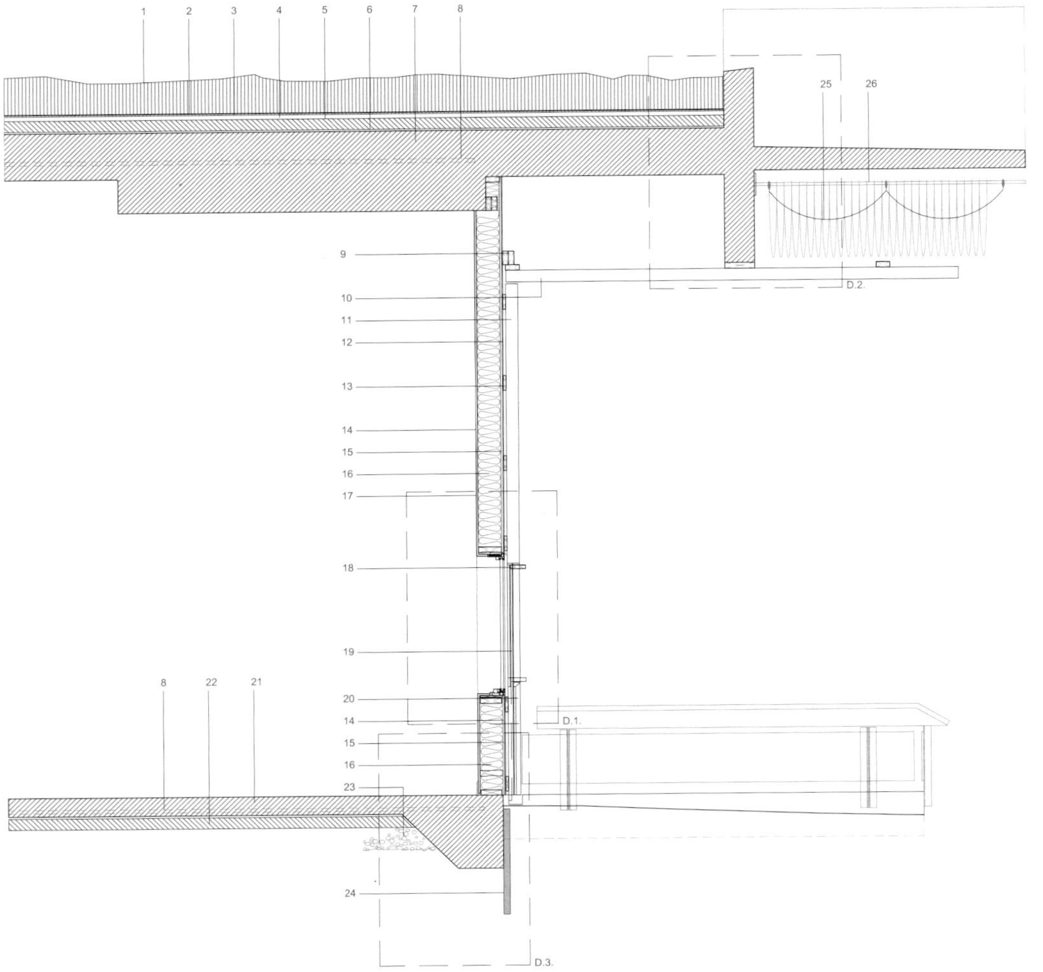

Blue Pine Wall Section Detail

0 1 2m

1:50

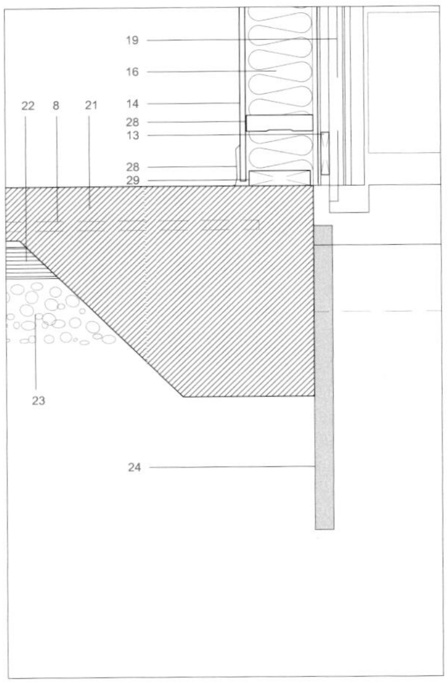

D. 3

0 10 30 50cm 1m

1:20

1. 23cm native soil
2. Microfiber root resistant sheet
3. "Sopradrain hd" drainage panel + filtering fabric
4. 10cm of rigid insulation layer (rsi 3.5)
5. Cap sheet
6. Base sheet
7. Concrete slab with mortar layer for creation of slopes
8. Mechanical conditioning pipes; Hot + cold radiant piping in slab
9. Wood strip, painted black prior to installation
10. 30mm x 80mm horizontal slats of Blue Pine
11. 30mm x 80mm vertical slats of Blue Pine
12. 6 mm g1s exterior grade plywood
13. 19mm x 89mm strips of wood, tinted in autoclave
14. 12.7 mm Plywood sheathing
15. 38 x 152 steel profile
16. Rsi 3.5 batten insulation
17. 12.7 mm protection layer
18. 30mm x 80mm strips of blue pine, window cap.
19. Steel security frame, stained and operable (shown closed)
20. 30 x 30mm vertical slats of VERT remilled blue pine
21. Concrete base slab
22. Vapor barrier
23. Gravel base on compacted soil
24. Rigid insulation
25. Retractable fabric protection
26. 20mm steel bar
27. Metal framing with insulating cavity
28. Double glazing with air chamber
29. Cap; wooden piece 140x35mm +150x20mm painted in autoclave + cover plate
30. Sliding ring ø 25mm
31. Metal flashing

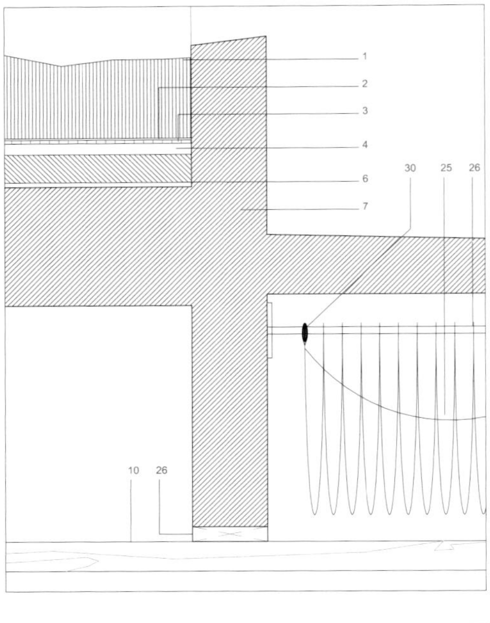

D. 2

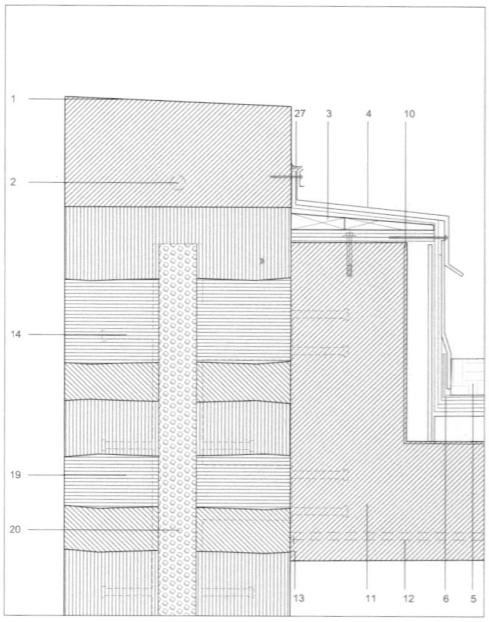

D. 4

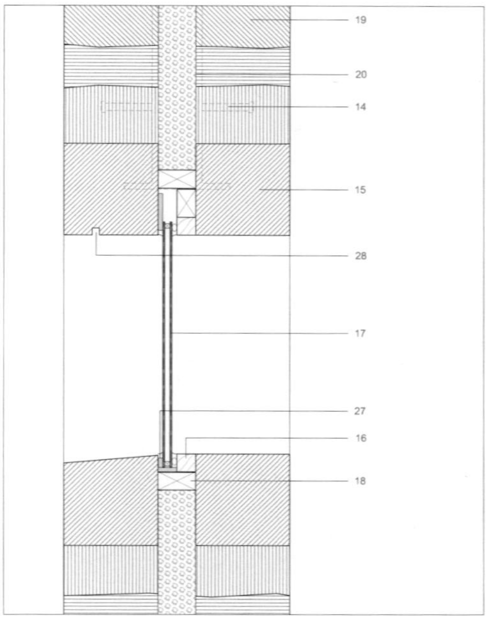

D. 5

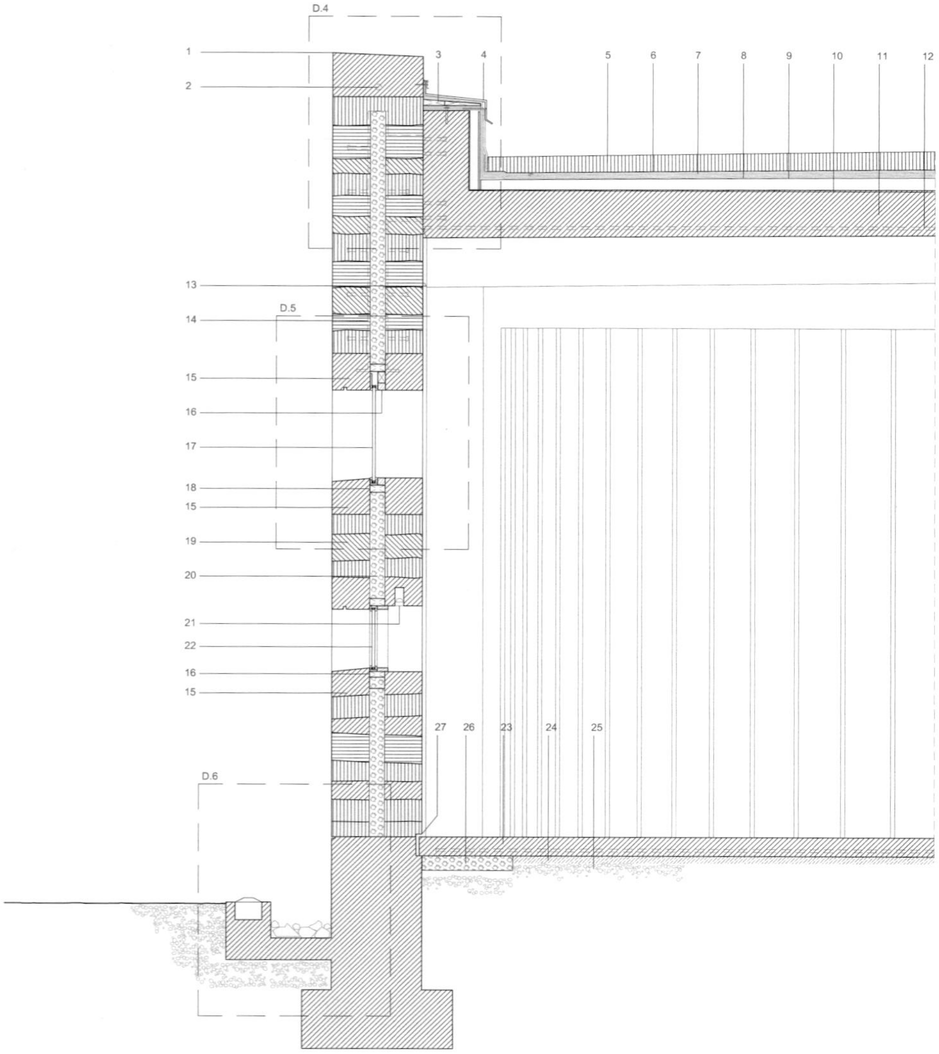

Adobe Wall Section Detail

0 1 2m

1:50

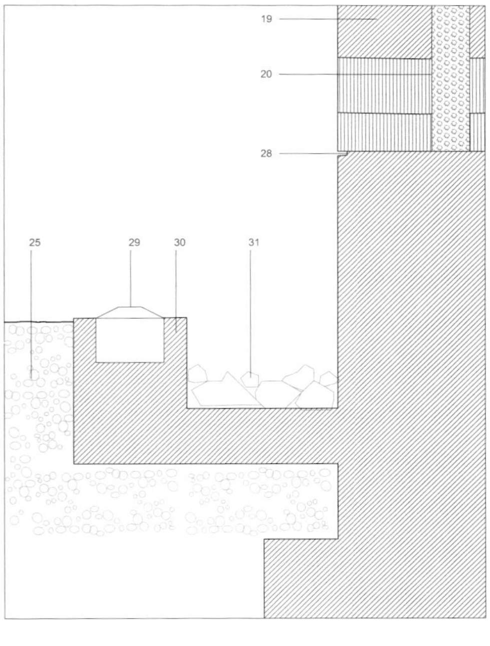

D. 6

0 10 30 50cm 1m

1:20

1. Layer of mortar sealant capping the parapet
2. Mechanical conditioning pipes; Hot + cold radiant piping in spandrel beam
3. Coarse finished wooden bar to connect insulation membrane and joint sealant
4. Metal flashing
5. 23cm native soil
6. Microfiber root resistant sheet
7. "Sopradrain hd" drainage panel + filtering fabric
8. 10cm of rigid insulation layer (rsi 3.5)
9. Cap sheet
10. Base sheet
11. Concrete slab with mortar layer for creation of slopes
12. Mechanical conditioning pipes; Hot + cold radiant piping in slab
13. Exposed Joint
14. Hollow profile frame built-in to wall
15. Earth molded in-situ
16. Solid ash wood window base and lintel
17. Double glazed sealed frameless window; hung and sealed with silicon on-site
18. 50mm x100mm piece of continuous plastic-sealed ('trex') wood
19. 250mm of earth + mineral color tints, tamped down mechanically
20. 100mm insulation panel of polyisocyanurate + 2 layers of paper
21. Recessed halogen light centered in 76mm diameter opening
22. 40cm x 40cm double glazed frameless window with air chamber; hung and sealed with silicon on-site
23. Concrete base slab
24. Vapor barrier
25. Gravel base on compacted soil
26. Rigid insulation
27. Sealed with silicon
28. 20mm dripstone formed by soil molded on-site
29. Light fixture @3200 o.c recessed in slab edge
30. Reinforced concrete strip footing
31. 40cm canal with slope for outdoor circulation of rainwater

05

Atelier Kempe Thill Architects

HEDGE BUILDING

ROSTOCK, Alemania

Atelier Kempe Thill

www.atelierkempethill.com

COLLABORATORS	André Kempe, Cornelia Sailer, Ruud Smeelen, Oliver Thill,Takashi Nakamura
PROJECT MANAGER	Matrix Architektur
BUILDER	Adviesbureau voor Bouwtechniek BV
PHOTOGRAPHY	Ulrich Schwarz

	COLLABORATING COMPANIES
Structure Analysis	Rob Nijsse, ABT Velp, NL
Landscape	Niek Roozen, Weesp, N
Video Concept	Leo Schepman Communicatie Projecten, Den Haag, NL
Screen	Mobilane, Nijmegen, NL
Metallic Structure	Manzke Stahlbau & Handel GmbH

	DATES
IMPLEMENTATION PROJECT	2002
BEGINNING OF WORKS	2003
WORK COMPLETION	2003

DESCRIPTIVE BRIEF

The project is an example of the logic and rationality of Dutch agriculture and of the quality we can find despite their limited conditions. The starting point, architecturally speaking, of the pavilion is basically the element that gives the building form: the 'smart screen'. The smart screen is formed by panels of ivy grown in Dutch glasshouses. It is produced in sections measuring 1.2 x 1.8 meters and is usually planted in gardens. Essentially an industrial product, the hedges can be arranged to build 'green walls'. Normally, ivy takes years to grow and cover a building, but with this screen system one can construct a green façade without this temporal limitation.

The dimensions of the building are 20 x 6.5 x 10 meters. The structure is, in fact, a pergola. Its compact shape, its translucent plastic roof and 4 meter high entrance doors give it the character of a house. At the same time, the ivy façade gives it a unique quality, providing it with semi-transparency which allows a filtered and soft light to enter. A steel frame gives shape to five rows of soil-filled channels, from which the screens grow and are nourished, while a computer-controlled trickle irrigation system supplies the hedges with the necessary water.

Site View

The structure has no conventional diagonal bracing but is stabilized by 4 star-shaped corner columns, 400N each, that withstand all horizontal forces. Vertical loads are absorbed by a multiplicity of 5cm-thick columns along the length of the facades. As a result, the edges are visually continuous, and it appears as if they support the structure. The ivy panels partially conceal the columns conferring the pavilion a light appearance.

The interior is surrounded on all sides by 10 meter high walls of green ivy. A screen of translucent plastic covers the top of the space. The quiet interior is sheltered from the surrounding, hectic IGA exhibition grounds. The neutral and modest space can be used to accommodate various functions. Natural light that prevails in the interior is a characteristic element of the pavilion. Light entering through the ceiling gives it the quality of a classical museum space, while light filtering through the ivy enclosure gives it the character of an exterior space. Moreover, the gentle movement of the ivy leaves and their shadows enhances the perception of the space. The result is an interesting play between inside and outside.

"Things perfected by nature are better than those finished by art"

Cicero (106-43 a.d.C.)

ENVIRONMENTAL ANALYSIS

1. Choosing the Site. Project and Development

1.1 Location

Latitude: 54º08'22"N
Longitude: 12º05'08"E

1.2 Urban Design and Site Improvement

As a part of the International Horticulture Exposition IGA 2003 in Rostock, Germany, it is located in the area designated by the organization of the event. Its character as an exceptional project is achieved with a simple solution with a powerful visual impact, making the most of industrialized garden techniques.

1.3 Project

The project is an original reinterpretation of the French garden, defined as nature which adopts the form that man desires. For the construction of this space, the interior of a Dutch greenhouse has been used, transforming it into a genuine pergola. Its geometric composition is prismatic and its proportion in floor plan makes its use ambiguous.

In relation to its surroundings and because of its double front door, the building has the character of a "vegetation threshold" that divides the park into two zones.
As you go through the building doors, at each side there are areas for expositions, but the spaces maintain the subjective sensation of horticulture spaces.

2. Consumption of Energy and Resources

2.1 Consumption of Energy

The project has opted for the prefabrication of ivy similar to those utilized in the Dutch garden industry. The level of industrialization achieved in this sector allows the construction of this unique project, using garden techniques consolidated in the region.

2.2 Consumption of Water

Through a computer-controlled system, the panels of ivy are watered by trickle irrigation.

2.3 Consumption of Materials

Three levels of materials can be differentiated:

Concrete is only used in the foundation with strip footing typical in Dutch greenhouses.

The façade of steel structure and prefabricated ivy panels is extensively used as gates for housing.

The plastic roof is similar to those used in greenhouses.

3. Environmental Load

3.1 Emissions

These are minimized by the used of prefabricated elements. The election of a steel structure, along with the symbolism as material of the very greenhouse, allows for the modulation of elements and the consequential savings of material.

3.2 Solid Waste

These are minimized by the prefabrication used in the construction of the pavilion.

3.3 Water Management

These are optimized with the trickle irrigation system, widely used in horticulture.

4. Interior Environmental Quality

4.1 Ventilation

The space is conceived as a pergola –greenhouse. Rather than isolate, the green screens delimit the space, allowing for natural ventilation of the space.

4.2 Natural Light

The four facades allows natural light into the interior of the pavilion. The light filtered through the ivy panels of the façade, creates a play of shadows that allows us to observe the faint contrast projected on the plasma screens located in the interior.

5. Control of Building Systems

5.1 Functionality and Efficiency

This is a simple project, with no major aspirations to exhibit, with a simple construction system; a modern reinterpretation of the greenhouse.

5.2 Control of Construction Systems

The elements of horizontal reinforcement, besides permitting the fitting of the ivy panels, through its form, allow containing the substrate that keeps it alive.

6. Long-term Performance

6.1 Flexibility and Adaptability

The open arrangement of the pavilion facilitates the development of different activities, besides that of pure exhibition. The facade elements are a good example of a domestic element adapted for a singular use.

The construction system is perfectly reversible. The metal elements can be unassembled, and the ivy modules can be reused in another project.

6.2 Maintenance and Operative Performance

The project has the temporal character of an expo; The IGA expo 2003 lasted from April to October, so that the useful life of the materials during the project were guaranteed. The ivy panels were maintained thanks to a trickle irrigation system that optimizes the consumption of water.

7. Economic and Social Aspects

7.1 Social Aspects

The quality of Dutch horticulture is a worldwide reference. Eight of the ten major companies of horticultural seeds of the world, have its main headquarters or important branch office in the Netherlands. This project demonstrates, in a simple but clear way, using industrial horticultural elements a singular building can be designed that represents the country, without the need for superfluous artifices.

7.2 Economic Aspects

The prefabrication decreases assembly time on-site, which translates into reduction of waste and economic and environmental savings. The importance of an appropriate singular project for an international event can be translated into the opening of new markets, as well as the maintenance of the existing ones.

8. The Eye of the Architect

There are two key moments in the development of the project; one is the election of the volume and proportion of the pergola in relation to its surroundings. Another very important point is the all-enveloping vegetation, which gives the visitor the sensation of being in the interior of a greenhouse.

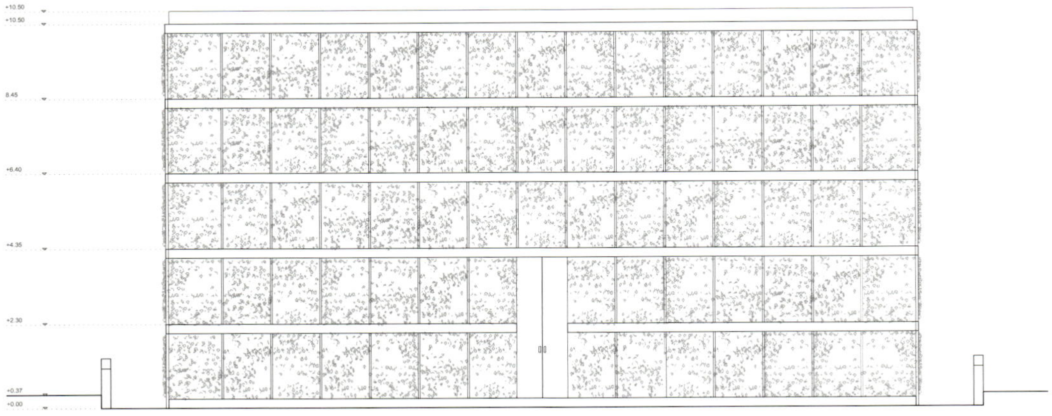

Longitudinal Elevation

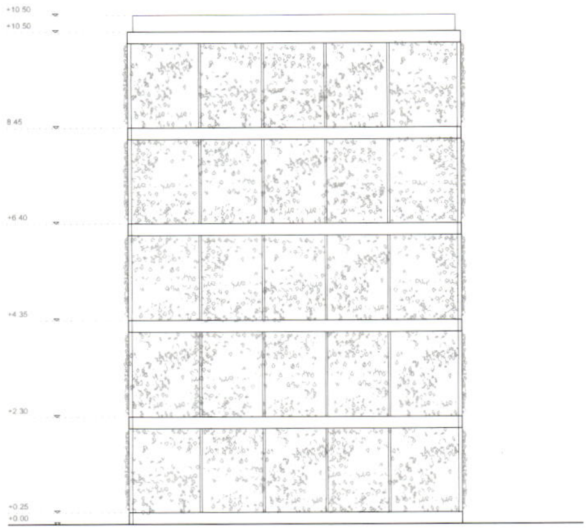

Cross Elevation

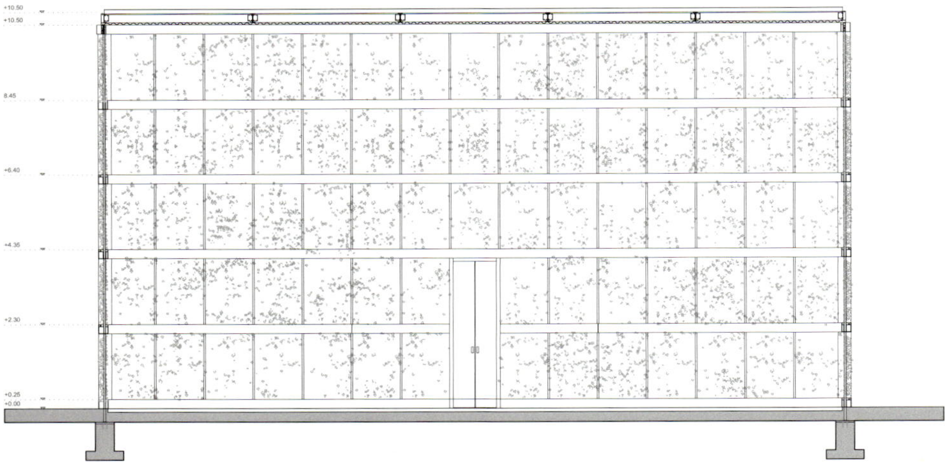

Longitudinal Section

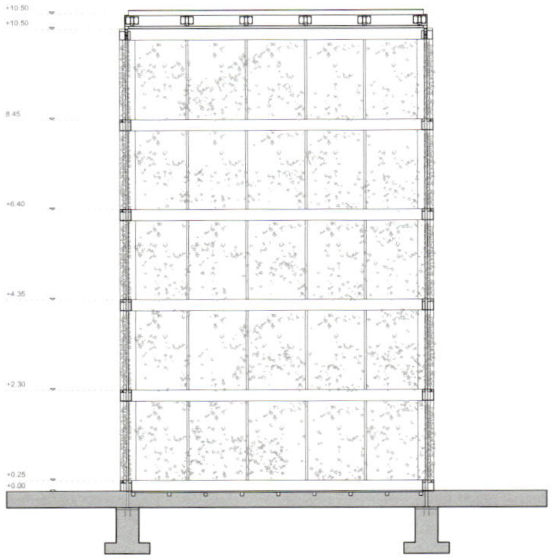

Cross Section

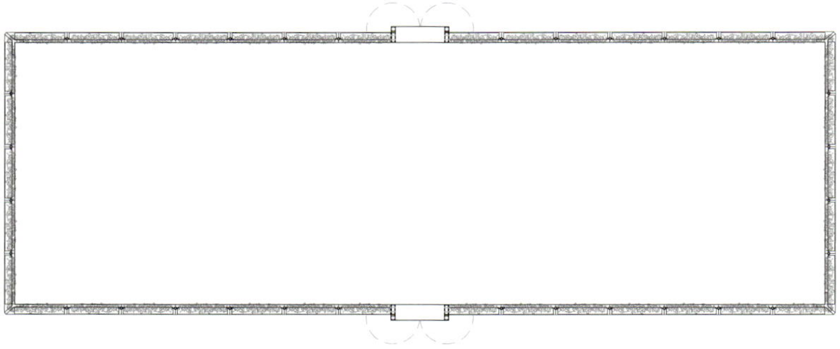

Ground Floor

1:200

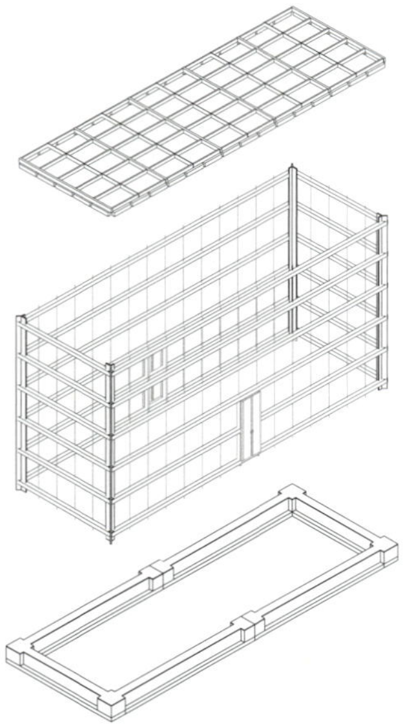

Axonometric View

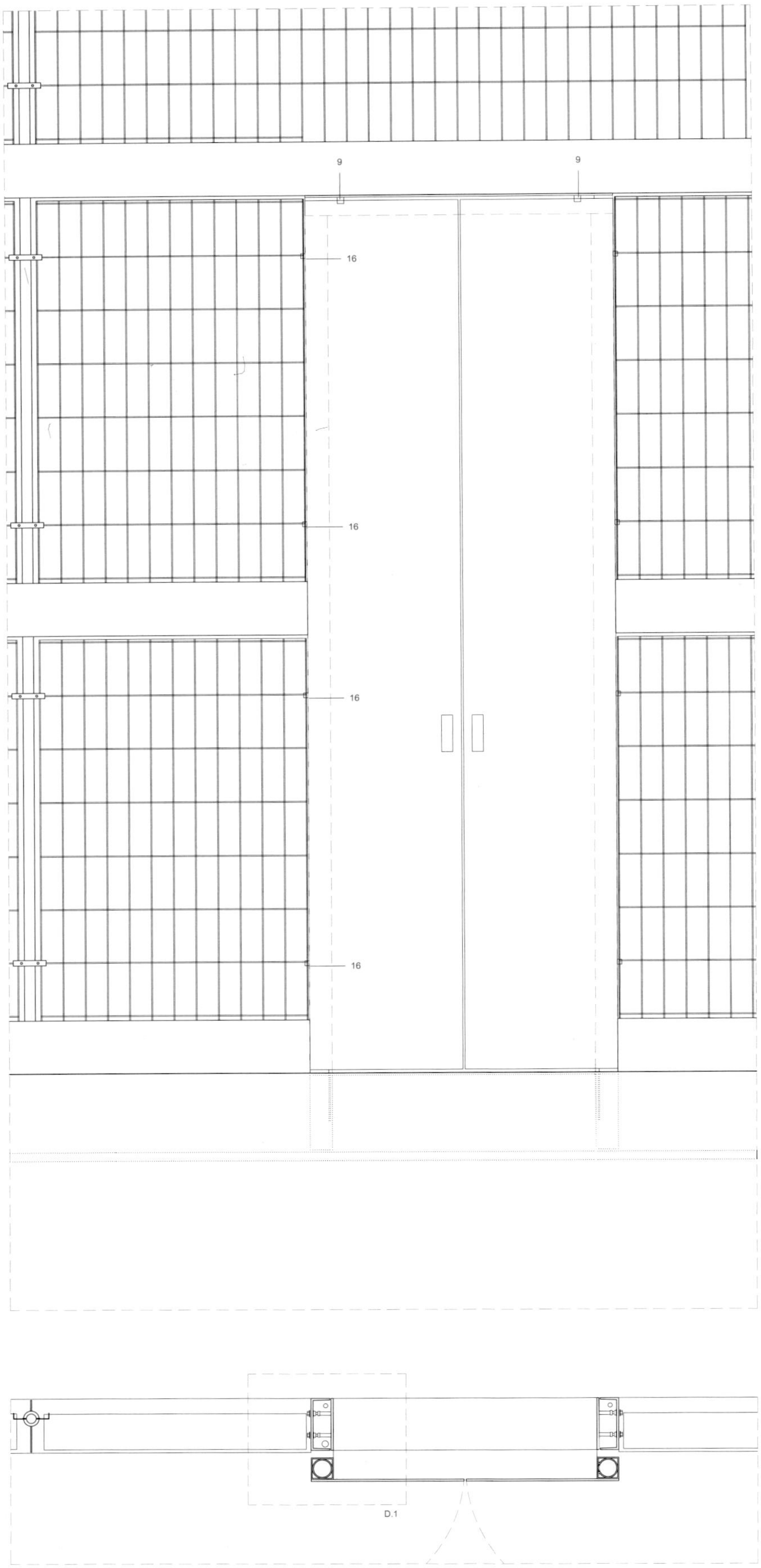

Entrance Detail

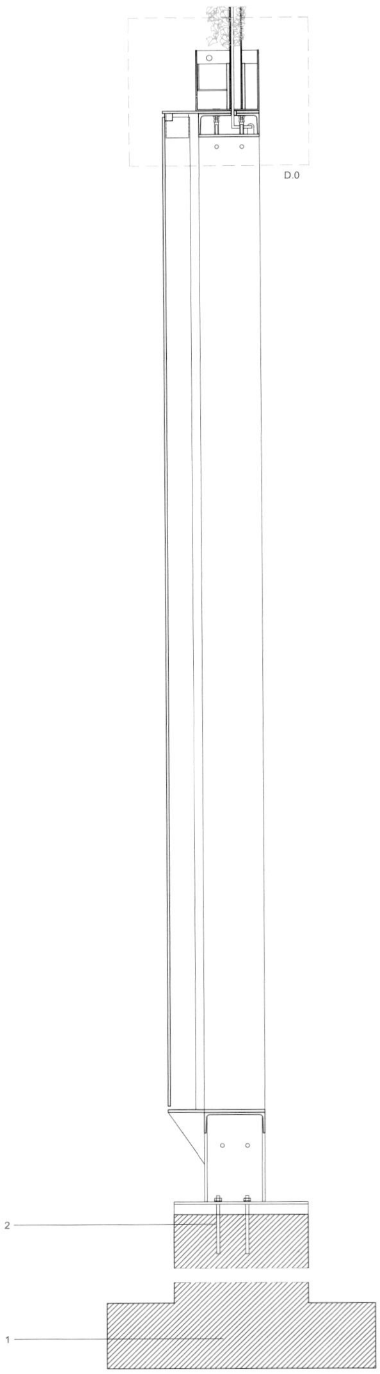

Section Detail 1

1:30

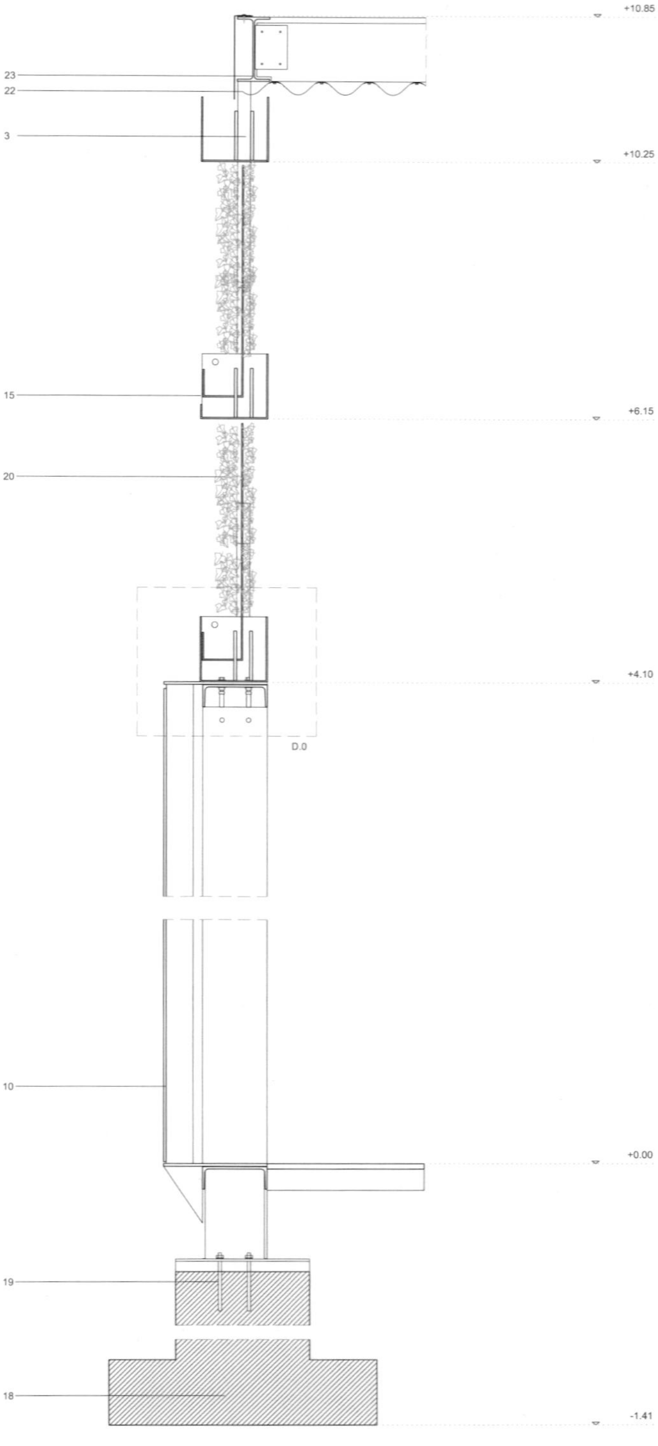

Section Detail 2

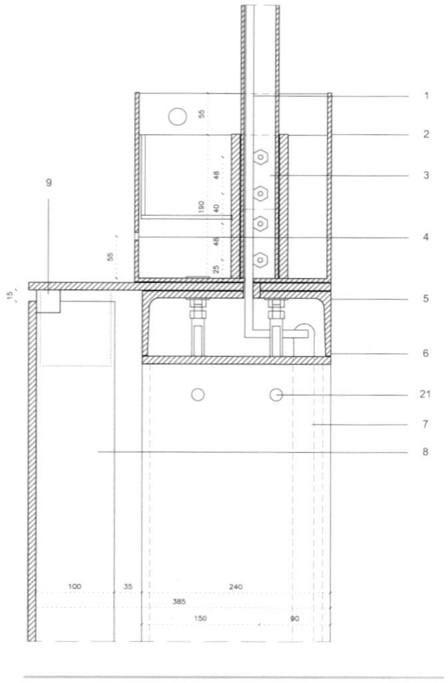

D. 0

1:10

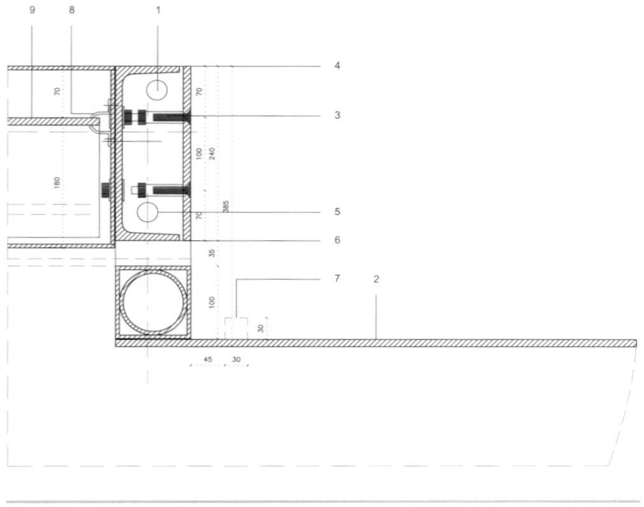

D.1

1. Electric line for lighting in door frame. Over circular support; opens vertically.
2. Steel box of 250x250X5 mm
3. Circular support of 2.6 mm thickness, Ø 48mm, welded to door
4. Drain hole drilled in boxes – flower beds of Ø 10 mm
5. Channel of 85x240 mm, UPN welded to steel plate of 10x1390x385 mm
6. Steel door frame of 85x240x8 mm. UNP S235JG2; Steel sheet of 10mm, screwed to frame.
7. Electrical installation which originates on the door frame, hole drilled on vertical support and box of Ø40mm
8. Door hinge: Hollow square leaf of 100x100x4mm section, steel thread of plate of 690x4060 x10mm, round profile fit into the square section
9. Profile of 30x30x30mm welded to upper plate
10. Steel sheet of 10mm thickness
11. Door hinge: Hollow square leaf of 100x100x4mm, sheet 690x4060 x10mm, round profile fit into the square section
12. Connection of the box to the doorframe, M12 screws
13. Atomizer irrigation line in the substrate, aerosol irrigation line on frame.
14. Irrigation line of Ø20mm, back or brown, hung to the door frame with clips, distance between clips 30 cm
15. Steel sheet of 30x30x30mm welded to upper plate
16. Connection to door frame with clips, hooked to pre-drilled holes
17. Element from the company "Mobilane" of 1025X1800 galvanized
18. Strip footing
19. Anchor bolts
20. Ivy panel
21. Mounting holes on door frames
22. Corrugated metal sheet
23. IPN 12

06

Bruno Stagno

Edificio Holcim

ALAJUELA, Costa Rica

Bruno Stagno

http//:www.brunostagno.info
http//:www.arquitecturatropical.org

COLLABORATORS	Carlos Araya FTL Design Engineering Studio
INDUSTRIAL ENGINEER	Juan Carlos Sotela
MECHANICAL ENGINEER	Juan Luis Flores
BIOLOGIST	Marco Gutiérrez
CONTRACTOR	RAE Ingenieros S.A.
LANDSCAPE	Jimena Ugarte
PHOTOGRAPHY	Bruno Stagno

	COLLABORATING COMPANIES
Aluminum and Glass	Sistemas de Ventanerías S.A.
Concrete	Holcim Costa Rica
Metallic Structure	Estructuras Madrigal S.A.
Fountains	Amanco Costa Rica S.A.
Electronics Installer	Instalec S.A.
Gardening	Ecosistemas S.A.
Textile Structures	Eurotoldos S.A.

PRIZES

Bienal de Arquitectura Santo Domingo Award

República Dominicana

	DATES
BEGINNING OF WORKS	2003
WORK COMPLETION	2004

DESCRIPTIVE BRIEF

In a devastated and rocky industrial ensemble, Holcim SA turned a desert into a green and pleasant industrial site. In order to achieve this, instead of designing "the great" corporate building that would cause a considerable environmental impact, the landscape and the various buildings were designed to compose a spatial ensemble with a pleasant scale, surrounded by courtyards and gardens. Holcim, which produces concrete and several other construction materials, commissioned a building that reflected the possibilities of their materials, without turning into, for that reason, a collection of samples. Different and new solutions were designed which illustrate the sophisticated uses of a rustic material, in essence, and they have been combined with very light cloths, which ease the tectonics of the most solid materials, as well as with light elements to control solar radiation and lower the building's thermal load, which has no air conditioning. The terrain's rocky character has been respected by using original rocks in the landscape design. These rocks are considered as a metaphor of the company's solidity and the toughness of the materials they produce. The trees that remained were respected, and more than 500 trees were planted to reforest and restore a natural habitat for the local flora and fauna.

The building's most significant achievement is the way it responds to a long series of requirements. For this, the building uses several passive design elements, instead of traditional systems with which a great expense for energy is generated. Built with a relatively modest budget, compared to the medium in the region (600 euros/m2), it has turned into a unique architectural piece, with a great symbolic power. The building responds to the purpose of creating attractive and functional spaces, developing to the maximum its occupants´ environmental conscience (under the slogan "passive building-active people") and enriches its environment with a landscape design completely integrated into the site's ecology.

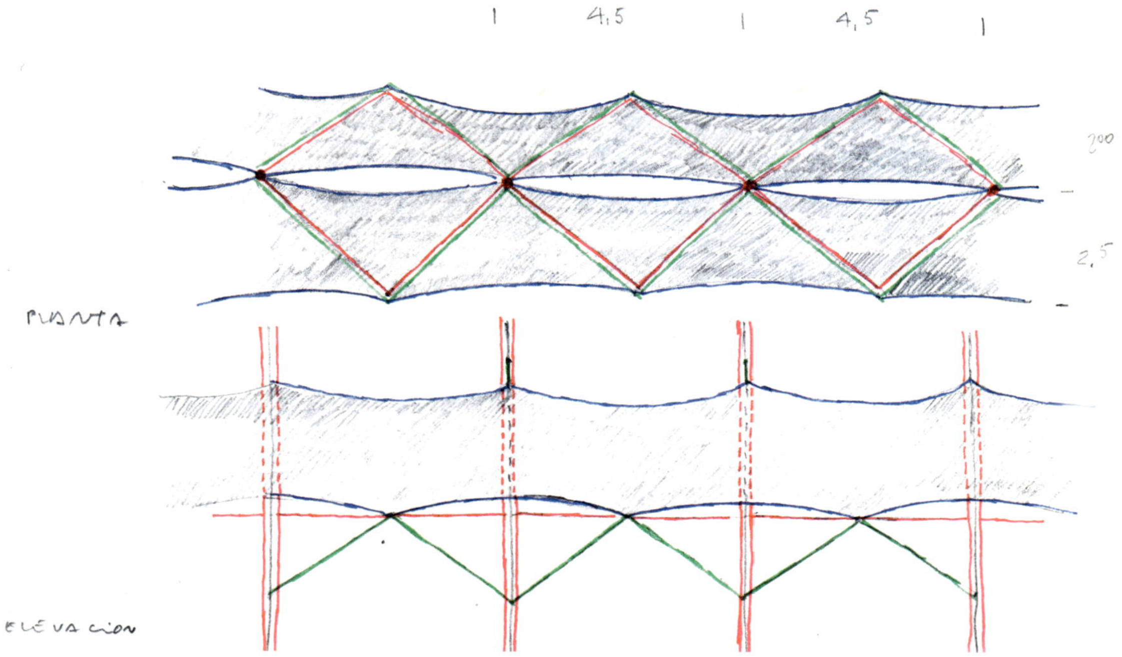

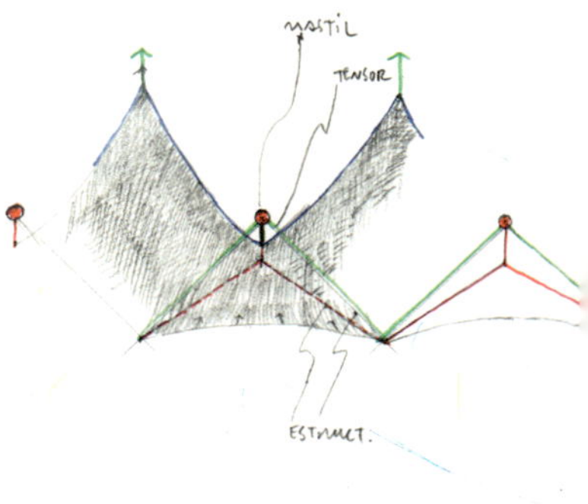

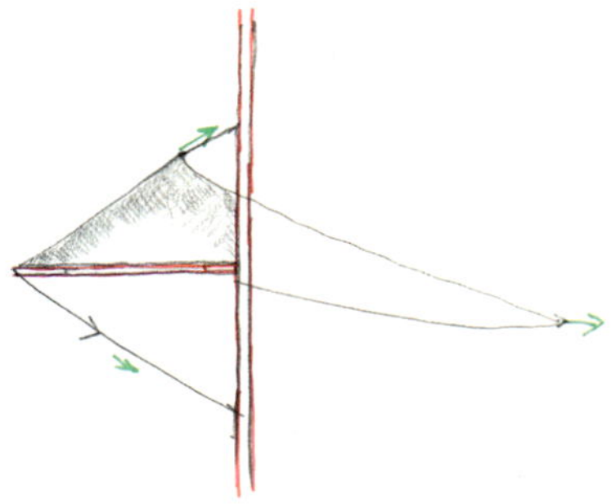

"Transferable ideas are those that are affordable, simple, and broadly applicable"
Bruno Stagno

1. Choosing the Site. Project and Development.

1.1 Location

Latitude: 09°58'N
Longitude: 84°13'W
Altitude: 800m above sea level

The site is found in an industrial complex exposed to breezes; located in San Antonio de Belén, in the province of Alajuela, on the west side of the Costa Rica Central Valley. The climate is hot in this area, sub-humid with a very defined dry season. Temperature and humidity are normally high (22°C and 78% average). Sunlight is intensive in this region, and despite not being a hurricane zone rain is normally abundant.

1.2 Urban Design and Site Improvement

The environment has been treated by sowing 174 trees, 1,100 coffee trees and a great variety of bushes and climbing plants, which were combined with the already existing ones. The majority of these species are endemic, planted intentionally to attract the existing local fauna. The internal vegetation plays an important role in the building's internal conditioning, contributing to block excessive solar radiation and reduce the settling of dust.

In order to accentuate the building's entrance, it is accessed through an area of fountains, channels, and vegetation, improving the urban quality of an environment of industrial use.

1.3 Project

The architecture of the ensemble intends to achieve internal environmental comfort, using natural energy as the main resource to avoid the use of air conditioning. This premise is materialized in a scattered ensemble of four strategically oriented buildings that enclose a central courtyard which acts as climatic regulator. Through fountains and narrow water channels one arrives at the access building, protected by a perforated concrete wall named by the author "wind tuner", which protects the ensemble from the dominating Northwest winds with gusts of up to 74 Km/h.

Two key environmental strategies can be identified in this project. The first one is that the ensemble has an isolated layout, which facilitates the ventilation between buildings. This permeability is reinforced by the effect achieved by the interior courtyard. The second strategy consists of using shade intentionally, incorporating textile elements that protect the facades and roofs from direct solar radiation, but they do not interfere in the air flow, necessary to condition interior atmospheres.

2. Consumption of Energy and Resources

2.1 Consumption of Energy

In the design stage, a simulation was made of the performance of the North and South buildings, with a great density of occupants. This simulation used the "COMFORT" program, supplied with climatic information obtained from the closest meteorological station, at an approximate distance of 10 Km to the North. This simulation exercise generated information that helped to improve the design, avoiding modifications during construction.

During the execution phase, the rocky material of the site was reused as a base for the landscape program. The entry of materials was reduced, and finishes were avoided which would increase the environmental load of the ensemble.

The most important challenge was to achieve an ensemble that would do without air conditioning, only used in the auditorium. To achieve this, the effects of solar radiation in the ceilings were diminished and its consequences on the interior temperature. The performance of the ceilings as an insulating element was developed, by means of tension structures that work as large umbrellas on the roof and on the glazed facades. The central courtyard facilitates this task thanks to tropical almond trees (Terminalia catappa) planted there. These trees have large 25 cm long and 14cm wide leaves, and can reach 30 m in height with a crown of symmetrical horizontal branches which face upward. In tropical areas it is used as an ornamental tree, because of the deep shade provided by its leaves.

East and West facades of the buildings are insulated by means of solid concrete walls and apertures were preferably located in the North and South facades to facilitate air flow. Thanks to this strategy, the annual energy consumption has been reduced to a third of the consumption of a typical office building in Costa Rica.

2.2 Consumption of Water

This project counts on a rainwater recovery system from the roofs, which are stored in a collection tank to be used for irrigation, in the nebulizers of the central courtyards, and in the fountains. Drinking water is obtained from a deep well. Besides economic saving, the need to extend the municipal water supply network to the site was eliminated.

2.3 Consumption of Materials

Use of long life and low maintenance materials were the premises to prescribe the materials used in constructing the Holcim building. Concrete, stone, glass, wood and fiber cement panels were use its construction; all of them manufactured in this region. Materials have not been clad with unnecessary finishes; surfaces are left to age naturally and, over time, they develop a patina of natural colors.

Land movement while building was limited and the reutilization of materials found in site was favored. Therefore, the central courtyard design has incorporated the recovery of enormous rocks that had previously been removed to build the industrial complex, and had remained useless in an area of the complex, which have been relocated and colonized by ivy and grass.

3. Environmental Loads

3.1 Emissions

Use of materials from the local industry and the use of stone resulting from the land conditioning, help diminish the environmental impact and emissions generated by the deposit in a rubbish dump, reducing the necessary transport to move material to and from the building site.

In the service phase, the project's major success lies in using local conditions to reduce energy consumption and the emissions attributable to its functioning. A proposal that favors crossed ventilation in the ensemble and the provision of shade by means of vegetation and auxiliary textile elements that allow reducing energy consumption devoted to conditioning.

3.2 Solid Waste

Construction waste has been used in the same location, for urbanization and landscape work. Material entries, the consequent waste, have been reduced to the maximum in building process.

3.3 Water Management

Rainwater is collected in a tank. It is later used for the fountains and channels of the entrance, courtyard irrigation system and plants. The use of rainwater, besides being a source of economic savings also avoids the use of communal water for irrigation, a limited resource and of high energy cost due to the infrastructure needed for its transport.

4. Interior Environmental Quality

4.1 Ventilation

Departing from conventional practice, the idea is that occupants control the interior air conditioning by operating the building's passive systems. In conventional buildings, with mechanical air conditioning systems, automatically controlled, people become passive and neither participate nor are given a choice of the quality of air conditioning of their work space.

The interior garden, designed as a conditioning garden, is located to capture the predominating winds. Air flows, keeping the courtyard fresh and humid. In the dry season, the aerosol type devices of the garden liberate mist for ten seconds every ten minutes, thus humidifying and cooling the courtyard microclimate, refreshing the whole.

Interior temperature and humidity conditions have been computer-controlled, simulated to evaluate the incidence of exterior fluctuations on the interior conditions. The results obtained demonstrate that with the above-mentioned strategies, the maximum and minimum interior temperature values have been reduced. Average temperatures during work hours (08:00 to 19:00) were of 24° - 25° C in both of the characteristic seasons of the area: dry and rainy[1].

4.2 Natural Lighting

North and South facades show the greatest surface area of apertures in the ensemble. This facilitates crossed ventilation, but it also creates problems because of direct sunlight. Strategies adopted were the provision of shade elements: textile screens and lattices to control direct sunlight. Interior light levels were homogenized with the ceiling's curved shape and white color. Measurements taken during its operation registered an average level of 1.500 lumens/m2 appropriate for the development of office activities which require a great visual effort[2].

4.3 Acoustics

As a result of the open approach of the edifications, the natural environment is included in the work area. Provision of open rest spaces allows employees to enjoy the breeze, natural shade, and the sound of native bird species which have repopulated the site as a result of the landscape program carried out.

1 http://www.brunostagno.info/ARTIC_CONFER.htm
2 Visual comfort is a complex concept that does not only depend on one's visual capacity. There are other factors such as temperature, the color of light, and the physical characteristics of the users that play an important role in determining this parameter.

5. Control of Building Systems

5.1 Functionality and Efficiency

The building systems used have a clear function that facilitated the construction and reduced construction expenses and maintenance.
Concrete; for structure
Glazing; for the enclosures
Steel, pre-fabricated concrete and fabrics; roof, connection bridges and shading elements.

5.2 Control of Constructive Elements

The project's design concept can be summed up as "passive building with active people". The idea is that users are aware that the can actively control air flows and heat transmission in their own spaces. That is why all control elements such as windows, lattices and fans can be operated by workers.

6. Long-term Performance

6.1 Flexibility and Adaptability

The challenge to design a building which would express the developer's corporate identity without falling into ostentation, has been materialized in a construction in which the most important symbolism lies in the adjustable elements (screens, courtyards). The open plan approach of the main buildings (North and South), allows layouts for different purposes, from a gymnasium or warehouse to offices. This open typology is liable to be transferred to buildings with similar programs: schools, health centers, markets. In this sense, the task of dissemination carried out by the designer and developer, at the same time, should be highlighted.

6.2 Maintenance and Operative Performance.

We highlight the architect's and developer's will to simulate the building's performance in operation. The measurements made have permitted to contrast the results forecasted by environmental design computer program. This has allowed the detection of places where comfort conditions are not appropriate and look for correcting mechanisms.
Low-tech mechanisms which use free energy sources and lasting and resistant materials allow reducing the building's energy and economic load while functioning. The users become aware of it when verifying that they can directly influence the internal comfort, by directly manipulating themselves the climatic control elements.

7. Economic and Social Aspects

7.1 Social Aspects

Used to active conditioning systems, the users had reservations to work in a building without air conditioning. Previous reunions took place in order to discuss the design of their work place. Once the ensemble was built, training sessions took place to teach employees how to adjust systems in reply to changes in climatic conditions.

The ensemble's open plan approach facilitates social interaction. The project has been provided with atmospheres such as a gym, cafeteria, and outdoor meeting points for relaxation.

Building contractors involved in the construction were required to give maximum levels of social responsibility, concerning workers' safety and environmental protection. Nearly 150 people were involved in the construction, and there were no accidents among workers.

7.2 Economic Aspects

The building was designed to incorporate Holcim products for two reasons: in order to save expenses and to express the company's corporate identity. The design, methods and processes of construction were adapted to the capacities of the Costa Rican building industry. Except for the expandable structures and wind tuner, the rest of the construction is conventional.

The building's construction cost has been 2 million Euros (a relatively modest cost of 600 Euros/m2 approximately), slightly over the original budget, but in line with the changes that arose during the project phase.

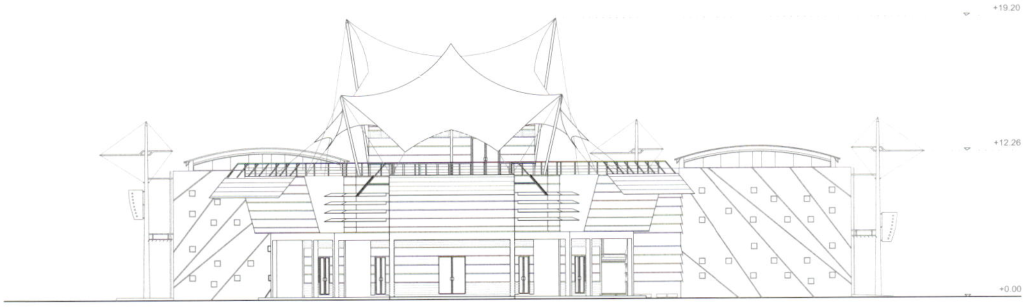

West Elevation

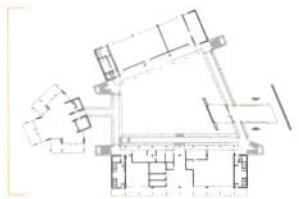

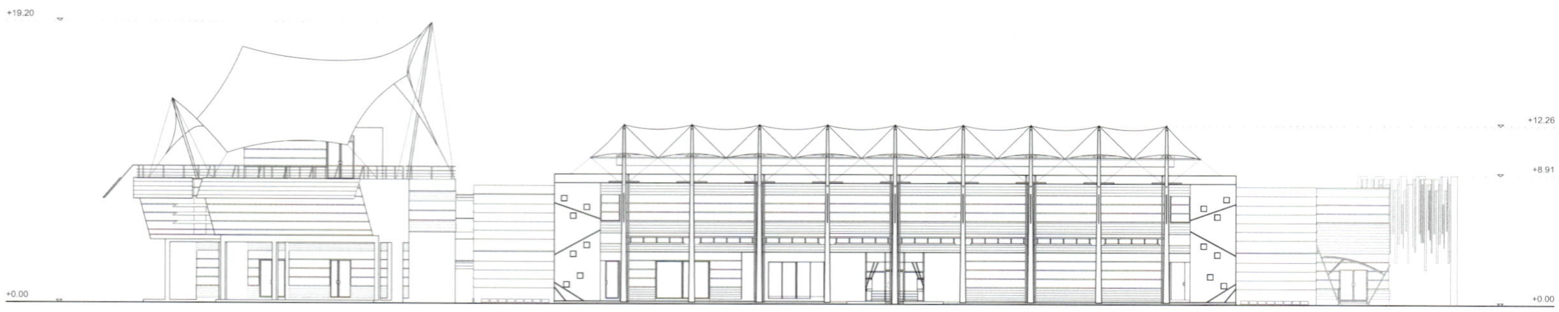

South Elevation

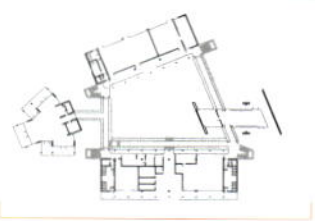

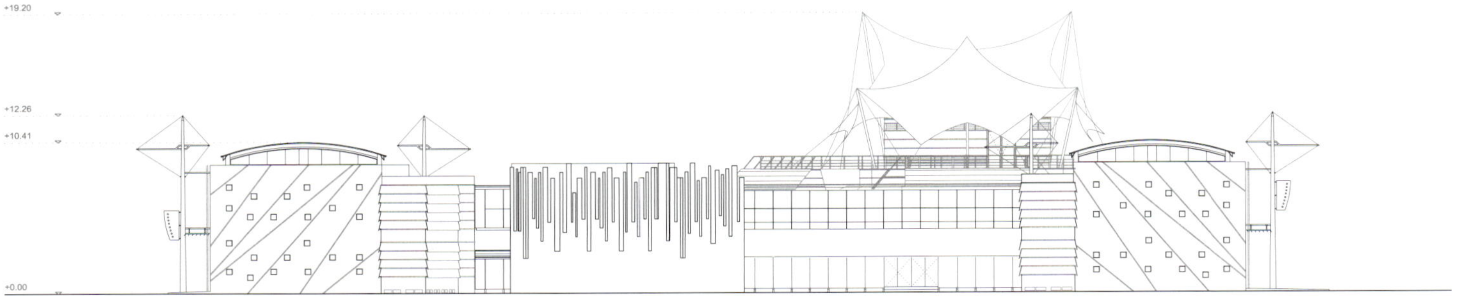

East Elevation

1:500

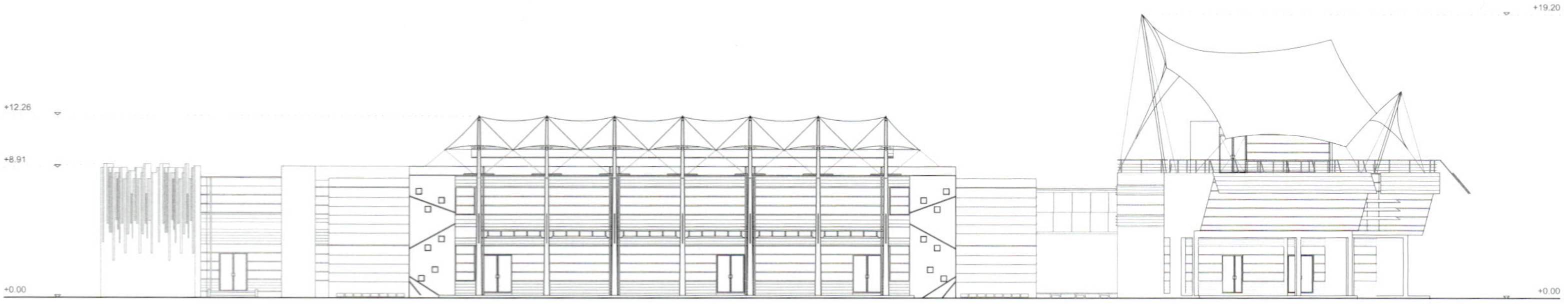

North Elevation

EDIFICIO HOLCIM
Bruno Stagno

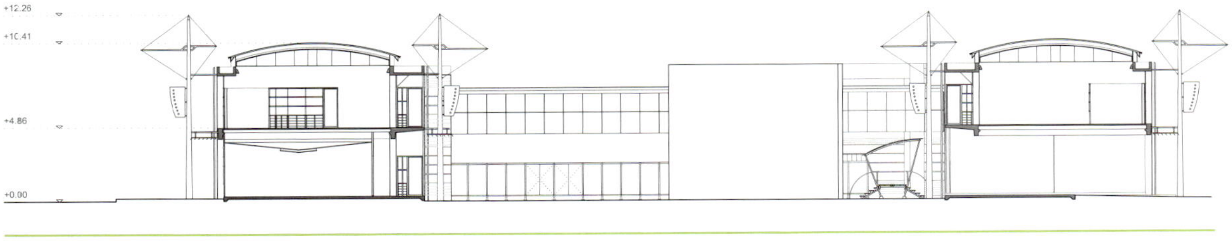

Section A

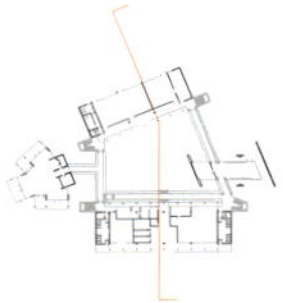

0 5 10m
1:500

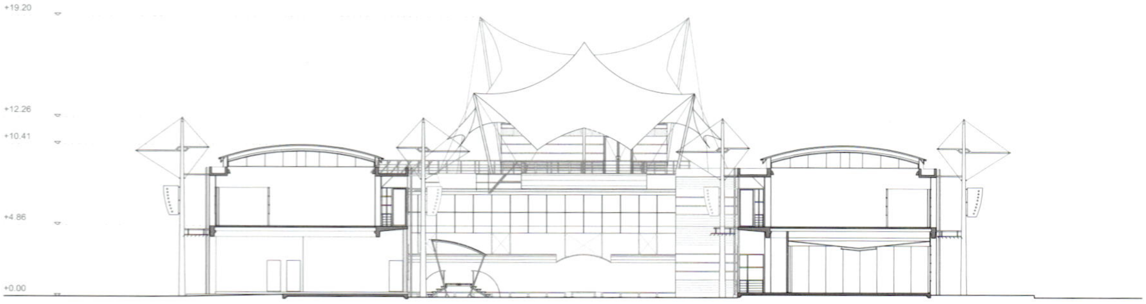

Section B

EDIFICIO HOLCIM

Bruno Stagno

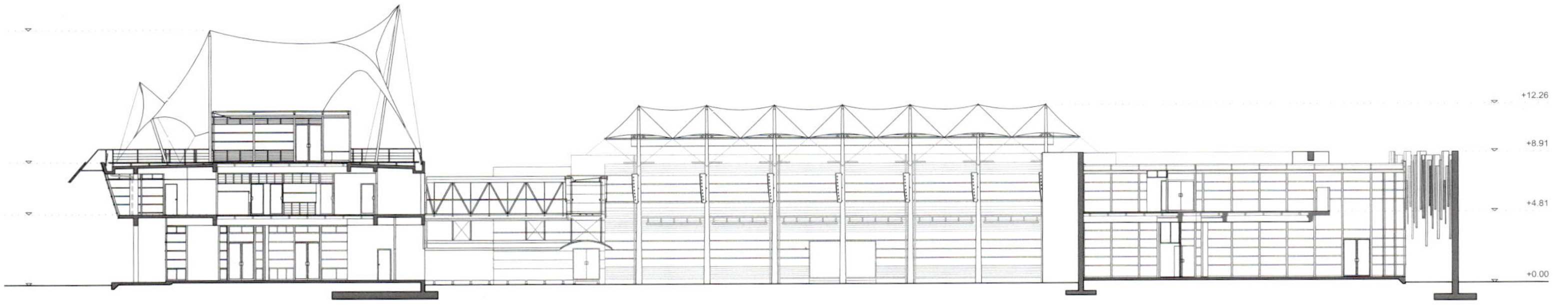

Section C

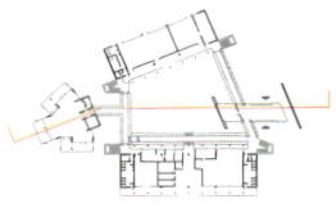

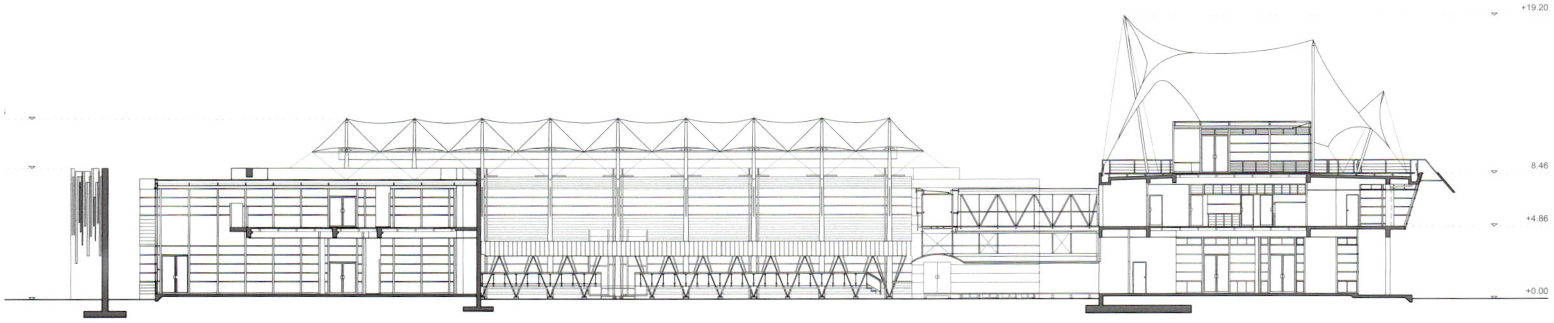

Section D

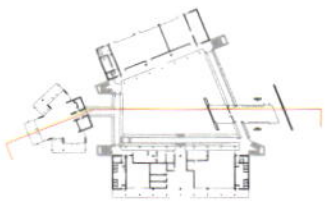

0 5 10m

1:500

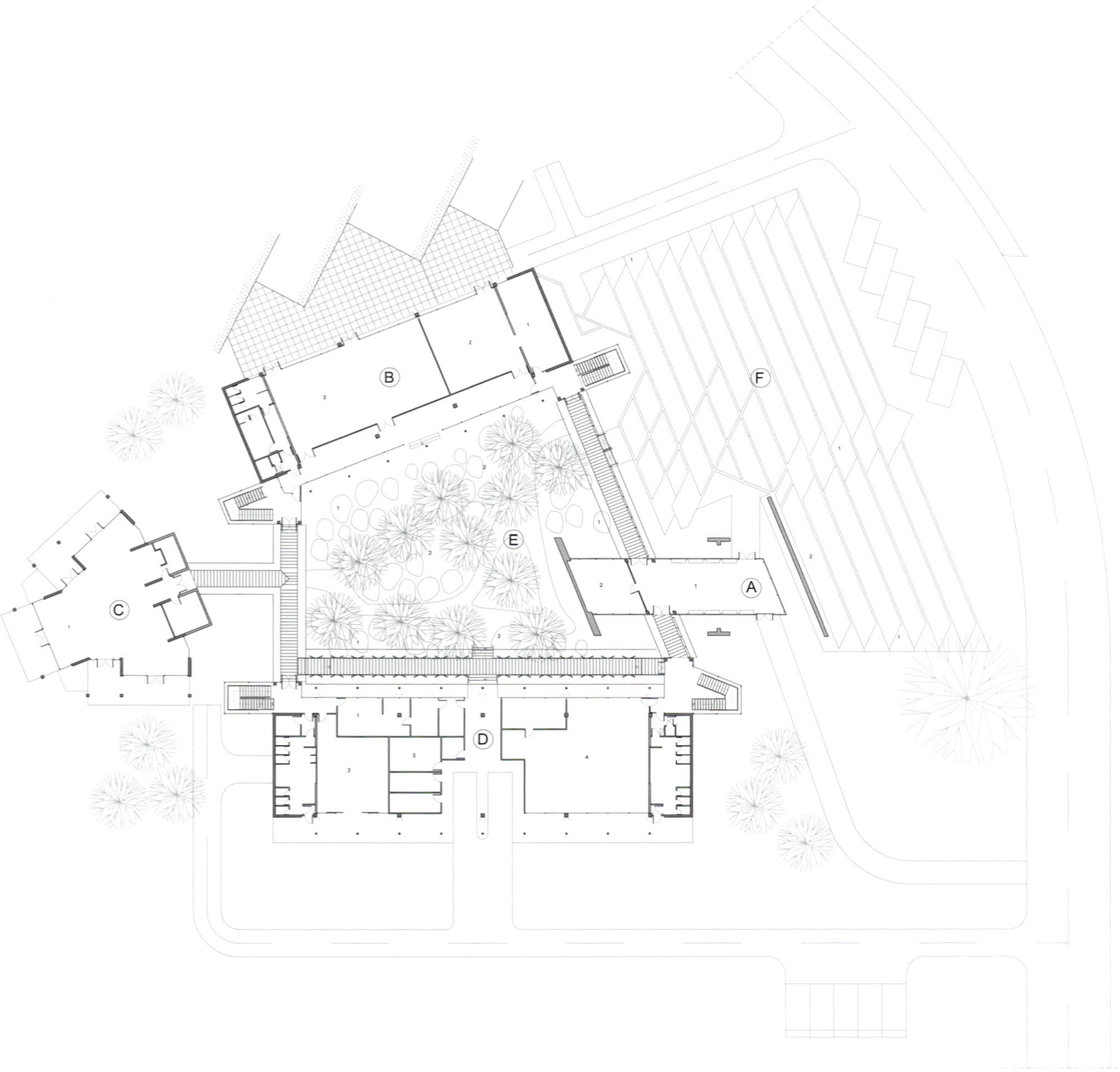

1. Vestibule
2. Marketing
3. Library
4. Exhibition
5. Auditorium
6. Cafeteria
7. Computing
8. Gymnasium
9. Archive
10. Engineering
11. Stones
12. Shading trees
13. Fountains
14. Windbreak

Ground Floor Level

0 5 10m

1:700

N

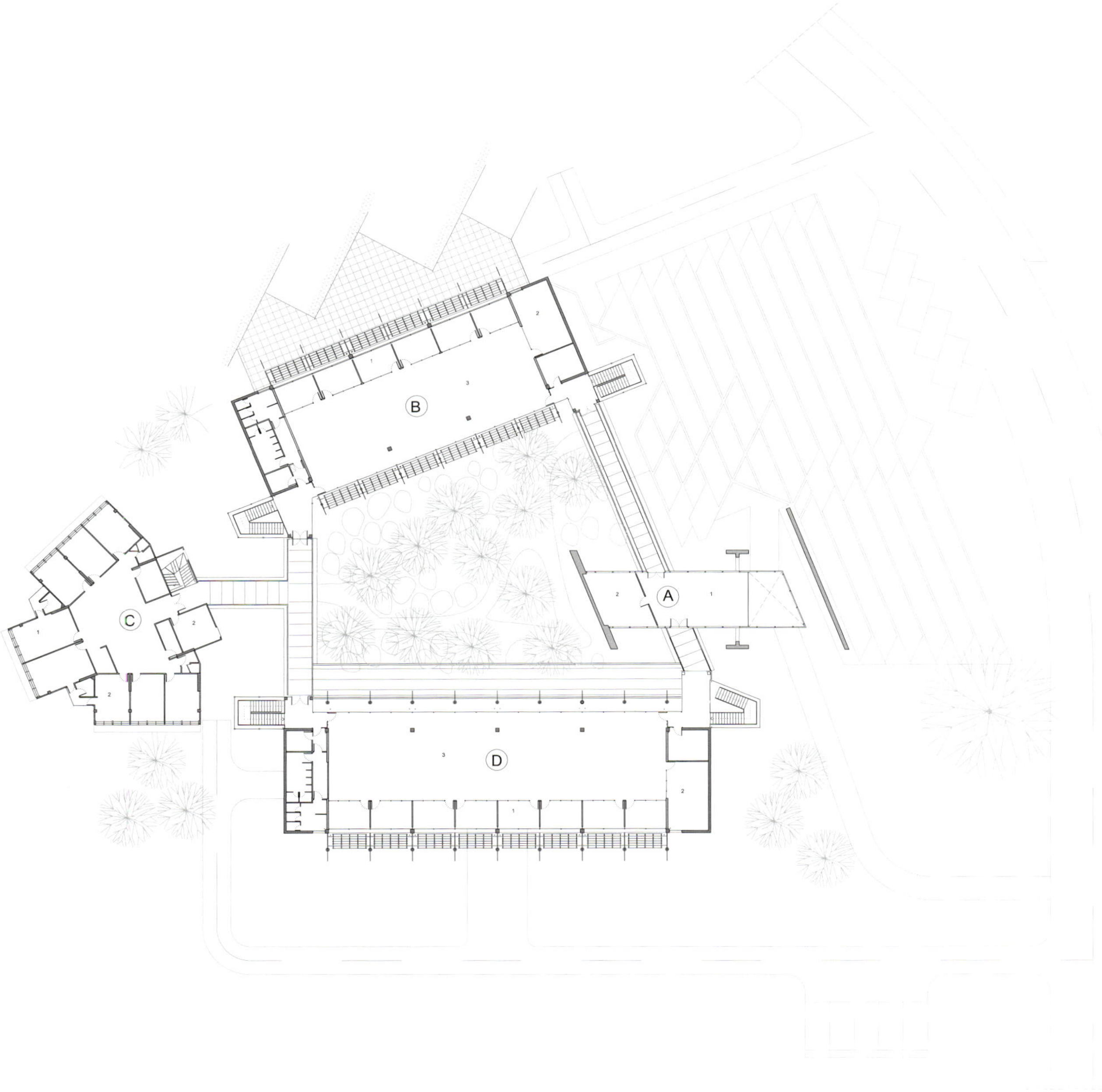

1. Secretary's Office
2. Radio
3. Offices
4. Meeting Rooms
5. Cubicles
6. Offices
7. Meeting Rooms
8. Offices
9. Meeting Rooms
10. Cubicles

First Floor Level

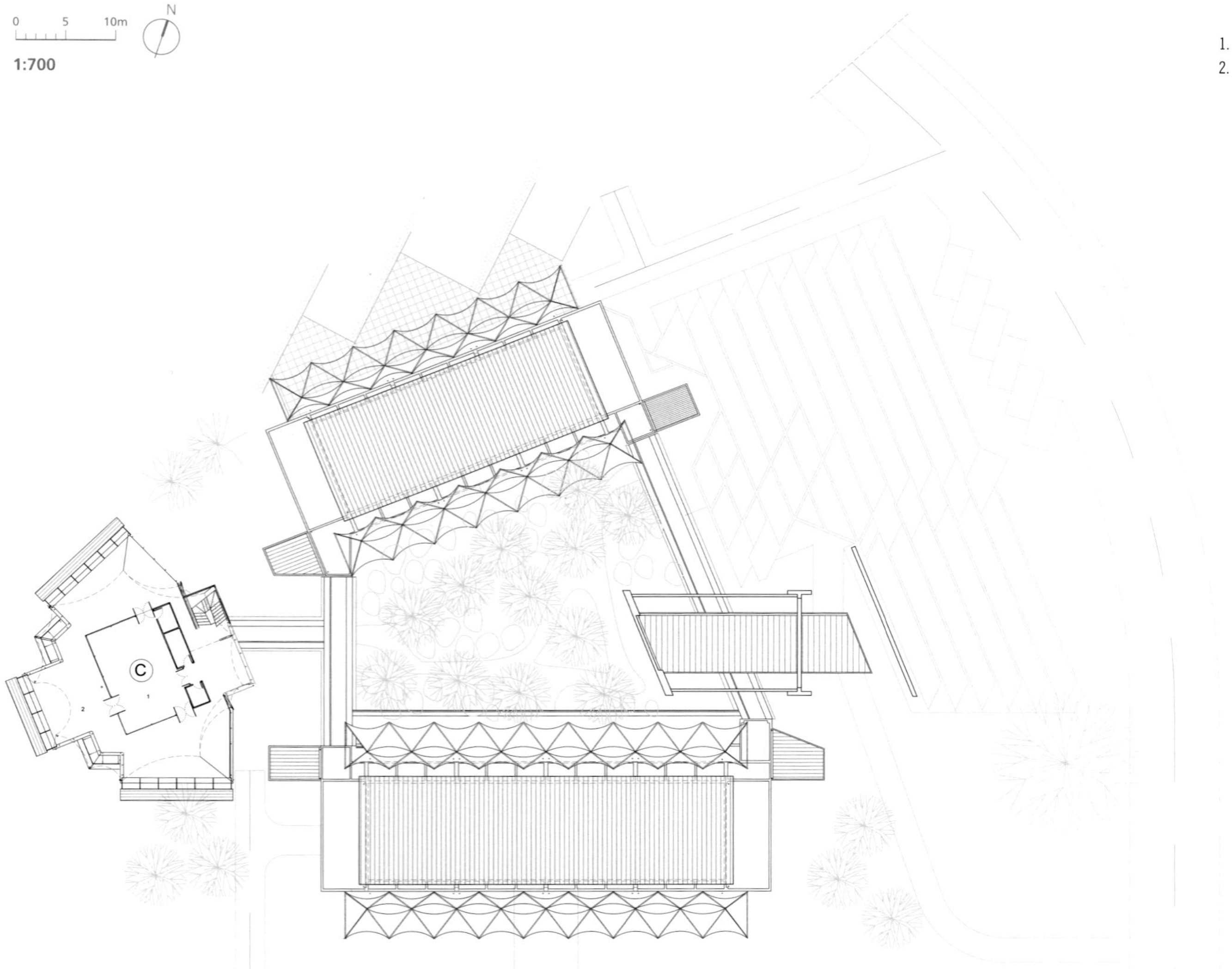

1. Board of Directors
2. Terrace

Second Floor Level

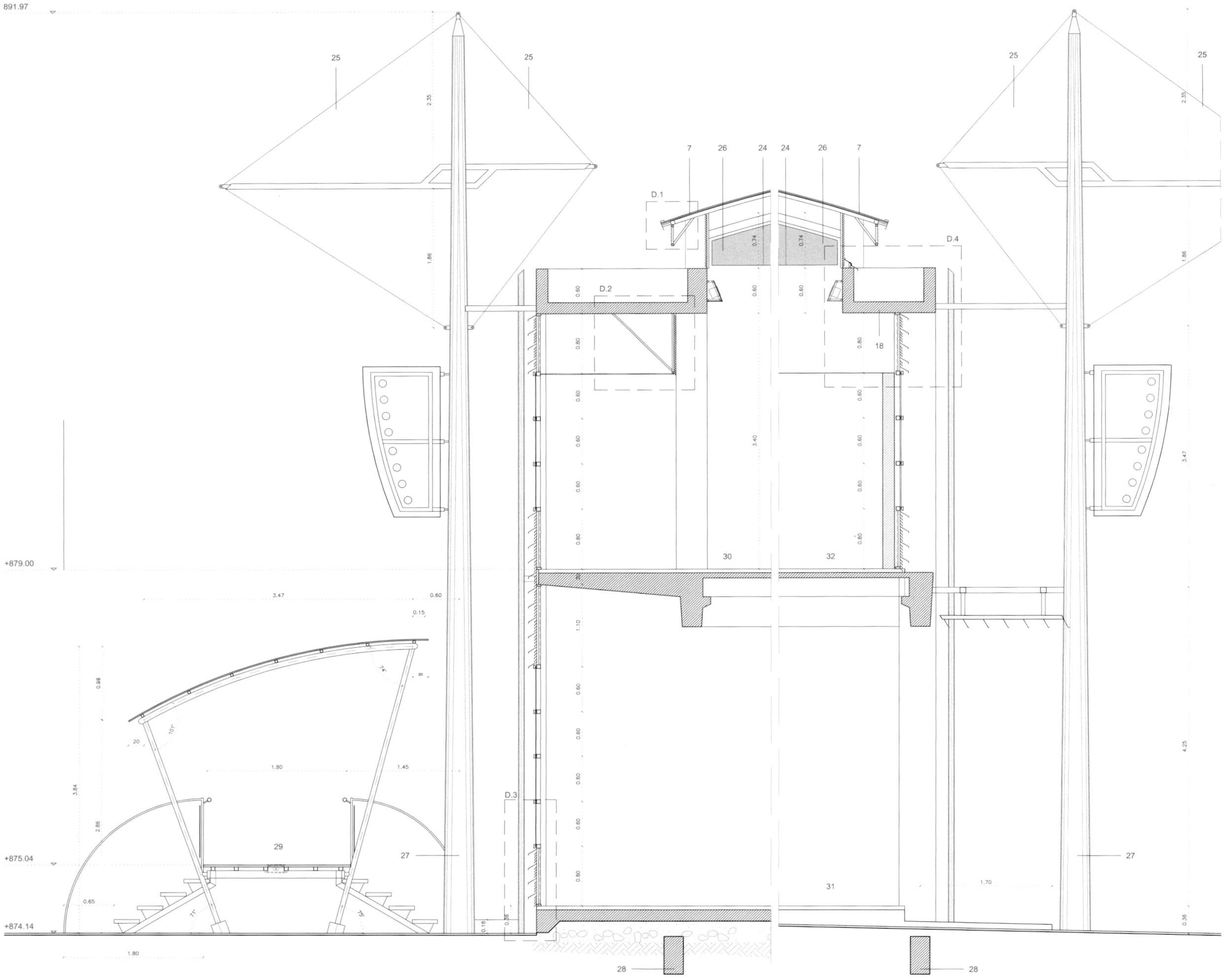

Section Detail

1. Slab
2. Tube of HN 2.5 x 2.5 x 0.15 cm
3. Pavement
4. Plate of 5 x 5 x 0.6 cm
5. Natural anodized aluminum parasol of de 5 cm
6. Fixed Glazing
7. Enameled corrugated sheet roof
8. Plate of 0.6 x 2.5 x 12 cm
9. IRT-2 # 11 cut and painted
10. Polyester sieve with aluminum frame
11. Aluminum mesh type Jordomex # 8, format 30 cm
12. Tube of 5 x 5 x 0.2 cm
13. Tube of 5 x 5 x 0.2 cm, painted
14. Aluminum square to fix
16. Aluminum tube connector of 2.5 x 2.5 x 0.16 cm
17. PVC hose of diameter 7.5 cm
18. Pipe beam
19. Dripstone
20. Rainwater drainspout
21. Drop Ceiling
22. Aluminum framing
23. Dining room lamp
24. Butt joint with silicone
25. Sunshade
26. VF1 - 6 mm.
27. Concrete post
28. Spandrel Beam
29. Covered pass
30. Cubicles
31. Vestibule
32. Offices

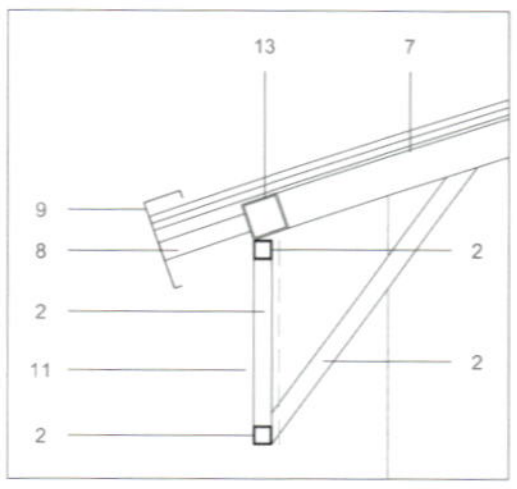

D. 1

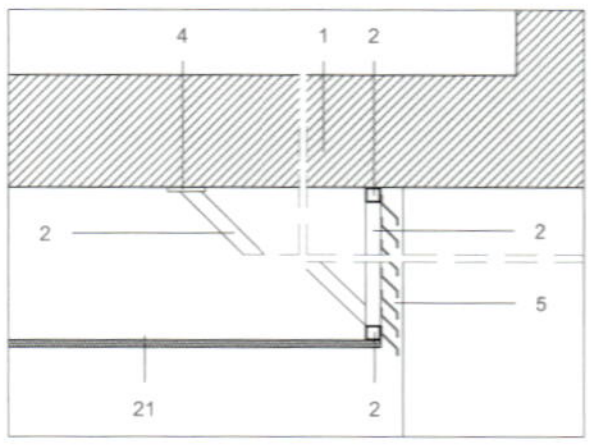

D. 2

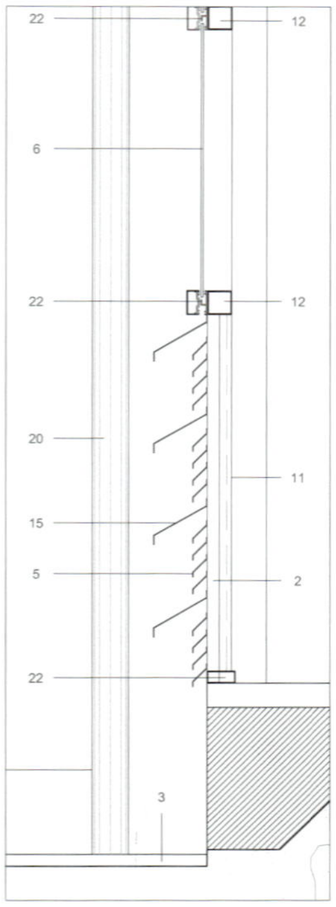

D. 3

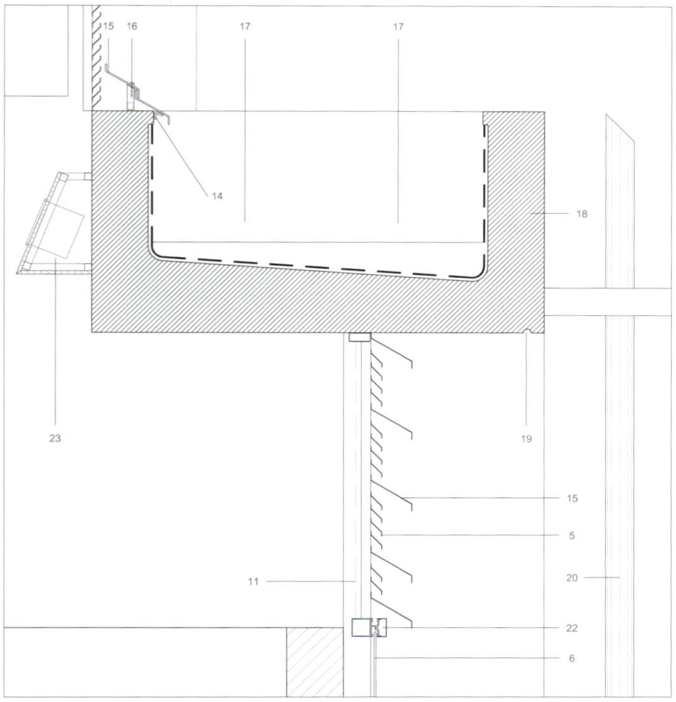

D. 4

07

MCA MARIO CUCINELLA Architects

SIEEB SINO-ITALIAN ECOLOGICAL AND ENERGY EFFICIENT BUILDING

Pekín, China

MCA Mario Cucinella Architects

http://www.mcarchitects.it

ARCHITECTS	Mario Cucinella Architects M. Cucinella, E. Francis, D. Hirsch, G. Altieri
ENGINEERS	Favero & Mlan Ingenieria S. Favero, F. Zaggia, G. Lenarduzzi, L. Nicolini
PROMOTERS	- Chinese Environment and Country Protection Ministry - Chinese Science and Technology Ministry
PHOTOGRAPHY	Gabriele Basilico, Andrea Cavazzuti, Alessandro Digaetano, Daniele Domenicale, MCA Archive

	COLLABORATING COMPANIES
Contractor	IMPREGILO SPA
Lighting	IGUZZINI
Facades	PERMASTEELISA SPA, VITTORIO VENETO
Heating	MERLONI TERMOSANITARI GROUP
Paving	GRANITI FIANDRE SPA
Cooling System	CLIMAVENETA SPA
Heating Celing Panels	PROTER IMEX SPA
Glazing	GLAVERBEL SPA
Photovoltáic Panels	ENITECNOLOGIE SPA

	DATES
BEGINNING OF WORKS	2004
WORK COMPLETION	2006

DESCRIPTIVE BRIEF

The Project

SIEEB building is the result of cooperation between the Ministry for Environment and Territory of the Republic of Italy and the Ministry of Science and Technology of the People's Republic of China. It is a platform to develop bilateral long-term cooperation between the two countries in the fields of energy and the environment and is a showcase for the potential for reducing C02 emissions in the building sector in China.

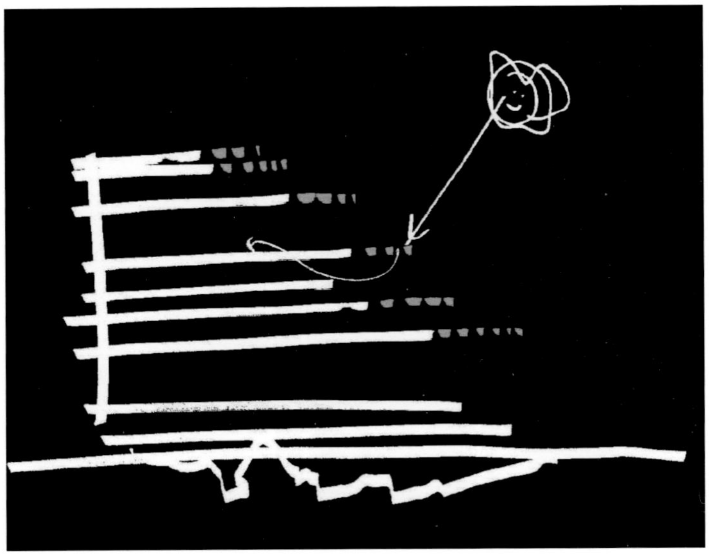

This building has been realized on the Tsinghua University Campus in Beijing and has been designed by the architect Mario Cucinella and the Politecnico di Milano.

The SIEEB faculty building is located on the Tsinghua University Campus. It hcuses a Sino-Italian education, training and research centre for environmental protection and energy conservation, offices and a 200 seat auditorium. It has a floor area of 20.000 m2 and is 40 meters high.

This project is the result of an integrated design process with collaboration between architects, consultants and researchers, a key issue in the design of green buildings.

Architectural Concept

The design philosophy combines sustainable design principles and state of the art technologies to create a building that responds to it's climatic and architectural context. The design uses both active and passive strategies through the design of its shape and of its envelope SIEEB to control the external environment in order to optimise the internal environmental comfort conditions.

The building design has been assessed through a series of testing and computer simulations of its performance in relation to its possible shape, orientation, envelope, technological systems and so on, finding a balance between energy efficiency targets, minimum C02 emissions, a functional layout and the image of a contemporary building. The design found a way to integrate tested and proven components with innovative systems.

Envelope components, control systems and technologies employed in the SIEEB represent the state of the art of the innovative Italian production in the building sector.

The building is closed and well insulated on the northern side that faces the cold winter winds and it is more transparent and open towards the south. On the east and west sides, light and direct sun are controlled by a double skin façade that filters solar gain and optimises the penetration of daylight into the office spaces.
Attractive green spaces, gardens and terraces are distinctive elements of the project. Cantilevered structural elements extend to the south, giving shade to the terraces

"The best way to predict the future is to design it"
Buckminster Fuller

1. Choosing the Site. Project and Development

1.1 Location

Latitude: 39°59'49"N
Longitude: 116°19'44"E
Altitude: 56 m

The SIEEB project emerges from the cooperation between the Ministry of Environment and Territory of Italy and the Ministry of Science and Technology of the People's Republic of China. It is also considered to be a joint work platform between both countries with regards to energy and the environment. It was built with the aim of becoming a research model to show the potential for reducing CO_2 emissions in Chinese constructions. It is located in the Tsinghua University Campus in Beijing.

1.2 Urban Design and Site Improvement

The building site was decided after an analysis of Beijing's climate conditions. The building was constructed in a 60x60m plot located in a dense urban environment, surrounded by 10-storey buildings. The way in which it was built allows for the provision of both private and public green spaces, to be used mostly during the spring and summer, and also to help configure an integrated urban image.

1.3 Project

The design of the building was generated with the help of a series of computer simulations, which evaluated its performance regarding shape, orientation, facade and technological systems. The resultant building is technologically advanced, environmentally integrated and energy efficient. Something as simple as a leaf was the idea that inspired this high tech project. The transformation of sunlight into energy was the leitmotiv of the design which directed the work of the project team.

The building's ground plan is U-shaped. Its two lower floors are for public use and it is here that the commercial spaces, exhibition spaces and an auditorium are located. Those spaces are physically connected with the urban environment. The North-South axis of the first floor is totally permeable to make accessibility easier and emphasize the integrating character of the institution it houses. The building is accessed through a translucent double-height space located in the North, through which the interior garden is visible from the street and the adjacent buildings. A combination of ramps, passageways and gardens allows the circulation to the second floor, which is also for public use.

The other floors house offices and laboratories belonging to the institution. The building has a regular shape, and as the floors go up they become smaller in size, making it easier for natural southern light to reach all of the rooms and the interior garden. The symmetrical shape of the building reduces the size of the areas exposed to the North facade. Vertical circulation is achieved through two staircases and elevator cores located in the East and West wings. These circulation cores, favor the structural stability of the building.

The building's simple volumetric distribution contrasts with the complexity of the facades. The North facade, entirely glazed and hermetic, is linked to the neighboring buildings through reflections. Climatic conditions require that the East and West facades have a double outer shell; the inner is fixed and the outer composed of horizontal slats. The southern façade, resolved with a system of horizontal protection, is characterized by a bold pergola with photovoltaic cells.

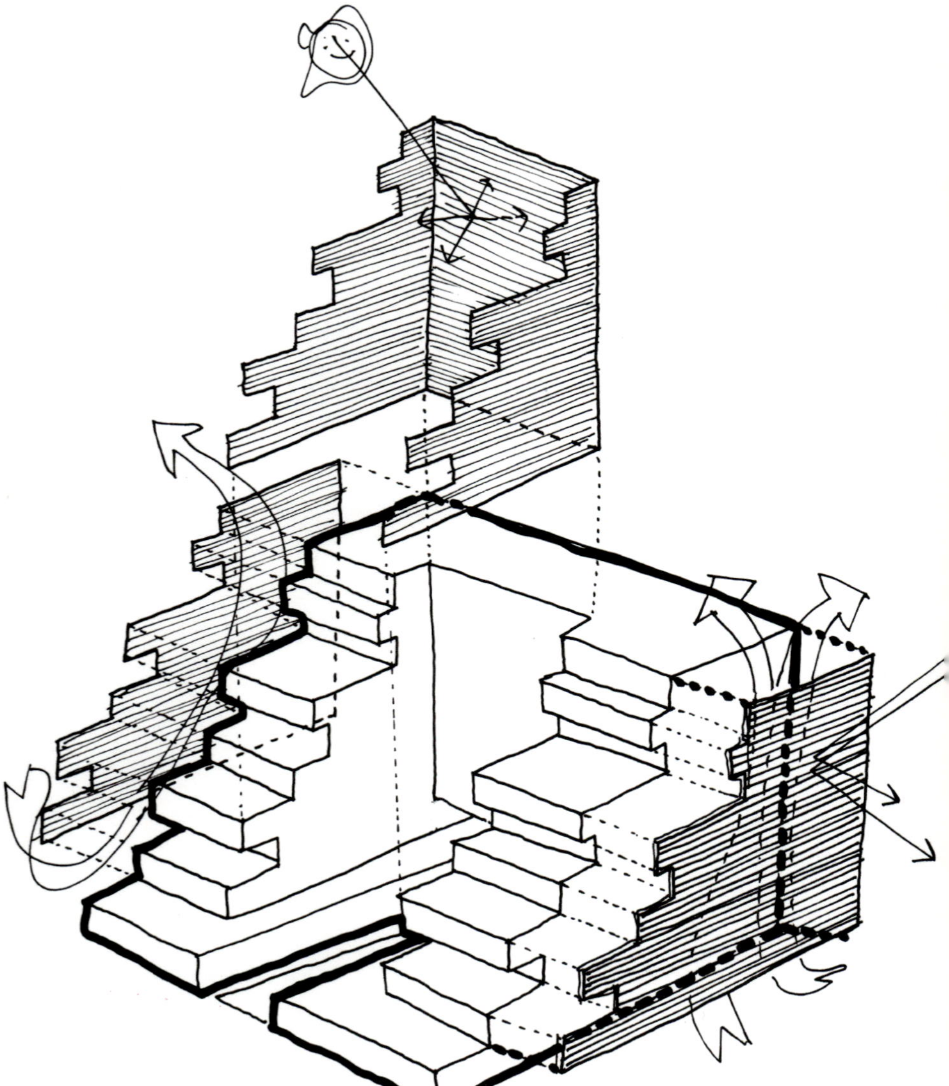

2. Consumption of Energy and Resources

2.1 Consumption of Energy

Thanks to its shape, it is possible to naturally light the offices and reduce the energy consumed to condition the building. The building's outside facade plays a fundamental role in the internal comfort. A design was adopted that adapts the outer shell to the orientation of the façade, optimizing the insulation. Four different kinds of facades can be distinguished in the building:

1. The North facade: exposed to the winter winds. It is basically opaque and closed, completely insulated with insulation panels and glass. This facade has a 43% solar factor and a U value=1.4 W/m2k[1,2].

2. The East and West external facades: naturally ventilated facades with an interior double-glass wall and an outer fixed glass skin. The external layer has a 76% solar factor and a U value=5,4 W/m2k, whereas the internal layer has a 43% solar factor and a U value=1,4 W/m2k.

3. The East and West internal facades: naturally ventilated facades, similar to the East and West external facades, but they include adjustable glass slats on the outside. The outer layer has a 57% factor solar and a U value=5,4 W/m2k, while the inner layer is the same as the previous one.

4. The South facade: with a glass outer shell and projecting structures which permit photovoltaic cells to serve a double function as solar protection and energy collection device. This outer shell has a 42% solar factor and a U value=1,3 W/m2k.

The building was fitted with a HVAC[3] air conditioning system, consisting of boilers, co-generators and heat absorption pumps, which receive energy through the combination of solar and natural gas systems. A radiant ceiling system, which consumes less energy than other technical solutions, recovers heat and distributes it during winter among all the rooms in the building. It is made out of 60x120cm modulated steel sheets, and thanks to the absorption pumps, sanitary water can also be heated.

During the summer, the recovered heat is used to work the absorption chillers[4], so that the temperature of the spaces can be reduced through the radiant ceiling.

2.2 Consumption of Water

All of the sanitary water is provided by reusing grey rainwater which is collected on the roof.

2.3 Consumption of Materials

The structure optimizes materials according to their location inside the building. Reinforced concrete poured in frames with 8x8 m modules and foundation beams, at a depth of 8 metres, were used for the underground levels. The structure from the street level upwards was built with recyclable steel framing, which is frequently used in China[5]. Glass and insulation panels were used for facades, optimising the quantity depending on the orientation. The floor slabs in the mezzanines were constructed with the combination of steel and poured concrete beams, a technique frequently used in China.

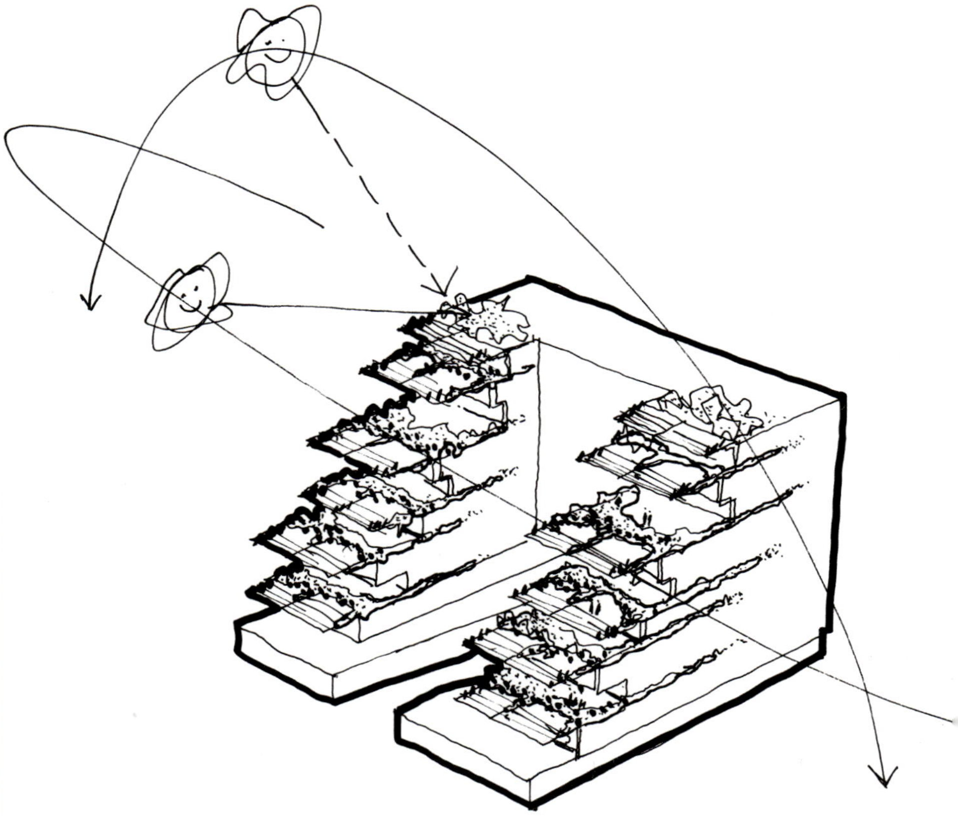

1 The solar factor is a coefficient which is calculated in transparent materials. It indicates the relationship between the quality of the solar energy which strikes the glazing, and the solar energy which actually passes through it. The lower the solar factor, the bigger the solar protection provided by the product.

2 Thermal transmittance (U): a heat flow in a stable regime, divided by the area and the temperature difference of the environments flanking the element being considered.

3 Heating, Ventilating and Air Conditioning: combined conditioning systems used in industrial or large-scale building projects, where humidity and temperature must be carefully regulated, maintaining internal conditions at safe and healthy levels.

4 Absorption chilling: is based on a simple chilling principle using lithium bromide as an absorbent element and water as a coolant. This technology offers an environmentally friendly solution for generating cold, because absorption chillers do not use HCFC compounds as coolants. These chillers also feature low electricital consumption, and consequently require less energy.

5 According to the International Iron and Steel Institute of China, China was the biggest steel producer in the world, totalling 418.8 million tons, and accounting for a third of the entire global production. In 10 years, Chinese production has quadrupled. After China comes Japan (116.2 million tones) and the United States (98.5 million), followed by Russia, South Korea, Germany and India.
http://www.worldsteel.org/index.php

3. Environmental Loads

3.1 Emissions

Form and function, constructive practice and technological innovation were all integrated into the project to achieve low levels of CO2 emission during its construction. To reduce the emissions caused by operating the air conditioning the following technologies were used: a tri-generation heating system, absorption chillers, condensing boilers and radiant ceilings.

A photovoltaic system was adopted to use solar light as an energy source, thereby reducing consumption from the local network which is supplied by coal operated centers. By connecting the system to the municipal network, surpluses can later be sold to the supplier. In this respect, the building produces more energy than it consumes.

3.2 Water Management

Rainwater is collected in deposits in the courtyards, where it passes through a sand filter and is then directed to a municipal treatment plant.

4. Interior Environmental Quality

4.1 Ventilation

During the spring, the strong winds bring sand to Beijing from the Northern Mongolian deserts, sometimes making the air unbreathable. Hence, the North facade is practically hermetic and the ventilated facades renew the air on the East and West sides.

4.2 Natural Lighting

Apart from the skin of the facade, which permits natural lighting, several metallised fabric elements in the East and West facades allow light to be controlled inside the building.

Highly efficiency fluorescent systems controlled by light intensity regulators were chosen to provide artificial lighting. A system of photo sensors allows for the regulation of light intensity in the different rooms depending on the time of day; it even turns off lights in areas where there is no one present, avoiding energy waste[6].

5. Control of the Construction Systems

5.1 Functionality and Efficiency

Materials are rationally used according to their requirements, as in the case of varying the exterior surfaces of the facades depending on their orientation. The 190 modules of photovoltaic cells, distributed in the East and West wings of the building, provide energy and, at the same time, passively control solar gain. The staircase and elevator cores, made with steel frames, meet the double function of allowing vertical displacement and providing structural stability.

5.2 Control of the Construction Systems

The skins in the East and West inner facades are operable elements, which can be positioned to regulate the interior lighting and insulation. The automatic systems to control the light are also manually operable to facilitate the development of specific activities.

6. Long-term Performance

6.1 Flexibility and Efficiency

The subdivision of the space between modules is facilitated by a rational structural arrangement of the floors intended for office use. On the other hand this makes the adaptation of industrial mass-produced elements into the facade easier.

The way materials are used with regards to their location and the differentiation of the facades according to their orientation can be applied to every kind of institutional or service project with a similar scale to that of this building.

7. Economic and Social Aspects

7.1 Social Aspects

It is worth emphasizing the collaboration of work between government organizations and private companies from both countries. Technical teams from the Asian country played an active role in defining the project, preparing the plans, construction and quality control, even though the technology was transferred to China from Italy. This fostered the use of local materials alongside the highly technological components contributed by the Europeans.

7.2 Economic Aspects

Applying environmental criteria to construction in countries with such a spectacular growth as China[7] will necessarily entail long-term economic benefits. Demonstrating, through large-scale institutional projects such as the SIEEB, that it is possible to reduce the consumption and demand of energy in buildings has a positive effect on a local scale within a fast-growing economy and also on a global scale with regards to environmental protection.

8. The Architect's Eye

The authors designed a unique and open building, which has a high didactic value within a developing constructive reality. They joined the simplicity of the volumetric approach with technologically advanced solutions for the facades, which were consequently adapted to the environmental conditions. Form and function are united in the pergola, an architectural element that, besides capturing energy and having a protective function, gives the building a great deal of character.

6 http://www.iguzzini.com/html/es/2288.html

7 After the United States, China is the second biggest energy consumer in the world. Energy is mostly obtained from coal-based generating plants. Therefore the government makes huge efforts to reduce the quantity of energy needed to maintain the economy, which grew 10.7% in 2006, the biggest growth in a decade. China Institute. University of Alberta, Canada. http://www.uofaweb.ualberta.ca/chinainstitute/

South Elevation

0 5 10m

1:600

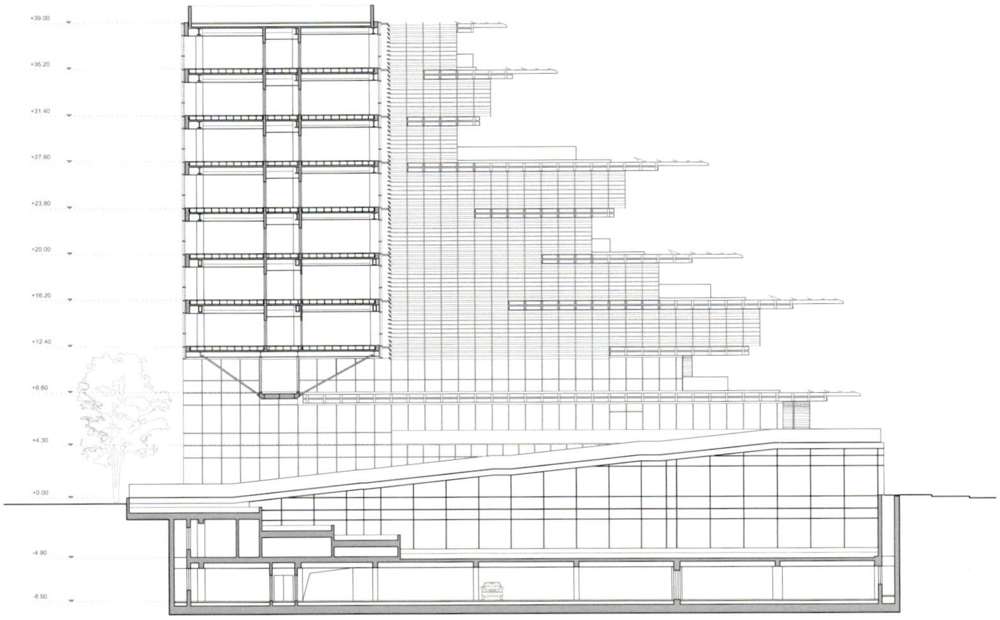

Longitudinal Section

0 5 10m

1:600

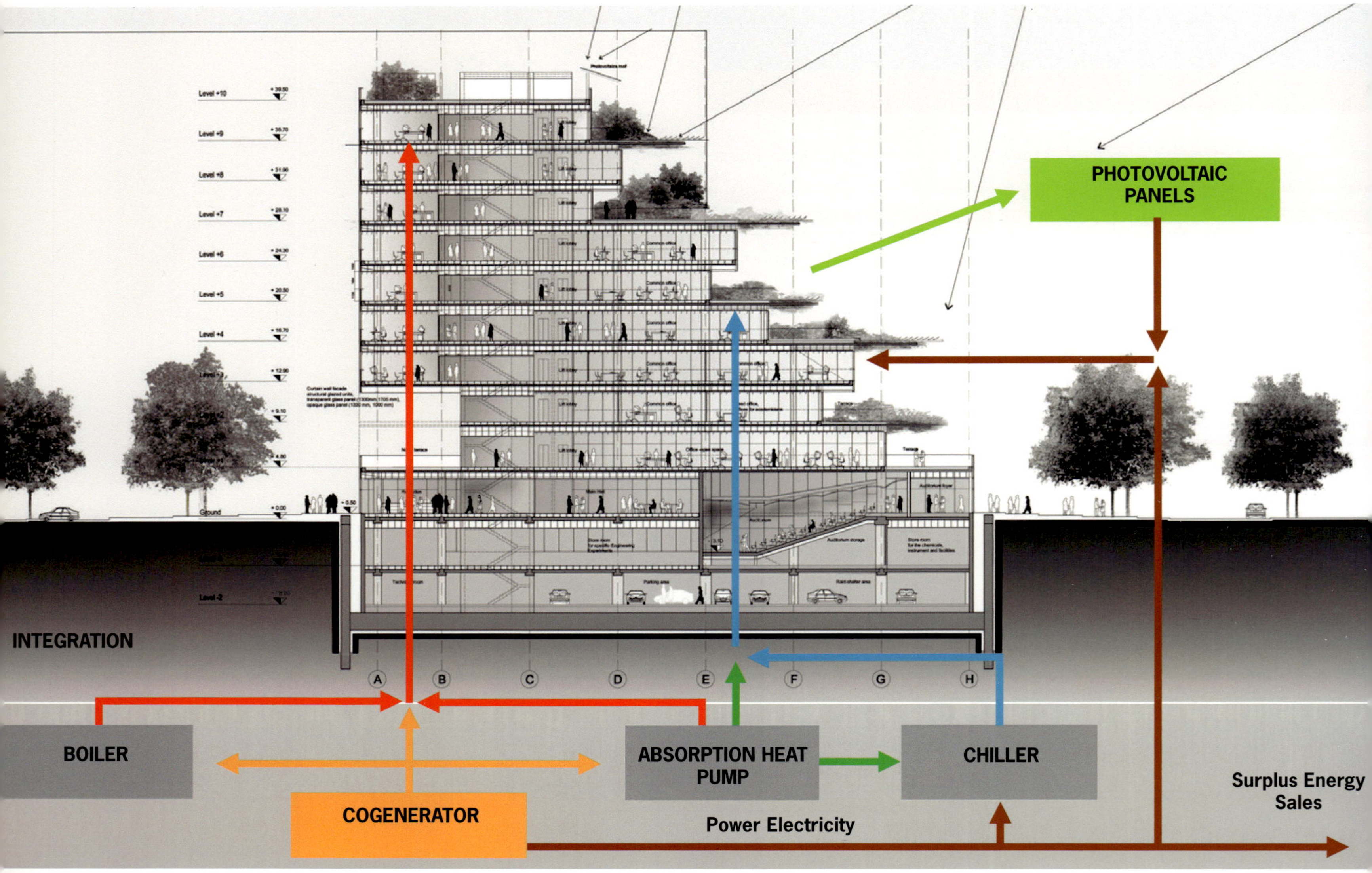

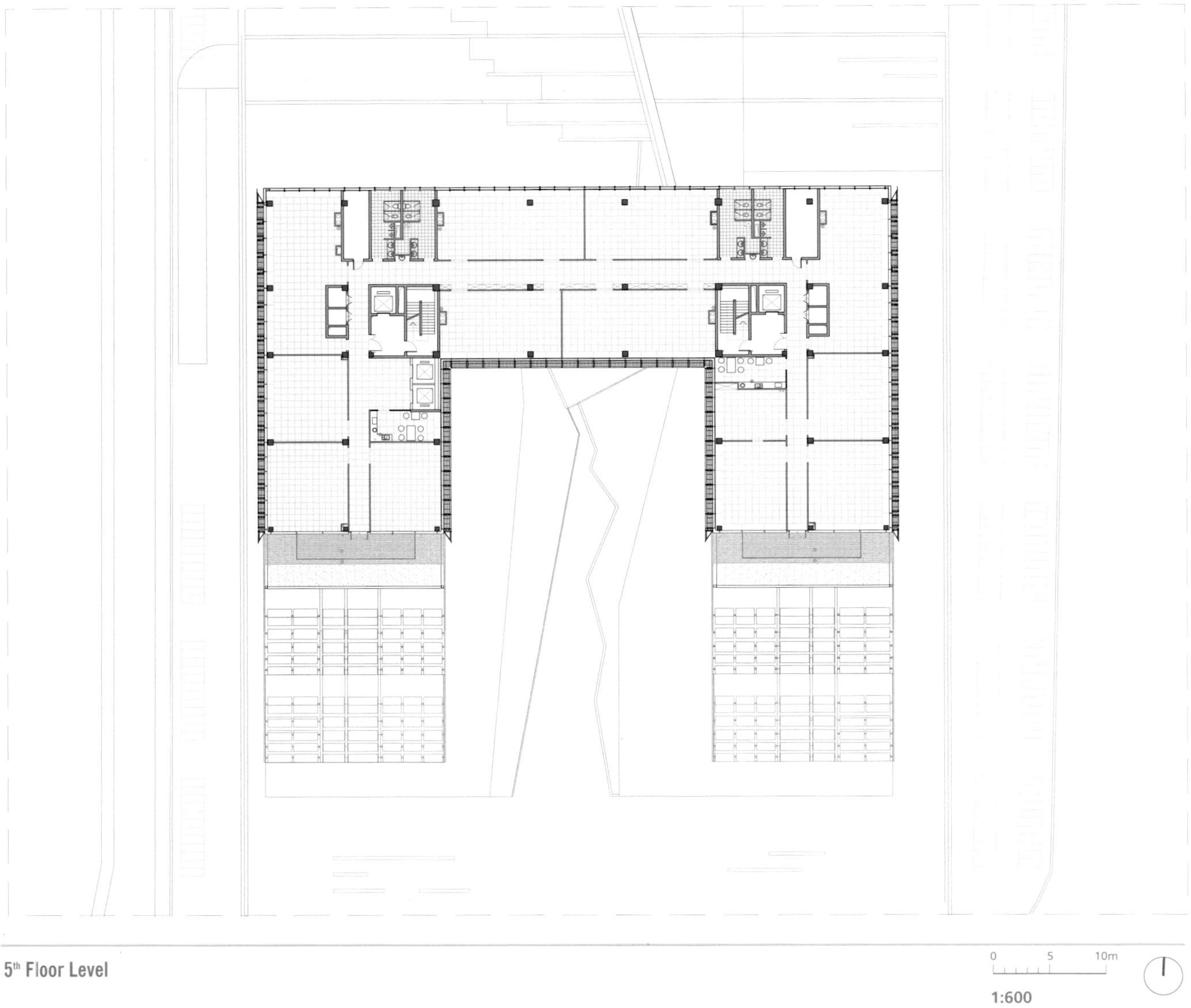

5th Floor Level

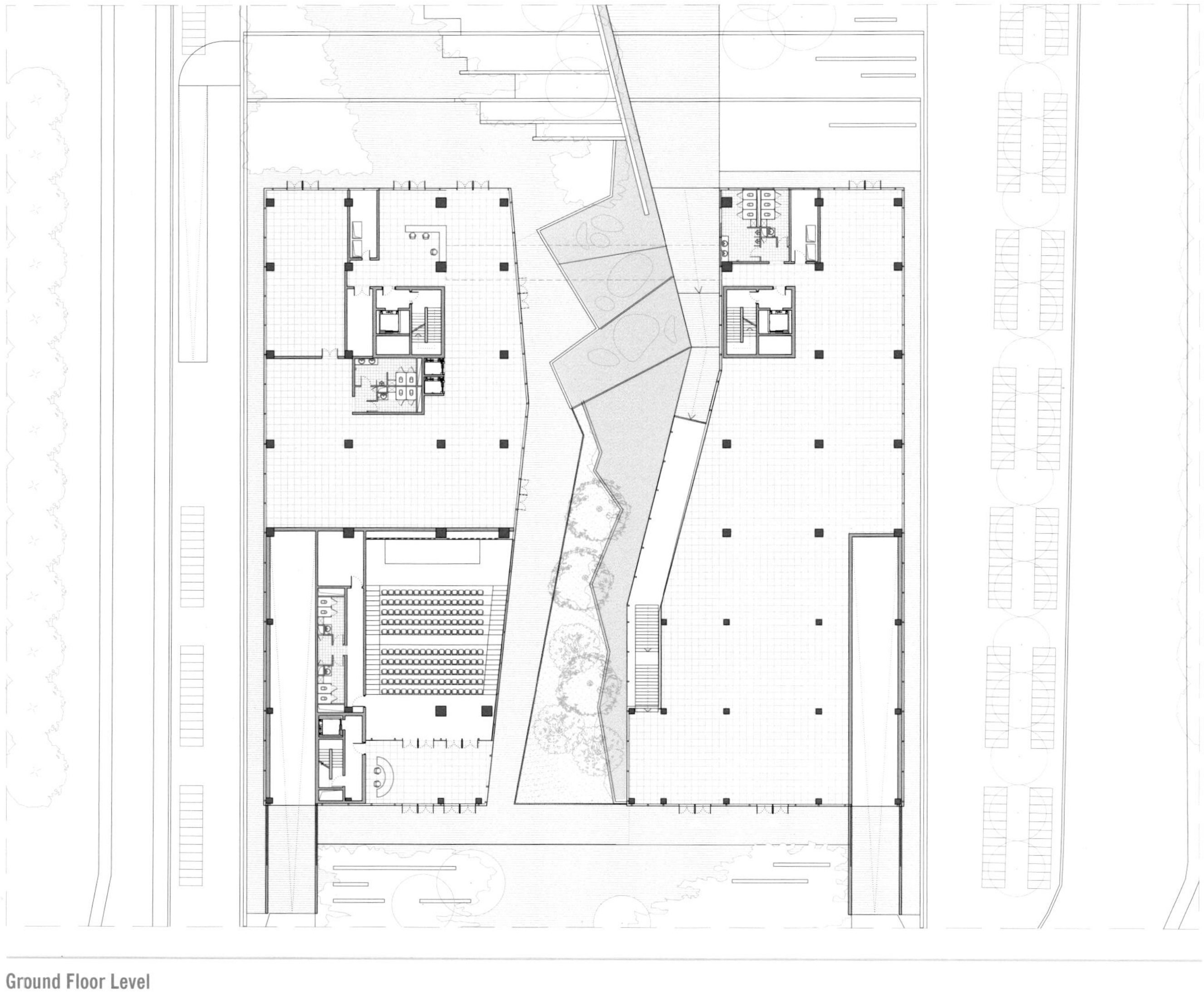

Ground Floor Level

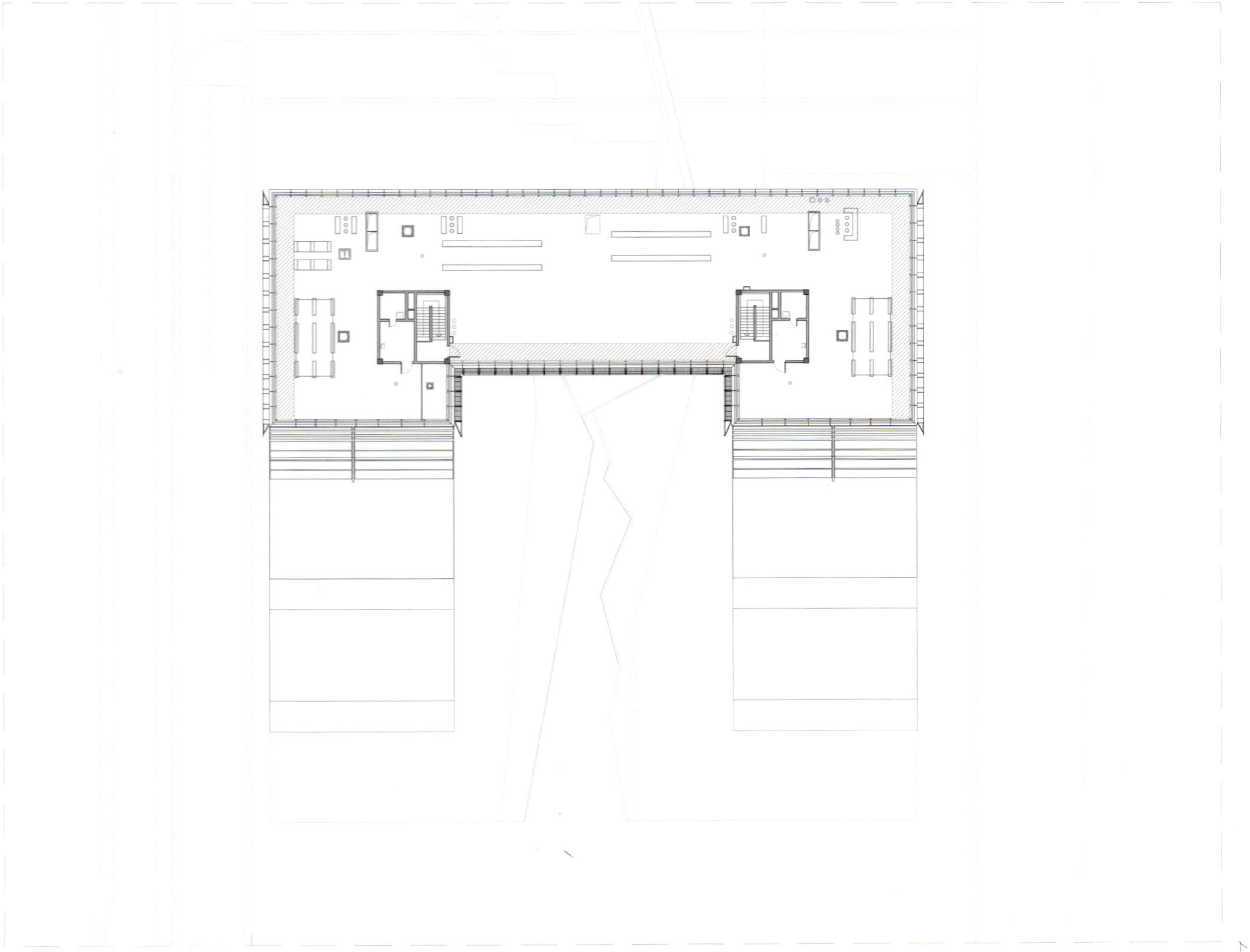

10th Floor Level

0 5 10m

1:600

SIEEB SINO-ITALIAN BUILDING
MCA Mario Cucinella Architects

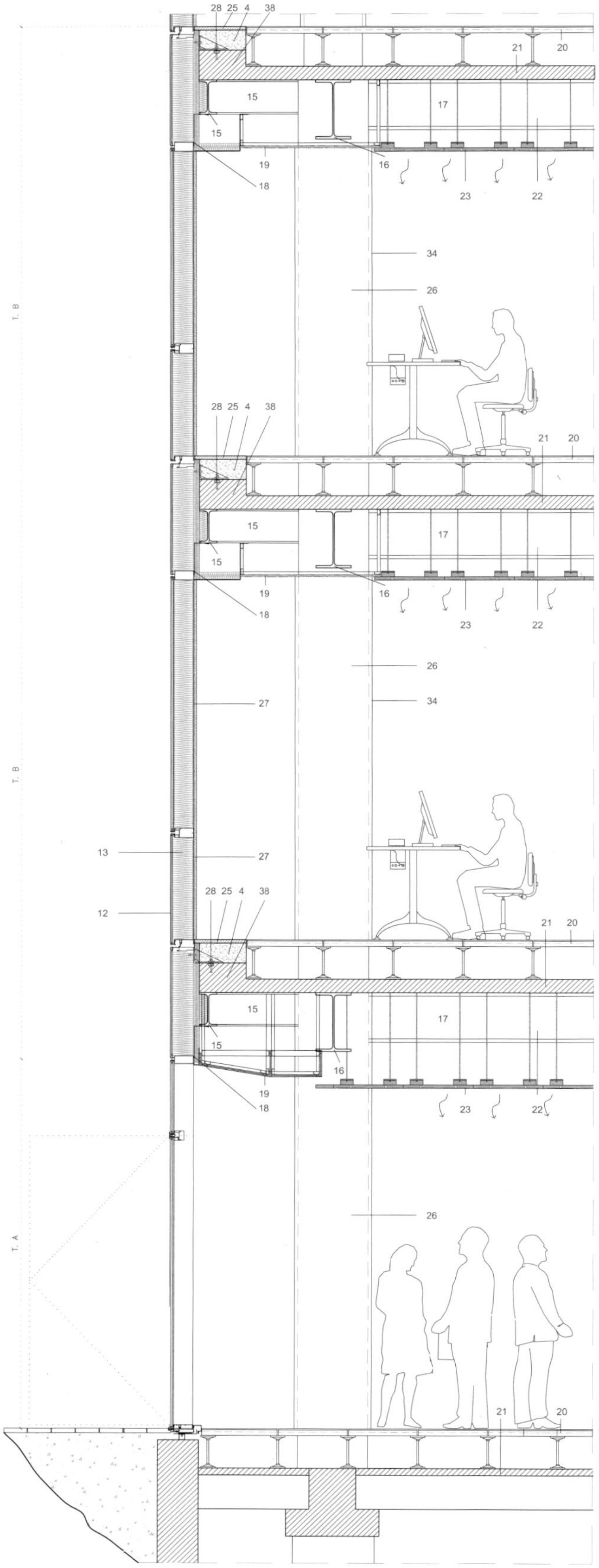

Section 1

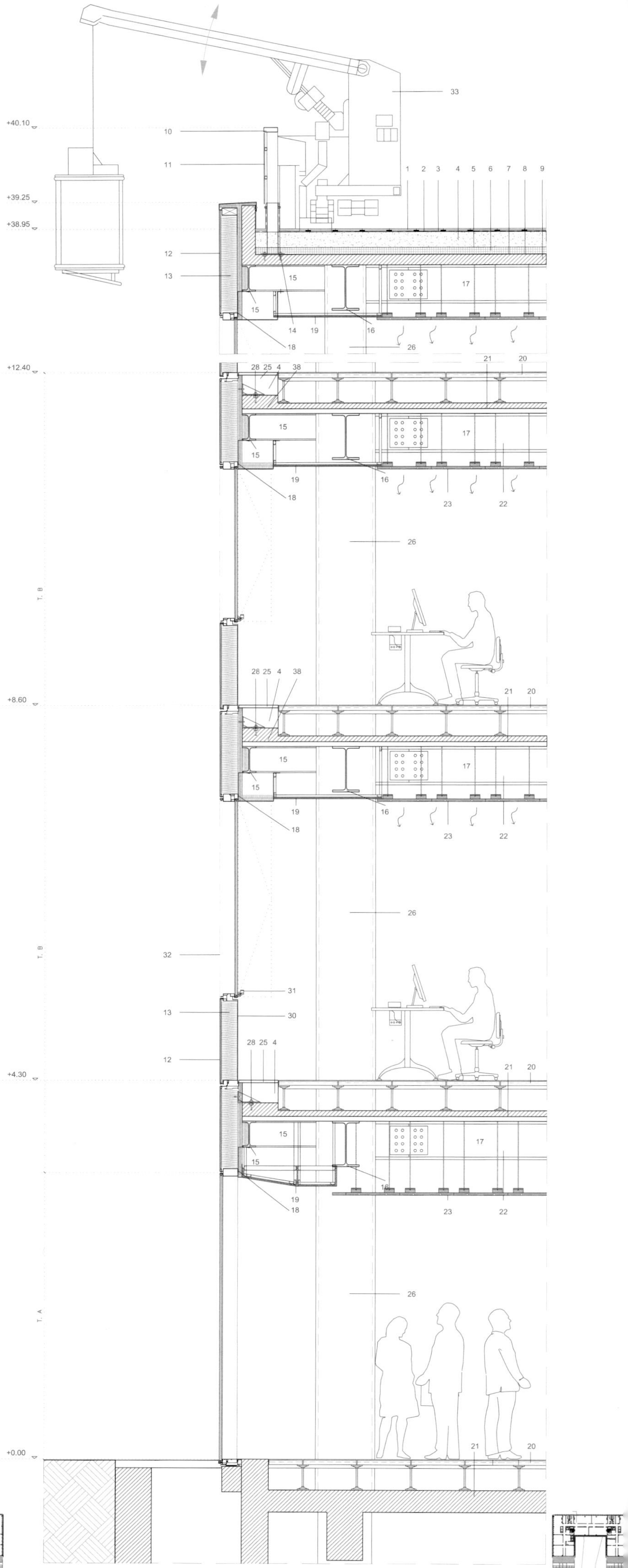

Section 2

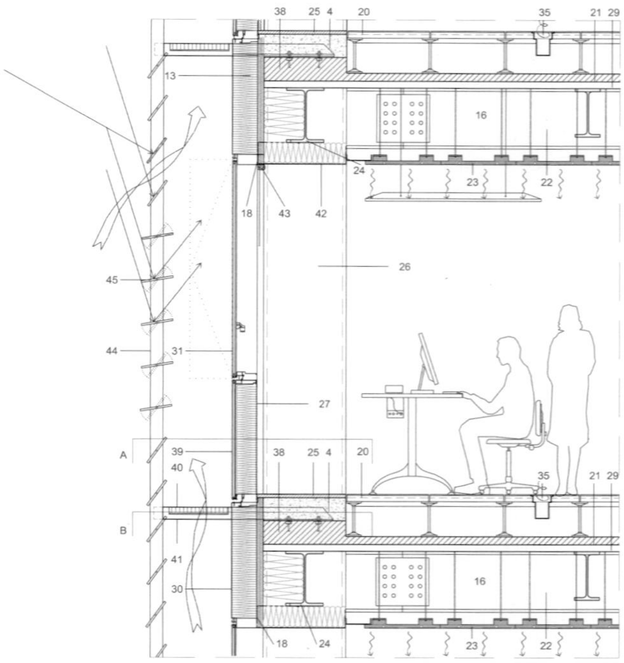

Section 3

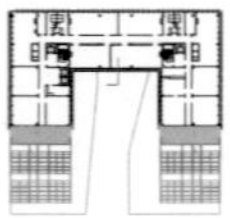

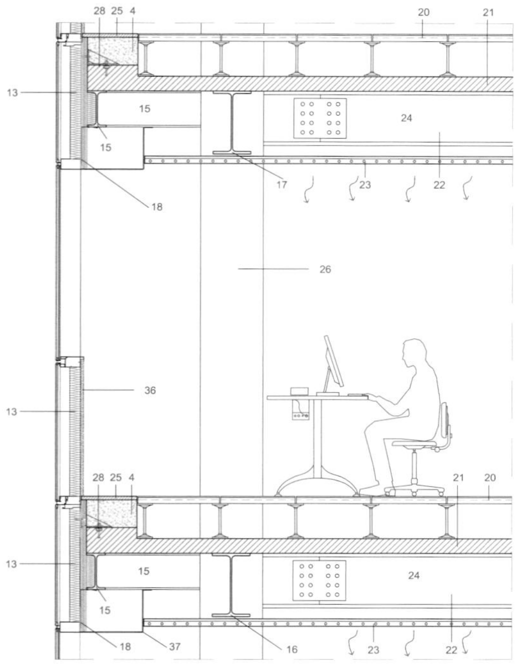

Section 4

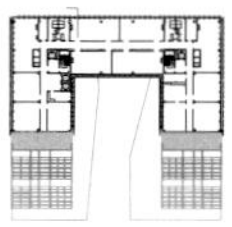

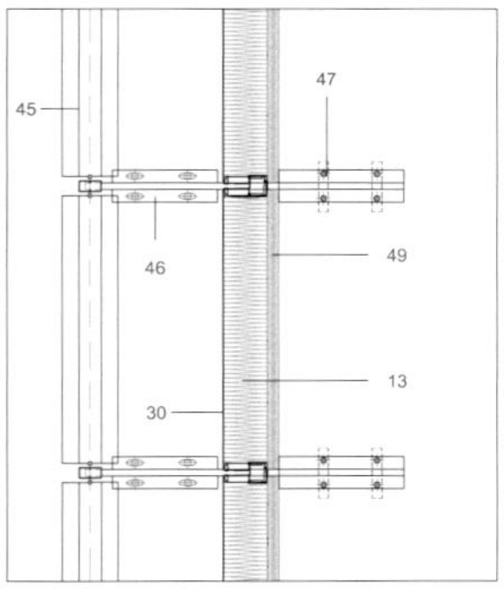

Section A

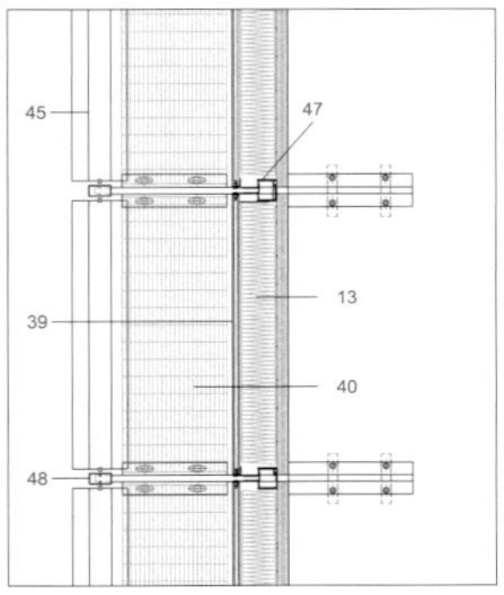

Section B

1. Prefabricated concrete paving
2. Separation layer
3. Waterproofing layer
4. Cement mortar
5. Separation layer
6. Insulation
7. Vapor barrier
8. Compensation layer
9. Compression layer
10. Steel handrail
11. Perforated aluminum panel
12. Enameled glass
13. Spandrel panels
14. Anchor bolt Halfen
15. HN 300x150
16. HM 500x300
17. HM 450x200
18. Metal sheet for fire protection
19. Gypsum board
20. Floating floor
21. Concrete slab
22. Steel beam
23. Radiant ceiling
24. HM 450x300
25. Stone finish
26. Steel column
27. Steel finished panel
28. "Halfen" brackets
29. Corrugated sheet
30. Aluminum finish
31. Tilt and turn window
32. Perforated metal panel
33. Glass cleaning machine
34. Fire protection
35. Fresh air floor diffuser
36. Laminated plaster board
37. Steel console
38. Built-up concrete slab edge
39. Double glazed enameled panel
40. Metal grated walkway for maintenance
41. Steel cantilever
42. Built-in ceiling
43. Built-in roller blind
44. Aluminum mullion for glass louvers support
45. "Double skin" external facade with glass louvers
46. Steel plates
47. Bolts connected to "Halfen" support
48. Mullion for support to glass louvers
49. Polyurethane panels between the cladding element

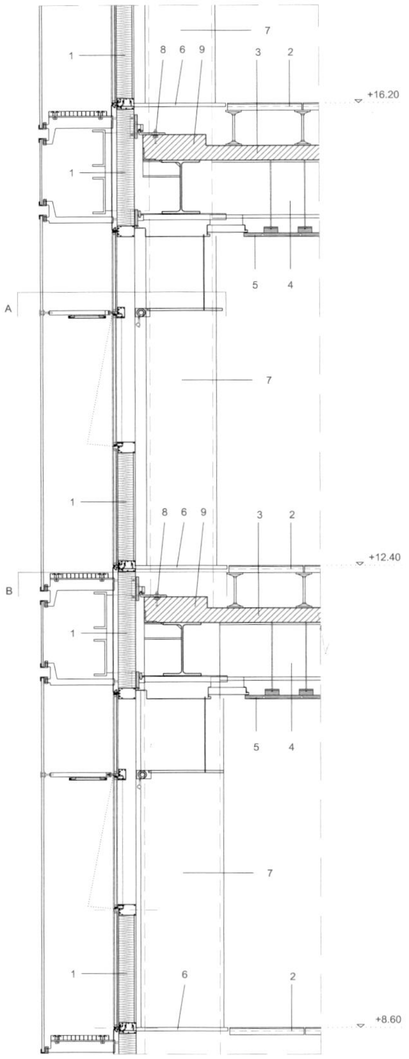

Section 5

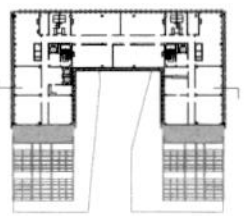

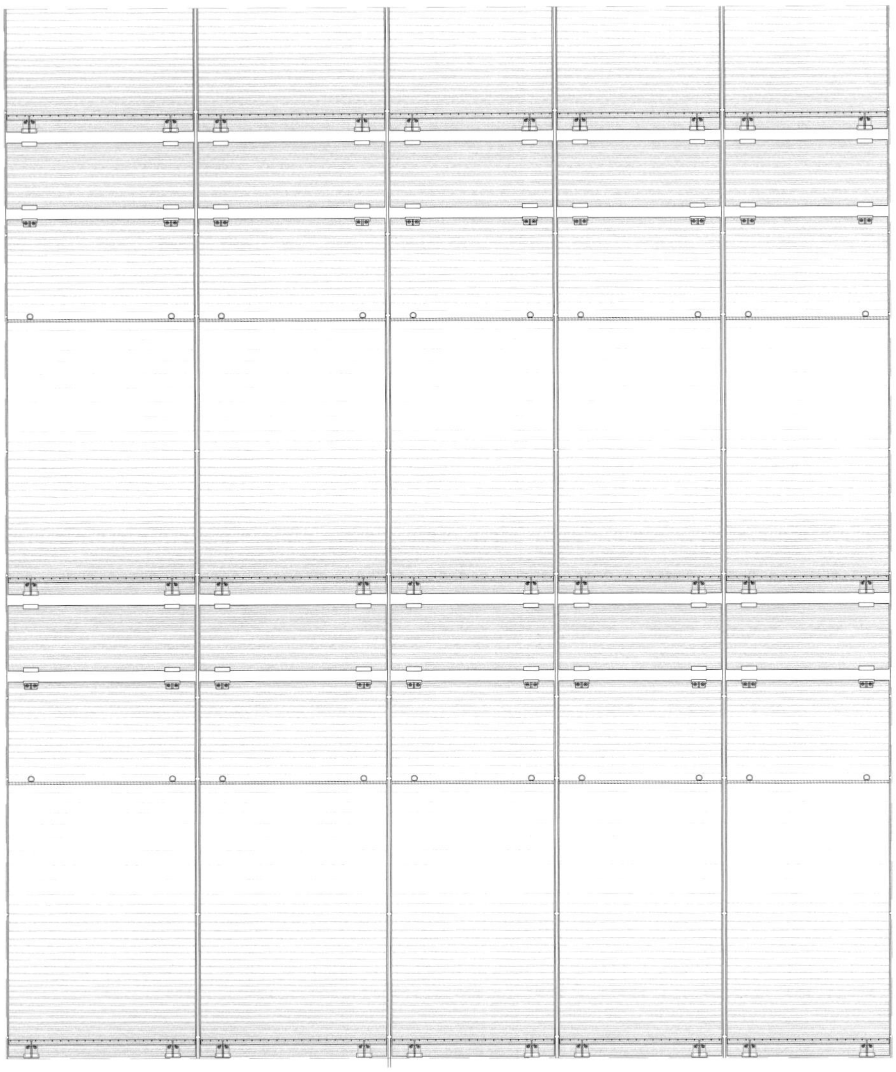

Elevation

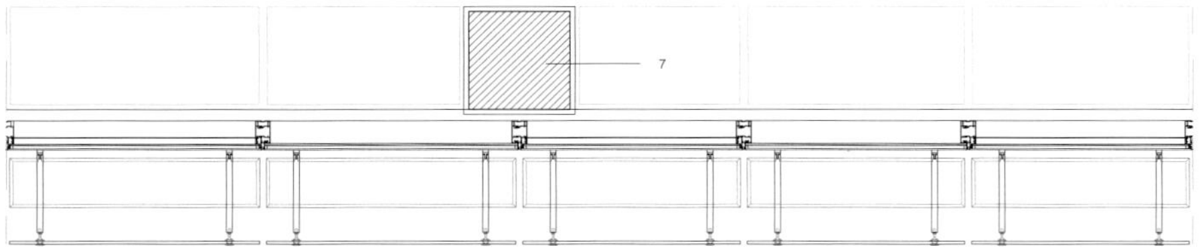

Section A

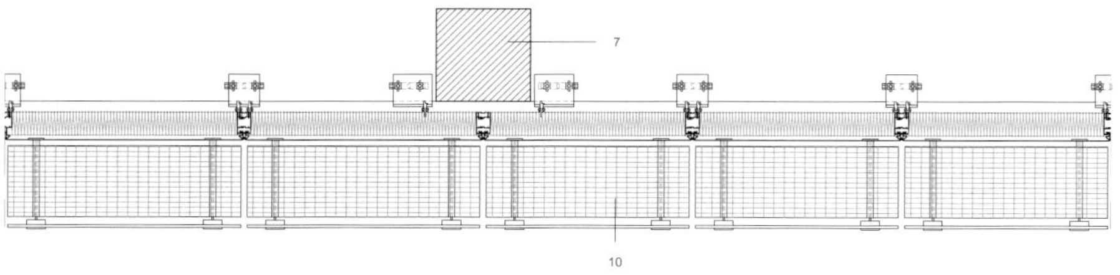

Section B

1. Spandrel panels
2. Floating floor
3. Concrete slab
4. Steel beam
5. Radiant ceiling
6. Stone finish
7. Steel column
8. "Halfen" brackets
9. Built-up concrete slab edge
10. Metal grated walkway for maintenance
11. Photovoltaic panels

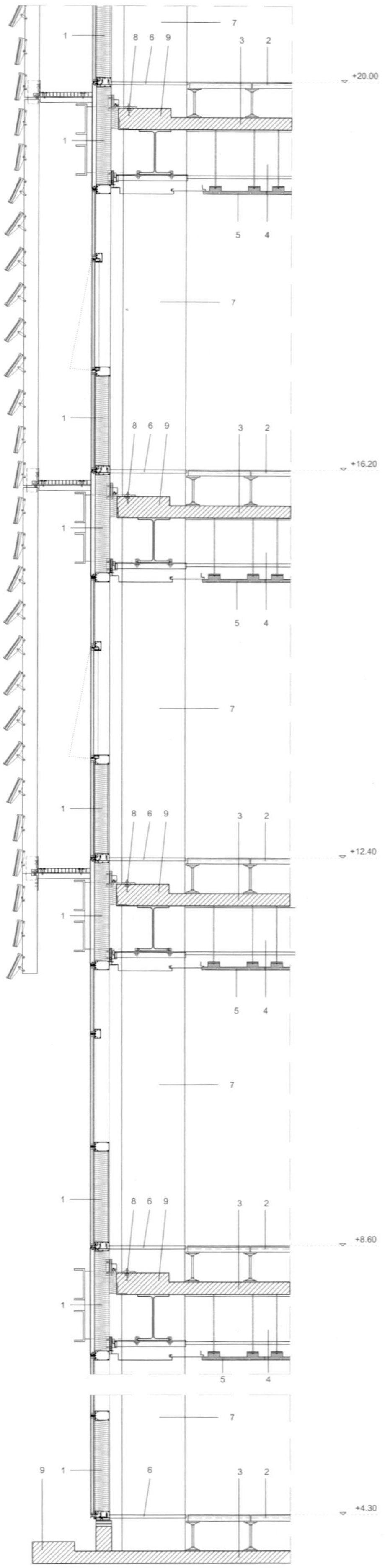

Section 6

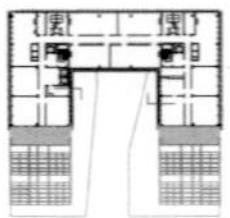

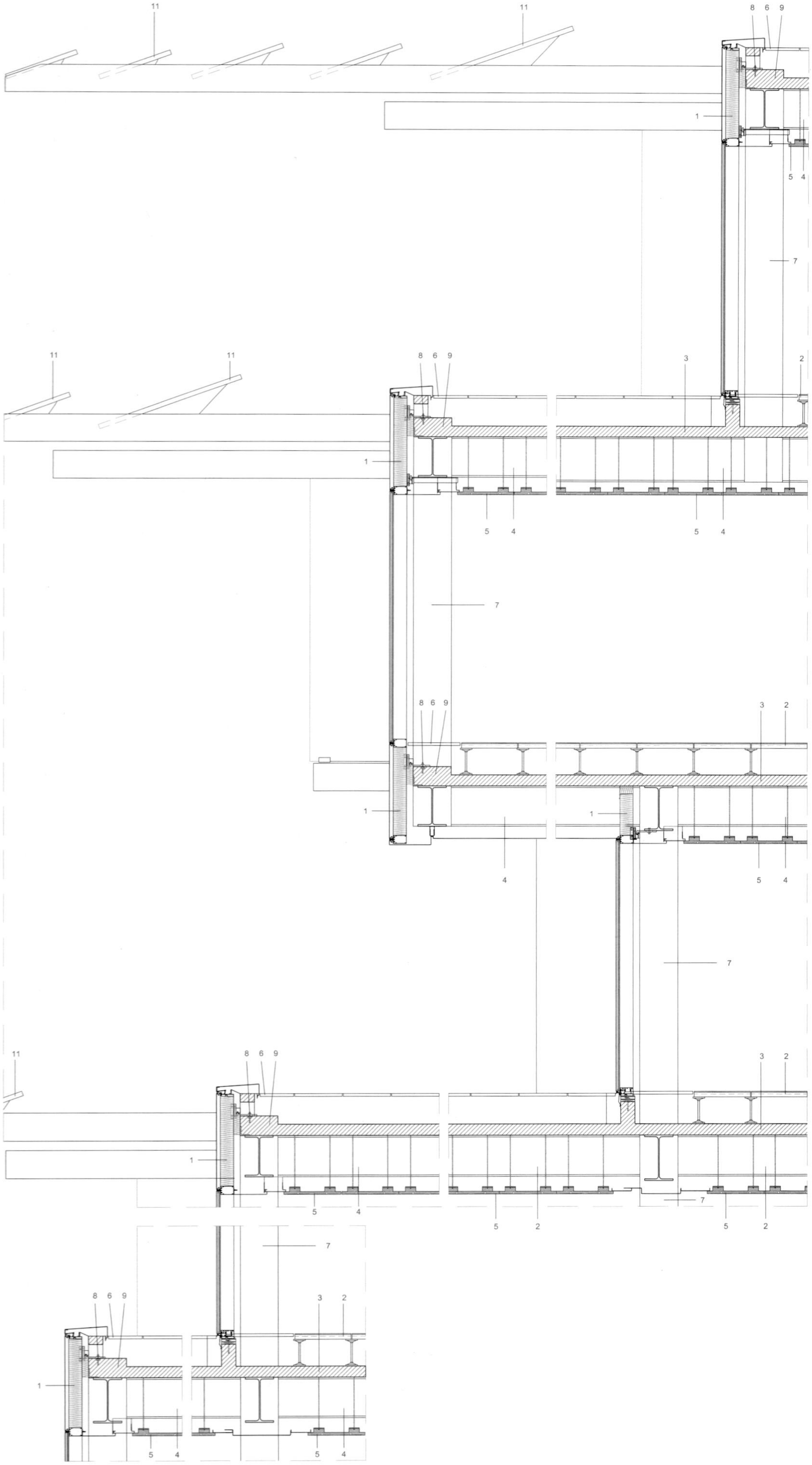

Section 7

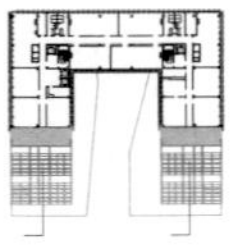

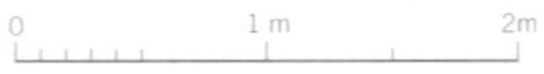

1:60

SARC Architects

METLA FOREST RESEARCH CENTRE

JOENSUU, Finlandia

SARC Architects

sarc@sarc.fi

ARCHITECTS	Antti-Matti Siikala Okke Kiviluoto
COLABORATORS	Sarlotta Narjus, Ville Hara, Niklas Lagerbohm, Anu Puustinen, Tuulikki Raivio, Niklas Sandås, Tiina Torna
CONTRACTOR	The Finnish Forest Research Institute Rakennusliike A.Taskinen Oy
PHOTOGRAPHY	Jussi Tiainen

	COLLABORATING COMPANIES
Interior Design	Arkkitehtitoimisto SARC Oy, Sarlotta Narjus
Landscape	Molino Oy
Electrics	Insinööritoimisto Olof Granlund Oy
Structure	Insinööritoimisto Magnus Malmberg
Geology	Savon Tekmi Oy
Fire prevention Plan	L2 Paloturvallisuus Oy
Acoustics	Arkkitehtitoimisto Alpo Halme Oy
Ventilation	ABB Fläkt Oy
Cooling System	Halton Oy
BMS	TAC Atmostech

	DATES
BEGINNING OF WORKS	2003
WORK COMPLETION	2004

DESCRIPTIVE BRIEF

The construction of The Finnish Forest Research Institute's (METLA) new building to accommodate the new office for Joensuu Forest Research Institute, which was expanding their workforce, started in April 2003 and was completed in October 2004. The building is located at the Joensuu University campus-area, in Joensuu's city center neighborhood.

The staff of Joensuu Forest Research Institute incremented towards the end of 2005 up to 150-170 employees, of which 100 were permanent staff members, 110 were employees, and 60 researchers at the Institute. This growth made it necessary to create new workspaces in the building, because of the insufficiency of the existing facilities.

The research institute's task is to undertake applied forestry research, which supports the regional activities of the companies and is the economic base for the region, as well as to promote the social and ecological development of the area. It is one of the research institutes with more areas of investigation on the topic of wooden materials.

The primary goal of the project, in its construction, was to use Finnish wood in an innovative way. Therefore, wood is the core material used in the building, from the structural system to the exterior cladding. The project perfectly adapts to its environment, in terms of size, which is similar to that of the surrounding buildings. However, the clear form of materializing the use of wood, converts it into an emblem for the city.

The workspaces in the building are arranged around a central courtyard and hall. The entrance to the courtyard is flanked by walls made of 100-year old timber. The courtyard is located in the immediate surroundings of the buildings, and together with the lobby and restaurant form a meeting point for the staff of the institute.

The courtyard is dominated by tall pine trees that grow in the terrace, a conference space that resembles a boat. The tilted wooden columns are inspired by a fish skeleton.

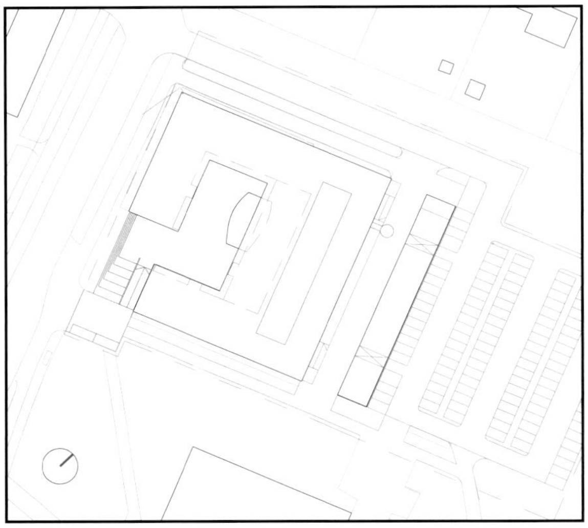

Site Plan

"Modern architecture does not mean the use of immature new materials; the main thing is to refine materials in a more human direction"
Alvar Aalto

ENVIRONMENTAL ANALYSIS

1. Choosing the Site. Project and Development.

1.1 Location

Latitude: 62º36'12"N
Longitude: 29º44'36"E
Altitude: 72 m

Joensuu is a Finnish town located in the province of Eastern Finland, in the region of Northern Carelia. It was founded in 1848. It is also the European forestry capital city, being a reference in research matters. It is the headquarters of the Forest Institute and of Joensuu European Science Park. The European Institute of Forests, the University and other institutions, as well as communication[1] and technology companies grant this town international presence. It has a population of 58.000 inhabitants.

1.2 Urban design and Site Improvement.

The site is on the edge of the Joensuu University Campus, and of a residential area of single-family homes. The setting is dispersed, without a consolidated urban fabric and borders the medium density areas with low density ones.

This project responds, with its proportions, to the other university buildings, and contrasts both because of its use of wood differentiating itself from the rest of buildings made in brick, and due to creating a contained exterior public space, such as an urban plaza that gives the surroundings an identity. The building's typology is defined by a closed exterior and a central courtyard. The courtyard is reinforced by its geometry in floor plan, and it volume open to the interior. On the whole, there remains a sensation of unity that is maintained although it is a public space.

1.3 Project

This project is originated when reinterpreting the typology of a cloister, with an open central space. The building opens towards this space, favoring apertures on the South and East facing facades. The central courtyard is divided, in one third, by a curtain wall. This third has been covered and conditioned to guarantee its use throughout the winter.

The exterior courtyard is accessed by one of the diagonal streets, flanked by wooden walls of more than 100 years old. In the center of the courtyard, a conference room is located, which looks like a boat and is finished with roofing tile of local fir. This figurative element is perceived from the outside as an attraction point that stands out of the rational setting of the ensemble. This courtyard will be dominated by three tall pine trees that have just been planted on the terrace.

The interior courtyard, as if the glass was an axis of symmetry of the exterior, is organized by four sets of laminated wood inclined columns which dominate the access vestibule and allow the triple height that facilitates sunlight into the interior rooms.

1 Perlos, Abloy y Timberjack. Companies for telecommunications, advanced security systems and forest machinery, respectively

2. Consumption of Energy and Resources

2.1 Consumption of Energy

This building is connected to Joensuu´s urban heating system by means of heat exchangers, where the water pipes distribute heating to the radiators of each space. By means of a centralized control system the performance of the system is monitored. This way any unexpected consumption can be detected and corrected.

As insulation, high insulation sandwich panels with wood finish are used. A considerable savings in energy consumption is achieved with this solution.

2.2 Consumption of Materials

This is the first office building of several floors built in wood in Finland. This material was used in load-bearing elements, in facades and finishes. The main objective of the designers was to use local wood in an original way, at the same time as its life cycle as material was coming to an end. This is why priority is given to the mechanical connections between elements, guaranteeing the building's reversibility.

Compared to a building with a reinforced concrete structure, this building uses 55% less non-renewable energies and 75% less non-renewable materials[2].

3. Environmental Load

3.1 Emissions

Use of local wood reduced emissions due to transport to and from the site. All of the wood is certified by the Finnish Forest Certification Council[3].

3.2 Solid Waste

Mechanical joints and the modulation of wood elements since the project stage, considerably reduce the waste on-site.

2 http://www.learn.londonmet.ac.uk/packages/euleb/es/p5/index.html
3 http://www.ffcs-finland.org/pages/english/finnish-forest-certification-council.ph

4. Interior Environmental Quality

4.1 Ventilation

The ventilation system in every room is achieved with refreshing beams controlled by adjustable thermostats (fan-coils)[4]. In cool periods ventilation is achieved through natural free-cooling without compressors. Mechanical ventilation systems count on a high efficiency heat restorer with which 80% of heat generated by the ventilation system is retrieved for room conditioning.

4.2 Natural Lighting

The building's exterior facades count on vertical, fixed protection. This is supported with interior operable solar and glare control systems. In the interior courtyard, facades with a greater surface area of glazing are facing towards the South and West, optimizing the solar gain of the ensemble. Direct solar incidence on glazed facades is controlled by a 2m cantilevered border which acts as a horizontal solar barrier in the summer.

For artificial lighting, lamps of direct and indirect emissions are hung from the drop ceiling. Luminescent lamps of greater performance and useful life than the equivalent incandescent units have been placed.

4 Fan-coils are small air treatment units (refreshing beams), used to filter and cool or heat the environmental conditions, facilitating the recirculation of the treated air.

5. Control of Construction Systems

5.1 Functionality and Efficiency

A simple layout around a courtyard allows the integration of the architectural program in a modulated building. This order is repeated on the building's three floors. Thanks to this, the incorporation of singular formal elements, conference room and vestibule columns gain a greater importance and constitute the mark of identity of the ensemble.

5.2 Control of Construction Systems

The structure is a flexible framing system (columns-beams-mezzanines) made of laminated fir tree wood, modulated to 7.20 m. It is the first time in Finland that a building of these characteristics and dimensions is built entirely with a wood structure.

The predominating forest species in Finland are the pine tree (Pinus Silvestris- 44 percent of total), the spruce tree (Picea excelsa- 36 percent) and the birch tree (Betula Verucosa and Betula pubescens- 18 percent); and this is reflected in the building:

. Windows, accessories and secondary structures have been built basically of pine tree wood.

. Drop ceilings are also made with pine tree wood and doors are veneered with birch wood.

. The conference room floor has been constructed using birch tree boards.

. All Finnish hardwood species have been used in the furniture manufacturing.

. The exterior has been clad with birch tree panels.

6. Long –term Performance

6.1 Flexibility and Adaptability

The simple volume saves heating costs while the vertical wood blinds on the façade protect against direct solar radiation. The long-span structure allows the building's flexible use. The secondary modulation at 1,20 m allows adapting wall partitions and generates changes in the facade.

6.2 Maintenance and Operative Performance

Use of local wood species facilitates the maintenance, replacement and recycling of constructive elements.

7. Economical and Social Aspects

7.1 Social Aspects

Finland is, in relation to its size, one of the most wooded countries in the world. Nearly three quarters of its surface area (22 million hectares) are covered by forest, which totals 5 hectares of forest per inhabitant. The social work carried out by METLA is the promotion, through research, of sustainable management and the economic, social and ecological use of the forests. Research is organized in projects oriented by multidisciplinary programs and they also realize projects commissioned to solve its customers' informational doubts. The building designed by SARC Architects clearly materializes the identity of the institution that it houses.

7.2 Economic Aspects

With a construction cost of 1700€/net m2 of building, a value was achieved very similar to the cost of 1600€ /m2 of a conventional building in Finland[5]. To this we must add the economic savings due to the optimization of the conditioning systems chosen, which will reduce the cost and energy load attributable to the building in operation.

8. The Architect's Eye

In this project, one can detect a tribute to one of the most important figures of architecture in the world: Alvar Aalto; as a reinterpretation of his proposal for Säynätsalo´s town hall, from the choice of the open cloister typology, passing through the definition of each detail, to rethinking the idea of how the Council Chamber is roofed in order to cover the courtyard. The architects have proven that architectural values go beyond the technological needs of the times.

5 Gardiner & Theobald. International Construction Cost Survey. January 2007. http://www.gardiner.com/Economics/images/ICCSgbp.pdf

METLA FOREST RESEARCH CENTRE
SARC Architects

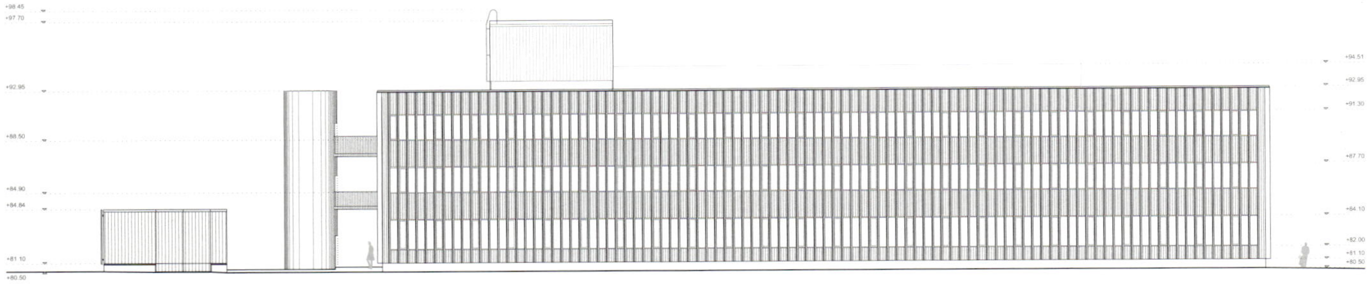

North Elevation

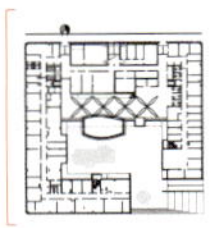

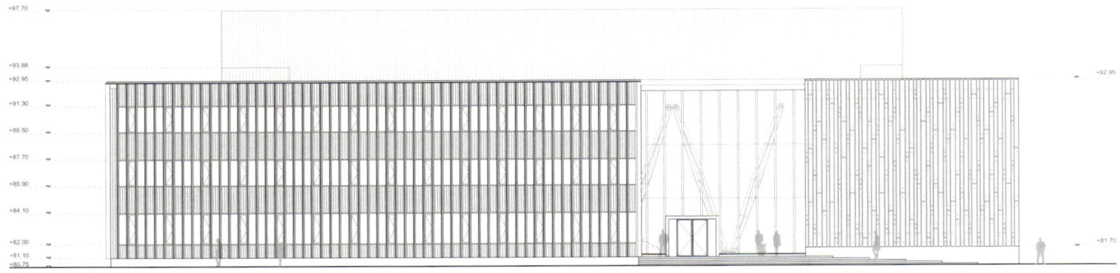

West Elevation

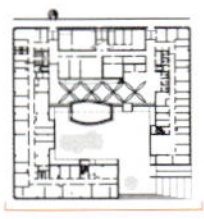

0 5 10m
1:500

METLA

METLA FOREST RESEARCH CENTRE
SARC Architects

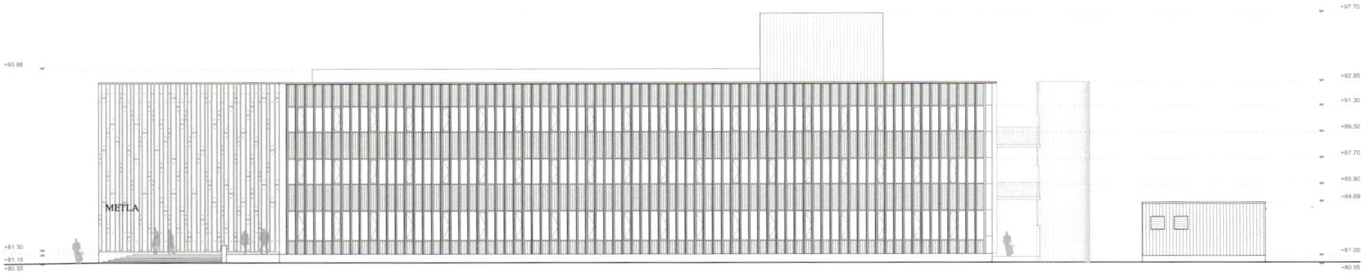

South Elevation

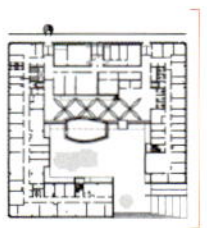

0 5 10m
1:500

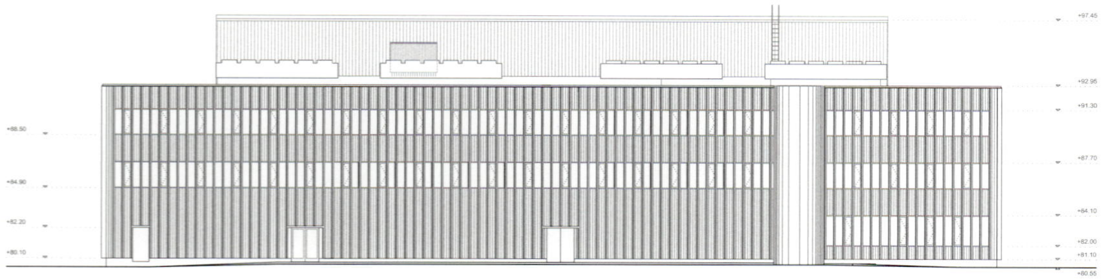

West Elevation

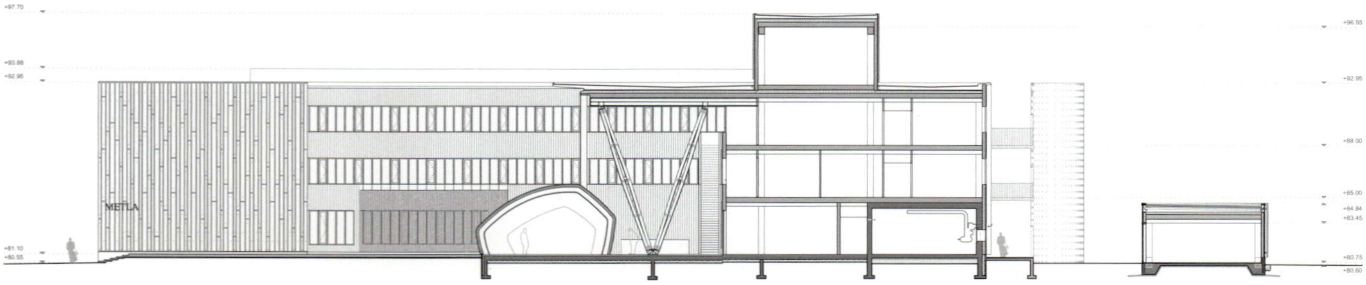

Longitudinal Section

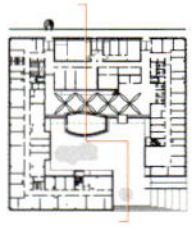

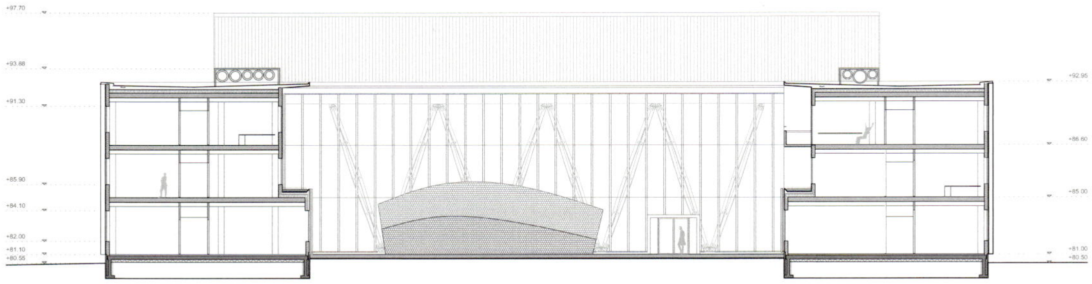

Transversal Section

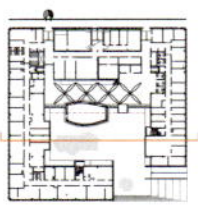

0 5 10m

1:500

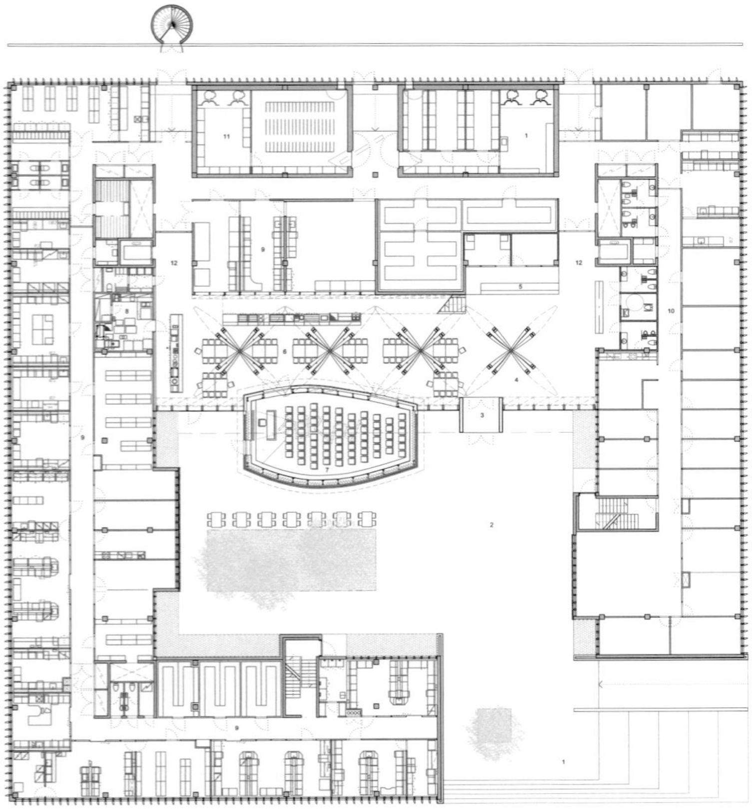

1. Access
2. Courtyard
3. Entrance
4. Vestibule
5. Reception
6. Restaurant
7. Auditorium
8. Kitchen
9. Offices
10. Offices
11. Storage
12. Elevators

Ground Floor Level

0 5 10m

1:600

METLA FOREST RESEARCH CENTRE
SARC Architects

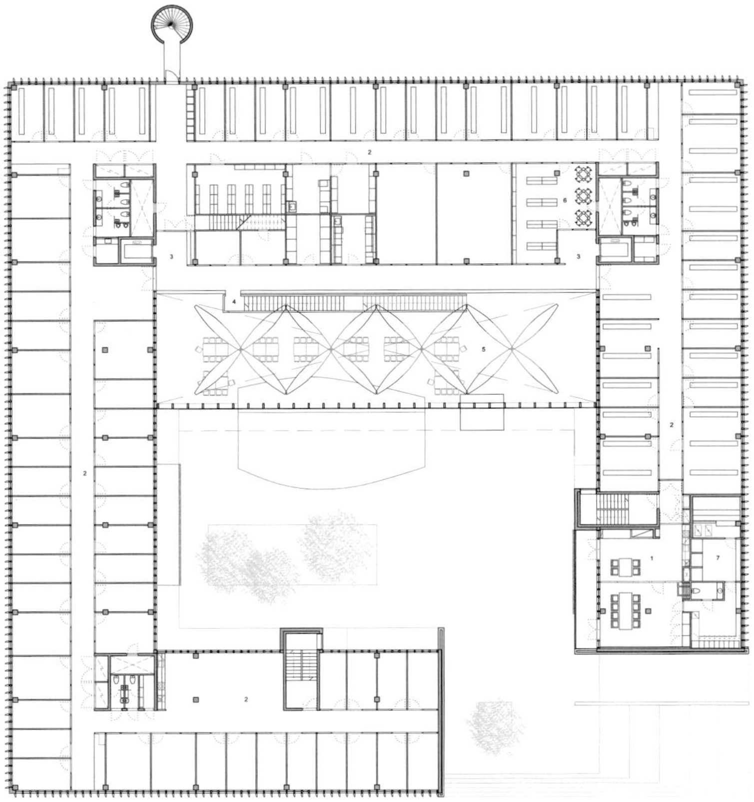

1. Conference Room
2. Offices
3. Elevators
4. Main Staircase
5. Vestibule
6. Library
7. Sauna

Second Floor Level

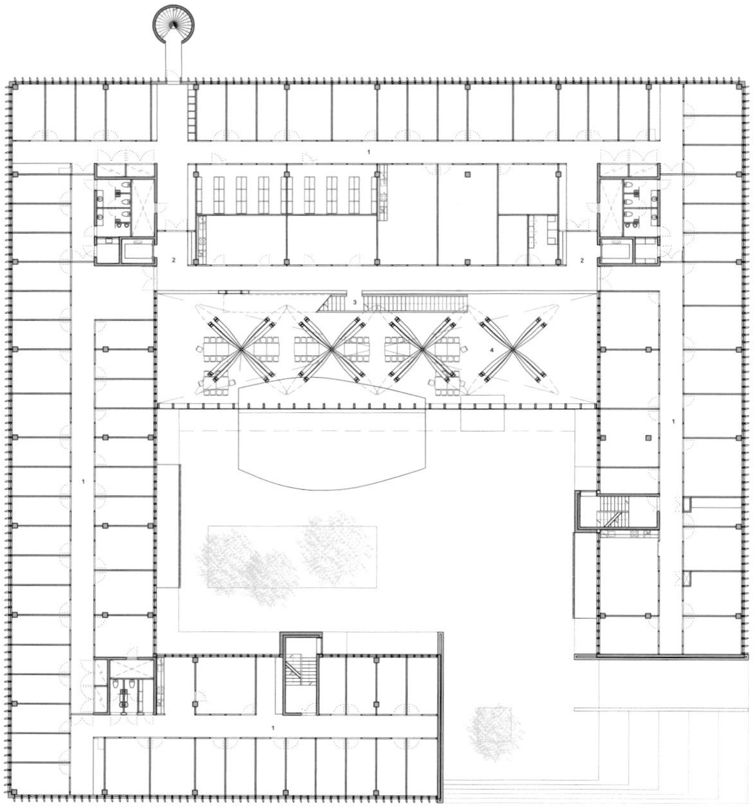

1. Offices
2. Elevators
3. Main Staircase
4. Vestibule

0 5 10m

1:600

First Floor Level

METLA

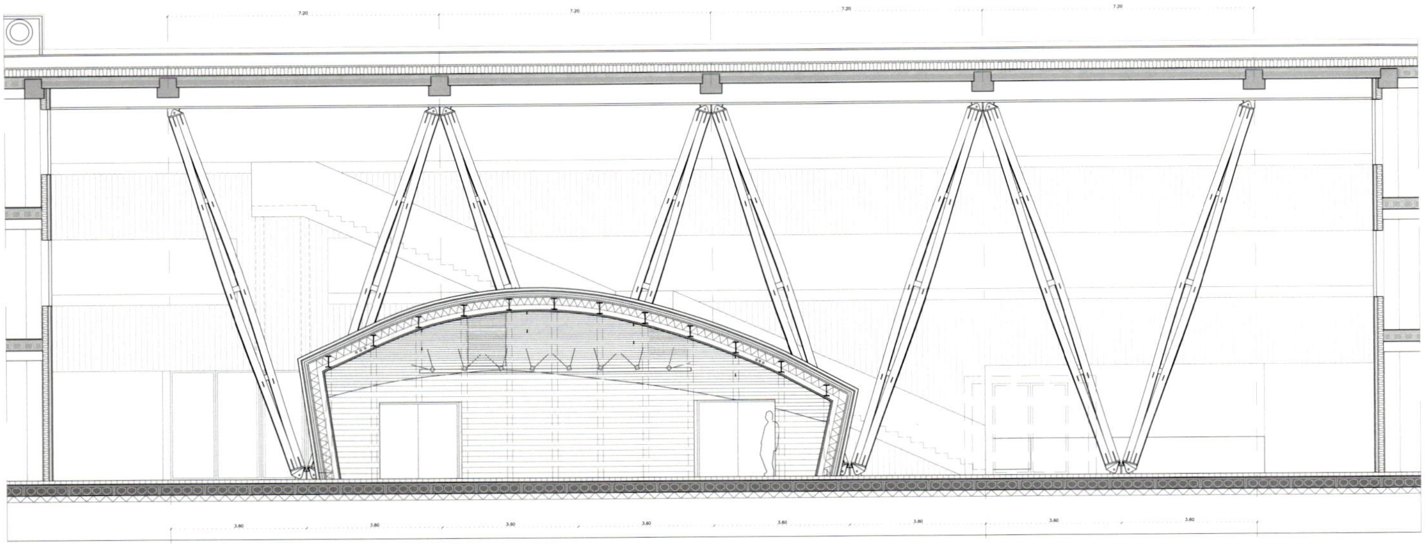

Detail Section

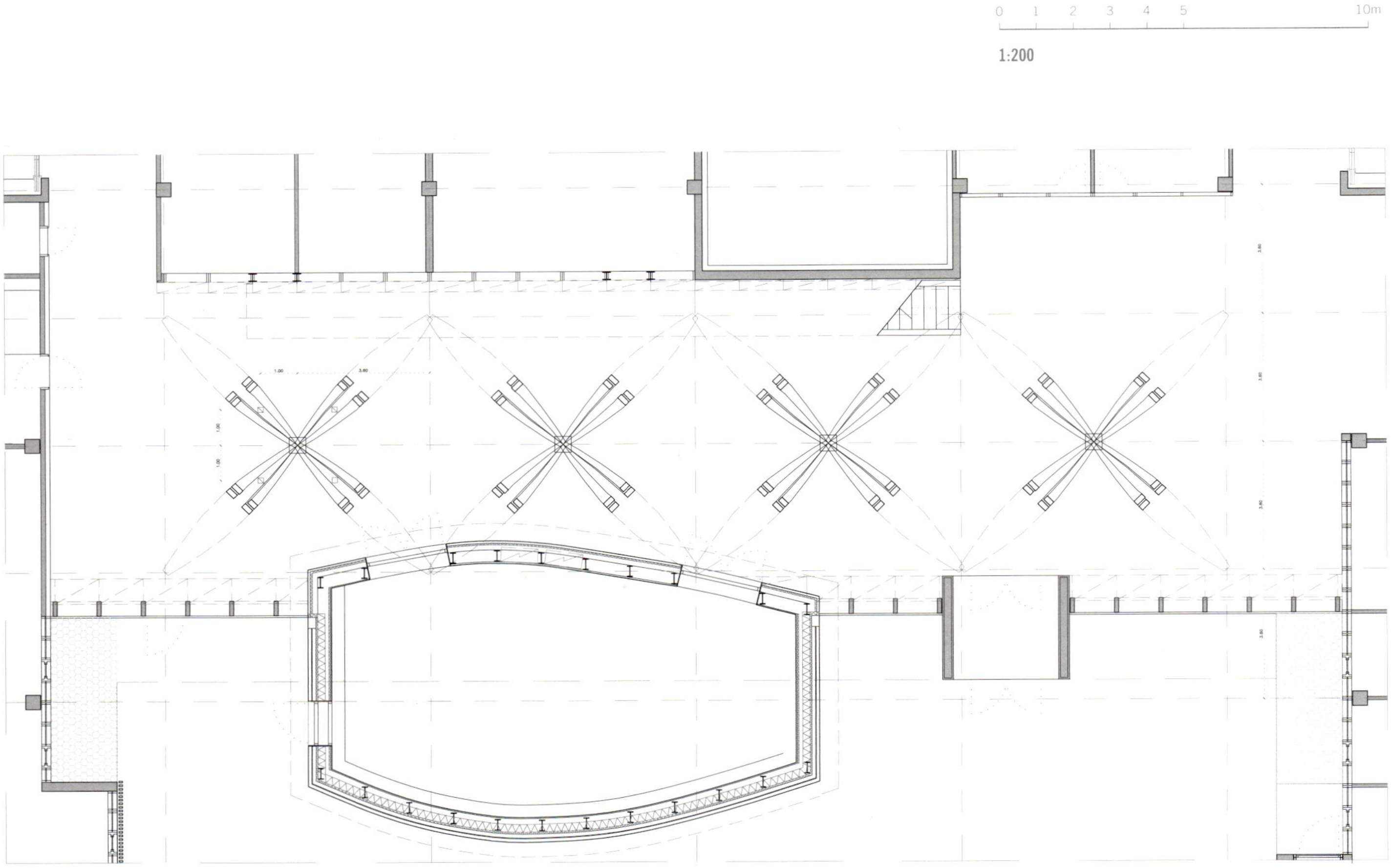

Detail Plan

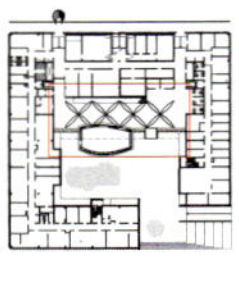

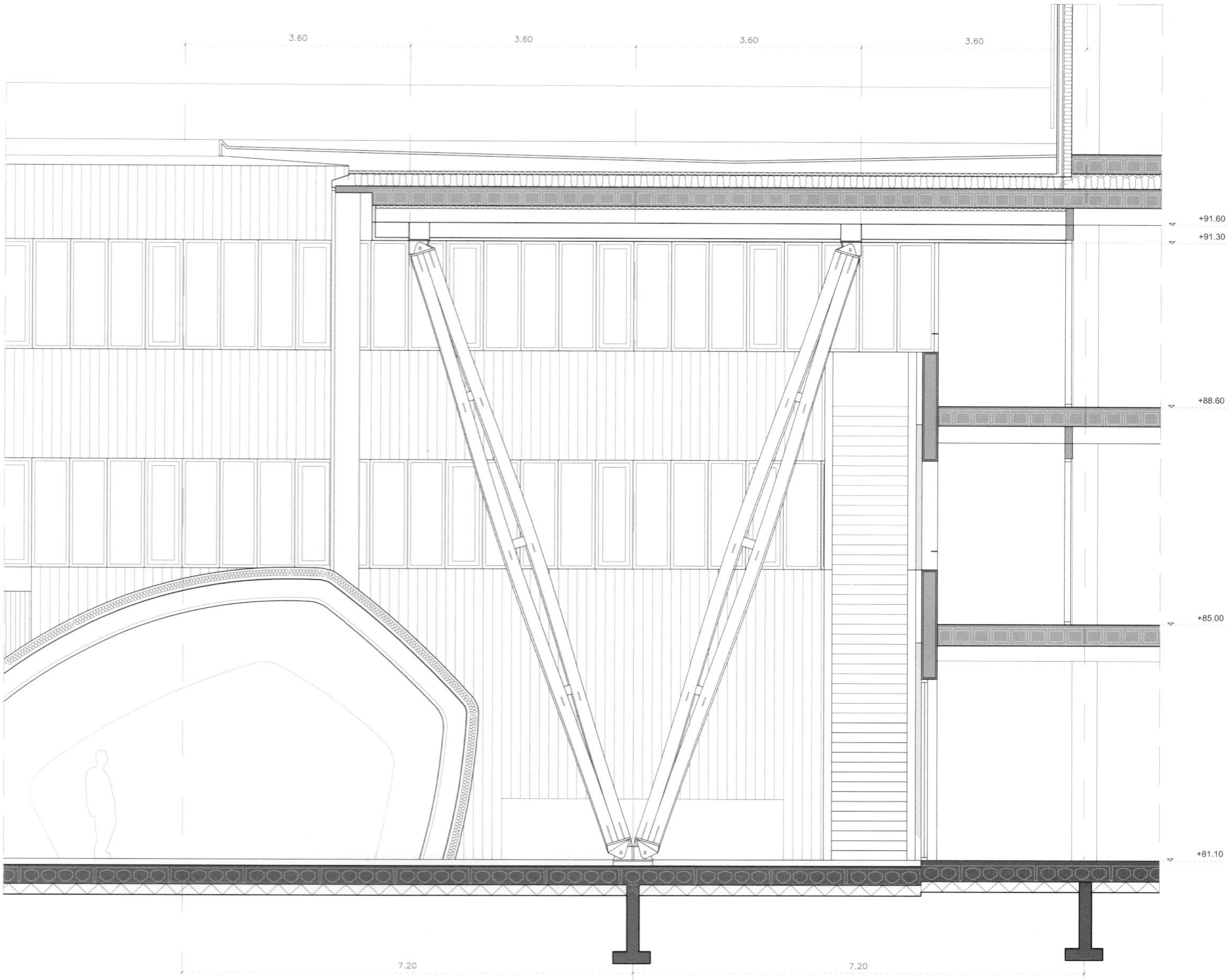

Column Detail

0 1 2 3 4m

1:100

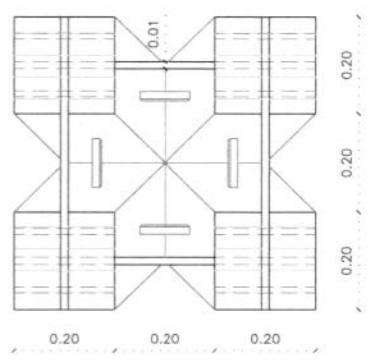

Column Transversal Section

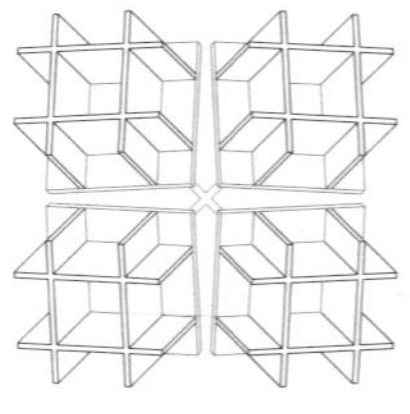

Upper View

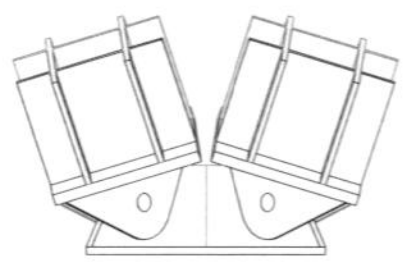

Cross View

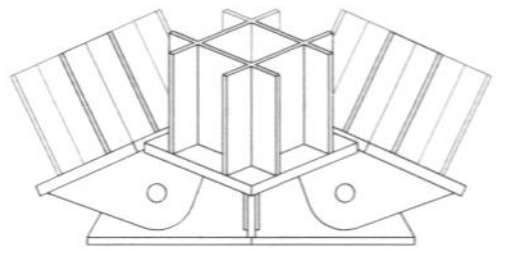

foreshortened view

4 Columns Iron ball-and-socket joint

0 25 50 75 1m

1:40

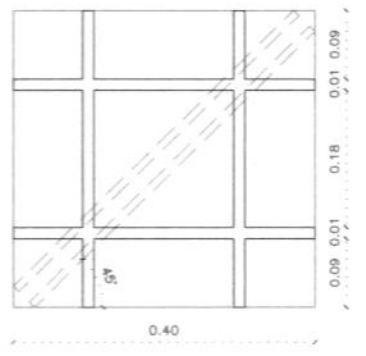

Upper View

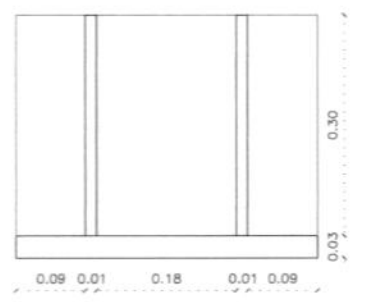

Cross View

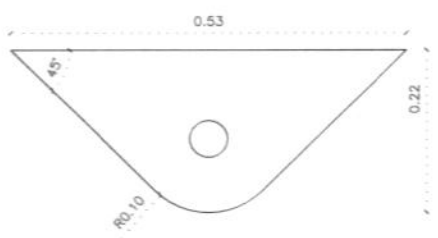

Cross View

column end Iron Conexion

0 10 30 50cm 1m

1:20

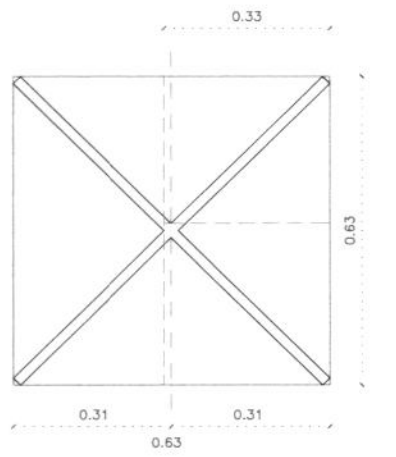

Upper View

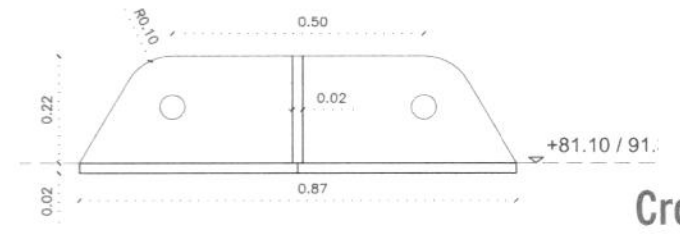

Cross View

4 Columns Iron ball-and-socket joint Base

0 0,5 1m

1:30

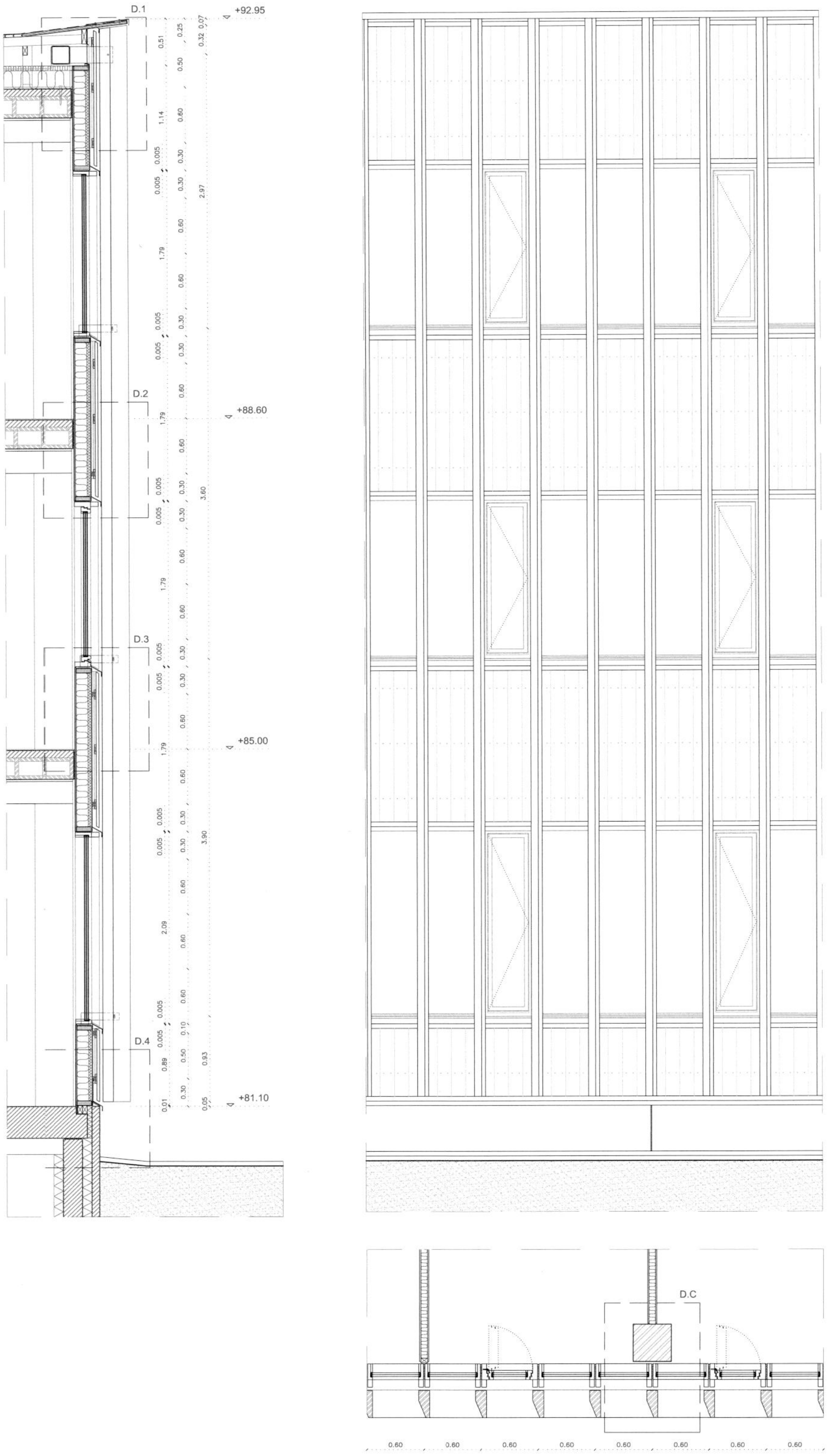

Section Detail

0 1 2 3m

1:75

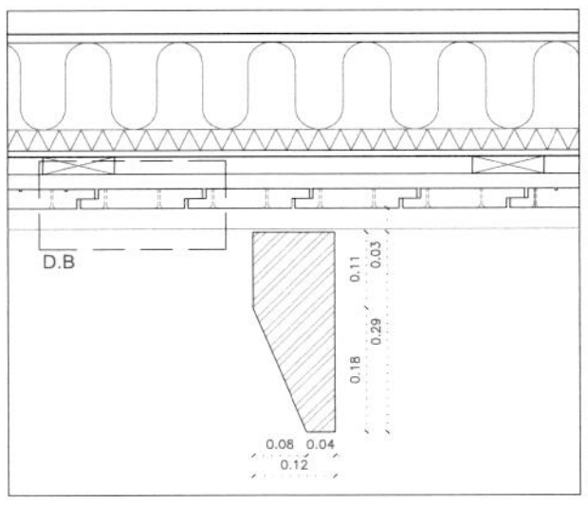

Detail A

0 10 30 50cm 1m

1:20

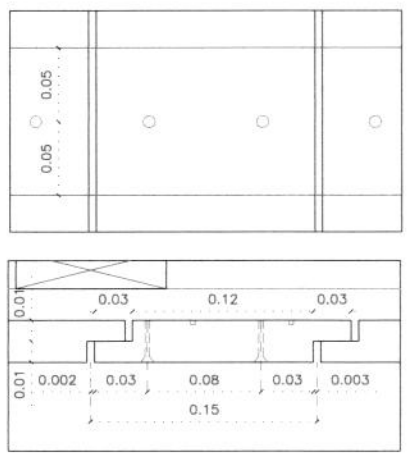

Detail B

0 10 20 30 40cm

1:10

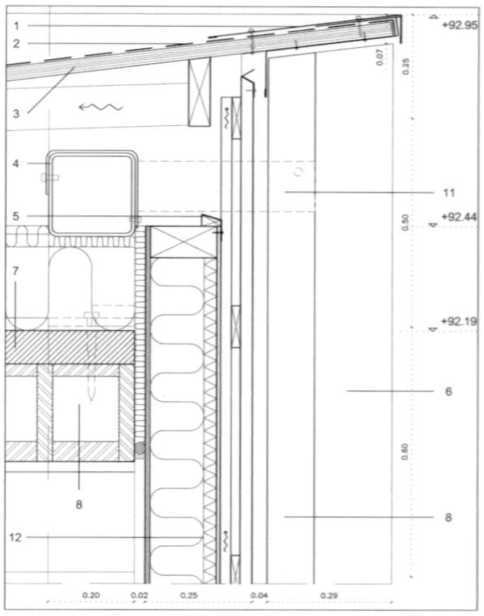

D. 1

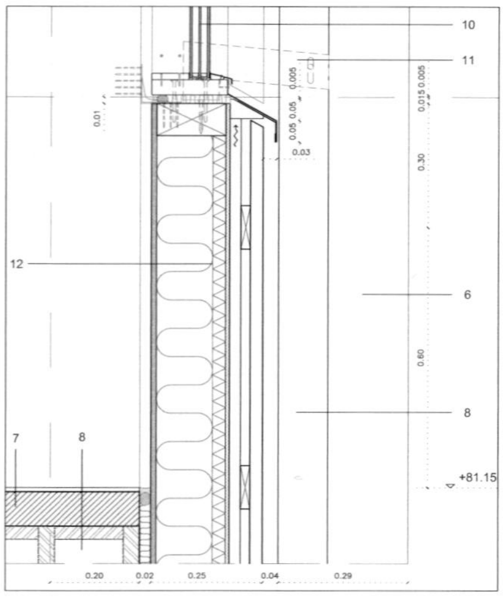

D. 3

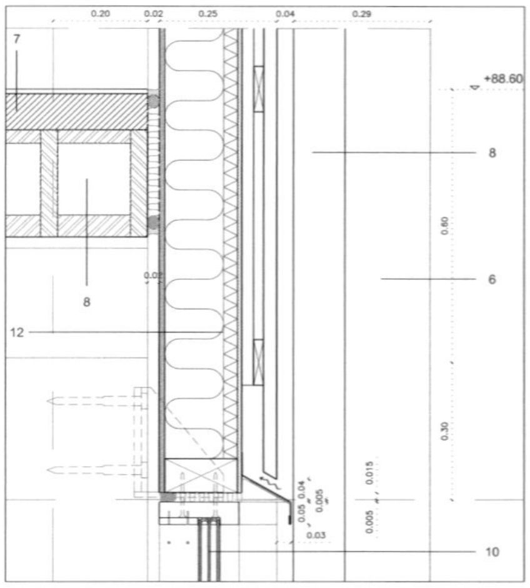

D. 2

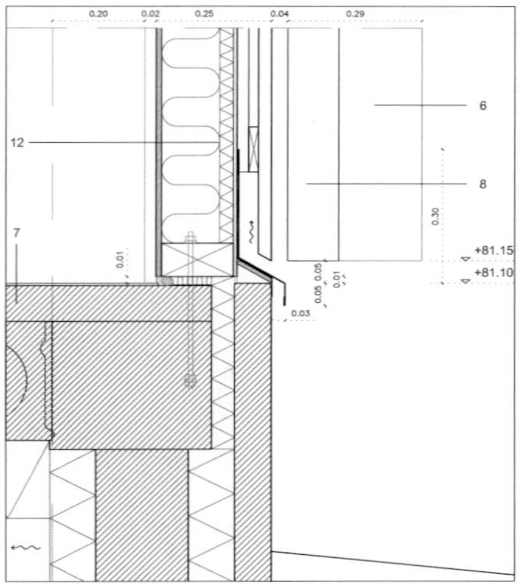

D. 4

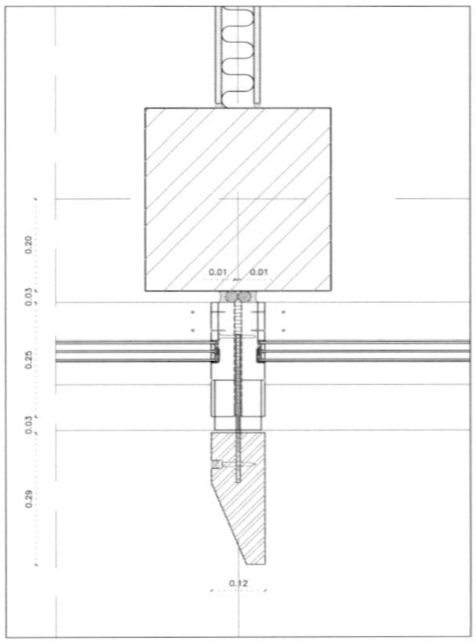

Section C

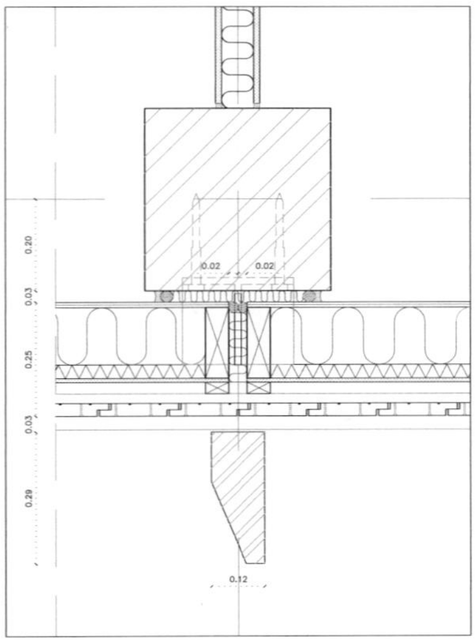

Section C'

0 10 30 50cm 1m

1:20

1. Copper sheet t=1mm
2. Waterproofing
3. Plywood t=3mm
4. Steel plate
5. Wood 14 x 28 x 45mm + corrugated copper sheet
6. Wall structure (from inside to out)
   - Plywood surface 12mm + vaporbarrier125mm
   - Vertical wood strips 125 x 50mm30mm for insulation
   - Horizontal wood strips 30 x 30mm for panel support of 9mm
   - 25mm cavity for ventilation
   - Vertical wood strips 25 x 50mm
   - 21mm cavity for ventilation
   - Horizontal wood strips 21 x 50mm for wood façade made with 28mm planks
7. 80mm concrete piece
8. Wood openings
9. Vertical façade element: laminated wood 115 x 290mm
10. Wood frame window
11. 8mm plate for support for vertical facade-elements
12. Insulation

09

Lyons

DPI QUEENSCLIFF

VICTORIA, Australia

Lyons

http://www.lyonsarch.com.au/

COLABORATORS	Carey Lyon Corbett Lyon Cameron Lyon
PROJECT MANAGER	Atkinson Project Management
CONTRACTOR	Kane Constructions
PHOTOGRAPHY	John Gollings, Gollings Pidgeon Arup

	COLLABORATING COMPANIES
Adviser	Arup
Bioclimatics	Arup
Structure	Arup
Hydraulic Design	Taylor Cullity Lethlean
Landscape	Arup

	DATES
IMPLEMENTATION PROJECT	2002
BEGINNING OF WORKS	2003
WORK COMPLETION	2005

DESCRIPTIVE BRIEF

This project was designed for Australia's Primary Industries Department, with the vision that the building function as an example of environmental design within the Government's work programs, and promote with it a new design, representative of what it predicates in terms of environmental policy.

This vision was enhanced by the land's location, adjacent to Swan Bay (a marine park included in UNESCO´s World Heritage list). This project has taken into account, within its program, the rehabilitation of the existing place, which had been used as a waste deposit for decades and exposed to great pollution levels.

The urban proposal, the architectural design and the landscape design make this building be the first to receive 6 stars according to the Green Building Council in Australia[1].

Predominating devices in the design and the use of materials which have generated important news in environmental functioning include:

- A concrete structure designed with the concept of thermal mass.
-Interior areas naturally ventilated, reinforced with the use of automated systems.
- Optimization of natural lighting using interior courtyards and a linear design.
- A method for rainwater reutilization, treating it before returning it to the bay.
- Maximum use of rainwater for a variety of in situ applications.
- A completely gardened roof to provide the building with thermal insulation and to rehabilitate native vegetation.
- Recycled wood, Classification A, for all windows and doors, including frames and window cladding.
- Use of certified wood for the rest of exterior cladding.

In addition to having received maximum qualification given by Green Building Council of Australia, this project's design does not only reply to the environmental necessities of the place, but it also directly replies to the design program requirements, both formal and cultural, and their relationship with the surroundings. With all of this, the design goes beyond than to just point to energy and it is based on creating the best possible practice through a wide range of environmental initiatives, including building design, use of native vegetation, control of the excessive rainfall, rehabilitation of local environment, use of materials and reducing the visual impact to a minimum .

This building has an optimum north facing orientation, maximizing passive solar design and providing areas with shade in a natural way. The natural environment literally "envelops" the building, going up towards the roof, giving the impression that it rises directly from the landscape.

1 http://www.gbcaus.org/

1. Service Building
2. Offices
3. Vestibules and Conference area
4. Laboratories
5. Center for Marine study
6. Reservoir fed by rainwater
7. Swan Bay

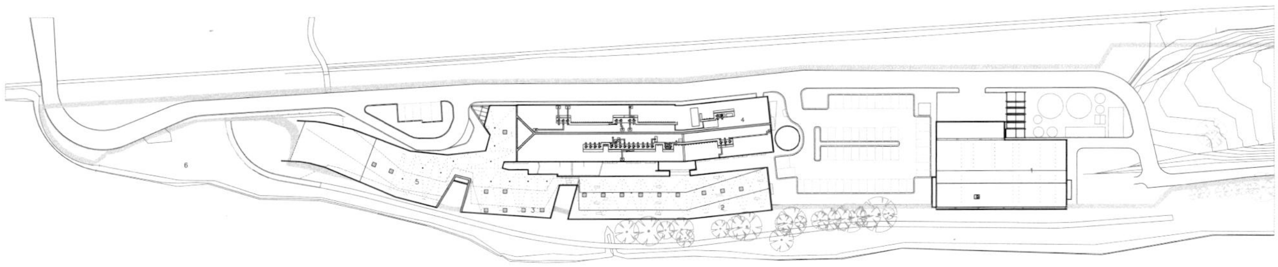

Site Plan

"El hombre se forma con las decisiones que configuran su medio ambiente."

Rene Dubos

ENVIRONMENTAL ANALYSIS

1. Choosing the Site. Project and Development

1.1 Location

Latitude: 38° 16' 09" S
Longitude: 144° 38' 73" E

The project is located on a spit of land joining the town of Queenscliff with Bellarine Peninsula, opposite Swan Bay in a marine park declared World Heritage. The recovery of an area exposed to degradation since its use as an oil and asbestos materials deposit, property of the local government, has been proposed.

1.2 Urban Design and Site Improvement

The design emphasizes the site's environmental wealth, by means of a low linear layout. The chosen proposal relates to the environment by its organic plasticity, with the intention of imitating it. With the purpose of avoiding filtrations of the contaminating material present in the site, a pile system was not used which would have been the first structural choice. Instead, the terrain was tamped down by means of a high pressure technique called Dynamic Compacting and a 30 cm layer of tamped terrain was placed, with enough load-bearing capacity to support the building's foundation, functioning also as a natural barrier against filtrations.

Landscape work carried out by the designers is the result of a careful study of native plants which delimitate a series of public paths and sidewalks. With this intervention, an area in a process of full degradation is provided with natural and public green spaces.

1.3 Project

The building is hidden as the topography is elevated and converted into roof. The access is discovered when reaching a roundabout, gaining access to the central hall, formed by a visual axis that allows the observer to discover a direct view of the sea.

The program is distributed in several rectangular-shaped buildings, forming a single unit, and arranged along a longitudinal axis parallel to the coast. Every building is connected by means of a corridor or a meeting room, allowing the absorption of geometric variations. The garden roof is the element that relates all of the buildings to the environment. In addition to its insulating function and recovery of native vegetation, it is used as a rainwater collector, later reused inside the project.

The façade cladding changes its rotation with the vertical axis, obtaining better use of the solar energy required in its interior and giving a formal identity to each part of the ensemble.

2. Consumption of Energy and Resources

This project has obtained a qualification of 6 Green Stars, maximum qualification according to the evaluation criteria of Green Building Council of Australia, which evaluates newly constructed projects for their environmental impact[1]. The strategies of energy savings can be found in the building's design, its impact in the landscape, rainwater management, use of materials according to their performance, and good environmental practice during construction.

2.1 Consumption of Energy

The orientation and insulation, due to the structure of great thermal inertia and its green roof, reduces energy consumption devoted to the building's indoor conditioning. Because of its shape, inclined walls in the office area function as solar controllers. On cold winter days, solar light with a low incidence angle penetrates the interior, heating the offices. During the summer, with a high incidence angle, the wall's shape provides shade and prevents overheating. An automated system controls the lights according to the occupation of the spaces.

2.2 Consumption of Water

This project is provided with a rainwater collection system, used as a substitute for the drinking water used for irrigation, and with a natural treatment system prior to the water's incorporation to the Bay. Both them are described in 3.3 Management of Water.

2.3 Consumption of Materials

Both the structure and materials have been chosen to achieve an adequate environmental performance, without increasing the project's economic cost. Concrete was only used because of its thermal inertia, to build the load-bearing structure of the office area. The façades are made of certified wood. Interior doors have been made from recycled wood, as well as the office furniture. In order to choose the rest of materials, their fabrication process was taken into account, and they were selected based on their energy cost.

1 http://www.gbcaus.org/
2 http://www.toolbase.org/Technology-Inventory/Plumbing/air-admittance-valves

3. Environmental Loads

3.1 Emissions

In order to control emissions due to laboratory activity, air admittance valves were used instead of conventional chimneys[2]. These devices increase the efficiency of the draining system. They permit material savings, as they eliminate the ventilation network associated to the draining systems. On the other hand, they reduce the common maintenance problems of the vents in a conventional system. With every domestic water release, the valve opens, liberating steam and admitting air into the system to facilitate drainage. The valve has a membrane that is kept locked the rest of time to avoid unnecessary emissions to the atmosphere.

3.2 Solid Wastes

During construction, the previous treatment of the site to avoid land movements, which would only have taken the problem to a different location, should be highlighted. During the operation of the building, the sedimentation treatment applied to the water for external use is very important (pavements, green areas), before incorporating it to the Bay.

3.3 Water Management

Rainwater is collected in a tank, with a capacity for 150.000 liters, and it is reused for the maintenance of the green roof and as a provision in case of fire.

Two artificial reservoirs have been created, which in addition to the integration in the landscape are used as filters in which rainwater from hard surfaces (pavements, buildings) is settled, before being incorporated, by filtration, to the bay. The first reservoir has a system of nets which act as a primary filter. The water flows to the second one and is then filtered through the sand to the Bay.

4. Interior Environmental Quality

4.1 Ventilation

Offices have the largest openings to the North, oriented towards the bay. With apertures towards the interior courtyards, a natural air stream is guaranteed. An automated system detects temperature variations, and controls the windows to permit air renovation and condition the building's interior. Because of technical determining factors, the laboratories use air conditioning systems.

4.2 Natural Lighting

The open façade has a clear northern orientation, optimizing solar gain. In the winter, the low sun penetrates through it. During the summer, the inclined walls, in addition to limiting space, provide shade to the ensemble. The linear arrangement of the ensemble guarantees natural light for all the offices. Three interior courtyards provide laboratories with natural light, also located linearly to the south.

4.3 Acoustics

The project's linear layout arranges the spaces according to their use. Offices with a larger occupation are separated by interior courtyards from the support spaces (pump rooms, tanks) and from the maintenance of the Institute's fleet of boats, which because of their characteristics have a higher acoustic level.

In the office area, the high index of acoustic reflection of the structure's exposed concrete is diminished with the placement of perforated wood panels.

5. Control of Construction Systems

5.1 Functionality and Efficiency

The construction systems were chosen according to the use of the spaces. For the office area, an exposed concrete structure with a great thermal mass was chosen. The garden roof acts as insulation and the façades were clad with certified wood. For the laboratory area, a lightweight system of steel profiles was used, with insulation panels as cladding.

5.2 Control of Construction Systems

This type of constructive system adapted to the density of occupation allows users to control the conditions where they are most needed. Façades with operable windows, although automated, also allow occupants to have direct control of the air streams in the office area.

6. Long-term Performance

6.1 Flexibility and Adaptability

The open interior structure of the office area permits freedom of the space layout.

6.2 Maintenance and Operative Performance

The provision of natural lighting and ventilation redounds to a lower energy cost in the building's functioning. The extensive green roof covering the project requires little maintenance, which is limited to three annual inspections of the waterproof membrane[3], while the native plants have enough with the environmental conditions.

3 http://www.apabcn.es/sostenible/castellano/castellano/news38cas.htm

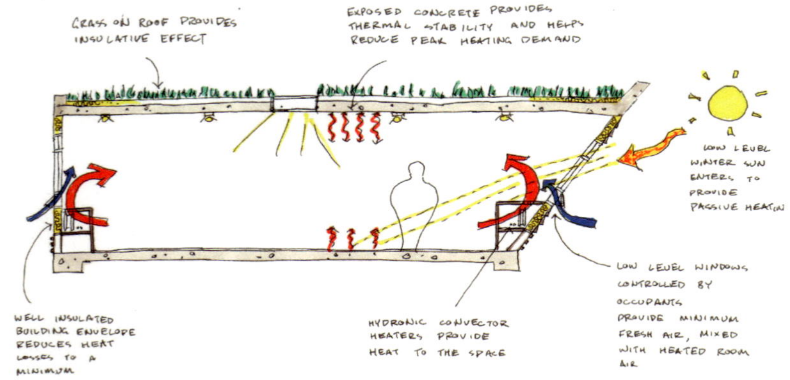

Winter Analysis

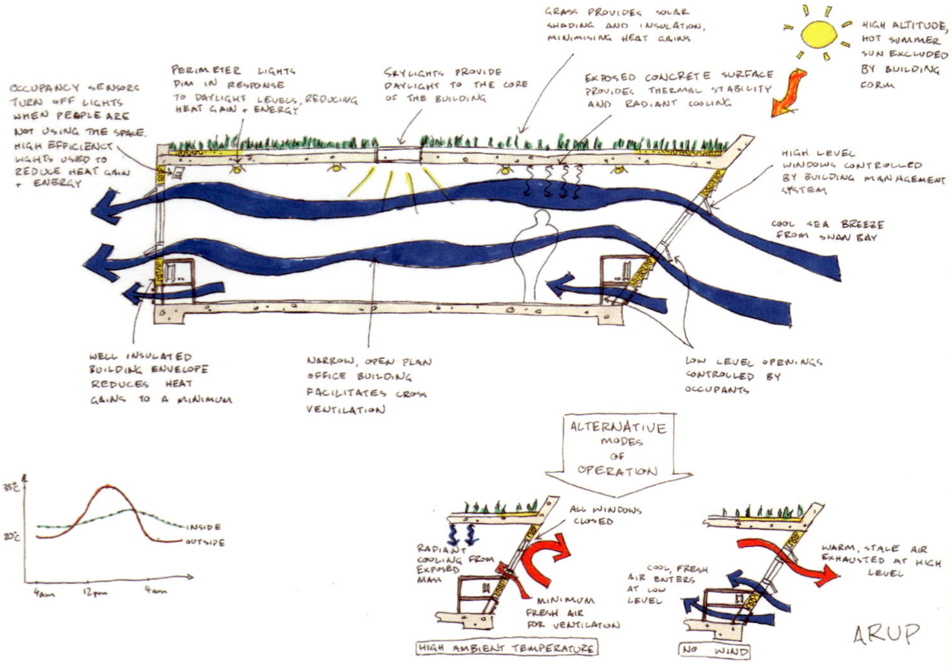

Summer Analysis

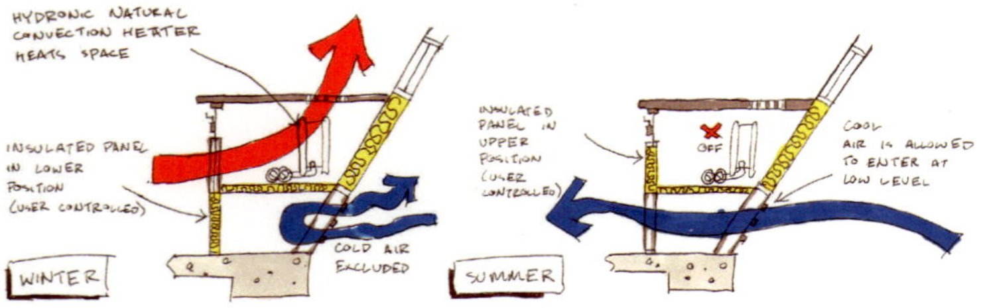

Façade. Ventilation and Heating

7. Environmental and Social Aspects

7.1 Social Aspects

A very important aspect for local community was constituted by the recovery of an area in danger of degradation, very close to a place declared as World Heritage. This project is a good example of the building's integration in the environment. While recovering plant species and providing the existing ecosystem with reservoirs, the design of a clear corporate image was achieved for the Institution it houses, appropriate to the work and marine research developed.

7.2 Economic Aspects

This project was built with the typical economic limitations of every construction promoted by a local government. The Industry Department contributed additional funds to finance novel environmental strategies such as the use of wastewater and the new artificial reservoirs. From the project phase until the final construction of the building, a rigorous audit was applied to control costs due to the incorporation of non-conventional environmental strategies. The incorporation of environmental strategies represented a 10% increase in cost above a conventional construction. However, a careful control of the building's global energetic consumption is being prepared, to demonstrate the economic savings due to the construction and functioning together.

8. The Architect's eye

The element that gives character to this proposal is its roof. The natural topography becomes a green layer that works as a substrate for the native vegetation and guarantees thermal insulation for the users.

Both topographies are articulated by a mirror of water; with two functions, an aesthetic one which is perceived as a reflection when approaching the building and another technical one, as a filter for water poured into the Bay.

One more success is the permeability achieved at the points where project's activities change. It allows long visuals towards the sea and facilitates the cross ventilation of the building.

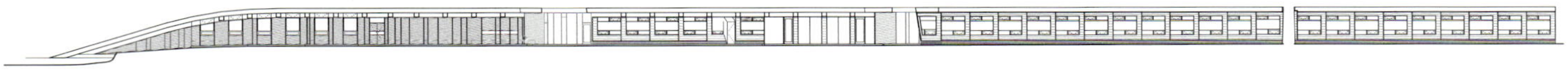

East Elevation

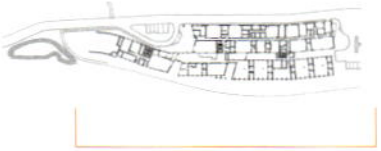

West Elevation

1:200

DPI QUEENSCLIFF
Lyons

1. Concrete element
2. Wood facade
3. Fixed glazing on wood façade
4. Wooden strips
5. Concrete columns + capitals
6. Roof slabs
7. PVC tubes
8. Metal railing and platform
9. Colorbond screen
10. Colorbond facade
11. Metal and wood solar protector
12. Offices
13. Corridor
14. Laboratories
15. Trial room

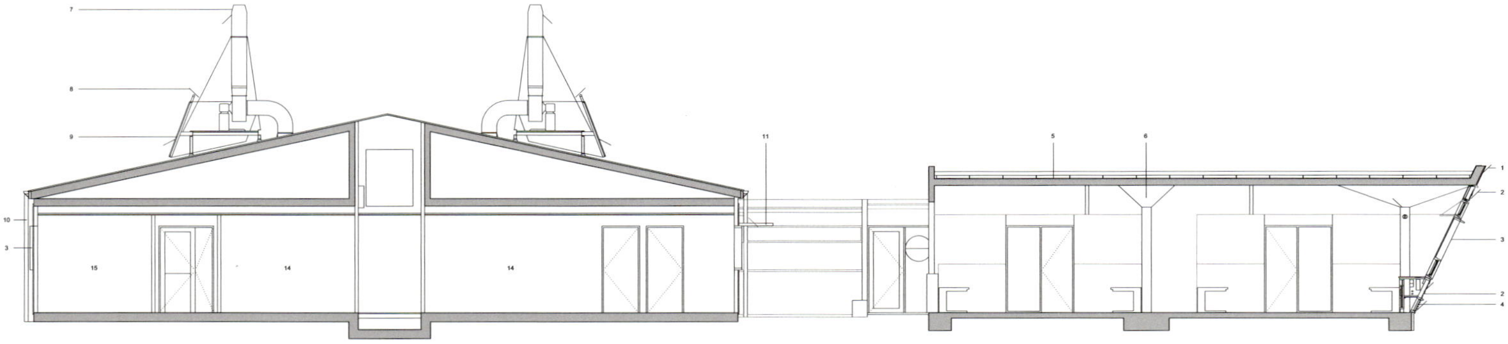

Transverse Section

0 1 2 3 4 5 10m

1:200

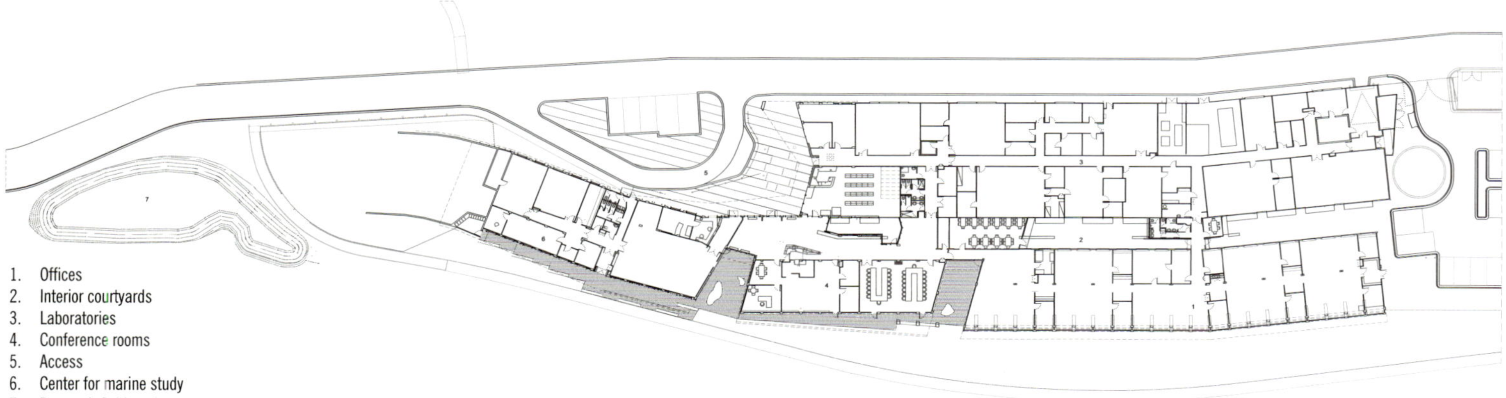

1. Offices
2. Interior courtyards
3. Laboratories
4. Conference rooms
5. Access
6. Center for marine study
7. Reservoir fed by rainwater

Floor Level

0 5 10 20 40m

1:1200

FIRE INDICATOR PANEL

DPI QUEENSCLIFF

Lyons

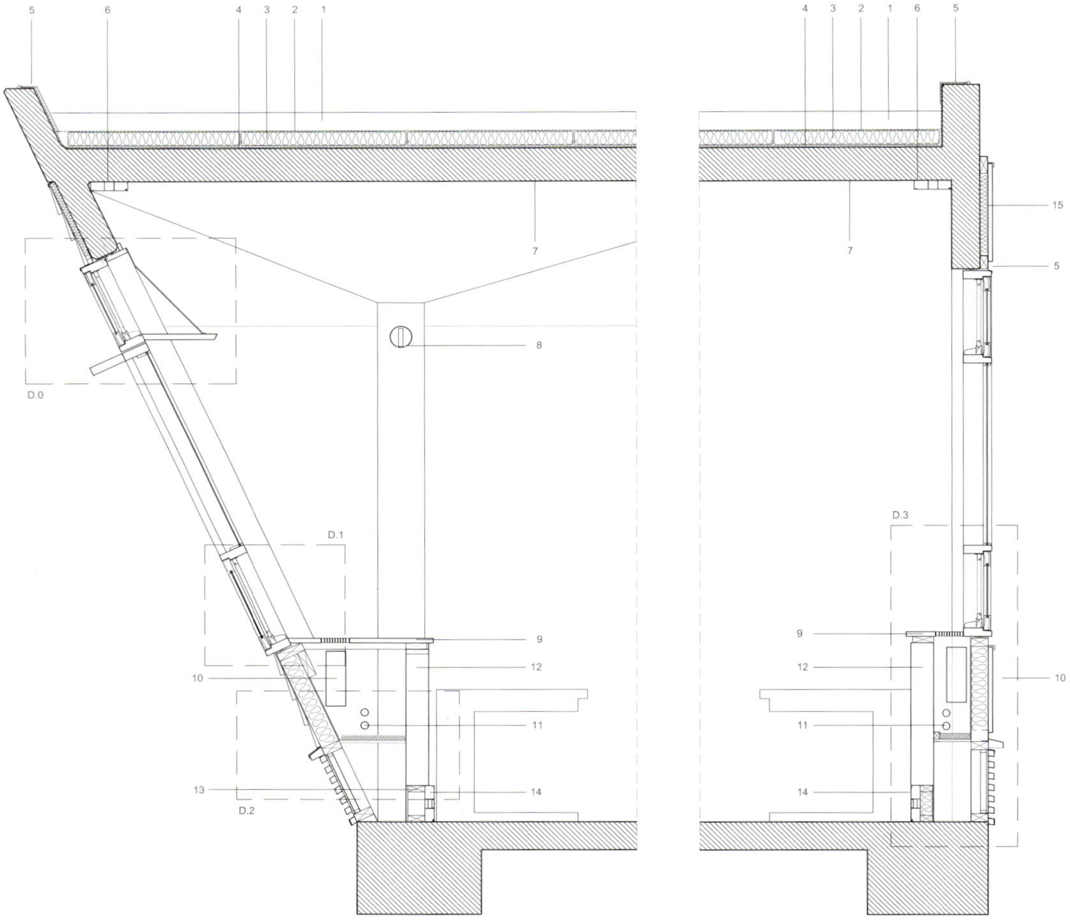

1. 100mm crushed rock
2. Geotech membrane
3. Insulation panels
4. Waterproof membrane
5. Colorbond metal flashing
6. 200x50 aluminum conduit
7. Class 2 interior finish
8. Hidden lighting fixture
9. Window ledge of 18mm with laminated finish
10. Heating unit
11. Hot water deposits
12. Window for natural ventilation
13. 6mm frame of fc sheet
14. Electrical cable
15. Spandek wall cladding

Wall Section

0 25 50 75 1m

1:40

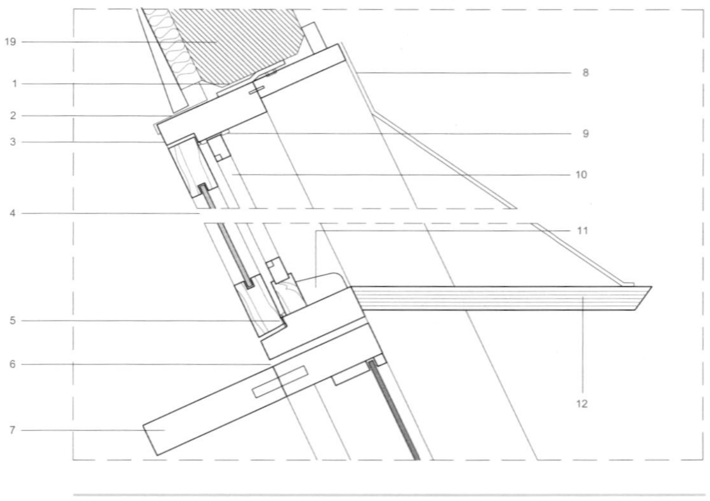

D. 0

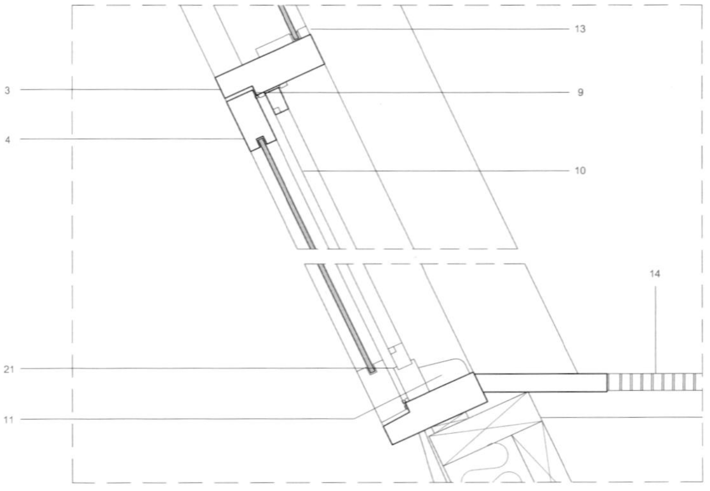

D. 1

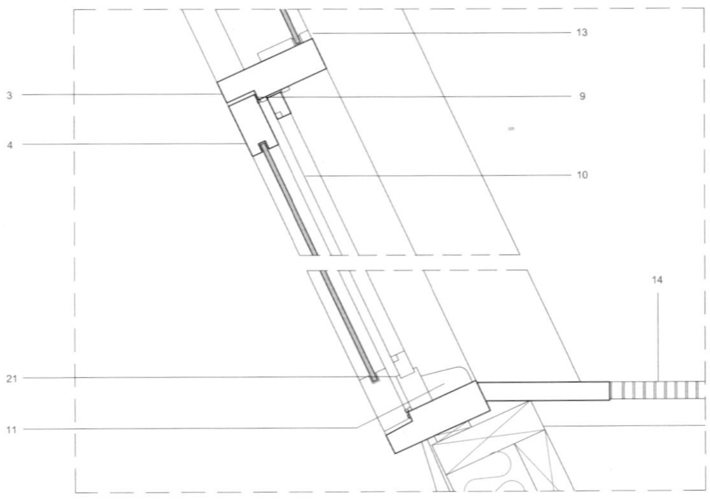

D. 2

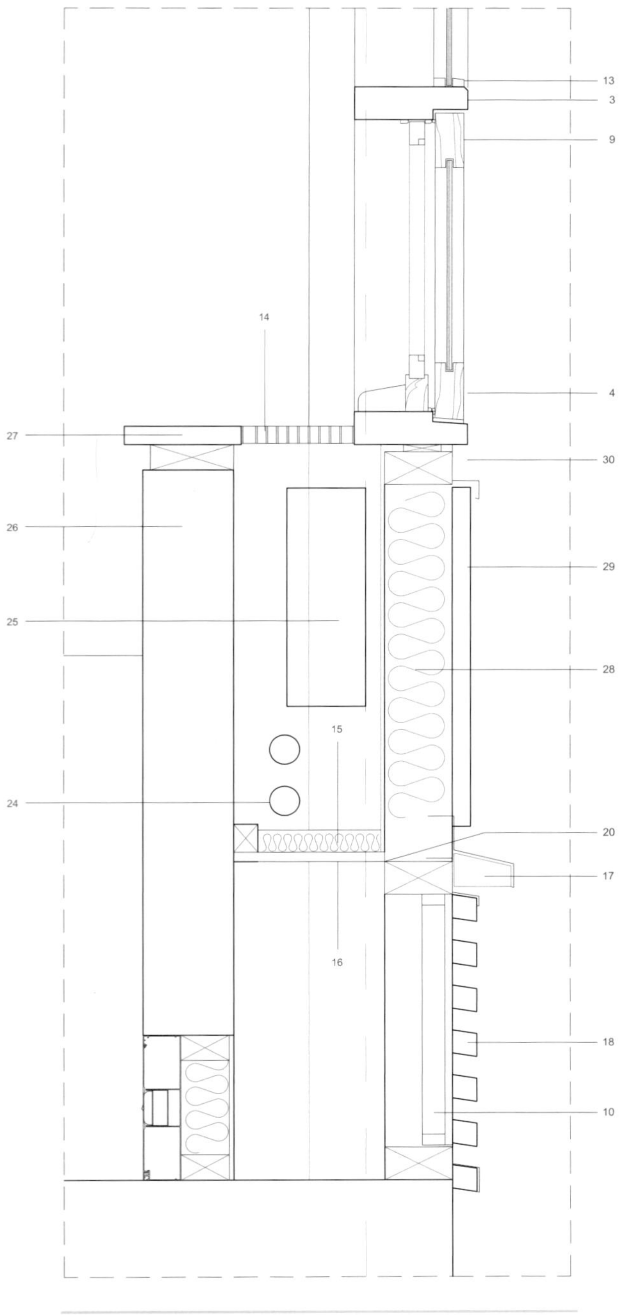

D. 3

1. Galvanized metal profile of 100 x 100 x 6mm bent fixed to window frame.
2. Colorbond metal flashing
3. Window frame of 140 x 45 of high durability kdhw with natural exterior finish
4. Awning of 75 x 40 of high durability kdhw with natural exterior finish
5. Schleigel or similar window seal
6. 10mm trickle vent
7. Sunshade of 190 x 45 high durability kdhw with natural exterior finish
8. 20 x 4mm steel suspension support
9. Schleigel or similar window seal
10. Insect screen
11. Electrically operated chain winder
12. 26mm plywood board with polished edges and white laminate finish
13. 3 x13mm glazing beads from same timber
14. 150 x 1200 black anodized aluminum grille
15. Caulk junction between 13mm insulation sheets and structure to ensure airtight seal
16. 6mm fc sheet weather seal, insulation with high thermal mass
17. 75 x 35 high durability kdhw weather protector with colorbond flashing
18. 45 x 45 kdhw eucalptus wood slats for exterior finish
19. 150 r. concrete wall
20. Caulk junction between insulation of 13 & 6mm fc sheets to ensure airtight seal
21. Screen locating bead
22. Insulation of 6 mm of fc
23. Electrical conduit
24. Hot water deposit
25. Heating unit
26. Window for natural ventilation
27. Window ledge from 18mm with selected laminate finish
28. 6mm fc sheet caulked to insure weather proof seal
29. Spandek wall cladding
30. Colorbond flashing trim

10

Javier de Antón

OLD PEOPLE'S HOME

CAMARZANA DE TERA, Zamora, España

Javier de Antón

cso@infonegocio.com

IMPLEMENTATION PROJECT	Javier de Antón Manuel Sánchez-Vera
PROJECT MANAGER	Javier de Antón
COLLABORATORS	Antonio San Hipólito, Laura Torres, Manuel Chirivella, Inés Fernández, Miguel Ubarrena, José Luís Serzo, Juan Valle y Bernardo Cummins
PHOTOGRAPHY	Esaú Acosta

COLLABORATING COMPANIES

Roofing	Intemper

DATES

IMPLEMENTATION PROJECT	2002
BEGINNING OF WORKS	2003
WORK COMPLETION	2005

DESCRIPTIVE BRIEF

A new land...

The intervention's setting, a small village in the province of Zamora, is the element which generates most of the guidelines that shape the project.

First of all, the existing ground was taken into account, a long and narrow lot, contained between two roads of unequal importance, squeezed between other lots of similar characteristics.

In second place, the surrounding landscape is fragmented in parallel bands of crop of different lengths, widths, thicknesses and textures.

In third place the project's program, an old people's home, with a special character due to its location, since the future residents are habituated to a very close contact with the rural environment.

All of these factors have given rise to the global conception of the intervention, which is a reconfiguration of the existing land. Therefore, we should talk in terms of new land and not of new building.

By deliberately manipulating the existing surface, the land is provided with a new meaning, according to the demanded needs. Therefore the intervention is a living land that responds in an active way to the different parameters applied to it. First of all, the need for the third dimension appears, introduced by the longitudinal cut of the surface into long bands and their subsequent vertical stretching. The new land seems to hide, below two long bands, the two biggest needs of the program; the private living room or night time area and the common living room or daytime area.

At the beginning and end of the bands, as well as in the areas where there exist height level changes, the surface turns diagonal, softly marking the aforementioned height level change. Because the new redefinition of the land is understood topologically, avoiding obstacles or interruptions. The new land rises and merges unto itself. And the difference of movement between bands is similar to the differences that appear when we fold the fingers of our hands.

To finish defining the new surface we must talk about texture. The applied texture appears from the will of turning the new land into a sort of new crop field, with its own vegetation incorporated. This aspect could be developed thanks to the ecological system TF of Interper. This vegetation (local covering plants) has been distributed over the surface like a pixel weft that slightly reminds us of the region's aerial pictures, which are divided into small fragments of vegetable life of various colors.

From the beginning, one of the fundamental issues was to obtain the maximum surface area of topsoil. This was achieved with the land stretching operation, increasing in that way the existing green surface, which before only occupied the horizontal projection; And with the density of vegetable pixilation, that has tried to optimize to the maximum the presence of vegetation between paths and the living spaces.

The spaces that result from the land operations are protected from the outside space, and at the same time they shelter it, with a vertical enclosure which asserts the tension generated by the surface's stretching. At the same time it is given a striated character, similar to the ground cuts that appear in the landscape on the other side of the road. This resemblance is stressed with the sort of finish these faces have been given, a diluted oxide treatment that reacts with the base mortar, dyeing it with the colors and the earthy shades of the region.

As can be appreciated, the new land is, in and of itself, an ecologic element that makes the most of all the advantages of the system used, such as the excellent thermal behavior of the garden roofs. The surface appears marked by a grove of metal elements, devoted to housing solar panels, that reminds us of the pieces of aluminum foil that the people of the region place in their crops to frighten away the birds. At night, the grove turns into an enigmatic field of lights and metallic reflections that surprise the observer.

"The longer I live the more beautiful life becomes."
Frank Lloyd Wright (1869 - 1959)

1. Choosing the Site. Project and Development

1.1. Location

Latitude:
Longitude:

Camarzana de Tera is a town of the province of Zamora, in the Autonomous Region of Castilla y León, placed on the bank of the Tera River. The building site is on the limit of the consolidated urban land, according to March 2003 Municipal. Its altitude is of 777m above sealevel. It is accessed by the Madrid-Vigo freeway, between Benavente and Puebla de Sanabria, 50kms away from Sanabria Lake and 30km away from Benavente and one hour by car from the border with Portugal.

The climate is continental, with winter temperatures slightly toned down in the valleys. Average temperatures in winter are from 6 to 9 degrees centigrade, and in the summer from 22 to 24; Not very high rainfall, more abundant in spring and winter, with an average from 500 to 600mm.

The town has two clearly delimitated zones and rich in fauna and flora; on the one side the mountain, where the holm oak tree predominates, and on the other side the Tera River. This area had been eminently agricultural until a couple of years ago, but now the service sector predominates.

1.2 Urban Design and Site Improvement

For this project, the land's potential has been reasonably exploited, a long and narrow lot, contained between two roads of unequal importance, and squeezed between other lots of similar characteristics; placed in a landscape with parallel bands of crop of different lengths, widths, thicknesses and textures. The building tries to keep this pattern and, to achieve it, uses the topography as the main drive of the project. The variation in ground level heights generates the necessary spaces for the architectural program.

1.3 Project

One of design proposals is to reduce the formal impact on the natural environment, and as such the designers choose to hide the building in the topography. The two volumes that define the program imitate the landscape. Both the textures of the materials that configure it and the area it occupies in floor plan are integrated into the crop areas.

With a specific program of an old people's home, its adaptation to the human environment is consolidated because future residents are used to a very direct contact with the rural environment. The sensation of belonging to nature is defined from its access where roof escapes towards the horizon. The surroundings resemble a flat carpet formed by different crops which change according with the seasons.

The designer has placed the building in the folds of this carpet. As such, the ground is converted into a garden roof with the thermal advantages that this represents. The system Losa Filtrón and plant surfaces used on the roof[1] generate a similar image to the one of the surrounding crops. By folding the terrain, the green surface of the site is increased, instead of reducing it with the edification. The side façade has the characteristics of an industrial façade, with exposed installations and piping.

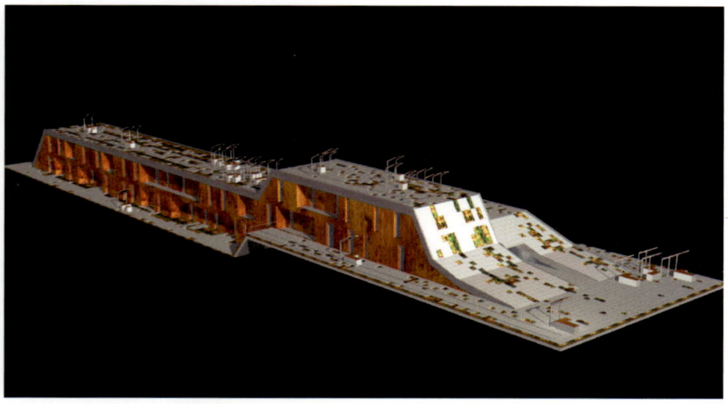

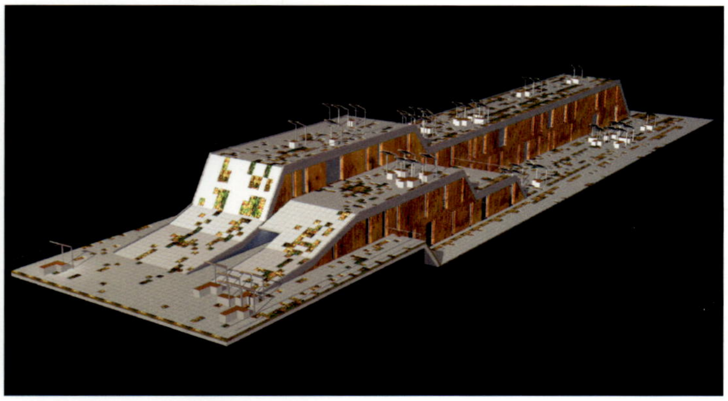

1 http://www.intemper.com/

2. Consumption of Energy and Resources

2.1 Consumption of Energy

With the use of solar panels part of the daily energy used is generated. These devices are supported on metal bases placed on the roof. This layout, despite seeming an added element outside of the architecture, is intentional and is inspired on the pieces of aluminum foil used by farmers to keep the birds away from their crops.

The garden roof favors the building's thermal insulation. According to the last industrial study that was provided by this mechanism, this system saves 37% more energy than traditional systems[2].

2.2 Consumption of Water

The building has been provided with a rainwater recycling system with water collection tanks, to be reused for the irrigation system.

2.3 Consumption of Materials

On façades and floor slabs, the materials used are manufactured in neighboring areas: windows with aluminum framing, perforated brick and ceramic vaults. With the addition of iron oxide, the earthy color of the area has been applied to the mortar finish of the facades.

3. Environmental Loads

3.1 Emissions

With the garden roof, the green surface of the site is extended, increasing the potential of this site to sequence the CO2 generated by its activity, improving the final balance of emissions attributed to the project. The level of insulation generated thanks to this element, avoids using heating systems therefore reducing the emissions created by conditioning[3].

Solar panels are also used as exterior light screens, diminishing the light contamination in the rural environment.

3.2 Solid Waste

Considering the building a "topographical operation", the line of the terrain is not modified; it is only reconfigured, avoiding, as such, the excess of waste during excavation and land leveling.

The use of pre-fabricated joists and ceramic vaults in floor slabs reduces waste derived from on-site assembly.

3.3 Water Management

On the building's roof, the TF System from Intemper has been used, formed by several elements that allow for a better evacuation of water. Losa Filtrón is a draining element with good saving properties because it allows rainwater to be channeled and later used for irrigation or sanitary water.

The facades clad with vegetation panels incorporate a trickle irrigation system integrated into the panel, therefore reducing water consumption for that purpose. This system is connected to an electronic timer in order to adjust irrigation times to the necessities at each moment.

4. Interior Environmental Quality

4.1 Ventilation

Because of the program, special care has been given to the arrangement of openings in every room of the building. With the greatest index of apertures in the East and West facades, crossed ventilation is generated on all three floors.

4.2 Natural Lighting

Due to its orientation, the greatest solar gains are obtained through East and West longitudinal facades. The bedrooms, with East facing windows to take advantage of morning sunlight, are arranged perpendicular to the North-South axis. Afternoon sunlight is filtrated through the circulation corridor that crosses the building. All the floors have access to green surfaces, to the terrain or the garden roof.

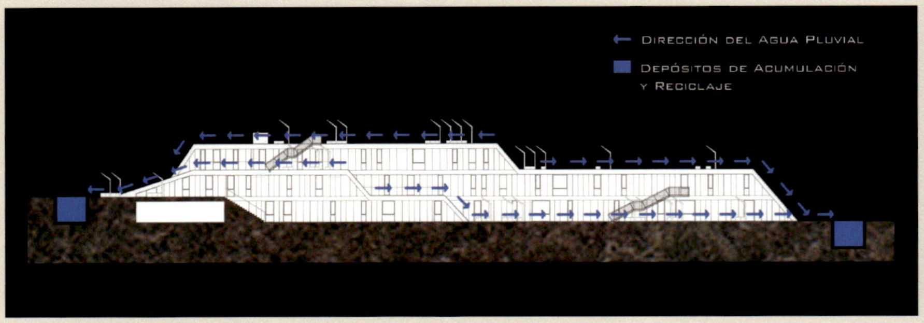

2 http://www.intemper.com/
3 Heating and the consumption of Hot Sanitary Water in offices represents between 50 and 60% average of total energy consumption, of which CO2 emissions are derived equivalent to between 700 kilos to 1 ton per worker and year. http://www.ceroco2.org/reducir/Ficha.aspx?id=15

5. Control of Constructive Systems

5.1 Functionality and Efficiency

Construction elements from the local industry have been used. There is a certain level of pre-manufacturing in floor slabs and façades. The elements of the garden roof need little maintenance, just limited to trickle irrigation.

6. Long- term Performance

6.1 Flexibility and Adaptability

Because of its typology, this building could be adapted to architectural programs with many rooms, and common leisure and administrative spaces, such as hotels and clinics. The environmental control strategies detected could be reproduced even in projects of a smaller scale projects, such as housing.

6.2 Maintenance and Operative Performance

Hydroponic crops placed on the roof require little maintenance. The trickle irrigation system and the reuse of rainwater facilitate this task.

7. Economic and Social Aspects.

7.1 Social Aspects

An important segment of the Spanish population requires services and equipments specifically for the elderly. And the previsions dictate that this percentage will increase in the mid-term[4]. With this project, a decision has been made to provide elderly people with sustainable equipment. In this sense, an architectural matter, that could be recurrent in the following generations, is solved in a pragmatic and positive way.

This building has been designed taking into account all of those details that permit achieving a comfortable stay for elderly people. For this reason, the natural lighting, thermal insulation, and the integration in the landscape structure the entire proposal. The rural character is highlighted with the provision of exterior spaces such as an ecological garden and game areas (pétanque, bowling) for the enjoyment of the users.

7.2 Economic Features

In a town of barely six-thousand inhabitants and with a decreasing demographic trend, it is important to diversify land uses and that new activities boost the town. The placement of the old people's home contributes to this purpose, and becomes an alternative to agriculture and the establishment of industrial estates, as the only way for a town's development.

8. The Architect's eye

Thanks to the simple gesture of folding the terrain and the use of technical elements on the roof, the building's impact on the rural environment has been minimized. The designer has generated this building thanks to the skill of complementing three basic architectural values; form, texture and color.

4 According to the United Nations, 37,6% of the Spanish population will be 65 or older in 2050 (13,4% will be in their eighties); Spin will be one of the oldest countries, together with Japan (36,4%), Italy (35,9%), Croatia or Czech Republic. www.imsersomayores.csic.es/estadisticas/informemayores/informe2002/index.html

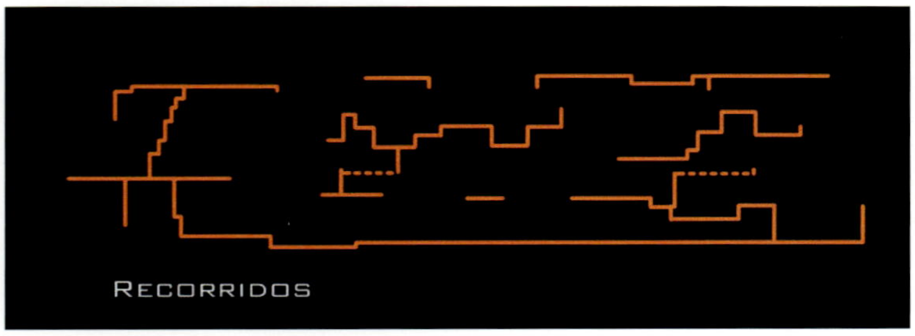

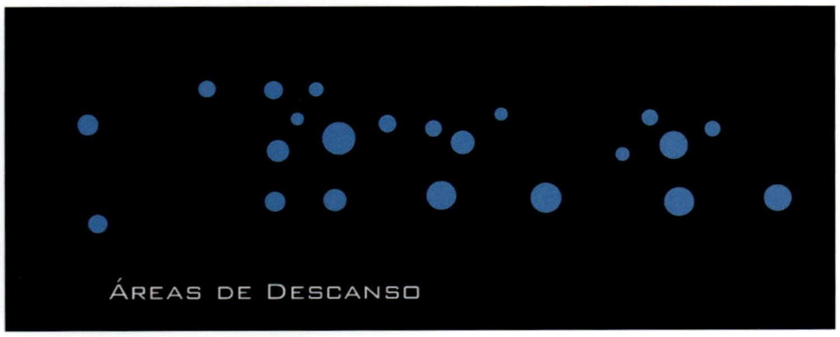

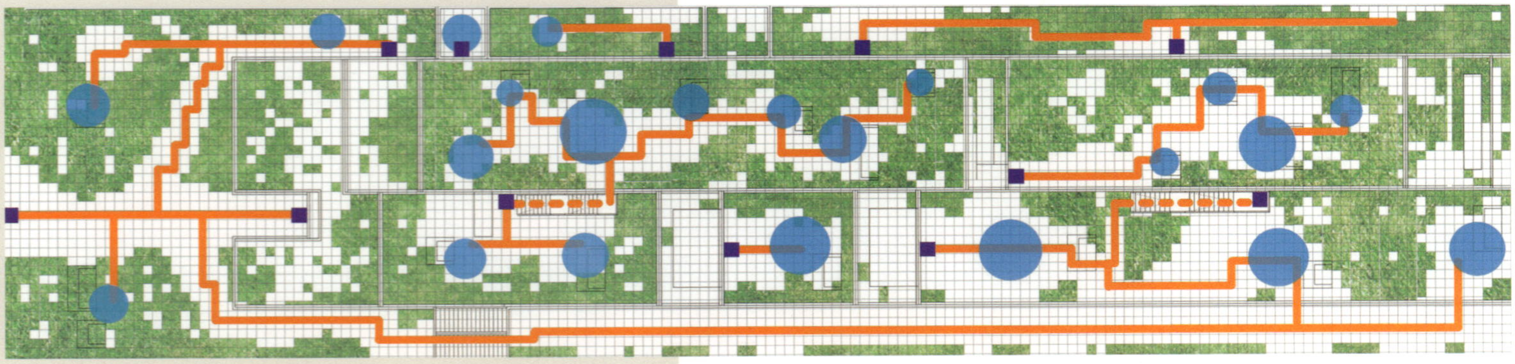

OLD PEOPLE'S HOME
Javier de Antón

North Elevation

East Elevation

0 5 10m
1:500

South Elevation

1:500

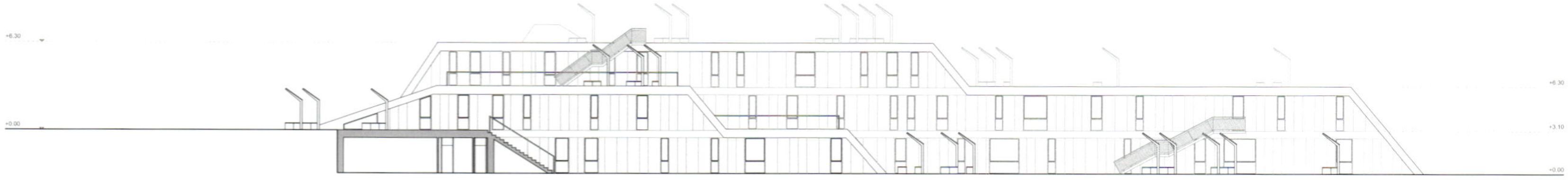

West Elevation

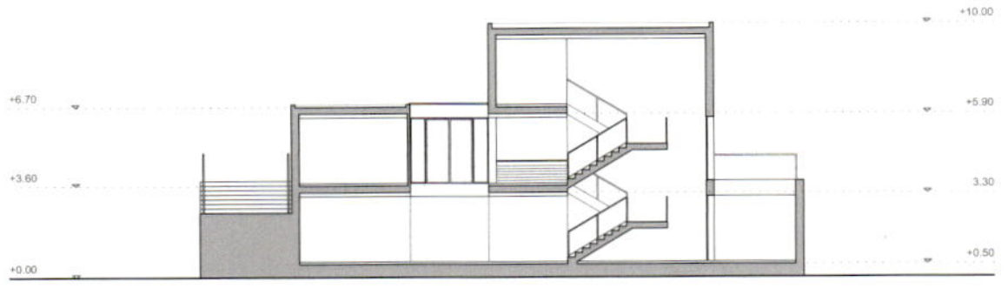

Section A

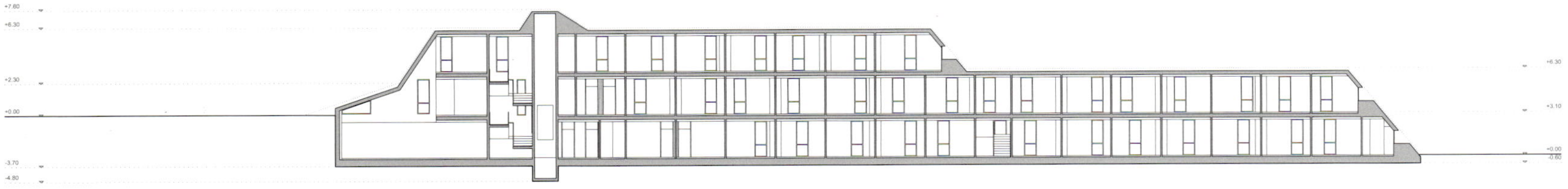

Section B

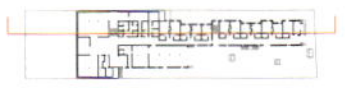

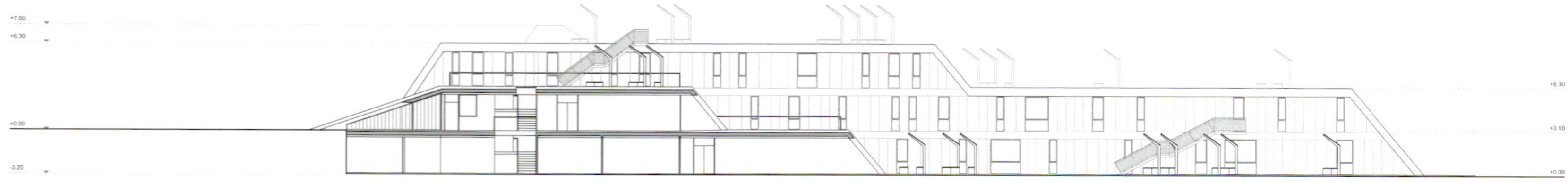

Section C

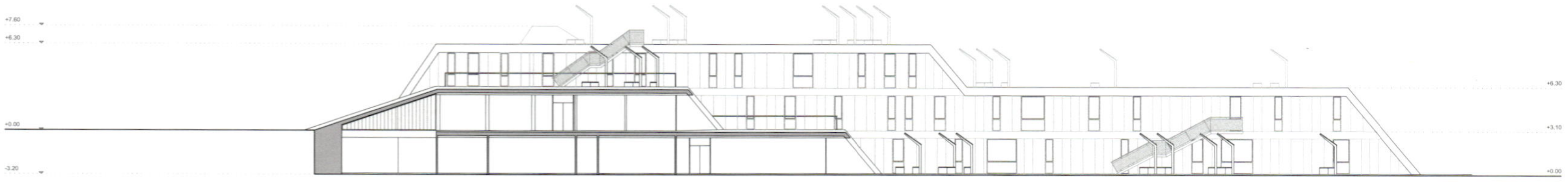

Section D

0 5 10m

1:500

Deployment Diagram

OLD PEOPLE'S HOME

Javier de Antón

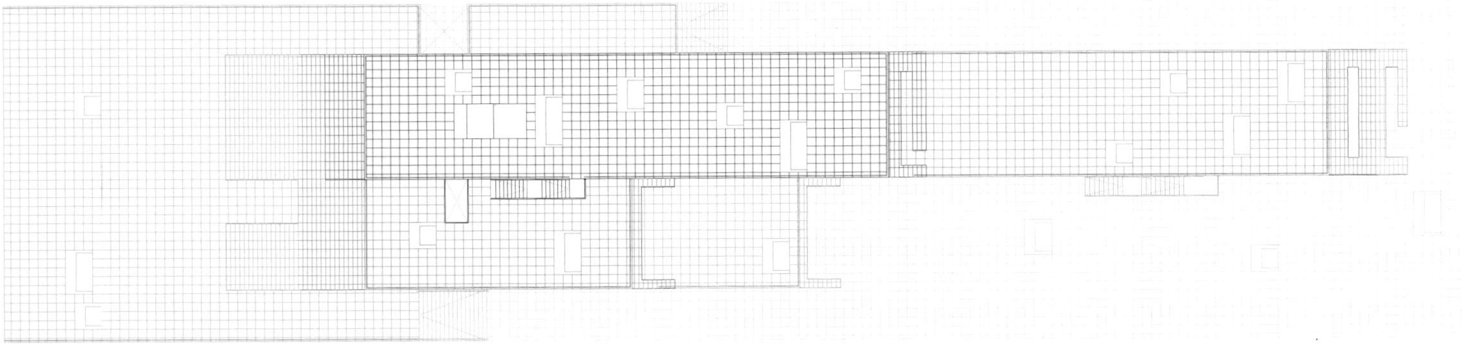

Roof Level

Floor Level Plan

1. Occupational Therapy Room
2. Staircase
3. Physical Therapy Office
4. Individual Room
5. Bathroom
6. Distributor
7. Double Room

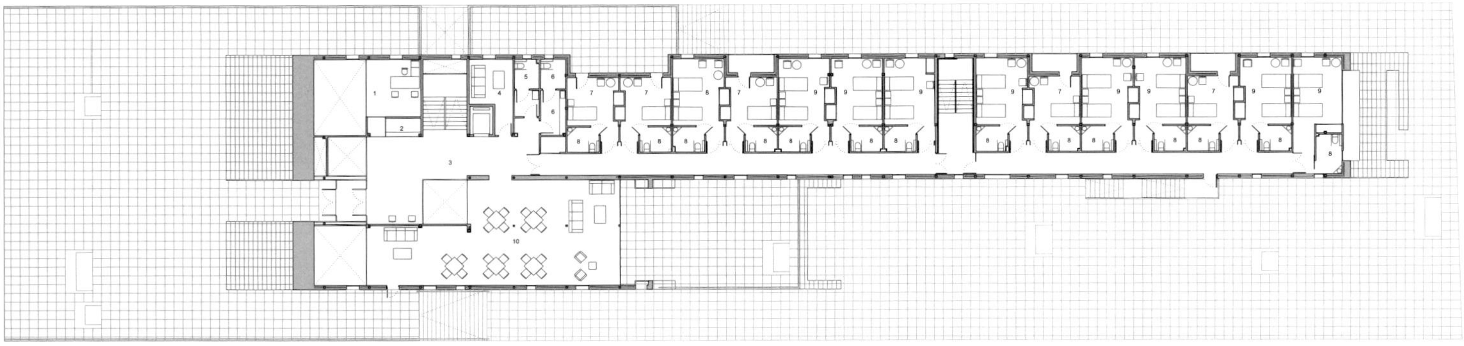

Ground Level Plan

1. Management
2. Reception
3. Entrance Hall
4. Waiting Room
5. Women's Bathroom
6. Men's Bathroom
7. Individual Room
8. Bathroom
9. Double Room
10. Living Room

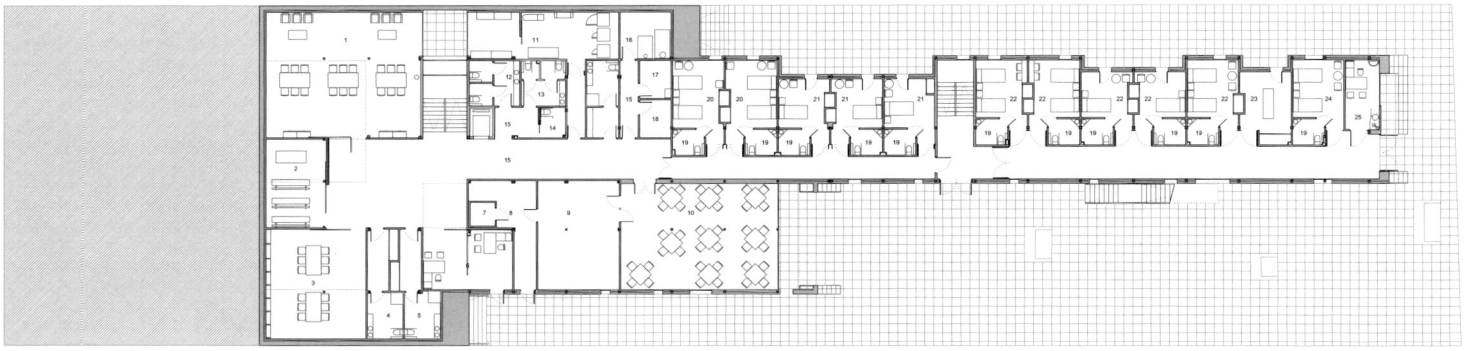

Basement Level Plan

1. Multipurpose Room
2. Chapel
3. Lounge for day center
4. Geriatric bathroom for day center
5. Women's locker room
6. Doctor's office
7. Cold-storage room
8. Kitchen storage
9. Kitchen
10. Dining Room
11. Laundry Room
12. Men's Bathroom
13. Women's Bathroom
14. Handicapped Bathroom
15. Distributor
16. Boiler
17. Cleaning storage
18. Electrical room
19. Bathroom
20. Double room
21. Individual room
22. Double room for special-care resident
23. Geriatric bathroom
24. Double room for infirmary
25. Nurses station

1:500

11

Felipe Pich-Aguilera -Teresa Batlle

EDIFICIO "CALL CENTER TELEFÓNICA MÓVILES"

TOLEDO, España

PICH AGUILERA ARQUITECTES

www.picharchitects.com

ARCHITECTS	Felipe Pich Aguilera Teresa Batlle
SUPERVISORS	Xavi Milanés Ángel Sendarrubias
PROJECT HEAD	Bruno Sauer Ute Müncheberg
COLLABORATORS	Iván Acevedo Pepe Vázquez
WORKS CONSULTANS	Manuel Santolaya Juan Francisco serrano Vicente Erguido
CONTRACTOR	Construcciones Ortiz
PHOTOGRAPHY	Eduardo Sánchez López

	COLLABORATING COMPANIES
Bioclimatic Architecture and Renewable Resources	Emilio Miguel Mitre, EMMA Consultores
Installers	PGI Grup
Mesurements	Tècnics G3
Structure	BD Consuktors

	DATES
IMPLEMENTATION PROJECT	2002
BEGINNING OF WORKS	2003
WORK COMPLETION	2005

DESCRIPTIVE BRIEF

The building is conceived as a big container where industrialized elements are assembled. Two, three-dimensional cores and a portico support large floor slabs as if it was an infrastructure of bridges placed at different heights. The environmental and energy load is not treated as an addition, instead determining, in essence, the architecture and the use of its materials.

The ensemble tries to avoid subsequent finishes, exhibiting the materials and industrial systems used in an apparent way and with their own plastic strength. The color has a special analysis in all the space.

The center of the building is a great open space, covered by a system that channels all of the air-conditioning as if it was an atmosphere and not a roof. Footbridges, five meter wide and seventeen meter long, cross through the space and rest on service and circulation cores; the space tries to give plasticity and flexibility to the entire central volume.

Functionally, the building is clearly differentiated in three areas:

- The first area houses the operators´ services. It works as a great conditioned atrium where the roof gathers the space and allows, with its different slopes, layers and mechanisms, an optimum energy gain and distribution of hot and cold air to all of the spaces. All of the natural lighting contributed to this area is through two lattice ceramic façades, studied together with the industry to be able to, on the one hand, control the solar light and to provide work spaces with enough natural light, and on the other hand, optimize their fabrication and assembly.

- A second area -intimately linked to the first one-, placed in the south, houses the rest area; as its name suggests, its function is to give the operators a rest place, which is an essential space required for good performance at work. It works as a big greenhouse that gives support to the winter comfort in the other spaces. This area is structured in a triple space with direct access to each of the working platforms.

- The third area holds offices, controls, training rooms and parallel services. It's made up of an ensemble of closed volumes and partially covered courtyards. In this area, the infrastructure of bridges closes onto itself, creating compartmentalized working areas which all face towards a courtyard, covered at all heights, and with a mainly climatic function. This north-facing space, with its courtyards and vegetation, functions as a thermal regulator providing coolness to all of the spaces.

Vegetation in this third area plays an essential role in the courtyards, giving a natural cooling effect and noise absorption. This vegetation is possible due to the terraces´ tank roofs. The roofs collect and store rainwater through the projections that overhang the structural frame and the enclosure, and are used as a hydroponic substrate for the vegetation.

The facilities support comfort and are designed to be able to fulfill the needs that cannot be met by the building's bioclimatic contribution.

The active conditioning systems are supported by thermal solar panels for the production of hot water, and controls that make the functioning of passive systems possible before the machinery of traditional air conditioning systems.

"We cannot resolve problems with the same type of thought we use when we create them"

Albert Einstein

1. Choosing the Site. Project and Development

1.1. Location

Latitude:	39°51'51.08"N
Longitude:	3°57'47.59"W

The building is located in the Industrial Estate of Santa María de Benquerencia, 6 km from Toledo. With a flat topography it is closer than 1 km to the Tajo River, in lands with an agricultural vocation. The site is determined by the developer.

Access to the complex where the project is located is reached by way of the N400. In addition to the car, there is a regular public bus service. Lines 6, 9, and circular of the company Unauto connect Toledo and some other neighboring towns with the Industrial Estate where the building is located.

1.2 Urban design and Improvement of the Site

This project responds to an isolated volume urban typology, because of the existing urban regulations.

The inclusion of afforestation provides an improvement of urban comfort to an industrial environment. The provision of trees on the exterior will create areas of natural shade and contribute to the CO2 sequencing of the area.

The water tank roofs on the terraces defined by the cantilevered footbridges provide a green layer to terrain hardened by pavement and edification.

Street furniture, created by the project designers, is incorporated. The Slope® bench is a landscape element used on the exterior and in the interior courtyards of the project.

1.3 Project

This project has an introverted character on the site. It is found as a single object isolated from the hostile border. The afforestation and covered parking work as border elements. The parking's void gives the central volume greater protagonism, from the pedestrian point of view. The access is defined by the reduction of the space when crossing the semi-covered gallery. Crossing the threshold, the surprise is visible when discovering a unique space where the offices are hanging elements.

The structure is determinant in its spatial conception; it is defined by a longitudinal axis made by two walls enclosing all services which are the lateral limits of the main space, with a regular floorplan composition (a,b,a,b). In the opposite direction, it is composed by the repetition of a rhythm (c), which has the freedom to be placed at different levels.

The three functional areas in which the building is divided also have an environmental function. The central area houses the building's main core; it works as a conditioned atrium, where the design of the roof and ceramic façades create an atmosphere with sufficient temperature and natural light to develop the building's main activity.

The second area, located in the South and functionally connected to the central area, contains the phone operator's rest areas. Environmentally, it works as a large greenhouse with a vocation to support winter comfort for the rest of spaces.

The third North-facing area is used for offices, training rooms and support areas. Here, the building's structural layout originates several covered courtyards with incorporated vegetation, working as thermal and acoustic regulators.

2. Consumption of Energy and Resources

2.1 Consumption of Energy

The roof, in addition to containing space, permits with its different slopes, layers and mechanisms, the capturing of energy and the hot and cold air distribution to all spaces.

Conventional conditioning installations are planned as support to the building's bioclimatic systems, which are the ones to assume the largest environmental load.

To generate hot water and as support for the heating pump, solar thermal panels are used, laid on the building's concave roof. The lights in the central work area are low consumption ones and are designed as support to natural lighting.

2.2 Consumption of Water

The covered courtyards of the North area are irrigated thanks to the rainwater collected in the roof water tanks of the terraces. The cantilevers that overhang from the structural portico capture and store the rainwater. These roofs are ecological water tank roofs.

The principle of the system consists of a water tank beneath several hanging slabs which support the substratum and vegetation. The plant substratum remains wet by capillarity thanks to a geotextile in direct contact with the water, which conserves the vegetation without any maintenance.

2.3 Consumption of Materials

Materials are used in two ways simultaneously; in the fist place, they have a technical role such as solving structural problems. The other one is a formal composition related to the man who observes the space.

The ensemble tries to avoid posterior finishes, exposing materials and industrial systems used with their own expressiveness. This way of using materials as composing elements results in a unit of spatial synthesis.

The use of pre-fabricated elements optimizes the material, reducing execution time and minimizing waste products.

The choice of materials and building systems, their formats, joints, and placement, require a narrow collaboration between the designer and manufacturer, with the purpose of using the materials correctly and optimizing both human and material resources, consumption, and waste products. Both in the genesis of the structure and façade, we counted on industrialists with the technology and products possible for its construction. Specifically, on the façade, we relied on the active interaction of local manufacturers, until finding the most adequate pieces for their texture, format and placement.

Unnecessary finishes are avoided in the interior. "Celenit" panels were used, made of fir tree fibres, in the interior of the central areas as protection for the footbridges, which have a decorative and acoustic function.

Interior partitions were made of screens, which reduce construction time and facilitates assembly and dismantling, as well as the changes in the layout of spaces, according to the necessities.

3.Environmental Loads

3.1 Emissions

Every project must be charged with gas emissions implicit in the fabrication of materials used. In this sense, this project, using prefabrication and eliminating unnecessary finishes, achieves the reduction of materials, therefore diminishing the total energy consumption used in its construction.

3.2 Solid Waste

The construction system used is based on the assembly of prefabricated material, which minimizes on-site dumping and waste. Dry joints used make dismantling easier in case of a hypothetical demolition, which facilitates separation and management of waste.

Pre-fabricated footbridges are supported by dry joints to corbels positioned at different levels on the load-bearing in-situ concrete walls.

The roof is supported on a structure of open-web steel joists which also have articulated supports on the dry load- bearing walls.

3.3 Water Management

Criteria for the reuse of rainwater for irrigation are incorporated by means of its storage in the water tank roofs of the terrace.

Waste products from the Industrial area are treated by the Residual Water Treating Station of Santa María de Benquerencia. This filtered water is later poured into the Castrejon reservoir, declared as "sensitive area" by the Ministery of the Environment.

4. Interior Environmental Quality

4.1 Ventilation

This building has two clearly different behaviors. In both cases the central space and roof play a prominent role when distributing ventilation to the rest of the building. During the winter the southern section of the roof works as a greenhouse. Several natural ventilation caps remain closed to facilitate hot air accumulation in the building's interior. The roof's central section works as a thermal collector, whereas the north section permits the direct entrance of radiation and lighting to interior courtyards. Two de-stratification columns, generated by the layout of the structural walls, facilitate air circulation towards building's upper floors.

In the summer, the sun has a closer incidence angle, and the south sector of the roof works as a parasol, facilitating light reflection towards its exterior. The natural ventilation caps are maintained open to facilitate the exit of hot air generated in the interior of the building. Apertures placed in the lower part of the north façade complete the system and permit the crossed ventilation of the complex, incorporating fresh air in the system. The roof's central section works as a thermal collector to feed a cooling absorption system. The north section of the roof works as a parasol thanks to the angle of the slats that cover it. The roof's north section works as a parasol-pergola made of vacuum tubes, capturer of solar-thermal energy. Radiation that penetrates the courtyards located in this part of the building allows, by pressure and temperature difference, to generate an air stream that circulates throughout the building through the de-stratification columns and comes out through the caps in the roof's south section.

4.2 Natural Lighting

The lighting of the building's central core is realized through the two ceramic lattice façades located in both the West and East side of the building. A study was made of the lighting necessities in the central space, and ceramic pieces were distributed -in a lattice in some points or avoiding the passing of excessive natural lighting- according to this previous study. The south façades receive7 light through the concave roof and the north area is illuminated through the roof and façade clad with translucent polycarbonate. The building's three main sections lit naturally. Absence of horizontal divisions in the central core facilitates a uniform distribution of light between the different work levels.

4.3 Acoustics

Although, structural elements with a low sound absorption coefficient and no finish have been use in the project, strategies have been adopted to avoid inadequate sound levels in the complex. The concrete's reflection level is attenuated by the addition of "Celenit" panels with a high acoustic absorption level. With the fibrous structure of these panels, the intention is to reduce the number of sound reflections produced by the activity of phone operators made in this part of the building, and to improve the listening quality in the room. The incorporation of plants in the north area of the building increases the equivalent absorption area, reducing reverberation time and definitively improving the ensemble's acoustic level. The monitoring on the type of furniture used by phone operators also contributes to the acoustic control.

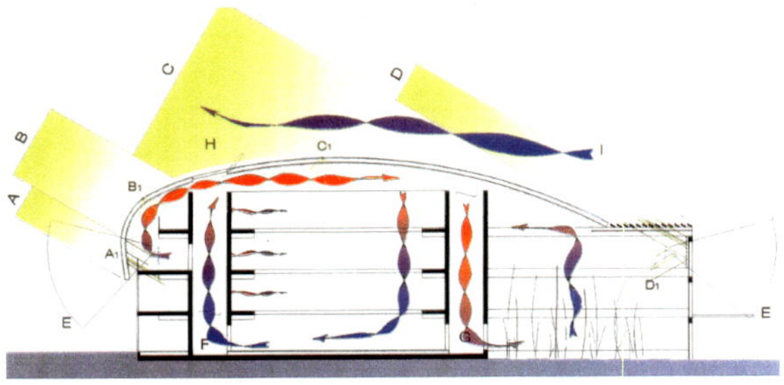

Winter bioclimaticanalysis diagram

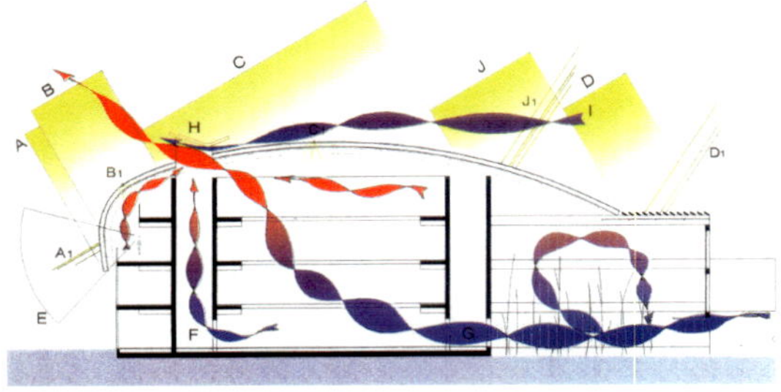

Summer bioclimaticanalysis diagram

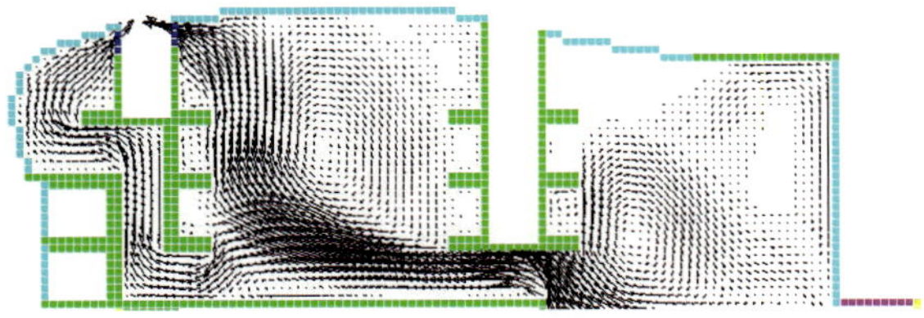

Winter winds analysis

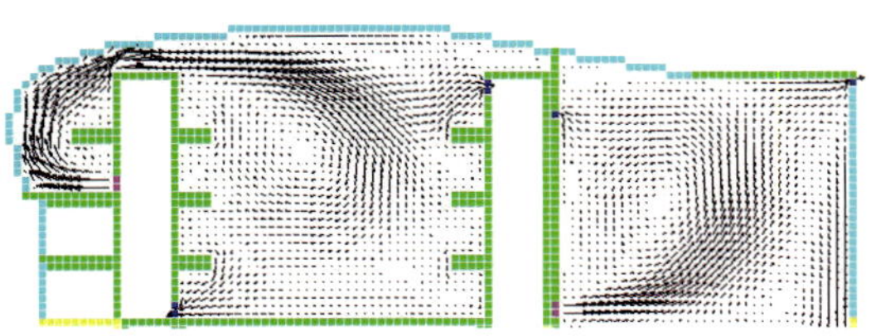

Summer winds analysis

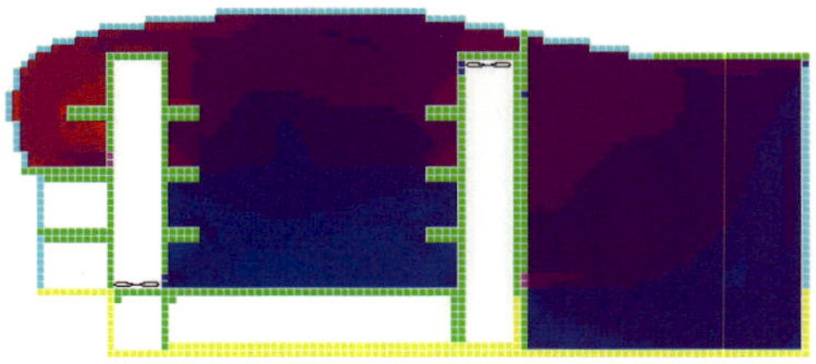

Winter temperatures Diagram

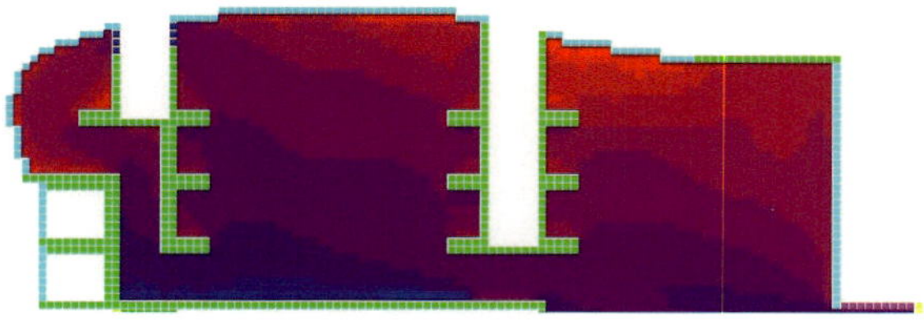

Summer temperatures Diagram

5.Control of Building Systems

5.1 Functionality and Efficiency

The building systems used take into account existing products of the industry and their processes. A high percentage of the work is manufactured in the factory and assembled on- site. Human resources and materials are controlled; consumption and waste are minimized. Work spaces are pre-existing large truss beams used in road bridges. Large format ceramic pieces were manufactured 10km away from the site by a local industry. The builders had extensive experience in the coordination of industrialized construction, therefore knowledge in the management of different construction entries and of their industrialists, without overlaps, without voids in time, and guaranteeing the quality and efficiency of each one of them.

The active conditioning systems are conceived to support the passive control achieved by means of the building's bioclimatic systems.

5.2 Control of Building Systems

The building systems used play an active role in the task of offering comfort to the building's occupants. The roof, in addition to its protective function, works as a channel for the conditioning system.

Thanks to its shape, materials, and feasibility, it creates an adjustable atmospheric effect according to the environmental conditions of each season. The structural footbridge-support cores are used as service and circulation containers. They facilitate, because of their shape, air circulation at different heights.

The east and west facades are resolved by a ceramic lattice, studied to control the natural light level and sufficient to develop the main activity in the building's central core.

6. Long-term Performance

6.1 Flexibility and Adaptability

Conceived as a large container, the building permits several layouts to solve architectural programs which require a great concentration of people in large open spaces.

6.2 Maintenance and Operative Performance

Avoiding the use of unnecessary finishes, maintenance is reduced to the structural materials.

Narrow partnership with industrialists from the project phase, allows controlling the performance of materials and systems. This will facilitate a hypothetic correction when necessary and the replication of the solution if correct.

7. Economical and Social Aspects

7.1 Social Aspects

All studies made about phone operator centers in member countries of the European Community reveal symptoms of organizational discomfort, among which great personnel movement and high levels of work and stress[1] should be highlighted. Phone operator centers normally follow a factory format. If we take into account the evolution of these centers, the organization of the work should support tools and structures of collaboration, professional development, and staff health.

Technical solutions are incorporated to this project which intend to provide these workers with a comfortable space in which to develop their activity. Phone operator work is a very widespread activity in the current labor system, which demands many hours of solitary work in front of a computer and telephone. The individual work of phone operators, with the furniture as their work space, forms part of a larger space with which they always interact and it must positively influence the worker's performance. The south space, rest area, was also designed in view of the light and its dimensions, considering it not only as another space, but from its function of visual, psychical and physical rest.

7.2 Economic Aspects

The use of pre-fabricated systems and a narrow collaboration with industrialists diminishes construction time and the final cost due to indirect savings.

Incorporation of passive systems of control permits a savings derived from the operation of conventional conditioning systems and definitive savings in environmental costs due to the building's operation. Phone operator centers constitute one of the forms of employment of greatest growth nowadays.

8. The Architect's Eye

The idea of the project is materialized when changing the context of a pre-fabricated element proper to road projects; compositional element that gives rhythm to the façade and interior space. Inside, it is used to support the work activities, and outside, it works as a rainwater collector.

[1] http://www.telework-mirti.org/reports/sum_ITES.htm

CALL CENTER BUILDING

Felipe Pich-Aguilera -Teresa Batlle

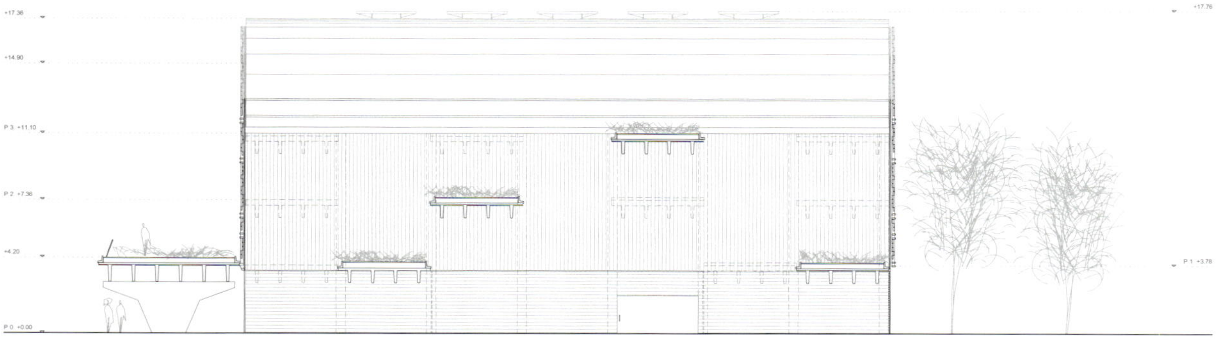

North Elevation

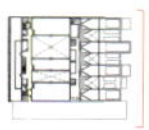

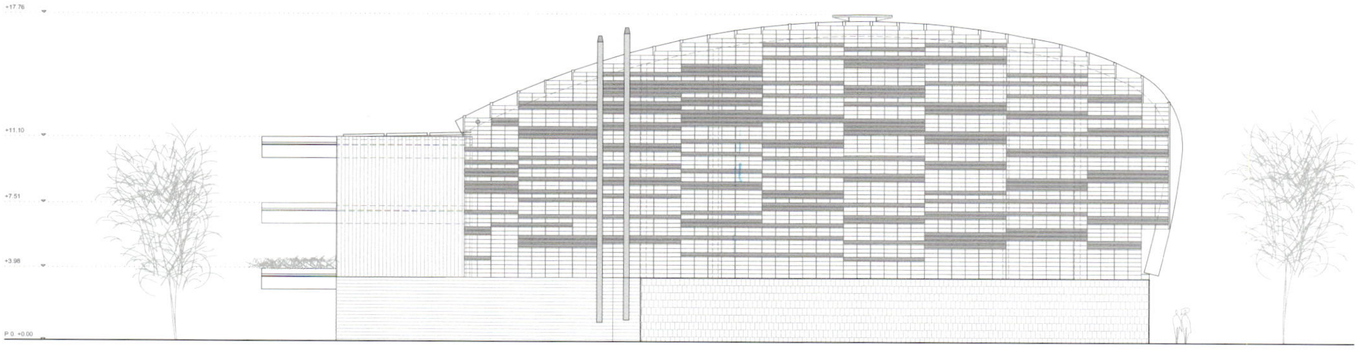

West Elevation

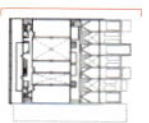

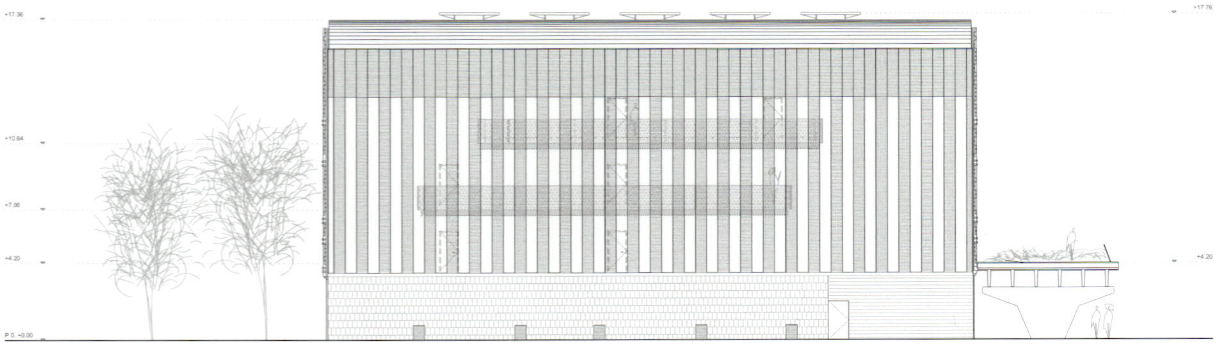

South Elevation

CALL CENTER BUILDING

Felipe Pich-Aguilera -Teresa Batlle

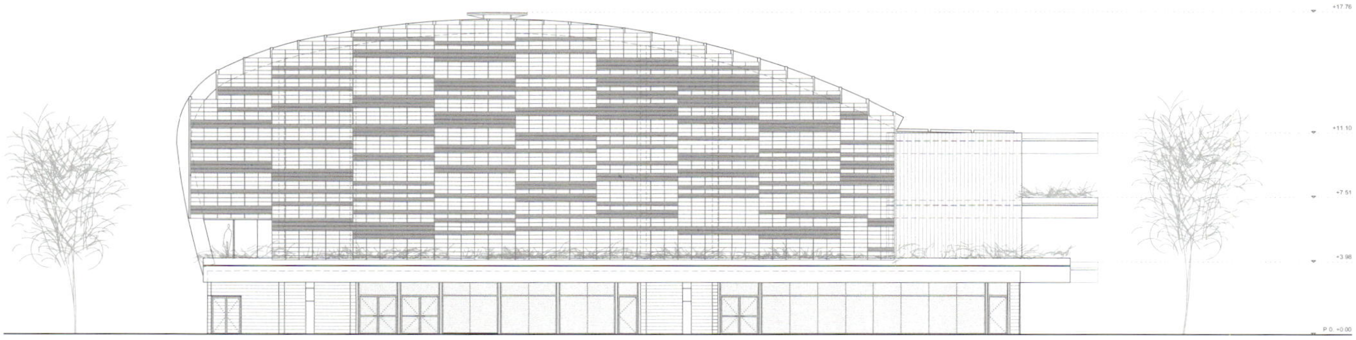

East Elevation

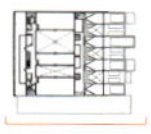

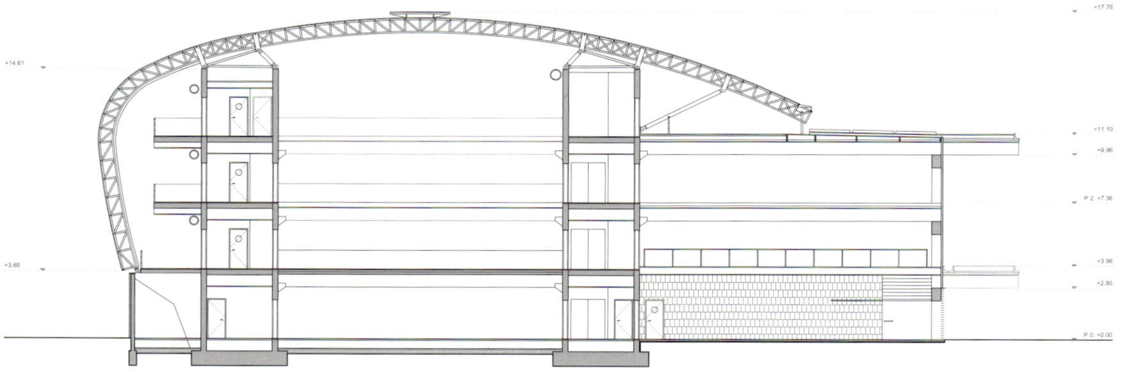

Section A

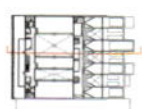

EDIFICIO "CALL CENTER TELEFÓNICA MÓVILES"
Felipe Pich-Aguilera -Teresa Batlle

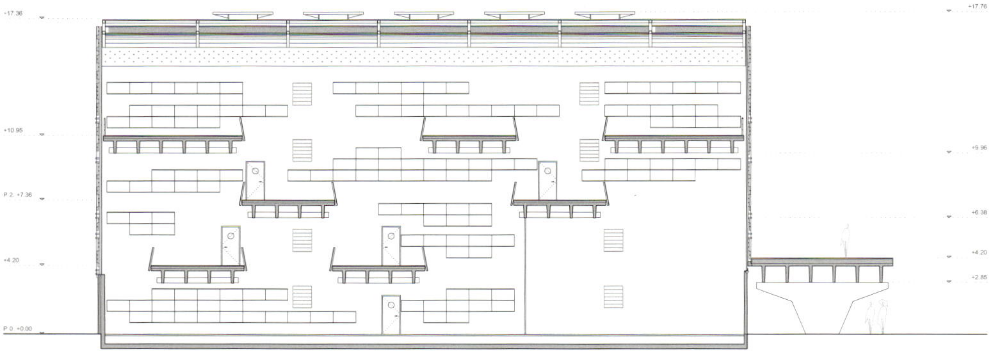

Section B

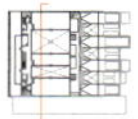

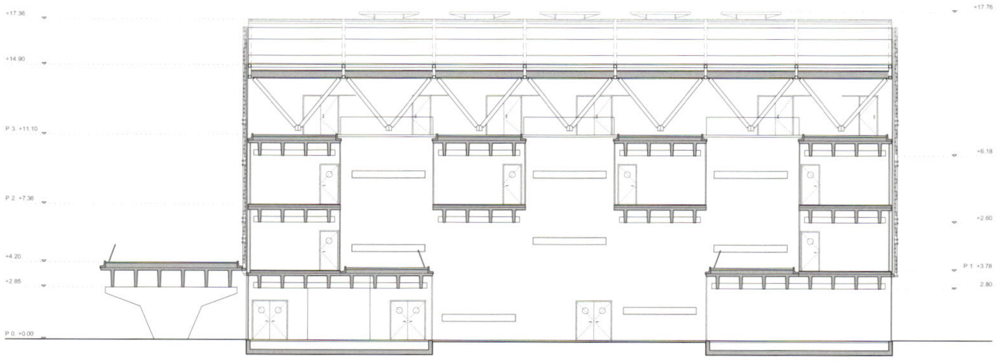

Section C

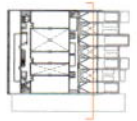

2. Handicapped bathroom
3. Elevator
4. Staircase
8. Ventilation
10. Bathrooms
11. Reception
13. Offices
16. Courtyard
17. Double height space

Ground floor level

1. Ventilation duct
2. Handicapped bathroom
3. Elevator
4. Staircase
5. Dining hall - rest
6. Kitchen
7. Dressing Room
8. Ventilation
9. Telemarketing phone operators
10. Bathrooms
11. Reception
12. Administration
13. Offices
14. Training
15. Cistern roof
16. Courtyard
17. Double height space
18. Solar panels

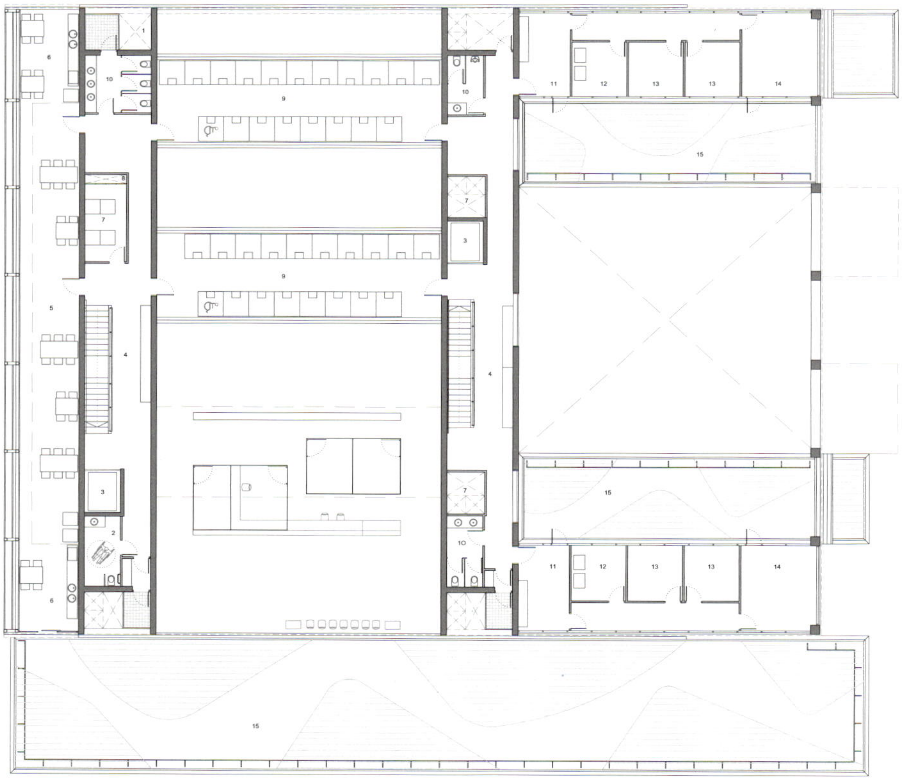

1st floor level

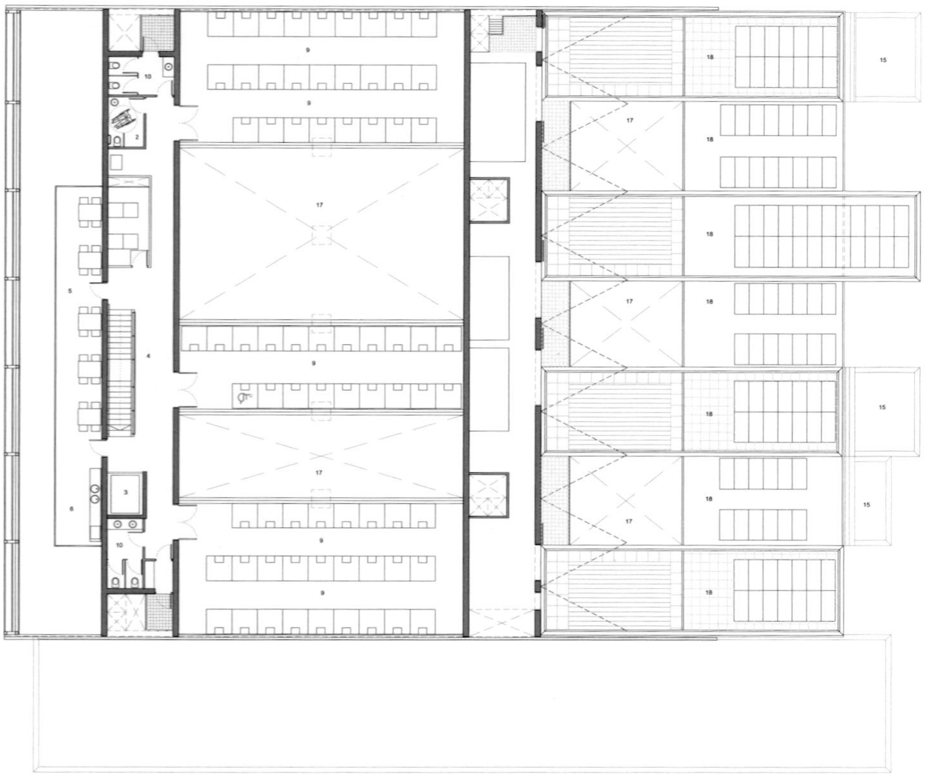

3rd floor level

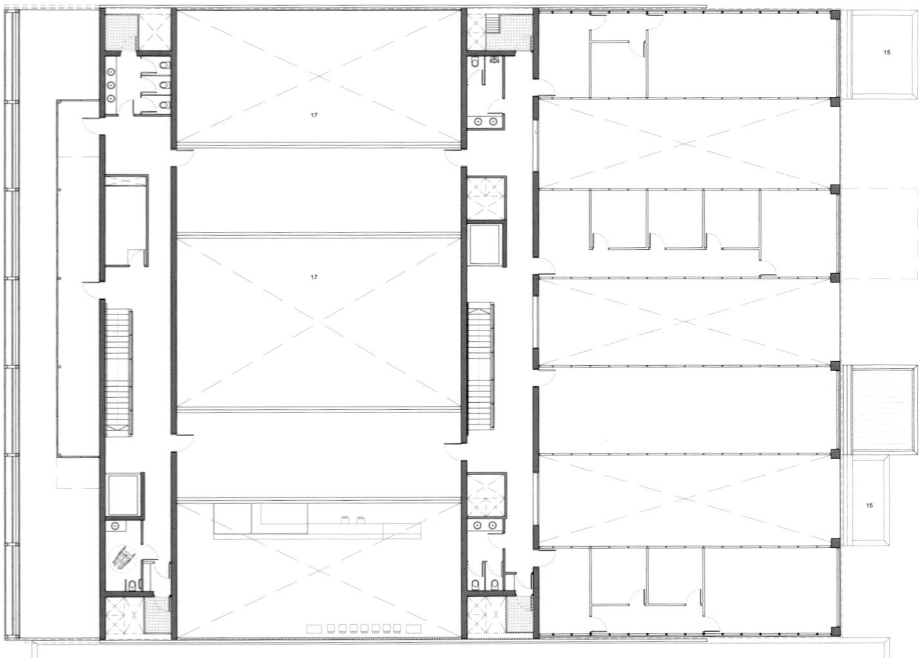

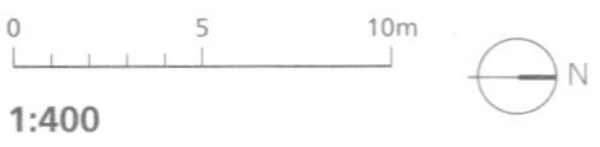

2nd floor level

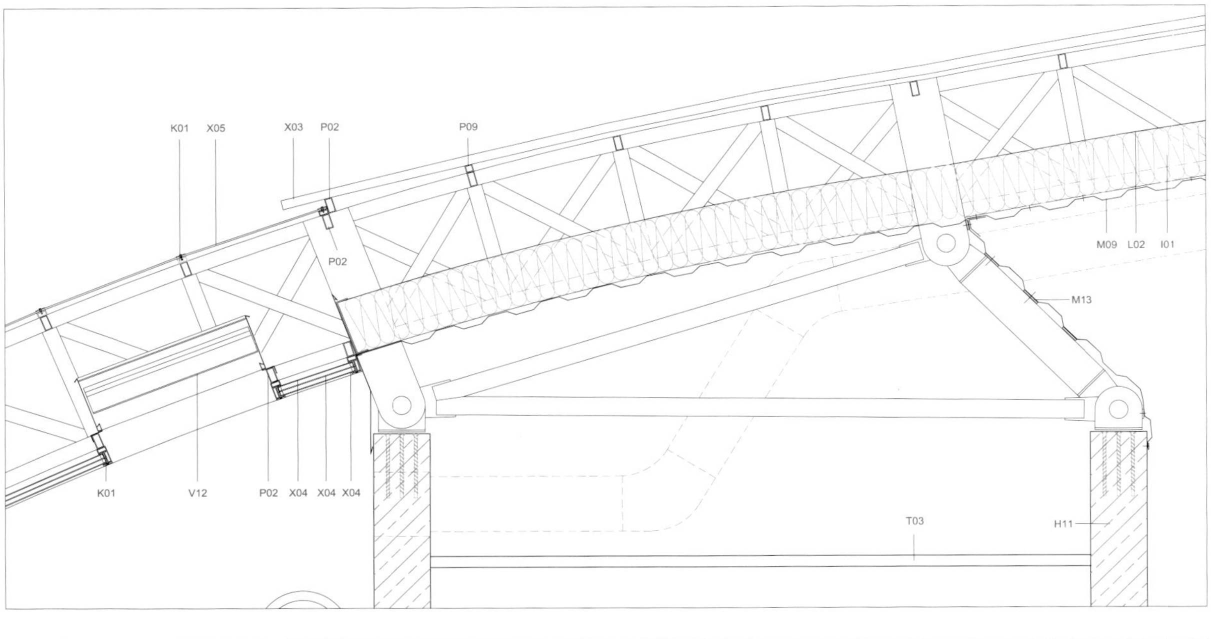

D. 1

0 25 50 75 1m

1:40

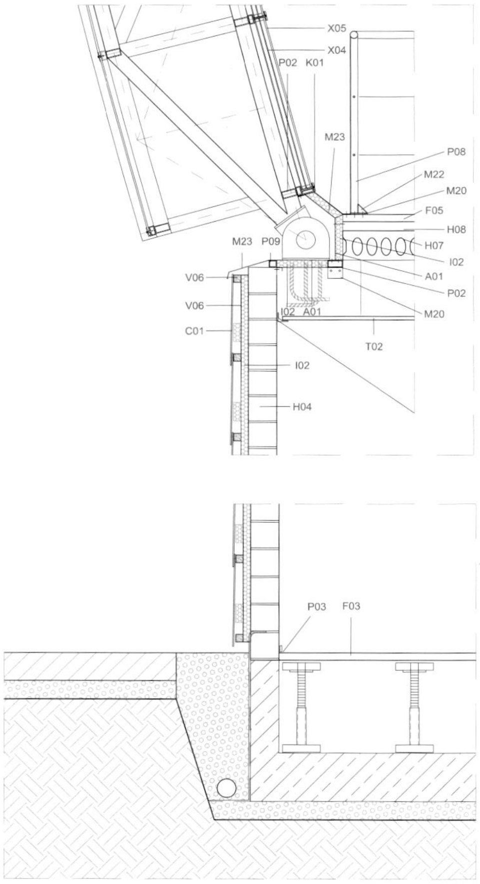

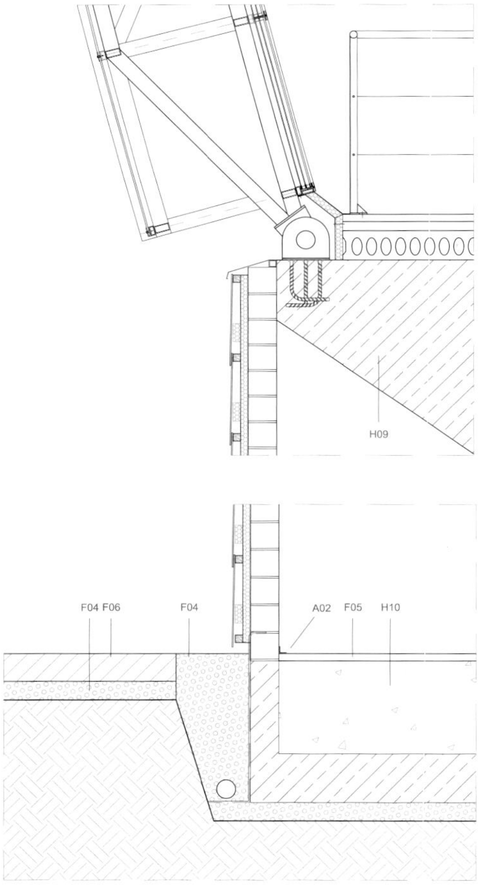

D. 2

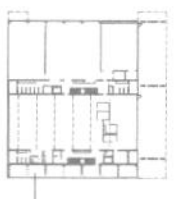

D. 3

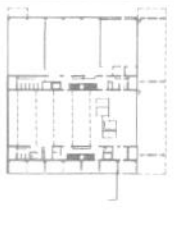

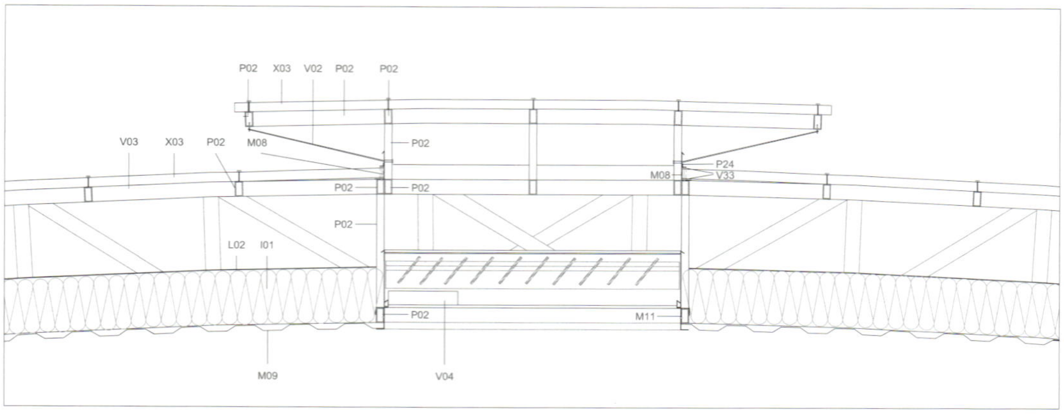

D. 4

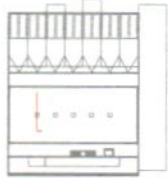

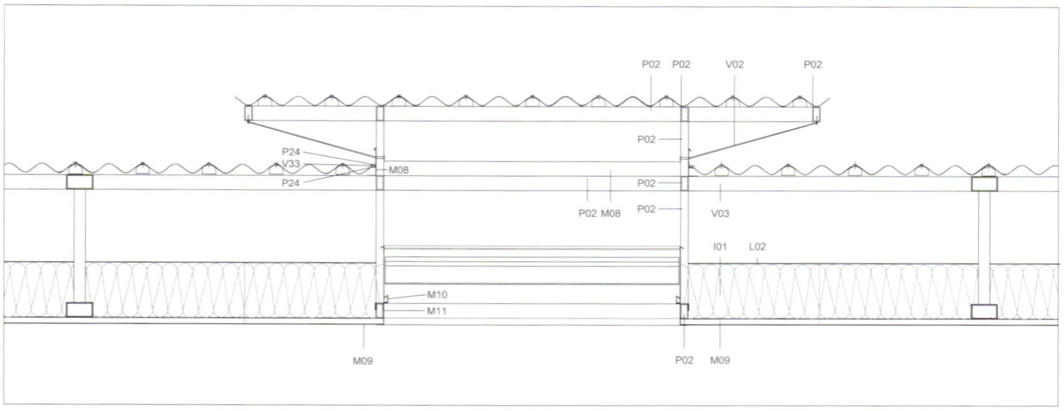

D. 5

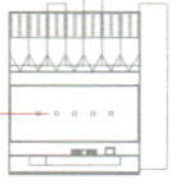

Metal Sheet
M08 Galvanized sheet 1750x (150x50)
M09 Folded perforated steel plate, Profiles "Trapezoidal MT-52" perforation type Hiansa, or, color to be defined
M10 Plate100x100x5, painted hammertone
M11 Folded galvanized steel plate (55+80)x1750, as end piece M09
M13 Plate 100x100x4
M20 Plate 100x80x6, painted hammertone
M22 Plate 50x50x4, in triangle, painted hammertone
M23 Folded galvanized steel plate, custom-size

Aluminum Sheet
A01 Aluminum cap, folded metal plate, anodized, silver color
A02 Aluminum tube 40x10 as baseboard, silver color, anodized

Drop Ceiling
T02 Celenit or equivalent, strips of 60cm, exposed guide
T03 Aluminum vertical louvers of 10cm, type Phalcel 100/100 of Gradhermetic, or equivalent

Concrete
H04 Concrete block 15x20x40
H07 Alveolar panel15cm, prefabricated Pujol or equivalent
H08 Compression layer 5cm
H09 Support for alveolar panel, concrete poured in situ
H10 Lightweight concrete refill
H11 Wall 30cm concrete poured in situ

Ceramic
C01 Flat vitrified roofing tile 14cmx28cm with various colors of Covallay or equivalent

Insulation
I01 Rockwool, 30cm, density to be defined
I02 Insulation panel of extruded polystyrene 4cm

Pavement
F03 Technical floor, slabs of 40cmx40cm, type DS/2 of Desmon or equivalent
F04 Gravel
F05 Tinted concrete 5cm, reinforced with fiberglass
F06 Tinted concrete 8cm, reinforced with fiberglass

Profiles
P02 Tube 40x80x4
P03 L 35x35x6
P08 T 40x40
P09 Tube 40x40x4
P24 L 40x40x4

Polycarbonate
X03 Opal corrugated panel, type 177/51 of GET or equivalent
X04 Solid panel 4mm, transparent of GET or equivalent
X05 Solid panel 8mm of GET or equivalent

Sheets

L02 Feltemper sheet from Intemper or equivalent

Various
V02 Braided steel cable diam.3mm
V03 Covered truss
V04 Machine for extraction of fumes type Euroco 16/16 of Colt or equivalent
V06 Wooden batten 40x40
V12 Machine for extraction of fumes type Euroco 16/07 de Colt or equivalent
V33 Neoprene

Window and door framing
K01 Standard profile for polycarbonate, according to installer

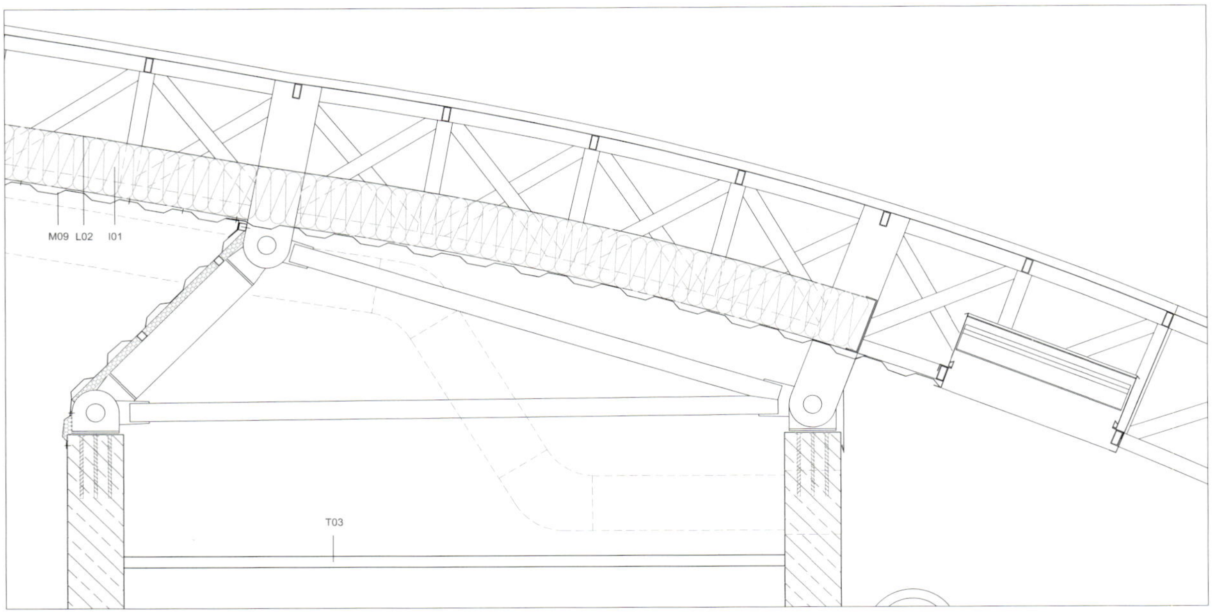

D. 6

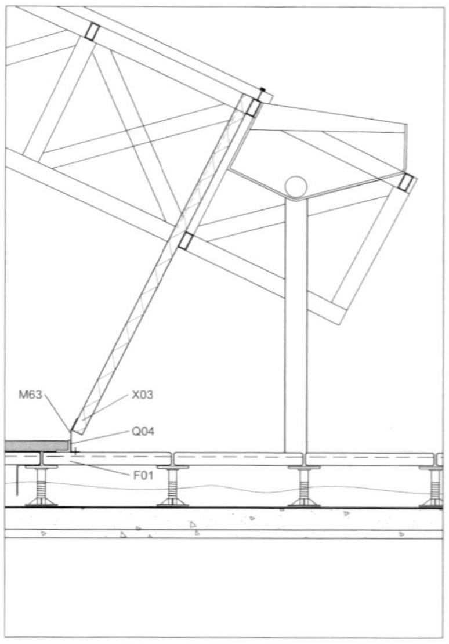

D. 7

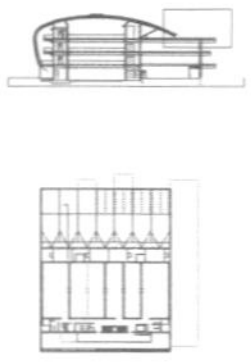

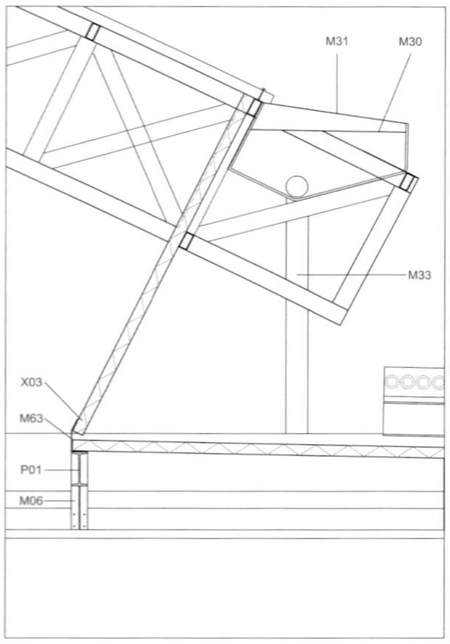

D. 8

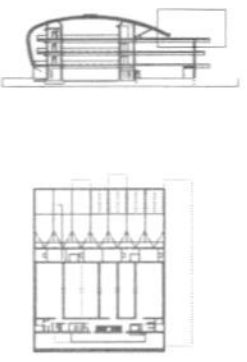

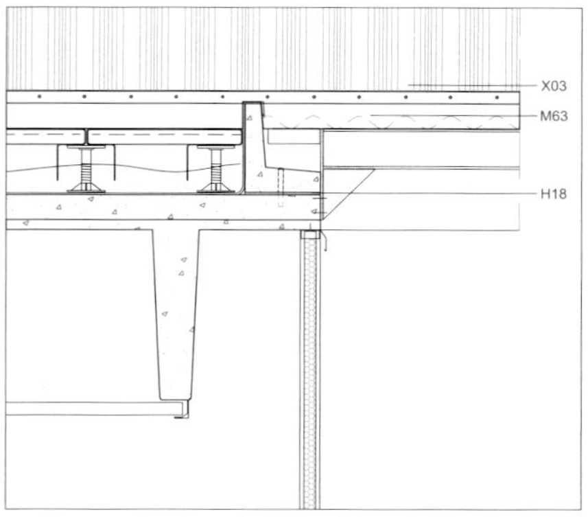

D. 9

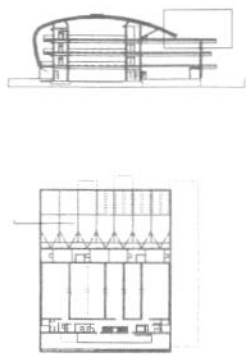

0 25 50 75 1m

1:40

Metal sheet
M01 Plate 74x200x6, painted hammertone
M02 Plate 140x300x4, in triangle, 1/m, painted hammertone
M03 Plate 2150x275x4, painted hammertone
M04 Galvanized steel weathering (180+50)x6700
M05 Galvanized steel weathering (120+50)x6700
M06 Plate 74x380x6, painted hammertone
M07 Plate 220x220x6, in triangle, painted hammertone
M09 Folded perforated plate, type Profiled plate "Trapezoidal MT-52" perforated of Hiansa, or equivalent, color to be designed
M30 Gutter of folded of galvanized sheet
M31 Triangular plate, reinforcement M30, galvanized
M33 Drainpipe Ø.160
M63 Galvanized folded sheet, cap X03

Aluminum Sheet
A01 Aluminum cap, folded metal sheet, anodized, silver color

Drop Ceiling
T03 Aluminum vertical louvers of 10cm, type Phalcel 100/100 of Gradhermetic, or equivalent

Concrete
H02 Panel TT 72, prefabricated Pujol or equivalent
H03 Compression layer 10cm
H14 Piece "L without dripedge" prefabricated, fastened to the slab with mechanical fixture
H18 Layer of Mortar

Ceramic

Insulation
I01 Rockwool, 30cm, density to be defined

Pavement
F01 Losa Filtrón of Intemper or equivalent

Profiles
P01 IPN160
P13 Pipe 60x40x4
P36 Pipę 4 cm, height 10 cm

Polycarbonate
X01 Transparent corrugated panel, type 177/51 de GET or equivalent
X03 Opal corrugated panel, type 177/51 of GET or equivalent

Divisions
W01 Dividing screen, hidden profile, double 16/450/16, metal profiles, thermal insulation, wood panels veneered with melamine, type Supra of Desmon or equivalent

Sheets
L01 Rhenofol CG sheet of Intemper or equivalent
L02 Feltemper sheet of Intemper or equivalent

Various
V01 Solar panel, vacuum tube, type Vitosol 200 of Viessmann, or equivalent
V32 Rubber cone adjusting to P36

Plastic profiles
Q04 Standard profile (PVC) of Intemper or equivalent

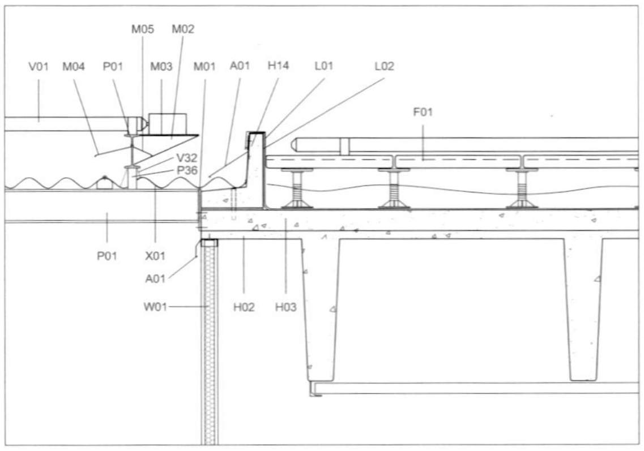

D. 10

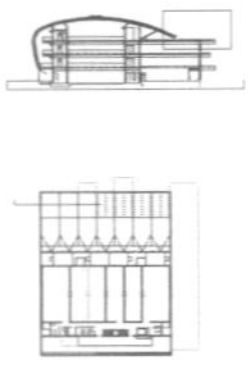

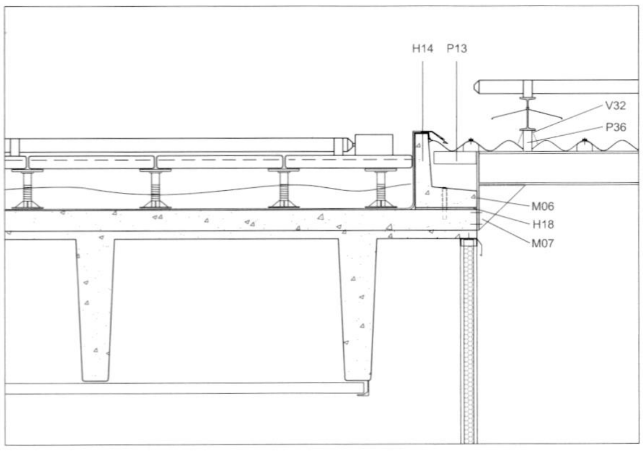

D. 11

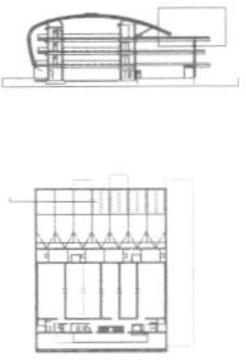

CALL CENTER BUILDING

Felipe Pich-Aguilera -Teresa Batlle

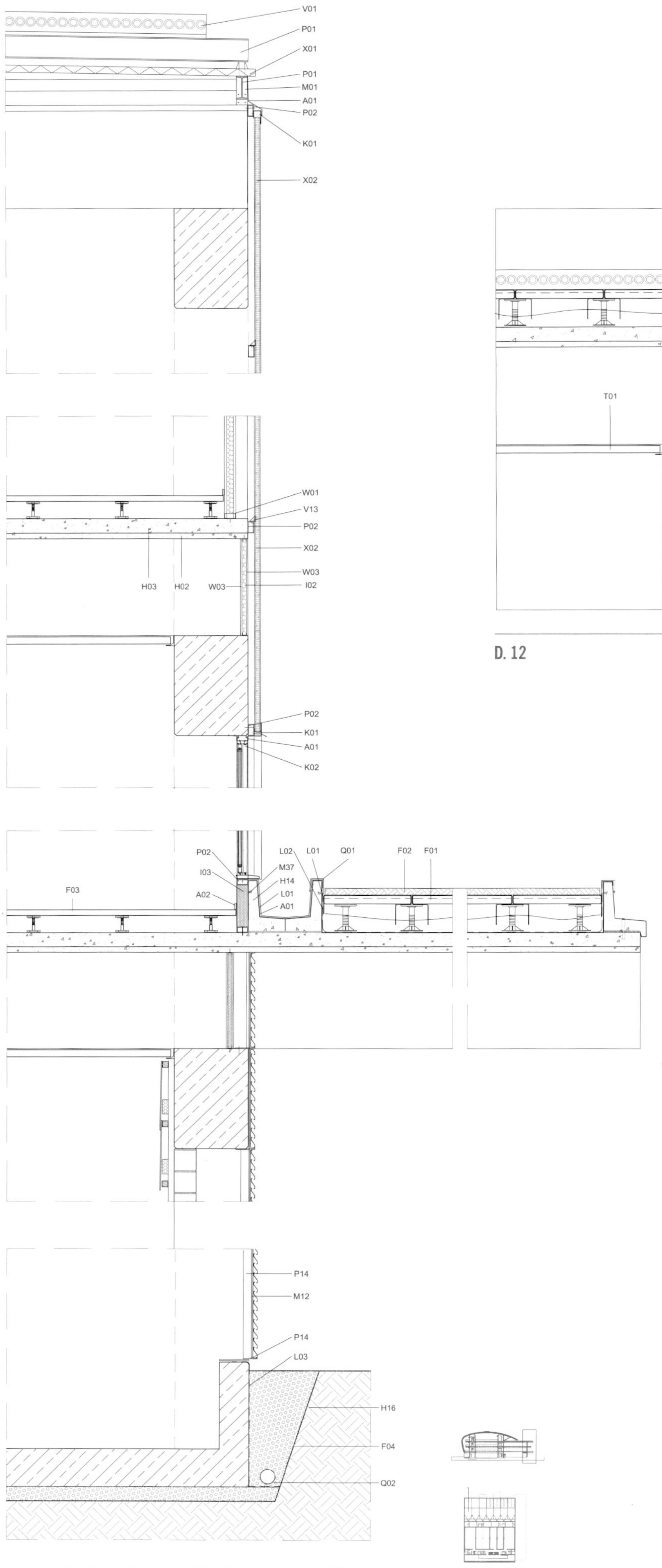

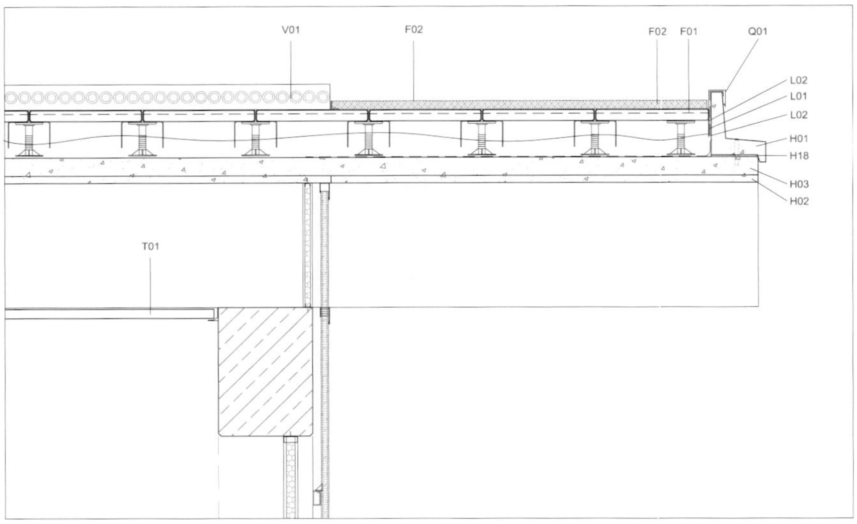

D. 12

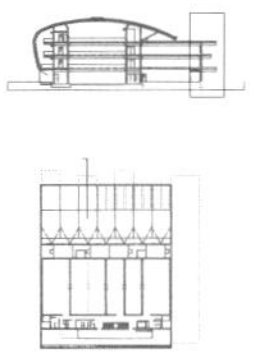

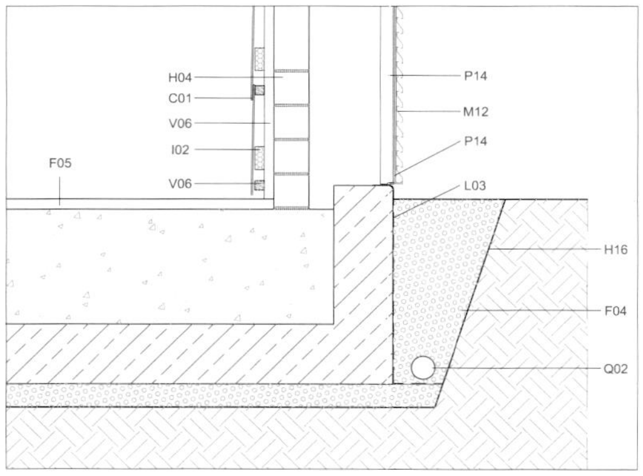

D. 13

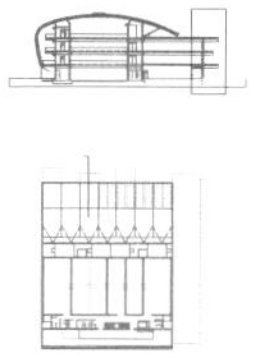

Section Detail 1

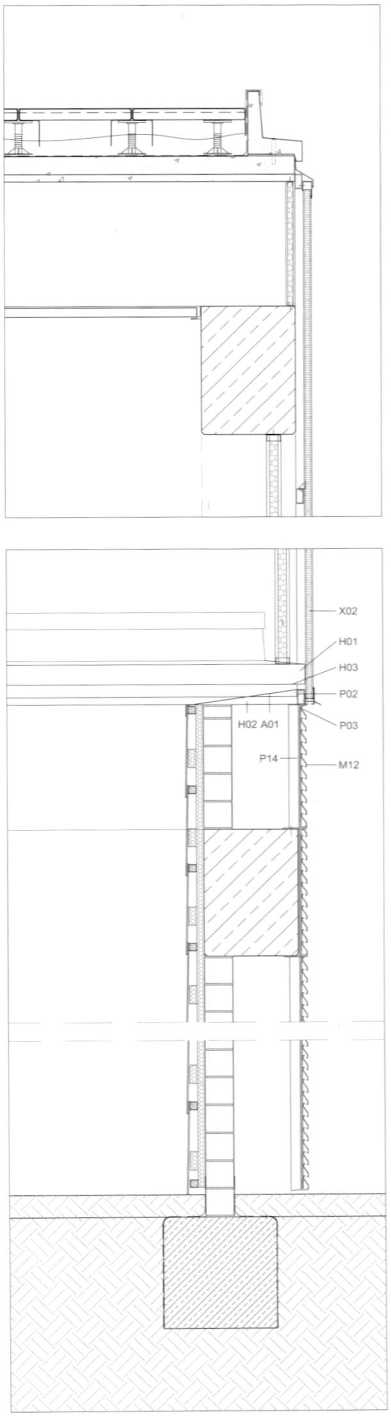

Metal Sheet
- M01 Plate 74x200x6, painted hammertone
- M12 Profile Z type PE-570 of Hiansa, or equivalent, painted hammertone
- M37 Smooth plate, galvanized

Aluminum Sheet
- A01 Aluminum cap, folded metal sheet, anodized, silver color
- A02 Aluminum tube 40x10 as baseboard, silver color, anodized

Concrete
- H01 Piece "L with dripedge" prefabricated, fastened to the slab with mechanical fixture
- H02 Panel TT 72, prefabricated Pujol or equivalent
- H03 Compression layer 10cm
- H04 Concrete block 15x20x40
- H14 Piece "L without dripedge" prefabricated, fastened to the slab with mechanical fixture
- H16 Mortar base
- H17 Prefabricated concrete step, 17,5x35x5cm, smooth upper face
- H18 Layer of mortar

Ceramic
- C01 Flat vitrified roofing tile 14cmx28cm with various colors of Covallay or equivalent

Insulation
- I02 Insulation panel of extruded polystyrene 4cm
- I03 Rockwool 8cm

Pavement
- F01 Losa Filtrón of Intemper or equivalent
- F02 Planting soil
- F03 Technical floor, slabs of 40cmx40cm, type DS/2 of Desmon or equivalent
- F04 Gravel
- F05 Tinted concrete 5cm, reinforced with fiberglass

Profiles
- P01 IPN160
- P02 Pipe 40x80x4
- P03 L 35x35x6
- P14 T 50x50

Polycarbonate
- X01 Transparent corrugated panel, type 177/51 de GET or equivalent
- X02 Panel from Lexan Thermoclick Sheet system LTC40/4RS3600 of GET, or equivalent

Divisions
- W01 Dividing screen, hidden profile, double 16/450/16, metal profiles, thermal insulation, wood panels veneered with melamine, type Supra of Desmon or equivalent
- W03 Water-repellant plasterboard, metal profiles, thickness

Sheets
- L01 Rhenofol CG sheet of Intemper or equivalent
- L02 Feltemper sheet of Intemper or equivalent
- L03 Waterproofing sheet (LBM40) with reinforcement FP-130 gr/m2

Various
- V01 Solar panel, vacuum tube, type Vitosol 200 of Viessmann, or equivalent
- V06 Wooden batten 40x40
- V13 Anchor for X02

Window and Door framing
- K01 Standard profile for polycarbonate, according to installer
- K02 Aluminum window and door framing, anodized 25 microns, silver color

Plastic profiles
- Q01 Standard cistern roof edge of Intemper or equivalent
- Q02 Drainage pipe

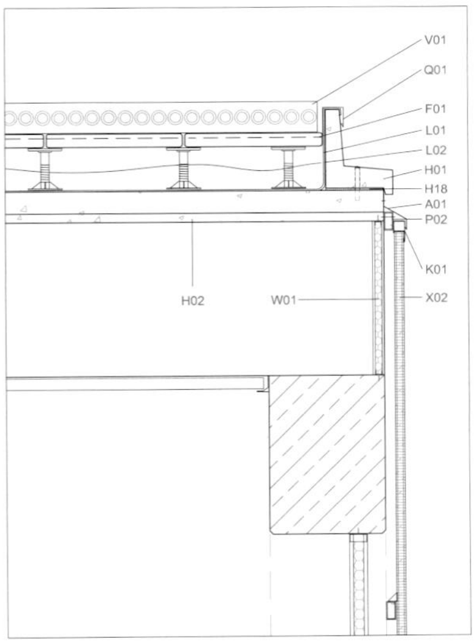

0 25 50 75 1m

1:40

D. 14 and 15

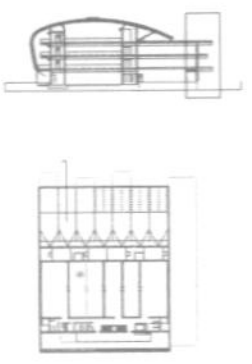

D. 16

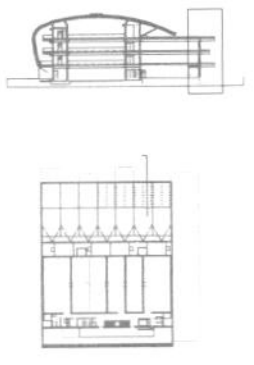

Metal Sheets
- M12 Profile Z type PE-570 of Hiansa, or equivalent, painted hammertone
- M14 Gutter of folded galvanized sheet
- M15 Plate 120x112x6, painted hammertone
- M16 Plate 140x50x6, 1/m, painted hammertone
- M18 Plate 140x70x7, painted hammertone
- M27 Anchor plate 75x75x5, painted hammertone
- M40 U Profile composed of 3 sheets of (2x120+1x140)x6
- M41 U Profile composed of 3 sheets of (2x70+1x140)x6
- M43 Plate (140+90)x200x7, painted hammertone
- M45 Plate 115x200x8, painted hammertone

Aluminum Sheet
- A01 Aluminum cap, folded metal sheet, anodized, silver color
- A02 Aluminum tube 40x10 as baseboard, silver color, anodized
- A03 Folded aluminum profile 40x20, siliconed, cap M14

Drop Ceiling
- T01 Aluminum, strips of 30cm, visible guide, type Orcal Pc Tegular of Armstrong, or equivalent

Concrete
- H01 Piece "L with dripedge" prefabricated, fastened to the slab with mechanical fixture
- H02 Panel TT 72, prefabricated Pujol or equivalent
- H03 Compression layer 10cm
- H06 Concrete support for cantilevered roof
- H10 Lightweight concrete refill
- H13 Panel TT 94, prefabricated Pujol or equivalent
- H18 Layer of Mortar

Ceramic
- C02 Large format piece 20x7x140cm type Bardeau of Guiraud Frères/St.Gobain or equivalent

Pavement
- F01 Losa Filtrón of Intemper or equivalent
- F02 Planting soil
- F03 Technical floor, slabs of 40cmx40cm, type DS/2 of Desmon or equivalent
- F04 Gravel
- F05 Tinted concrete 5cm, reinforced with fiberglass
- F06 Tinted concrete 8cm, reinforced with fiberglass

Profiles
- P02 Pipe 40x80x4
- P03 L 35x35x6
- P05 T 140
- P12 L 90x90x10
- P14 T 50x50
- P15 L 40x40x4
- P18 Pipe 80x80x4
- P19 Pipe 140x80x5
- P21 HEA 140
- P23 HEA 120

Polycarbonate
- X01 Transparent corrugated panel, type 177/51 de GET or equivalent
- X02 Panel from Lexan Thermoclick Sheet system LTC40/4RS3600 of GET, or equivalent

Divisions
- W01 Dividing screen, hidden profile, double 16/450/16, metal profiles, thermal insulation, wood panels veneered with melamine, type Supra of Desmon or equivalent

Sheets
- L01 Rhenofol CG sheet of Intemper or equivalent
- L02 Feltemper sheet of Intemper or equivalent
- L03 Waterproofing sheet (LBM40) with reinforcement FP-130 gr/m2

Various
- V03 Covered truss
- V09 Lighting for cantilevered roof
- V10 Channel for 10x10cm continuous for collection of rainwater, with stainless steel grate
- V13 Anchor for el X02
- V34 Mechanical anchor with neoprene for C02

Window and Door framing
- K01 Standard profile for polycarbonate, according to installer
- K02 Aluminum window and door framing, anodized 25 microns, silver color

Plastic profiles
- Q01 Standard cistern roof edge of Intemper or equivalent
- Q03 Drainpipe

1:40

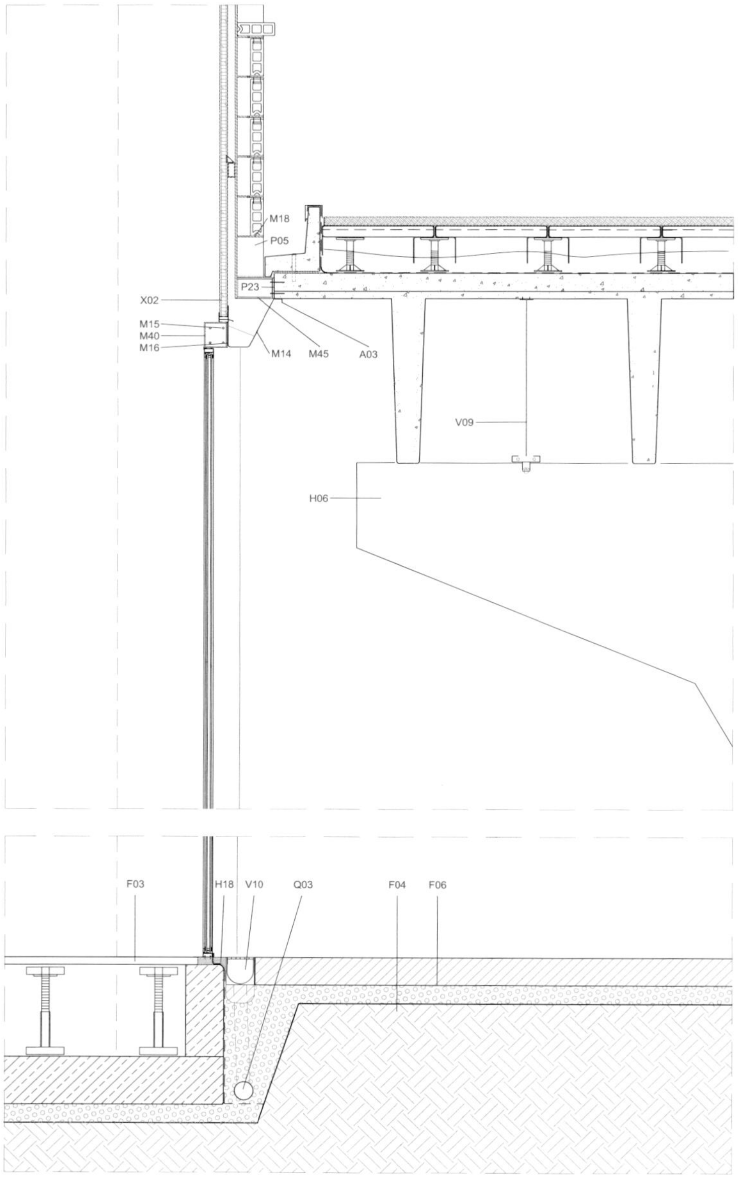

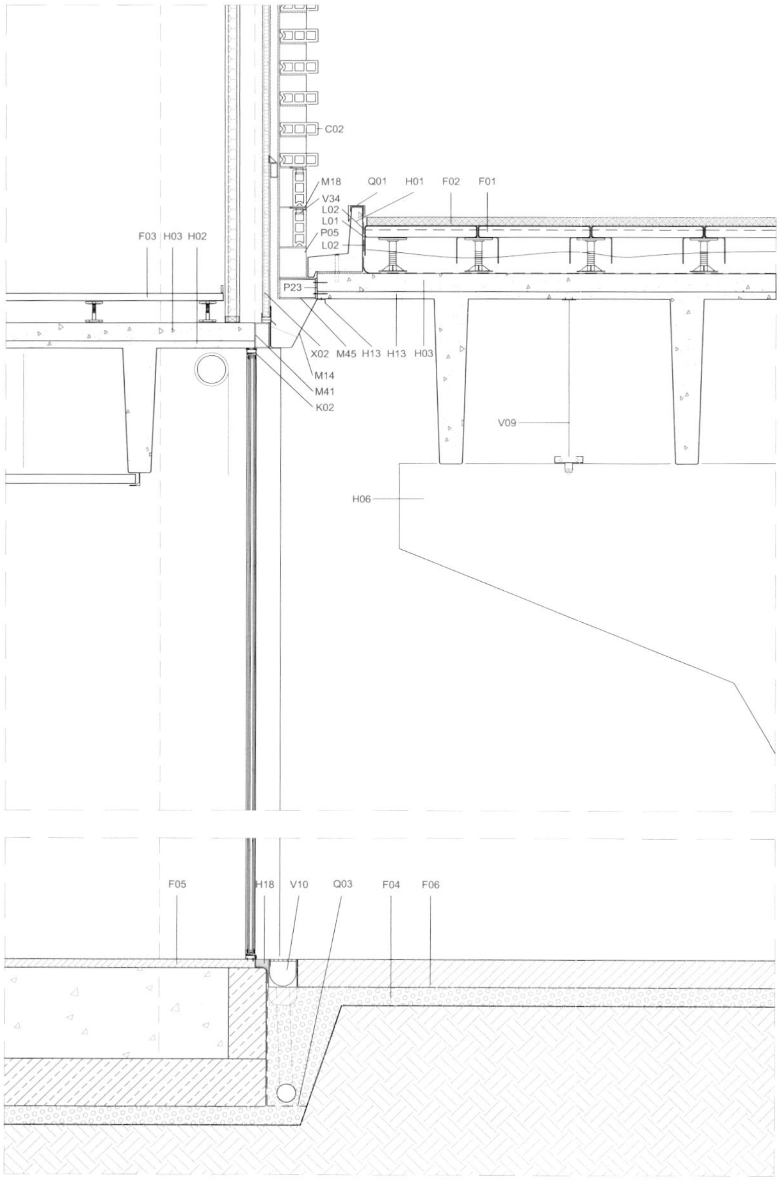

D. 17

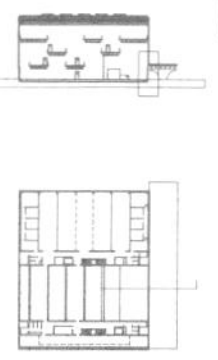

D. 18

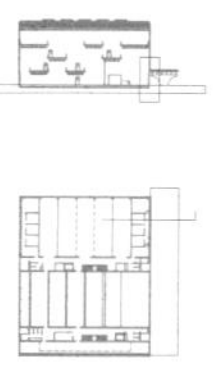

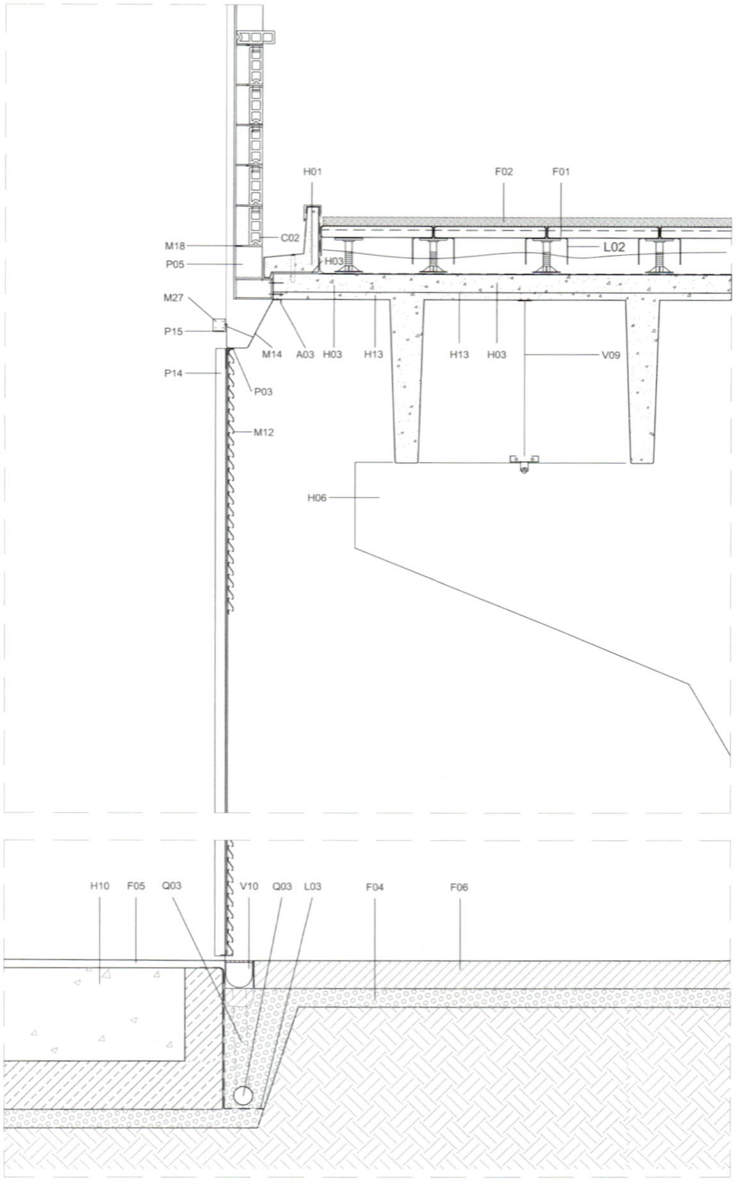

D. 19

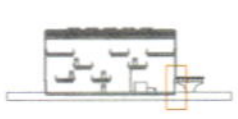
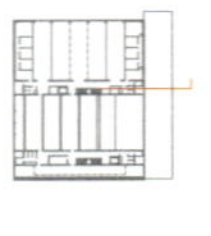

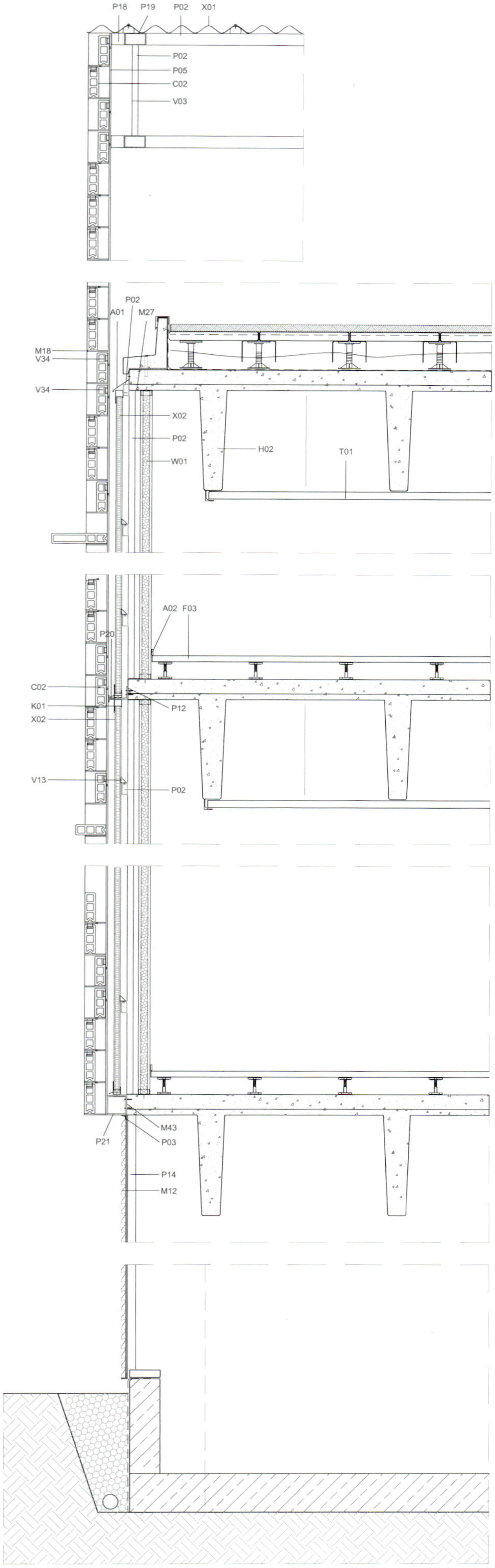

Section Detail 2

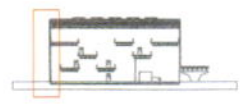
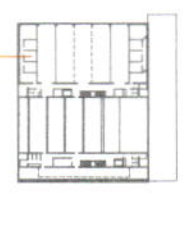

12

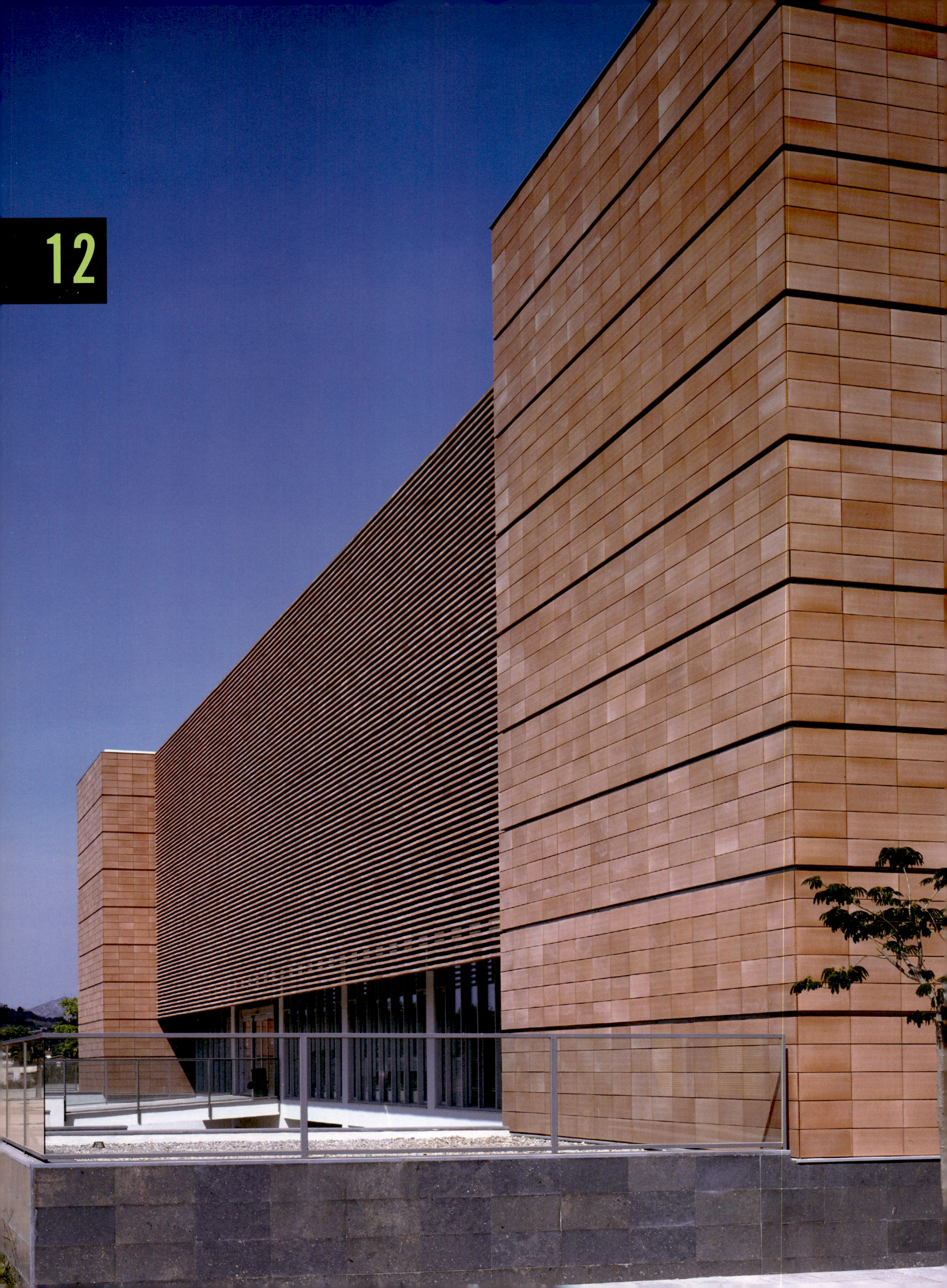

Roberto Ercilla - Miguel Ángel Campo Arquitectos

SERVICES BUILDING
UNIVERSITAT POLITÈCNICA DE CATALUNYA

CASTELLDEFELS - BARCELONA - España

Roberto Ercilla
Miguel Ángel Campo
Manuel Enríquez
Javier Barcos

eyc@infonegocio.com

COLLABORATORS	César Besada Agustín de la Tajada Carmen Orbañanos
TECHNICAL ARCHITECTS	Josep Molero Javier Valdivielso
PHOTOGRAPHY	César San Millán

	COLLABORATING COMPANIES
Structure	Eduardo Martín
Contractor	Construcciones Serom
Ceramic Pieces	Sannini Impruneta

PRIZES

Primer premio concurso restringido

	DATES
IMPLEMENTATION PROJECT	2002
BEGINNING OF WORKS	2003
WORK COMPLETION	2006

DESCRIPTIVE BRIEF

The Services Building of the UPC - Castelldefels is articulated from the existing buildings.

The plan is organized by means of two protected sectors on the East and West faces which contain the accesses, facilities, storage spaces, etc., and a North-South central space that regulates the open program.

From the existing bank, a green slope is proposed which relates with floor level -1 in a natural way, connecting the cafeteria and the Student hall directly with the campus.

The ground floor houses the main access, notice boards, conference halls, shops and the dinning room.

Floor levels 1 and 2 are exclusively for the library and classrooms, designed with central and front filtered light.

This simple scheme guarantees evacuation, separates the noisier activities from the quiet ones and, by means of an economical 7x5.50m grid, also allows making flexible use of the central space.

The East-West arrangement of the opaque bands, the double thermal façade, the relation between floor level -1 and the terrain's profile, all provide a pleasant image of the building while contributing to optimize the building's bioclimatic conditions.

The library's ventilated façades are clad with ceramic pieces, anchored with auxiliary stainless steel elements. The insulation is placed on the outside face of the enclosure, mechanically fastened. Fixed ceramic lattices fixed on auxiliary stainless steel frames, are also included.

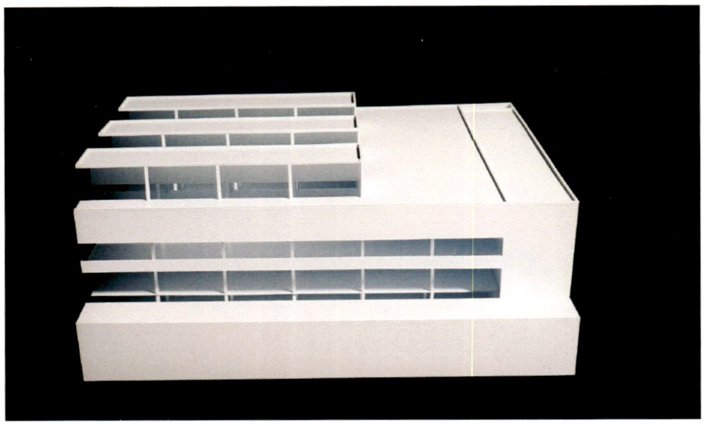

Floor Level +1

Floor Level +1

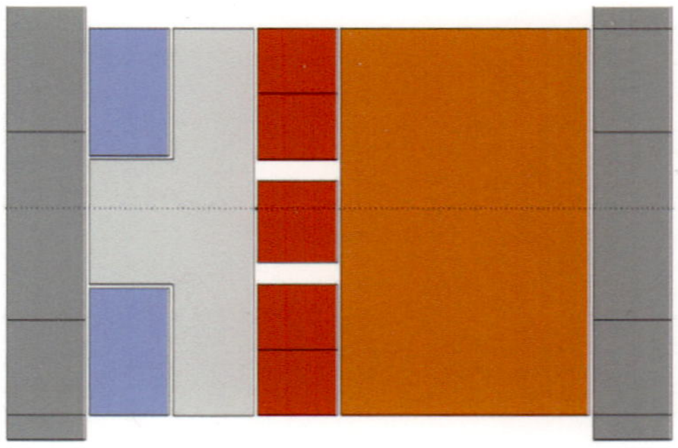

Ground Floor Level

Floor Level -1

TECHNICAL DATA

GROSS SURFACE AREA

FLOOR LEVEL -1	
Total net surface area:	1.379,90 m2
Total gross surface area:	1.466,75 m2
GROUND FLOOR LEVEL	
Total net surface area:	1.601,25 m2
Total gross surface area:	1.743,00 m2
FLOOR LEVEL +1	
Total net surface area:	1.512,45 m2
Total gross surface area:	1.616,60 m2
FLOOR LEVEL +2	
Total net surface area:	1.165,65 m2
Total gross surface area:	1.327,20 m2
Total surface area / net:	5.659,25 m2

divided on 4 floors, of which 3.000 m2 are library

- 300 reading stations
- 77 reference PCs
- 40.000 volumes
- 10.000 magazine titles
- WIFI access in all spaces
- 6 group study rooms (6 personas)
- 3 individual study rooms (1-2 personas)
- 32individual silent study stations
- 1 research room
- 1 training and presentation classroom
- 1 computer classroom
- 1 meeting room and celebration of official functions
- 2 personal meeting rooms

ZONING DIAGRAM

- Green space
- Circulation core, services, installations and storage
- Exhibition area, student area
- Bar cafeteria
- Reception, relax area, control and information
- Conference rooms
- Commercial services
- Dining Room
- Library, magazine area
- Classroom
- Mediateca
- Study rooms (1/6 personas)
- Offices

"Listen to the man that works with his hands. He will be able to show you the best way to do things"

Louis Khan

ENVIRONMENTAL ANALYSIS

1. Choosing the site. Project and Development

1.1. Location

Latitude: 41°16'30"N
Longitude: 01°59'05"E
Altitude: 5 m

The building for UPC Services is located on the Baix LLobregat campus, which forms part of Parc Mediterrani de la Tecnología (Mediterranean Park of Technology[1]), which encompasses an area of 38 Ha and houses other educational centers, university services, investigation centers and companies.

Located beside the Olympic Channel, the campus has excellent connections with Barcelona and its metropolitan area: Castelldefel's railway station is only 300m away from the campus, and there are several bus lines that reach the grounds, amongst them number 95, 96 and 97. It can also be accessed by the C-32 motorway and Castelldefels highway.

1.2 Urban design and Improvement of the site

The building is located in a new urban development; there exists a scarce relation with the surroundings as it finds itself in the midst of a complete transformation, conferring the building an introverted character.

The access is situated on the future pedestrian boulevard that crosses the volume as if it were a city street.

1.3 Project

As a part of PMT[2], the building incorporates the entire design program required with an environmental commitment based on the Environmental Plan of the Campus of Castelldefels. The proximity to the Baix LLobregat motorway makes it essential to incorporate several proceedings to the plan which help reduce the acoustic level and guarantee the comfort of the building's users.

The building consists of 4 floors in one single volume; the program has been thoroughly broken down, which permits a wide range of spaces beginning with very public ones and reaching exceptionally private spaces. Morphologically, the building has a symmetrical composition along its two Cartesian axes, shored up by a modular structure. Each floor level has little subtleties, such as on level -1 where toilets and bathroom fixtures are placed in the least favorable areas, topographically speaking, leaving the best orientations and expansions for the noble areas.

The second floor level is spatially rich with double height spaces lit from above with skylights.

[1] http://www.pmt.es/homePage.html
[2] http://www.upc.es/mediambient/recerca/lreal1.html

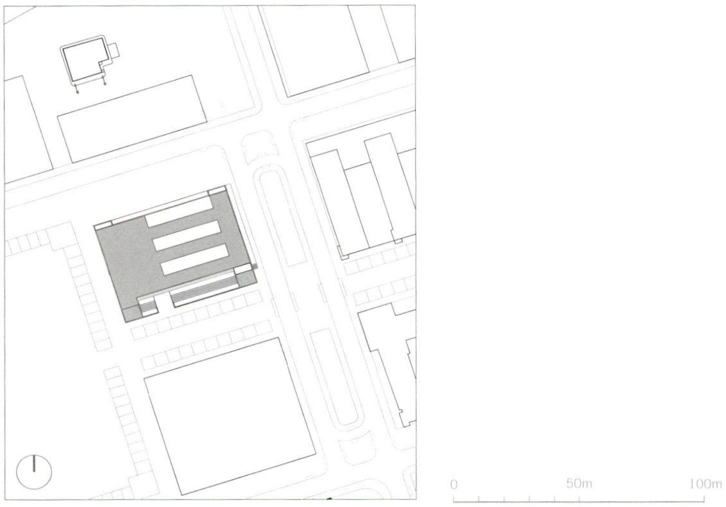

Site Plan

2. Consumption of Energy and Resources

2.1 Consumption of Energy

The use of passive solar gain systems has been established. The South façade has a double enclosure system of glass and shutters which enables the penetration of low sun in the winter. Deciduous trees have been planted to the south which allows solar gain during the winter.

It also relies on an indoor thermal storage system that works by way of a gravel layer below the basement level.

The access areas have been designed with stone pavement and solid enclosures with concrete interiors, which due to their high thermal inertia are ideal for heat storage. The movement and distribution of air is generated through vertical installation shafts and the pipes that pass through the service areas in the wings.

2.2 Water Consumption

The design considers water consumption from the urban development until each of the campus´ buildings, and therefore, counts with a number of micro-irrigation or trickle systems, humidity detectors and the sowing of native covering vegetation.

The building also comprises a rain water collection system, which is reused for irrigation.

All of the bathroom fixtures are low consumption and have controlled unloading; taps have volume reduction systems, and a leak detector has been installed in order to prevent excessive consumption generated by damages in the system.

2.3 Materials Consumption

The materials used have been chosen due to their low impact in the manufacturing process. They are renewable and recyclable materials which produce a low environmental impact.

An example of this are the ventilated ceramic façades, with an interior finish that incorporates galvanized steels anchors. The façade with ceramic slats also has the same kind of anchors and they are combined with a steel framing and laminated glass of easy assembly.

3. Environmental loads

3.1 Emissions

Using modular and prefabricated elements has reduced material waste, thereby reducing energy consumption generated during the construction of the building.

3.2 Solid waste

Due to the construction system used, based on modular systems, solid wastes have been reduced to a minimum at the construction site.

The placement of exterior ceramic tiles with steel anchor systems permit the reuse of each piece, the type of steel framing, the outdoor treated wood pavers, the interiors with cellulose wood or removable panels, are aspects that make the buildings disassembly possible and therefore recyclable.

3.3 Water Management

The building has been designed with a system of permeable areas to subterranean water and trees that hardly need water for their maintenance which allows filtering all of the rainwater.

At an urban level, in order to make the circulation of rainwater on the campus easier, a surface run-off system was designed to guide surface water through the slopes of the PMT terrain and towards the lake.

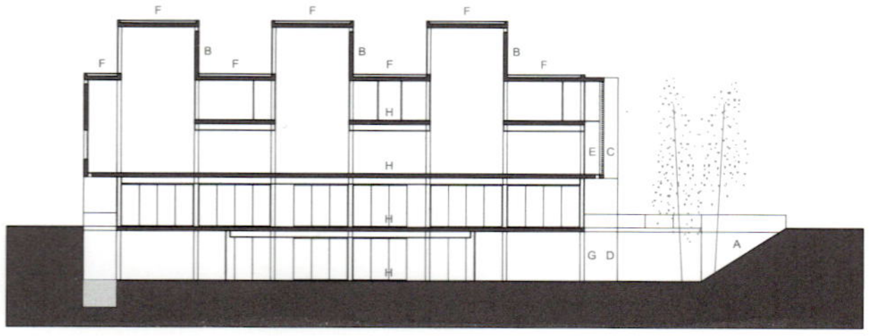

Materials

A. Previous works
B. Ventilated ceramic facade
C. Ventilated ceramic facade
D. Thermal control gallery
E. Inverted roof
F. Reinforced concrete structure
G. Finishes
H. Installations

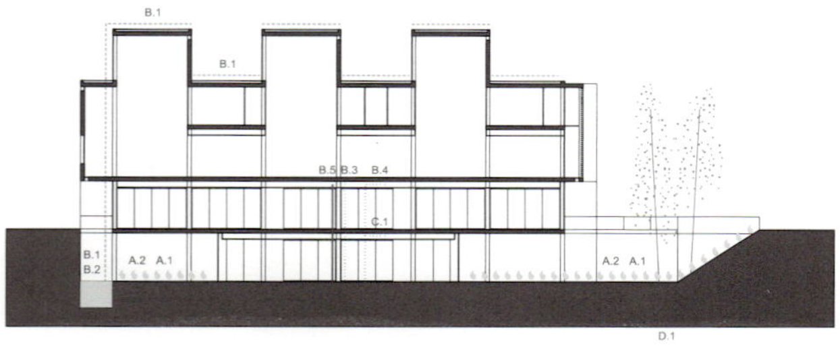

Water Consumption

A Development of low consumption
- A.1 Tapestry plants, before native vegetation
- A.2 Micro irrigation or trickle irrigation
- A.3 Humidity detectors

B Separation systems
- B.1 Collection of rainwater and phreatic storage
- B.2 Reuse for trickle irrigation
- B.3 Separation of waters

C. Low consumption installation
- C.1 Low consumption bathroom fixtures with controlled release
- C.2 Volume reduction system
- C.3 Mixing faucet and Flush valves in the rest of fixtures
- C.4 Installation with register

D. Equilibrium of the terrain
- D.1 Permeable subterranean water zones

E. Waste treatment
- E. 1 Recuperate, recycle, reuse
- E.2 Separation of origin of garbage
- E.3 Possibility of pretreatment of water

4. Interior Environmental Quality

4.1 Ventilation

The building has operable window systems which are activated by means of smart systems and make the direct ventilation of the premises easier.

The radiant heating system allows cool water circulation during the summer, which helps the indoor cooling. The library, according with current regulation, also has a forced ventilation system with primary outside air; with this, air from the fresher Northern areas is captured, passed through the gravel bed, and then introduced through the shaft towards the inside of the building.

4.2 Natural Lighting

Favoring natural light has been one of the design premises. The use of skylights oriented to the North allows the entrance of natural light while avoiding glare in the reading areas.

The low energy lighting system is complemented with a sensor-based control system for closed areas, such as the offices.

4.3 Acoustic

The concrete is no recommended in large spaces because of is low acoustic absorption. To reduce the level of reflection, parts of the interior walls have been veneered in wood, which has a high absorption coefficient.

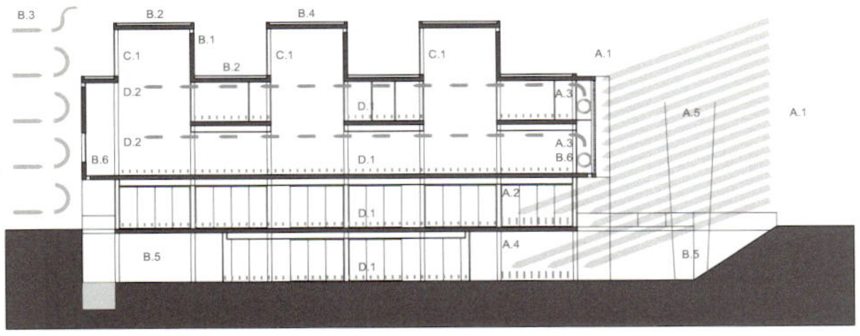

Analysis of a Winter Day

A Solar gain
- A.1 Direct gain through south facade
- A.2 Storage and conservation
- A.3 Distribution of heat
- A.4 Support with natural accumulation
- A.5 Support with deciduous trees oriented to the south

B. Protection of cold areas
- B.1 Ventilated façade, walls with thermal inertia
- B.2 Ventilated roof with insulation
- B.3 Protection from cold winds
- B.4 Good form factor
- B.5 Support with inertia of terrain
- B.6 Adapted glazed closures

C. Protection of natural lighting
- C.1 Lighting of work areas

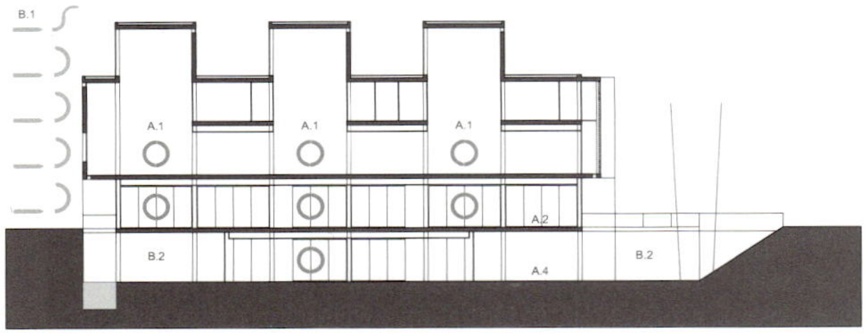

Analysis of a Winter Night

A. Maintenance of heat
- A.1 Maintenance of heat

B. Protection of cold areas
- B.1 Protection from cold winds

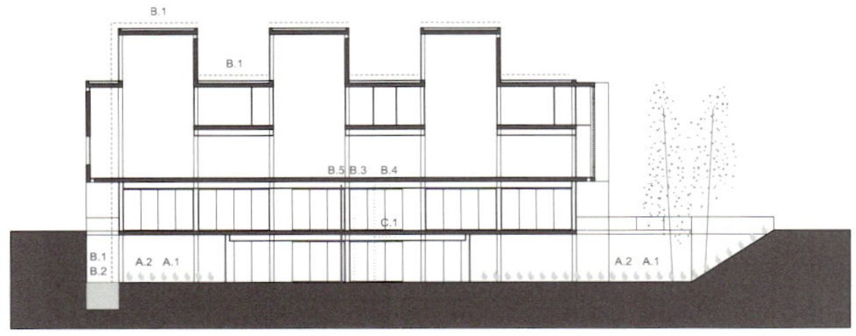

Analysis of a Summer Day

A. Solar protection
- A.1 Protection of the south facade
- A.2 Protection of the east and west facades
- A.3 Support with natural accumulation
- A.4 Support with gain by deciduous trees to the south

B. Protection of hot areas
- B.1 Ventilated façade, walls with thermal inertia
- B.2 Cubierta ventilada con aislamiento
- B.3 Protection from winds
- B.4 Introduction of cold air
- B.5 Good form factor
- B.6 Support with inertia of terrain
- B.7 Adapted glazed closures

C. Power of natural lighting
- C.1 Natural light of work areas

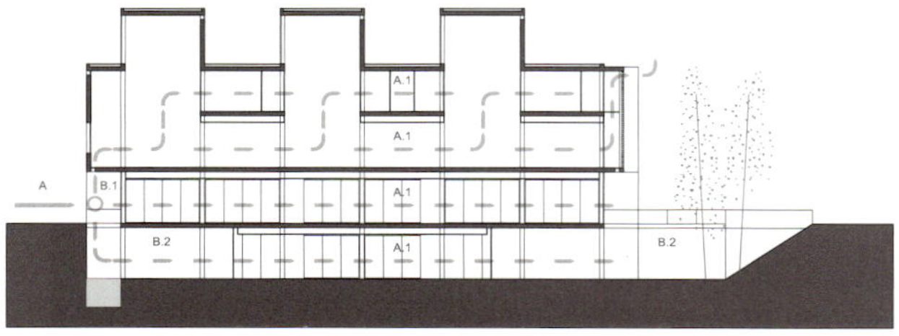

Analysis of a Summer Night

A. Cross ventilation

B. Protection
- B.1 Introduction of the cold air
- B.2 Support with inertia of terrain

0 5 10m

1:750

5. Constructions Systems Control

5.1 Functionality and Efficiency

The building adopts a basic and simple geometrical form: the cube. It is modulated in such a way that it allows various arrangements and uses.

5.2 Control of Construction Systems

Due to its arrangement and organization in plan and the use of prefabricated materials, pleasant and well conditioned spaces are created, according to the seasons. Air circulation and natural lighting are enabled through the interior courtyards.

The facade's enclosure with brick shutters is used to control the natural light levels necessary inside the building.

6. Long- term Behavior

6.1 Flexibility and Adaptability

Having been designed with an open program allows the adaptability of different areas depending on the needs at each moment.

The central area has been planned as a flexible use space. The open spaces on floor levels 1 and 2 permit a great variety of uses and ephemeral divisions when needed.

6.2 Maintenance and Operative Behavior

The operative behavior is simple due to a spatial distribution through an open program and central space, from where all of the program is distributed.

7. Economic and Social Aspects

7.1 Social Aspects

The most important social aspect is, basically, the use of the building. Being a university campus library, means it's also a meeting and service place for a great number of users, aside from counting with conference halls, cafeteria and shops, which support the program.

Furthermore, it is a place designed for education, investigation and technology transfer between different institutions inside the park.

7.2 Economic Aspects

The use of prefabricated systems reduces the project costs since it minimizes execution time and waste at the construction site.

The foresight of all passive systems considered has been developed according to the season and time of day required which results in considerable savings in energy costs. In addition we must add the use of smart systems to control the library's air conditioning.

8. The architect's eye

The project is clear and rigorous like a Cartesian coordinate system, that arranges the construction system and the inside activities. The façade, with a clear vocation for thermal and visual control, facilitates the activities typical of a library.

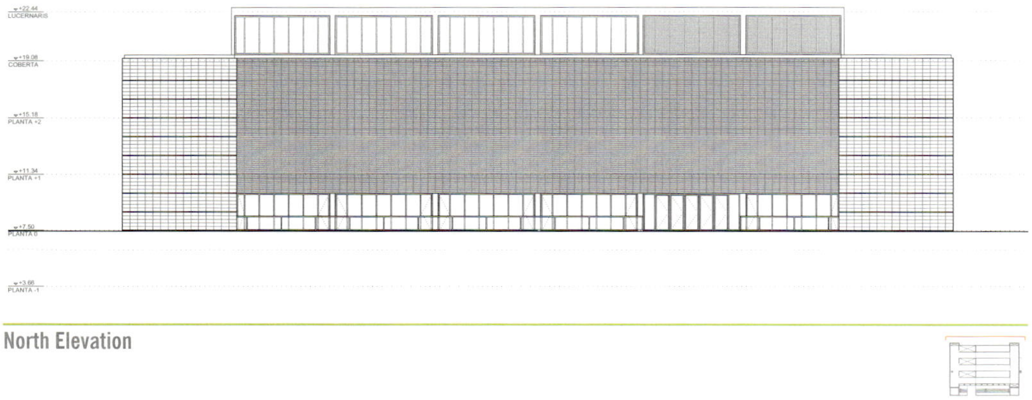

North Elevation

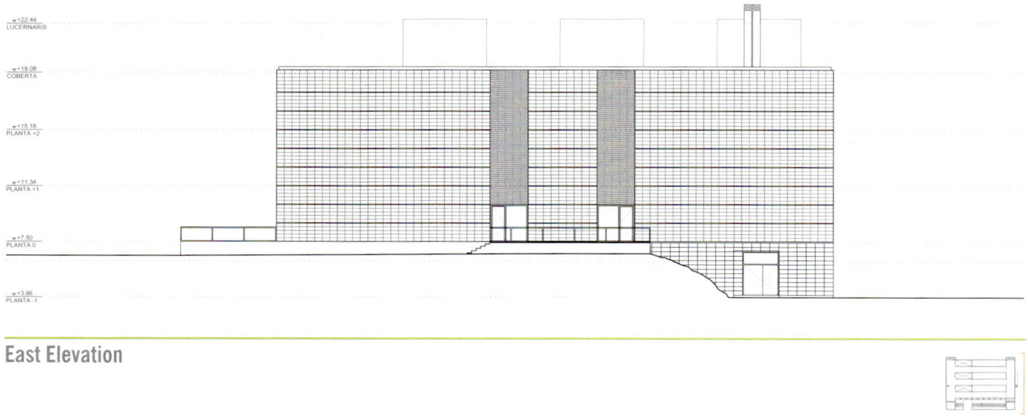

East Elevation

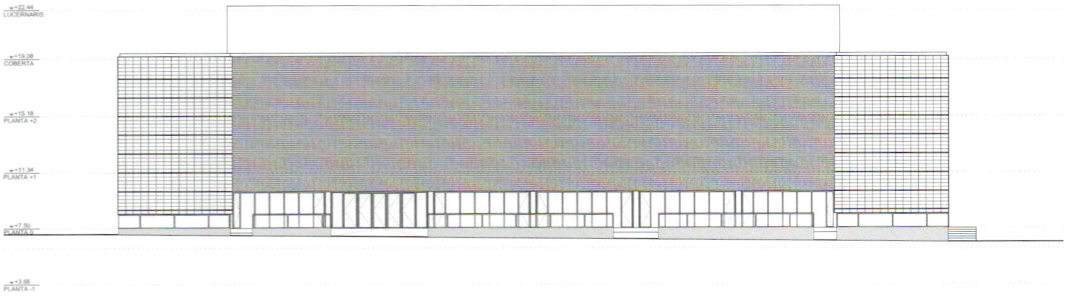

South Elevation

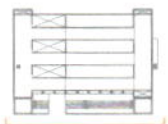

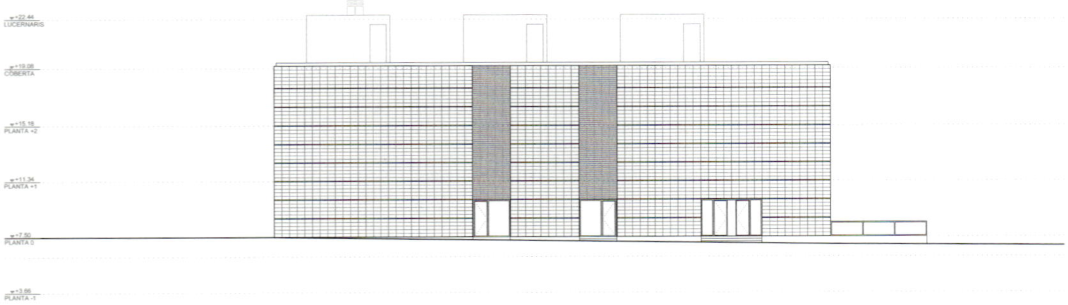

West Elevation

0 5 10m

1:500

SERVICES BUILDING UPC
Ercilla-Campo arquitectos

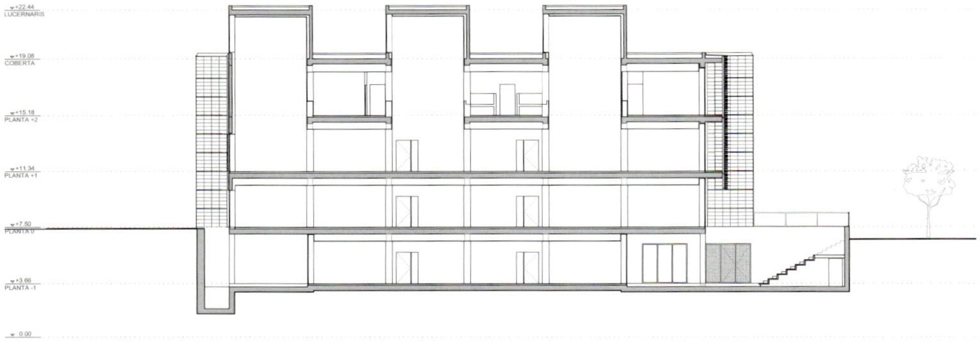

Section AA'

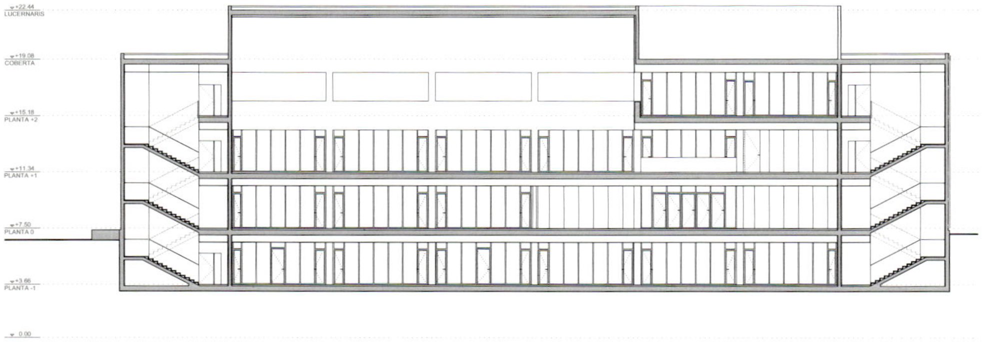

Section BB'

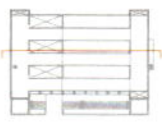

0 5 10m

1:500

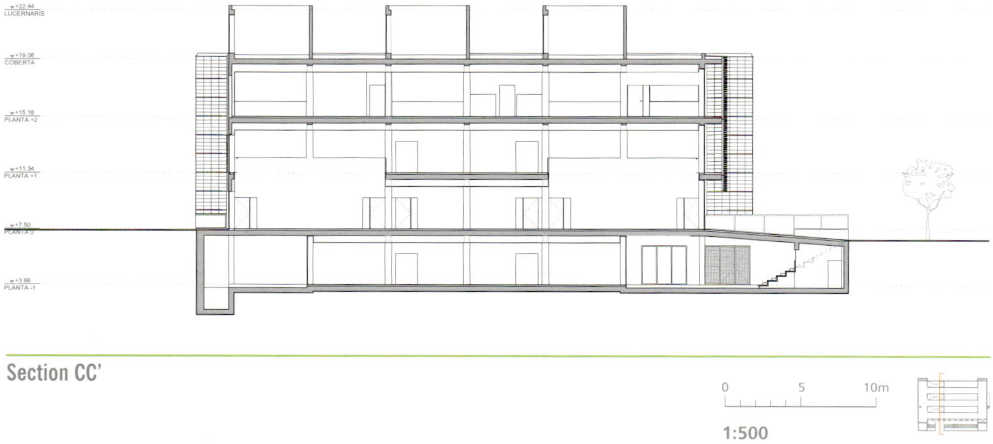

Section CC'

SERVICES BUILDING UPC
Ercilla-Campo arquitectos

1. Courtyard
2. Bathrooms
3. Circulation core
4. Public elevator
5. Internal elevator
6. Rest area
7. Service management
8. Vestibule / relax
9. Exhibition area
10. Control desk
11. Anti-theft
12. C.T.T.
    12a. Institutional relations
13. Campus manager
    13a. Office of the campus representative
    13b.Office of the coordinator
    13c.Secretary's office
    13d.Meeting rooms
14. Student association
15. Services (bookstore, copyroom)
16. Academic management
17. Installations
18. Installation shaft
19. Public access
20. Emergency exit
21. Campus lounge
22. Security / control

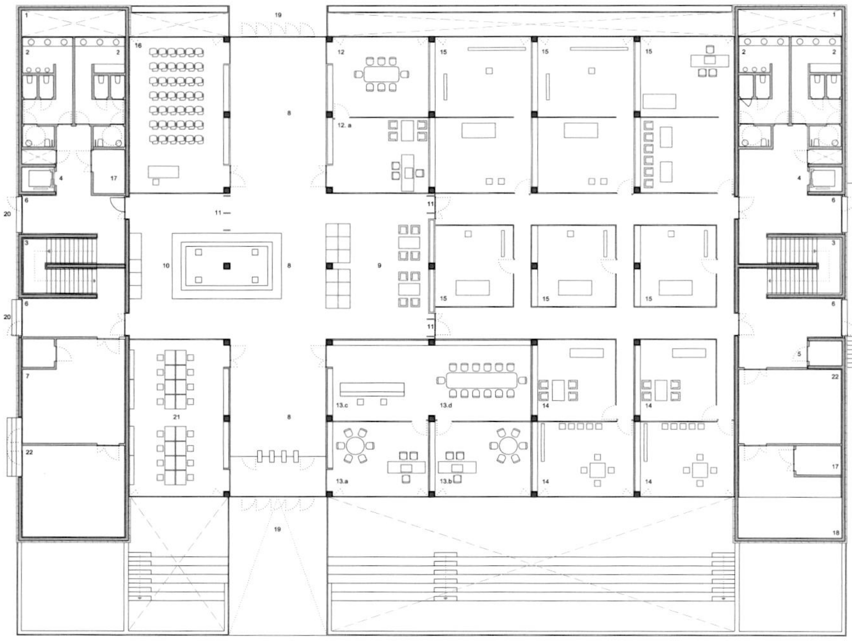

Ground floor level

1. Courtyard
2. Bathrooms
3. Circulation core
4. Public elevator
5. Internal elevator
6. Rest area
7. Maintenance
8. Cafeteria / bar
9. A la carte dining room
10. Menu dining room
11. Self-service
12. Staff bathrooms / locker rooms
13. Kitchens
14. Office
15. Storage
16. Installations
17. Porch
18. Sheet of water
19. Tiers
20. 8 PC posts

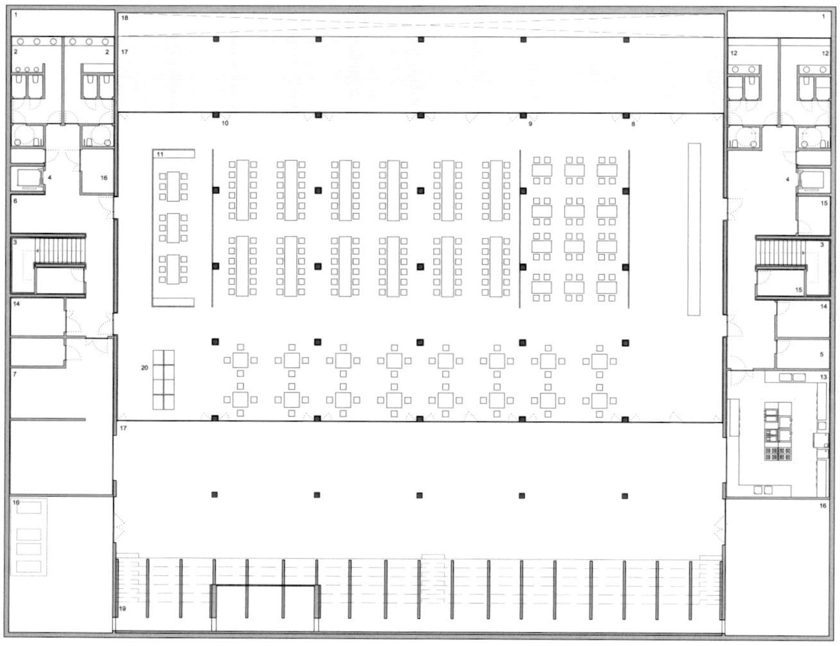

Basement floor level

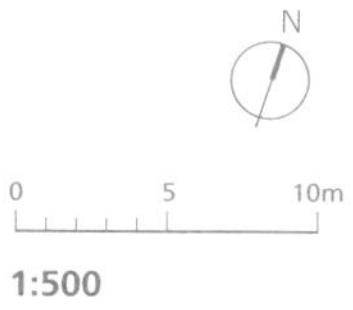

1. Courtyard
2. Bathrooms
3. Circulation core
4. Public elevator
5. Internal elevator
6. Rest area
7. Compact storage
8. Factory
9. Control
10. Reading Areas
11. Computer areas
12. Photocopies
13. Installations
14. Installation shaft
15. Antique funds
16. Training and self-learning

First floor level

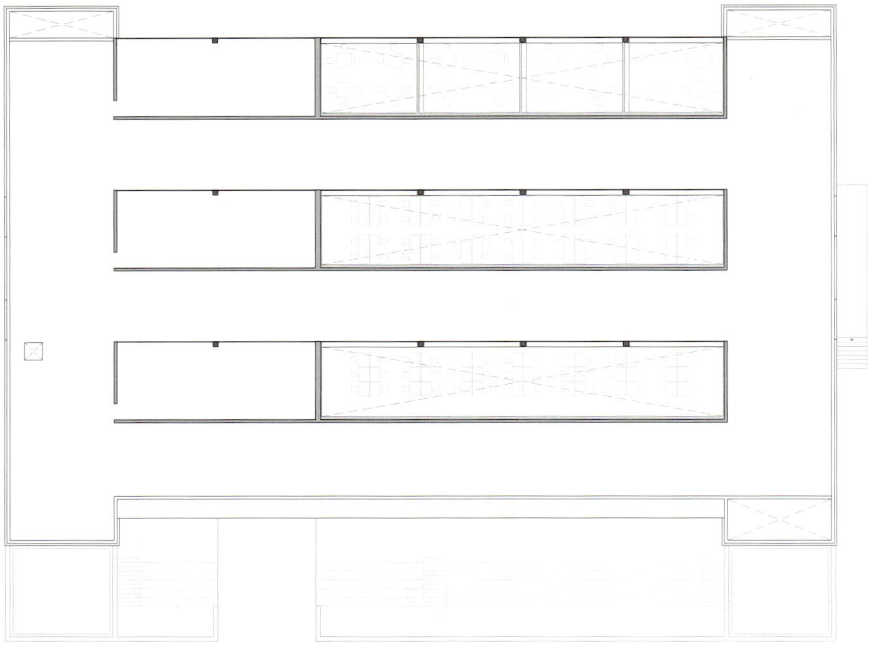

Planta Tercera

1. Courtyard
2. Bathrooms
3. Circulation core
4. Public elevator
5. Internal elevator
6. Rest area
   6a. Photocopies
7. Compact storage
8. Control desks
9. Magazine storage
10. Computer area
11. Magazine area
12. Study room for 4/6 persons
13. Individual study room
14. Director's office
15. Meeting room
16. Customer service
17. Mediatheque
18. Library storage
19. Installations
20. Installation shaft

Planta Segunda

N

0 5 10m

1:500

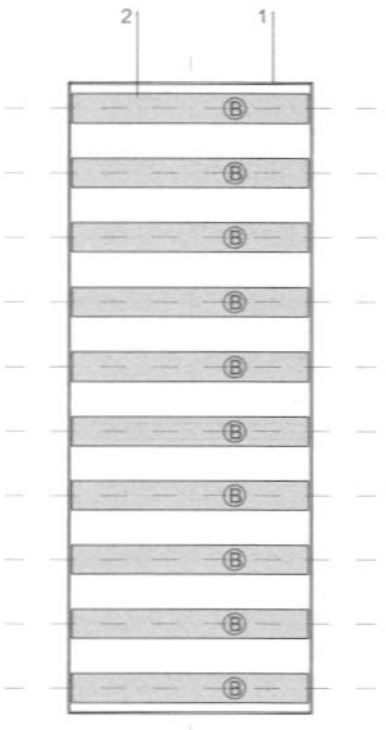

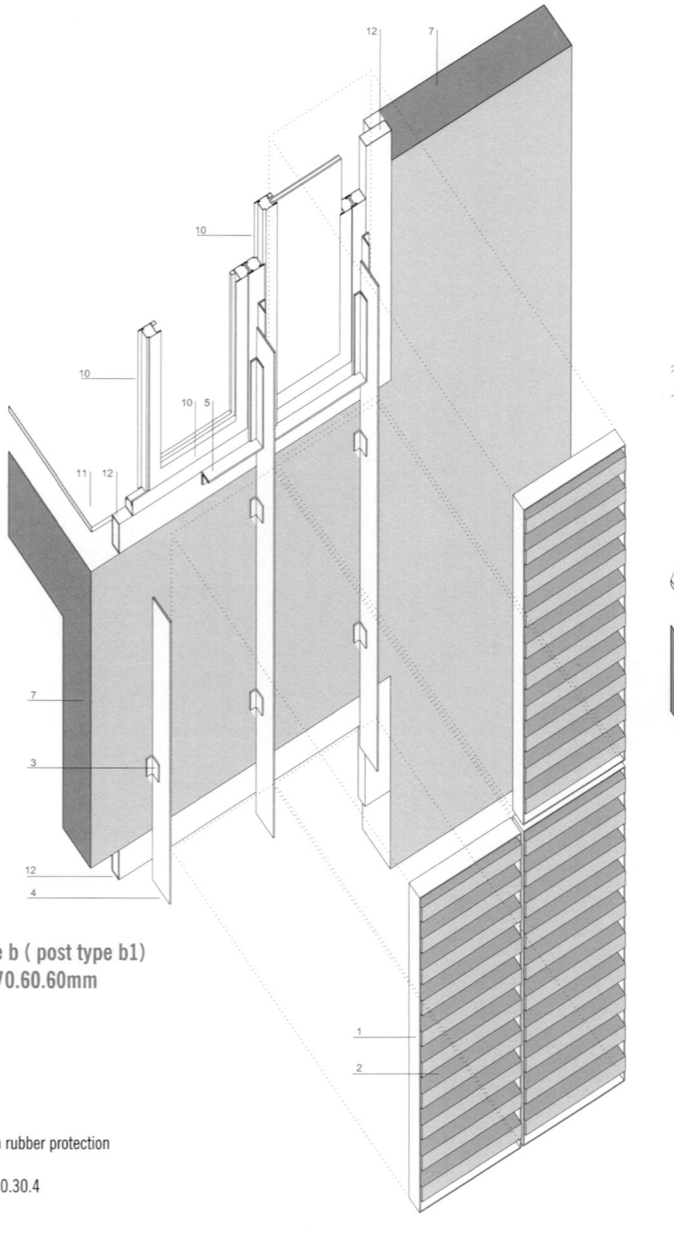

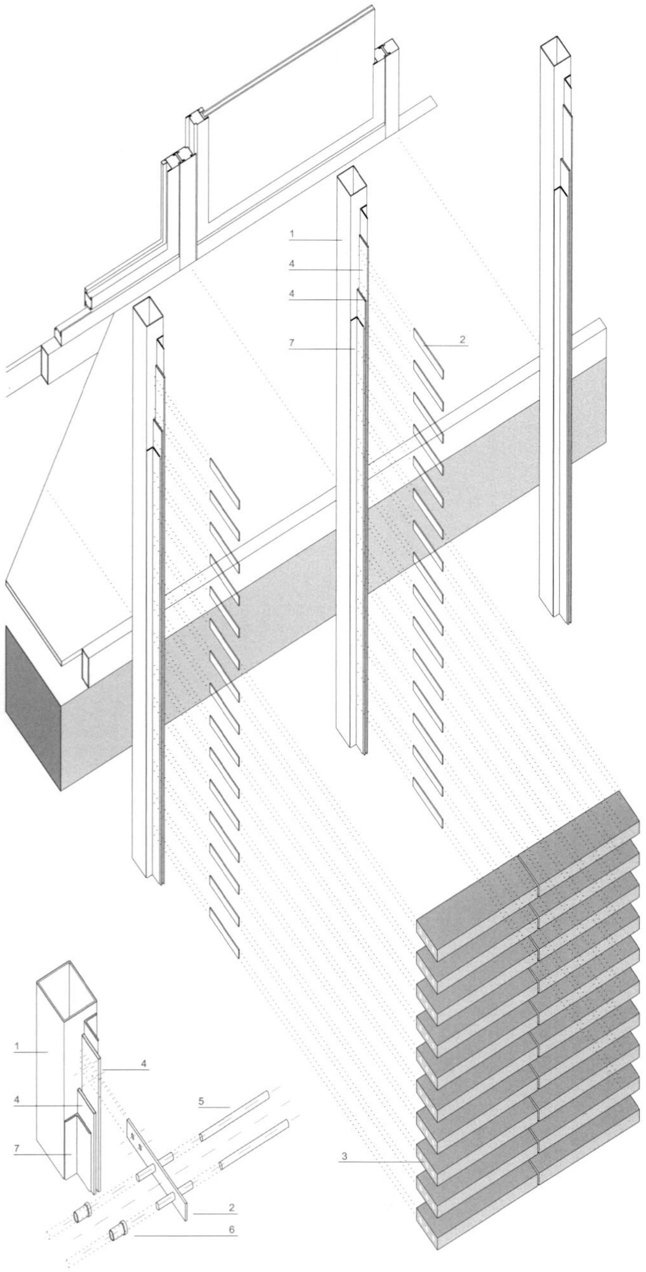

Module of ceramic slats type b (post type b1) east and west facade. slat 470.60.60mm

1. Stainless steel post, t: 4 mm
2. Ceramic slat type b . d: 470.60.60
3. Stainless steel anchor, t: 4 mm
4. Stainless steel post, t: 4 mm
5. Stainless steel profile. l.50.50.4
6. Anchor piece for slat with joint with rubber protection
7. Reinforced concrete wall
8. Stainless steel finishing profile. u.40.30.4
9. Insulation
10. Stainless steel framing
11. Interior pavement
12. Profile #120.50.3 (stainless steel post)

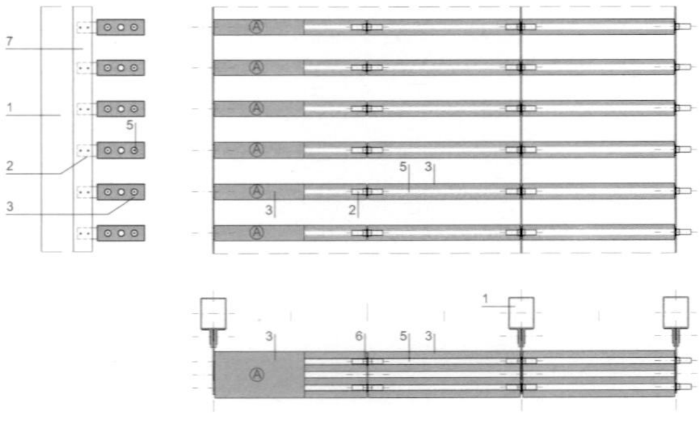

Module of ceramic slats type a (independent slat without framework) South facade. slat 480.150.50 mm

1. Stainless steel structure
2. Stainless steel anchor, t: 4 mm
3. Ceramic slat type a, d: 480.150.50
4. Stainless steel post
5. Stainless steel profile ø15, t: 2 mm double interior slat
6. Anchor piece for slat with joint with rubber protection
7. Profile l.50.30.3 for post fastener

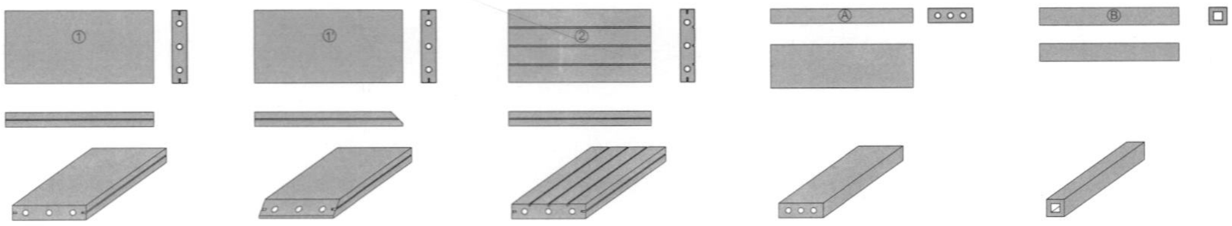

Ceramic pieces (left to right)

- Ceramic piece type 1 (smooth)
- Ceramic piece type 1' (smooth from corner)
- Ceramic piece type 2 (grooved)
- Ceramic slats type a
- Ceramic slats type b

SERVICES BUILDING UPC
Ercilla-Campo arquitectos

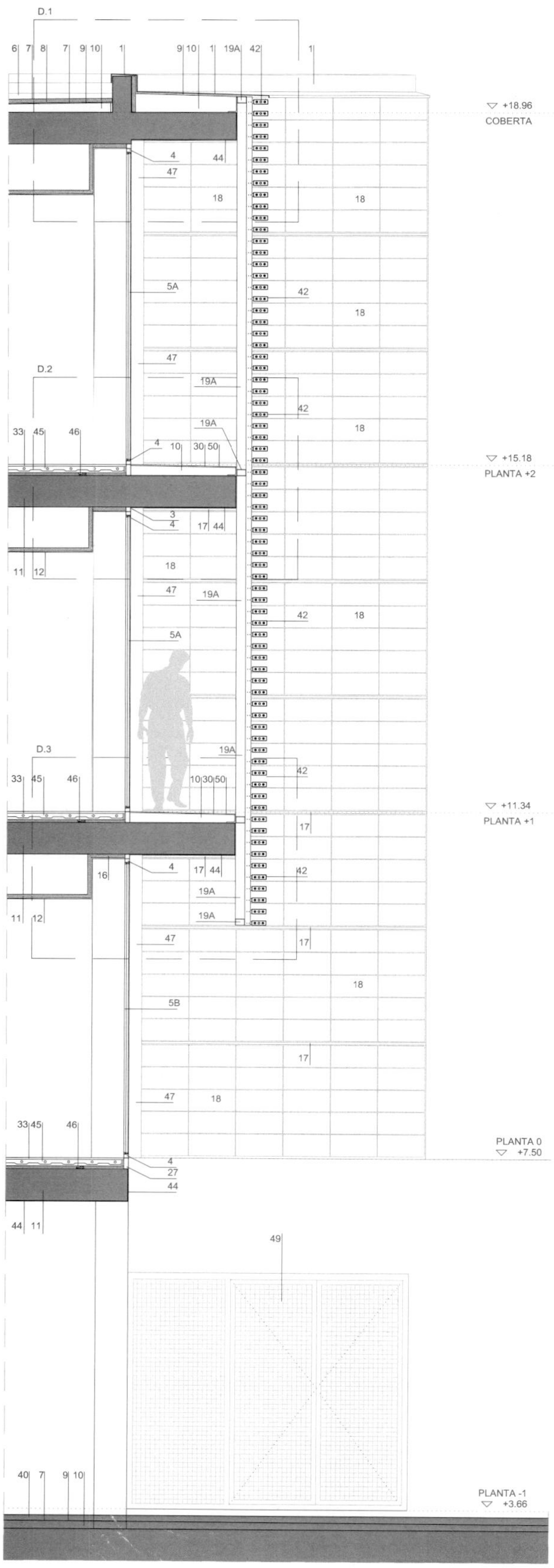

Section Detail 1

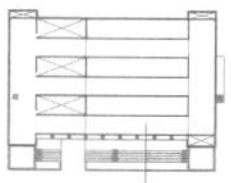

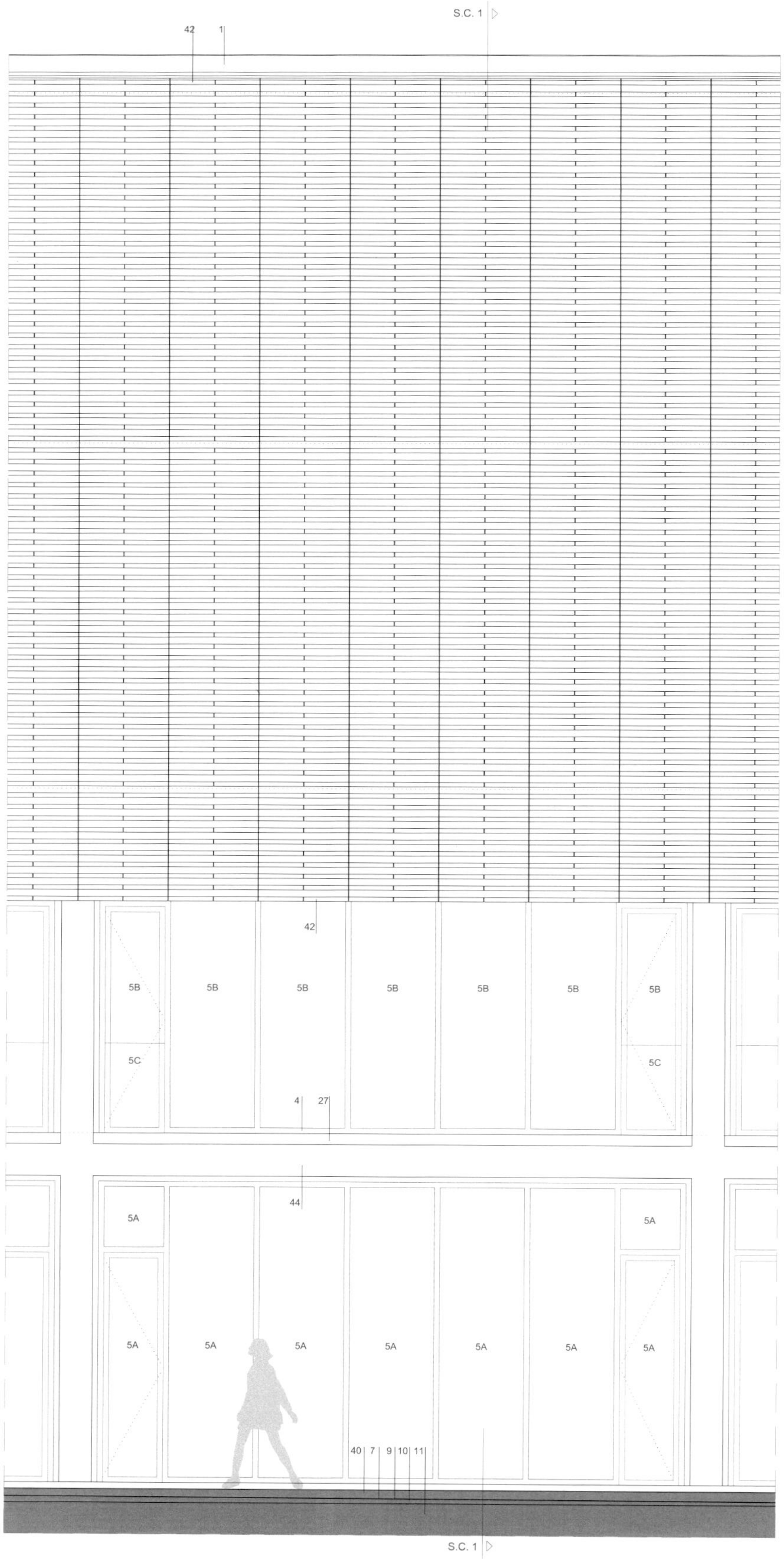

South Elevation

0 1 2 3m

1:75

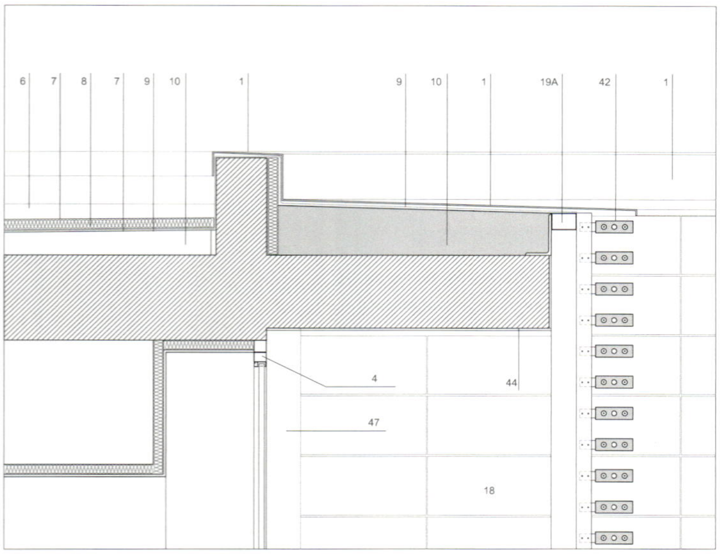

Detail 1

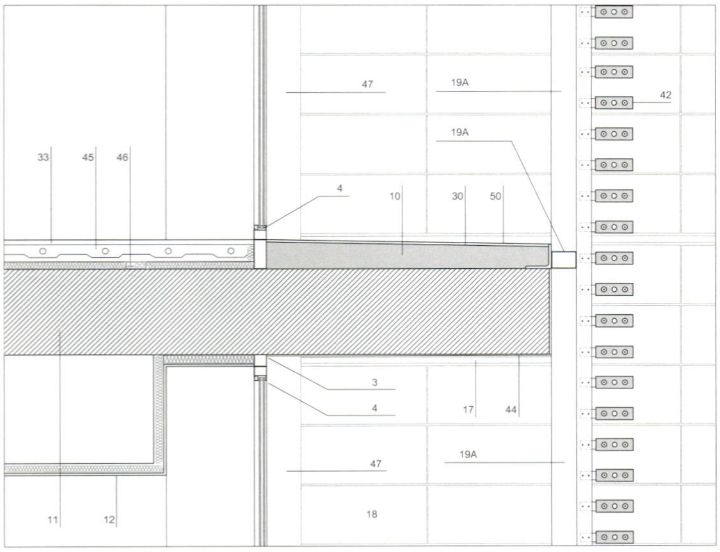

Detail 2

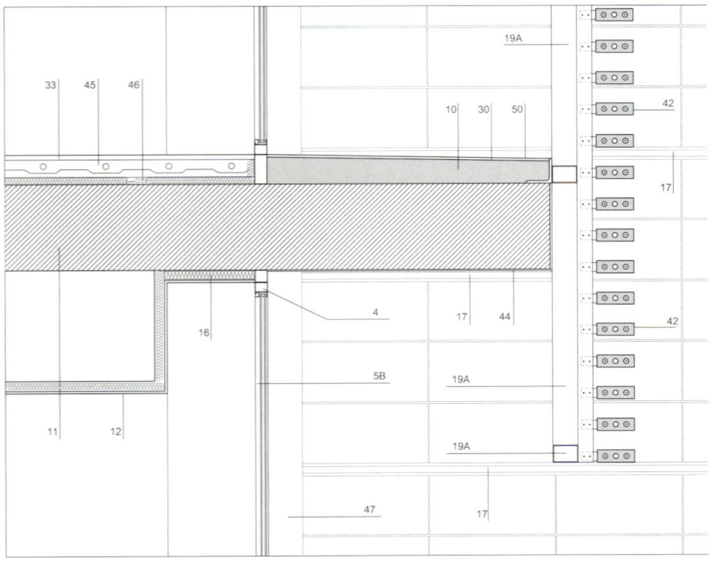

Detail 3

1. Finished with galvanized sheet
2. Reinforced concrete parapet
3. Subframe of galvanized steel and paint
4. Fixed steel framing type Jansen
5. Glazing:
   - 5A: Double glazing with chamber
   - 5B: Double glazing with chamber with transparent butyral
   - 5C: Security glazing
   - 5D: Double glazing with chamber with translucent butyral
6. Washed boulder d=16-32 mm
7. Separation sheet
8. Insulation of extruded polystyrene
9. Waterproofing
10. Lightweight mortar for slopes
11. One-way floor slab

12A. Laminated and perforated plaster drop ceiling
12B. Fire resistant drop ceiling
13. Wall cladding
14. Rainwater drain
15. Thermoclay block t: 20 cm
16. Insulation
17. Stainless steel profile U40.30.4
18. Ceramic piece type 1: 500.240.50
19A. Support for ceramic facade
19B. Fastener for ceramic facade
20. Stainless steel anchor
21. Adjustable wall anchor
22. Stainless steel profile L50.50.2
23. Fixed steel piece type Jansen
24. Ceramic piece type 2: 470.60.60
25. Stainless steel frame
26. Stainless steel sheet fencing
27. Galvanized steel subframe
28. Rainwater drainpipe
29. Pond-water tank
30. Waterproof rubber paint
31. Reinforced concrete wall
32. Reinforced concrete beam
33. Indoor flooring of polished terrazzo
34. Exterior galvanized steel railing
35. Steel sheet flower bed
36. Outdoor flooring of continuous polished concrete
37. Lightweight reinforced concrete built-up floor
38. Reinforced concrete retaining wall
39. Ceramic piece type 2: 470.240.50
40. Topsoil + plantation
41. Stainless steel profile L100.100.8
42. Ceramic slat type A:480.150.50
43. Stainless steel slat grille
44. Lime mortar stucco
45. Radiant-coolant
46. Floor piping
47. Galvanized sheet cap t:1,5 mm
48. Galvanized steel gargoyle
49. Galvanized steel Tramex grill
50. Finished in gravicolor t:8mm
51. Built-in weatherproof light
52. Galvanized steel pre-lacquered sheet t: 3 mm

0 0.5 1m

1:30

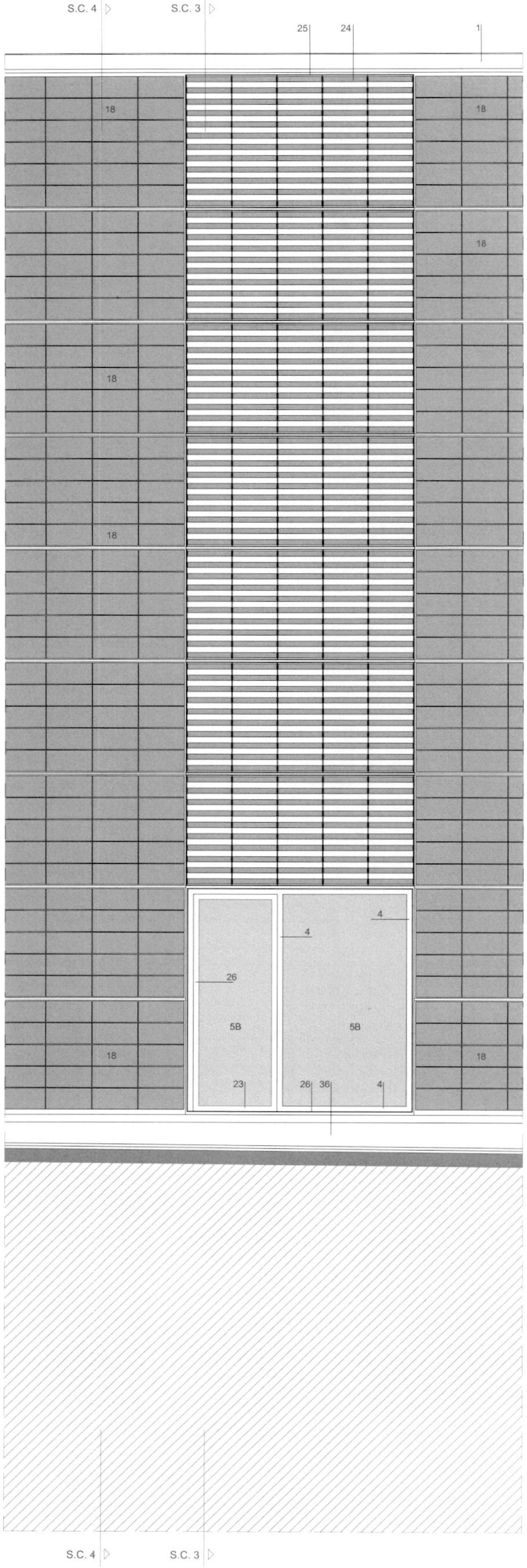

East Elevation

1:75

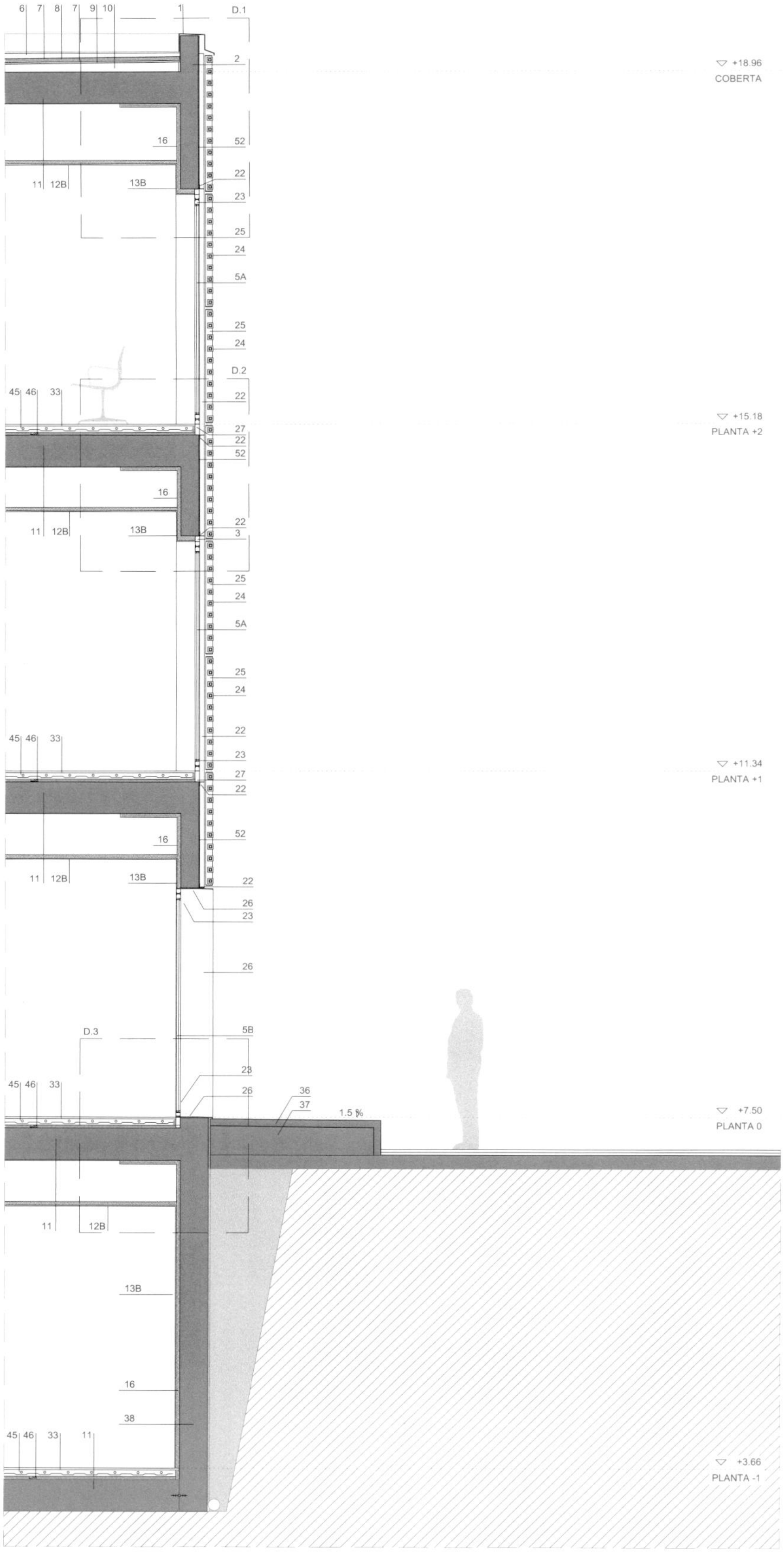

Section Detail 3

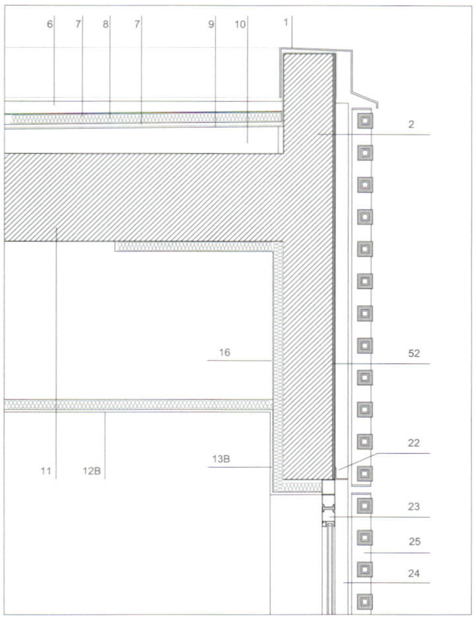

Detail 1

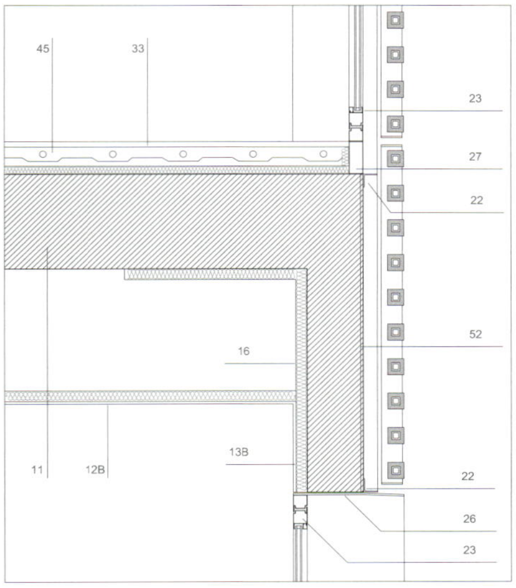

Detail 2

1. Finished with galvanized sheet
2. Reinforced concrete parapet
3. Subframe of galvanized steel and paint
4. Fixed steel framing type Jansen
5. Glazing:
   5A: Double glazing with chamber
   5B: Double glazing with chamber with transparent butyral
   5C: Security glazing
   5D: Double glazing with chamber with translucent butyral
6. Washed boulder d=16-32 mm
7. Separation sheet
8. Insulation of extruded polystyrene
9. Waterproofing
10. Lightweight mortar for slopes
11. One-way floor slab
12A. Laminated and perforated plaster drop ceiling
12B. Fire resistant drop ceiling
13A. Wall cladding
14. Rainwater drain
15. Thermoclay block t: 20 cm
16. Insulation
17. Stainless steel profile U40.30.4
18. Ceramic piece type 1: 500.240.50
19A. Support for ceramic facade
19B. Fastener for ceramic facade
20. Stainless steel anchor
21. Adjustable wall anchor
22. Stainless steel profile L50.50.2
23. Fixed steel piece type Jansen
24. Ceramic piece type 2: 470.60.60
25. Stainless steel frame
26. Stainless steel sheet fencing
27. Galvanized steel subframe
28. Rainwater drainpipe
29. Pond-water tank
30. Waterproof rubber paint
31. Reinforced concrete wall
32. Reinforced concrete beam
33. Indoor flooring of polished terrazzo
34. Exterior galvanized steel railing
35. Steel sheet flower bed
36. Outdoor flooring of continuous polished concrete
37. Lightweight reinforced concrete built-up floor
38. Reinforced concrete retaining wall
39. Ceramic piece type 2: 470.240.50
40. Topsoil + plantation
41. Stainless steel profile L100.100.8
42. Ceramic slat type A:480.150.50
43. Stainless steel slat grille
44. Lime mortar stucco
45. Radiant-coolant
46. Floor piping
47. Galvanized sheet cap t:1,5 mm
48. Galvanized steel gargoyle
49. Galvanized steel Tramex grill
50. Finished in gravicolor t:8mm
51. Built-in weatherproof light
52. Galvanized steel pre-lacquered sheet t: 3 mm

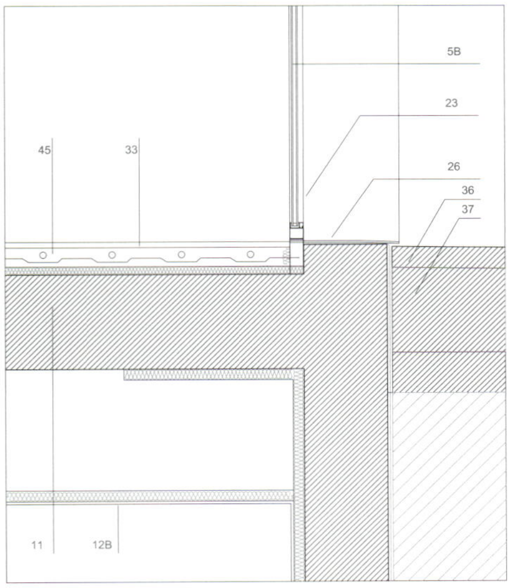

Detail 3

0 0,5 1m

1:30

SERVICES BUILDING UPC

Ercilla-Campo arquitectos

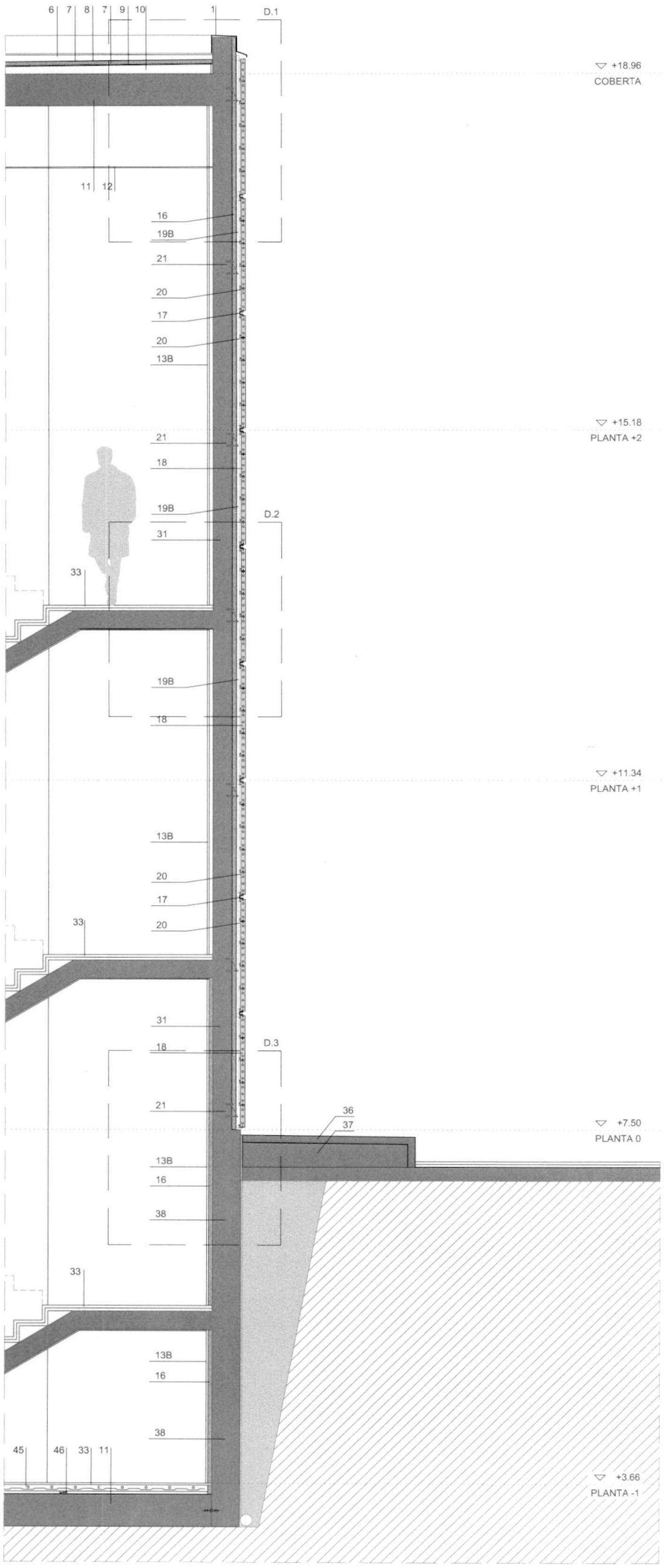

Section Detail 4

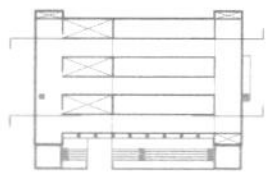

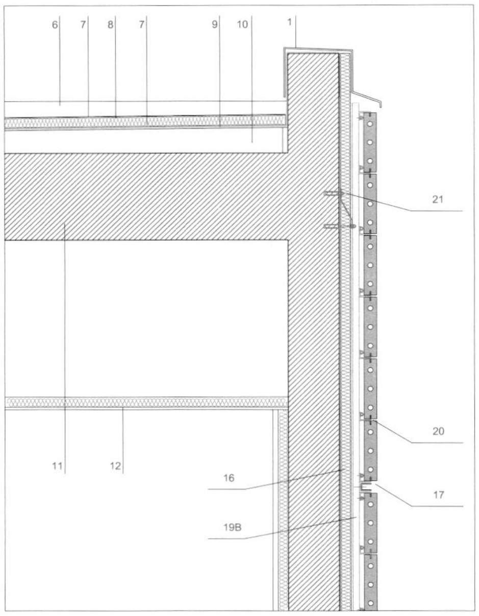

Detail 1

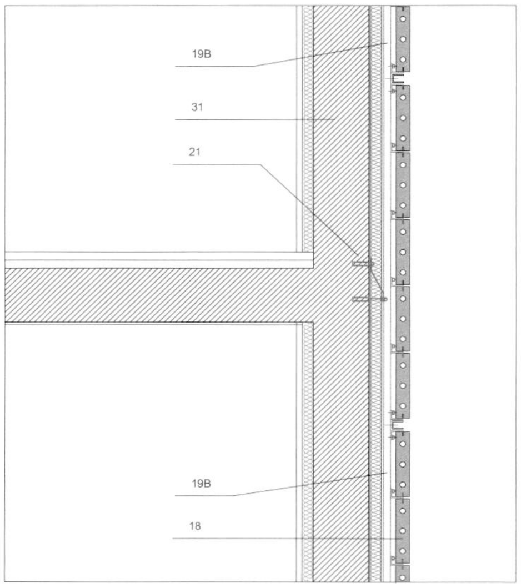

Detail 2

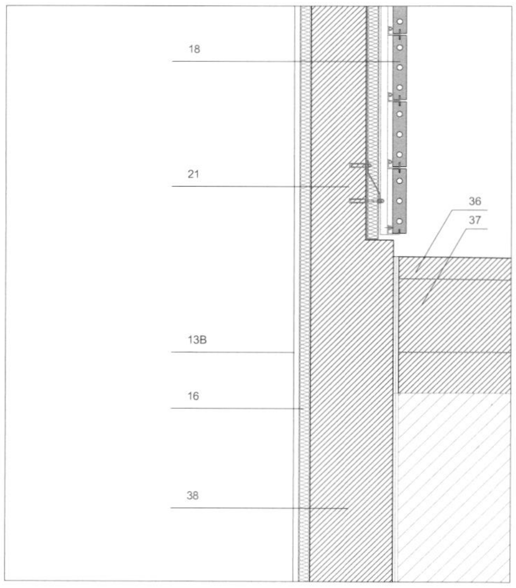

Detail 3

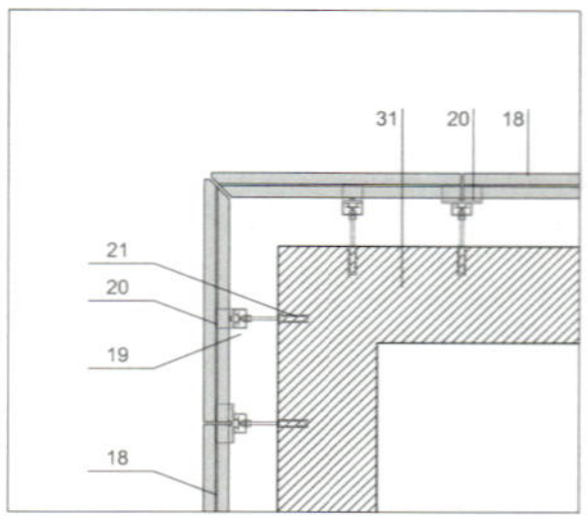
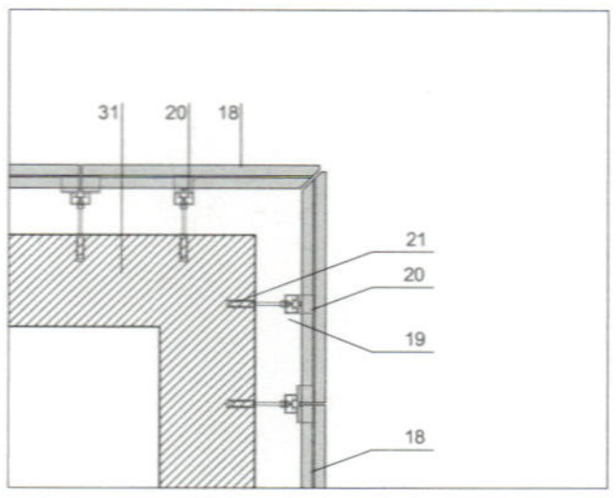

1. Finished with galvanized sheet
2. Reinforced concrete parapet
3. Subframe of galvanized steel and paint
4. Fixed steel framing type Jansen
5. Glazing:
   5A: Double glazing with chamber
   5B: Double glazing with chamber with transparent butyral
   5C: Security glazing
   5D: Double glazing with chamber with translucent butyral
6. Washed boulder d=16-32 mm
7. Separation sheet
8. Insulation of extruded polystyrene
9. Waterproofing
10. Lightweight mortar for slopes
11. One-way floor slab
12A. Laminated and perforated plaster drop ceiling
12B. Fire resistant drop ceiling
13. Wall cladding
14. Rainwater drain
15. Thermoclay block t: 20 cm
16. Insulation
17. Stainless steel profile U40.30.4
18. Ceramic piece type 1: 500.240.50
19A. Support for ceramic facade
19B. Fastener for ceramic facade
20. Stainless steel anchor
21. Adjustable wall anchor
22. Stainless steel profile L50.50.2
23. Fixed steel piece type Jansen
24. Ceramic piece type 2: 470.60.60
25. Stainless steel frame
26. Stainless steel sheet fencing
27. Galvanized steel subframe
28. Rainwater drainpipe
29. Pond-water tank
30. Waterproof rubber paint

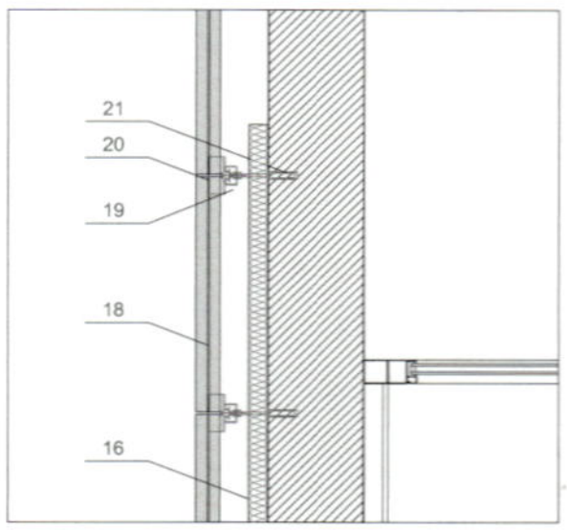
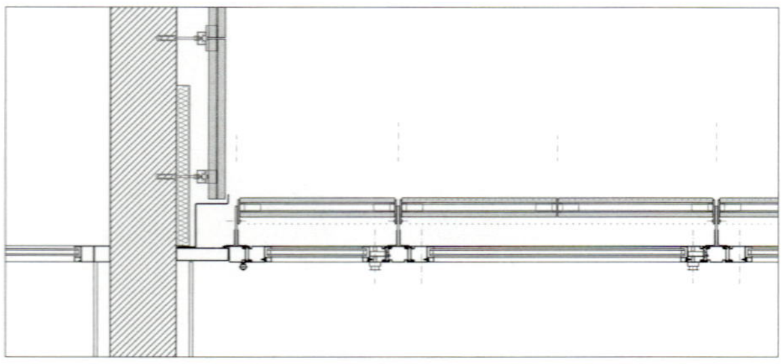
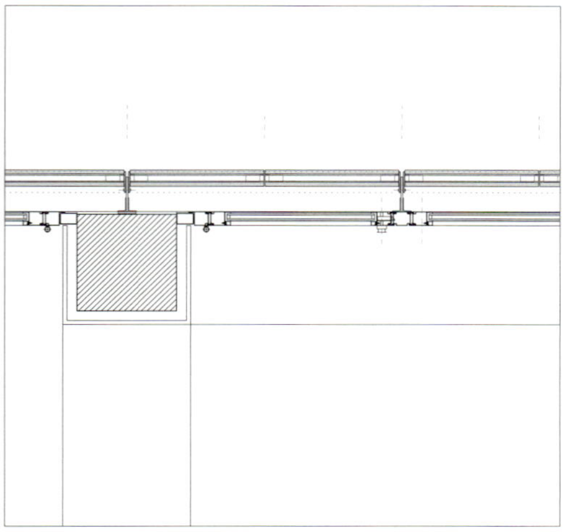
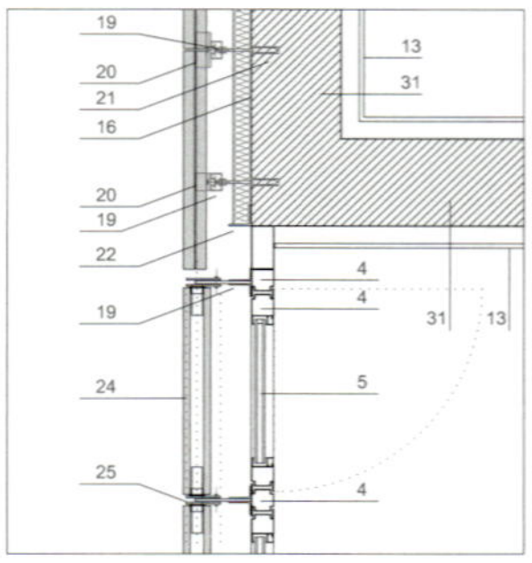

31. Reinforced concrete wall
32. Reinforced concrete beam
33. Indoor flooring of polished terrazzo
34. Exterior galvanized steel railing
35. Steel sheet flower bed
36. Outdoor flooring of continuous polished concrete
37. Lightweight reinforced concrete built-up floor
38. Reinforced concrete retaining wall
39. Ceramic piece type 2: 470.240.50
40. Topsoil + plantation
41. Stainless steel profile L100.100.8
42. Ceramic slat type A:480.150.50
43. Stainless steel slat grille
44. Lime mortar stucco
45. Radiant-coolant
46. Floor piping
47. Galvanized sheet cap t:1,5 mm
48. Galvanized steel gargoyle
49. Galvanized steel Tramex grill
50. Finished in gravicolor t:8mm
51. Built-in weatherproof light
52. Galvanized steel pre-lacquered sheet t: 3 mm

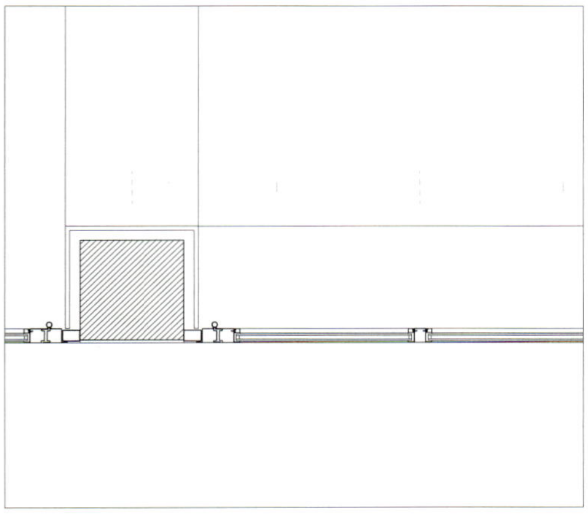
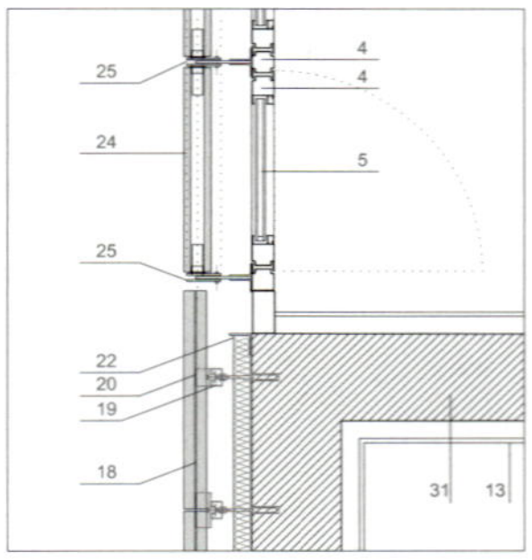
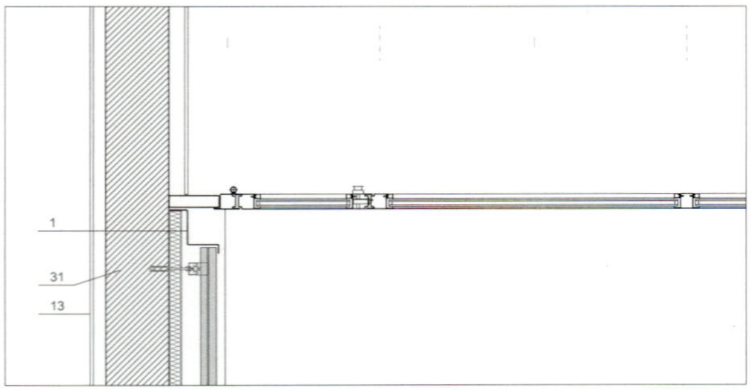
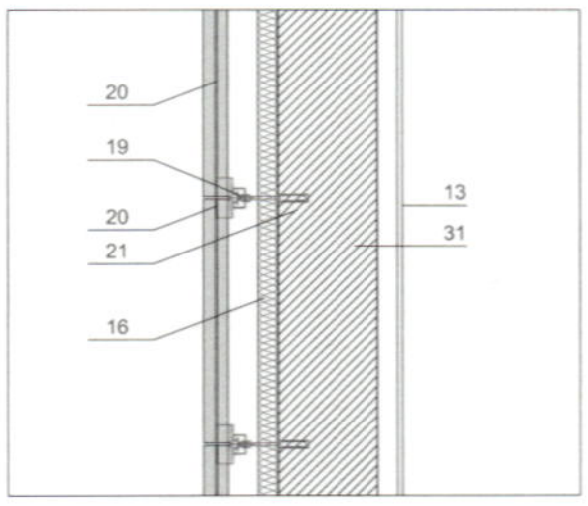
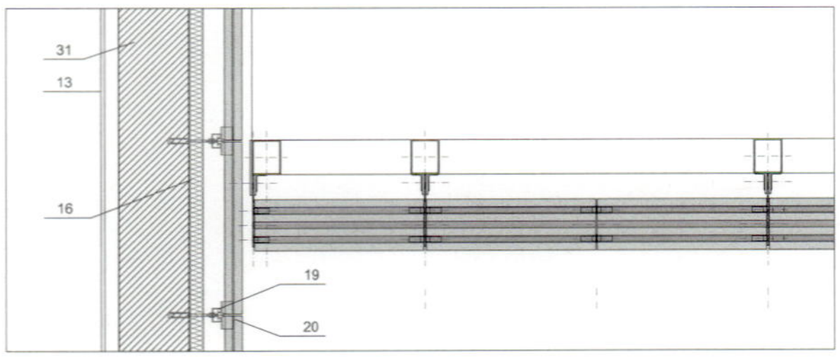
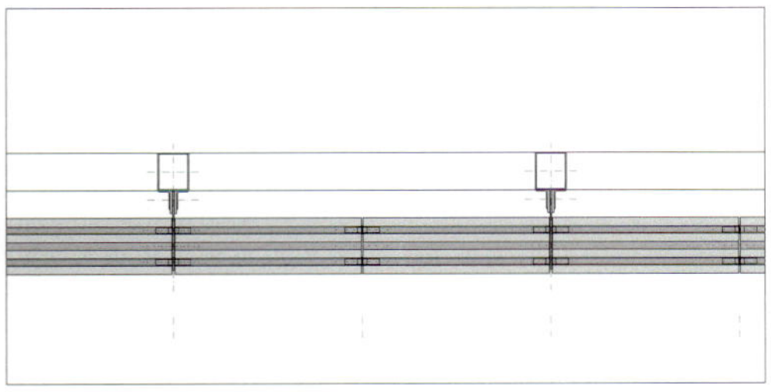
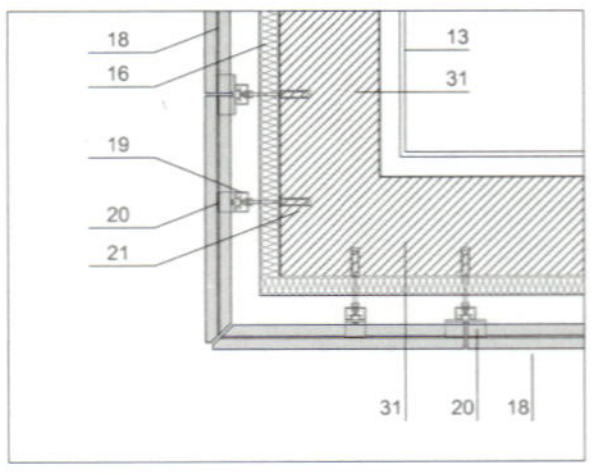
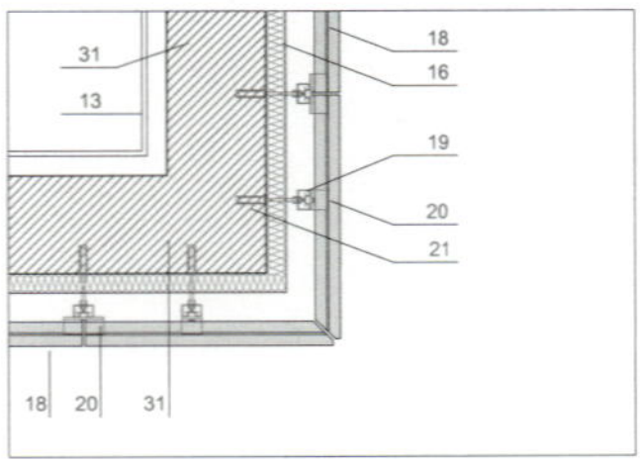

1:30

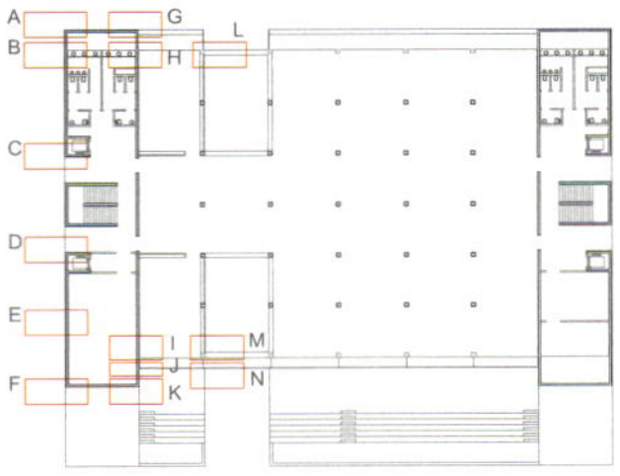

13

Javier Peña Galiano

TWO COLLECTORS HOUSE

LOS ALCÁZARES, Murcia, España

Javier Peña Galiano

xpiral@xpiral.org

ARCHITECT	Javier Peña Galiano
COLLABORATORS	Antonio Abellán, proyecto Lola Jiménez, ejecución
INSTALLATIONS	Oliver König
QUANTITY SURVEYOR	Luis Fernando Perona, Miguel Ángel Cárceles
ENERGY	Federico Salmerón
PHOTOGRAPHY	Juan de la Cruz Mejías

	COLLABORATING COMPANIES
Domotics	Medios Avanzados
Structures	L&P
Video	Oliver Hadfield
Layout	Jesús Galera Agostino Pilloni

Awards	Edificación Ward, XIII Premios Arquitectura Región de Murcia Mention on 2004 Residencia Singular Contest

	DATES
IMPLEMENTATION PROJECT	January 2001
BEGINNING OF WORKS	April 2001
WORK COMPLETION	September 2003

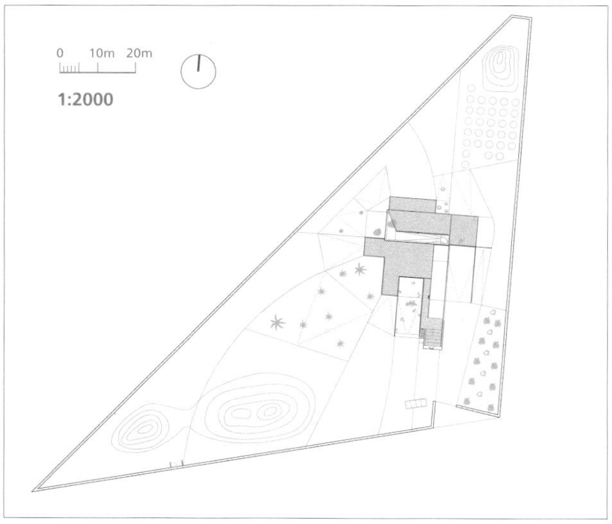

DESCRIPTIVE BRIEF

One of the few things about which architects apparently have agreed throughout the ages, is the difficulty of creating a single-family house, understood as a tailored suit; therefore it is a tense wrestle between the owner, a specific character who tries to solve diverse needs (personal, social, public, private, emotional,...), and the architect who tries to create an architectural program which is capable of proposing, beyond the consolidated culture of inhabiting.

It has been a long process in which we have already been through five years, that began with the search for a place to settle this "logistic center" in a setting that is communicated, at most, twenty minutes away by car from their workplaces, and in which we are still today continuing to place the art collection, the furniture, talking with different artists...enjoying time.

It would almost be better to write a novel rather than an architecture brief. How many events, problems, surprises, discoveries, trials and many mistakes have appeared during this journey; nevertheless I find it interesting to recover this e-mail sent on May 2001, at the beginning of the structure, to arrange thing before starting the garden:

ACUPUNCTURE AS LANDSCAPE

This document appears with the intention of explaining the current situation of the house and above all the garden, as a result of a call Avelino made to buy some centenary olive trees: which are the factors that articulate it?

The Setting

The land's definition: barren, scarce and dry; where the distance to the sea makes it very abstract, cosmic, a flat topographic relationship. The only rule that we could draw is the relationship with the sun, just as the rural architecture that shapes Cartagena's fields does.
The plot is quite big and is waiting for a future re-parceling of the land, designated as not- for-building, and most probably will be shortly absorbed by the nearby built-up lands (Lomas del Rame).

It would be interesting to propose the garden from the idea of proximity and maintenance of the territory.

The House

It is the prism that we all more or less know: a unique space that contains the different collections (painting, drawing, sculpture) terraced from the roof (for large format sculptures) throughout a spiral journey capable of holding different events, exhibition storage and crossed views that sense the numerous possibilities of use of this space: rest, study, chamber music, recitation, food and wine tasting, parties, multimedia projections, facilities...

With a similar territorial structure to those of the tower-farms of the colonization (like Rame´s tower, el Negro, etc.) in which the tanks, farmyards and stores make up a base from where mass prisms emerge, stored or pierced by dovecotes.

It has a base in its lower area that contains the small program: the swimming pool and the gym, as well as what would be the guests or relatives bedrooms and living-kitchen from where, following their trajectory, the courtyards open, defined at mid-height, approximately one meter forty from the terrain's grade, establishing a half-buried relationship with the outside.

The transition between these outside courtyards, which are at the same level as the bedrooms, and the ground is done throughout a series of ramps, inclined planes that, once landscaped, give a similar view from the inside to the one we would have if we had a mountain or small green hill nearby, removing the feeling of being half-buried.

Textures

There would be different types of surfaces between the inner space and that outer space without qualifying that it forms part of the territory, and it is partly located inside the site.

Those outside surfaces which are at the same level as the gym and bedrooms -that is -1, 40 m from the original terrain level- are horizontal, lands without vegetation made up of white gravel, which partially act as drainage or dry places, and partially as areas where one can take a chair outside and read the newspaper or sunbathe.

The four courtyards are thematic, according to their orientation and size: cactus and xerophytes in the South (your bedroom), palm trees in the guests´ courtyard (it's wider and the evening projected shadows would function well on the walls and ground floors), olive trees in the West courtyard, do olive trees go to the gym?, and different kind of shadows in the north one with dychondra repens on the slope (cooler and shadier).

Some small trees could appear on these surfaces which, with their closeness, also accentuate the color change and the seasonal change between the inside space and the garden.

In these courtyards there is a sloped surface that should be more gardened, in a more classical sense. A green and thick surface with herbaceous plants, which is well watered and which transmits the idea of coolness, with the different trimming heights.

The possibility of buying those centenary olive trees would be very interesting, because that would allow us to have a garden with different ages from the beginning, that is, that there would be trees that have already been established and plants that are still growing. With this the garden will always, from the beginning, seem finished. And on the other hand, I think that the olive tree is a suitable tree for this environment, because it can be uprooted, and there is possibility of success in the uprooting, and on the other hand, it has very strong formal and expressive qualities.

We could start searching for some other trees to place them on this stretch of green grass, adapted to this dry climate we live in, such as palm trees or the cactus collection you have, which are already adapted to the environment.

Controlled Landscapes
These sloped planes have, along their edges, concrete walls of variable height, where openings of different sizes appear.

These walls begin with orthogonal perimeters linked to the house, but right away they begin to distort and to take on curved trajectories that continue afterwards with plant designs, stone paths or other colonization elements.

This "landscape formatting" is also going to be seen from the inside of the house, through the gaps in the ceramic bard grid, creating numerous views of unique and apparently monotonous landscapes from 7:1 to 1:1 formats. This process is repeated in a similar way with the pool's water, trimmed, photographing its activity and light from the water hall and the entrance vestibule.

From the outside, the ceramic prism also tries to capture the sky (like the great drying places for fish that existed around here when we were children). We have three skies: the real one, the one painted by the insulation, and the one reflected on the glazing.

Colonization
The idea is that this land which is at height level zero, with stones, thistles, and weeds continues being that way, and the only thing will be done to it is an acupuncture exercise, like needles on a body on which we are going to stick plant elements and other architectural, even technologic elements.

Those needles could be similar elements to the ones the land contains, but organized in a different way, like wefts of stone, rosemary, and thyme which, when cut, appear or disappear allowing to create different spaces or crossings, paths. Well-organized on the plot, the house would have different scents depending on which direction the wind blows.

Planting aromatic plants or some big evergreen and deciduous trees would depend on the views from inside the house, acting as low visual obstacles, and especially from the terrace which is on level +1,40m. Therefore they should be placed near the fence, so that the distance between the observer inside the house and the trees, creates a sensation of distance.

The architectural elements would be:

-The use of the land, the slope or the accumulation of the remaining land to create a small hillock, which would be in the southern part of the garden, double with a small isthmus, complemented with another one maybe in the northern area, which constitute two smooth transgressions of the landscape's horizontality.

-The fences and car access road, as well as the swimming pool's walls, that with the blue mosaic tile wrapping around the outside and the horizontal overflow, revalue this water sheet designed for swimming, like an active reflection of the house.

- The third element of which we talked about before are the installations, the possibility of placing some technological elements that qualify the land. They could be fiber optic elements or lamps that also gave spaces of vision through the night. The image of stellar constellations as groups of light mass would give distance and scale.

Besides lighting, I think it might be interesting to place solar panels facing south and that they be hot water collectors for the swimming pool during the winter. Although they could also be used for the house's hot water supply, not only in winter, but also in summer, without consuming any energy and converting themselves, besides, into qualifying elements like those acupuncture needles that would mark out the territory.

The fourth element could be some artistic installations like the horse that Xavier Mascaró has to do, and that marked out that barren territory with isolated actions.

Another important place would be the access slab (like a mixed terrain with prefabricated concrete and grass), which is considered an exterior vestibule, where the access to the house is located. From this exterior entrance hall you can see the house's front and back, the northern area of the garden and everything that is formed to the south.

Conclusions
It would be a very controlled garden that responds functionally to basic concepts, intention of views and of relationship with the architecture through sloped planes which seek to give continuity between the inside and outside space.

It's economical: with little water consumption and maintenance, little ground occupation and the possibility of enjoying the garden from the first minute that the house begins to work, as a finished place, still growing but thought out. It is not left to chance. In this sense, buying or searching some plant species such as those olive trees is interesting. We'll take as many as there are available.

Another interesting reflection is that the garden is really important to consider the house's original idea, a little center of your universe.

It starts from a rectangular and cubic shape which then opens up and begins to deform, from its orthogonal nature adjusting to those curves that the garden generates, which can be parabolas or hyperbolas, infinite trajectories.

They open themselves from that controlled and personal feeling which is a house (a reference center) to an open and broken world, chaotic; that is why it is so necessary to finish the garden in order to complete the house. The house has no value without the garden and the garden is part of the house's program.

"Technology is the answer, but what was the question?"
Cedric Price

ENVIRONMENTAL ANALYSIS

1. Choosing the site. Project and development

1.1 Location

Latitude: 37º43'55"N
Longitude: 00º52'35"O
Altitude: 8 m

The region where this project is placed is part of the coastal plain skirting Mar Menor, in Murcia. A little rough relief placed 8 meters OSL. With a dry and warm sub-desert Mediterranean weather, arid due to scarce rainfall that hardly ever is over 300mm/year. On the other hand hydrographical net in all the town is nearly void.

1.2 Urban design and site improvement

Volume highlights plain environment, reminding of lookout fortresses in Arabian citadels which were built in this region during the Middle Age.

An unfinished ceramic prism, with holes in its upper side, which in a way of contemporaneous battlements, allow occupants to observe the horizon. This position closed to exterior is softened by presence of water mirror and vegetal mantles at the bottom of the prism, thus contributing with green surface which helps reduce environmental emissions.

1.3 Project

The house, a rational volume with parallepiped shape, can be entered by pedestrians from street level or through parking place in lower ground floor. In this half-buried floor are located bedrooms, one kitchen and a sitting-room; with a scattered layout, following perpendicular axis among themselves.

In the social area located at street level, space longitudinally opens. Wide open volume holds the owners´ art collection. South facing windows open the prism facilitating natural lighting. Kitchen and lounge equipment is repeated, a decision attributable to the owner´s requirements with a clear intention of social use.

Vertical circulation generates a spiral walkway that allows different visuals of the exposed art work. It is reached and attic where the library is placed, a half-insulated space that allows absorption as well as it provides with full interior visuals and works as antechamber of the cover, raised as a passable gardening space, from where scene can be watched through holes left by façade ceramics.

2. Consumption of Energy and resources

2.1 Consumption of energy

The strategy of semi-burying private areas has been adopted in order to take profit on land´s insulating qualities and thus reduce energy consumption in conditioning. At the cover level a passable garden over stairs is raised, a strategy with a clear insulating wish.

Besides, electrics are adapted to incorporate photovoltaic panels to generate energy for the house in service period.

2.2 Consumption of water

Rainwater captured by cover and vegetation platforms is reused for irrigation.

2.3 Consumption of Materials

Closing is raised as a series of clearly differenced layers: pre-made concrete panels, projected polythene, air layer and ceramic placated over metallic profiles. Proposed assembly is easily reversible, except for projected polythene, being alternatives in market such as extracted polythene sheets or organic materials sheets such as cork[1], coconut or hemp.

Use of pre-made elements in forgings and closing, reduce execution time and building waste.

3. Environmental loads

3.1 Emissions

They are minimized by the type of materials used in closing and by provision of vegetal mantles around the house.

Projector, when choosing ceramic placated for closing has opted for a low emission material in its manufacturing process and in its service stage. Since 1990 ceramic industry in Spain, has managed to reduce an 18% CO_2 specific emissions whereas it has increased production a 70%.

3.2 Solid waste

Closing allows installations to go through layers with no need of channels which increase building waste.

3.3 Water management

It has been taken into account to provide the house with separating nets which allow reusing grey waters for green areas maintenance. This strategy acquires higher sense in a dry environment.

4. Interior environmental quality

4.1 Ventilation

Natural ventilation, guaranteed by prevision of openings in all atmospheres, even the underground ones, and by a wide open interior allowing fresh air to flow.

4.2 Natural lighting

Social area is open to south by means of large windows in street floor. Radiation and light access in summer time is controlled by roll-up curtains placed in interior.

In order to provide lower ground floor with light it has been chosen the interesting solution to use as gardens the soft slopes rising above level difference. This way spaces open to vegetal mantles that change perception of being half-buried.

The pool is used as a water mirror and because of its location opposite south façade allows interior reflections that generate a positive visual and subjective effect.

4.3 Acoustics

Interior divisions are solved by chipboard panels, with a high level of acoustic absorption. This way reflections provoked by flat pre-fabricated concrete and main metal beam are reduced, low absorption materials used without interior cladding.

1 http://www.cork-2000.com

5. Control of building systems

5.1 Functionality and efficiency

This architectural programme has been divided in two areas (private and social) providing each one with different spaces. Internal prism is diaphanous, with kitchen and sanitary laid under vertical circulation, what allows freedom for interior layout.

Gardens and pool have a specific an important specific weight in this project and provision of vegetation in different maturation stages (old olive trees, cactus, palm trees, new implantation aromatic plants), will help create a series of visual, acoustic and olfactory sensations as well as having a thermal and sunstroke controlling function.

5.2 Control of building systems

This is the section where it can be identified a great knowledge of constructive systems and their possibilities as tools to materialize sustainable projects, never neglecting promoter's singular requirements.

Intensive use of pre-fabricated materials and austerity in finishes, combined with a correct use of scene. Simple settings that might guarantee habitability comfortable conditions and that allow reversibility in actuation.

6. Long time performance

6.1 Flexibility and adaptability

The way of using technical resources has allowed creating a flexible space that permits many uses: living space, domestic wellness[2], art gallery, party room, chamber music room, library or rest garden. All of them appropriate to promoters' life style.

This setting of technically sustainable house thanks to its materiality, with the intention to get temporarily adapted to any use variation, is comparable to any architectural project.

6.2 Maintenance and operative performance

Use of material without finishes, visiting installations inside skin and frugal vegetal species[3] own of this area used to configure landscape around the house; reduce maintenance as well as they optimize building´s performance inside environment.

7. Economical and social features

7.1 Social features

It becomes necessary example of projects with a clear environmental intention in a region featured by unstoppable estate development, joined to a growing population, a desert land and with a total coastal occupation prevision for 2008.

8. Architect´s eye

Social space layout, library and vertical circulation remind of the solution used by Le Corbusier in Ville la Roche in 1923. Respect for natural and historical condition of implantation site; joined to the possibilities of use flexibility spaces, solved by the simplicity of constructive systems and development of the programme in a narrow collaboration with promoter; have given as a result a domestic architecture singular and sustainable.

2 Word used to define the generic concept of welfare

3 Vegetation of Murcia. Digital Cartography of the region http://www.carm.es/siga/mnatural/medbioti/mbvegeta.html#Vegetacion

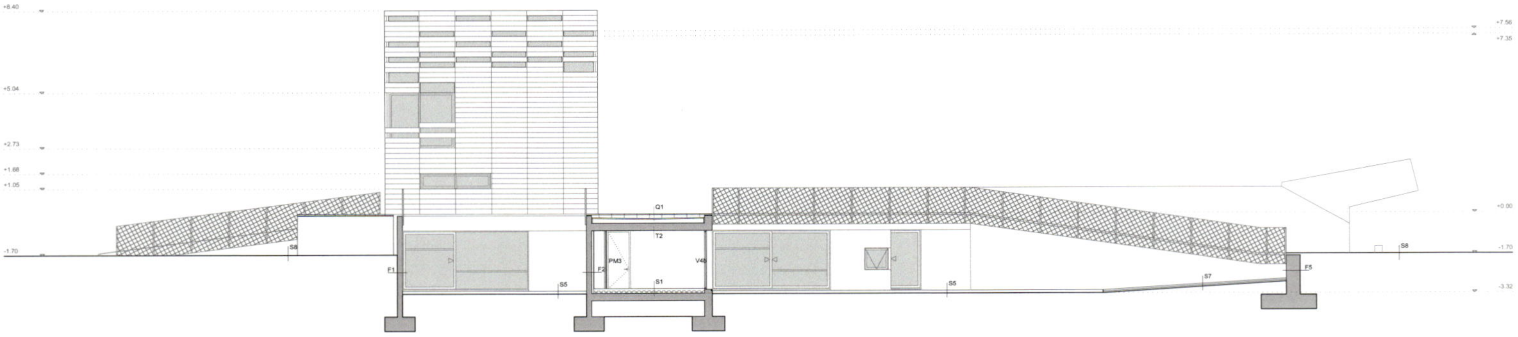

East Elevation

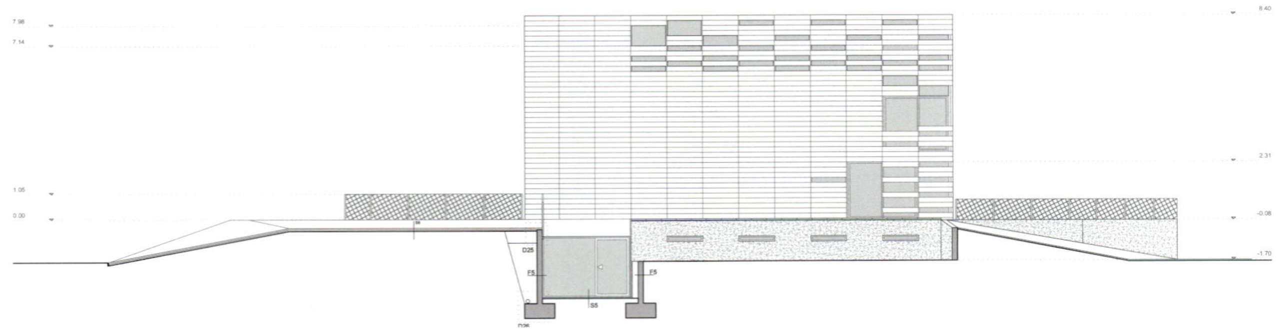

South Elevation

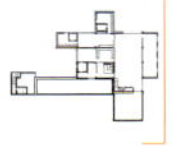

0 5 10m

1:300

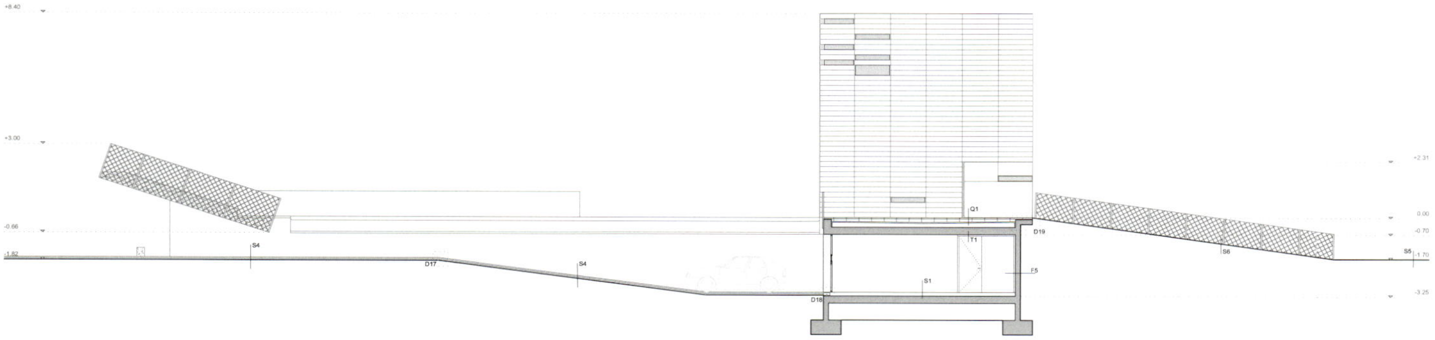

West Elevation

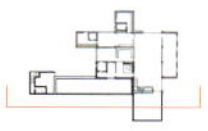

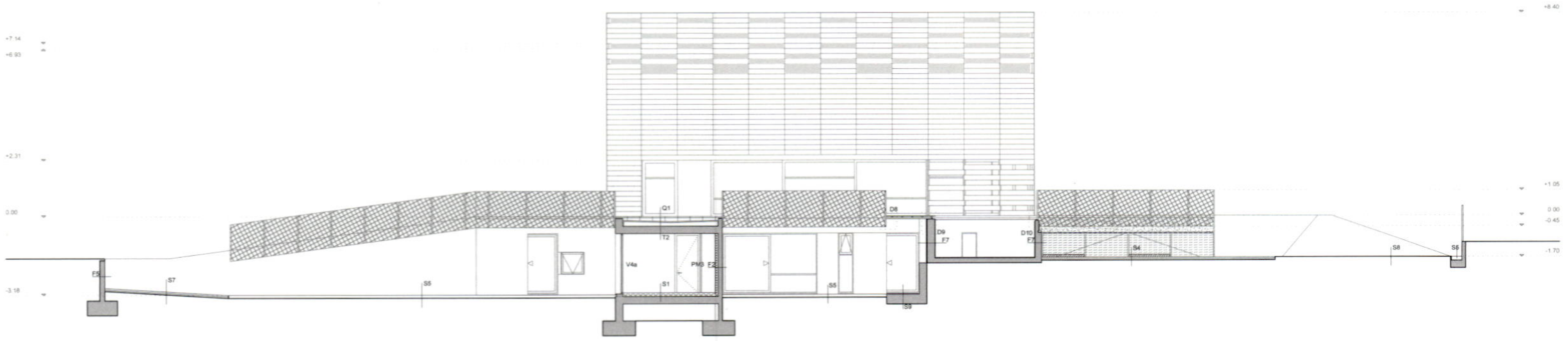

North Elevation

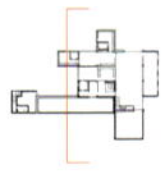

0 5 10m

1:300

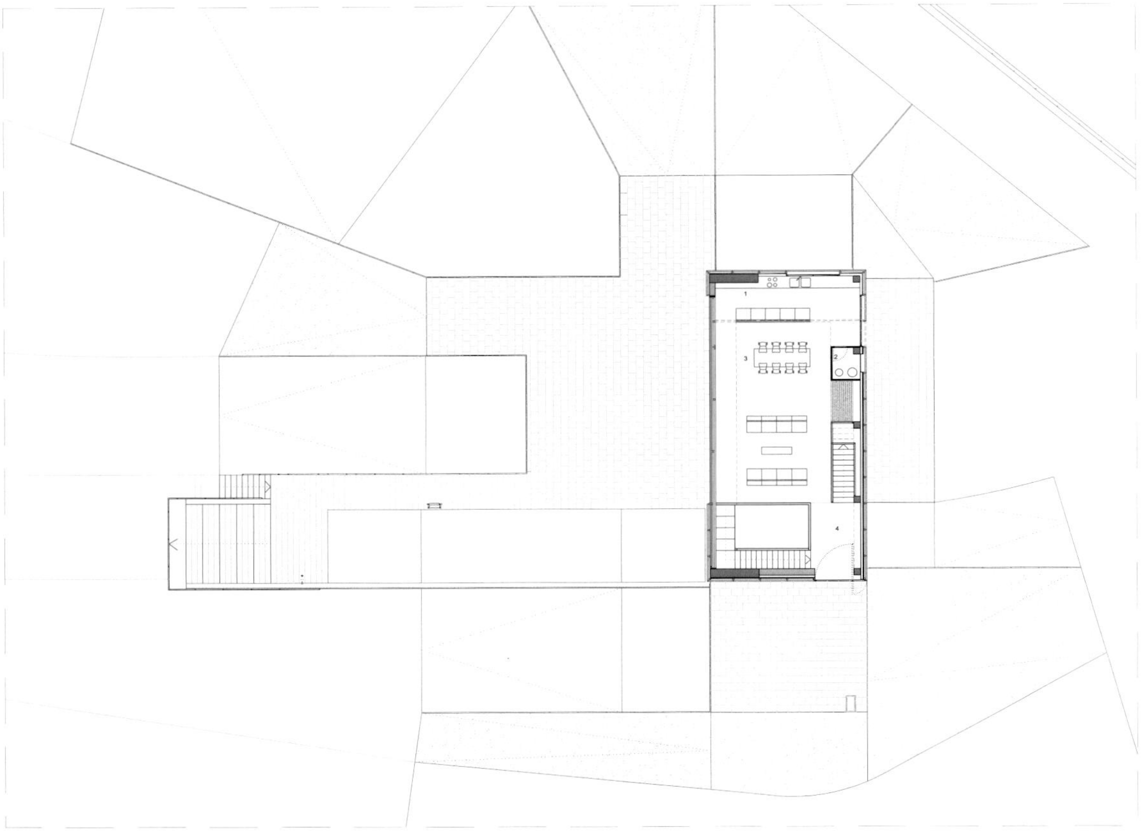

1. Kitchen
2. ½ bath 2
3. Living - bedroom
4. Entrance

Ground Floor Level

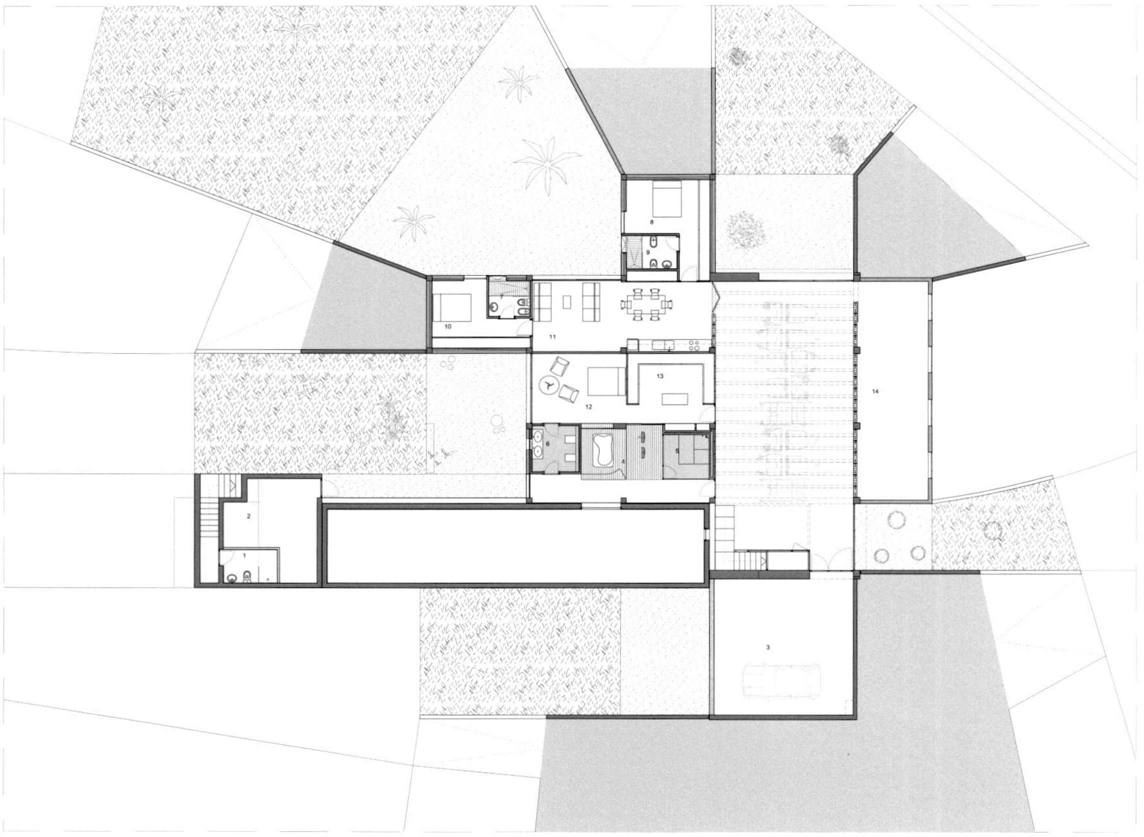

1. Swimming pool bathroom
2. Installation room
3. Garage
4. Water area
5. Sauna
6. ½ bath 1
7. Bathroom 2
8. Bedroom 1
9. Bathroom1
10. Bedroom 2
11. Living – dining room
12. Bedroom 3
13. Passage and dressing room
14. Wine cellar - storage

Basement Floor Level

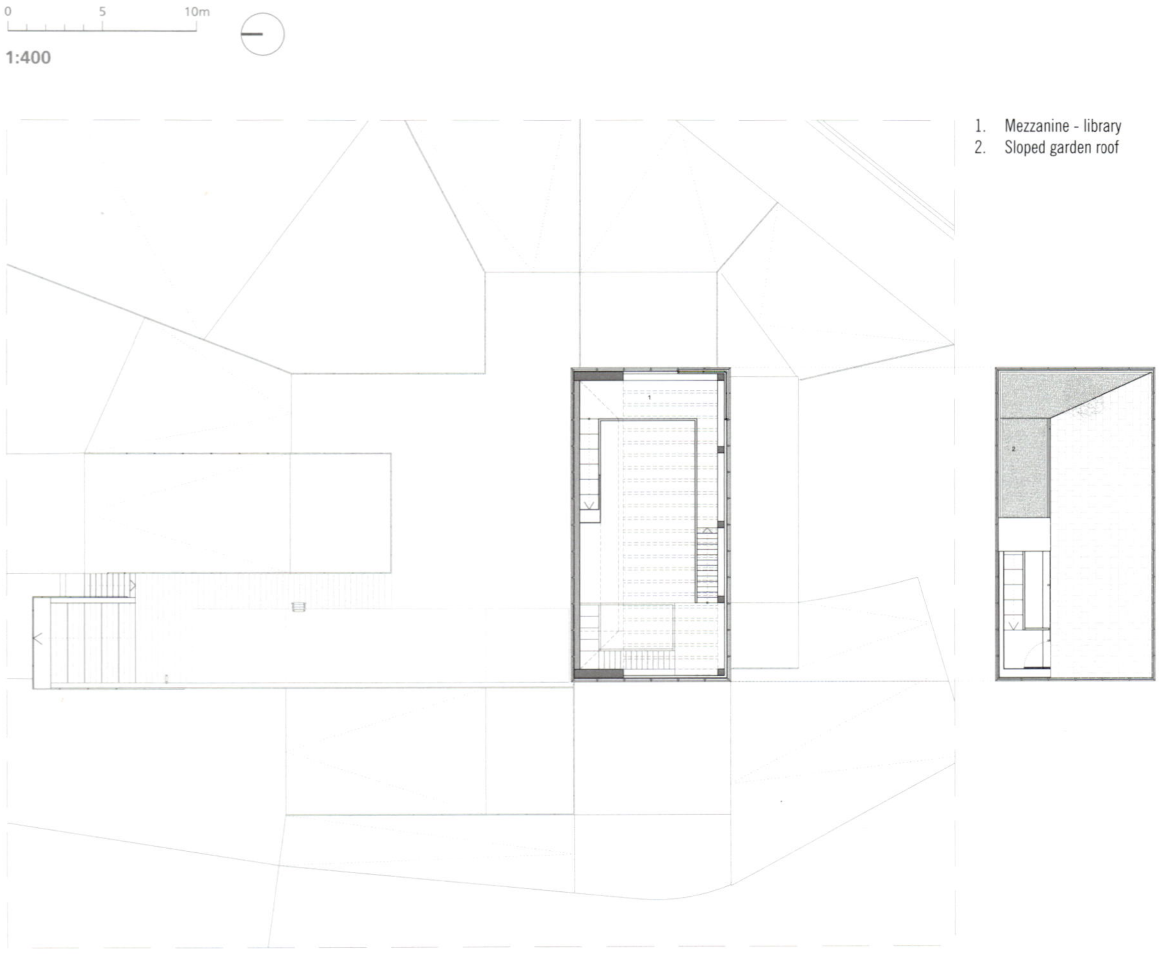

1. Mezzanine - library
2. Sloped garden roof

Roof and 1st Floor Level

TWO COLLECTORS HOUSE

Javier Peña Galiano

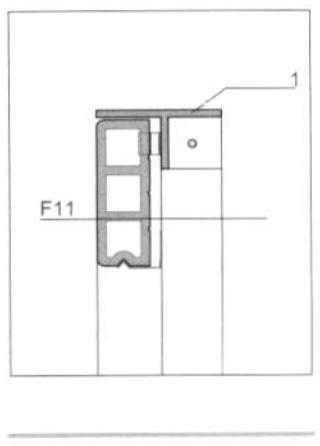

D. 1

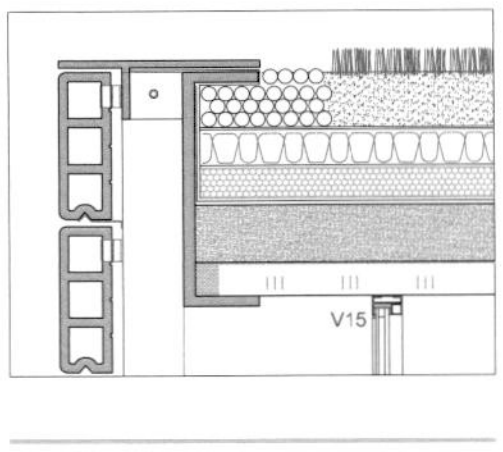

D. 2

0 10 30 50cm 1m

1:20

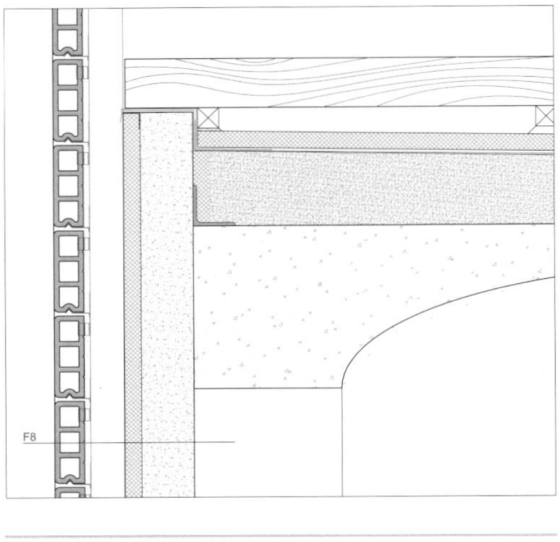

D. 3

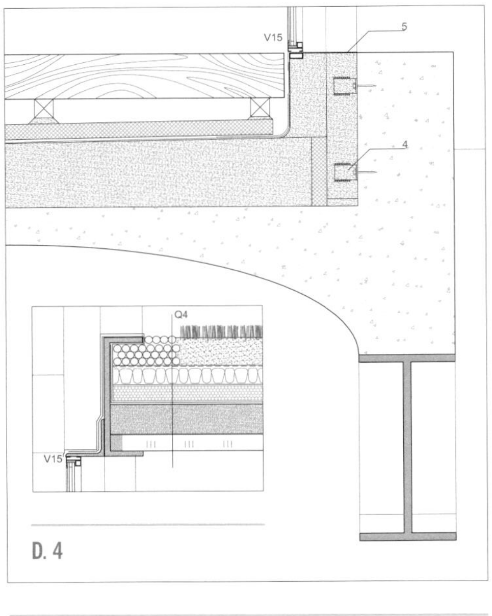

D. 5

D. 4

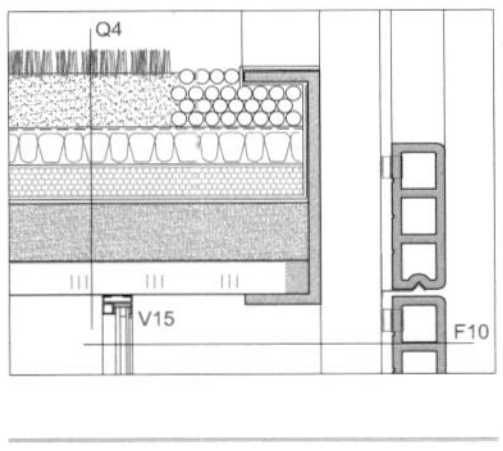

D. 6

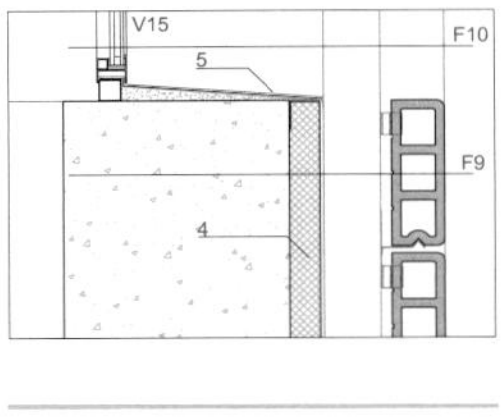

D. 7

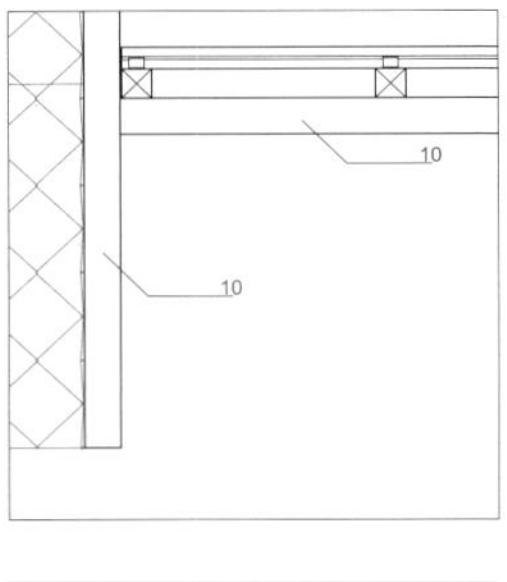

D. 8

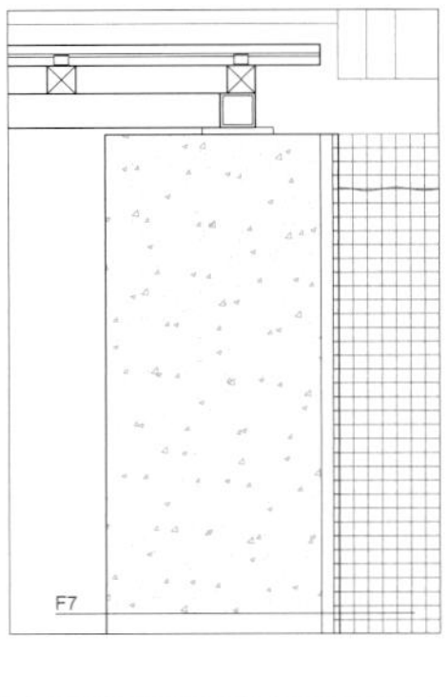

D. 9

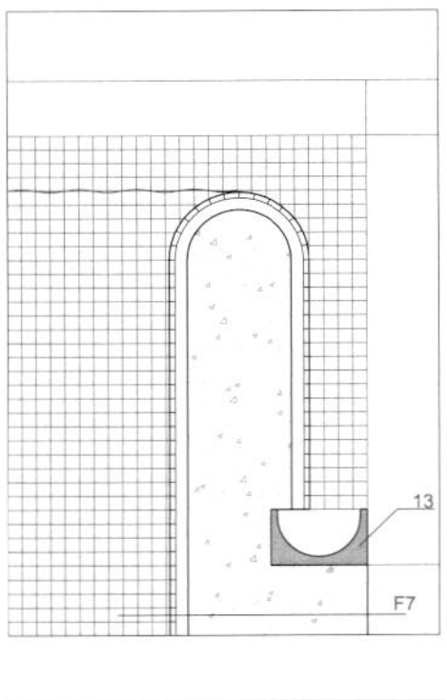

D. 10

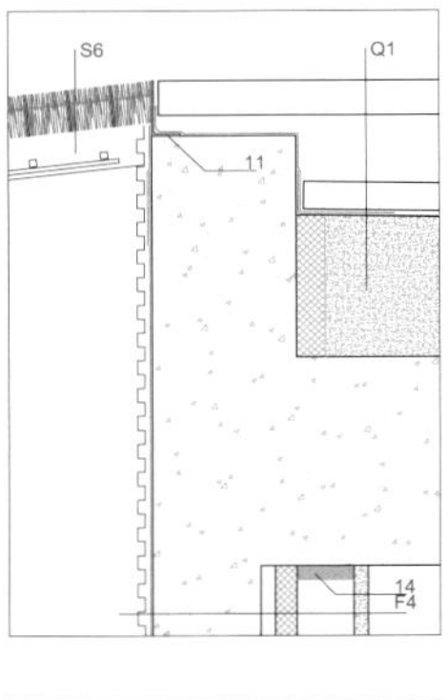

D. 11

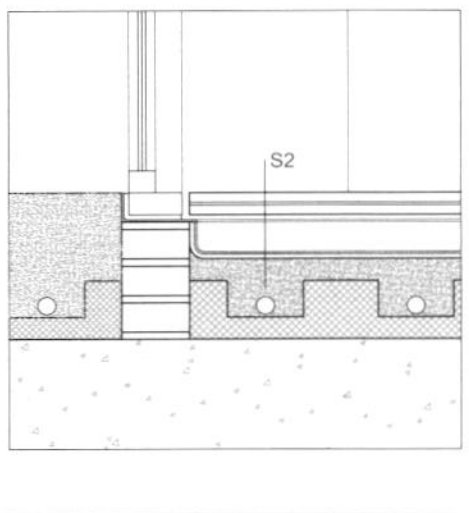

D. 12

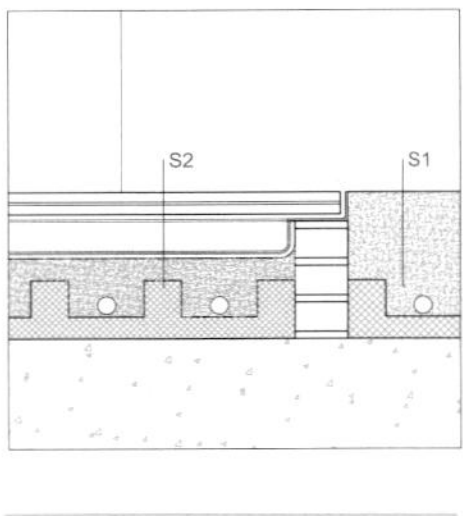

D. 13

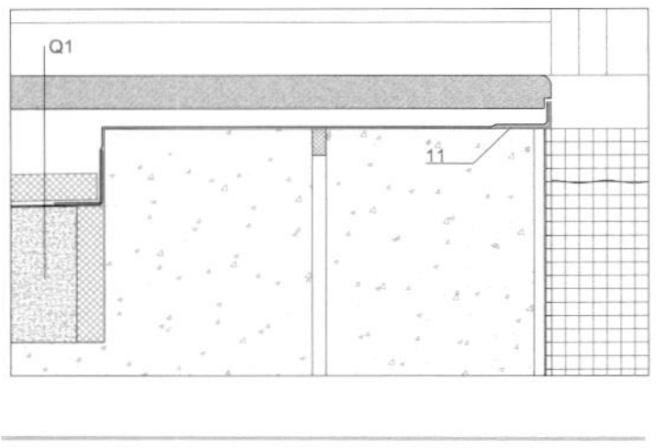

D. 14

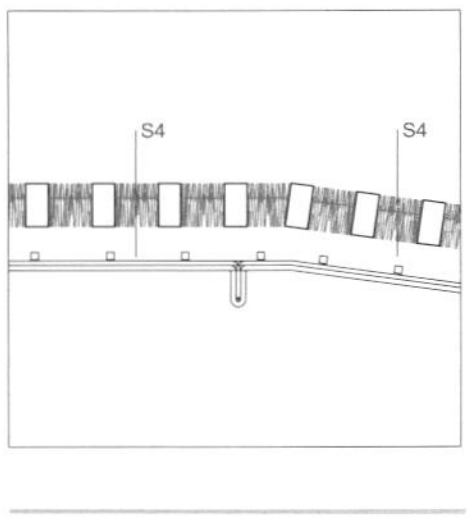

D. 17

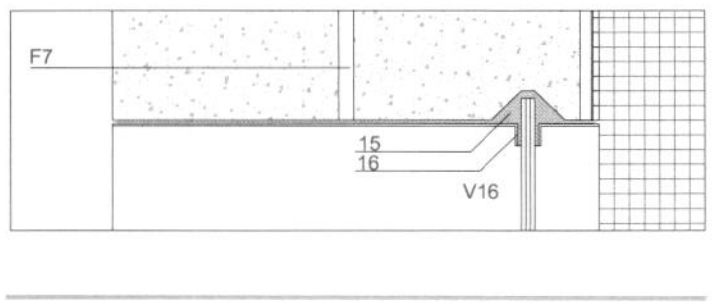

D. 15

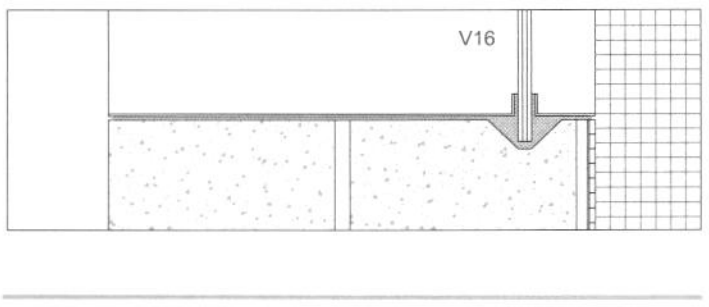

D. 16

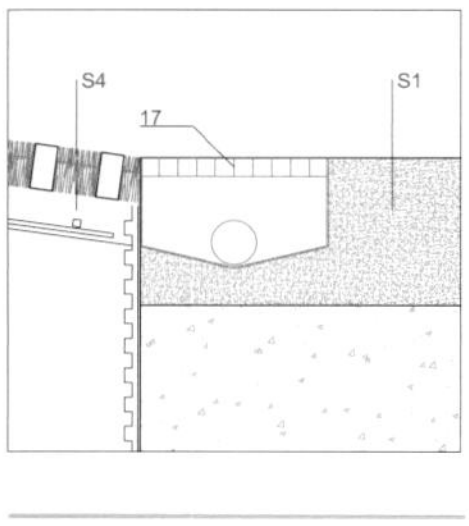

D. 18

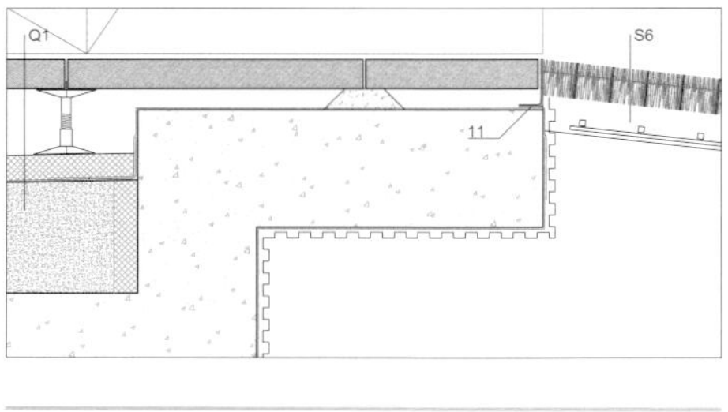

D. 19

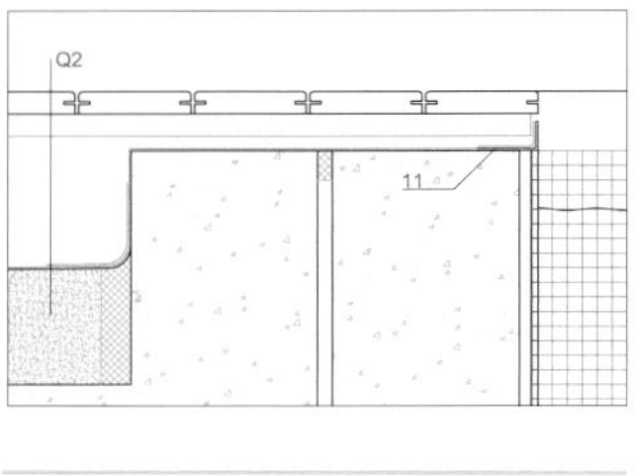

D. 20

1. Stainless steel plate cap 80.10
2. Angle edge profile l.120.120.4 screwed to pre-fabricated concrete panels
3. Railing composed of:
   - Aluminum profile u.60.40.2 to house florescent tube + methacrylate cover 35.4 mm
   - Aluminum profile u.40.40.2
   - Stainless steel finish plate 100.3 mm
4. Anchor for metal structure by means angular profile cuts l.80.80.4 welded to the post and screwed with hilti pegs to the concrete beams
5. Cap of corrugated aluminum sheet with drip edge
6. Substructure of steel tubing 30.30.3 welded for the support of framing v15 and edge of roof slab. Clad with plywood board
7. Angular edge profile l.90.90.3 screwed to prefabricated concrete panels
8. Cap of galvanized corrugated steel sheet to define edge of projected insulation and formation of dripedge
9. Edge profile for exterior railings to hold fluorescent light. Angle l.100.50.4
10. Exterior railing formed by steel tube 0.4 and simple torque galvanized mesh
11. Longitudinal edge profile for beams and walls. Angle l.80.40.3
12. Reinforced concrete weathering
13. Ceramic piece for collection of water
14. Wall closure with black plaster
15. Silicone sealant
16. Stainless steel profile screwed to concrete wall, prior placement of glazing with projected silicone sealant
17. Prefabricated linear drain with stainless steel 'tramex' grill
18. Corrugated stainless steel sheet 80.40.2 mm to hide back face of concrete panel, and for support for sheet 8
19. Porous draining tube
20. Stainless steel window edge

FLOORING

- s1. Continuous flooring - Suesco- concrete poured 'in situ'
- s2. Accessible treated wood flooring, elevated over basin of mosaic tile in showers and wet rooms
- s3. Floating floor of tripli board16 mm. over MDF 19 mm. over metal structure, varnished with satin finish with color
- s4. Flooring -Checker block- from 'Escofet', slab filled with reinforced concrete as resistant reinforcement for the plant soil of format 610x610mm laid over 5cm of sand.
- s5. Flooring of whitewashed boulders from 'Lorca' of 80/100mm over geotextile of 150 gr/m2 over compacted terrain
- s6. Planting soil with PVC panel framing, extended over sandbed
- s7. Planting soil cultivated in angled fowerbeds
- s8. Natural plowed soil
- s9. Polished concrete groundslab

EXTERIOR FACADES

- f1. Reinforced concrete structure, exposed on both faces
- f2.
  - Smooth plastic paint
  - Plastered 2 cm
  - l.h.d. 7 cm.
  - Thermal insulation of fiber glass panels
  - Air chamber
  - Concrete wall on exposed on outer face
- f3.
  - Stoneware tile 20x20

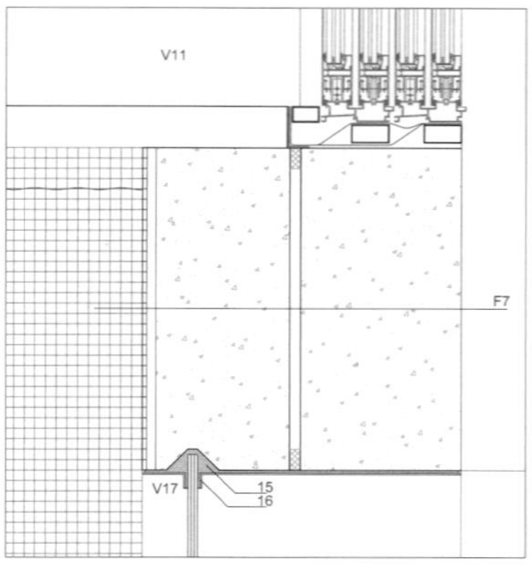

D. 21

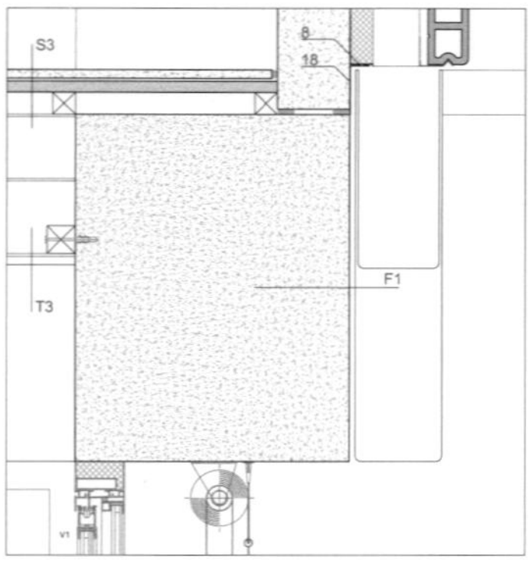

D. 23

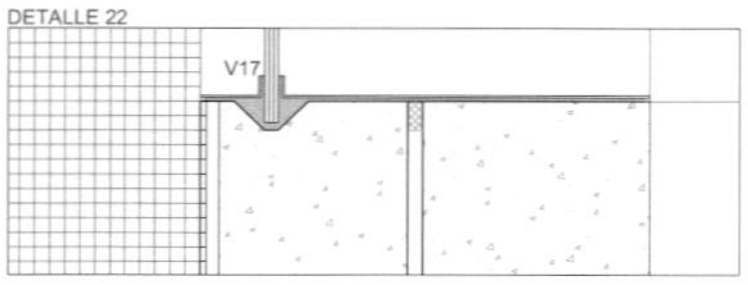

D. 22

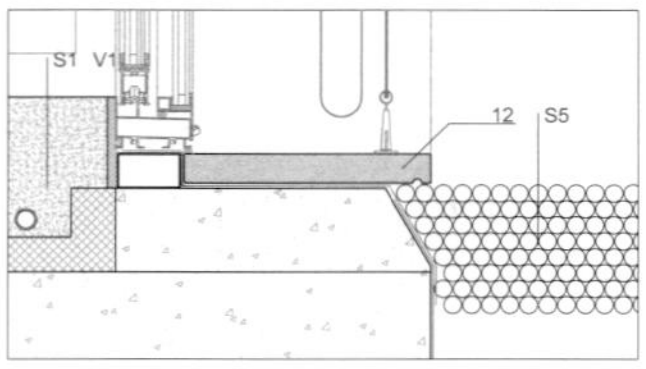

D. 24

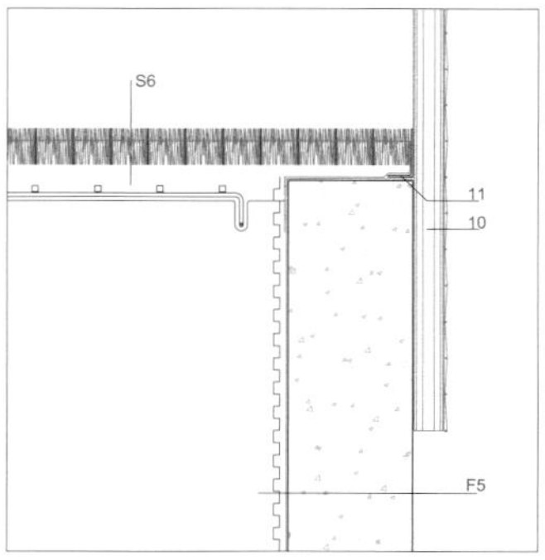

D. 25

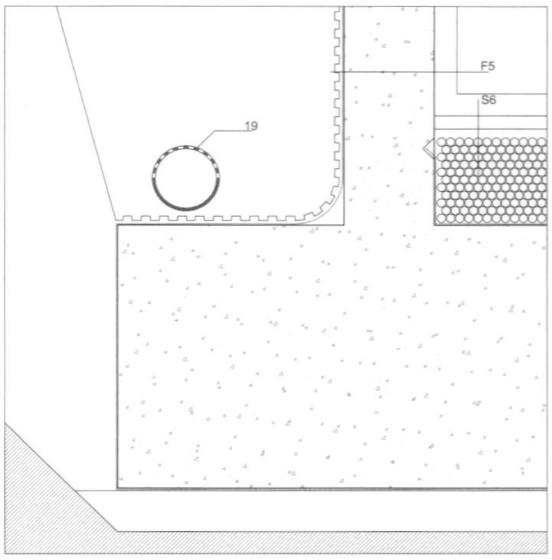

D. 26

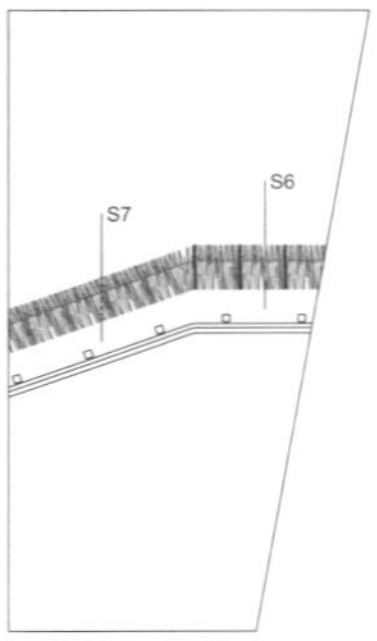

D. 27

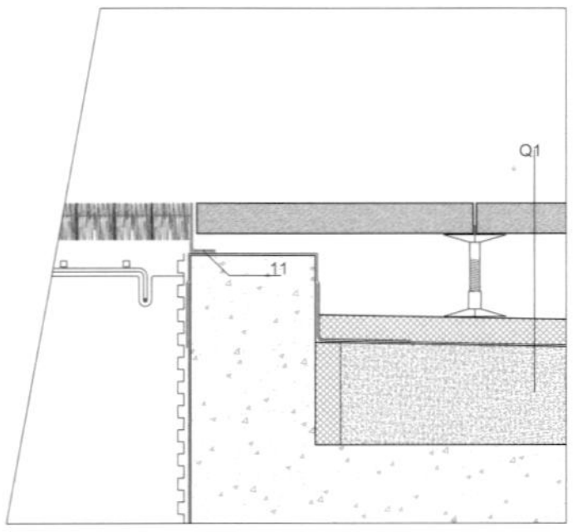

D. 28

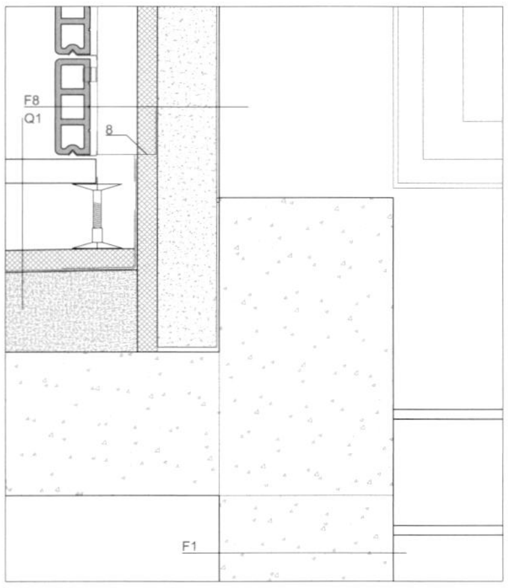

D. 29

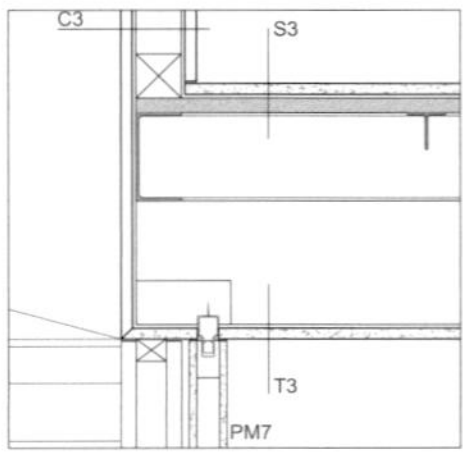

D. 30

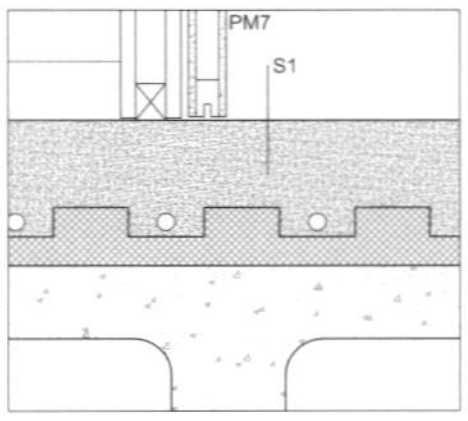

D. 31

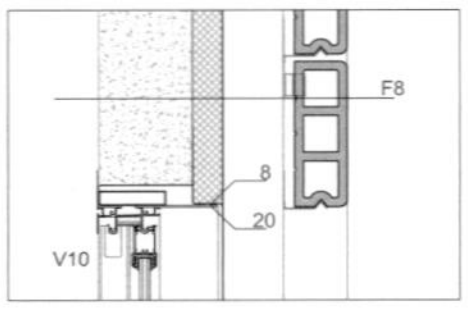

D. 32

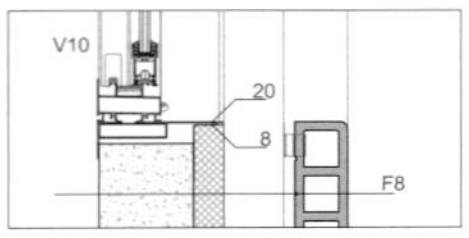

D. 33

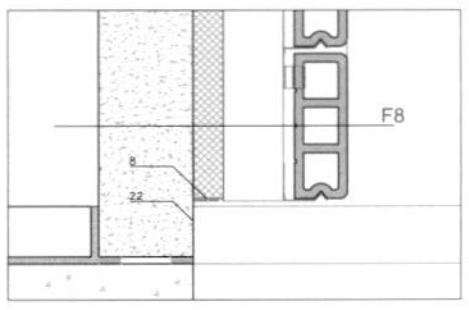

D. 34

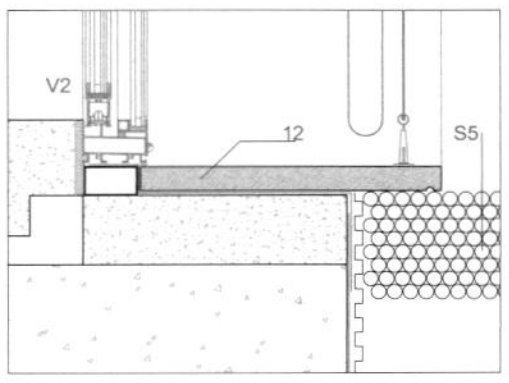

D. 35

- Screeded render coat 2 cm
- l.h.d. 7 cm.
- Thermal insulation of fiber glass panels
- Air chamber
- Concrete wall on exposed on outer face

f4.
- Smooth plastic paint
- Plastered 2 cm
- l.h.d. 7 cm.
- Thermal insulation of fiber glass panels
- Air chamber
- Reinforced concrete retaining wall
- Bitumen primer
- Draining membrane -Fondaline-

f5.
- Concrete wall on exposed on inner face
- Bitumen primer
- Draining membrane -Fondaline-

f6.
- Ceramic phonic panel – BMA – placed with vertical joint, supported on suspended floor
- Air chamber
- Reinforced concrete retaining wall
- Bitumen primer
- Draining membrane -Fondaline-

f7.
- Mosaic tile 2x2 cm.
- Reinforced shotcrete wall with exposed outer face

f8.
- Prefabricated concrete panel 12 cm with exposed inner face
- Projected polystyrene 4 cm.
- Ventilated air chamber 9 cm.
- Ceramic cladding -Bardeau- with stainless steel anchors over stainless steel batten profile #80.80.3

f9.
- Concrete structure, exposed on inner face
- Projected polystyrene 4 cm.
- Ventilated air chamber
- Ceramic cladding -Bardeau- with stainless steel anchors over stainless steel batten profile #80.80.3

f10.
- Security glazing with air chamber
- Ceramic cladding -Bardeau- with stainless steel anchors over stainless steel batten profile #80.80.3

f11.
- Ceramic cladding -Bardeau- with stainless steel anchors over stainless steel batten profile #80.80.3

INTERIOR FACADES

c1.
- Smooth plastic paint
- Plastered 2 cm
- l.h.d. 7 cm
- Plastered 2 cm
- Smooth plastic pain

c2.
- Stoneware tile 20x20
- Screeded rendercoat 2 cm
- l.h.d. 7 cm
- Plastered 2 cm
- Smooth plastic paint

c3.
- Structure of laminated steel tube
- Lined with tripli board 16 cm. lacquered finish in own color
- Flush doors on registers and passes

c4.
- Structure of laminated steel tube
- Lined multilaminate board 16 cm. finished with lacquered birch in own color
- Flush doors on registers and passes

CEILINGS

t1. Exposed concrete ceiling
t2. Plastered ceiling over concrete structure. Smooth plastic paint.
t3. Ceiling of tripli board 16 mm. adhered to metal structure. Lacquered with satin finish in own color
t4. Ceiling of corrugated galvanized steel sheet with concrete slab that makes up the ceiling of bulkhead for roof access

ROOF

q1.
- Formation of slopes. Cellular concrete
- Waterproofing sheet with cement mortar system of polymeric bitumen 4kg/m2
- Geotextile 135 kg/m2
- Thermal insulation of rigid panels of extruded polystyrene, density 32-35 kg/m2 thickness 3 cm.
- Floating floor, Compostalosa pieces 1606 de 60x40x5 cm. from 'Escofet' elevated on plots

q2.
- Formation of slopes. Cellular concrete
- Waterproofing sheet with cement mortar system of polymeric bitumen 4kg/m2
- Geotextile 135 kg/m2
- Thermal insulation of rigid panels of extruded polystyrene, density 32-35 kg/m2 thickness 3 cm.
- Floating floor, boards of iroco wood installed over batten with clamps and sufficient room for drainage and ventilation

q3.
- Formation of slopes. Cellular concrete
- Waterproofing sheet with cement mortar system of polymeric bitumen 4kg/m2
- Geotextile 135 kg/m2
- Thermal insulation of rigid panels of extruded polystyrene, density 32-35 kg/m2 thickness 3 cm.
- Floating floor, wood crossbeam sectioned in two halves, placed over batten with sufficient room for drainage and ventilation

q4.
- Collaborating galvanized steel sheet
-Reinforced concrete with slopes according to details
- Framework of pine batten 4x4 and infill of fiber glass insulation 4 cm.
- Lined with zinc sheet with plates of the total length of the roof, with lateral cogging

14

Fran Silvestre

HOUSE IN AYORA

AYORA, España

FRAN SILVESTRE

http://www.ecosistemaurbano.com/#

ARCHITECT	Fran Silvestre
	DATES
IMPLEMENTATION PROJECT	2003
BEGINNING OF WORKS	2004
WORK COMPLETION	2005

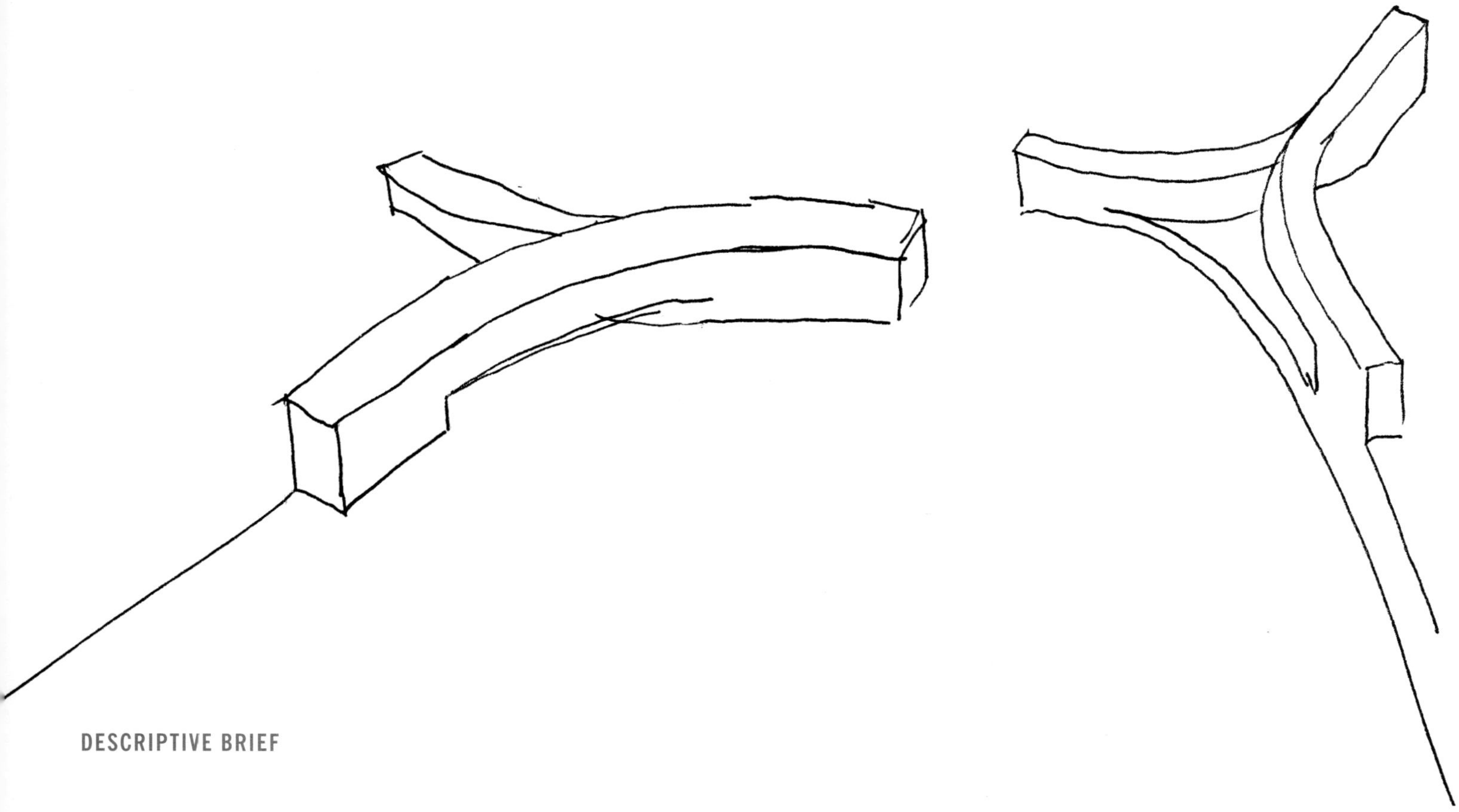

DESCRIPTIVE BRIEF

A natural landscape with a privileged view in all directions, in which a path, respectful and sufficient, takes us to a field with 167 olive trees. The project arises from the commitment between the will to be a part of the landscape and the desire of capturing it.

The proposal is located in the upper area of the field, providing a dynamic reading that transforms its proportions when one moves around it. The establishment sets bounds to three different fields, the portico-like access, the private atmosphere of the area facing the pine grove, and a belvedere overlooking the olive tree tops.

The relationship with the exterior is increased by maximizing the contact perimeter, what will facilitate that the wind decrease the summer heat. The geometry of the floorplan enhances exterior tangential views that along with the suction effects generated by the curvature disperse the limits of the inside of the house, which always seems to have something more to show us. At the same time, the human proportion of the spaces creates a feeling of privacy and protection.

In the upper level, each of the nighttime areas frames a different view of the landscape. The main room controls the only access. The distribution hall, facing south, works as a Trombe wall and invites us to a journey of which only the supposed end (or beginning) can be seen when arriving to the stair atrium, lit from the east.

In the lower plan, you can find the daytime areas; the stairs and the wet areas are attached to the wall, leaving free the maximum space possible, where the uses will be arranged according to appeals, seasons or circumstances...

The water tank and a chimney, supplied with the olive trees pruning waste, .demonstrate a will to be self-sufficient; on the other side the necessary parking makes patently clear the dependence with the exterior.

The construction is made with the repetition of elements in "sardinel", which permits materializing its geometry in a natural and simple manner, utilizing the same criteria in all of the construction elements, including the concrete structure, insulated from the exterior. That way all of the curvature is absorbed by the mortar between bricks, the space between the wooden vertical strips that make up the ventilated façade...wood that time will help to humbly imitate the colors of the surroundings.

"You can never learn less, you can only learn more"
Buckminster Fuller

1. Choosing the Site. Project and Development

1.1 Location

Latitude: 39º03'35"N
Longitude: 01º03'37"O
Altitude: 613 m

Situated at 600m above sea level, the region where this project is located is characterized by a continental climate. A rough and sometimes abrupt landscape, with multiple gullies and hills in which important extensions of pine tree forests still remain, configure the physiognomy of the landscape.

1.2 Urban Design and Site Improvement.

The edification is approached as a sculptural element of curved outlines high up on a hill, from where rural environment can be distinguished.

1.3 Project

It constitutes an interesting example of environmental planning in its project stage. At this point, the designer has resolved the layout and orientation of the spaces that form the house.

On the ground floor, the social space is resolved in a longitudinal strip along the North-South axis. With this, the main façade surface is oriented towards the East-West axis. Window apertures, placed from floor to ceiling, are positioned in such a way that the morning sunlight penetrates the living/dining room and study room. The afternoon sunlight filters through a large window in the west, bearing on a covered terrace and lights the kitchen and the living/dining room by reflection.

On that façade, internal control systems should be positioned in order to avoid excessive levels of radiation. An isolated space to the west is used as a parking area. It will function as a barrier against direct solar exposure, which is why it could be counterproductive in winter because it would block low angle incidence solar rays.

On the upper floor, there are three rooms aligned on the East-West axis. The master bedroom opens towards the West, whereas the other two open towards the North. The South façade is the one that receives the best sunlight, especially in the winter, and despite this it is nearly closed. The architect takes advantage of the best visuals of the West and North façades, facing the pine tree forests... but he turns his back on the South. The designer justifies this approach, since he will utilize the South façade as an energy capturing element.

2. Consumption of Energy and Resources

2.1 Consumption of Energy

The architect proposes to use the South façade to place a Trombe[1] wall, to capture energy to condition the bedroom area.

Although he neither yet has detailed the materials nor the construction method he will use to resolve the façade, this strategy has great potential and in someway helps demythologize the attitude of taking environmental criteria as simple recipes that should be followed literally. With this proposal the architect demonstrates that, though desirable, it is not imperative that all openings always face the area of most sunlight, and that if the best views are in a different position, the best lit facade can be given a different environmentally correct use.

1 The Trombe wall –called like this in honor of its designer, is the engineer Félix Trombe- consists of a wall, painted black to better absorb the solar radiation facing a window, such that the rays of light that hit the wall generate heat, which the glass prevents from escaping, and introduces itself into the house by way of by an opening above.

2.2 Consumption of Materials

Load-bearing concrete structure and brick façades with edge bond (sardinel). The window materials and possible Trombe wall are yet to be resolved.

3. Environmental Loads

3.1 Solid Waste

Despite their particular geometry, the regular width of the two curved prisms that form the project allows the use of floor slabs with pre-fabricated joists, thus reducing construction waste. As an alternative to concrete columns and beams poured on-site, a structure of pre-fabricated metal frames built in the workshop could be used.

4. Interior Environmental Quality

4.1 Ventilation

By curving the façades the surface of exposure to the wind is increased, which is greater at the top of the hill. This strategy of using shape as a support for indoor conditioning is complemented with the provision of openings on both sides of the facades to facilitate indoor air renovation.

4.2 Natural Lighting

Floor to ceiling apertures have been planned on all façades, except for the South one that is approached as a thermal accumulator. They must be complemented with interior control elements (curtains or shutters) in order to avoid high light and solar radiation levels in the interior of the house.

5. Control of Construction Systems

5.1 Functionality and Efficiency

Pure, non-eaved edges, which afford the project a sculptural quality, are justified in a dry environment. Ayora Valley, being enclosed by mountains that create a screen effect, is charactized by low rainfall[2].

6. Long-term Performance

6.1 Flexibility and Efficiency

The approach of closing the South facade and using it as a thermal accumulator is quite original, and despite its potential it has been relatively used in bioclimatic buildings in Spain[3].

7. Economical and Social Aspects

7.1 Social Aspects

Construction of single-family houses in Spain represented 75% of the total construction in 2005. This is why we highlight the didactic value of the development of bioclimatic projects at a domestic scale. The repetition of good practice in the design and construction of housing can have a very positive repercussion, by reducing the environment load generated by this activity.

8. The Architect's Eye

Formal plasticity and environmental care are combined in this proposal in project phase.

2 www.chj.es/cgi-bin/geomorfo.asp

3 Exceptions exist, like the Titus House (Solà Diaz-García Ferrer), Les Planes House, House in Terrassa y House in Vacarisses (Frutos Sanmartín)

4 www.ine.es/inebase/cgi/axi

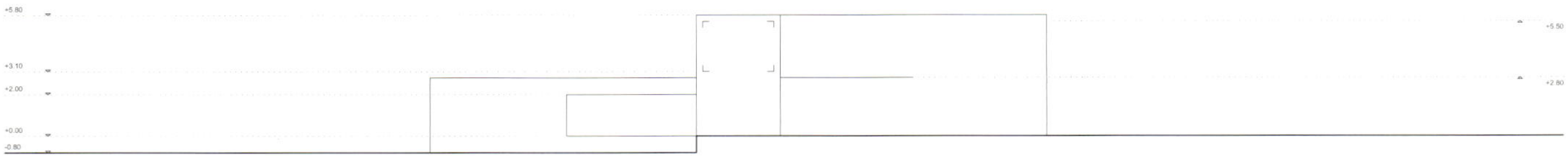

Elevation 4

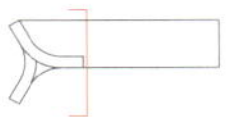

Elevation 3

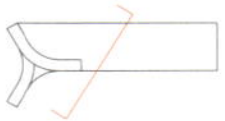

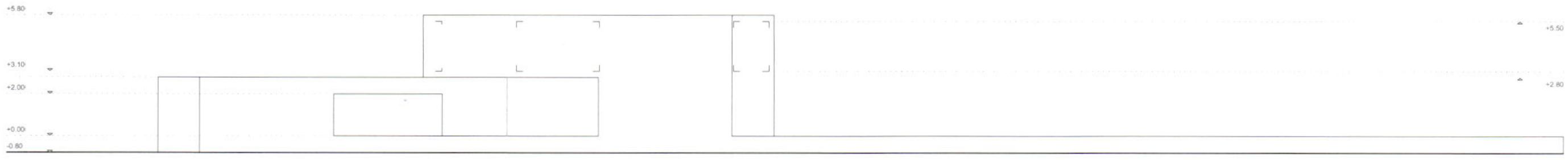

Elevation 2

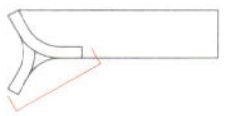

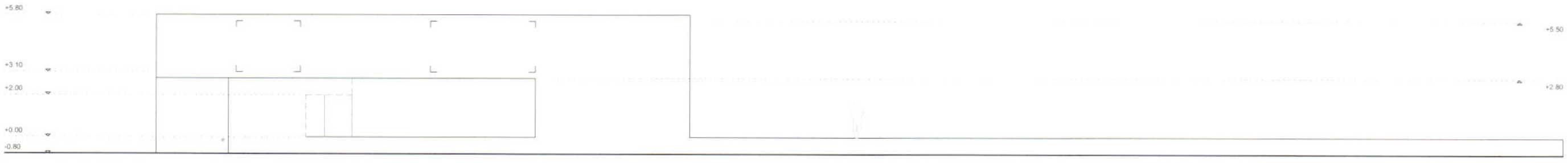

Elevation 1

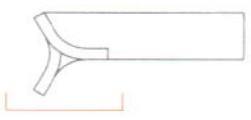

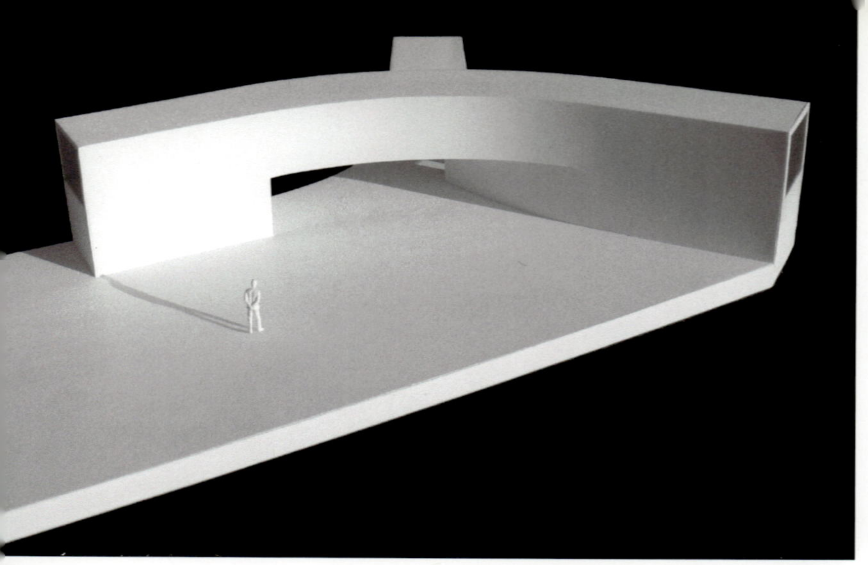

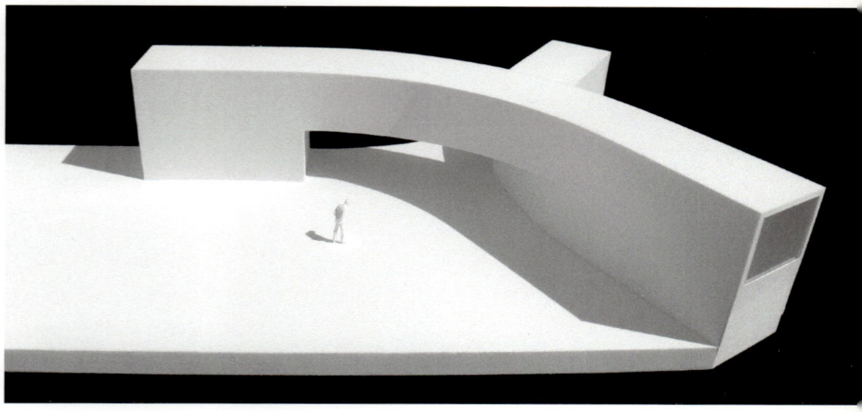

0 5 10m

1:400

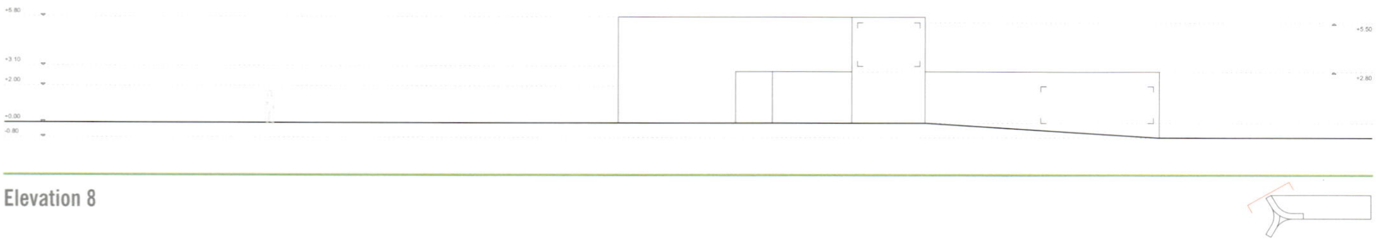

Elevation 8

Elevation 7

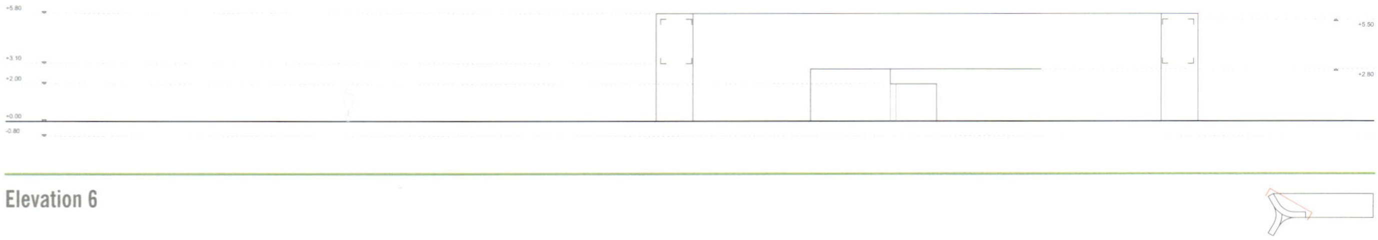

Elevation 6

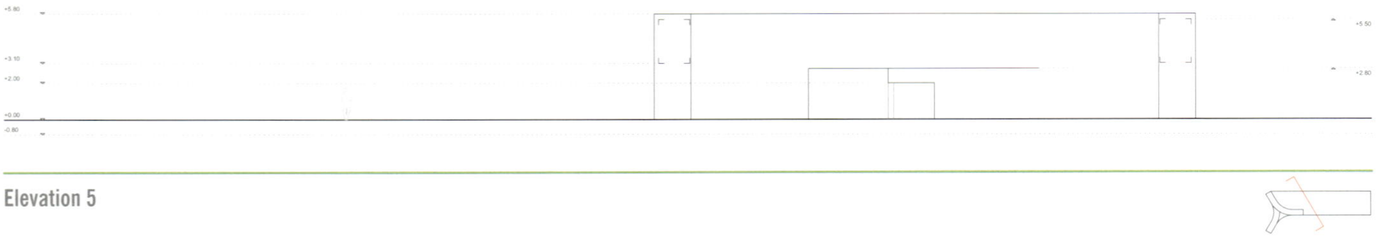

Elevation 5

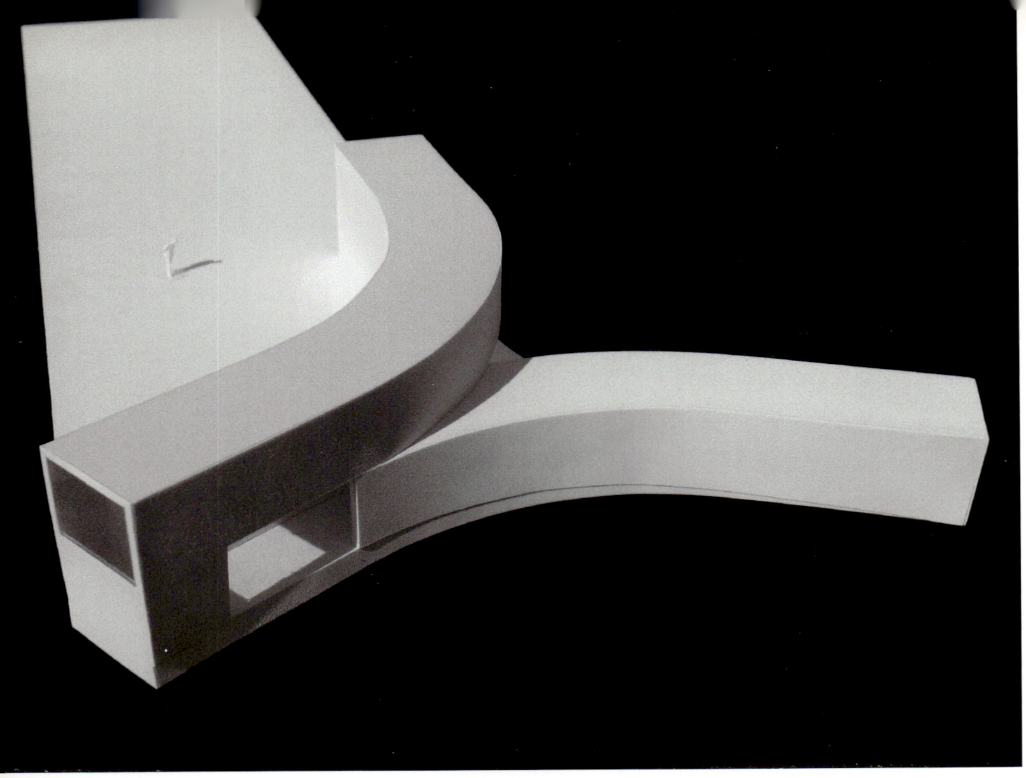

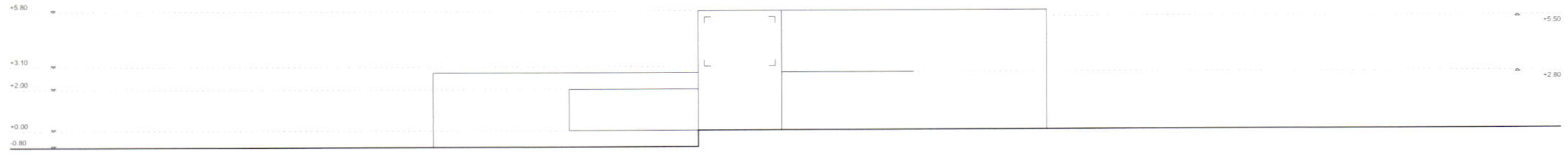

Elevation 12

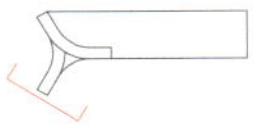

Elevation 11

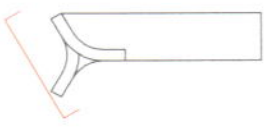

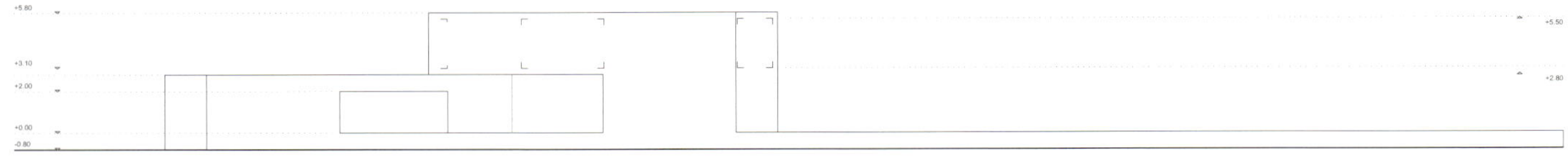

Elevation 10

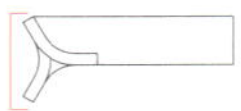

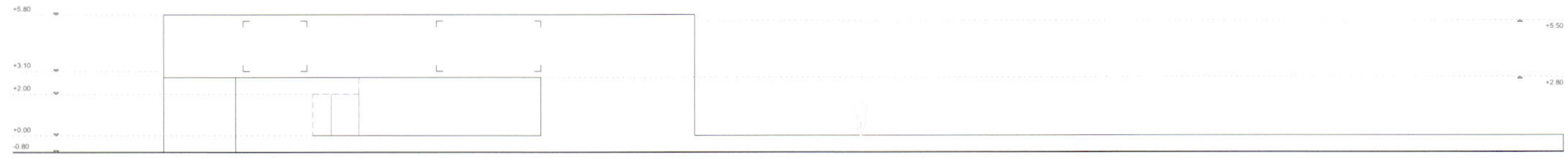

Elevation 9

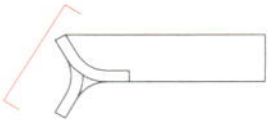

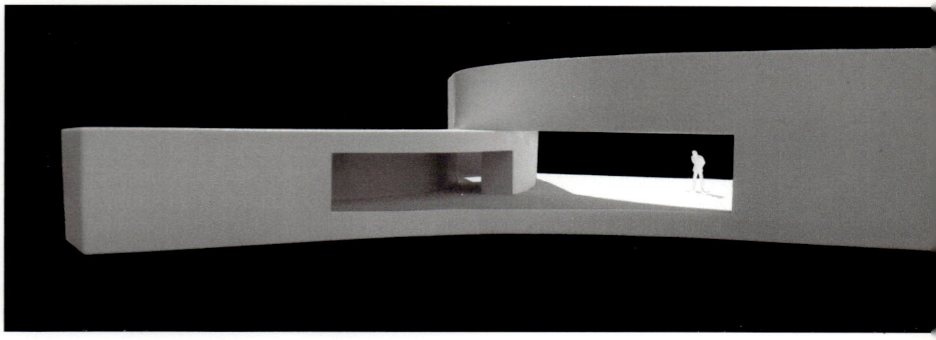

0 5 10m

1:400

Section 1

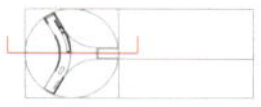

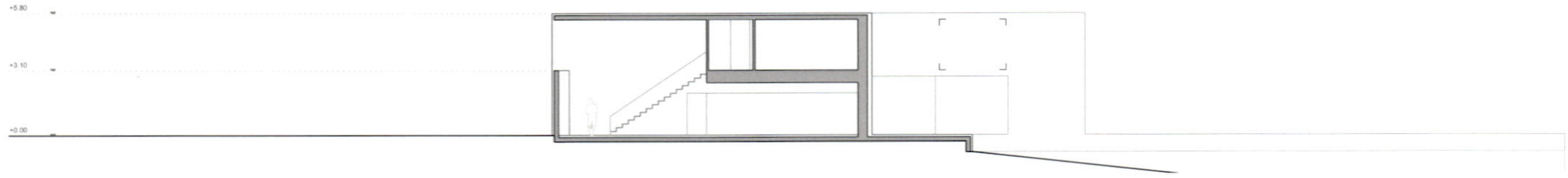

Section 2

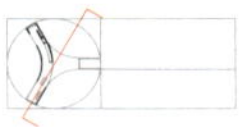

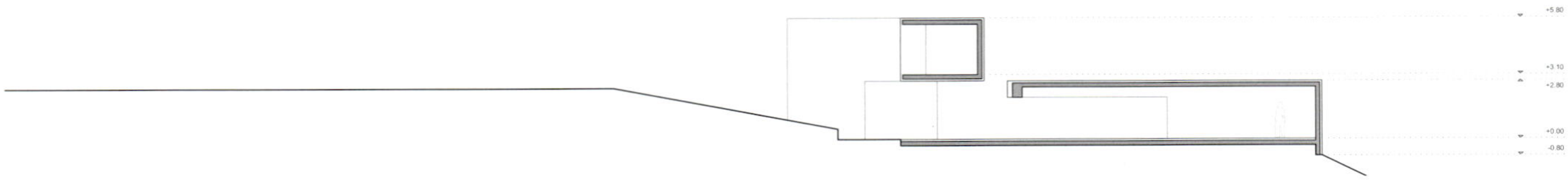

Section 3

HOUSE IN AYORA

Fran Silvestre

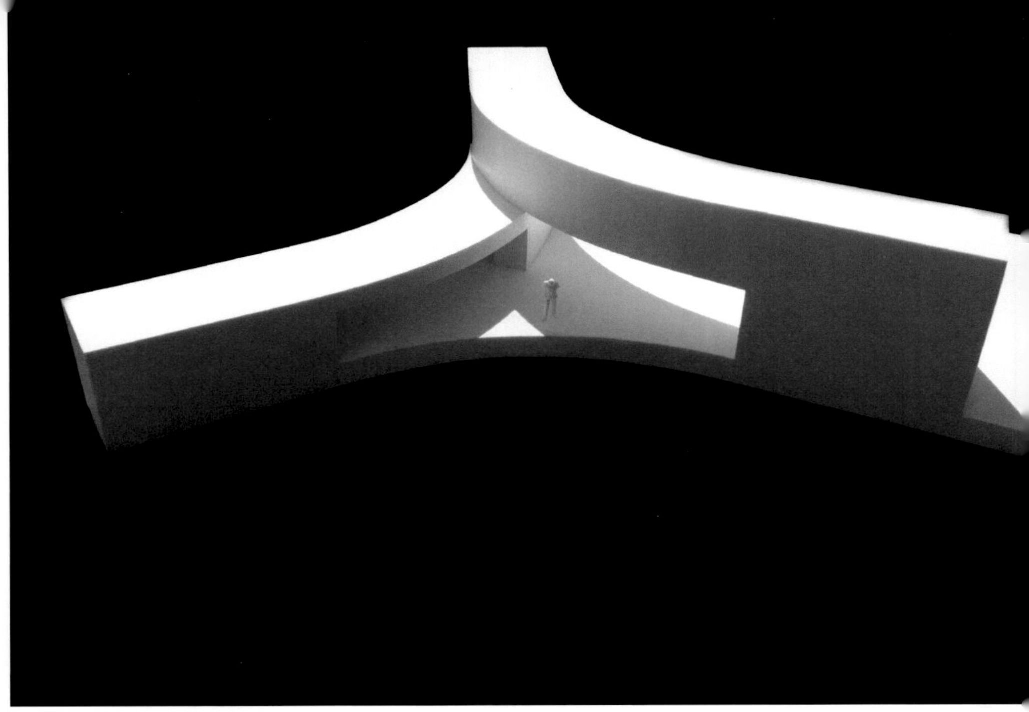

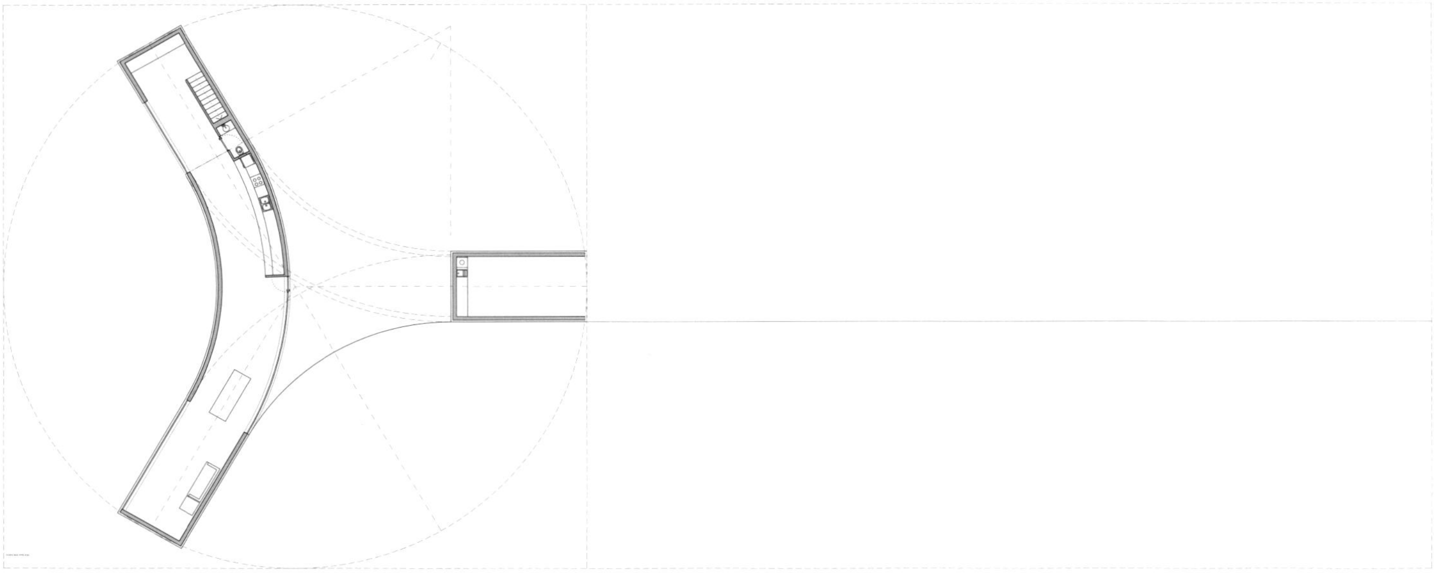

1st Floor Plan

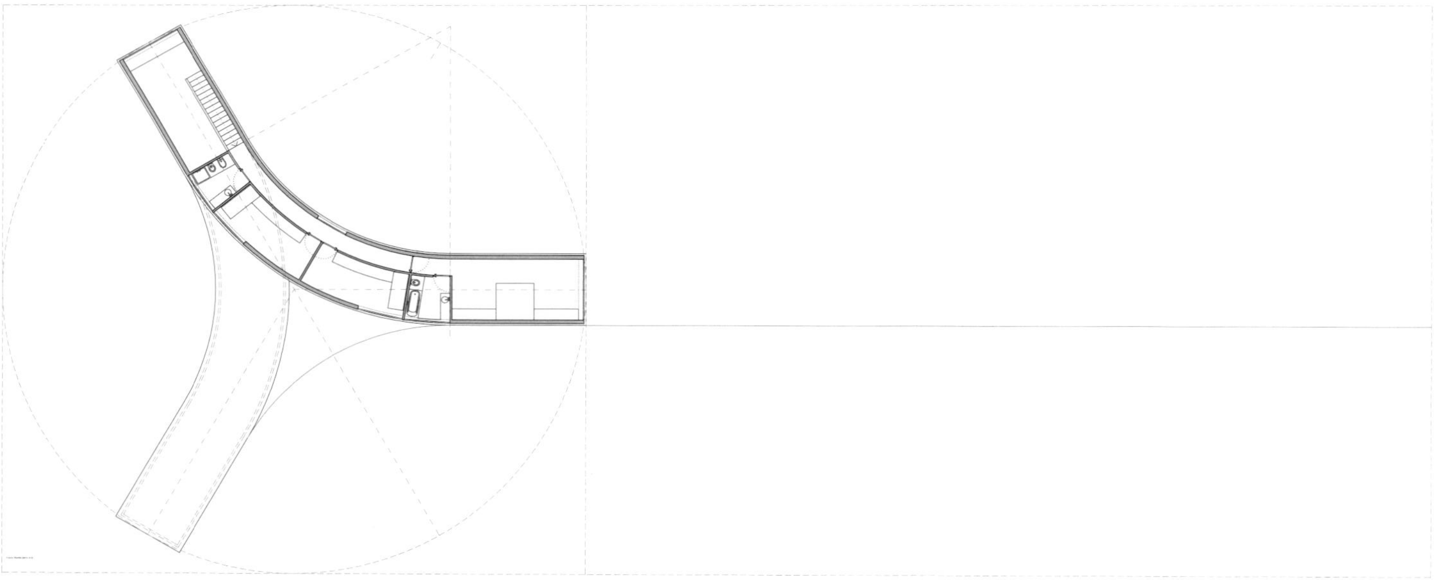

Ground Floor Plan

0 5 10m

1:400

1. Natural cedar wood shutter. guide type Klein
2. Wooden windows and doors
3. Cellular concrete for formation of slopes
4. Waterproofing
5. Extruded Polystyrene
6. Geotextile sheet
7. Gravel
8. Natural cedar wood amortissement
9. Metal amortissement with a 1% slope
10. Anchor for pipe 30x30x3
11. Concrete wall 15 cm
12. Bonding mortar. insulation Coteterm_m
13. Thermal insulation 4 cm type 3
14. Reinforced and pigmented mortar: layer coteterm-m, mesh Coteterm, layer Coteterm-m, finishing mortar
15. Anchor
16. Natural cedar wood. transventilated facade
17. Double wire mesh at the junction between materials
18. Bonding mortar
19. Wall of hollow brick 4 cm on edge
20. Rendercoated and smooth plaster finish 1 cm
21. Wood baseboard 5 cm
22. Dripedge profile 9011-2154
23. Wood flooring
24. Regularization
25. Radiant floor type Movinord
26. Selected earth
27. Reinforced concrete base slab
28. Floor finish type Marmorite
29. Gypsum board
30. Concrete Slab

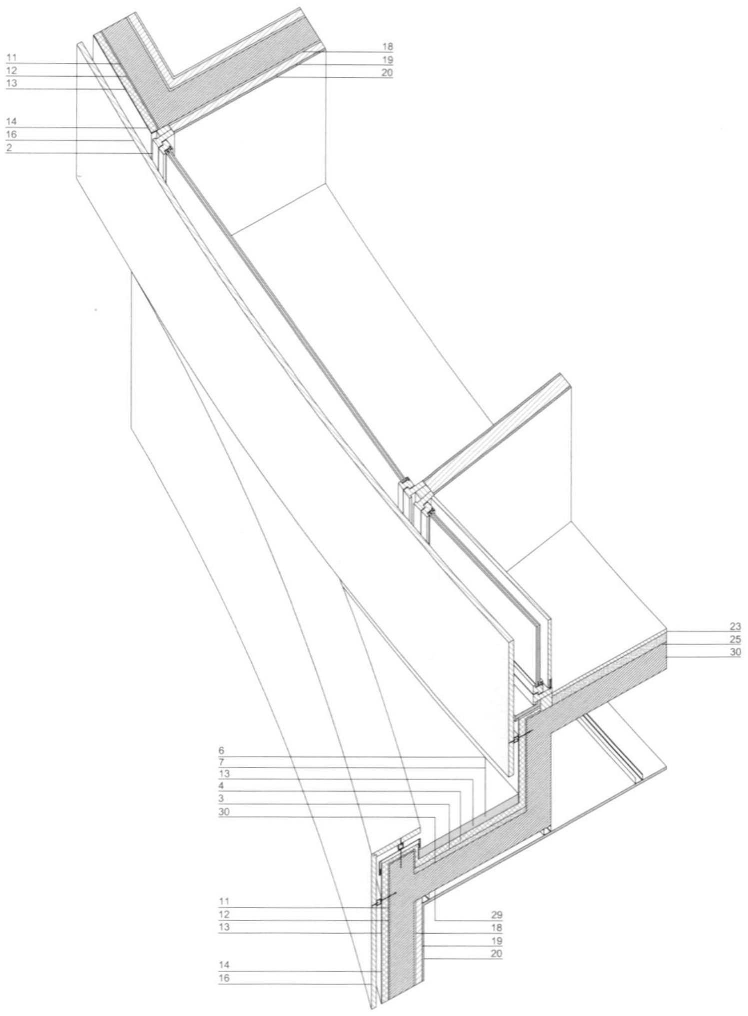

Façade Construction Detail

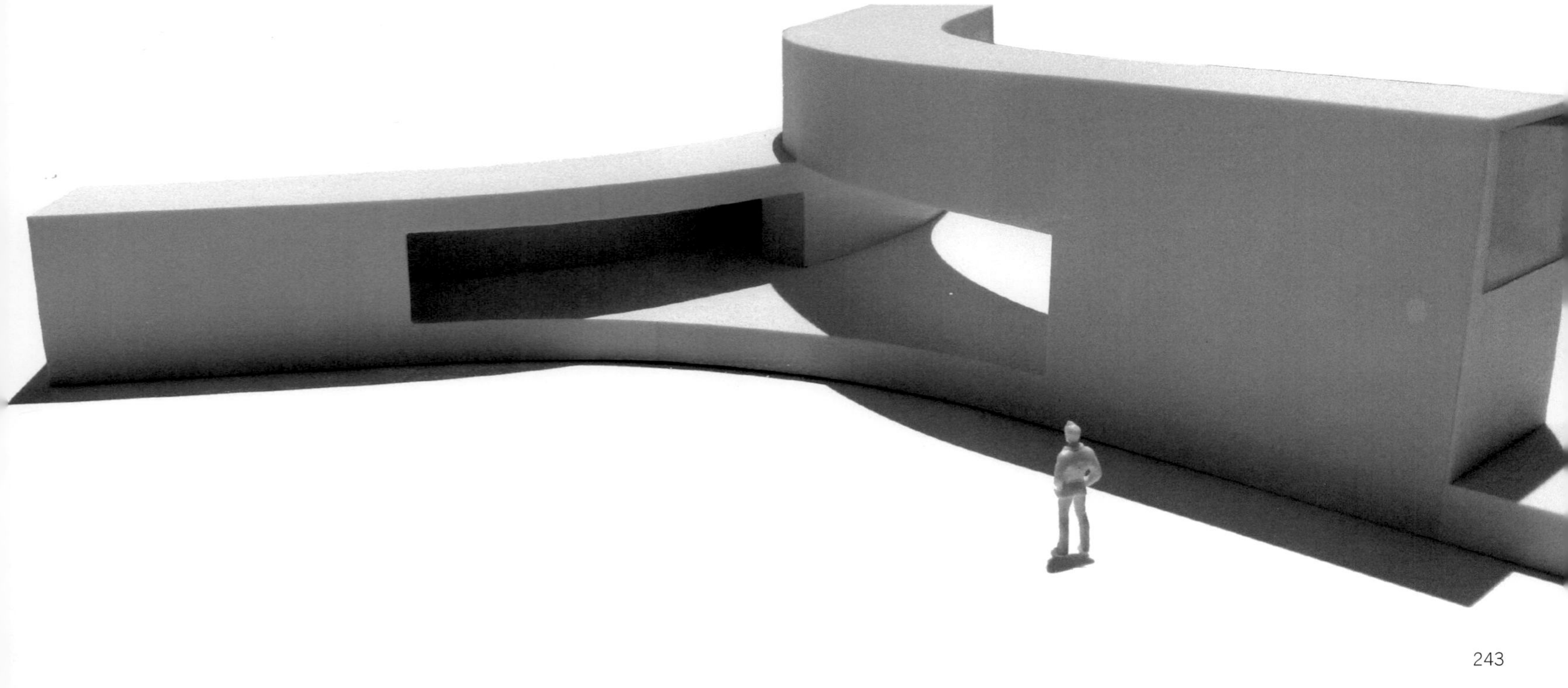

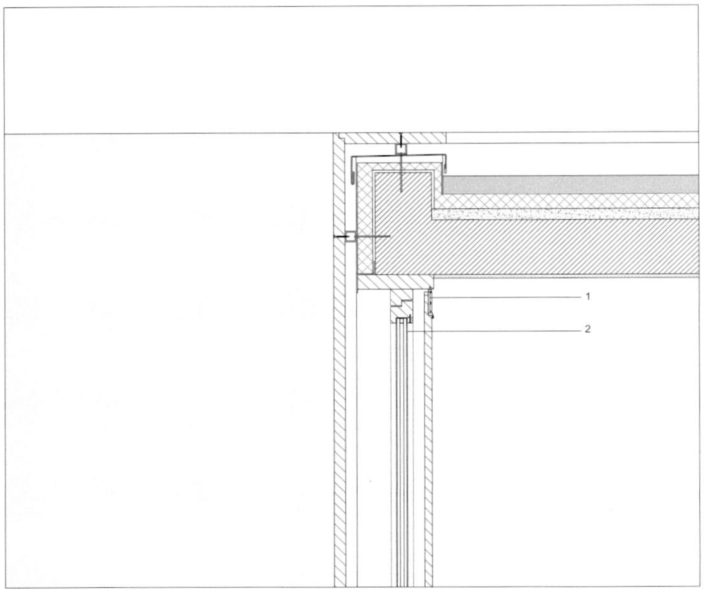

D. 1

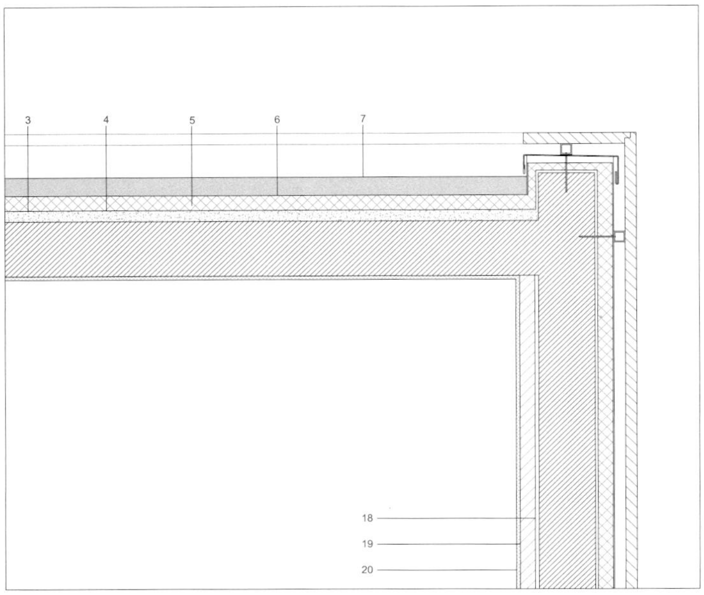

D.2

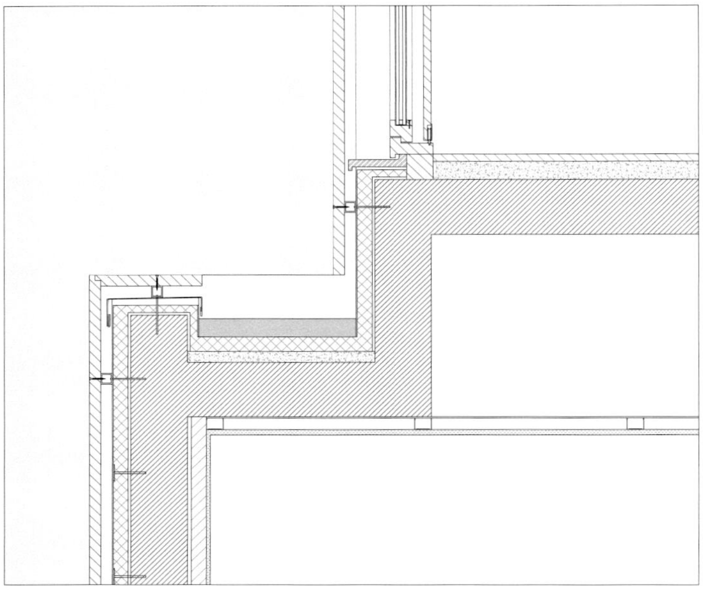

D. 3

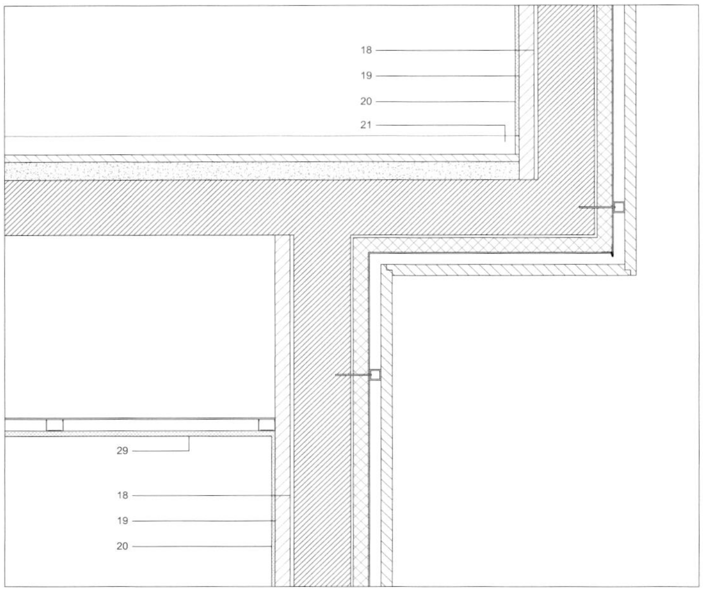

D. 4

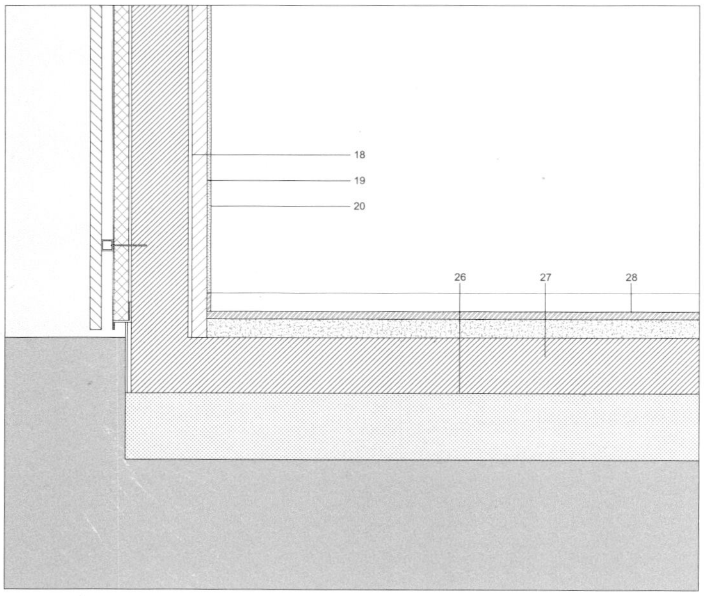

D. 5

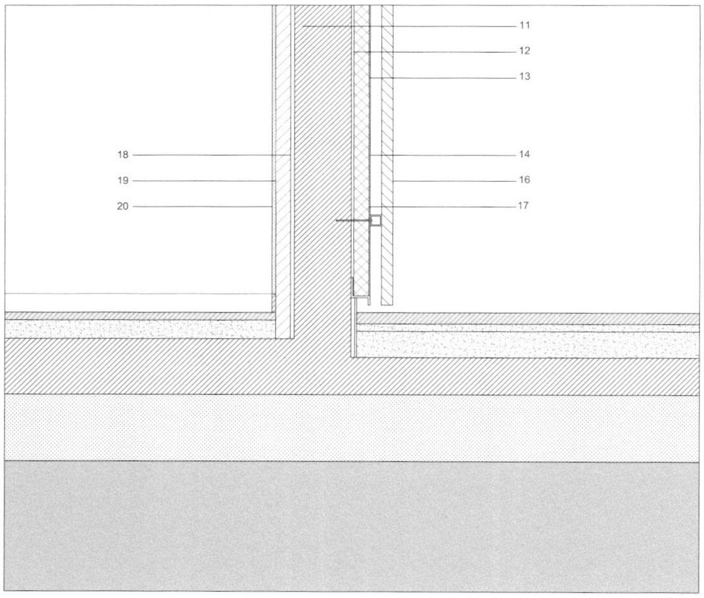

D. 6

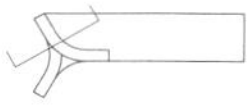

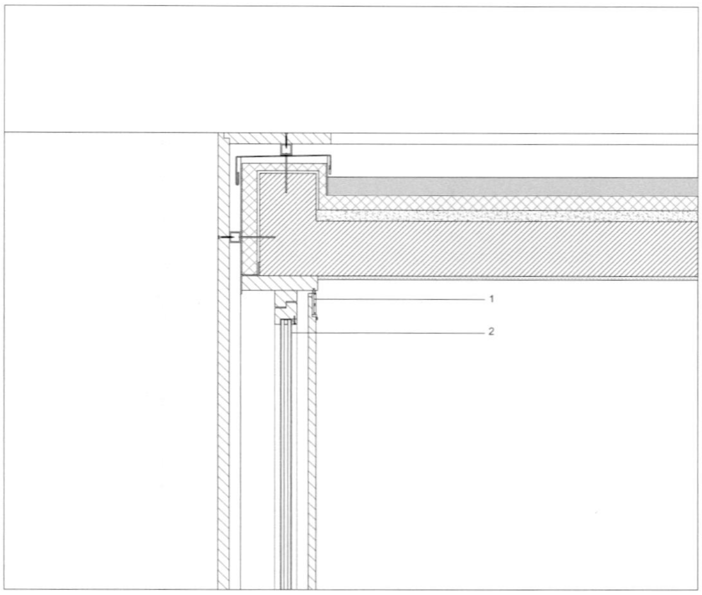

D. 7

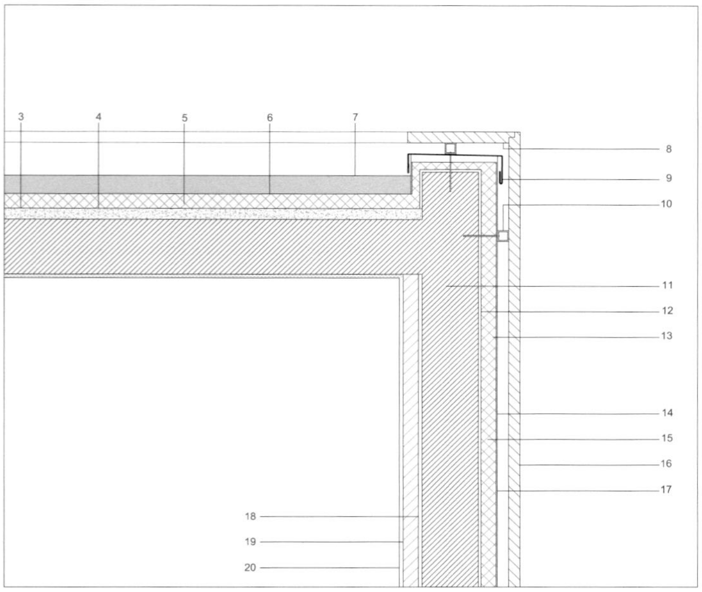

D. 8

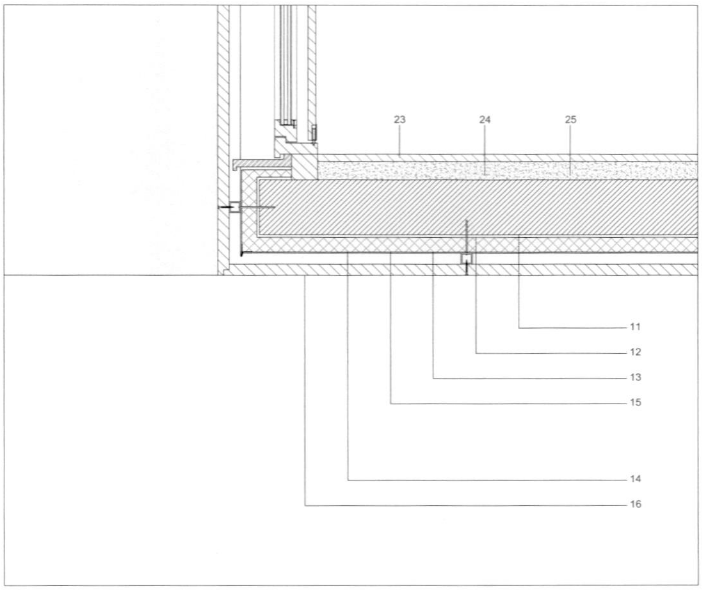

D. 9

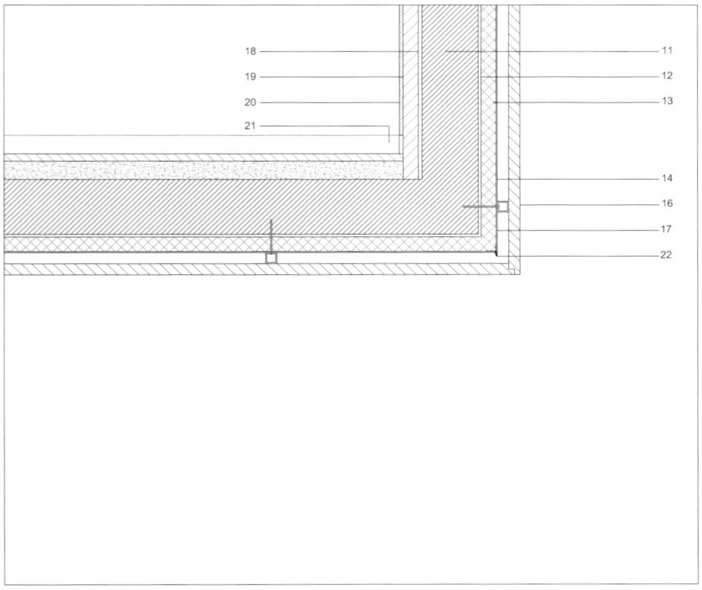

D. 10

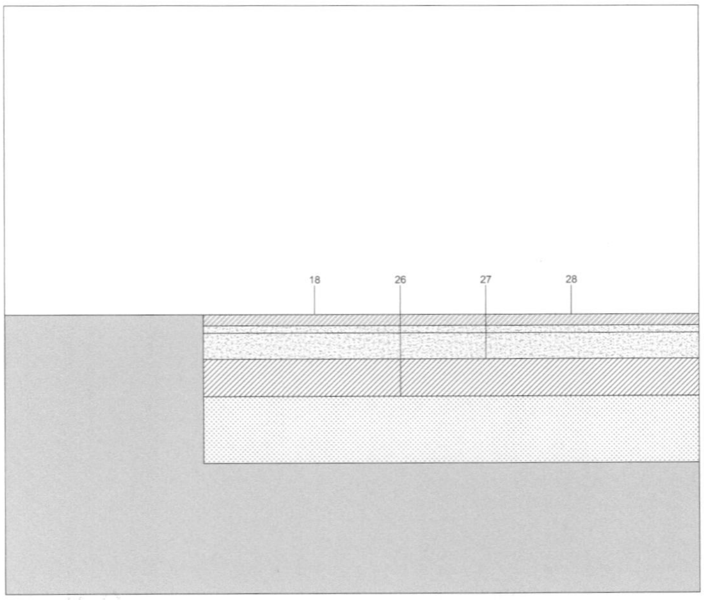

D. 11

0 10 30 50cm 1m

1:20

1. Natural cedar wood shutter. guide type Klein
2. Wooden windows and doors
3. Cellular concrete for formation of slopes
4. Waterproofing
5. Extruded Polystyrene
6. Geotextile sheet
7. Gravel
8. Natural cedar wood amortissement
9. Metal amortissement with a 1% slope
10. Anchor for pipe 30x30x3
11. Concrete wall 15 cm
12. Bonding mortar. insulation Coteterm_m
13. Thermal insulation 4 cm type 3
14. Reinforced and pigmented mortar: layer coteterm-m, mesh Coteterm, layer Coteterm-m, finishing mortar
15. Anchor
16. Natural cedar wood. transventilated facade
17. Double wire mesh at the junction between materials
18. Bonding mortar
19. Wall of hollow brick 4 cm on edge
20. Rendercoated and smooth plaster finish 1 cm
21. Wood baseboard 5 cm
22. Dripedge profile 9011-2154
23. Wood flooring
24. Regularization
25. Radiant floor type Movinord
26. Selected earth
27. Reinforced concrete base slab
28. Floor finish type Marmorite
29. Gypsum board
30. Concrete Slab

15

Norberto Beirak - Bibiana Ulanosky

ENVIRONMENTAL RESOURCES CENTRE

RIVAS VACIAMADRID, Madrid, España

NORBERTO BEIRAK
BIBIANA ULANOSKY

2b@byuarquitectos.com

ARCHITECTS	Norberto Beirak Bibiana Ulanosky
COLLABORATORS	Fernando Andrés Verónica Seldas
PROMOTER	Ayuntamiento Rivas Vaciamadrid Consejalía de Medio Ambiente
COTRACTOR	Abalos S.A. Grupo San José
PHOTOGRAPHY	Beirak & Ulanosky

	COLLABORATING COMPANIES
Heating	ROCA York S.A.
Installator Gas	CEVIGAS S.A.
Bathroom Fittings	ROCA S.A
Geotechnics	CONES S.A.
Lighting	LAMP S.A.
Exterior Panels	PRODEMA S.A.
Interior Partition Walls	PLADUR S.S.
U-glass Partitions	SAINT GOBAIN CRISTALERÍA S.A.
Air Extractor	SOLER & PALAU
Air Conditioning	POLITHERM S.A.

	DATES
IMPLEMENTATION PROJECT	Junio 2002
BEGINNING OF WORKS	Noviembre 2002
WORK COMPLETION	Junio 2005

DESCRIPTIVE BRIEF

The CHICO MENDES Environmental Resources Center has been developed by the Environmental Council of the City Council of Rivas-Vaciamadrid. It is an Educational and Exhibition center.

It is located in Cerro del Telégrafo, a natural space for education and leisure, and replaces the ruins of an old Gliding Flight School. That way, a location that has already been altered by construction is reused; the building design is adapted to the pre-existing platforms and a building is designed with a linear configuration, in cascade, and with a moderate transverse dimension, due to its location near a narrow and very sloped stream bed, reinterpreting the topography in architectural terms.

We opted to design a building with a double character. On the one hand, there is a traditional construction that adapts itself to the pre-existing platforms, redrawing the demolished building's floorplan with the new project. This construction is devoted to administrative, educational and services program; for the exterior panes of the enclosures, klinker ceramic bricks have been utilized, with a similar color to that of the nearby ground. On the other hand, downstream from the previous construction, the empty sites are occupied, with cascading volumes intended to house the exhibition halls and the greenhouse. The exterior panes of the enclosures are cellulose-fiber panels impregnated with thermohardened phenolic resins and a protected natural wood surface. In any case, it is a building that has accesses at different levels, corresponding to the natural ground level at each point, and it is integrated both physically and landscape-wise with the immediate and distant surroundings. The starting height for each volume has been placed on the lowest height level of each section in order to reduce the building's visual impact.

The exhibition halls form a sequence of spaces on independent platforms internally joined by ramps; they are lit from above and from the north to avoid direct sun over the displayed material. The jagged profile of the section features 15° inclined roof planes to the south, where integrated photovoltaic panels are installed. The building's section synthesizes, in this way, the varied programmatic requirements. A concrete base defines the platforms and becomes the transition between the natural terrain and the building itself.

At the lower height levels a greenhouse is designed, and on the outside the re-creation of an ecosystem at the pool's border is developed. The whole of the existing woodland is preserved.

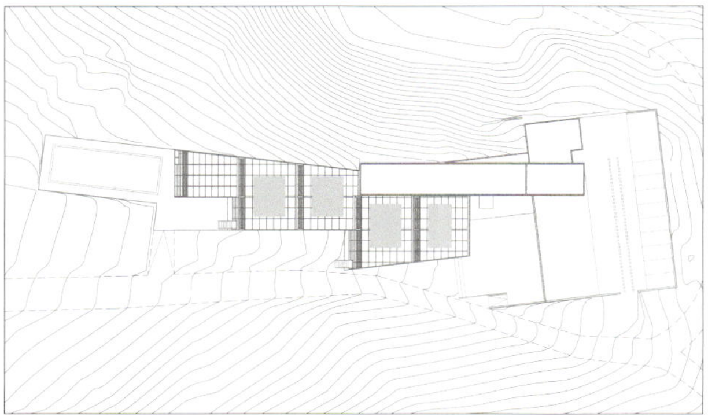

Site Pla

"In the long-term, the economy and the environment are the same thing. If something is unnatural it is uneconomical. This is nature's rule."
Mollie Beattie

ENVIRONMENTAL ANALYSIS

1. Choosing the Site. Project and Development

1.1 Location

Latitude: 40º22'00"N
Longitude: 03º31'28"O
Altitude: 646 m

It is a building devoted to house both educational and broadcasting activities related to the natural environment and its conservation, concentrated in the geographical area of the town of Rivas – Vaciamadrid, a recent and important urban development area near the city of Madrid. The center is located in Cerro del Telégrafo, natural leisure and sport area used by this and other nearby towns.

1.2 Urban Design and Site Improvement.

Rivas-Vaciamadrid´s City Council had not defined a precise location for the building in the Cerro area, this being one of the purposes of the commission. On one side of the Cerro we could find the old Gliding Flight School ruins, a degraded site but close to one of the exterior accesses. The choice of this location to build the Resource Center allowed the reuse of a topography already altered by edification, degraded in its landscape, stitching the topographical wound and maintaining at the same time the memory of the site, conserving the original platforms of the old building. The proposal is conceived from the addition of volumes, which keeps the linearity of the topography. On the other hand, special care was taken in keeping all of the existing trees.

1.3 Project

The proposal is implanted in a pre-existing construction. When reusing a former settlement, the impact on the natural environment is minimized. The building's functional program differentiates everyday and singular activities. All of this originated a building with a double character:

- On the one hand, a traditional construction adapted to platforms, in great measure tracing the floorplan of the demolished buildings, devoted to administrative, educational and services program
- On the other hand, the occupation of a vacant lot downstream from the former, devoted to exhibition rooms with a singular volume

The building is arranged in cascade, with accesses to different levels corresponding to the natural terrain levels, integrated physically and landscape-wise in both the immediate and distant environment. The configuration of the Center reflects the topography of the location, with a marked longitudinal slope in the North-South axis, manifested in its exterior volume and its moderate transversal dimension.

The longitudinal section of the building provides the backbone for the architectural proposal and it is an answer to the different factors considered:

- Apertures oriented to the North in the exhibition spaces to guarantee natural light without solar radiation, which would deteriorate the work displayed.
- A 15 degree rotation in the added volumes permits the incorporation of photovoltaic panels, oriented to the South, without secondary elements.

. Fragmentation of the exhibition rooms, permitting their access from the terrain's natural levels

2. Consumption of Energy and Resources

2.1 Consumption of Energy

This project has been provided with the necessary protection from excessive heat gain in summer, with the purpose to counteract it with refrigeration systems, above the heat gain in winter, which is cheaper to be counteracted through central heating. This fact, combined with the necessity to avoid direct sunlight in exhibition areas, urged a well insulated construction from exterior temperatures, exclusively lit from the North in exhibition areas.

In order to achieve adequate energy savings, the building has been insulated with double façade, double glazing and absorbent glass. Moreover, installations are controlled by electronic regulation systems with temperature sensors. On the other hand, photovoltaic panels are integrated into the roof and air conditioning systems work with water in radiant floors for heating, and cold floor and ceilings, above the drop ceiling, for refrigeration.

For artificial lighting, low consumption lamps are used; made by fluorescent tubes with minimal mercury content. Timers and presence sensors have been installed in bathrooms to activate lighting, with the purpose of saving energy.

2.2 Consumption of Water

For the irrigation and humidification of plants, a sprinkler fog-system[1] has been installed and a system of pipes with interlinear drip.

2.3 Consumption of Materials

The consumption of foundation materials has been eliminated, thanks to the strategy of reusing the existing concrete platforms.

The structure of the exhibition rooms and greenhouse was constructed of laminated steel frame. As far as the rest of the building is concerned, the structure is made of reinforced concrete columns and flat concrete beams.

The use of the same material on the façade planes and the roof, give the volumes a more emphatic image, as well as making the on-site assembly easier.

3 Environmental Loads

3.1 Emissions

The use of pre-fabricated and modular elements reduces material waste and thus, energy consumption generated during construction.

3.2 Solid Waste

Special attention has been paid to reutilization, construction and demolition. This means, when designing this building, construction systems and materials have been employed that permit:

. the reuse of pre-existing elements in the site
. quick assembly
. diminishing waste during the phases of material preparation and construction
. the choice of materials according to the necessary energy for their fabrication and building assembly
. minimization of wet construction.

3.3 Management of Water

PVC has not been used in the installation design, replacing it for polyethylene (PE) or polypropylene (PP). Thermal insulation has been provided in the main cold water network avoiding condensations, and standard insulation has been used in the hot water piping.

1 Fog system formed by micro-drops of water which allows reducing temperature, humidifying atmospheres, and controlling dust suspended in the air with low water and energy consumption.

4. Interior Environmental Quality.

4.1 Ventilation

Both natural air renovation by motorized mobile slats and complementary renovation forced by extractors has been provided; both systems triggered by air quality sensors placed in the upper areas of the volumes. Air infiltration is produced by pressure difference.

The adopted system for heating is low water temperature radiant flooring; for refrigeration cold water circuits through both ceiling and floor are used. This system refrigerates the space without air movement or acoustic discomfort and with a drastic reduction in energy consumption. Distribution circuits have been installed above the drop ceilings, in ventilated chambers to avoid condensation, and the floor circuits are used for heating.

Both systems are built with high density polyethylene pipes and are regulated by a switchboard which processes all of the information received from outside air temperature, water temperature, condensation sensors, and inside air temperature, determining at each instant what the caloric or refrigeration contribution to the building must be.

The heating system incorporates an anti-inertia system which permits the rapid heating of the radiant surface. An air condensation water freezer has been used, a low resonance version with ecological refrigerant.

4.2 Natural Lighting

The section defined for the exhibition spaces permits lighting the space from the upper areas of the façade oriented to the North (1/3 of the planes), with maximum light gain and zero solar interference. The remaining 2/3 of the Northern façades are interior, and the 4 exhibition platforms are interrelated through them. There are no apertures towards the West, East and South sides in the exhibition spaces. For security reasons, and being an isolated building in the middle of nature, no glazed plans have been designed in low areas of the exhibition spaces.

4.3 Acoustics

The volumes of the exhibition spaces and greenhouse have double-leaf lightweight façades with thermal and acoustic insulation. The exterior leaves are made of a high density, fire-proof panel composed of a cellulose fiber core impregnated with phenol, thermo-hardened resins and natural, treated wood surface, assembled by an exposed fastened system.

The thermal and acoustic insulation is formed by two 6cm flexible panels made of water-proof fiberglass agglomerate mixed with thermo-hardened resins in an air chamber. Low sound emission refrigerating machinery has also been used.

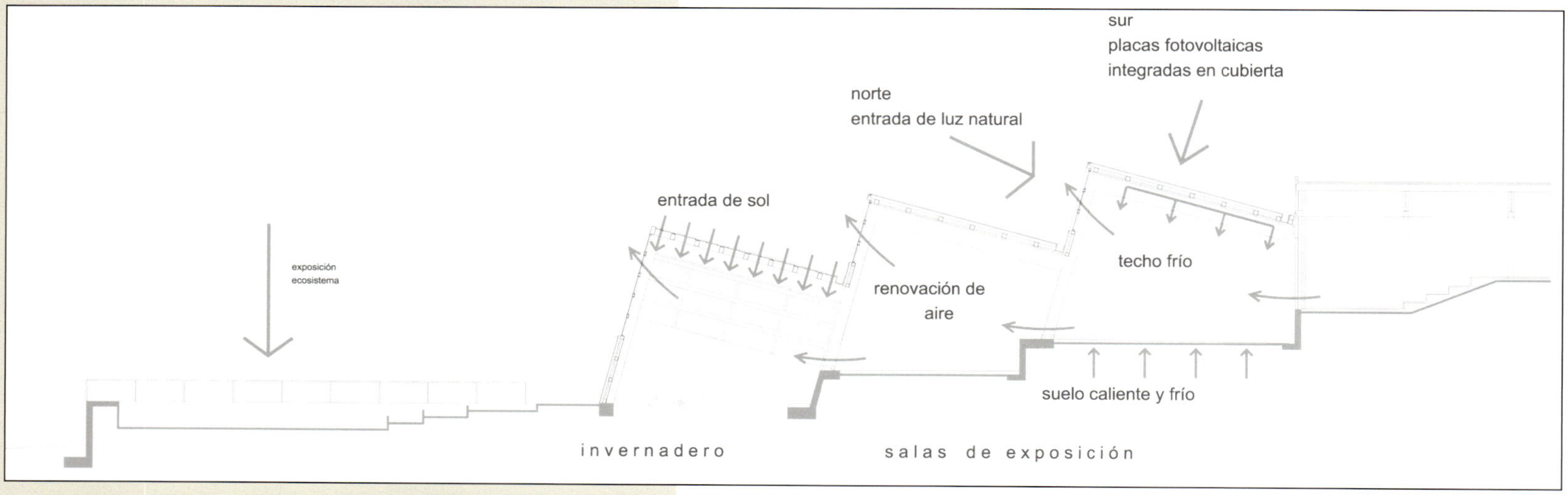

Natural Lighting Diagram

5. Control of Construction Systems

5.1 Functionality and Efficiency

The integration of the landscape has been considered in the construction of the building aiming for the minimum environmental impact. Ruins of a former building have been revalued, giving them a new function.

5.2 Control of Constructive Systems

The type of construction that has been designed, conceived more as an assembly rather than a construction, permits the dismantling and reuse of a very high percentage of the building's construction components.

6. Long –term Behavior

6.1 Flexibility and Adaptability

Conceived as a large container, this building allows giving an answer, over time, to the different requirements of the permanent or temporary exhibitions according to the necessities of its programs, to organize events with a large concentration of public in open spaces.

Special care has been taken to avoid architectural barriers. One can travel through the entire Center, using ramps of a uniform 8% slope.

6.2 Maintenance and Operative Performance

Lasting and standard materials have been used, which require a less maintenance and can be easily replaced.

Heating and cooling installations are regulated by environmental probes which control ambient temperature and humidity, reducing energy consumption and facilitating its management.

7. Economical and Social Aspects

7.1 Social Aspects

The Center for Environmental Resources "Chico Mendes" is a referential space in environmental matters for this town. Built with non-aggressive materials for the environment, it is named "Chico Mendes" in memory of the leading Brazilian ecologist who was killed for his commitment to the defense of the Amazon. It counts on a permanent exhibition, "Rivas-Vaciamadrid: on the way towards sustainability".

7.2 Economical Aspects

We should highlight the prevision and energy consumption in service by the developers and designers, with the intention of reducing the economic and environmental costs. The installation of photovoltaic units on all of the roofs of the exhibition spaces is foreseen in the near future; such that, once completed, the Center will produce as much energy as it consumes.

8. The Architect's Eye

He has concentrated on minimizing man's intervention in nature, thus the decision to position the building on an old settlement. The unique volume of the ensemble comes defined by the necessary orientation to incorporate sunlight and photovoltaic devices into the project.

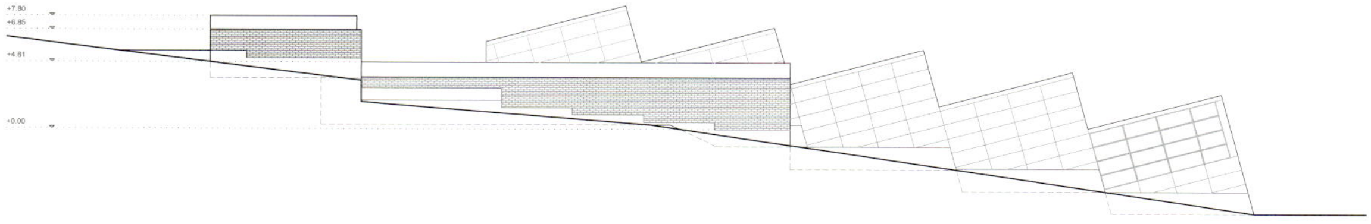

East Elevation

0 5 10m

1:600

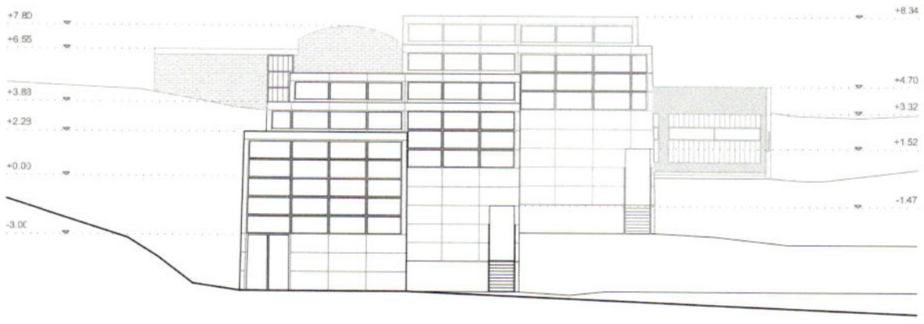

North Elevation

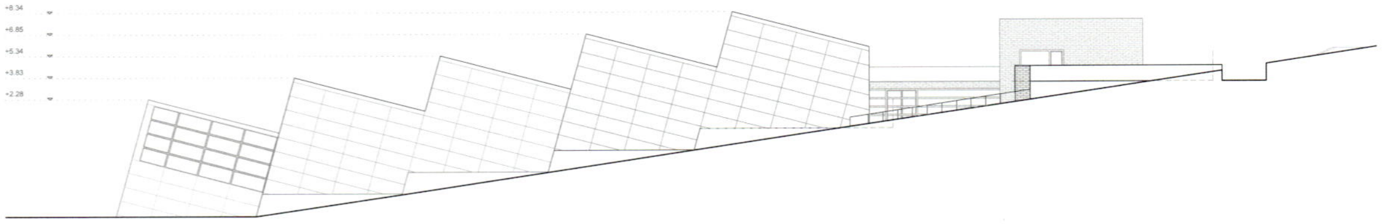

West Elevation

ENVIRONMENTAL RESOURCES CENTRE

Norberto Beirak - Bibiana Ulanosky

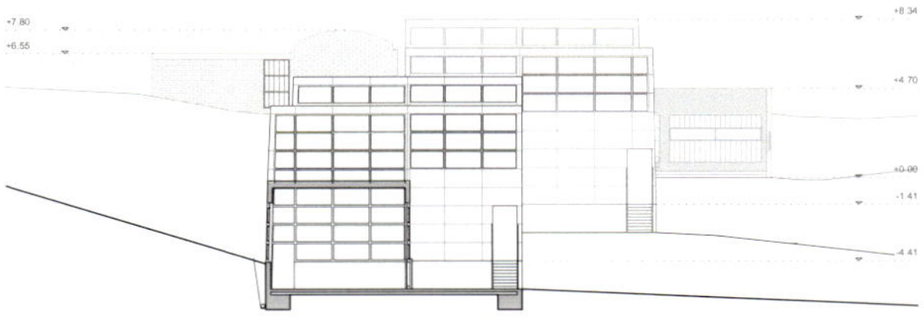

Section 1

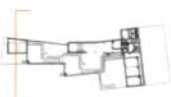

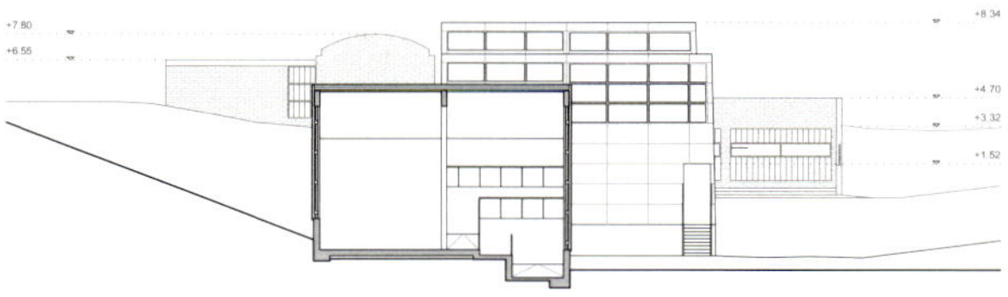

Section 2

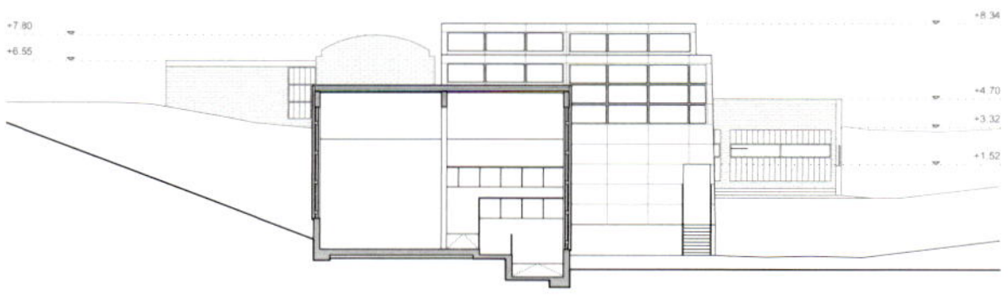

Section 3

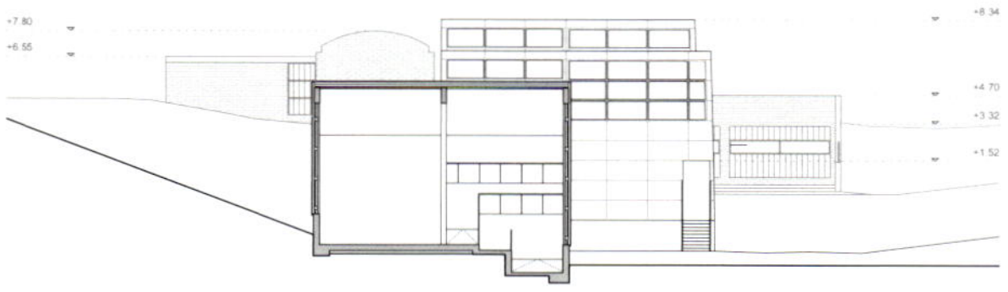

Section 4

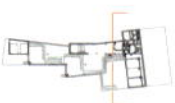

0 5 10m

1:600

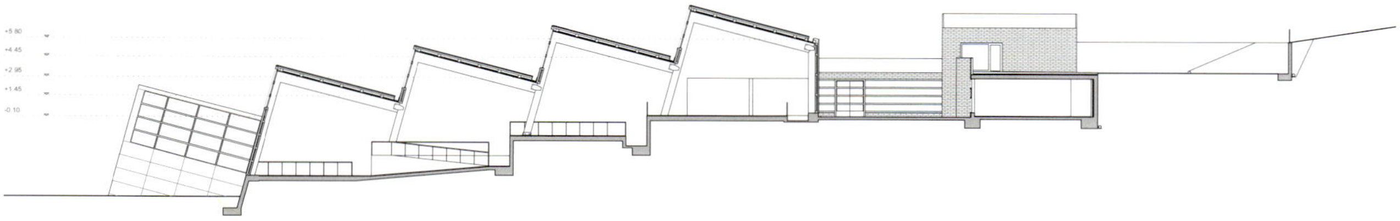

Section 5

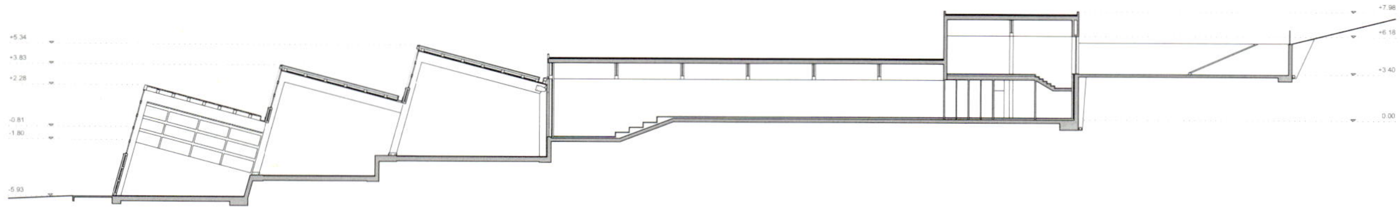

Section 6

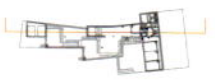

ENVIRONMENTAL RESOURCES CENTRE

Norberto Beirak - Bibiana Ulanosky

1. Terrace - balcony
2. Parking lot
3. Installations
4. Storage
5. Cafeteria
6. Bathrooms

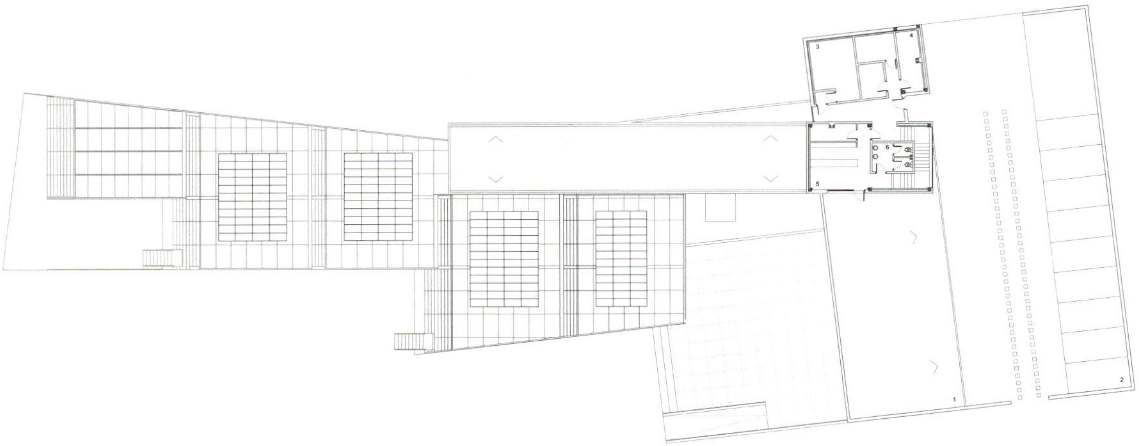

1st Floor Level

1. Greenhouse
2. Exhibition Hall
3. Projection Area
4. Access/information
5. Administration
6. Administration storage
7. Changing Rooms
8. Kitchen
9. Access to educational area
10. Classroom
11. Laboratory
12. Access plaza

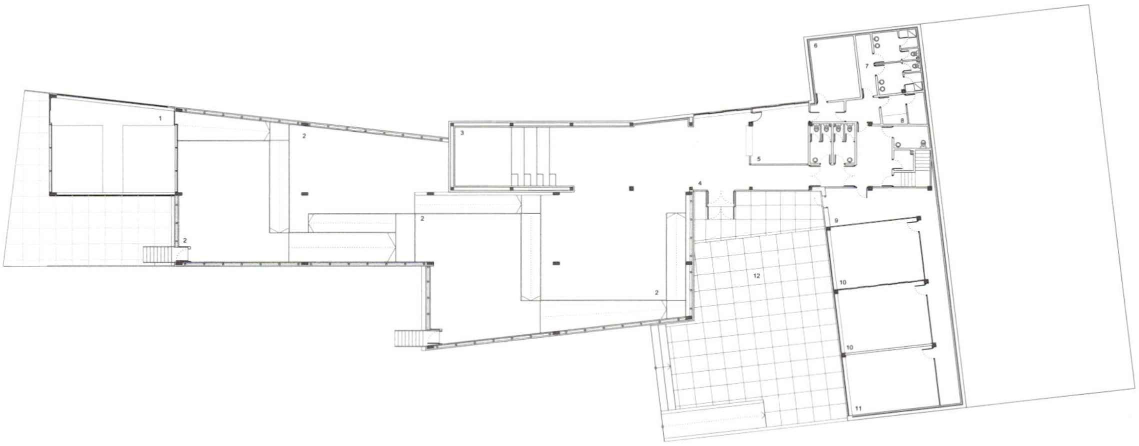

Ground Floor Level

0 5 10m

1:600

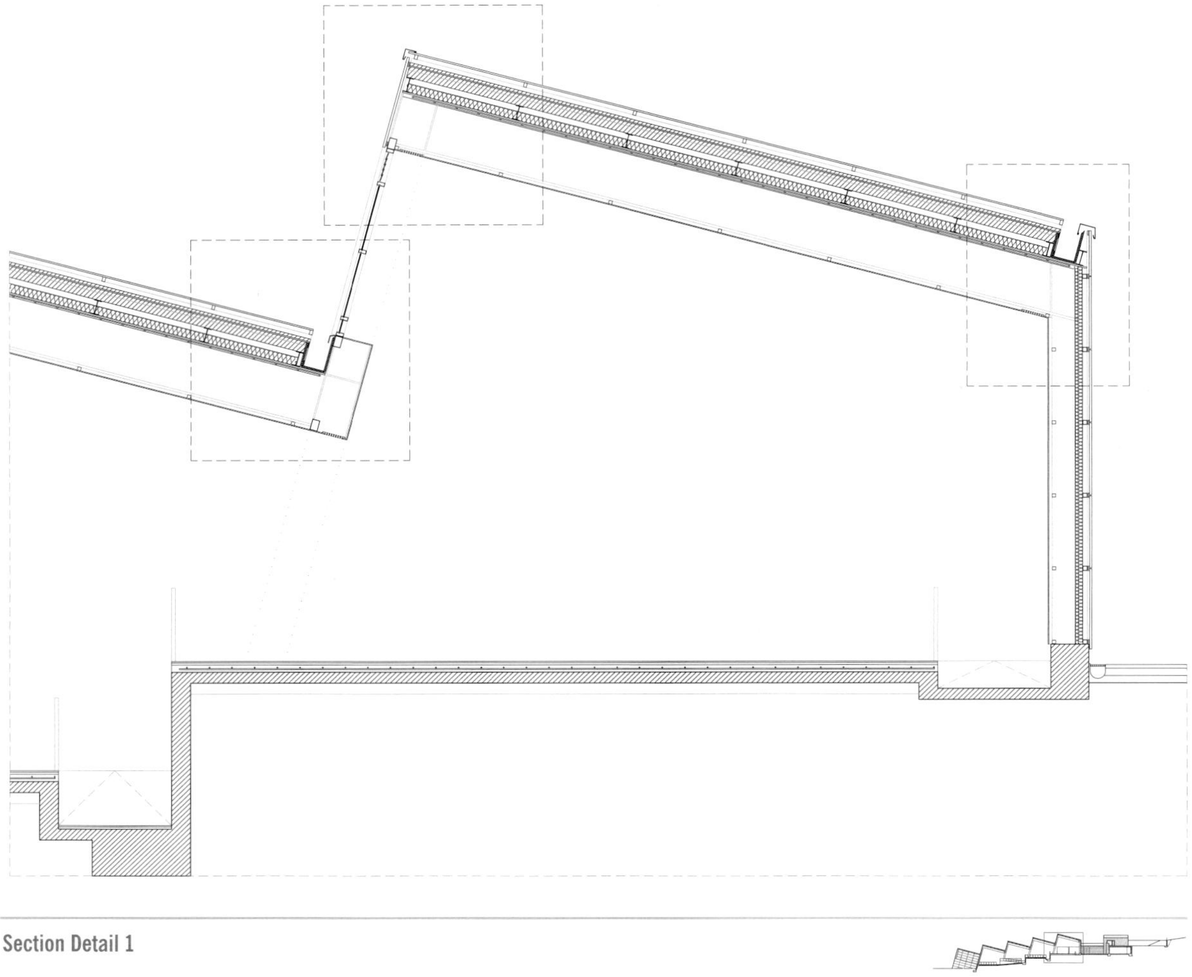

Section Detail 1

1:100

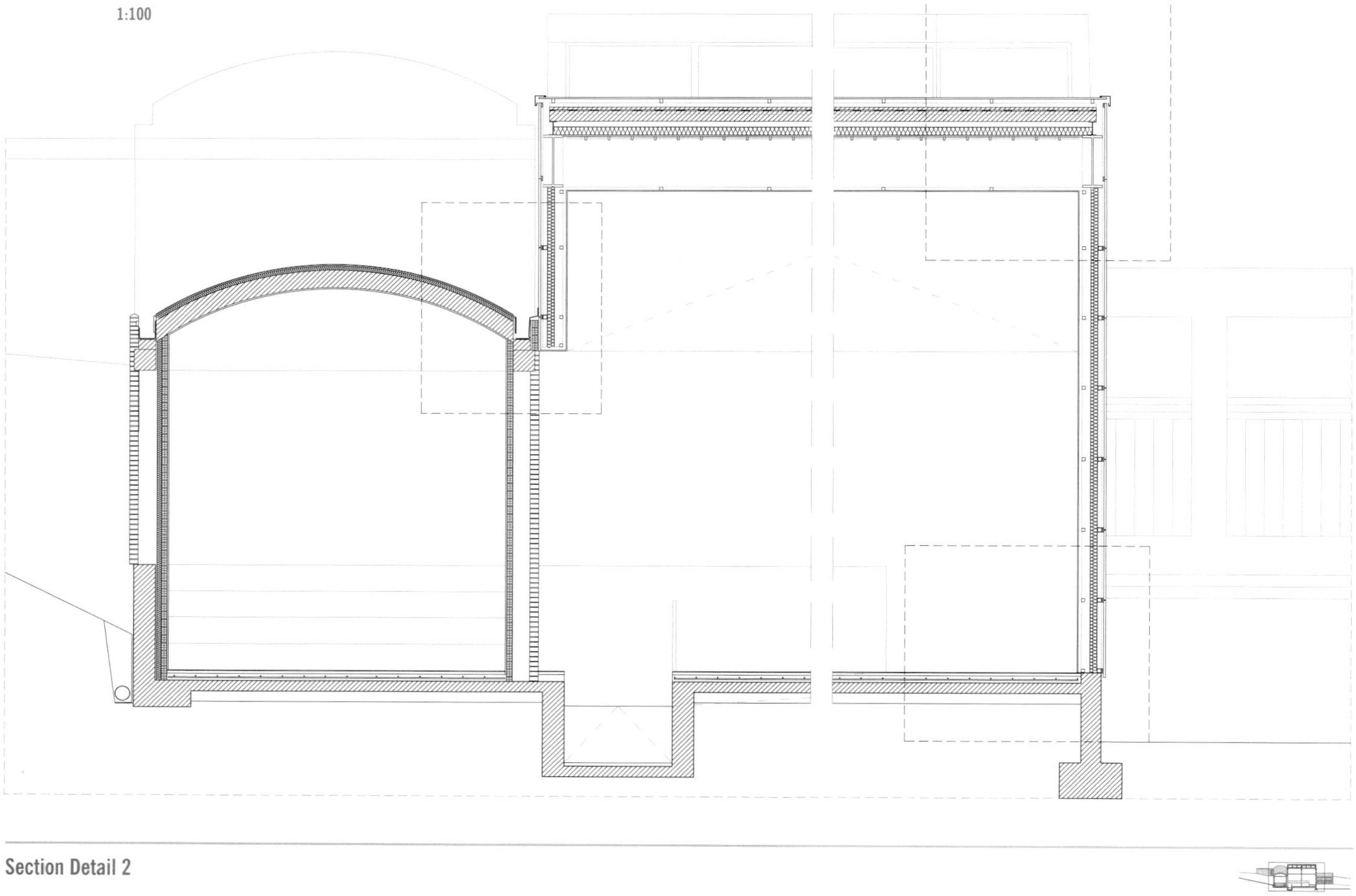

Section Detail 2

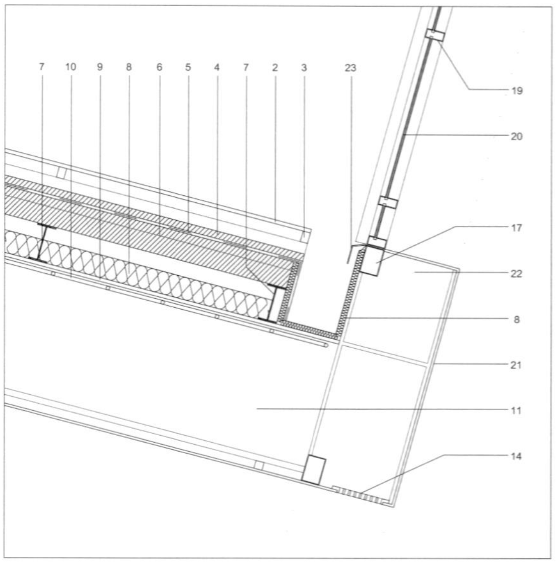

D. 1

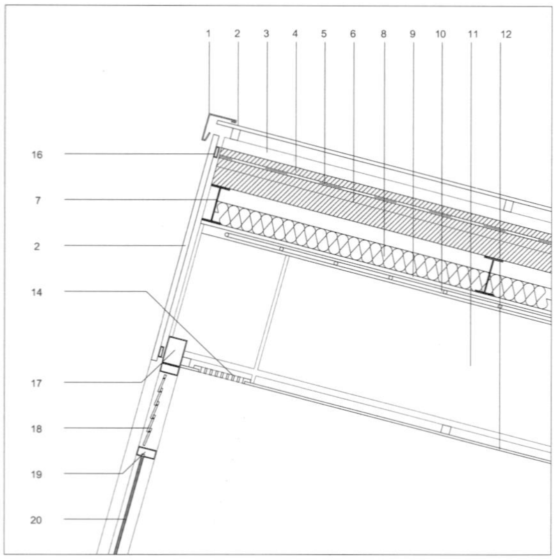

D. 2

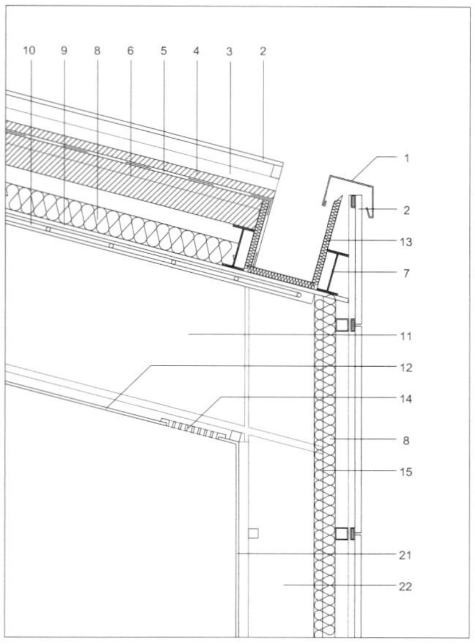

D. 3

1. Corrugated metal cap.
2. Cellulose fiber panel, finished in natural wood
3. Galvanized steel batten
4. Cement and sand mortar
5. Sand-covered asphalt waterproofing.
6. Floor slab of collaborating corrugated metal decking with concrete compression layer
7. Steel binding rafter, profile IPE 200.
8. Thermal insulation; 2 panels PV of 60mm
9. MDF panel for fastening of insulation
10. Cooling coil
11. Metal portico
12. Drop ceiling of plasterboard with vapor barrier
13. Corrugated metal gutter with thermal insulation
14. Ventilation grating
15. Vertical steel post
16. Galvanized steel batten
17. Horizontal metal post
18. Glass louvers for natural ventilation
19. Aluminum window framing.
20. Insulated glazing with security glass
21. Plasterboard panel with vapor barrier (130 mm)
22. Metal portico
23. Corrugated metal dripedge
24. Gravel15 cm.
25. Concrete base slab 15 cm
26. Radiant flooring
27. Cement and sand mortar
28. Polished terrazzo
29. Perforated metal sheet railing.
30. Corrugated metal gutter.
31. Cement mortar + sand.
32. Reinforced concrete driveband.
33. Klinker face brick.
34. Double building brick wall.
35. Rough coated and rendered in plaster and plastic paint
36. Floor slab of concrete joists and ceramic brick vault
37. Ceramic tile brick

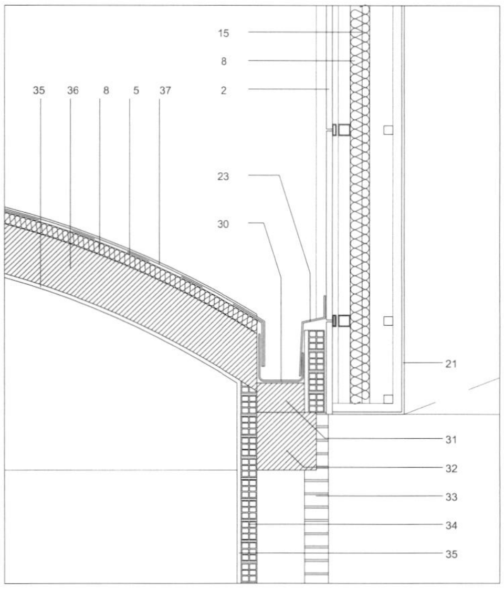

D. 4

1:40

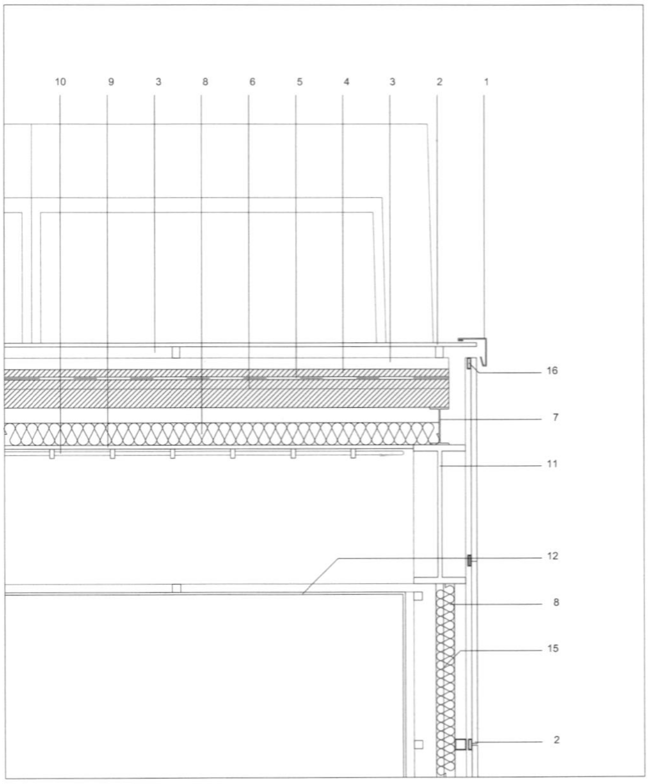

D. 5

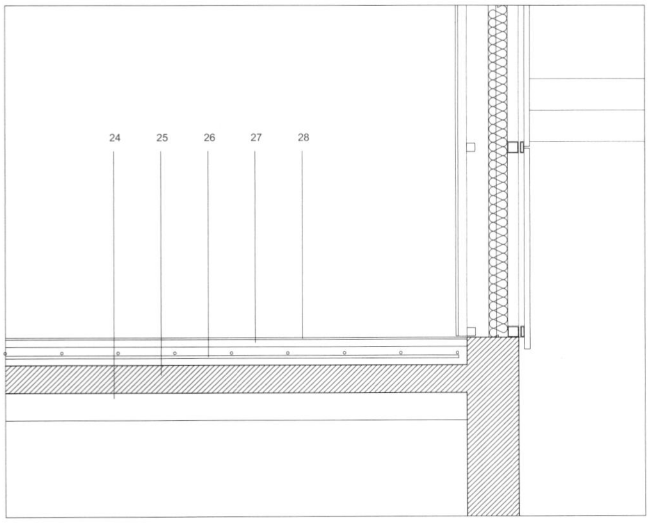

D. 6

16

Angel de Diego Rica

METROPOLI FUNDATION BUILDING

ALCOBENDAS, Madrid, España

ANGEL DE DIEGO RICA

http://www.fundacion-metropoli.org/

COLLABORATORS	Blanca Diez Diez, Arquitecto Vicente Olmedilla Ramos, Arquitecto
OWNERSHIP	FUNDACION METROPOLI
CONTRACTOR	AVALOS (Grupo Constructora San José)
PHOTOGRAPHY	Carlos Lozano

	COLLABORATING COMPANIES
Bioclimatic advising	MIYABI LAAB (Laboratorio Avanzado de Arquitectura Bioclimático de la Fundación Metrópoli)
Installators	ACCIONA ENERGIA(Aesol)
Solar Panels	VIESSMANN
Photovoltáic Paneles	SAINT- GOBAIN
UTC + Gas boiler	VIESSMANN
Heat Pump	THERMAX
Refrigeration Device	BALTIMORE
Heated Floor	UPONOR
Domotic Control	SIEMENS
Natural-Stone Façade	NATURPIEDRA

	DATES
IMPLEMENTATION PROJECT	2002
BEGINNING OF WORKS	2003
WORK COMPLETION	2005

16 Angel de Diego Rica , Arquitecto

METROPOLI FUNDATION BUILDING
ALCOBENDAS, Madrid

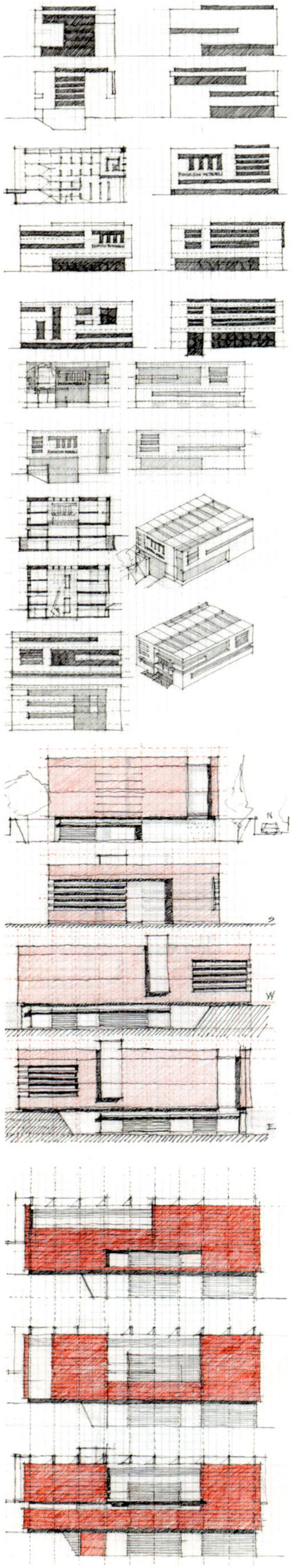

DESCRIPTIVE BRIEF

The headquarters of the Fundación Metrópoli in Madrid, with an experimental design, attempts to combine two basic criteria: the creation of a space for innovation and creativity where architecture and bio-climatic commitment play a leading role.

The design of the ECOBOX building is approached with architectural criteria, bio-climatic installations and construction systems that foster energy savings and efficiency.

The aim was to design an experimental building that would clearly favor innovation and sensitivity towards sustainable energy, always paying heed to sound construction guidelines.

The building has three levels with large diaphanous spaces around an atrium or central street of two and three floors high that link together the parts of the program.

At the access floor from the street, or level 1, there are workshops devoted to urban research and idea incubators for urban development. On level 0, with direct access from the plot, the space is unitary and is devoted to the concept of art and territory. Lastly, level 2 houses the more private and smaller spaces also devoted to research.

Beneath level 0, a huge energy storage of gravels significantly improves the thermal performance of the building. Finally, on level 3 are the bio-climatic installations and energy sensors, visible and accessible from a mineral roof, which also act as storage for energy.

A solid base of exposed concrete walls connects the stone, steel and glass box of the ECOBOX to the ground, supporting itself on a layer of gravel that acts as a huge energy storage for the building. Well insulated and weatherproofed, this stony mass significantly improves the thermal conditions of the interior spaces, acting as an energy and geothermal exchange that provides, through controlled ventilation, natural heating or cooling.

From this base emerges an exposed modular steel structure that sustains several prefabricated concrete floor slabs with a grand atrium or central opening in its intermediate space that, like an indoor street, crosses through the entire length of the building.

From this module of 3.20 meters, a series of open and flexible spaces are designed.

The exterior façades act as energy storage: a double sheet of concrete block with intermediate gravel ventilated natural stone facade with great insulation and warmer birch wood interior finishes. Its huge mass generates a thermal inertia that allows the temperature of the spaces to be controlled.

"In the long term, economy and the environment are the same thing. If something is anti-nature, it is anti-economic. That is the rule of nature".
Mollie Beattie

ENVIRONMENTAL ANALYSIS

1. Choosing the Site. Project and Development

1.1 Location

Latitude: 40°31'50"N
Longitude: 03°38'27"W

The building located on Avenida Bruselas 28, 28108, Alcobendas, Madrid, at an altitude of 670 meters above sea level.

The town is situated to the North /Northeast of Madrid at 16 km. point of the A-1. Access to the complex where the project is developed, is via the A-1, exit 16. Apart from arriving by car, there is also a regular public bus service and regional trains to and from Madrid. Alcobendas is a town in which the residential use (65%) coexists with four other well-balanced uses: Industrial use (9%), service industries (9%), non-residential amenities (9%), green zones and other uses (8%).

1.2 Urban Design and Site Improvement

An Urban Plan has existed in Alcobendas for the last 10 years that consists of designing a flexible, consensus-based planning, taking into account all the different points of view and initiatives from all the city's agents. The construction of the Fundación Metrópoli building falls within the framework of this plan.

The project offers green zones around the site on which it is located. The idea of surrounding the site with trees will provide areas of natural shade and will contribute to the CO2 sequencing in the area.

In a consolidated area of isolated buildings, this proposal perfectly suits the site due to the volumetric relationship it has with the existing buildings. The building is situated in a section of high density, accessible either by vehicle or on foot.

1.3 Project

Approaching the building using either means, the formal totality of the building is revealed. Access is gained directly from the public road. Upon entering, the visitor is surprised by a succession of double height spaces that are linked together along the same linear axis, until they visually cross through the building.

The building is organized into spaces defined by activities that occupy longitudinal sections. In the center is the access and central courtyard, to the left all the services are concentrated in line, and to the right are the activity classrooms.

In the central space, the natural interior light is soft and uniform, allowing all social activities to be incorporated.

The building spatially interprets the commitment to innovation through the design of meeting points and the visual and functional interaction of all the spaces that make up the Eco-Box. The entire project revolves around the atrium, its central element. This is an open space that connects all the rooms and simplifies the understanding of the building as a whole.

In designing the building, architectural solutions based on traditional and bio-climatic concepts are proposed, such as orientation, controlled exposure to the sun, the arrangement of apertures in the façade, which provide and adequate thermal control of the building, etc. All of the exterior apertures are

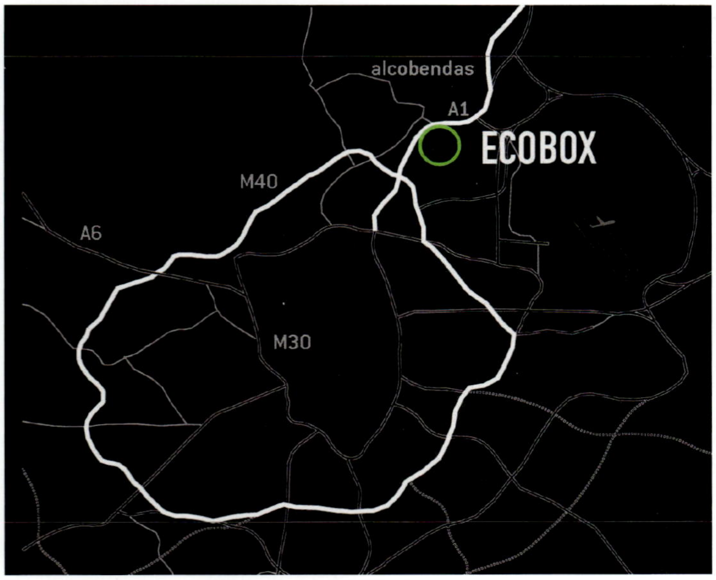

Situation

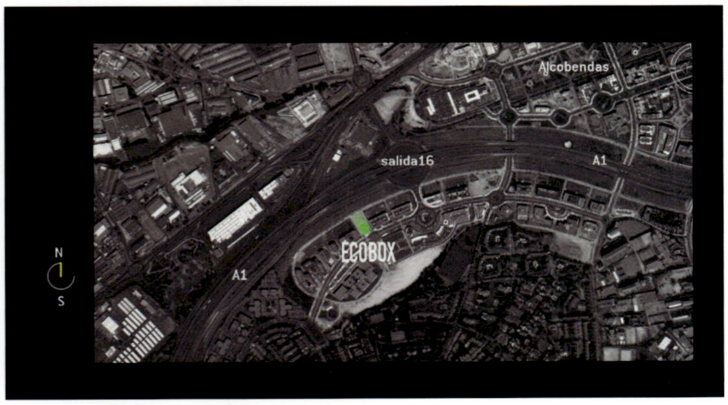

Location

protected from direct exposure to sun by operable metal slats, triggered by photoelectric cells with the aim of regulating the passage of solar energy depending on the energy necessities of the spaces.

2. Consumption of Energy and Resources

2.1 Consumption of Energy

A solid base of exposed concrete walls connects the stone, steel and glass box of the building to the ground, supported on a layer of gravel that acts as a huge energy storage for the building. Well insulated and weatherproofed, this stony mass significantly improves the thermal conditions of the internal spaces, acting as an energy and geothermal exchanger.

The installation is equipped with high-performance glass-to-glass photovoltaic panels that act as natural generators of electrical energy vertically arranged as a blue glass curtain wall on the south facade.

It is also equipped with 72 m2 of efficient, high technology, solar collectors positioned on the building's roof. These collectors heat the water that accumulates, centralized in two tanks (6,000 liters) which receive the solar heat by means of an external panel exchanger. Depending on the type of demand, the hot water accumulated in the tanks is directly used for heating and hot sanitation water in winter (40 a 45ºC), or for refrigeration in summer, through an absorption machine capable of transforming hot water (70 ºC) into cold water (8ºC).

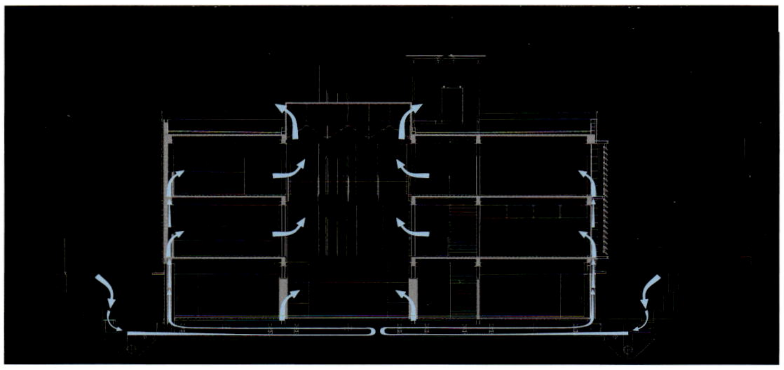

Chimney effect in atrium

2.2 Consumption of Water

The annual forecast for the building's water consumption is 1,100 m3.

The car parking areas have permeable paving. The retaining walls are formed of gabions made up of stones and gravel material taken from the waste of granite quarries. This provides the natural irrigation of the external areas of the building by means of recycling wastewater.

2.3 Consumption of Materials

The building's materials are in harmony with the bio-climatic technology employed. The existence of radiant heat floors and cool ceilings has, particularly, determined the materials, which are continuous concrete paving and concrete roof formed by the prefabricated elements of the floor slabs themselves. Inside, the walls of the building are of glass and wood.

Non-polluting materials that incorporate little energy in their manufacturing have been used. An example of this is the stone cladding of the façade, which is cut by a system employing a controlled blow, allowing that each piece have a natural rough cut finish without using the energy that is usually employed in saw cutting.

The façade is resolved by a combination of materials organized according to the modulation of the structure. This composition proposes a contrast of opaque material textures, where color is provided by the nature of the chosen material itself.

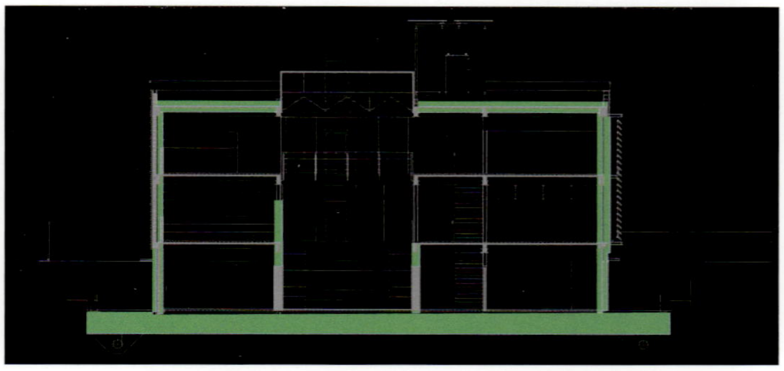

Energy Storages

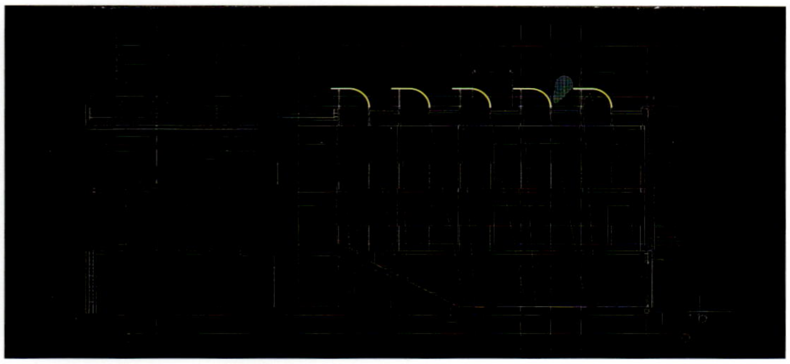

Energy Capturers

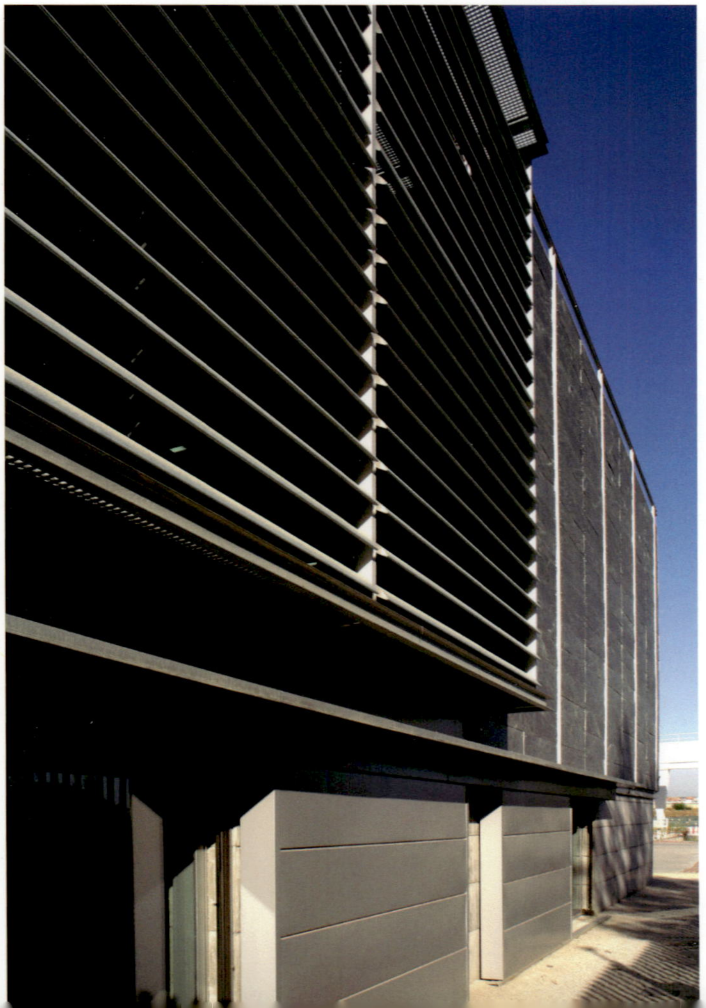

3. Environmental Loads

3.1 Emissions

Today, boilers are to a large extent responsible for emitting contaminating gases and numerous particles in suspension that significantly pollute metropolitan areas. The installation of a solar system in the building, in addition to providing savings in energy will produce a huge reduction in the emissions to the surrounding area.

The use of modular and prefabricated elements reduces material waste and, thus reducing the consumption of energy generated during construction.

3.2 Solid Waste

Due to the building system employed, based on exposed floor slabs, prefabricated elements, and modular systems, waste from construction has been minimized.

The use of gravels as material in the energy storage at the base of the building, in the walls, in the gabions, and in the mineral garden, permits the reuse of this material. The fastening of the external stone with screws, allowing the reuse of each of the panels, the fastening of the internal wooden panels also with screws, the prefabricated and exposed floor slabs, the metal structure itself, the glass panels, both inside and out, are aspects that have an impact on the ease of dismantling of the building for recycling.

3.3 Water Management

A mineral garden with gravels of different color tones and trees that scarcely need water for their maintenance and that enable all rainwater to filter through, have been proposed.

4. Interior Environmental Quality

4.1 Ventilation

Two types of ventilation are proposed:

1. An over-pressured building, with permanent and controlled ventilation or air renewal of the space, depending on the different atmospheric conditions.

2. Ventilation of energy storage, the aim of which is to condition the outside façade walls and floors in such a way that these great masses can act as energy storage.

All radiant heat floor circuits are equipped with individual temperature control systems, with the aim to independently condition each of the spaces according to their needs. This system is optimum for radiant floors, making use of the same emission panels for heating in winter and for cooling in summer.

The geothermal energy of the subsoil is transmitted to the energy storage situated under the building. From there, it is introduced into the interior spaces and exterior enclosures by means of a system of ducts through which the outside air circulates, driven by small fans on the collector elements that are arranged in the courtyards of the building.

4.2 Natural Lighting

Light is the central axis of the project. The atrium's skylights, which function simultaneously as energy collectors, introduce the diffused light into the core of the building, and illuminate the working spaces. The distribution of openings on the façade has been designed in relation with the specific needs of each space.

Likewise, the use of solar protection slats on the façade serves to diffuse the natural light into the building, and allows it to be regulated, depending on the time of day, through a smart system incorporated into the design.

4.3 Acoustics

The two basic techniques for controlling noise in the buildings are insulation from external sound sources and the absorption of internal noise. The first of these control systems is achieved in the building through the use of outdoor vegetation that forms an enclosure around the entire site, reducing, in this way, the noise levels that reach it.

Concrete, of low absorption, facilitates reflection, so it is not advisable in large spaces and for office use. To diminish the level of acoustic reflection, parts of the interior walls are clad with wooden plates which, due to their fibers and porosity, possess a high sound absorption coefficient.

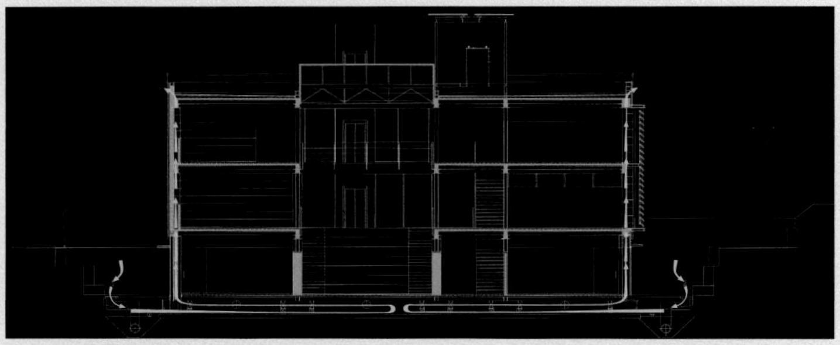

Ventilation and geothermal energy

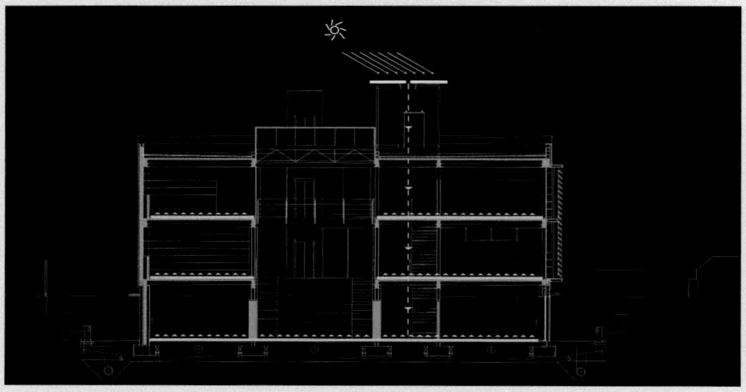

Heated floors

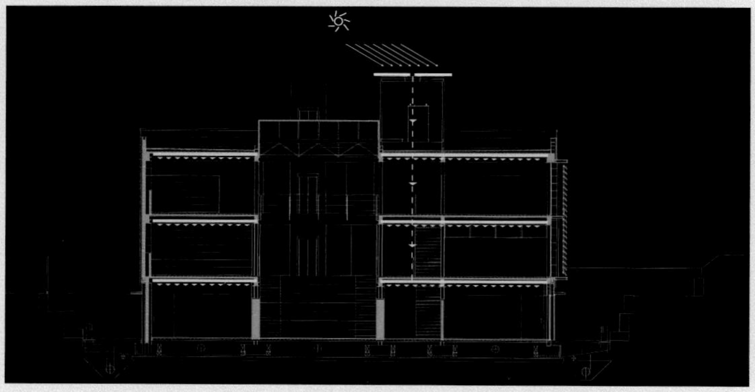

Cold Ceilings

5. Control of Building Systems

5.1 Functionality and Efficiency

The building adopts a very simple and modulated geometric form, allowing diverse layouts and uses. It parts from the conviction that innovation comes about from the combination of diverse disciplines and a confluence of different ideas.

The process of building, architectural and aesthetic integration of the solar systems is revealed in the choice of solar and photovoltaic collectors, providing a harmonious solution for integrating them into the architecture and design of the visible installations on the roof, supported on a metallic substructure that directly transmits the loads to the columns.

5.2 Control of Building Systems

The building systems employed are basic for achieving appropriate comfort in the building.

The façade enclosure, clad with natural stone and dry fasteners, functions as a thermal control system and diffuses the entrance of natural light into the building.

Most of the air conditioning systems are housed on the roof. This is complemented by electronic systems for regulating and controlling the environment, which make it adaptable to the climatic conditions throughout the year.

6. Long-term Performance

6.1 Flexibility and Adaptability

Due to its initial conception, in which the whole program is perceived both for office use and for public access spaces, and because of the use of dry-assembly systems both in the interior and exterior, the spaces can be easily modified, enabling their adaptation depending on the requirements of space at any given moment.

6.2 Maintenance and Operative Performance

Due to its clean design with no unnecessary finishes, the maintenance of the building is limited to the maintenance of the structural materials themselves.

7. Economic and Social Aspects

7.1 Social Aspects

Socially speaking, the main space for interaction is the atrium. Its essence is scale, transparency and light. It is a meeting place for important reunions, celebrations, communication and exchanges.

Inside the building, partitions do not reach the roof, facilitating visual transparency. A great part of the building's area is devoted to Art Halls, Classrooms and Terraces, which facilitate the interaction between the staff who work in the building and the visitor.

The Fundación Metrópoli is an international institution with its headquarters in Spain, whose aim is to contribute to the innovation and development of cities and territories from an international perspective. The building reflects that vision, both in its bio-climatic design and in the use of the same, by providing spaces that interact with the visitors.

7.2 Economic Aspects

The use of modular and prefabricated systems reduce construction time, waste on-site, and the cost of the project.

The incorporation of passive control systems, such as the façade enclosures, allows savings in the operation of traditional conditioning systems. This, combined with the smart systems that complements the air-conditioning of the building, produce savings in environmental cost.

8. The Architect's Eye

The structure is arranged on a Cartesian grid of steel columns that give rise to the distribution of the functional modules of the building. The facade, rich in textures, functions as an energy collector, and moreover, provides a backdrop for the corporate identity of the ensemble.

South Elevation

0 5 10m

1:300

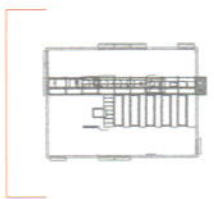

METROPOLI FUNDATION BUILDING

Angel de Diego Rica , Arquitecto

East Elevation

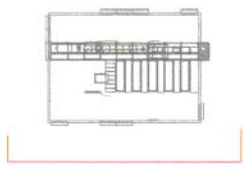

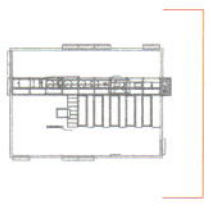

North Elevation

0 5 10m

1:300

West Elevation

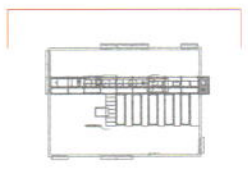

METROPOLI FUNDATION BUILDING

Angel de Diego Rica , Arquitecto

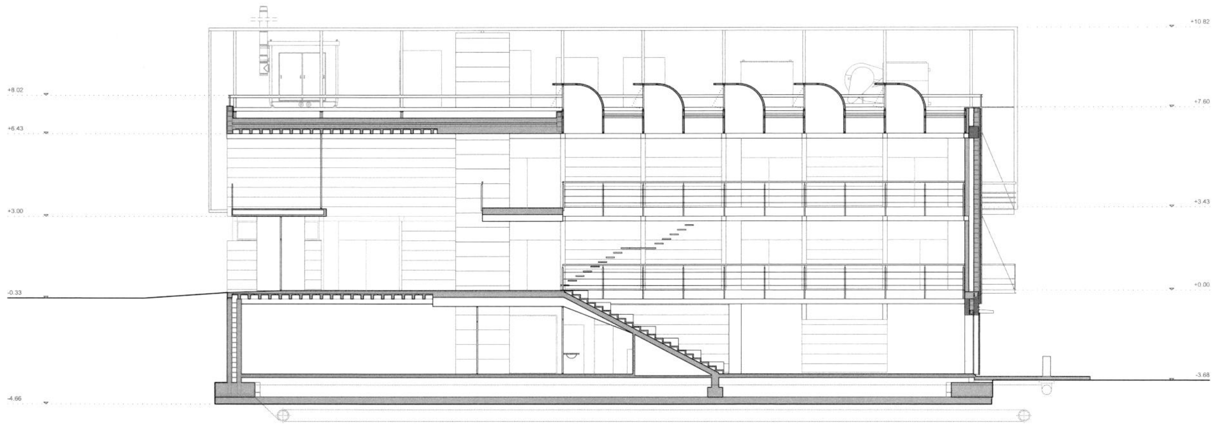

Section 1

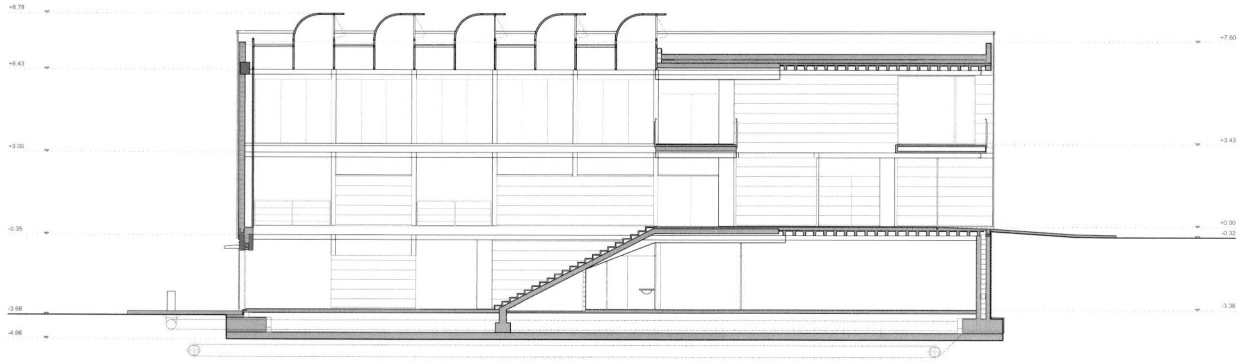

Section 2

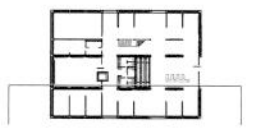

0 5 10m

1:300

Section 3

METROPOLI FUNDATION BUILDING

Angel de Diego Rica , Arquitecto

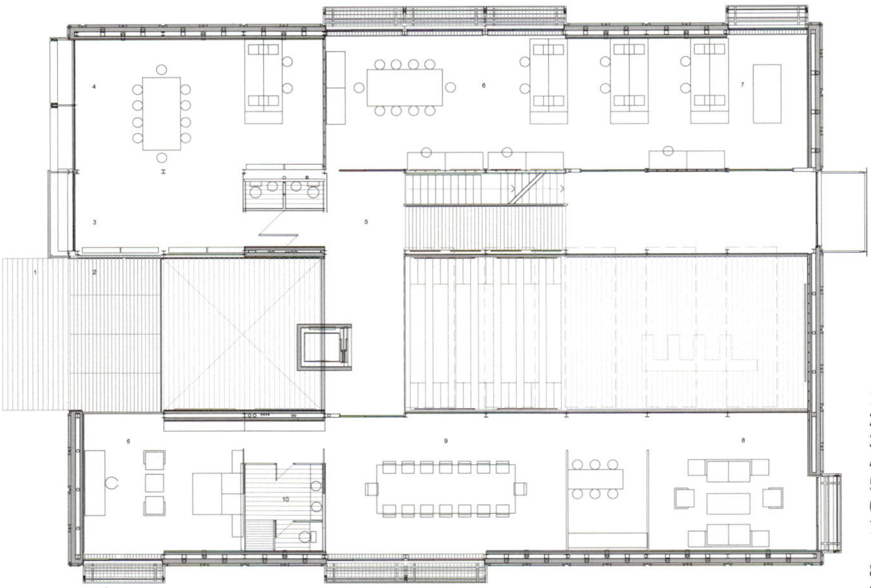

1. Access
2. Terrace
3. Library
4. Chairmanship
5. Circulation core
6. Work area
7. Area for responsible personnel
8. Living room
9. Coordination
10. Bathroom

2nd Floor Level

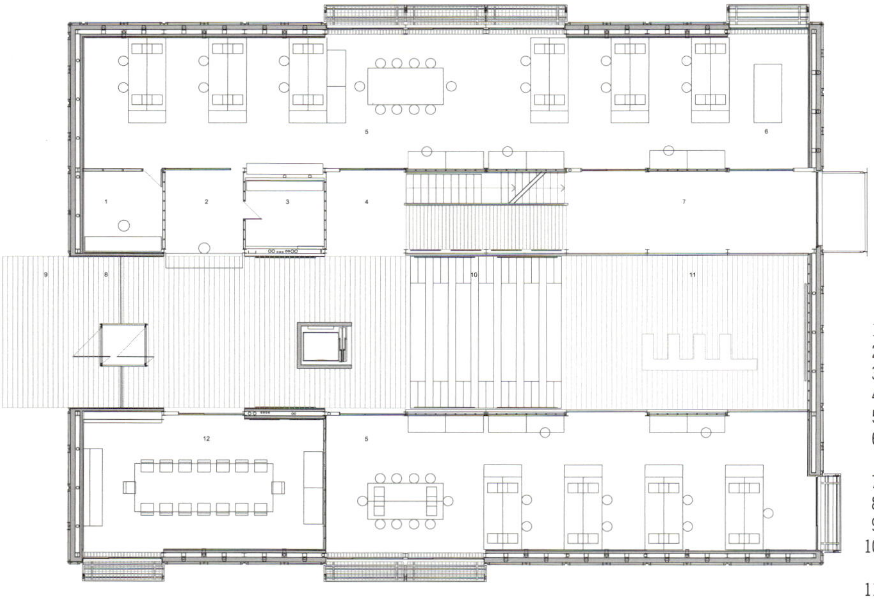

1. Management
2. Administration
3. Storage - control
4. Circulation core
5. Work area
6. Area for responsible personnel
7. Meeting point
8. Vestibule
9. Access
10. Central atrium / classroom
11. Void / art hall
12. Meeting room

First Floor Level

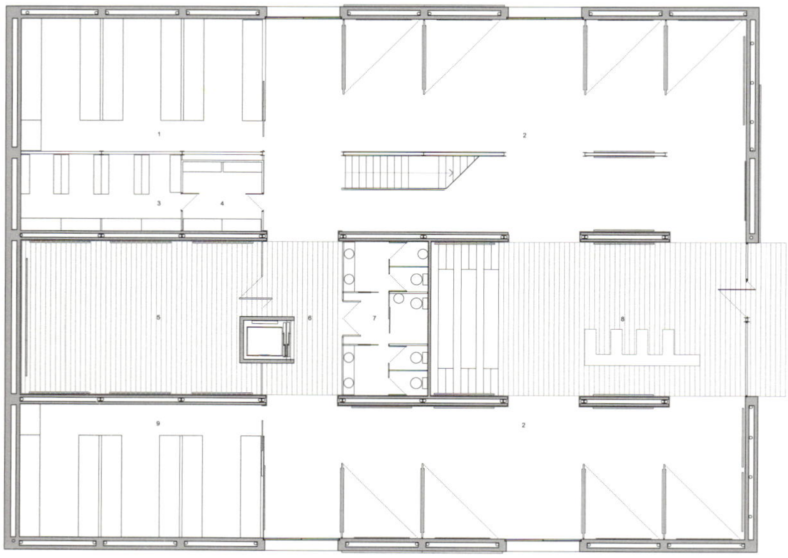

1. Art storage / general
2. Art hall
3. Archives
4. Storage, installations
5. Audiovisual rooms
6. Vestibules
7. Bathrooms
8. Art hall / central atrium
9. Multipurpose hall

Ground Floor Level

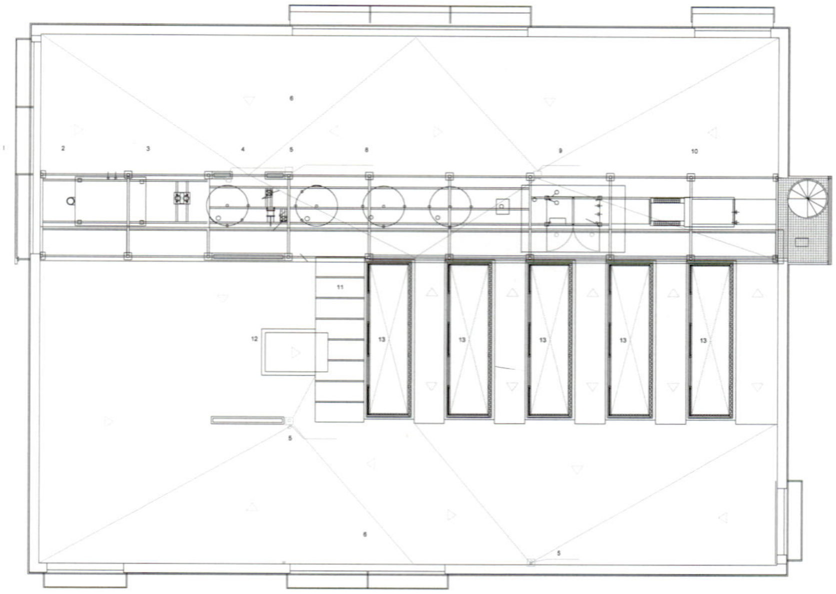

Roof Floor Level

1. Photovoltaic panels
2. Boilers
3. Pumps
4. Solar tank 2 x 3000 liters
5. Drain
6. Gravel
7. Bathroom
8. Cold tank 2 x 2500 litros
9. Absorption machine
10. Cooling tower
11. Concrete slab flooring
12. Elevator core, roof exit
13. Lightwell aperture

0 5 10m

1:300

METROPOLI FUNDATION BUILDING
Angel de Diego Rica , Arquitecto

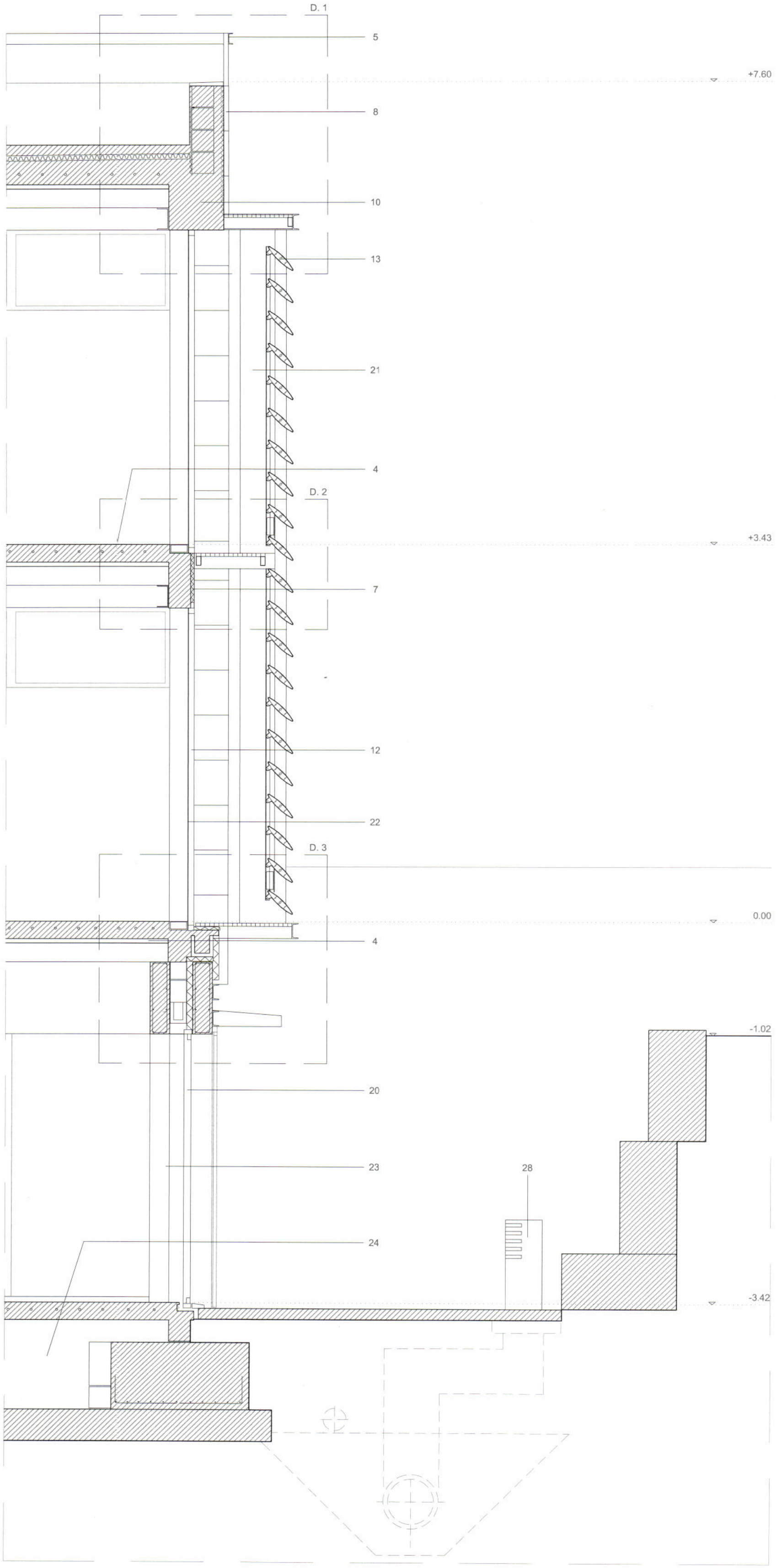

Section Detail 1

1:60

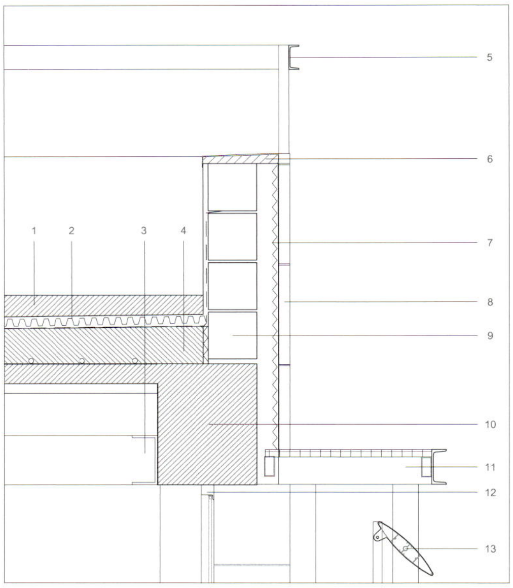

D. 1

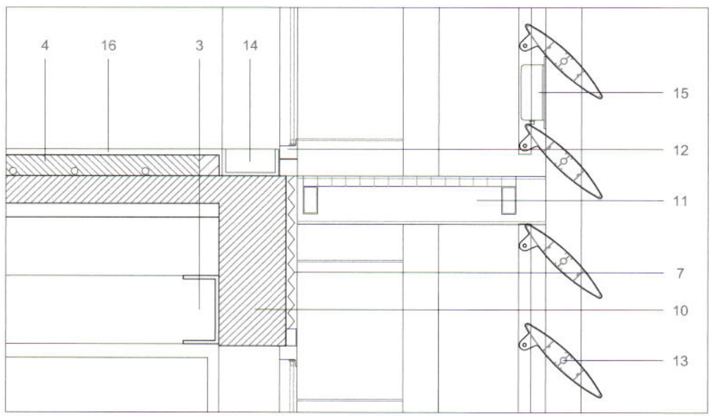

D. 2

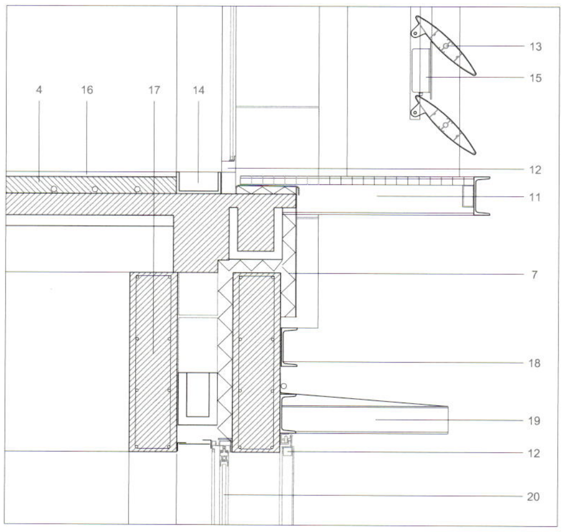

D. 3

1:30

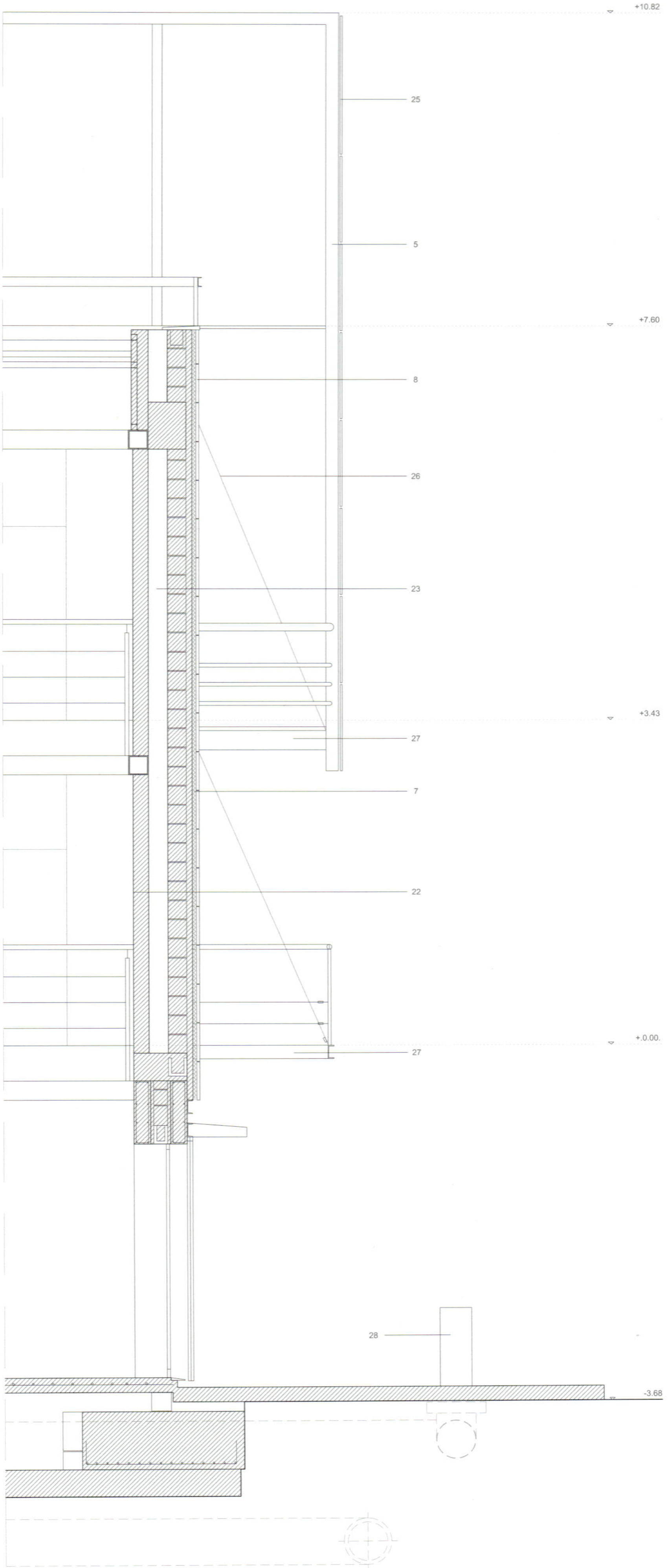

1. Pavement
2. Insulation
3. Metal beam c 200.100.10
4. Cool ceiling / radiant flooring system Uponor
5. Metal beam c 100.40.4
6. Metal parapet on roof
7. Thermal rockwool insulation
8. Natural stone facade, positioned with screws
9. Concrete block wall
10. Concrete beam
11. Metal beam
12. Aluminum window and door framing
13. Adjustable metal louvers for solar protection, triggered by electric cells
14. Metal piece c 160.80.10
15. Motor for control of louvers
16. Wood flooring
17. Reinforced concrete beam
18. Metal beam c 140.60.7
19. Metal canopy for solar protection
20. Glass access door
21. Air cushion for ventilated facade
22. Radiant flooring
23. Interior wood finish
24. Structure with steel columns
25. "Ecobox" sign
26. Metal strut
27. Balcony
28. Ventilation system

Section Detail 2

1:60

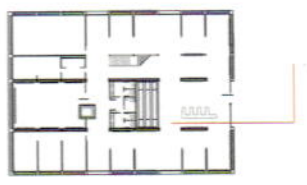

17

Francisco José Mangado Beloqui

2008 EXPO ZARAGOZA PAVILION

ZARAGOZA, España

FRANCISCO MANGADO BELOQUI

http://www.fmangado.com/

COLLABORATOR	Richard Kralovic. Hugo Mónica José Mª Gastaldo
TECHNICAL ADVISOR	Cristina Chu
STRUCTURE ANALYSIS	NB 35
INSTALLACION ANALYSIS	Fundación Cener-Ciemat (asesoría ahorro energético y sostenibilidad) Iturralde y Sagüés

	COLLABORATING COMPANIES
Contractor	Constructora San José
Topography	Servicios Topográficos Zaragoza
Metallic Structure	Martifer
Plumbing	Instalaciones y Montajes San José S.L.
Steel Supply and Assembly	Hierros Ayora Hierros J. Pombo

AWARDS

1er premio concurso ideas

	DATES
BEGINNING OF WORKS	2005
WORK COMPLETION	2008

DESCRIPTIVE BRIEF

The main objective has been to reproduce the space of a poplar grove or an ensemble of bamboo over a surface of water. On the one hand a municipal mechanism is created, capable of generating incredible possibilities from the viewpoint of the logic of energy and environmental commitment. This is basic, but in any case fundamental and emblematic for the future Spanish Pavilion in the International Expo in Zaragoza, but on the other hand this also transfers to the architecture one of the most attractive spaces we can come against, both physically and in terms of lighting. Variable spaces, full of suggestions and nuances, where concepts like verticality and depth play a fundamental role.

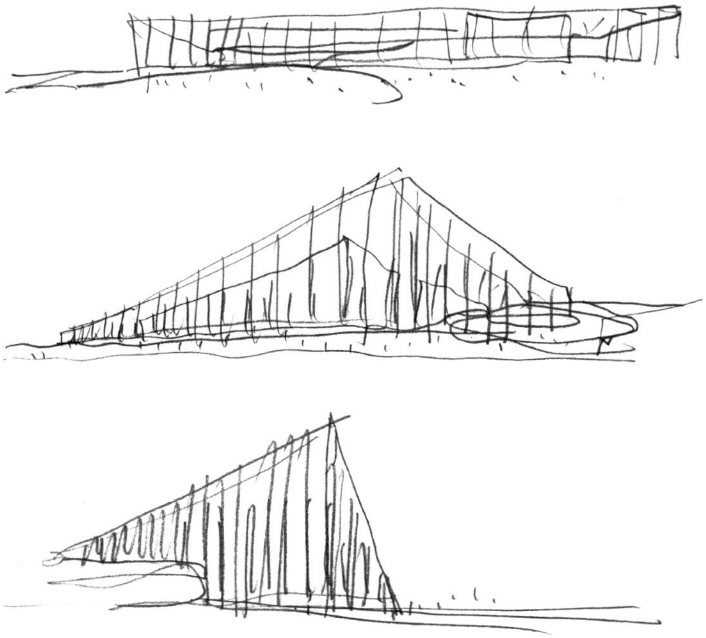

Is it possible to artificially reproduce a natural occurrence? An old frustrated aspiration in architecture. In either way in this case an approximation is possible, considering that the geometric strength of the metaphor is in our favor. On the other hand, the proposed image provides of a necessary symbolism to what should be the function of a Pavilion; in this case that of Spain in a universal expo. The metaphoric reference where water is present through the reference of landscape is strong and evident.

The execution is easy and clear. The vertical elements can be manufactured in the workshop. They have a metal nucleus, lined with pieces elaborated like botijos, earthenware drinking jugs, identical pieces which in contact with water, absorbs it and generate air currents which function as microclimates.

Its bracing, with the objective of guaranteeing its structural unity is very easy and simple, and is based on the same scheme found in many tree nurseries, maintaining the trunks in a vertical position.

A large roof, supported by all of these profiles, covers the pavilion. A very useful roof, as its thickness (3 m) permits housing of energy saving systems, and simultaneously calibrates the light using this depth, which allows the very controlled rays of sunlight to be drawn and reflected on the columns and the surface of water at the base. The roof is covered with panels of recycled wood shavings.

The exhibition spaces are excavated voids. Its floor slabs are hung from the roof and are only braced to the columns. They are built with wooden beams, also from recycled shavings and resin. The exterior enclosure is glass, and although well anchored to the structure, mobile partitions are provided, with acoustic insulation that achieves the visual and acoustic tightness that is necessary for some of the exhibitions, as well as for its future use as a cinema center.

"Modernity has domesticated the water, erasing its evoking characteristic. It is referred in economical or biological terms and few people can recognize its symbolic qualities"

José Ángel Bergua

ENVIRONMENTAL ANALYSIS

1. Choosing the Site. Project and Development

1.1. Site

Latitude: 41°40'04"N
Longitude: 00°53'51"W
Altitude: 193 m

The building is located within the complex of the International Exhibition of Zaragoza 2008, in the left margin of the Ebro River, in the northwest of the city of Zaragoza. The region has a Mediterranean climate, arid with a continental tendency, characteristic of the Ebro Valley. Winters are fresh and summers are warm, with little rains that are concentrated in the spring. The wind blows continuously and intensely in Zaragoza, with an average speed of 19Km/h; its intensity grows when it blows from the West and Northwest, reaching speeds of up to 100 Km/h (Cierzo).

1.2 Urban Design and Site Improvement

The Pavilion is a singular object within a new grid generated for the International Exhibition, located on grounds that are part of the flood plain of the Ebro River, and on their own alluvial deposits, in a parcel whose current use was the cultivation of cereals. As plantations in a swamp, or like poplars on the bank of the Ebro River, the authors have conceived a building with great symbolism which contributes to improve the environmental conditions of the site.

Aside from the symbolic load of a Pavilion itself, the designers have equipped the building with an original conditioning system that uses water and the structural columns to regulate the environmental conditions inside and around the building. With this strategy it is intended to improve the comfort of the people who wait to access the Pavilion, or simply for those who want to rest under the shade.

1.3 Project

The Pavilion is formed by volumes of glass immersed in a forest of 700 columns located along the entire perimeter and the interior of the building. The multiple columns, covered by porous ceramics, reinterpret the spaces like the Hypostyle Halls of old Egypt or the Mosque of Cordoba. As in a dream, the visitor will live sensations with water, in a crossing reflections between the pools, crystals and the audio-visual spaces designed.

The building has a 5,000m2 roof, like a great visor that covers the columns forest. Its main function is to give shade to all of the building. In addition, it expands at the center to a height of about three meters to lodge the equipment for the air conditioning systems. Using its depth, the roof allows graduating the light, controlling it so that it outlines and reflects on the columns and the water surface at the base. The architectural program, with a surface of 5,400 m2, is distributed in three plants: basement, ground floor and first floor.

At the access level, a water sheet of thirty centimetres of depth will serve as starting point for the forest of columns (some structural and others only with climatic function), that together with the circulation cores serve as part of structural support for the building.

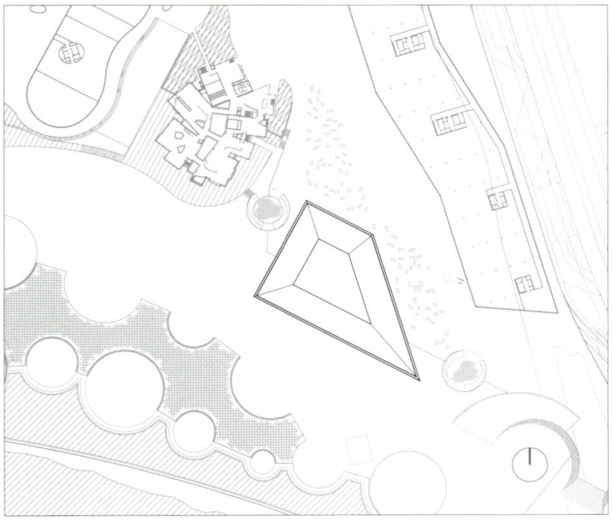

Site Plan

1:4000

2. Consumption of Energy and Resources

2.1 Consumption of Energy

The forest of columns functions as a great conditioning system that works due to the water and characteristic winds of the area. Inside the columns, water will circulate, which filtered through the pores of the ceramic pieces will dampen and refresh the atmosphere in summer, a physical phenomenon that can be observed in the clay pitchers called botijos which have been used from immemorial times to cool water in a simple way.

During the winter, hot water will circulate through the columns from a power station that combines a gas plant with 4000m2 of solar panels. Winter wind, called Cierzo, circulating through the hot water columns will increase the air temperature and will generate a thermal layer around the inner pavilions, diminishing the need for heating.

2.2 Consumption of Water

The roof is developed like a photovoltaic energy collector and will also have a system for rainwater accumulation, with a deposit of 150m3 where the water will be stored to later be used in the columns.

2.3 Consumption of Materials

The materials will be differentiated according to their structural function within the building. Concrete has been used for the load-bearing walls of the vertical circulation and for the floor and roof slabs. A glazed curtain wall supported on metal structure has been designed. Metal columns are covered with ceramic pieces by means of reversible mechanical connections. The roof is clad in its interior with panels of recycled wood shavings.

3. Environmental Loads

3.1 Emissions

The Pavilion was designed as a "battery building", that is, a building that accumulates energy fed with totally renewable energy sources like the sun and the wind. This energy will be used in the indoor conditioning system; whereas its external energy supply is obtained from a plant that combines gas and solar energy[1]. The challenge is to reduce the dependency from energy plants that operate using fossil fuels.

3.2 Solid Waste

The columns, characteristic element of the project are solved with prefabricated metal and ceramic elements assembled on-site. Due to this, the waste of construction will be reduced.

3.3 Water Management

The entire concept of the building design is based on efficient water management. This valuable resource is used to generate and to condition both inner and outer spaces.

4. Interior Environmental Quality

4.1 Ventilation

Instead of insulating itself from prevailing winds, the project adopts the intelligent strategy of using them as a fundamental element of the conditioning system:

The summery South wind, called Bochorno, after contacting with the ceramic columns, loses its heat as the water that suppurates from the columns vaporizes and refreshes the atmosphere. The suction effect generated by this summer wind will be used to extract the interior air from the building and to naturally ventilate the space that will be visited by up to 50.000 people per day.

The North winter wind (Cierzo) will absorb the preheated water from the columns to warm the same spaces during the cold seasons.

4.2 Natural Lighting

The forest of columns will filter the direct solar radiation that otherwise would arrive directly to the glazed prisms. Glazing, with a low solar factor and reduced transmission coefficient, has been chosen. The enormous visor of the roof works like passive horizontal control mechanism, providing the pavilion and its surroundings with shade.

4.3 Acoustics

In an analogous way to other emblematic constructions in which the water is a part of the composition of spaces, like The Alhambra in Granada, in this project the presence of water as a mirror at the base of the building or vaporized between columns will generate a series of reverberations that will subjectively contribute to improving the comfort of the visitors.

Interiors will be divided by movable panels with acoustic isolation which will permit the development of different exhibition activities within a same space.

1 The system that will provide energy for the Exposition is formed by a gas plant (cogeneration) and an enormous solar park (4000m2) for hot water production, and a high efficient network that will connect the plant with each one of the consumers. It is estimated that the insulated pipes of the network will have losses of only 5% in hot water, and 3% in cold water.

5. Control of Building Systems

5.1 Functionality and Efficiency
It is detected in the double function of the roof, as protector and energy collector. The columns that support the building act simultaneously as structural and conditioning elements.

6. Long-term Performance

6.1 Flexibility and Adaptability
The spaces generated by the project of the Pavilion can be reused to house architectural program of institutional or corporate buildings. As a result, it has been contemplated that after the end of the Exhibition, the site can be used as headquarters for the City of Cinema and Image, institutional project in definition phase.

6.2 Maintenance and Operative Performance
The strategies used to facilitate the maintenance of the building and to guarantee the reversibility of the construction are: the simplicity of the building system, the differentiation of materials according to function within the building, the use of mechanical unions between materials of a different nature.

7. Economic and Social Aspects

7.1 Social Aspects
With the carrying out of international events, there usually is generated a positive civic climate in the host cities, which favors citizen reflection, and except for certain negative effects like the increase of the real estate market and the possible environmental affection if the project is not well[2] managed, it unites the citizens in a common cause: to make their city a perfect host for an international event. In that sense, the building represents the aspirations of the organizers as it combines technical solutions with environmental care.

7.2 Economic Aspects
The construction of singular buildings for international exhibitions can be associated to certain wastefulness justified only with the argument of displaying the advances of the exhibiting country[3]. In that sense, the provision of elements of passive control based on simple ancestral systems, the use of solar collecting devices on the roof, and the will of reusing the building once the International Exhibition is completed, demonstrates that it is possible to build self-sufficient pavilions, that simultaneously save energy and money in its maintenance while expressing the spirit of the represented country[4].

8. The Architects eye

Mangado has been able to capture the symbolic value of water in architecture, the wellness that can be provided by a simple clay pitcher with fresh water, materializing this sensation within a space with historical and natural reminiscence. The pavilion achieves, through a constant draw and redrawing of spaces and sensations, combining technological advances with environmental respect.

2 The master plan of the Zaragoza Exposition has been criticized by some ecologist organizations because of the selected site, which is located in a meander of the Ebro River and because a floodgate designed to regulate the river volume.

3 The Lisbon Exposition in 1998 marked a difference in the spirit of the International expositions. The optimistic will of progress was substituted by a tough critique about the problems of the planet.

4 In this line, it is important to highlight the work of Zumpthor in Hannover 2000 for the Swiss Pavilion, or the nomad character of the Pavilion Shigeru Ban + Dean Maltz in 2005.

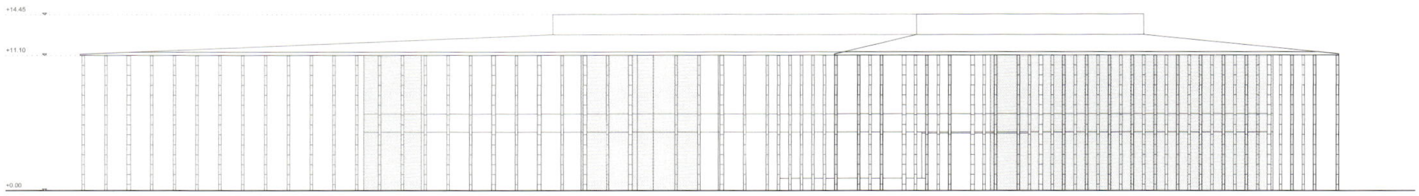

East Elevation

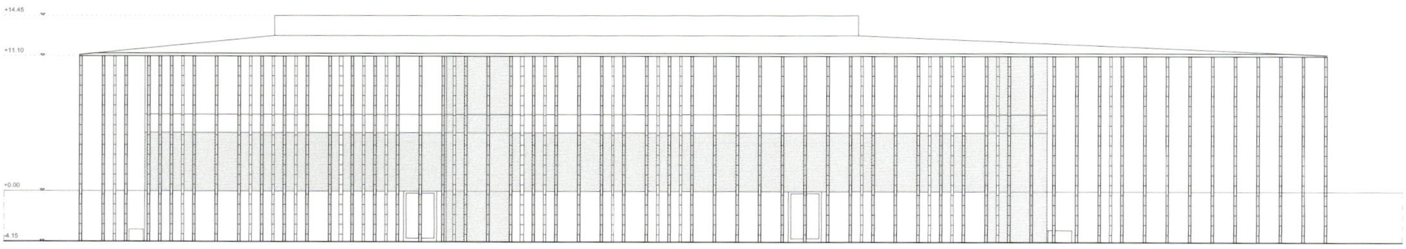

North Elevation

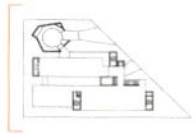

0 5 10m

1:600

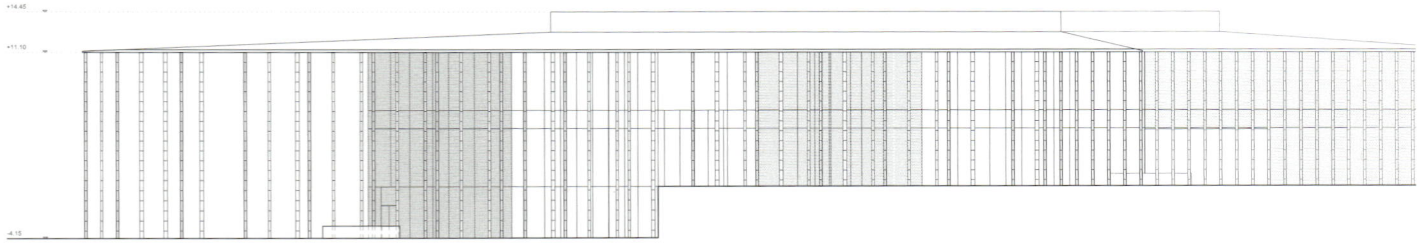

Southwest Elevation

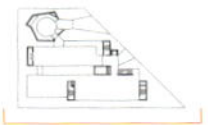

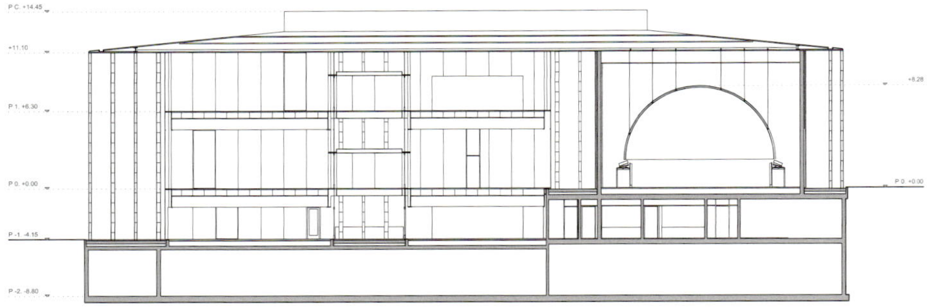

Section A

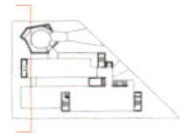

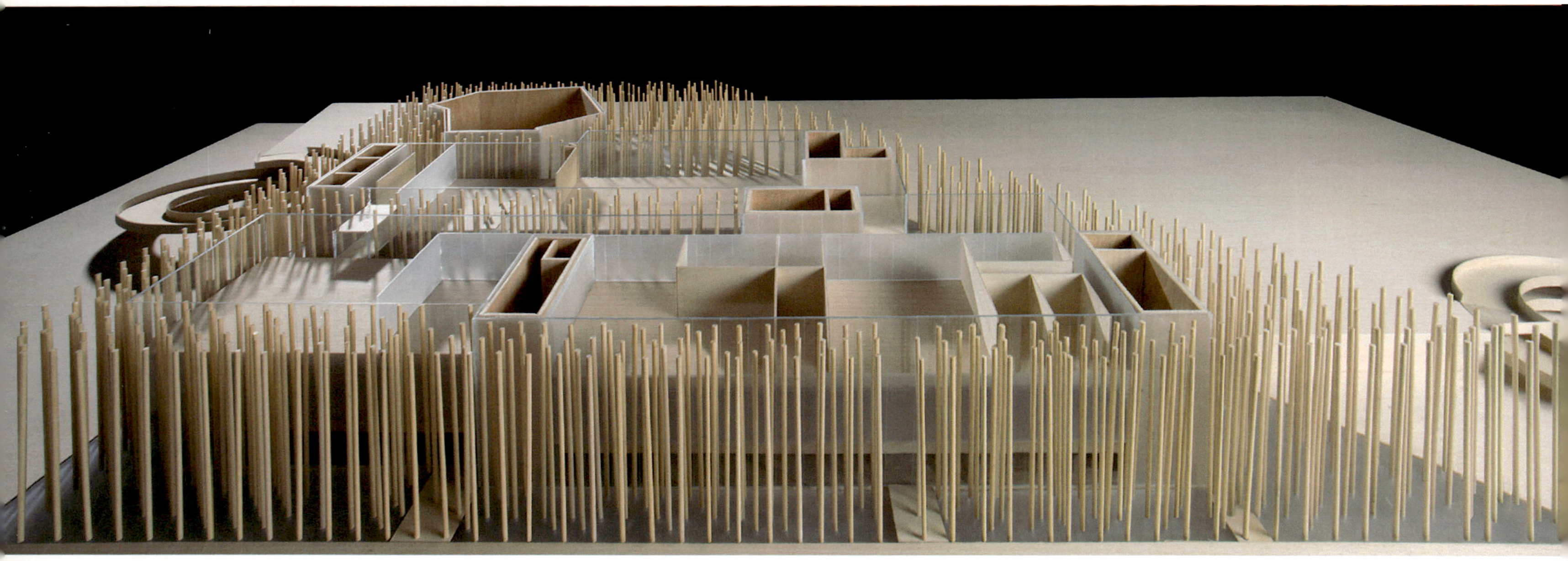

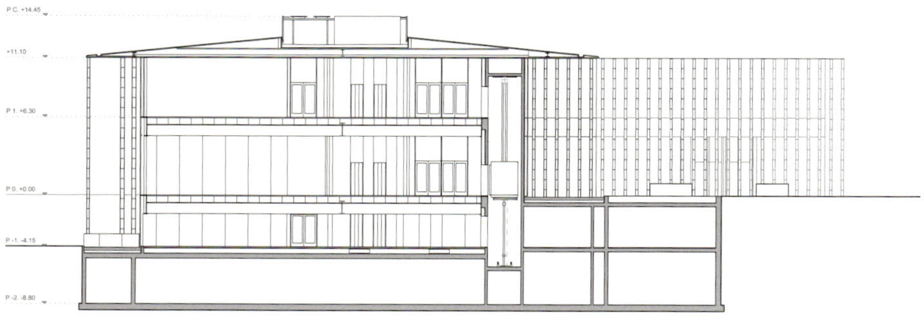

Section B

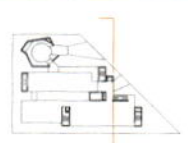

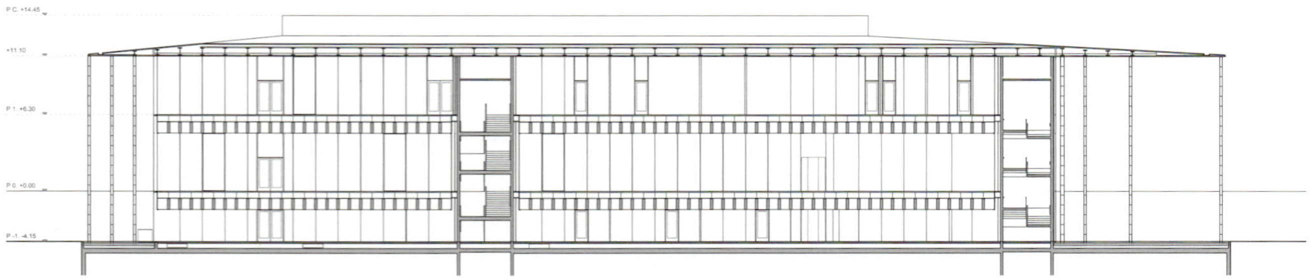

Section C

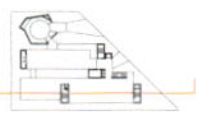

0 5 10m

1:600

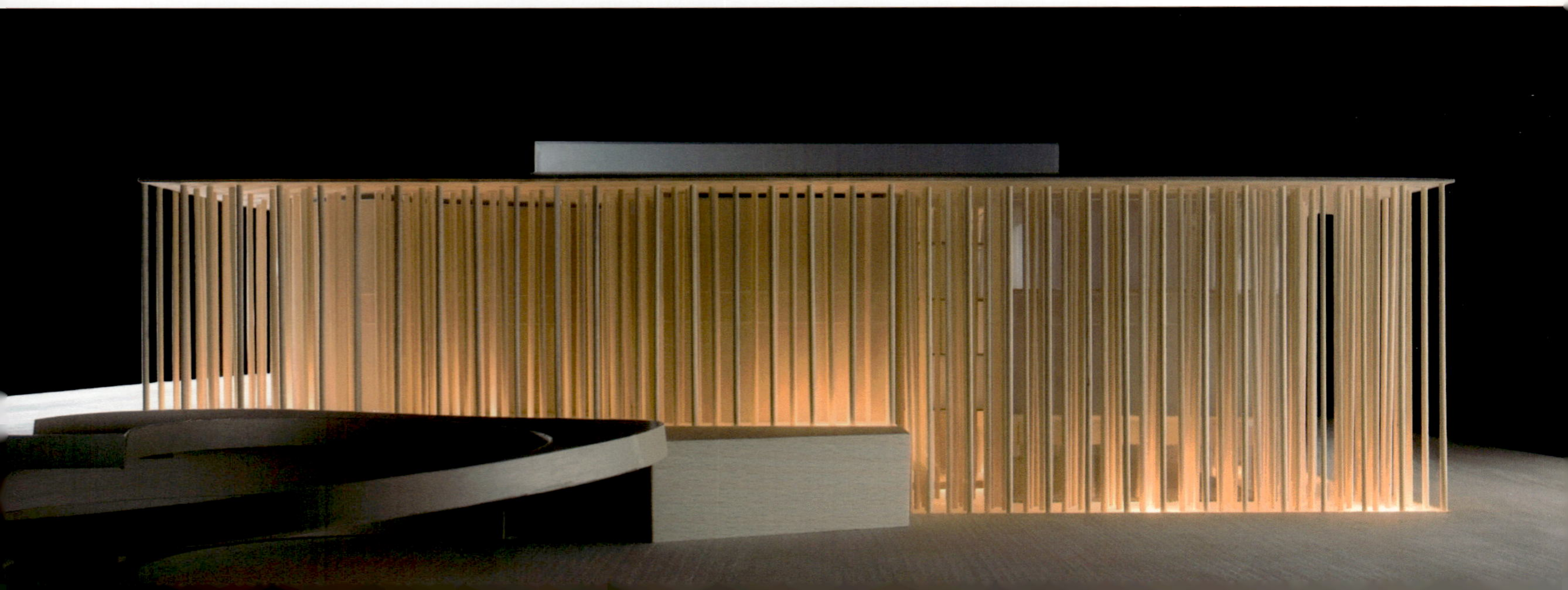

2008 EXPO ZARAGOZA PAVILION

Francisco José Mangado Beloqui

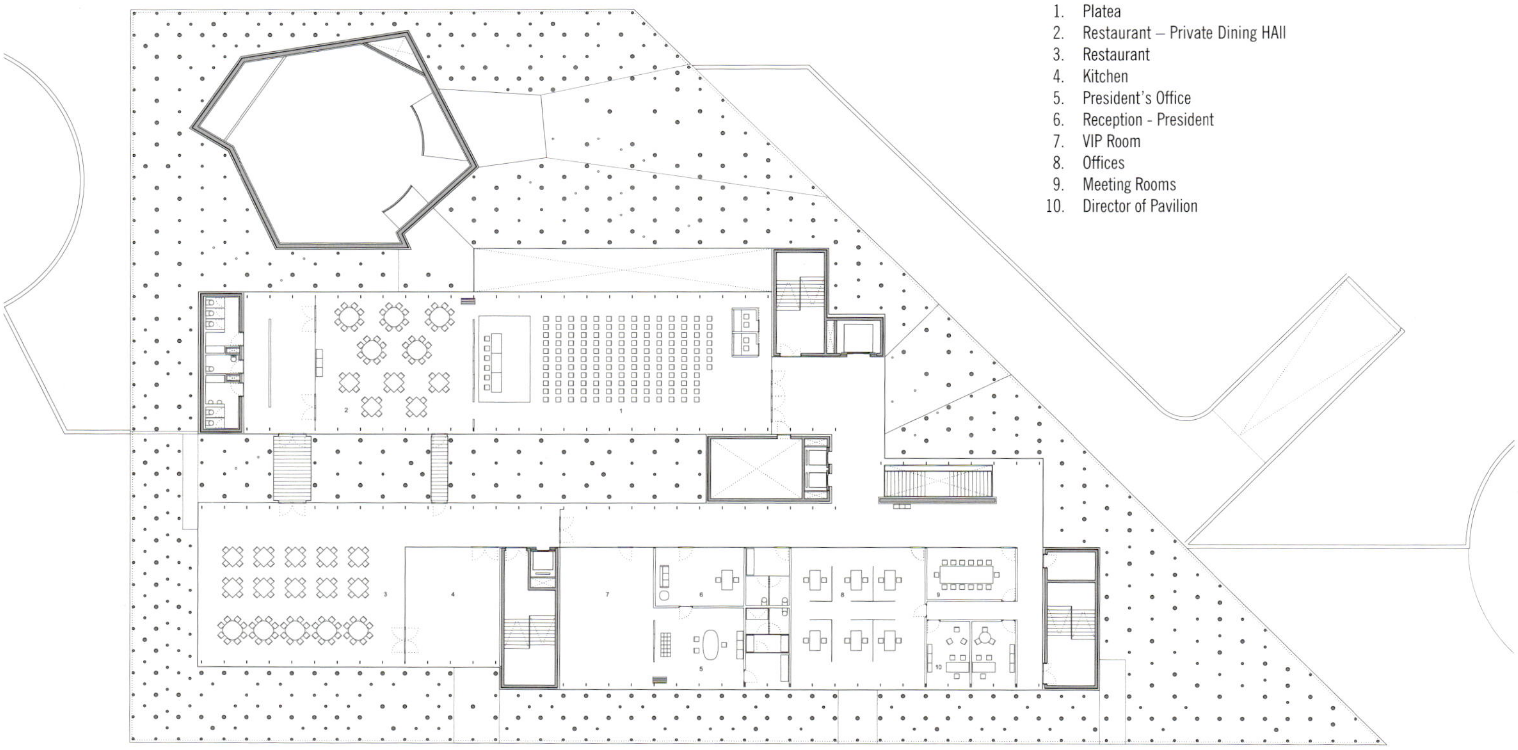

1. Platea
2. Restaurant – Private Dining HAll
3. Restaurant
4. Kitchen
5. President's Office
6. Reception - President
7. VIP Room
8. Offices
9. Meeting Rooms
10. Director of Pavilion

First Floor Level

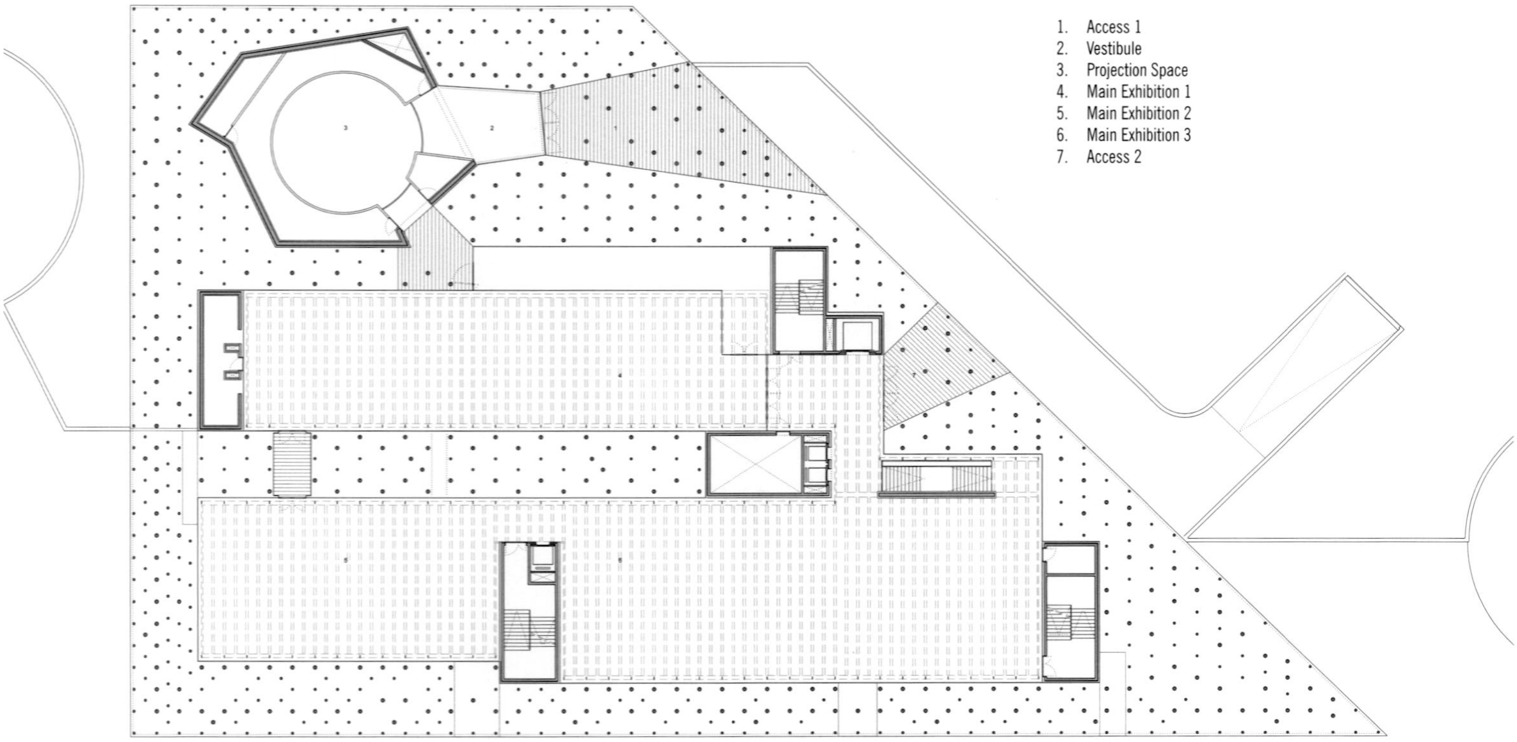

1. Access 1
2. Vestibule
3. Projection Space
4. Main Exhibition 1
5. Main Exhibition 2
6. Main Exhibition 3
7. Access 2

Ground Floor Level

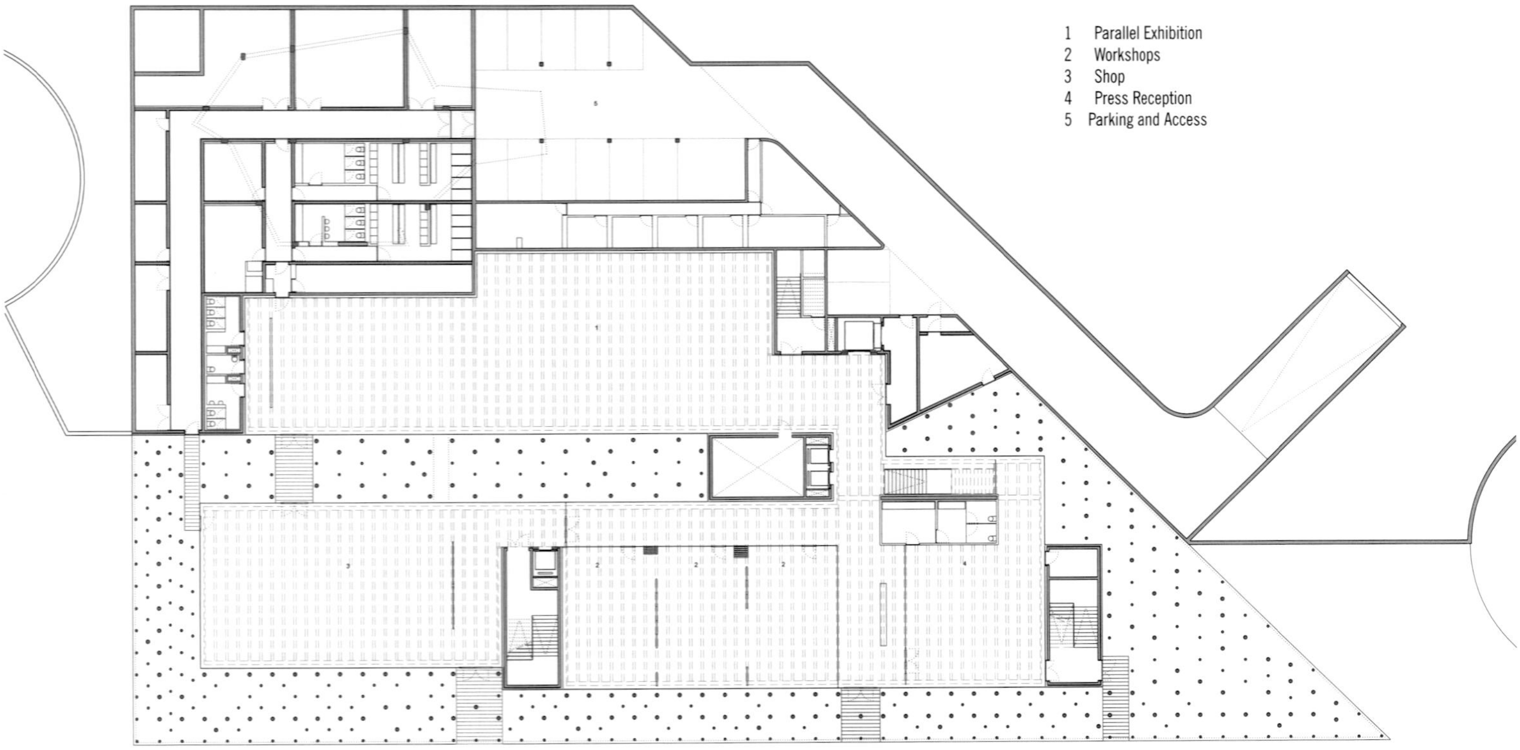

1 Parallel Exhibition
2 Workshops
3 Shop
4 Press Reception
5 Parking and Access

Lower Ground Floor Level

0 5 10m

1:600

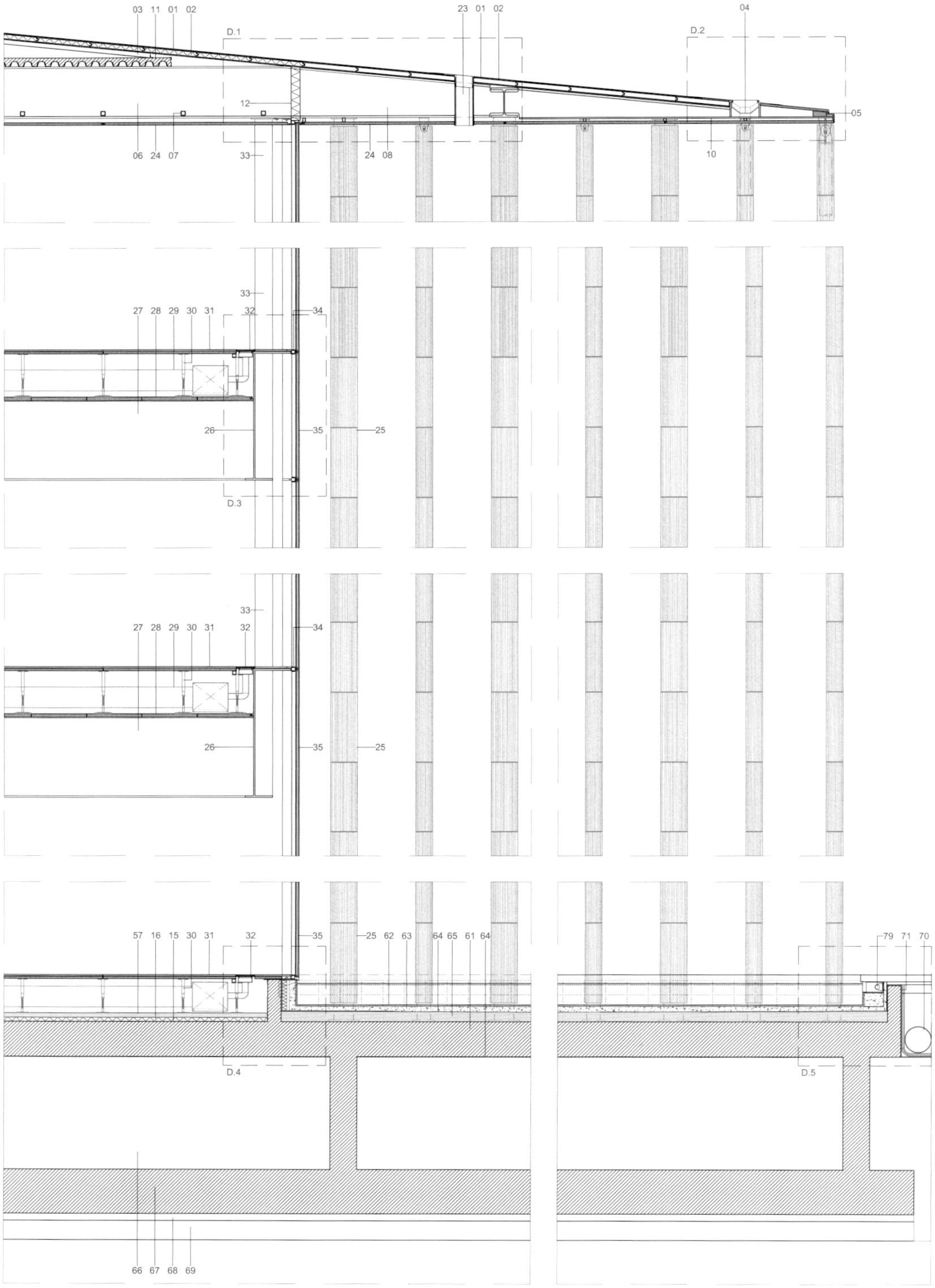

Section Detail 1

0 1 2 3m

1:75

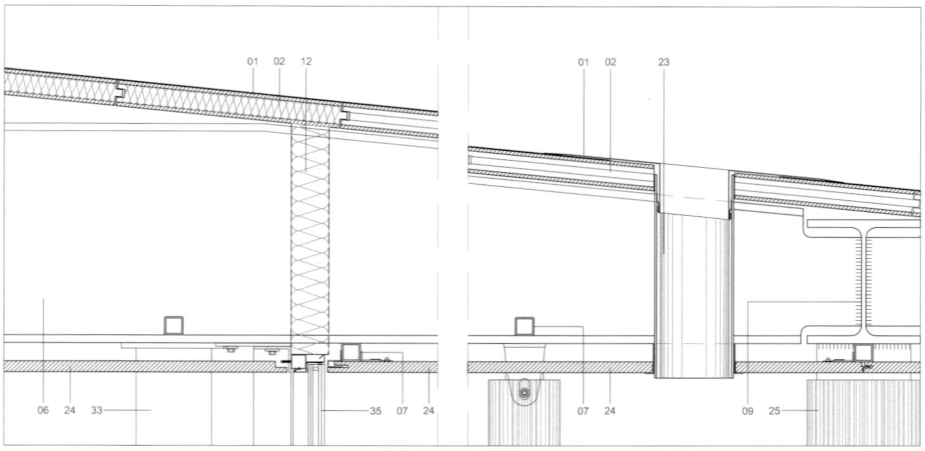

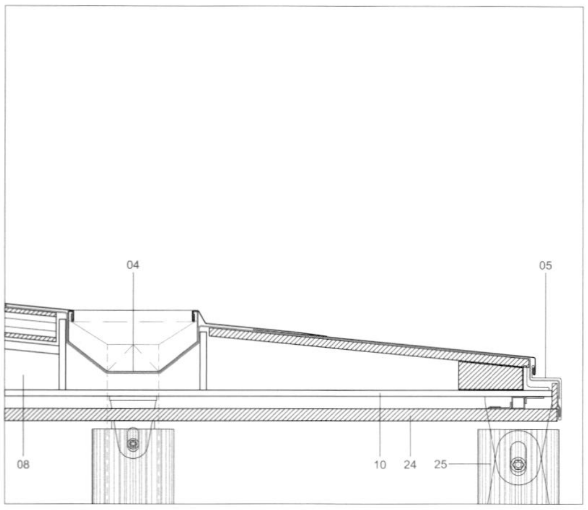

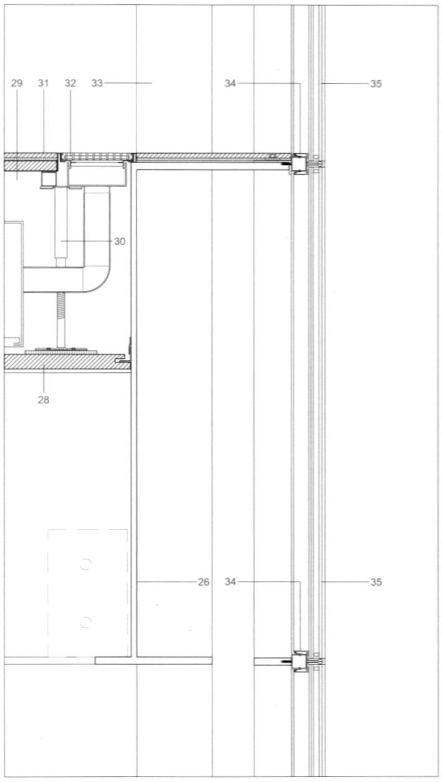

1. Waterproofing roofing sheet of synthetic rubber
2. Sandwich panel with upper face of water-repellant plywood
3. Structural formwork for sloped roof.
4. Formation of hidden galvanized steel gutter
5. Lined with corrugated galvanized steel sheet
6. Steel beams for roof: HEB 600
7. Tubular profile binding rafter
8. Reinforced metal ribbing: variable height plate
9. Confinement profile HEB 340
10. Metal sheet
11. Collaborating corrugated metal slab.
12. Rockwool insulation
15. Waterproofing membrane
16. Thermal insulation of sheet of agglomerated cork
23. Interior finish of galvanized sheet in form of opening
24. Dovetailed boarding of wood fiber board
25. Iron tube lined on outside by ceramic piece
26. Structural perimeter of floor slabs: galvanized iron plate
27. Pine wood beam
28. Wood board ceiling
29. Technical space for installations
30. Metal plot for compact technical flooring
31. Elevated pavement with MDF board
32. Air conditioning / heating intake grill
33. Metal brace
34. Galvanized steel perimeter framing.
35. Double thermal glazing
57. Leveling groundslab
61. Reinforced concrete slab
62. Floor tiling – Stoneware tile, non-slip, glazed finish
63. Formation of swimming pool basin: layer of concrete
64. Waterproofing sheet
65. Formation of slopes with concrete.
66. Infill, extension and compacting of earth
67. Reinforced concrete foundation slab.
68. Layer of concrete
69. Gravel base
70. Perimeter draining and basement walls with PVC tubes
71. Wall waterproofing
79. Submerged weathertight light fixture

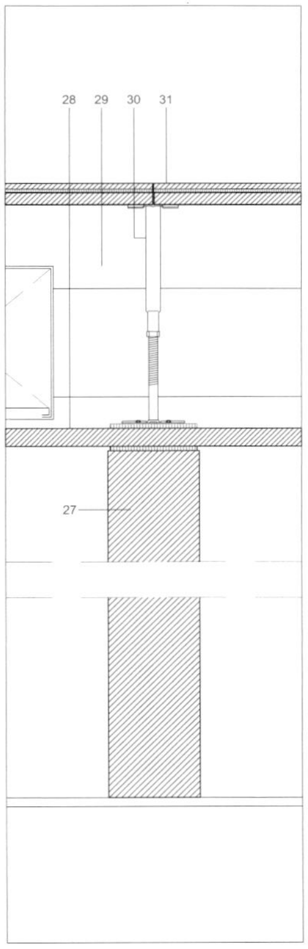

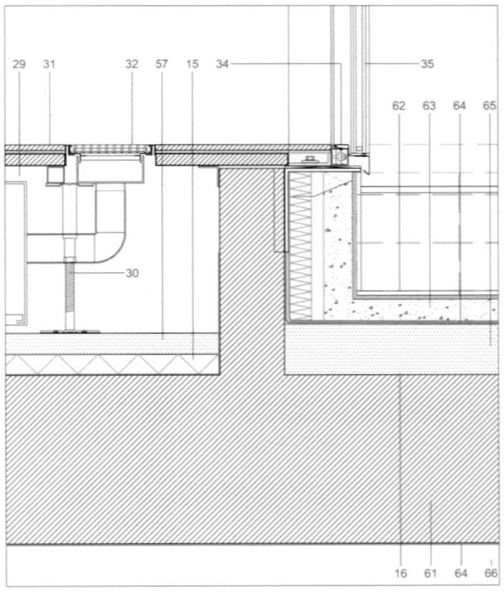

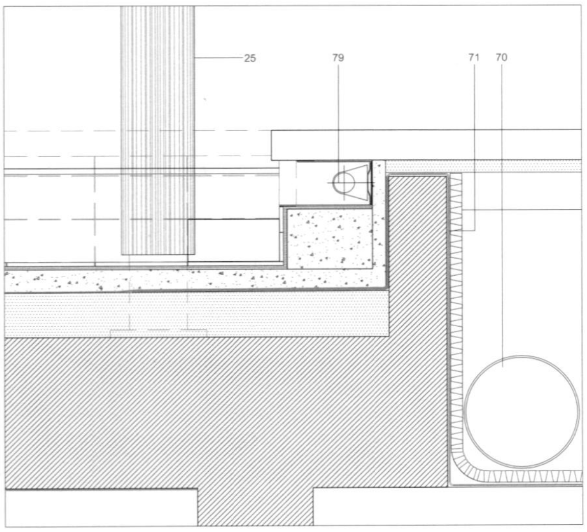

Section Details

0 10 30 50cm 1m

1:20

Roof Detail

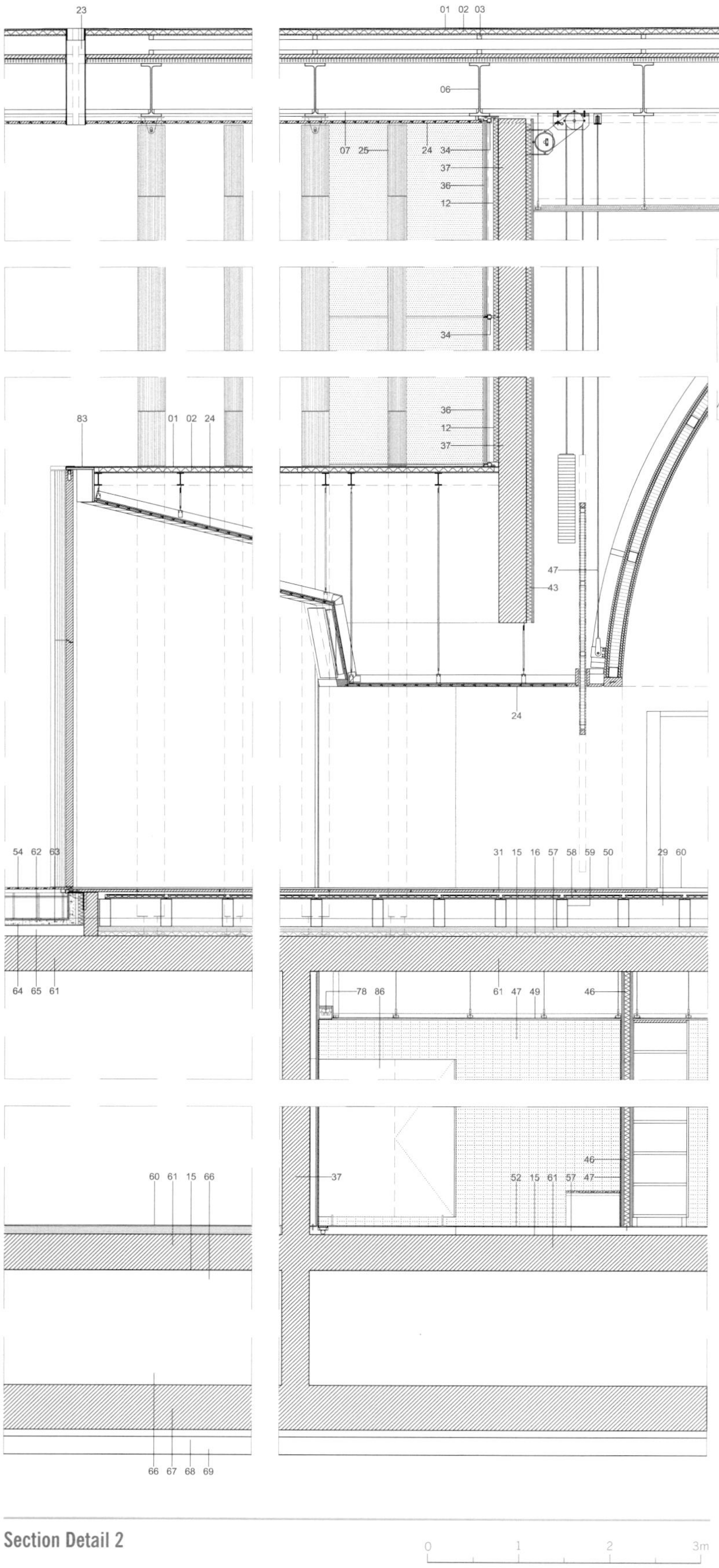

Section Detail 2

1:75

1. Waterproofing roofing sheet of synthetic rubber
2. Sandwich panel with upper face of water-repellant plywood
3. Structural formwork for sloped roof
5. Lined with corrugated galvanized steel sheet.
6. Steel beams for roof: HEB 600
7. Tubular profile binding rafter.
8. Reinforced metal ribbing: variable height plate
11. Collaborating corrugated metal slab
12. Rockwool insulation
13. Formation of upper level of photovoltaic panels
14. Structural framework of upper roof
15. Waterproofing membrane
16. Thermal insulation of sheet of agglomerated cork
18. Galvanized metal lattice grill with steel plate.
20. Structural steel roof column
23. Interior finish of galvanized sheet in form of opening
24. Dovetailed boarding of wood fiber board
25. Iron tube lined on outside by ceramic piece
26. Structural perimeter of floor slabs: galvanized iron plate
27. Pine wood beam
28. Wood board ceiling
29. Technical space for installations
30. Metal plot for compact technical flooring
31. Elevated pavement with MDF board
32. Air conditioning / heating intake grill
33. Metal brace
34. Galvanized steel perimeter framing
35. Double thermal glazing type 'Climalit' with interposition of butyral of translucent polyvinyl in interior pane
36. Reinforced concrete wall
41. Double laminated security glazing type Stadip
43. MDF baseboard to paint.
46. Interior wall of double layer of gypsum board
47. Stoneware tiling of white vitrified paste
49. Continuous suspended drop ceiling of gypsum board
50. Floor of dovetailed board of baked oak wood.
52. Flooring of ceramic stoneware tile of vitrified white paste
54. Exterior floor type EXTERPARK Classic of solid wood decking
57. Leveling groundslab.
58. Elevated groundslab of dovetailed prefabricated concrete board
59. Low hollow brick wall
60. Leveling groundslab, polished in color and polyethylene sheet.
61. Reinforced concrete slab
62. Floor tiling – Stoneware tile, non-slip, glazed finish
63. Formation of swimming pool basin: layer of concrete
64. Waterproofing sheet
65. Formation of slopes with concrete
66. Infill, extension and compacting of earth.
67. Reinforced concrete foundation slab
68. Layer of concrete
69. Gravel base
74. Steel bridge structure: HEB fixed on extremes with profile reinforced with laminated steel L
75. IPE binding rafter for pavement of bridges.
76. Security glazing formed by double laminated glass
77. Laminated steel calibrated plate
78. Formation of ceiling light: weathertight fixture.
82. Semi-sphere of projections of interior metal structure
83. Metal plate in form of side lock
84. Dividing screen in bathrooms and water-repellant MDF board

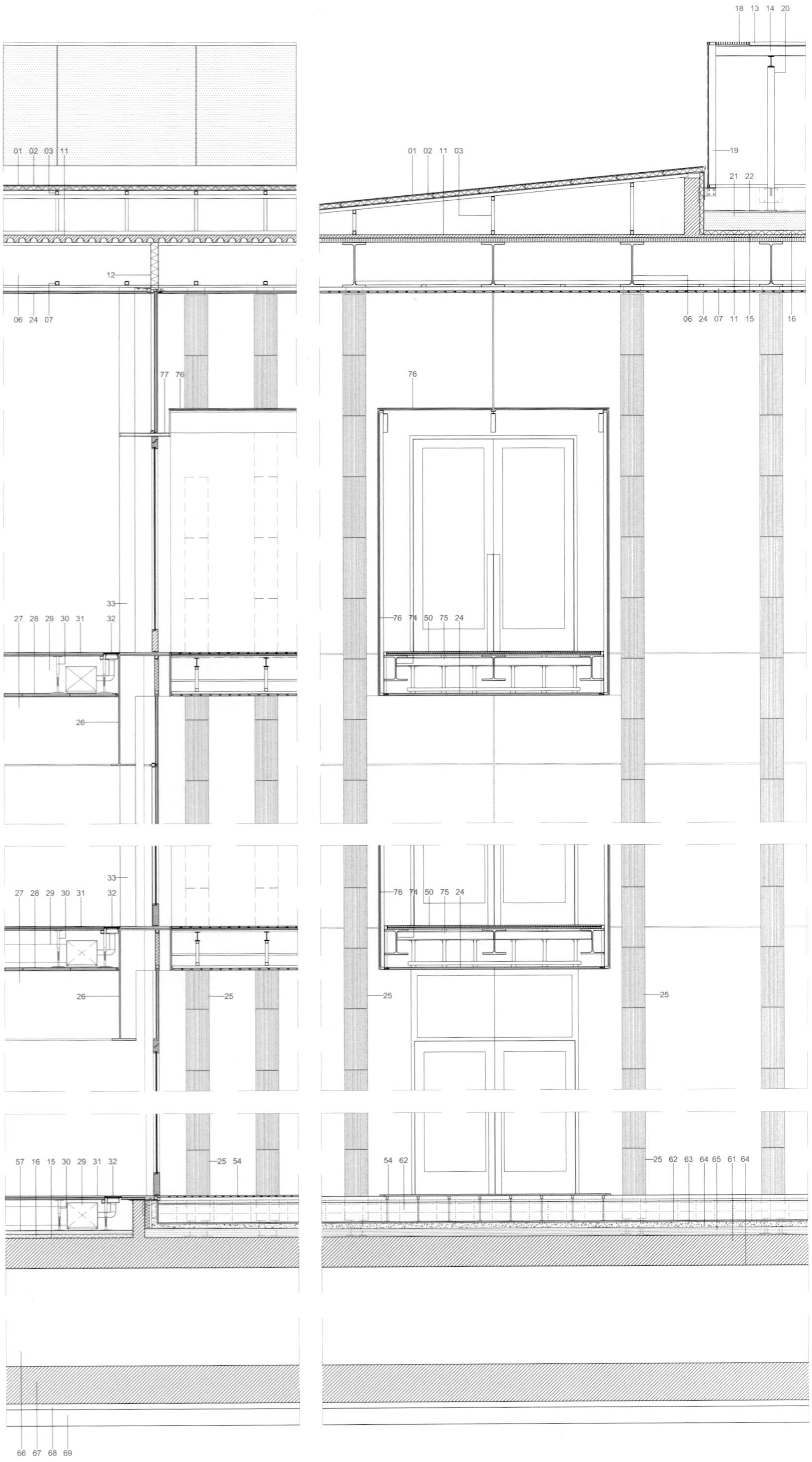

Section Detail 3

0 1 2 3m

1:75

18

Albert de Pineda Alvarez
Manuel Brullet i Tenas

BIOMEDICAL RESEARCH CENTRE

BARCELONA, España

MANUEL BRULLET I TENAS
ALBERT DE PINEDA ALVAREZ

http://www.pinearq.com/

PROJECT HEADS	Toni Montes, Raúl García, Volker Zimmermann, Estefanía Aguado, Josep Roure, Marc Muntané, Eva Tamayo, Jaume Piñol
CONSTRUCTORS	UTE Dragados-COMSA UTE Axima-Klimacal UTE Cobra-Elecnor
PROJECT MANAGER	GPO Ingeniería
OWNER	El Consorci de la Zona Franca Ajuntament de Barcelona Generalitat de Catalunya (DURSI)
PHOTOGRAPHY	Jordi Miralles

	COLLABORATING COMPANIES
Structue	Manuel Arguijo
Installations	Grupo J.G.
Health and Safety	Servei de Prevenció Gaudí
Quantity Surveyor	Imma Casado Francesc Xurigué

	DATES
IMPLEMENTATION PROJECT	2000
BEGINNING OF WORKS	2001
WORK COMPLETION	2005

DESCRIPTIVE BRIEF

The Biomedical Research Park is located on Barcelona's oceanfront, beside the Hospital del Mar.

The surroundings of the site are characterized by a proliferation of singular buildings (the two large towers of the Villa Olímpica, the new building of Gas Natural, the small housing tower and 'mono-block' tower of Hospital del Mar, the fish of Frank Ghery, a sport's centre in the process of restoration, etc...)

In view of these surroundings, the strategy has passed, in the first place, through absorbing the sport centre in process of renovation, inside the complex of buildings of the Biomedical Research Park, placing it below, and secondly, through looking for a volume which does not compete in height with the surrounding buildings, but formally relates and dialogues with all of them.

The proposal of a great platform that organizes the site, in a very irregular way, and the placement above an over-elevated building in the shape of a diagonally truncated elliptical cone, has allowed us to organize the environment and to calmly mix with the closest volumes.

The elliptical shape arises from the need to adapt a building of large dimensions (about 35.000m2 above ground level) to a very small site, of a sensibly irregular shape, and surrounded by very different volumes.

The building is created necessarily compact to adapt itself to the site, but it is terraced towards the sea, softening the seafront and adapting itself to the buildings on the boardwalk, which in this area are low in height; and because of the space available is lifted along its back side towards the city. This terraced shape towards the sea, facilitates the placement of solar panels on the roof for the production hot water and electricity.

The building's interior is emptied to create a new reality, independent from its surroundings, which will frame and control ocean views, and allow the regulation of solar gain.

The building's structure is cantilevered about 7 meters along all of its perimeter.

The façade cladding is designed in natural wood, lightweight, floating above the floor, trying to lighten a building that presents a considerable size for its compact and unitary conception. This second skin must allow a good control of the light and energy of the building.

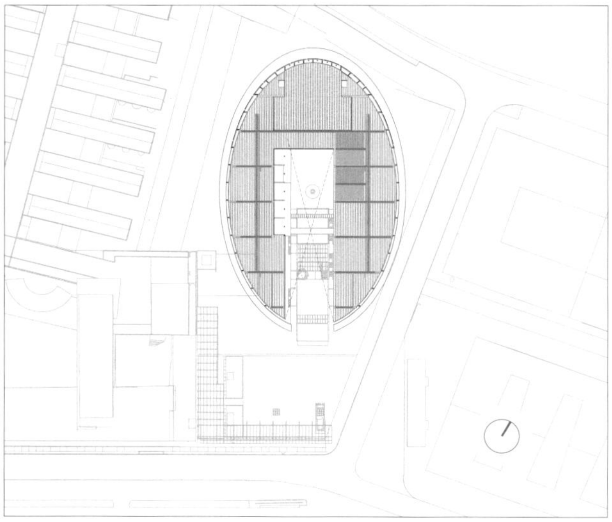

Site Plan

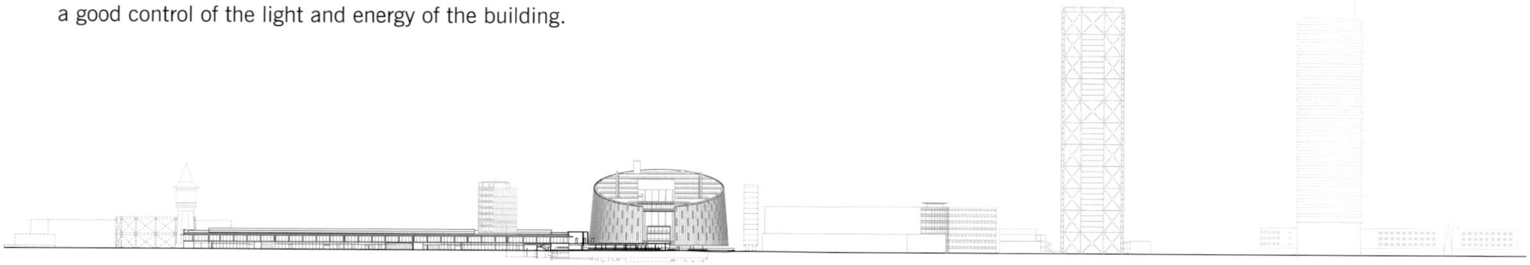

"Of a line architecture is born"

Oscar Niemeyer

ENVIRONMENTAL ANALYSIS

1. Selection of the site. Project and Development

1.1. Location

Latitude: 41°23'07"N
Longitude: 02°11'40"W

The project is located in Barcelona's promenade, in Spain. In this city, a new building typology has emerged since the city opened up urbanly to the sea in 1992. The "Terrain Vague"[1], placed between the maritime border and the littoral bypass is characterized by the proliferation of singular constructions, such as the two tower in the Olympic Villa, the new building of Gas Natural, the mono block tower of the Hospital del Mar and the Frank Gehry´s fish shaped pergola-sculpture amongst others, which in some cases are only related to the coastal border.

1.2 Urban design and site improvement

The project has been built on sports centre in process of restoration that has been absorbed in the ensemble's undergrounds. The general volume has an elliptic cone trunk shape, diagonally shortened, similar to a boat hull, and it does not compete with the surrounding building's height.

In a street level, a great open atrium, facing the promenade, articulates the relationship between the building and the adjacent constructions. This square is part of the architectural ensemble's visible face, whereas in the floors below the ground level, you can find the sports centre, the parking and some of the common scientific facilities of the PRBB´s new building. In the building's central square, three examples of Tijuana tipu have been planted. These trees are typical of South America, but are adapted to the Mediterranean's climatic conditions, and part of the structure has been arranged for them. Those examples can reach a height of 25m. In the atrium in front the building, four examples of phytolacca dioica have been planted. These species, of South American origin, are part of Barcelona's littoral landscape for decades now.

1.3 Project

The building, which is put up on a 9000 m2 lot, has a total surface of 55000 m2, distributed in ground floor, seven storeys plus two attic floors for facilities and two more storeys under the ground level. The plan has an elliptic shape and a high level of functional polyvalence. The elliptic shape arises from the need to adapt a big size building (over 35000 m2 above the ground level) to a very irregular lot, and with very different volumes around it. The building is terraced in the direction of the sea, softening its meeting with the maritime front, whereas its back stands up facing the city in order to have enough space to take in the architectural programme.

The volume has a groove in its verticality that allows to ventilate and illuminate the inside rooms. This way, a free space is created, around which the labs and offices are distributed. This gap is independent of the social setting, and is visually related to the distant sea.

In the underground floors there is a 300 places car park and a 1600 m2 sports centre. There is also here a facilities area to support the labs, the main stores and the merchandise receptions stores. You can gain access to these spaces through a patio which is also used as a supplying access for the adjoining Hospital del Mar.

The building's general accesses as well as the reception areas of the different institutions located in the Park are placed on the ground floor. The rest of the floors hold the offices and labs, which are arranged under clear rational concepts of work space organization.

1 The term Terrain Vague is part of an urban analysis alternative to the models of structuralist origin. Models that have proved their ineffectiveness when facing the contemporary urban facts. The vacuum to rebuilt is an interruption of the grid, a vacuum linked to other times of the city and region's economy.

2. Consumption of energy and Resources

2.1 Consumption of Energy

The building's terraced shape towards the sea makes easier placing in the roof solar panels for sanitary hot water production. The façade's cladding consists of natural wood (Red Cedar from the Pacific[2]) fixed on aluminium structure. This second skin allows a good light energetic control of the building. Each lath is 1.20 metre long, less than ten centimetres wide and a diamond shape cross section that will allow a good visibility from inside and a proper absorption of solar radiation. The choice of this semitraslucent natural skin, that won't even reach to touch the ground, visually reduces, from outside, the volume's weight above the ground level.

The water mirror that covers the auditorium's prism, make's air conditioning easier, as it refreshes the cloister's environment during the summer, and at the same time, it is used as an isolating layer of the space it holds.

2.2 Consumption of Materials

The building is supported by a load-bearing structure which is based on two big T shaped pillars from where all the other floors hang out, supported by metal struts. Between each floor, these struts are connected by a semi-rigid system that allows it to adapt to the stress variations the structure suffers. The struts are distributed so that they cover all the building's perimeter: 46 hold the slabs from the inside, and 66 do it from the outside. This way, the in situ concrete wet work is reduced, which would have required an inside pillar system.

Glass and metallic carpentry were used for the enclosures, as well as an exterior wood skin, which seams to cover all the exterior of the building, when it represents actually, only the 18 % of a façade that has an area of 8800 m2.

3. Environmental loads

3.1 Emissions

Even though its high density, and being considered as rot-proof due to its high content of tannic substances, the wood that covers the building has been treated with lasur[3], which guarantees its durability in saline environments with a high sun and humidity exposure. This substance, with water base, doesn't produce toxic emissions to the atmosphere.

This wood has the FSC (Monte Stewardship Council) certification created by environmental organizations (specially World Wildlife Foundation; the CSA-Z809, a Canadian quality standard that certifies a sustainable forest management developed under auspices of the Canadian Association of Standards, and the ISO 14001, an internationally recognized certification for the management of environmental systems, which has been developed by the International Standardization Organization ISO.

3.2 Solid waste

Above all, it has been tried to homogenize materials depending on their use, distinguishing the structure's materials from the enclosure's materials. With this strategy, the systems are simplified promoting enclosures with homogeneous materials (metal carpentry) that besides being prefabricated in factory, also adapt to the variations this flexible structure can suffer in the service phase.

4. Interior environmental quality

4.1 Ventilation

The horseshoe layout, and an open inner space with light modular partitions, permit the cross ventilation of the offices. Practicable carpentry in the inside façades, and pivoting carpentry in the outside façades, allows the users to regulate manually the ventilation conditions.

4.2 Natural lighting

The building's original horseshoe layout allows natural lighting for all sections, while guaranteeing sea views.

Using wooden slats as the external skin, the designers have recovered a typical element of Mediterranean architecture, applying it in contemporary style. The dark green or brown vernacular Mediterranean shutters serve a double function, regulating both temperature and light. The dark color absorbs heat through radiation, thus having an insulating function while at the same time permits the entrance of light through reflection within the spaces. This light, reflected through the slats inclination, generate spots of light on spaces' the interior ceiling. Thanks to the second reflection a level of half-light is caused, in which the eye's pupil rests and adapts better to the visibility conditions[4].

4.3 Acoustics

A series of strategies improve the building's acoustic comfort. The first one was to close up the volume on the back side towards the freeway and open it up towards the sea. The second one was the supply of trees and a water mirror in the atrium, which isolate from the surrounding street noise, generating pleasant reverberations on the complex's interior.

2 (Thuja gigantea) The red cedar of the pacific is a wood with a great density, a low number of knots and a good elasticity. The laths are vertically separated every ten centimetres and, laid out all over the structure, space-windows can be appreciated, this is, spaces without wood. This is due to the security regulations that the fire brigade of Barcelona has specified in the PRBB building.

3 Lasurs are water-based stains that give wood the properties of hardness, resistance and elasticity. Lasur colours and decorates wood thanks to its pigments which without transmitting opacity to wood, present a high resistance to UV rays and they give it a prolonged durability avoiding that it acquires greyish shades. The new development water-repellent rays, once they have been polymerized, permit water steam formed inside the wood go out, without allowing in rain or humidity. At the same time (in turn), the active elements that contain, avoid fungus actions over its surface.

4 Thanks to this phenomenon apparently simple, values of internal lighting of approximately 900 lux are obtained sufficient to realize reading and writing activities.

5. Control of Building Systems

5.1 Functionality and Efficiency

The diagonal terracing of the roof, on top of lending the building a singular urban character, was designed in order to place the sanitary hot water solar panels with optimized orientation.

5.2 Control of Building Systems

Heterogeneous enclosures were avoided. The two skins covering the building are clearly divided, something which facilitates its maintenance and repairing.

6. Long term behaviour

6.1 Flexibility and adaptability

The adopted structural planning has allowed open floors, making it easier to vary the interior distribution according to necessities.

6.2 Maintenance and operative behavior.

The different nature of structure and enclosure materials makes its maintenance easier, considering that the joints of mechanical type simplify repairing and reduce waste.

The lasur treatment employed on the wooden skin permits a open pore finish, without a film which could rip. The absence of the film allows the wood to breathe, guaranteeing its longevity and extending the treatment period to 3 years between applications.

7. Economic and social aspects

7.1 Social Aspects

Maintaining the sports center as part of the project, a blend of apparently non-related uses arises, generating a positive social interaction for the city. On the one hand a high level institution is being brought closer to a neighborhood facility and on the other hand it gives the complex's users, high level scientists, the possibility to practice sports next to the inhabitants of the city which shelters them.

The building is equipped with computer and highly advanced communications infrastructure, disposes of common and relation spaces, a modern auditorium and, in terms of technology, one of the most advanced animal farms. On the other hand the building also includes additional spaces for its marketing[5]. It's a high level investigation complex, but at the same time opens to the city and to its inhabitants.

The scientific synergies have been considered in the internal disposition. In investigation centres as big as the PRBB, where up to eighty investigator teams work simultaneously, the best ideas often emerge during relaxed conversations the scientists of different groups have while on work-breaks. With this in mind the designers came up with the central cloister, the perimeter terraces, the terraces and the staircases which lead to the auditorium, as meeting areas which encourage this productive idea exchange.

5 http://www.prbb.org/cas/part01/p08.htm

7.2 Economic aspects

Barcelona's Biomedical Investigation Park building is carefully designed to host internationally high level investigational and teaching institutions. Through this initiative Barcelona is looking to put itself in the leading position of biomedical investigation in the south of Europe. The critical mass generated by the activity of more than a million persons, originating from 30 countries, can only have a multiplying effect.

It was looked after writing off the cost of 100 million euro in construction and annual 50 million for its operation, with contributions from institutional organizations and private companies which locate their activity right here. It was aspired to obtain another part of the budget through competitive contracts with the biomedical industry.

8. The architect's eye

In terms of urbanism, the [concept] of singularity which characterizes the surrounding buildings is maintained. In this sense the littoral reminds us of the proceedings [realized acts] of the American west coast. On the other hand the architect has been able to reinterpret Mediterranean architecture concepts like the patio and the blinds, applying them with care on a contemporary construction.

BIOMEDICAL RESEARCH CENTRE
Albert de Pineda Alvarez - Manuel Brullet i Tenas

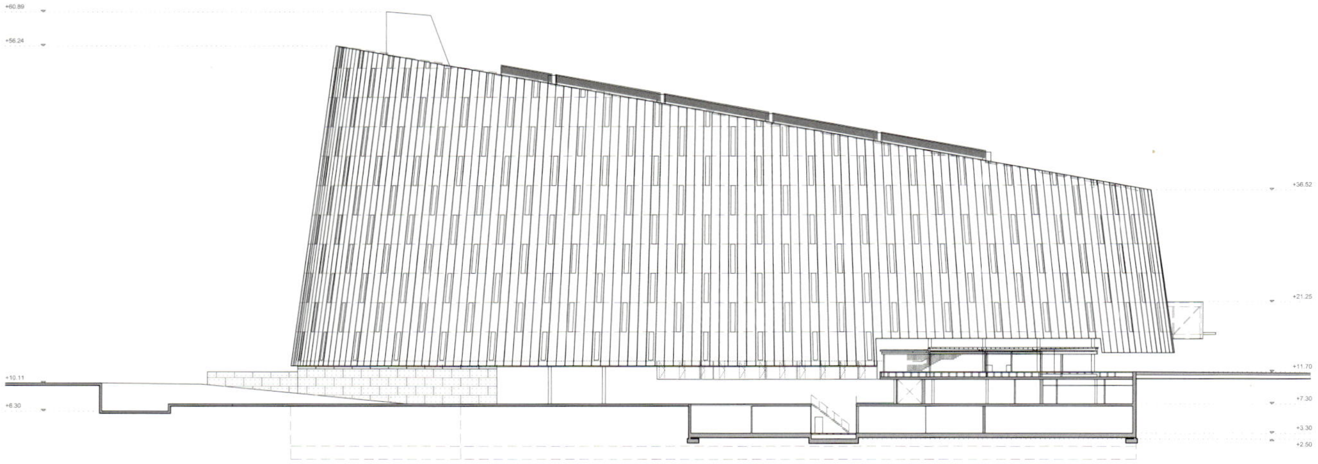

South Elevation

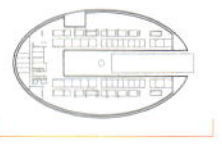

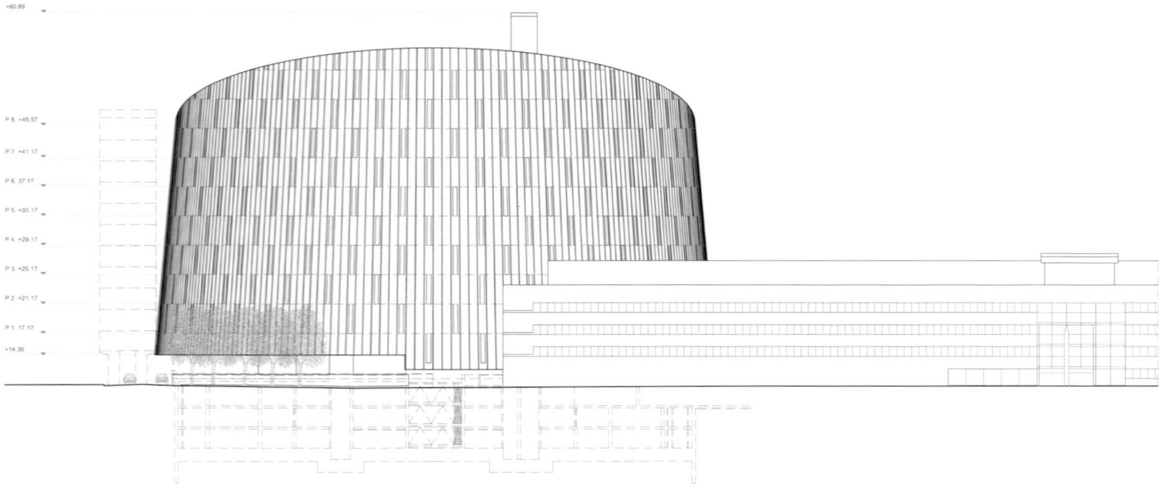

West Elevation

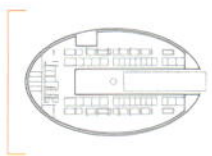

0 5 10m 20m

1:1000

BIOMEDICAL RESEARCH CENTRE

Albert de Pineda Alvarez - Manuel Brullet i Tenas

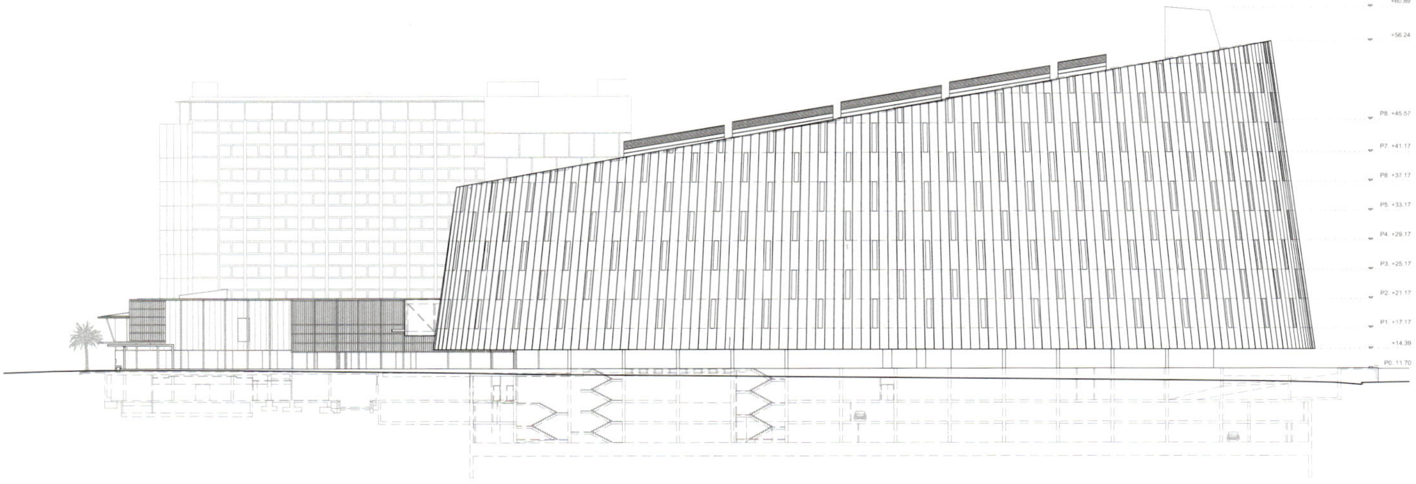

North Elevation

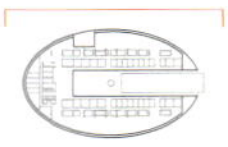

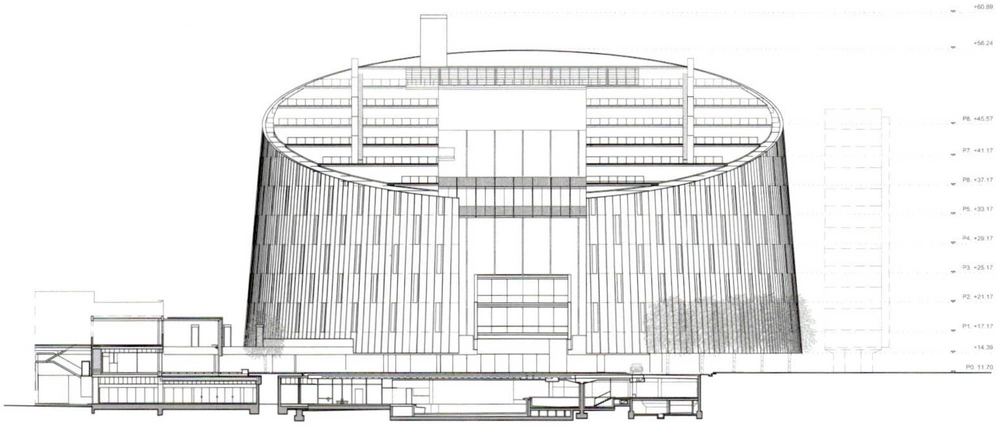

East Elevation

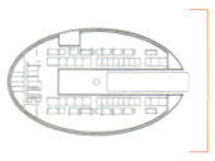

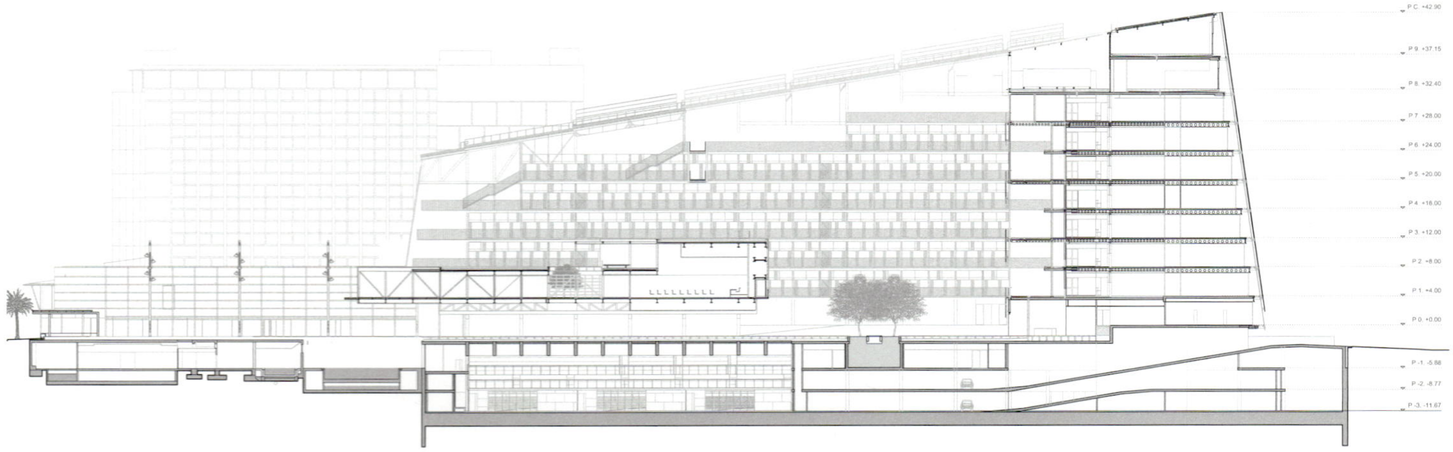

Longitudinal Section

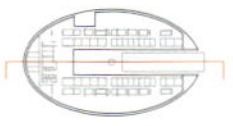

0 5 10m 20m

1:1000

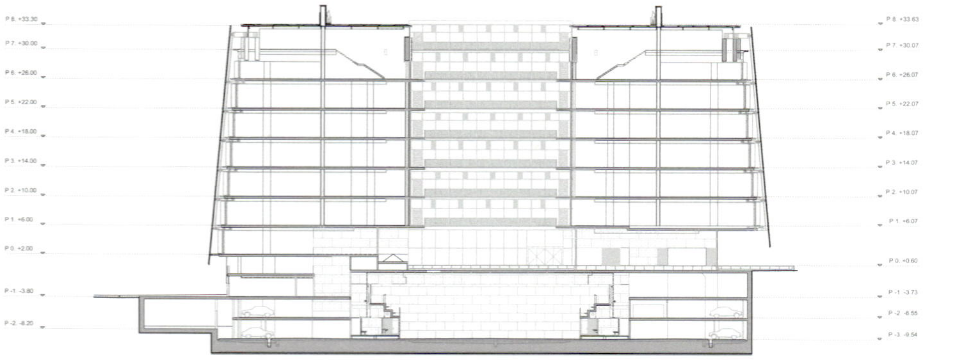

Transversal Section

0 5 10m 20m

1:1000

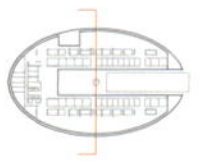

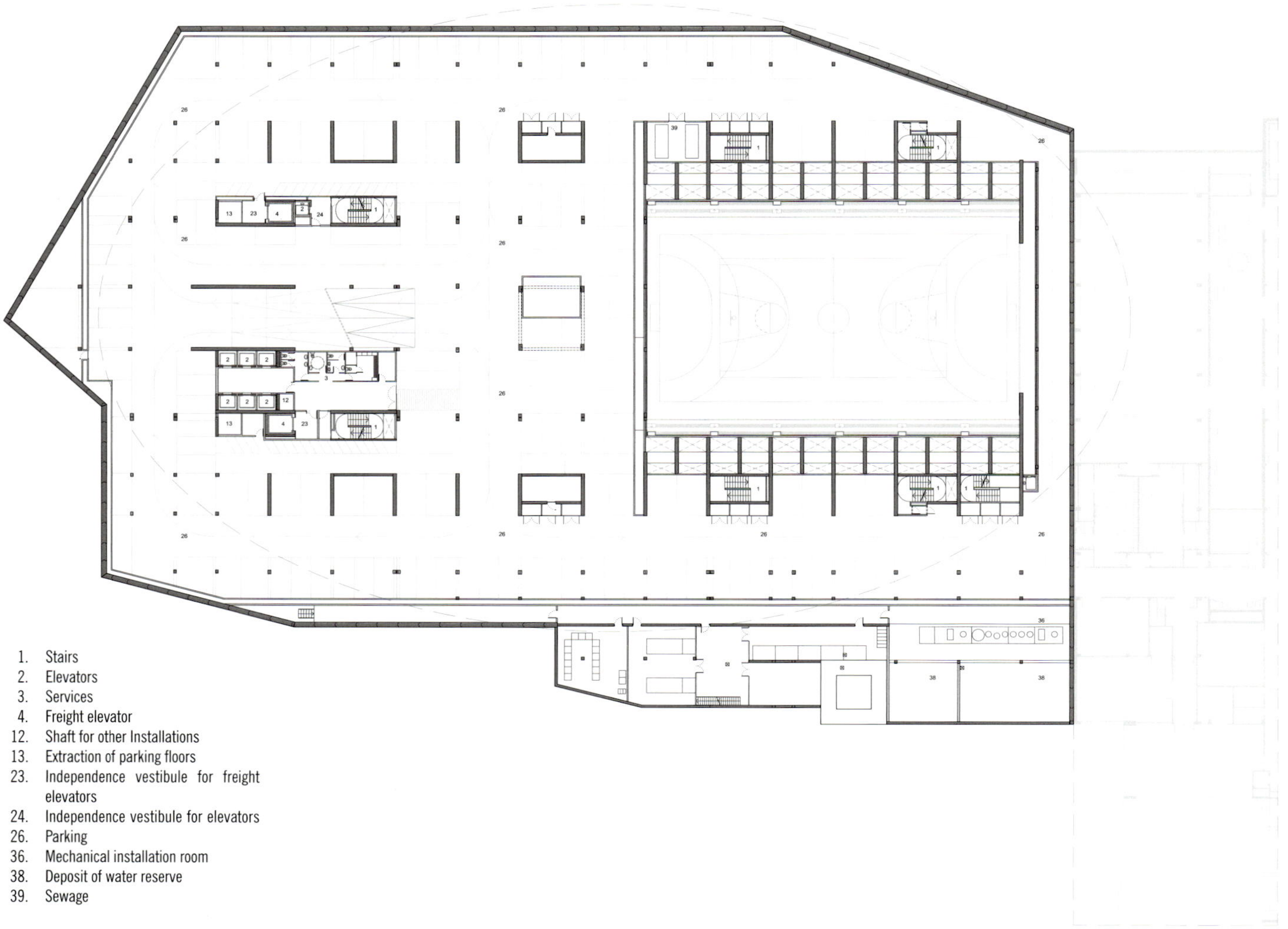

1. Stairs
2. Elevators
3. Services
4. Freight elevator
12. Shaft for other Installations
13. Extraction of parking floors
23. Independence vestibule for freight elevators
24. Independence vestibule for elevators
26. Parking
36. Mechanical installation room
38. Deposit of water reserve
39. Sewage

Floor Level -2

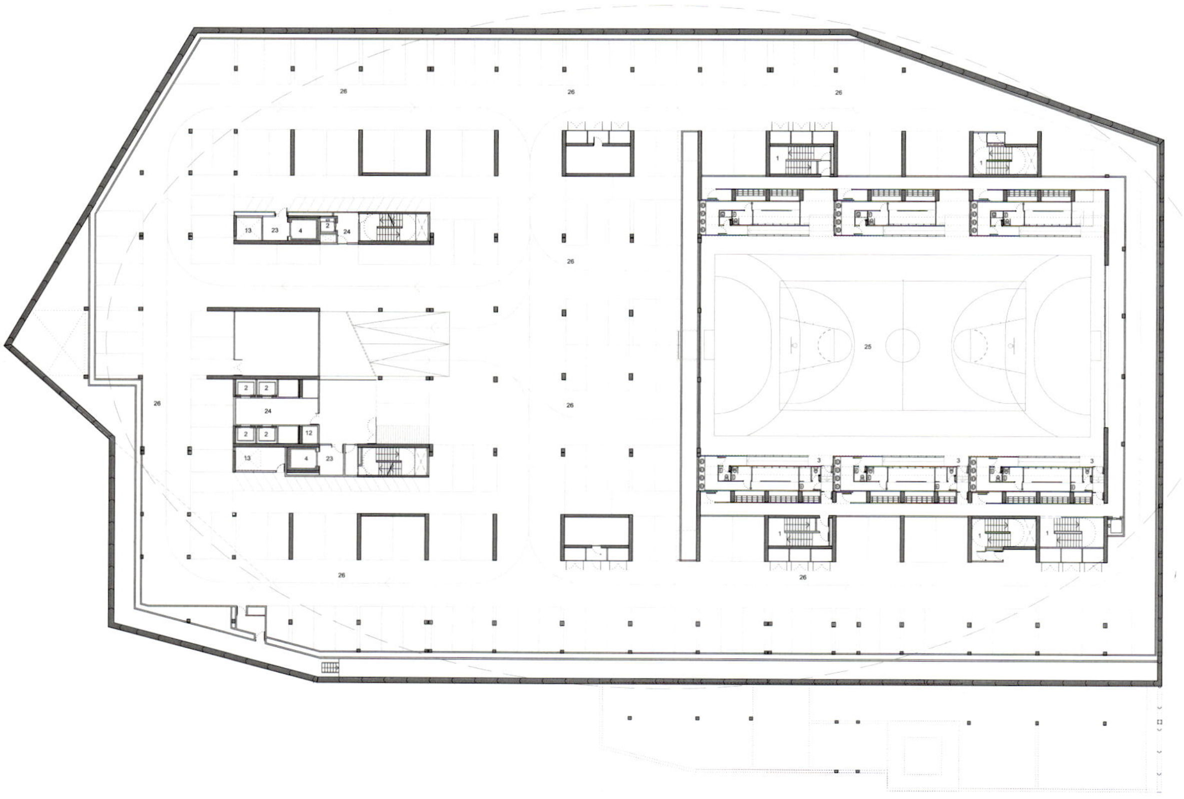

1. Stairs
2. Elevators
3. Services
4. Freight elevator
12. Shaft for other Installations
13. Extraction of parking floors
23. Independence vestibule for freight elevators
24. Independence vestibule for elevators
25. Sports center
26. Parking

Floor Level -3

0 5 10m

1:800

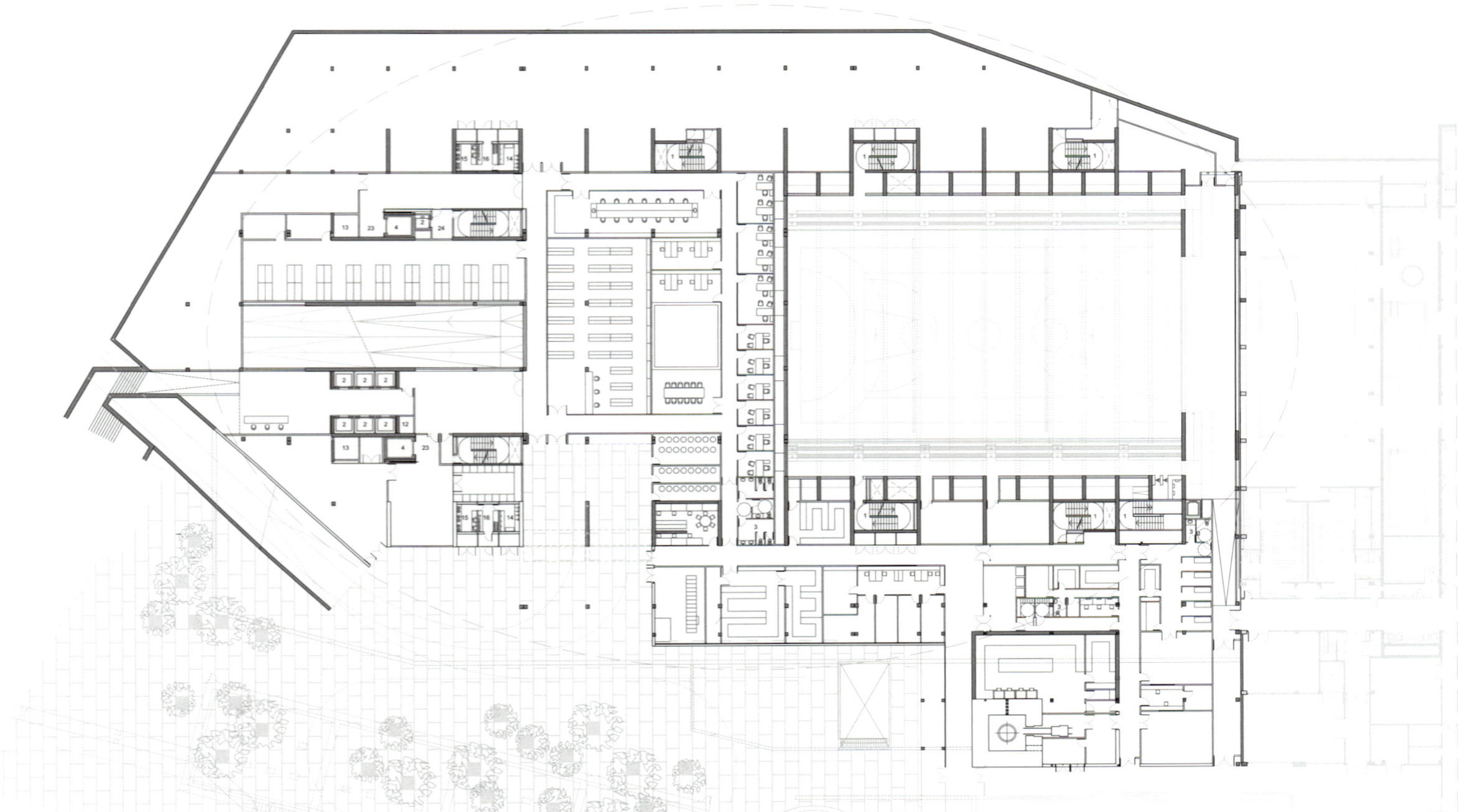

1. Stairs
2. Elevators
3. Services
4. Freight elevator
12. Shaft for other Installations
13. Extraction of parking floors
14. Shafts for electricity, sound and data
15. Shafts for water for air conditioning and fire protection
16. Shafts for sanitary water
23. Independence vestibule for freight elevators
24. Independence vestibule for elevators

Floor Level -1

BIOMEDICAL RESEARCH CENTRE

Albert de Pineda Alvarez - Manuel Brullet i Tenas

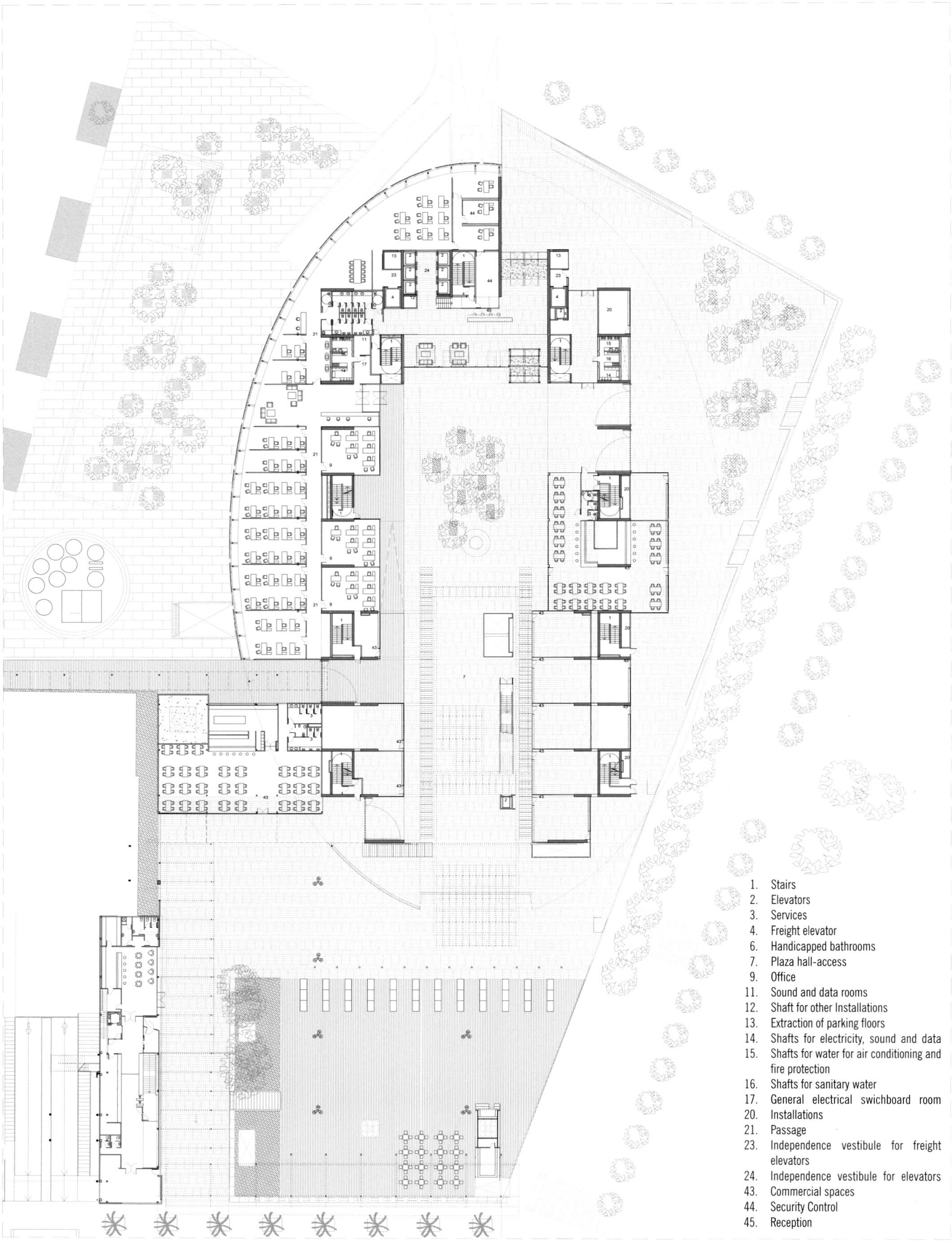

1. Stairs
2. Elevators
3. Services
4. Freight elevator
6. Handicapped bathrooms
7. Plaza hall-access
9. Office
11. Sound and data rooms
12. Shaft for other Installations
13. Extraction of parking floors
14. Shafts for electricity, sound and data
15. Shafts for water for air conditioning and fire protection
16. Shafts for sanitary water
17. General electrical swichboard room
20. Installations
21. Passage
23. Independence vestibule for freight elevators
24. Independence vestibule for elevators
43. Commercial spaces
44. Security Control
45. Reception

Ground Floor Level

0 5 10m

1:800

BIOMEDICAL RESEARCH CENTRE

Albert de Pineda Alvarez - Manuel Brullet i Tenas

1. Stairs
2. Elevators
3. Services
4. Freight elevator
5. Laboratory machines
6. Handicapped bathrooms
7. Plaza hall-access
8. Seminars - meeting rooms
9. Offices
10. Laboratories
11. Sound and data rooms
12. Shaft for other Installations
13. Extraction of parking floors
14. Shafts for electricity, sound and data
15. Shafts for water for air conditioning and fire protection
16. Shafts for sanitary water
17. General electrical swichboard room
18. Extraction chimneys
19. Exterior terrace
21. Passage
23. Independence vestibule for freight elevators
41. Cleaning
42. Maintenance

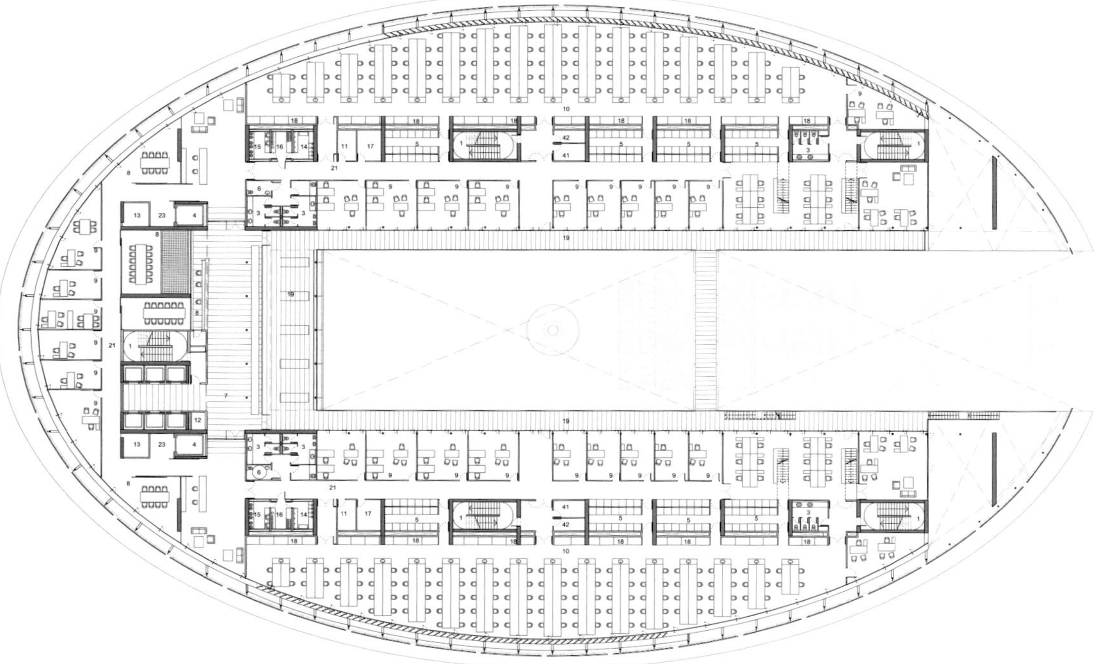

Floor Level 5

1:800

1. Stairs
2. Elevators
3. Services
4. Freight elevator
5. Laboratory machines
6. Handicapped bathrooms
7. Plaza hall-access
8. Seminars - meeting rooms
9. Offices
10. Laboratories
11. Sound and data rooms
12. Shaft for other Installations
13. Extraction of parking floors
14. Shafts for electricity, sound and data
15. Shafts for water for air conditioning and fire protection
16. Shafts for sanitary water
17. General electrical swichboard room
18. Extraction chimneys
19. Exterior terrace
21. Passage
22. Assembly room
23. Independence vestibule for freight elevators
41. Cleaning
42. Maintenance

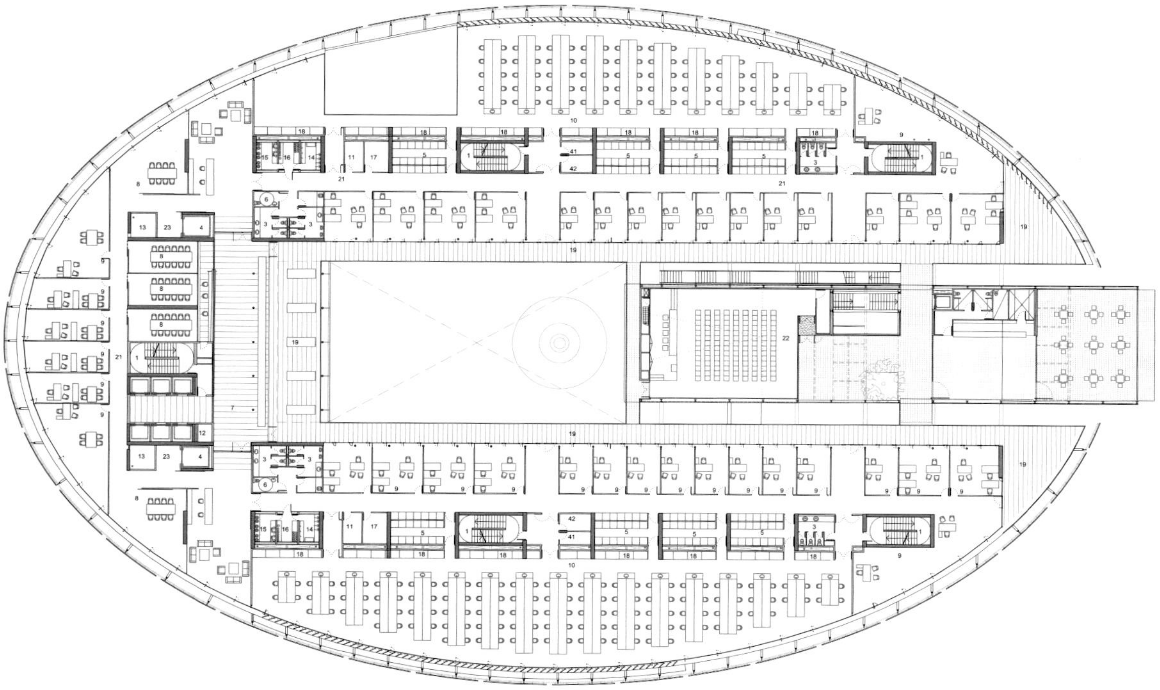

Floor Level 1

prbb
Parc
Recerca
Biomèdica
Barcelona

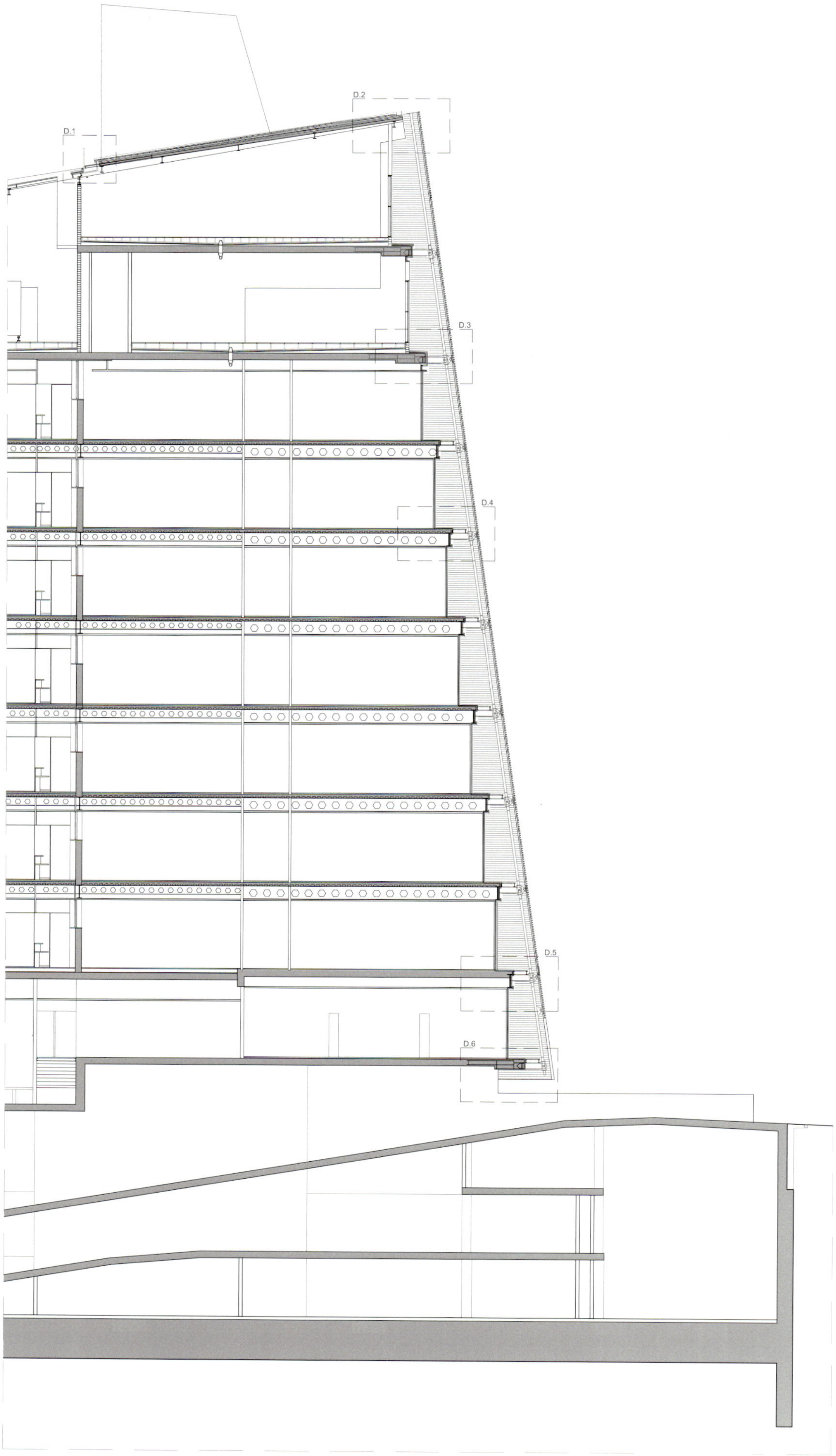

Construction Detail 1

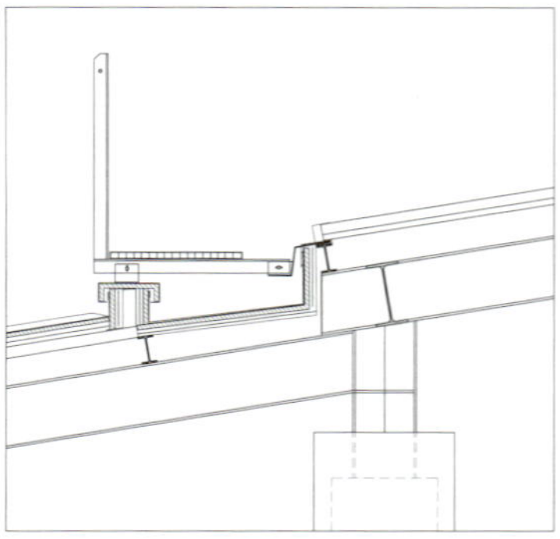

D. 1''

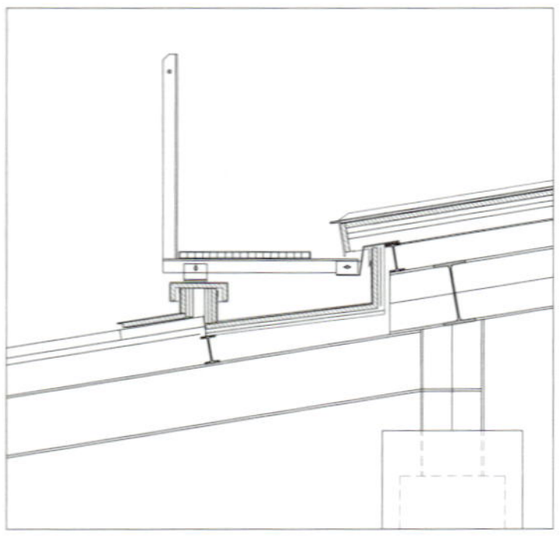

D. 1

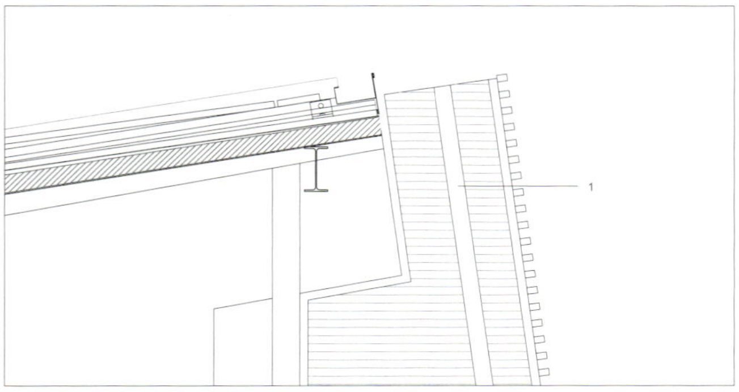

D. 2

1:50

1. Solid steel bar ø120
2. Steel counter-pipe with bolt fasteners
3. IPE 280
4. Embossed pavement
5. IPE 160

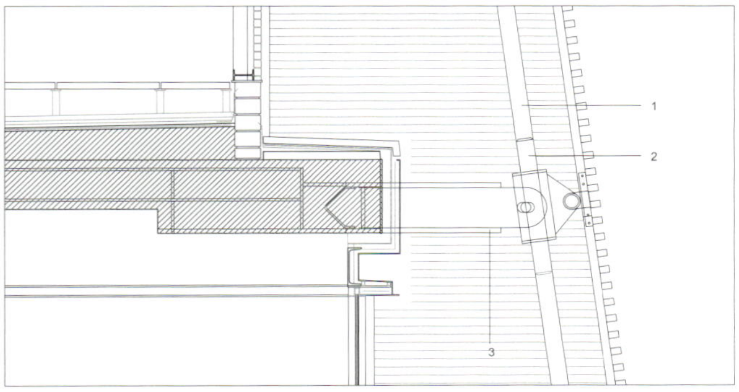

D. 3

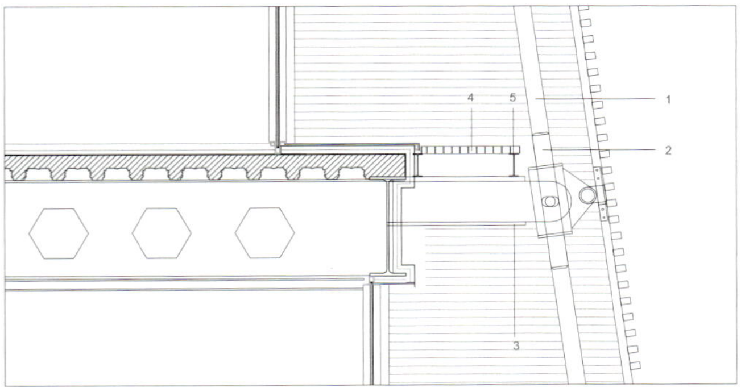

D. 4

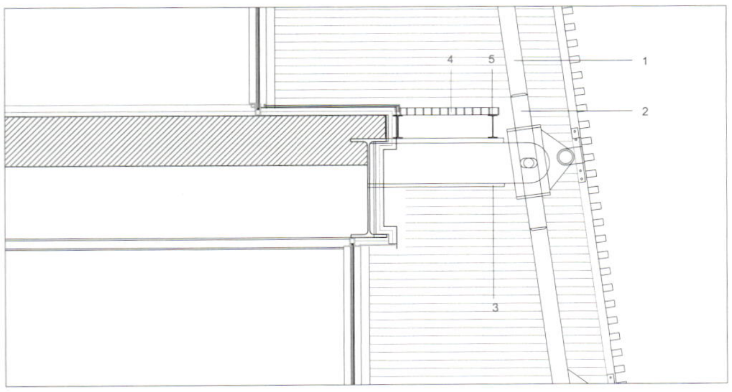

D. 5

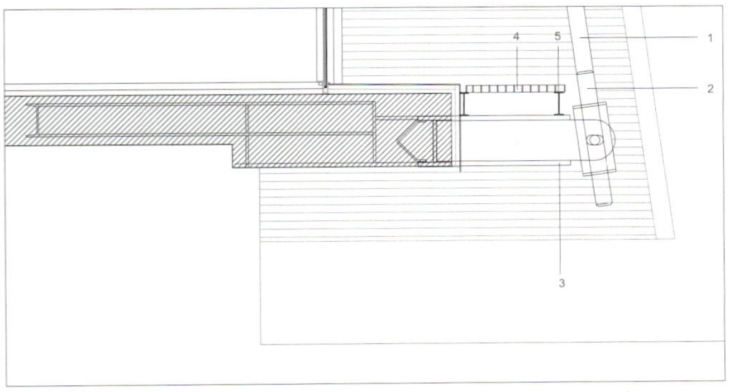

D. 6

BIOMEDICAL RESEARCH CENTRE

Albert de Pineda Alvarez - Manuel Brullet i Tenas

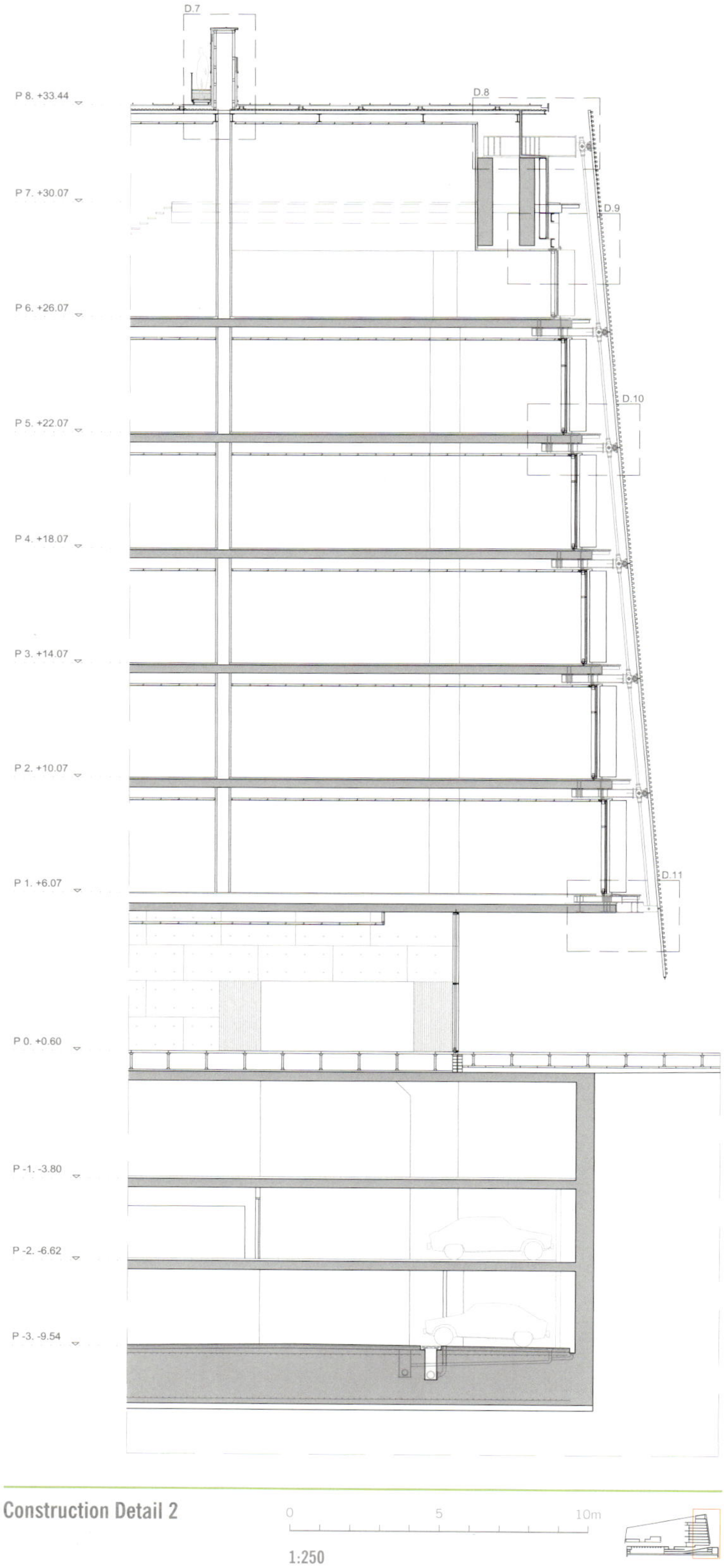

Construction Detail 2

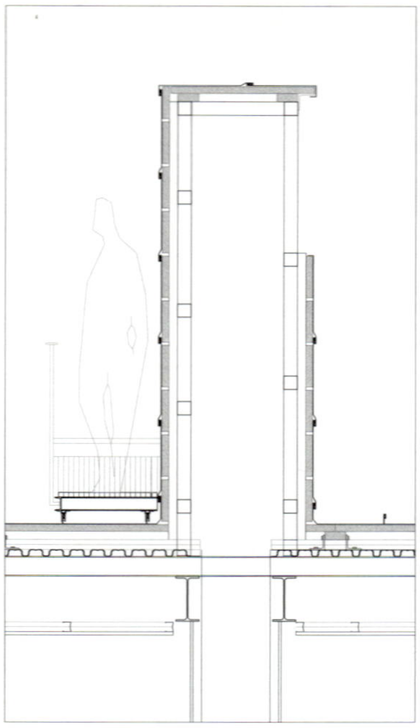

D. 7

1. Solid steel bar ø120
2. Steel counter-pipe with bolt fasteners
3. IPE 280
4. Embossed pavement

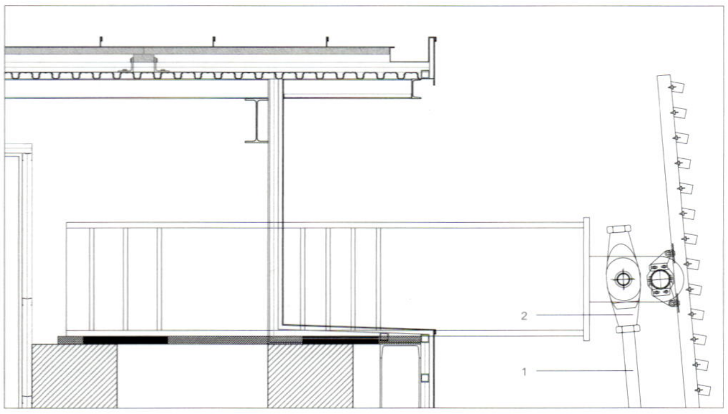

1:50

D. 8

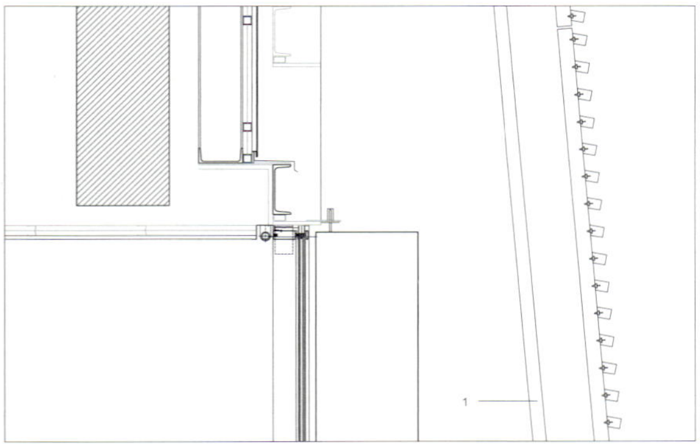

D. 9

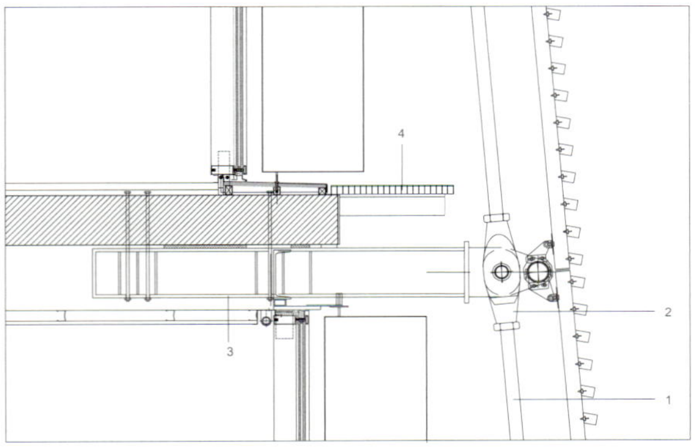

D. 10

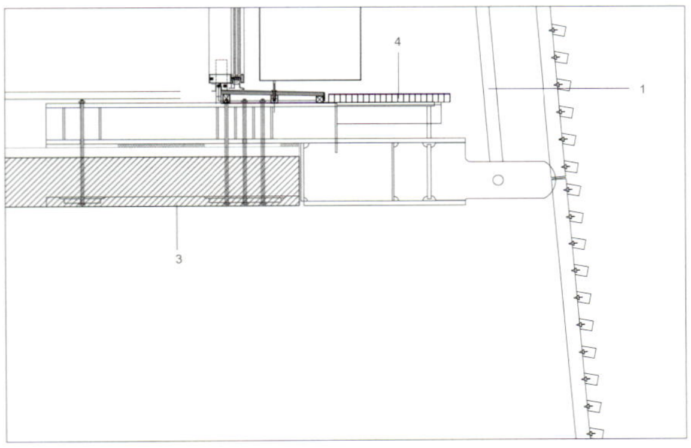

D. 11

Box
3

Miguel Palmero

VILADECANS HOSPITAL

VILADECANS, España

HOSPITAL SANT LLOREÇ VILADECANS

www.palmeroarquitectos.com

COLLABORATORS	Alon Eldar 2 Arq
PHOTOGRAPHY	Eugeni Pons
	COLLABORATING COMPANIES
Bioclimatic Advice	Grupo JG Ingenieros Consultores
Structure	BOMA
	DATES
IMPLEMENTATION PROJECT	1998
BEGINNING OF WORKS	1999
WORK COMPLETION	2000

DESCRIPTIVE BRIEF

The Sant Llorenç de Viladecans hospital of the Institut Català de la Salut (ICS), forming part of the XHUP, covers the population of the municipalities of Gavá, Viladecans, Castelldefels, St. Climent and Begues.

The hospital was initiated in the industrial saga of the Roca iron and steel industry, and is situated on Gavá Avenue next to the new axis of development of city services, which is made up of Marqués de Estella Street and begins with this extension.

The extension of San Llorenç de Viladecans Hospital rises from the necessity to resolve the current overload.

A force of emergency services is planned, adjunct to the existing hospital, that together with the old services and the radiography core, will form a single element.

The adopted solution is based on a volume placed perpendicularly to the existing hospital, creating an access plaza, landscaped and paved, along with the parking lot and vehicular accesses to the emergency services.

In order to speed up the execution time, a construction system using prefabricated elements was chosen, avoiding unnecessary finishes and highlighting the plasticity of the materials, as well as the building's flexible character.

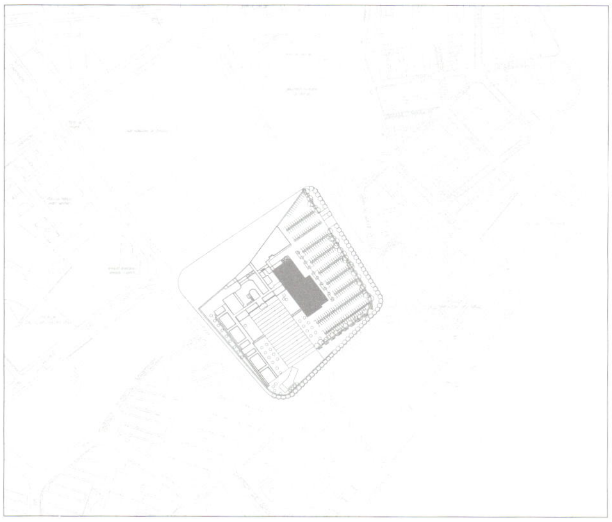

Site Plan

"All should be made so simple as it is possible, but not simpler"
Maurice Freehill

ENVIRONMENTAL ANALYSIS

1. Choosing the Site. Project and Development

1.1. Location

Latitude: 41°18'13"N
Longitude: 02°00'52"E

1.2 Urban Design and Site Improvement

The project responds to the necessity of extending the Sant Llorenç de Viladecans Hospital.
It was designed as one emergency service volume, adherent to the existing hospital, which forms a singular element along with the old services and radiography core.

The intervention derives from a formal concept; the building is positioned on the central axis of the city block and differentiates two public zones, the parking lot and the pedestrian access.

On the urban scale, the proposal is oriented according to classic concepts, defining in the fabric two types of uses within the block. The city block, of public use, is characterized by the locating the building in the center and the open spaces on the border, guaranteeing better visual perspectives and a greater representation of the hosting institution.

Along with the extension project, the opportunity was taken to renovate the hospital's surroundings, integrating the parking and green areas which were separated, and generating a single environment which serves both functions, while also improving the surroundings. With this aim, a tree-covered parking lot was proposed to provide shade, contribute to the CO_2 reductions of the area, and to the control of the building's temperature, eliminating the circulation which divided the location in two parts.

The extension is solved with a rectangular volume, designed like a skin which serves as protection from the exterior, controlling the solar incidence according to the necessities in each season of the year.

1.3 Project

The project is made up of a volume which annexes to the pre-existing, like a wing of the same building. The new extension is organized through the definition of an access which joins the two public zones, and from which different circulations part towards the different program spaces.

Each circulation is treated with a different type of sunlight; Lateral lighting for public zones and overhead lighting for the hospital's internal zones. This differentiation in the lighting of the spaces is organized based on different symbolic connotations of light in culture[1].

1 Skylight has had a subjective component related to mystical and religious manifestations in various cultures. We want to emphasize the architect's ability to make use of this resource in the hospital's internal spaces, where this subjective component can support the intern's recuperation in a decisive way.

Design Process

Concept

Perforate

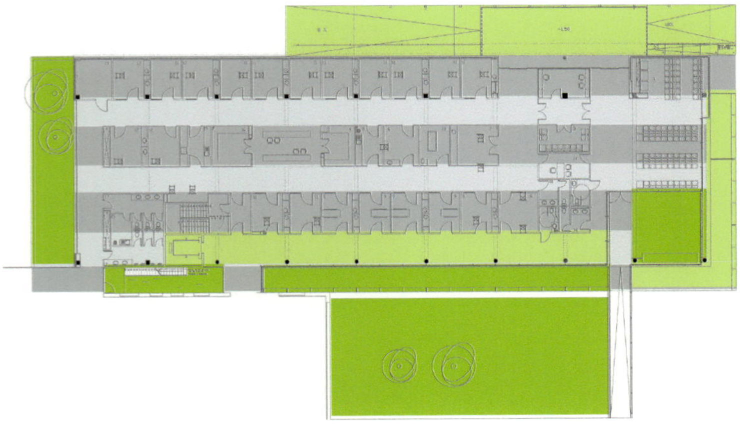

Adapt

The intervention is divided into four zones:

Zone 1
Based on the analysis of the solar incidence during each season of the year, the public space includes the main access and the ambulance's emergency access, vestibule, waiting room and reception. It is here where, during the winter, the air which circulates through the building is heated by way of the greenhouse effect. For optimum air-distribution, interior gardens are used to generate a microclimate which humidifies and regulates sudden temperature changes in summer.

Zone 2
The work and medical revision spaces are where treatment, exploration, first aid, nursing station, storage rooms etc. are located. It is an open space which permits flexibility for future circulation and usage modifications. The roof, solved as a bar code, generates corridors which illuminate and ventilate the interior.

Zone 3
The floor below grade will house the laboratory spaces, which are currently almost entirely underground, awaiting a second phase of construction. This area is illuminated and ventilated through inclined slopes on the south and west sides.

Zone 4
The current emergency area which will be devoted to the doctor's private area, where bedrooms, bathrooms and rest areas will be located, connected to the extension volume through a corridor with access to both the public and the work area.

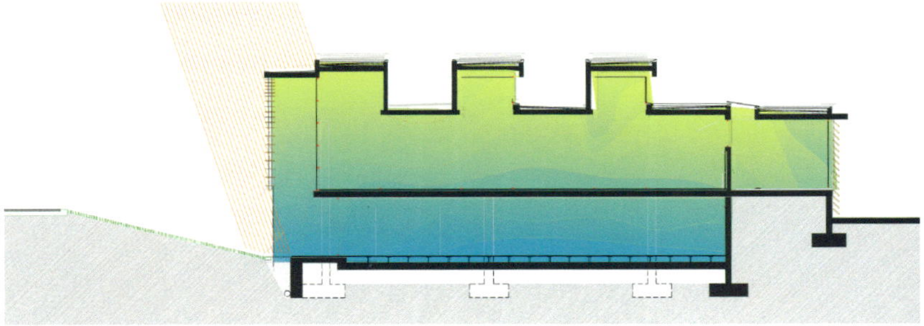

Air temperature analysis: Summer solstice

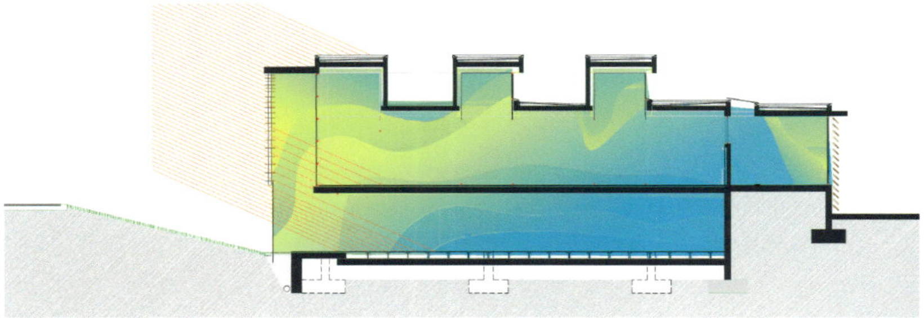

Air temperature analysis: Winter solstice

2. Consumption of Energy and Resources

2.1 Consumption of Energy

The active air conditioning systems are designed to support the natural ventilation system, operating during extreme temperature conditions in the warmest or coldest periods of the year.

The roof has been designed to reduce the energy consumption to a minimum. Gravel was placed on the surface, absorbing and dispersing the heat caused by the rays of sunlight, avoiding the transmission of heat towards the interior and reducing the necessity of air conditioning during the warmer months. Skylights with openings oriented to the north were also provided, with the aim of naturally lighting the interior. All spaces have natural lighting and ventilation, reducing the use of energy and maintenance.

As support systems, low energy lights have been used in interior working areas, power controllers in every zone, condensers and transformers, and power compensation batteries.

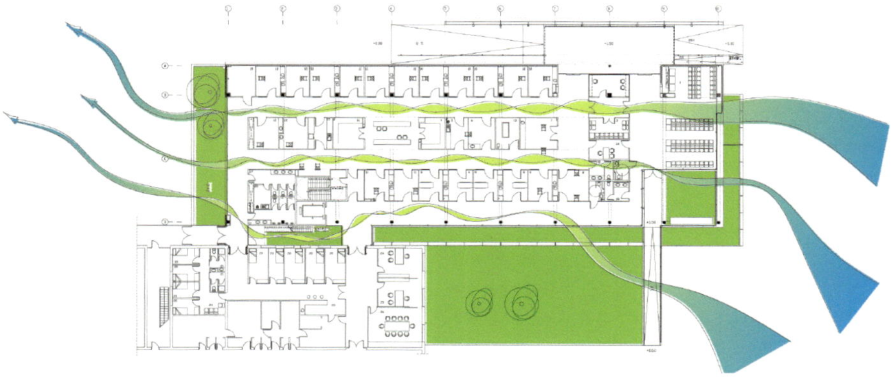

Wind blows : Acces floor level

2.2 Consumption of Materials

An efficient system was chosen to reduce execution and maintenance times. The project made use of prefabricated elements and industrial systems, favoring the natural aspect of each element. In this way its use is optimized, the waste is minimized, and the affectation to the site is reduced.

High quality wooden slats were placed, which in addition to regulating the solar incidence, grants warmth to the façade's industrial aspect.

All interior partitions are made of prefabricated modules which permit high flexibility and adaptability.

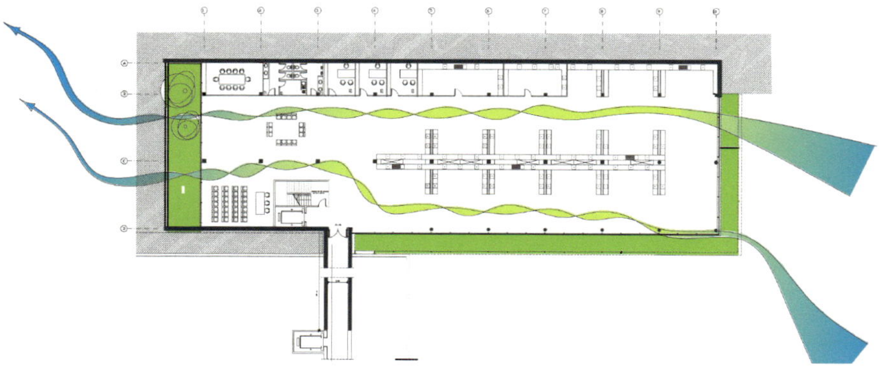

Wind blows: Lower ground floor level

2 In order to improve the power factor of an electric installation, the simplest system locates condensers which provide the reactive power needed by the installation receptors; in this way one decreases or even cancels (technically: compensates) the reactive energy demanded by the supply network and therefore improves the power factor.

3. Environmental Loads

3.1 Emissions

It was decided to construct using prefabricated elements with the intention of helping to reduce emissions caused by the industrialization of the posterior-finish materials, as well as reducing the use of mechanical units and energy resources during the construction phase.

3.2 Solid Waste

Thanks to the application of prefabricated systems, waste caused by the construction is considerably reduced, as is its environmental impact. Through the joint and assembly systems applied, the dismantling, modification or demolition is facilitated.

3.3 Water Management

In general, consumption reduction systems were installed, such as: taps with water volume reducing mechanisms, low volume and rainwater-collecting lavatories.

4. Interior Environmental Quality

4.1 Ventilation

Based on the favorable climate which prevails on location, a design was chosen which takes advantage of the natural wind situation, along with an artificial ventilation system as support for days of extreme temperature.

In the space which makes up the corridors, reception and waiting rooms, glazed surfaces oriented to the south were designed, serving as temperature regulators for the air of the building and acting as a thermal collector. In this way the air, which later flows through the corridors into the interior, is heated by way of the greenhouse effect.

For the summer months, green areas towards the south were designed which serve to maintain the wind's ideal temperature before filtering to the interior. This design strategy is enhanced through the remaining systems on the roof, which allow the air to maintain its temperature during its passage through the different spaces.

The openings on the building's back side and on the roof, along with the arrangement of spaces, allow the crossed ventilation of the complex and the system's continuous fresh air supply.

The mechanical systems are provided with machines with screw compressor, module burners, free-cooling air-conditioners, variable speed ventilators, individual room control, and proportional electronic control3.

4.2 Natural Lighting

The ensemble's lighting is solved through the tinted, glazed surfaces orientated to the south, which provide the public area of the building with natural light. The interior disposes of two openings towards the north in the roof, through which all interior corridors are lit. The floor below grade is lit through glazed sections located in the English style courtyard.

All of these measures allow the majority of the spaces to receive natural lighting, reducing the consumption of electricity.

4.3 Acoustics

Sound absorbing materials were chosen for walls and ceilings, along with special glazing in apertures which help to considerably decrease noise pollution, from or towards the building.

3 The screw compressor needs less maintenance than a conventional compressor, and it is adequate for the air conditioning of large areas. The free-cooling system consists of lattices which open up and permit the entering of exterior, cool air, which is then injected into the inside area through the air conditioning unit, reducing the use of compressors.

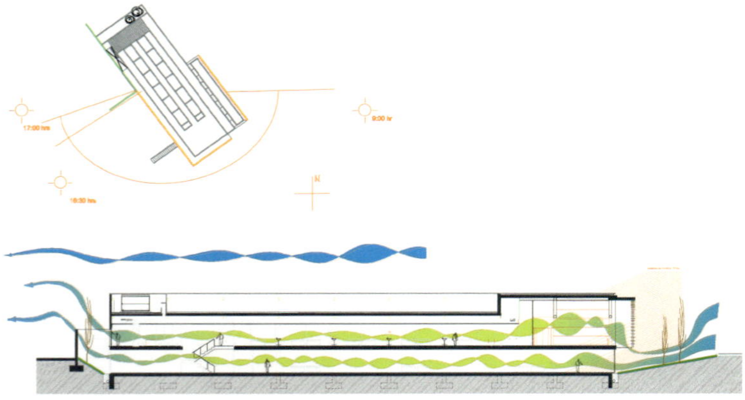

Analysis of solar incidence and winds: Summer solstice
Longitudinal section

an·lisis de incidencia solar y vientos

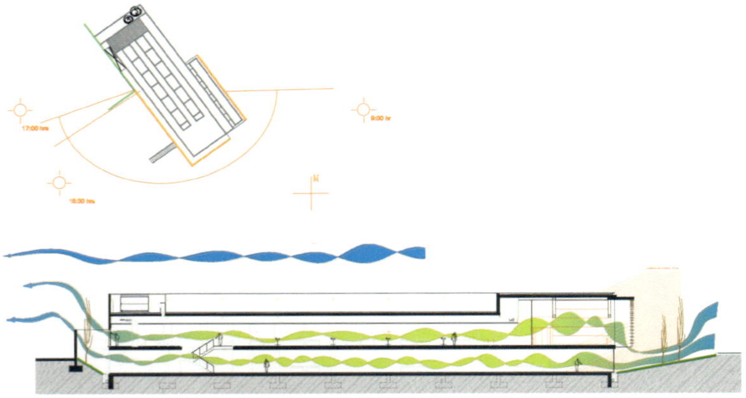

Analysis of solar incidence and winds: Winter solstice
Longitudinal section

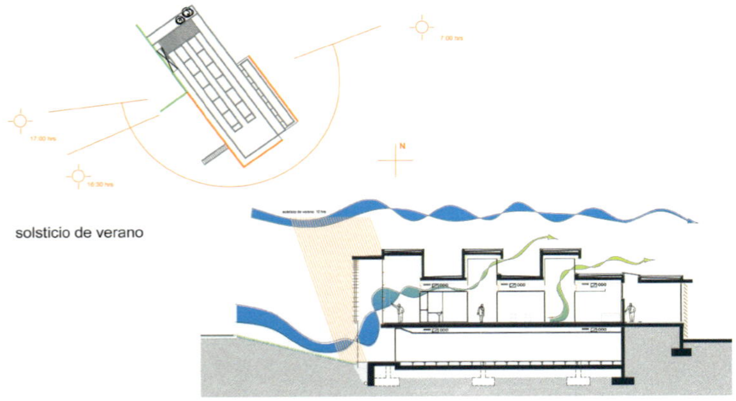

Analysis of solar incidence and winds: Summer solstice
Transversal section

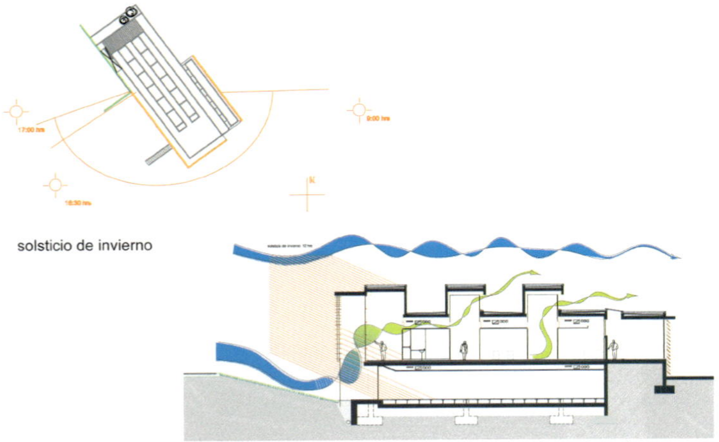

Analysis of solar incidence and winds: Winter solstice
Transversal section

5. Control of Building Systems

5.1 Functionality and Efficiency

The constructive system was planned with prefabricated materials in mind. The building's foundation is made up of concrete columns and retaining walls below grade. From then on, the central columns disappear giving way to an open ground floor, achieved thanks to a large truss and prefabricated concrete elements.

The facades have been distinguished; in the south they are solved through glazed façades, protected by Prodema louvers, and in the north with prefabricated concrete elements with smaller openings, in order to protect from the lowest temperatures during the winter.

6. Long-term Performance

6.1 Flexibility and Adaptability

The open floor plan and centralized installations allow future adaptations to new architectural program or extensions.

6.2 Maintenance and Operative Performance

The maintenance tasks are considerably reduced, having avoided the application of unnecessary finishes.

Green areas view: Pedestrian entrance

7. Economic and Social Aspects

7.1 Social Aspects

Considering the necessities for a optimum work space for the emergency service personnel and users, technical solutions were chosen which offer a high level of comfort. This provides an adequate space which facilitates the development, and therefore improves the quality, of the medical service offered.

7.2 Economic Aspects

Thanks to intense planning during the project phase, the design of an economically sustainable building was achieved by incorporating different passive ventilation and natural lighting systems, along with thermal insulation and solar radiation control. The incorporation of these systems allows savings in the operation of conventional systems. In this way the energy cost of the building's operation, throughout its lifespan, is reduced.

8. The Architect's Eye

Working with an existing building, the architect was able to identify the values which originated it. In this case, the original building has a classic composition. In his proposal, the architect continues with this disposition from the urban scale up to the building's organization. The formal representation has changed both in its abstract language, as in its material composition. Moreover, he was capable of contributing extra value to the space: the study of natural lighting with its cultural connotations and positive subjective influence on the hospital program.

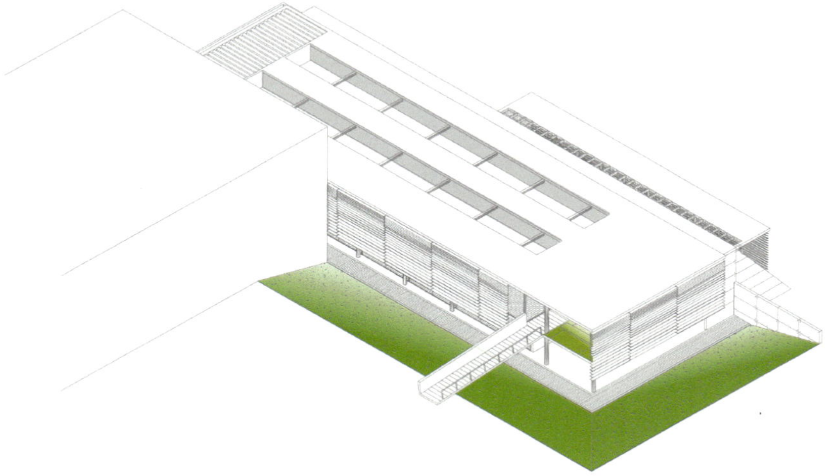

Green areas view: General axonometry

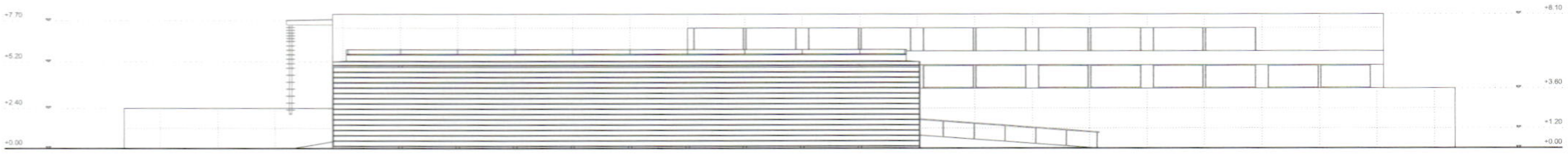

North Elevation

Southwest Elevation

1:500

Southest Elevation

0 5 10m

1:500

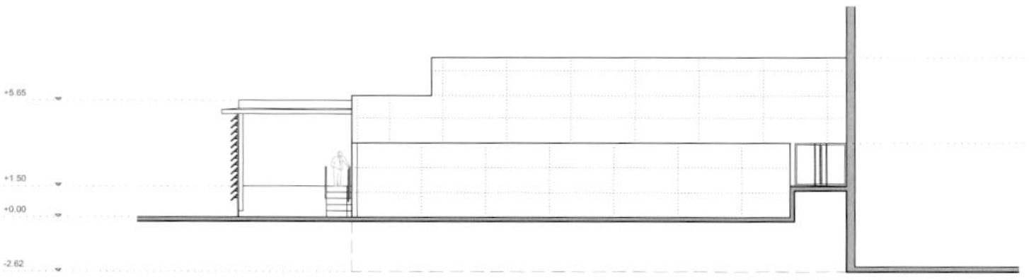

Northwest Elevation

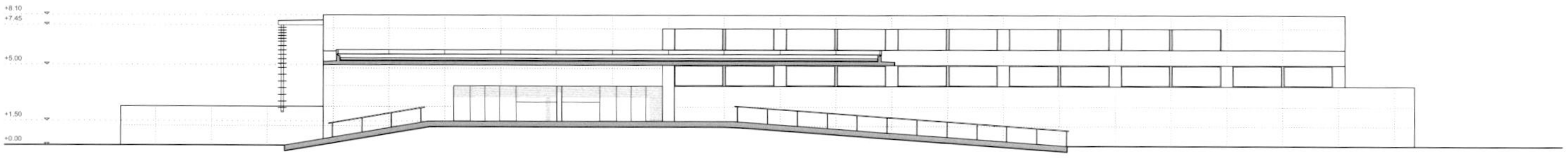

Section 1

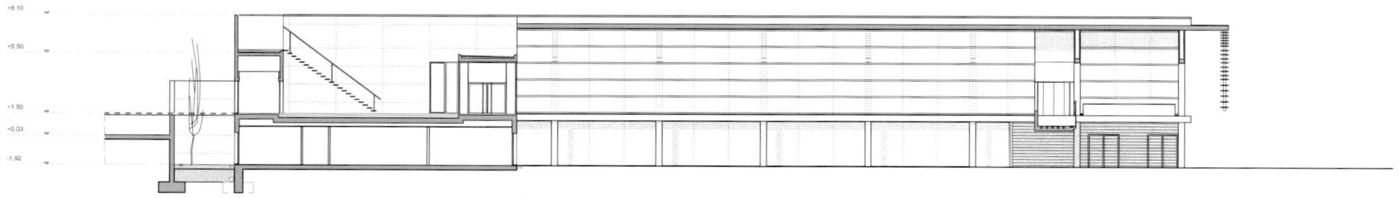

Section 2

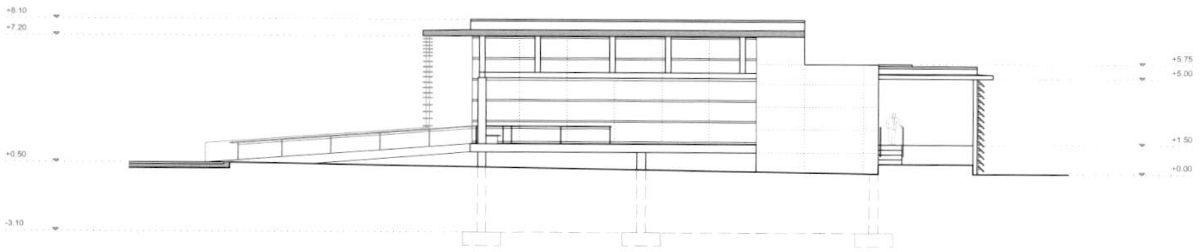

Section 3

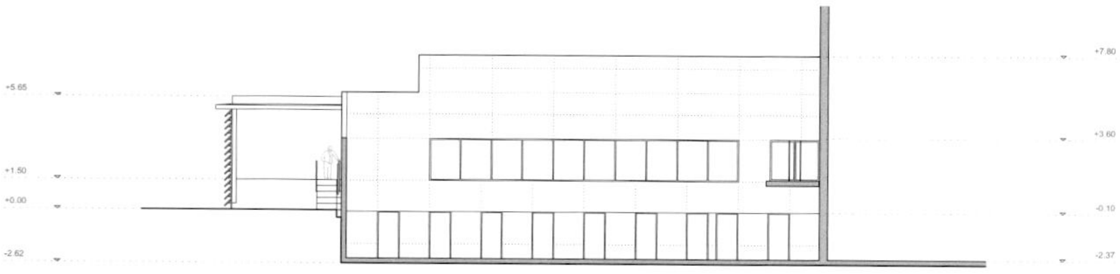

Section 4

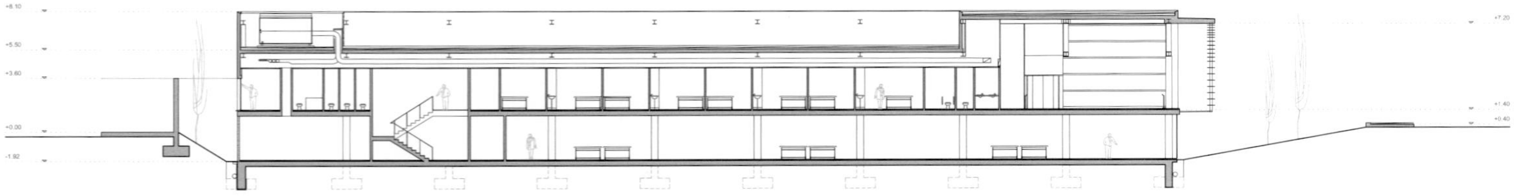

Section 5

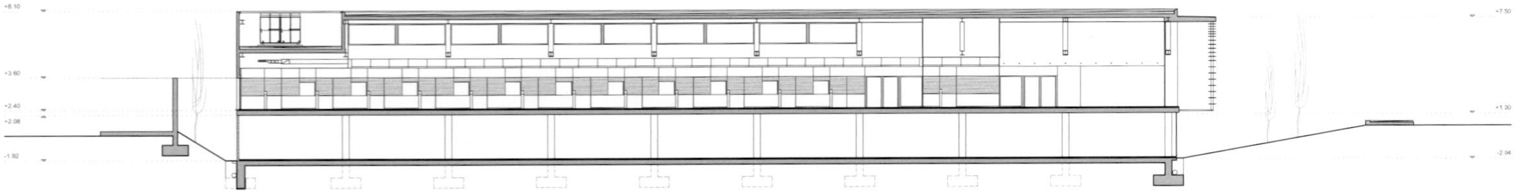

Section 6

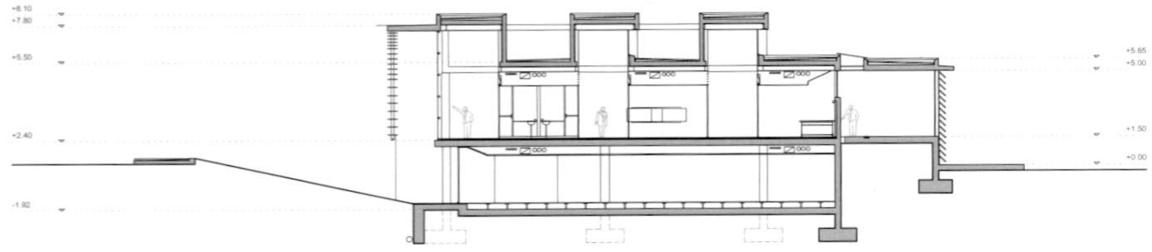

Section 7

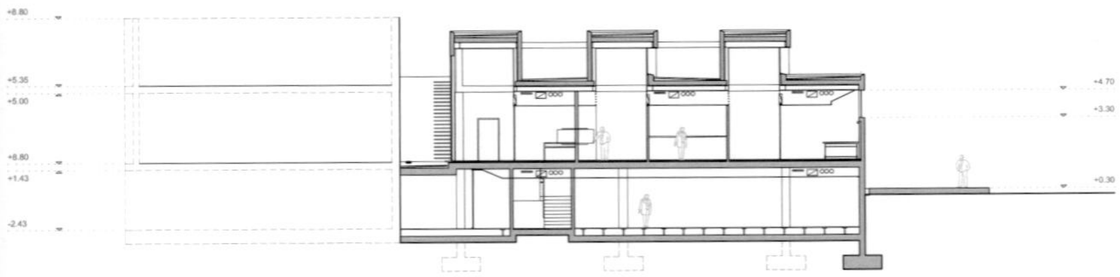

Section 8

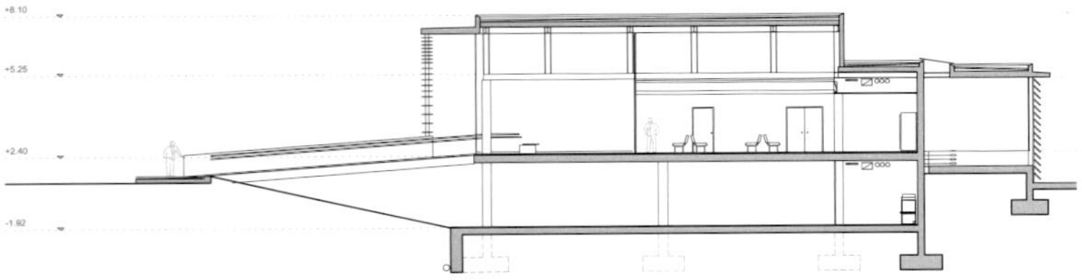

Section 9

Section 10

0 5 10m

1:500

VILADECANS HOSPITAL
VILADECANS, Spain

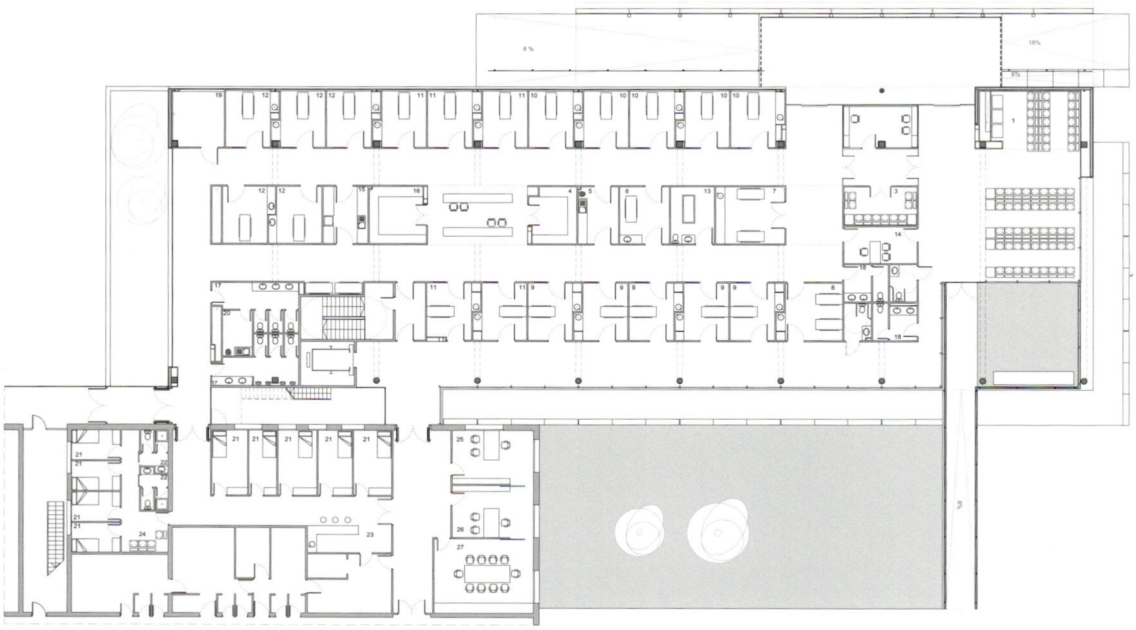

Ground Floor Level

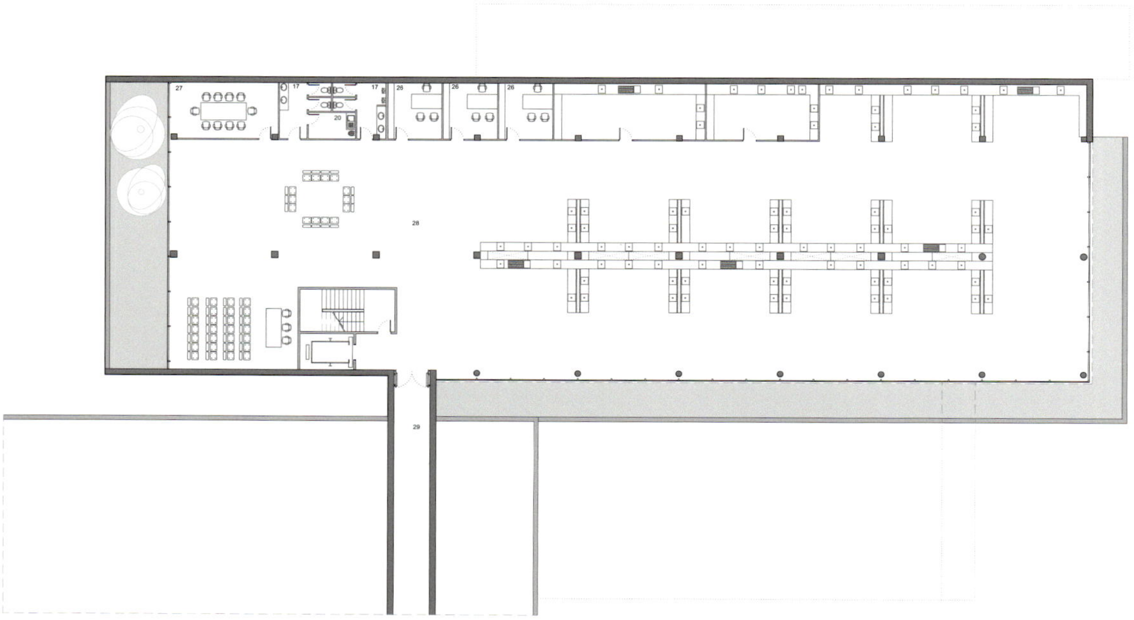

Floor Level -1

1. Waiting Room / Vestibule
2. Reception / Control
3. Waiting room for plaster casts
4. Laundry Room
5. Dirty Laundry
6. Curing Room
7. Plaster casts box
8. parado box
9. External exploration box
10. First aid box
11. Observation box
12. 24 hour area
13. Handicapped bathrooms
14. Information office
15. Office
16. Nurses station / Storage
17. Personnel bathroom
18. Public bathroom
19. Electrical installation
20. Cleaning room

RENOVATED BUILDING

21. Doctor's bedrooms
22. Doctor's bathrooms
23. Doctor's offices
24. Doctor's rest area
25. Office of service headquarters
26. Adjunct offices
27. Meeting rooms
28. Reserve for installations
29. Subterranean passageway

0 5 10m

1:500

Sortida
Box 18

VILADECANS HOSPITAL
VILADECANS, Spain

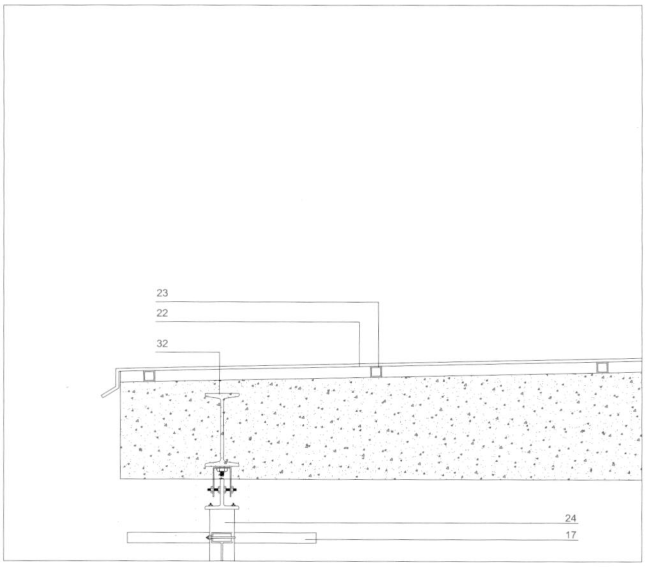

D. 1

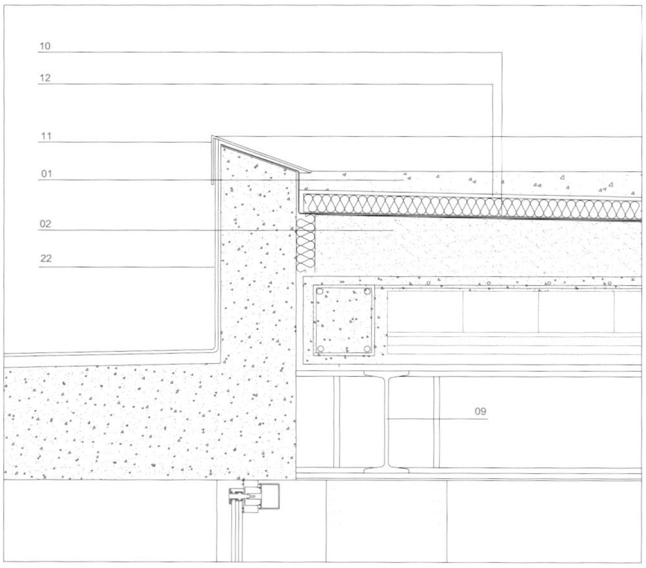

D. 2

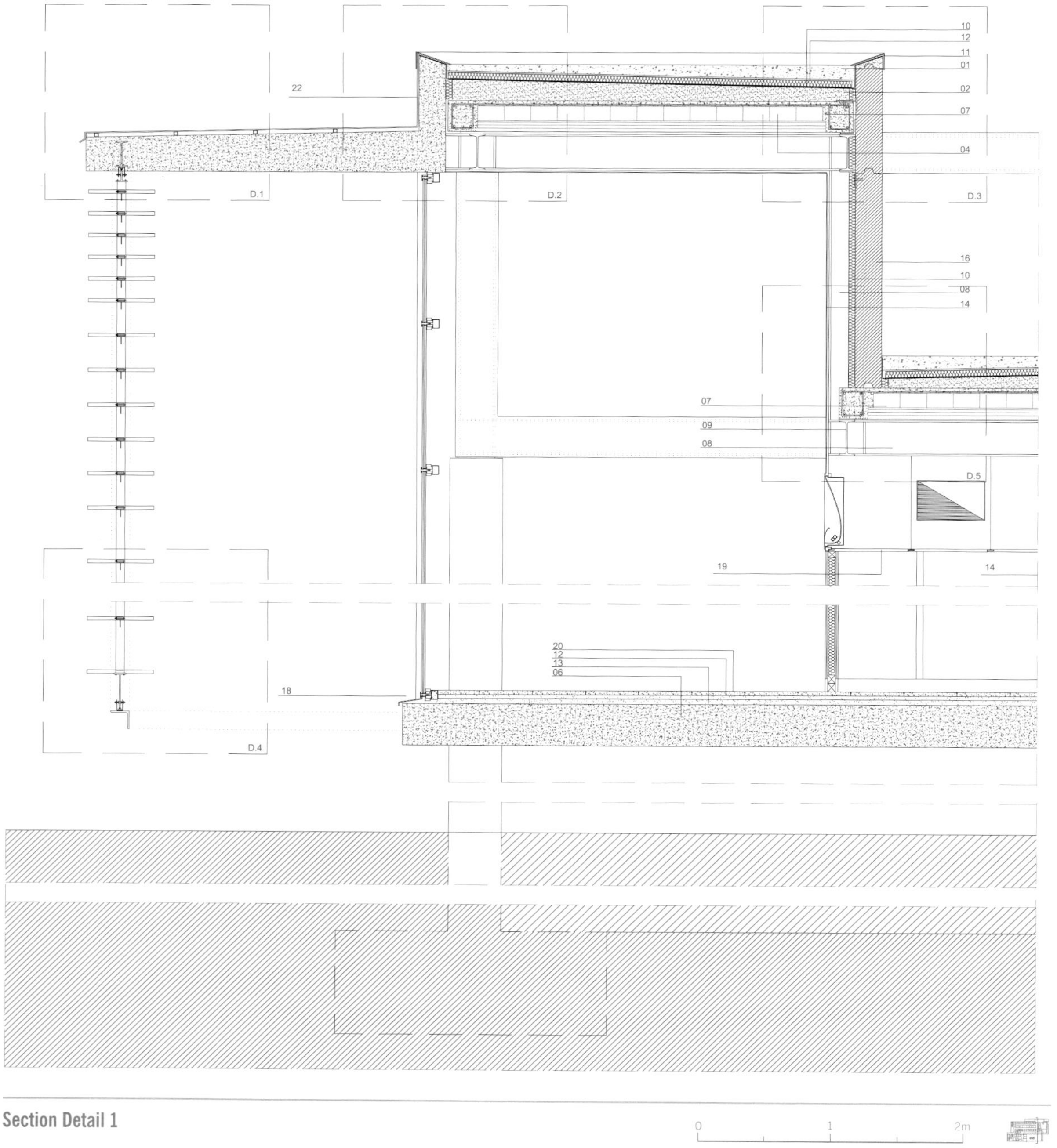

1. Gravel layer, of20cm. thickness
2. Layer of slopes, formed with cellular concrete
3. Welded wire mesh 15 x15 d.3
4. Ceramic coffer of 20cm
5. Steel profile I 600 x190
6. Steel tie type HEB 10. Floor slab 32cm
7. Steel profile in U of 250. One-way floor slab
8. Steel profile type HEB 280
9. Steel profile type IPN 280
10. Insulation with extruded polystyrene plates of density 12kg/cm of 50mm
11. Cap of galvanized steel sheet t=0.7mm
12. Layer of mortar
13. Acoustic insulation of glass wool 3cm
14. Gypsum board wall
15. Laminated glazing with transparent butyral 6+6
16. Prefabricated concrete wall
17. Prefabricated reinforced concrete louvers.
18. Galvanized steel plate
19. Drop ceiling of gyptone nº1 panels with sharp edges screwed to concealed structure placostil, in accordance to dtu 25.41
20. Polished grey granite 40 x 40
21. Metal ventilation grill.
22. Galvanized steel sheet t=10mm
23. Anodized aluminum I profile
24. Galvanized steel u profile
25. Galvanized steel cleat
26. Galvanized steel t profile of 50 x 50
27. Galvanized steel grate for water collection
28. Wall light fixture
29. Screw thread
30. Profile IPE 80
31. Profile I 30 x 30
32. Steel profile type IPN 200
33. Profile I 140.12

Section Detail 1

1:50

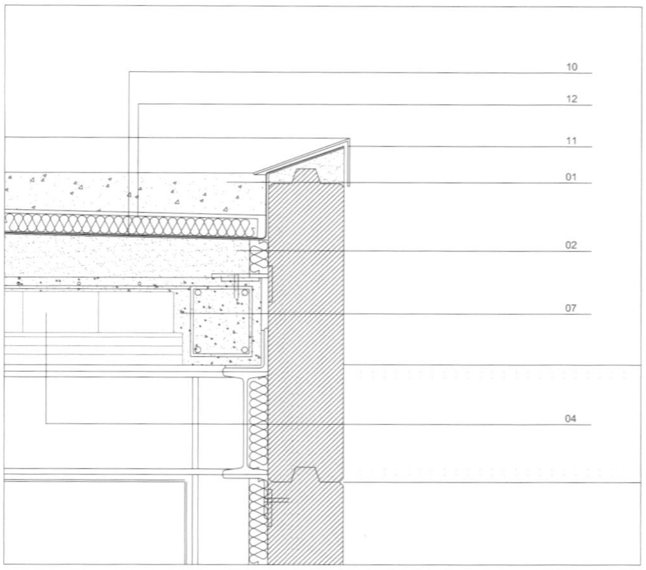

D. 3

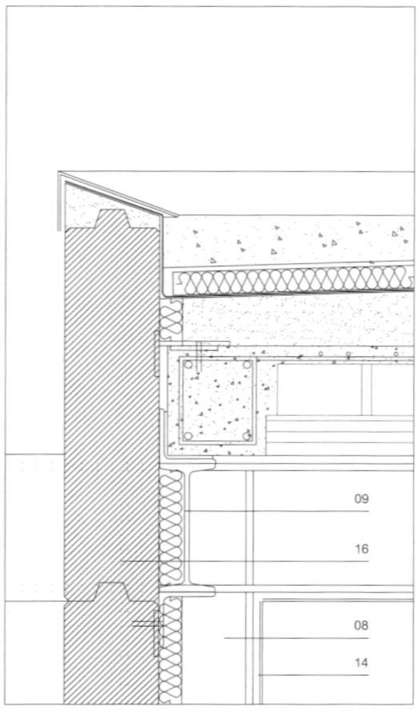

D. 6

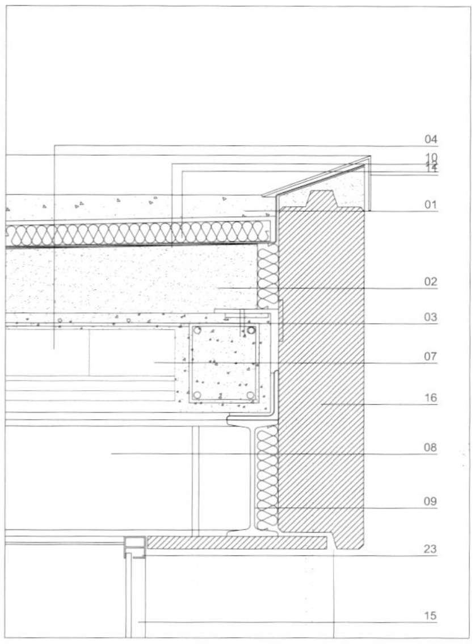

D. 7

0 10 30 50cm 1m

1:20

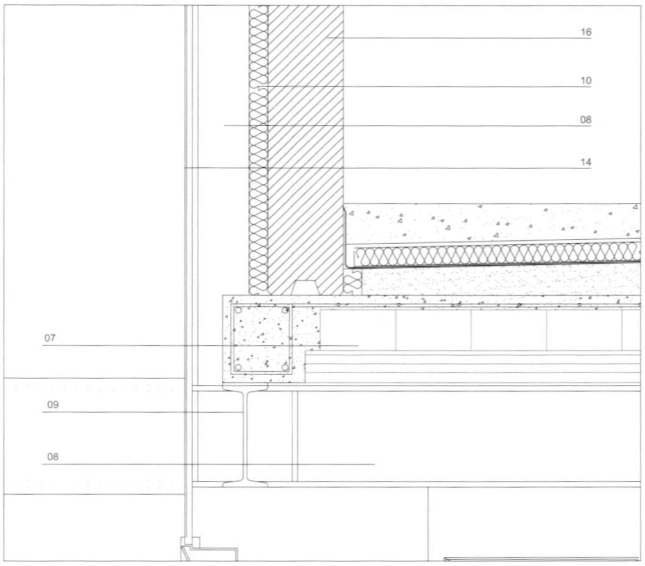

D. 5

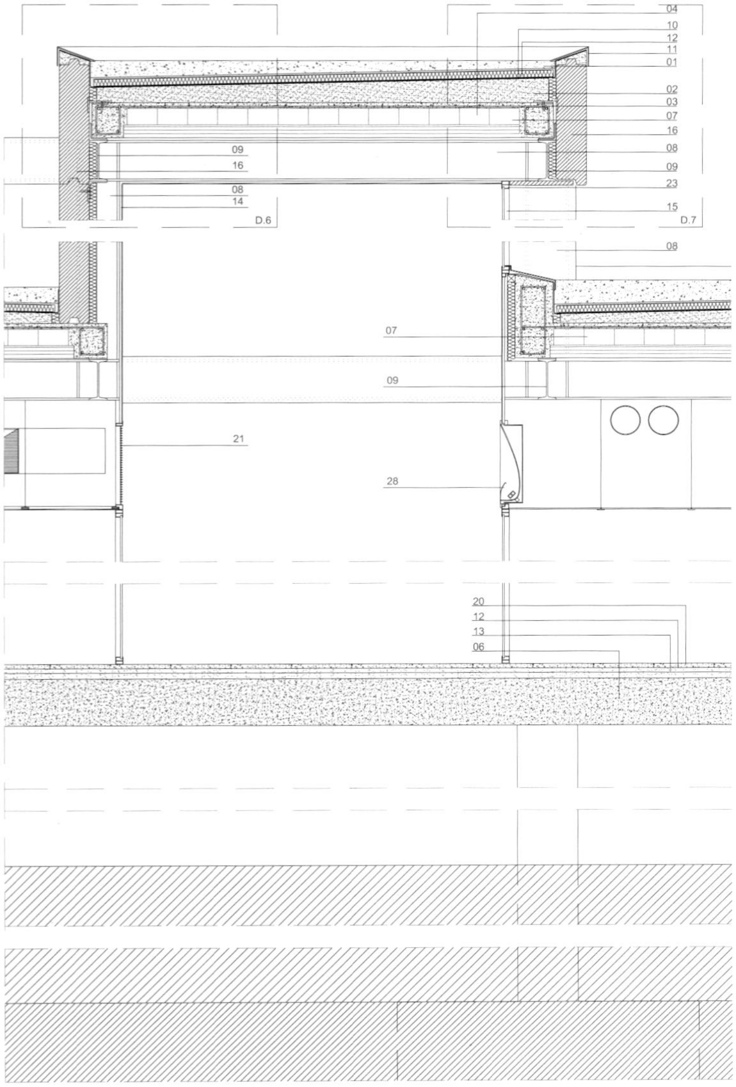

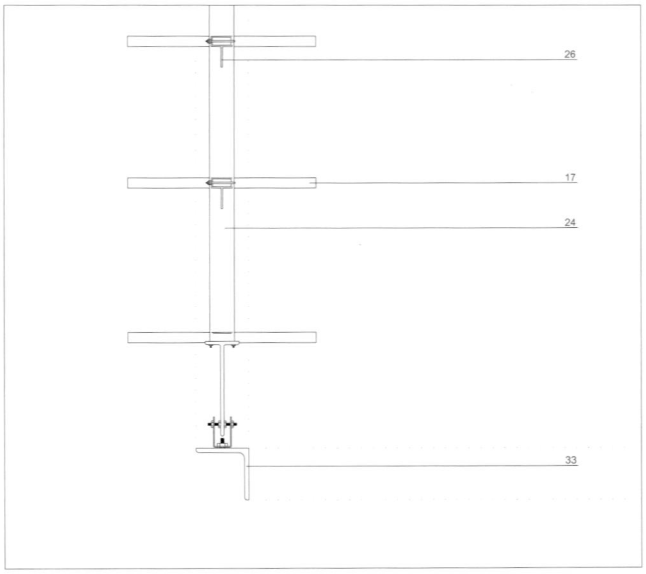

D. 4

Section Detail 2

0 1 2m

1:50

VILADECANS HOSPITAL
VILADECANS, Spain

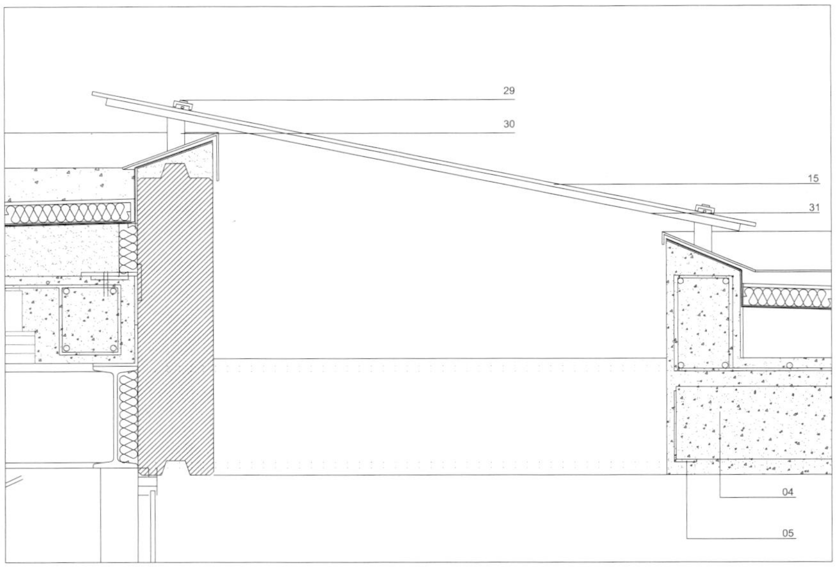

D. 8

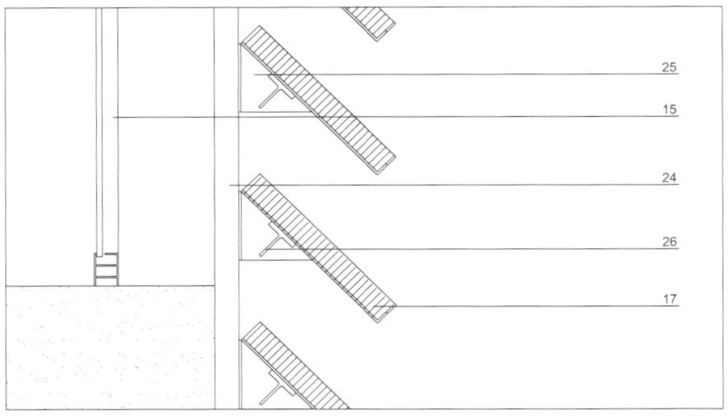

D. 9

0 10 30 50cm 1m

1:20

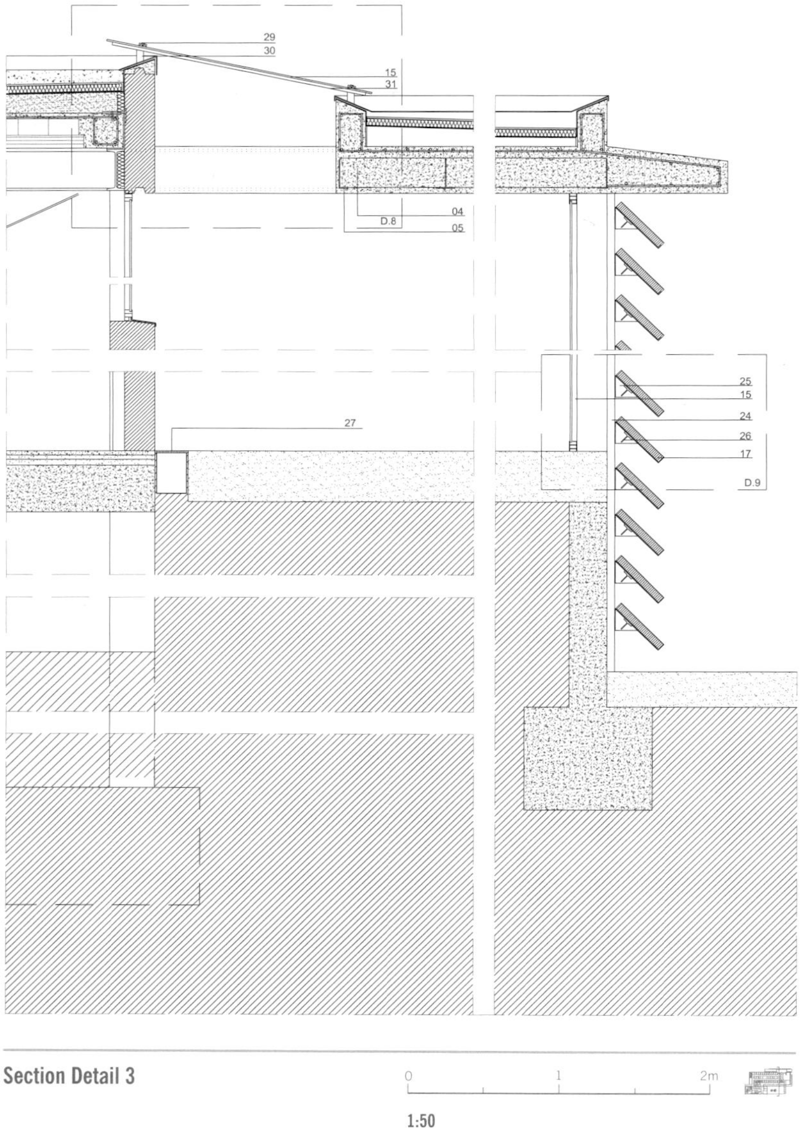

Section Detail 3

0 1 2m

1:50

1. Gravel layer, of20cm. thickness
2. Layer of slopes, formed with cellular concrete
3. Welded wire mesh 15 x15 d.3
4. Ceramic coffer of 20cm
5. Steel profile I 600 x190
6. Steel tie type HEB 10. Floor slab 32cm
7. Steel profile in U of 250. One-way floor slab
8. Steel profile type HEB 280
9. Steel profile type IPN 280
10. Insulation with extruded polystyrene plates of density 12kg/cm of 50mm
11. Cap of galvanized steel sheet t=0.7mm
12. Layer of mortar
13. Acoustic insulation of glass wool 3cm
14. Gypsum board wall
15. Laminated glazing with transparent butyral 6+6
16. Prefabricated concrete wall
17. Prefabricated reinforced concrete louvers.
18. Galvanized steel plate
19. Drop ceiling of gyptone nº1 panels with sharp edges screwed to concealed structure placostil, in accordance to dtu 25.41
20. Polished grey granite 40 x 40
21. Metal ventilation grill.
22. Galvanized steel sheet t=10mm
23. Anodized aluminum I profile
24. Galvanized steel u profile
25. Galvanized steel cleat
26. Galvanized steel t profile of 50 x 50
27. Galvanized steel grate for water collection
28. Wall light fixture
29. Screw thread
30. Profile IPE 80
31. Profile I 30 x 30
32. Steel profile type IPN 200
33. Profile I 140.12

20

Ecosistemaurbano

STEEL AND WOOD HOUSE

ASTURIAS, España

Belinda Tato
José Luis Vallejo

http://www.ecosistemaurbano.com/#

COLLABORATORS	Patricia Arroyo Silvia Sánchez
CLIENT	Alejandro Ribot
BASIC PROJECT	Belinda Tato, José Luis Vallejo, Jorge Lobos
STRUCTURE	Constantino Hurtado, TECTUM INGENIERÍA
QUANTITY SURVEYOR	Lorena García
CONTRACTOR	ESPINAREU
PHOTOGRAPHY	Emilio P. Doiztua

	DATES
IMPLEMENTATION PROJECT	2003
BEGINNING OF WORKS	2004
WORK COMPLETION	2005

STEEL AND WOOD HOUSE
Asturias, España

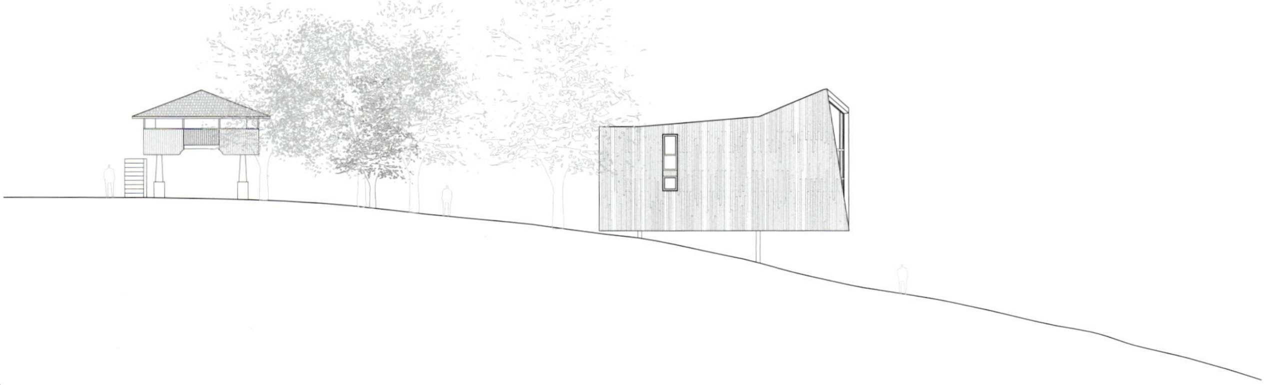

DESCRIPTIVE BRIEF

Contemporary revision of vernacular architecture models (raised granary and glazed gallery, application of wood in structure and cladding). Combination and reinterpretation of formal and constructive typologies of popular local architecture.

Placement which adapts to the climatic conditions and integrally respects the tree-covered site. It minimizes its impact on the terrain and the landscape; the construction is lifted off of the ground and only rests on four points. The original slope is maintained, the green layer of the terrain passes below the house once again, without any interferences.

It is a mixed steel and wood structure, detachable and recyclable; Reversible architecture.

The cladding is resolved with the combination of two types of woods (north pine and douglas pine) with two different widths. Random combination of elements which integrate the house into the landscape, like the bark of a new tree. Building which mixes with nature.

Space adapted to the climatology, designed without heating or cooling systems. Orientation, geometry and folds which adapt to the climatology, solar orientation.

We committed to a double-height space, totally glazed and oriented towards the south. We substituted a conventional system of adjustable louvers as solar protection, for a system of operable apertures of varying positions and combinations, which acts as a hygrothermic regulator, and responds more adequately to the microclimate of the area.

Facades of greater dimension are almost entirely opaque, avoiding thermal loss.

Ventilation apertures facing all directions. Cross ventilation in all spaces.

The north façade protects itself through a preliminary space and a lattice windbreaker.

The double height is not conceived with a spatial or compositional purpose; it is a fundamental bioclimatic mechanism to regulate the thermal behavior of the house. It acts as a temperature regulating center.

Compact space, optimization of the form factor.
Functional flexibility, transformable house, temporarily compartmentalized (the ground floor integrates different uses in one single space which can be configured in various ways by the user; the upper floor can be transformed from a single bedroom, up to two or three).

"Who is more foolish, the child afraid of the dark or the man afraid of the light?"

Maurice Freehill

ENVIRONMENTAL ANALYSIS

1. Choosing the site. Project and development

1.1 Location

Latitud: 43º55'N
Longitud: 06º03'E
Altitud: 140 m

1.2 Urban design and site improvement

The urban ecosystem team has reinterpreted the raised granary and the glazing gallery, two of the representative constructive typologies of the site. Asturian raised granary is a wooden granary raised over pillars that insulate it from soil and it is used grain and farming tools store. The glazing gallery is featured element of traditional house.

The building defined in a single volume is integrated in landscape as an element of rural environment. This proposal joins conceptually two types of edification to project a house that barely touches the land where it settles. With only four bearing points the house gets adapted to land's original slope and respects vegetation in the plot.

1.3 Project

Volume is simple, compact and closed. By means of folds in geometry it is achieved a simple bioclimatic device. Four out of five sides are closed to avoid thermal loss. The open frontage is faced south and totally glazed in order to maximize solar contribution in Summer time, when solar height incises with 24º.

The enveloping of opaque frontage is the most complex element in the project. its shape changes when covering necessities of the house: sitting-room, lounge, bedroom, courtyards. Building's carrying structure and thermal-acoustic insulation is held there: like an organic membrane, which transforms not committing interior microclimate.

By means of folds in South frontage it is achieved to avoid direct solar incidence in Summer time. In this wall section fixed and practicable glasses are combined through which internal ventilation can be regulated.

Without partitions, interior space facilitates the building's conditioning. In North frontage, exposed to dominating winds it has been incorporated a windbreak lattice and filter space working as insulating gap.

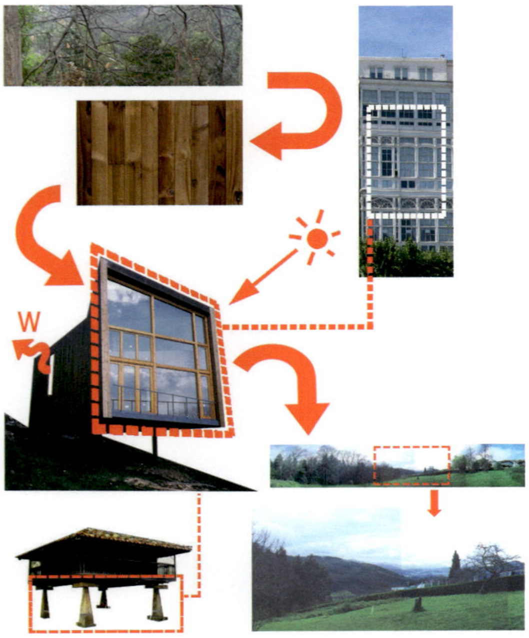

2. Consumption of water and resources

2.1 Consumption of energy

Compact design, with all architectural programme adapted inside a prism facilitates interior heat conservation. Closed frontages minimize thermal bridges, thus reducing energetic necessities for conditioning. The only glazing frontage is raised as heat accumulator in winter time. Double interior height placed south and located by glazing frontage facilitates heat circulation inside the house.

2.2 Consumption of materials

One of the most significant features of the raised grainer is that it can be moved from one place to another with a relative easiness because of the type of joints used in wood. In this direction, Steel and Wood House reinterprets tradition using a mixed, detachable and recycling structure. Use of dry joints in assembly shop and building place reduce consumption of auxiliary materials like plank mould.

3. Environmental charges

3.2 Solid waste

Because of the type of implantation solid waste due to dismantling are reduced to the four ones of foundation pillars. Thanks to their structure of assembly type waste in building site have been reduced to the maximum. This constructive approach also allows resulting material from a hypothetic demolition to represent a reusable product in anew building.

4. Interior environmental quality

4.1 Ventilation

Despite its compact and closed design, interior environmental ventilation is carefully solved. South frontage with practicable large windows allows air flow, whereas small apertures in rest of frontages grant air circulation by means of pressure difference. Double interior height facing south allows air renovation among floors, thanks to temperature change generated by solar radiation that penetrates through the glazing frontage.

Wooden lattice and transitional space located in North frontage work as windbreak protection.

4.2 Natural lighting

Natural lighting is achieved through the glazing frontage, completely south facing, and interior double height, which allows recovering and distributing directly natural light to the house interior.

1 Robles Otero R. http://usuarios.lycos.es/grado/horreo/Horre.htm

5. Control of building systems

5.1 Functionality and efficiency

We can identify a clear use of materials according to their function: steel for structure and wood for closing. Denying any use as decorative artifice and though achieving an aesthetical quality result.

5.2 Control of constructive systems

We are in view of a completely reversible and reusable construction example. This constructive system is based on laminated steel detachable elements, to which secondary structure is anchored and also wood coatings by means of screws, what facilitates their dismantling and use of materials to be reused in the future.

South frontage has practicable windows which can be manually operated by users, according to thermal and ventilation interior necessities.

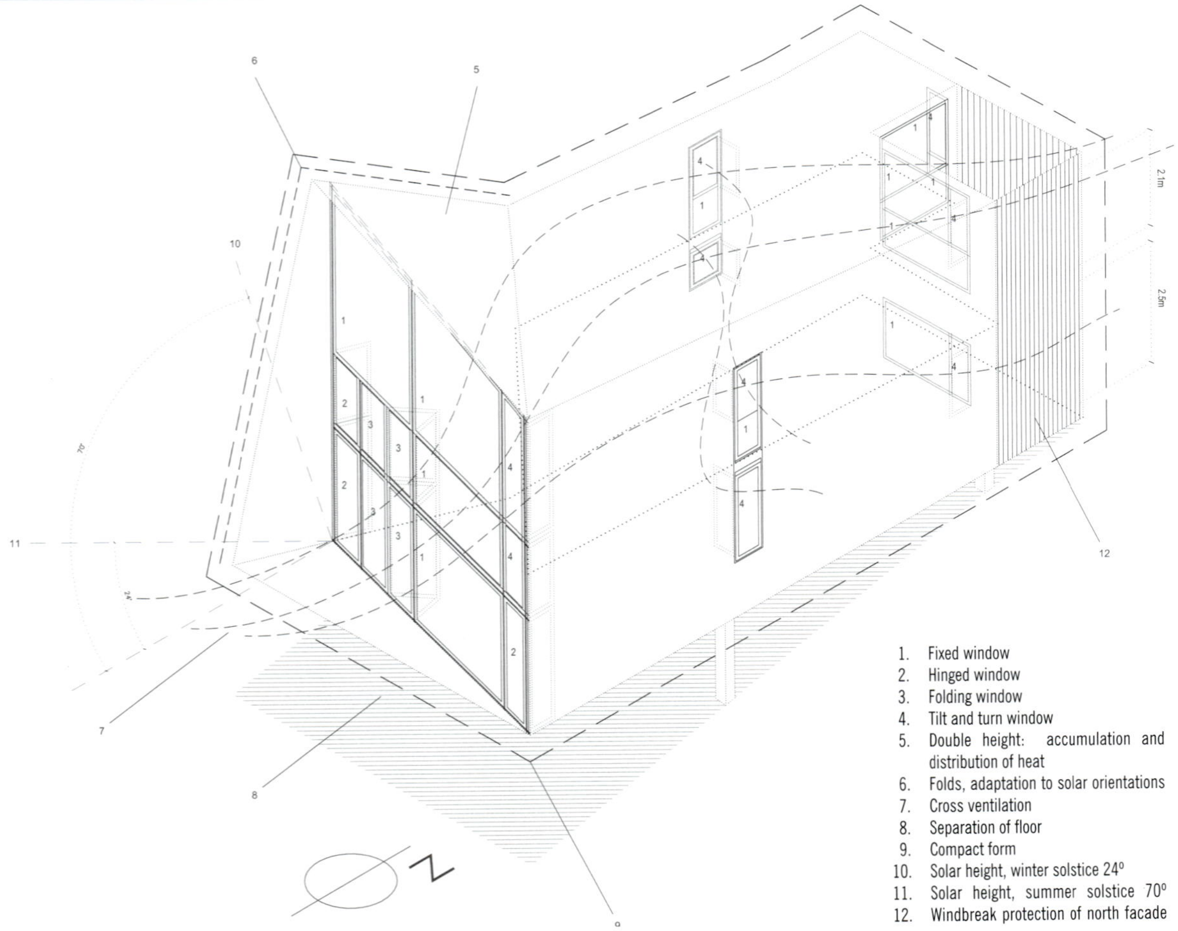

1. Fixed window
2. Hinged window
3. Folding window
4. Tilt and turn window
5. Double height: accumulation and distribution of heat
6. Folds, adaptation to solar orientations
7. Cross ventilation
8. Separation of floor
9. Compact form
10. Solar height, winter solstice 24°
11. Solar height, summer solstice 70°
12. Windbreak protection of north facade

Axonometry

6. Long time performance

6.1 Flexibility and adaptability

Transformability feature of the house and its capacity to be compartmentalized according to inhabitant necessities provide the house with a great flexibility. Lower floor has no intermediate closings, what facilitates layout changes according to user's needs.

In lower floor a sole space capable to contain a big dimension bedroom which can be divided into two or three smaller bedrooms is located, by means of collapsible closings.

6.2 Maintenance and operative performance

Maintenance is simplified thanks to reduction of finishing materials: wood treatment, exterior antioxidant protection in base structure and glass cleaning.

7. Economical and social features

7.1 Social features

This house proves that tradition and sustainability are nor quarrelled with good architecture. In an original way typology native elements are reinterpreted, adapting them to contemporaneous edification. Didactic sense of this experience can become a reference for new edification in the area.

7.2 Economical features

Building's quick assembly based on steel and wooden pre-made pieces reduce production indirect expenses. Energetic saving due to orientation and treatment of closings is reflected in economical and environmental charges terms. Reversibility of this edification makes possible that, in case of demolition generated sub products can be incorporated to new constructive processes.

8. Architect's eye

Projectors have managed to understand the future inhabitant of the house, who has got a contemplative relationship with rural environment. This is why space of the house is defined with a linear orientation that runs away in south horizon.

Both formally and aesthetically two rural typologies have been joined thus granting the minimum visual-environmental impact. This duality relationship is represented in frontage materialization. Both industrialized and manufactured elements are integrated in it, which were measured out by a professional, who observes from an architectural artisan job towards a total design.

South Elevation

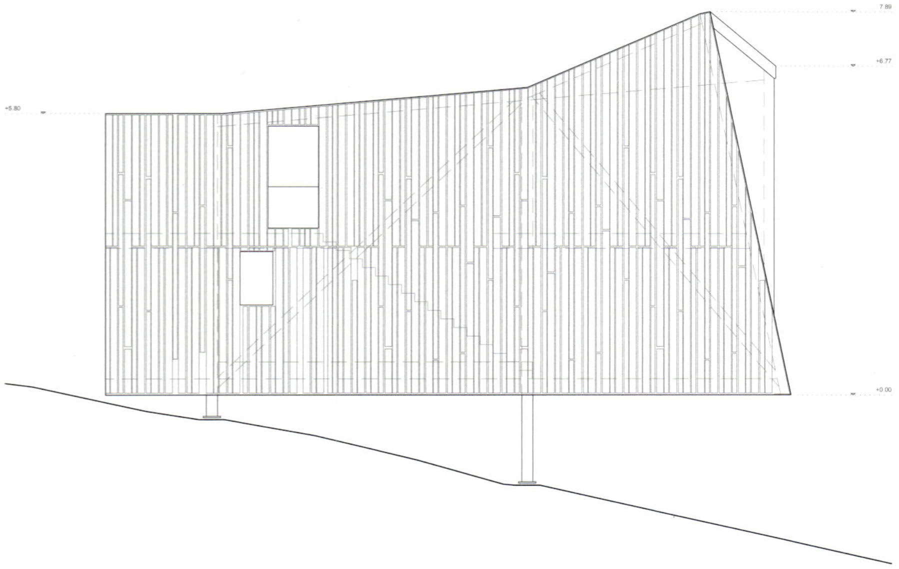

West Elevation

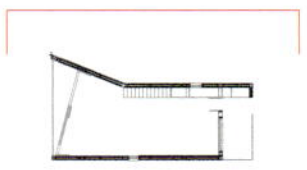

0 1 2 3 4 5m

1:150

STEEL AND WOOD HOUSE
Ecosistemaurbano

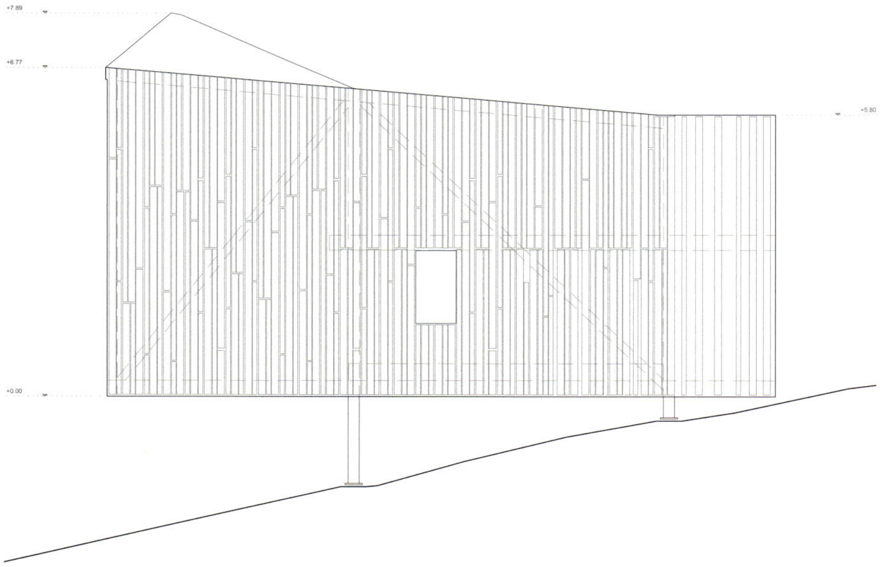

East Elevation

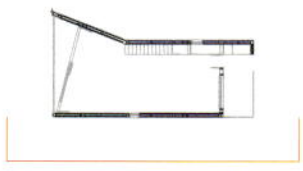

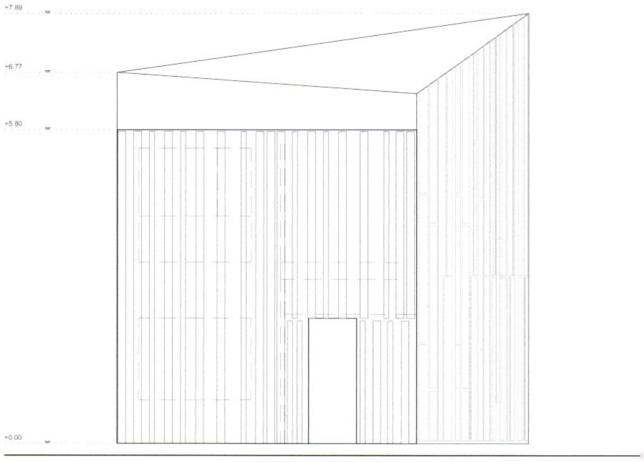

North Elevation

0 1 2 3 4 5m

1:150

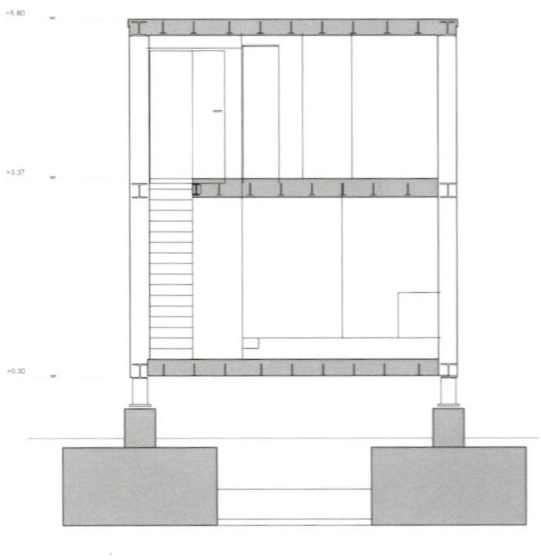

Transversal Section

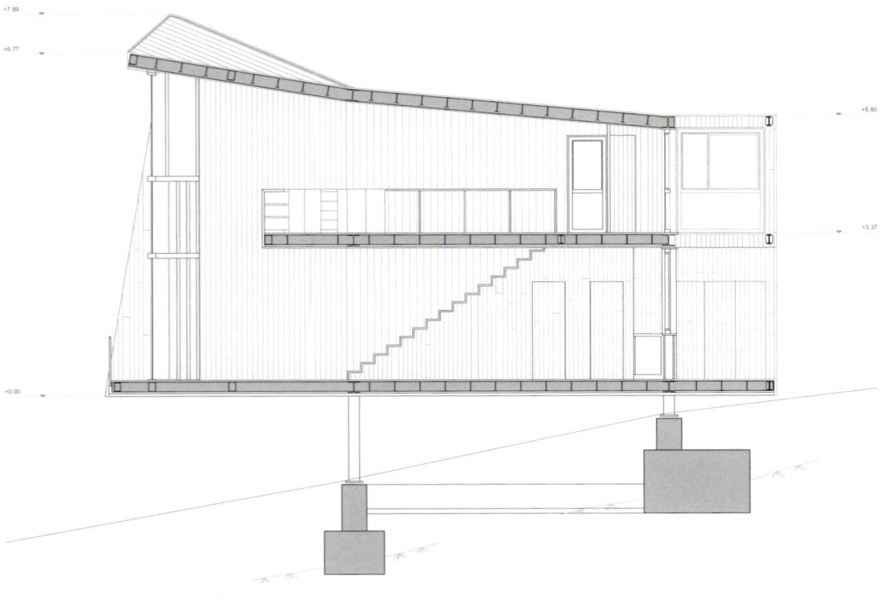

Longitudinal Section 1

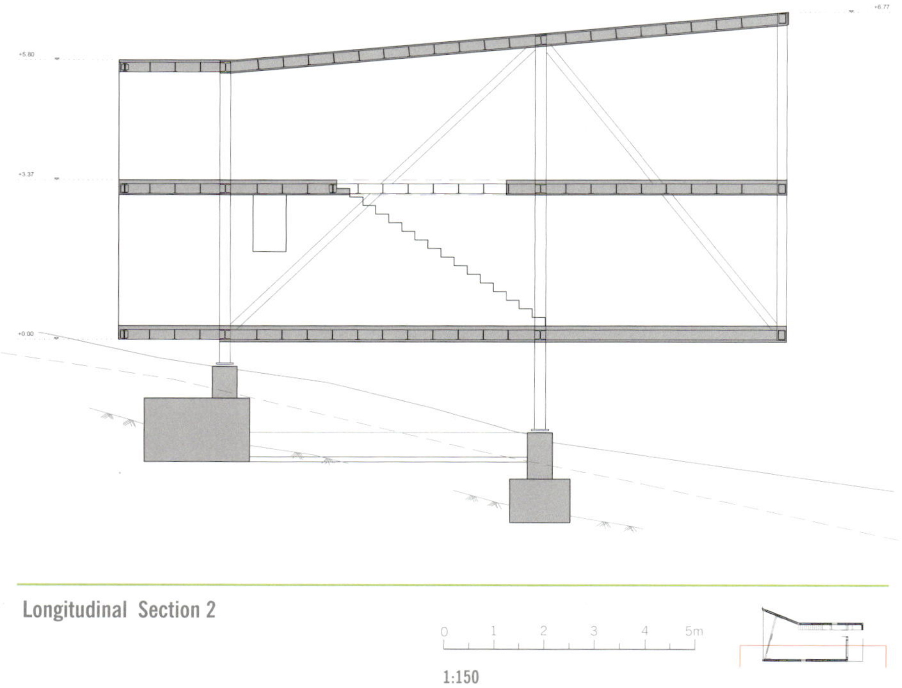

Longitudinal Section 2

STEEL AND WOOD HOUSE
Ecosistemaurbano

Roof Floor Level

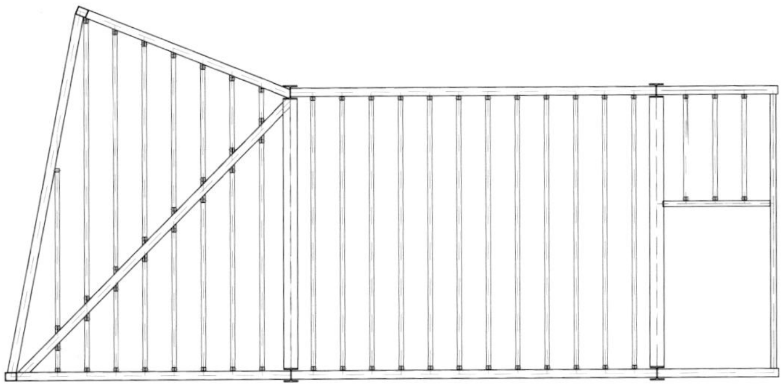

Steel Frame. Level +10,08 m

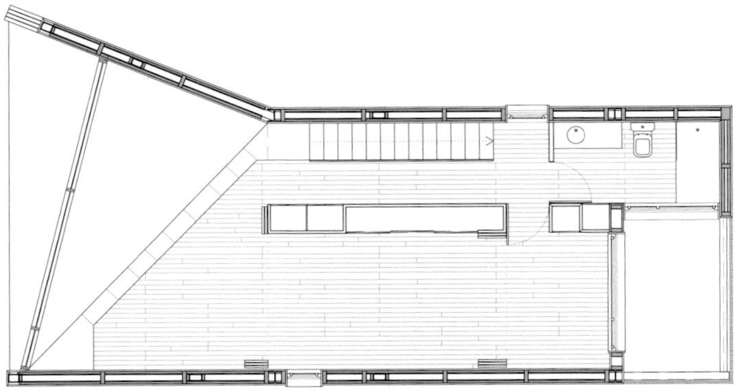

First Floor Level

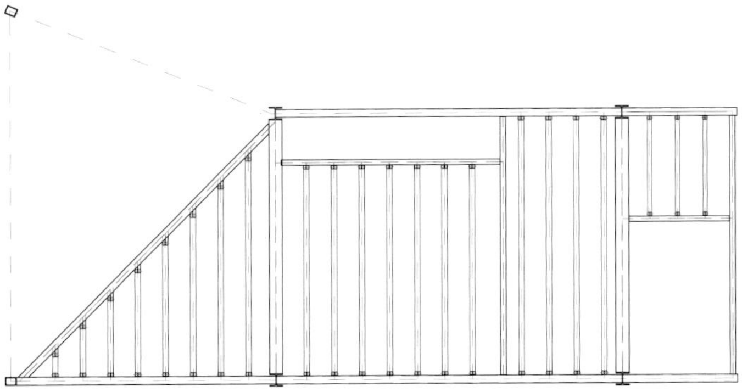

Steel Frame. Level+5,50 m

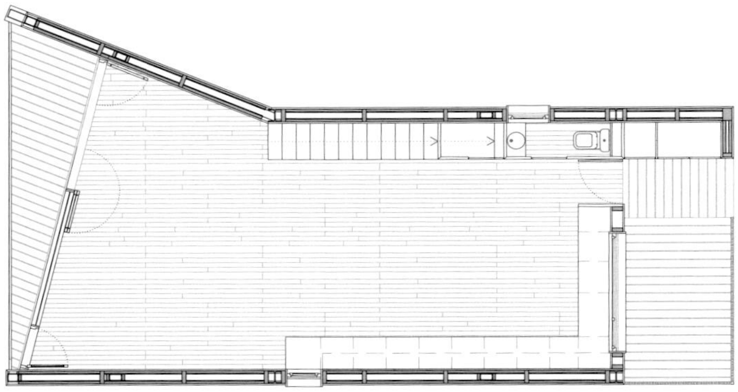

Ground Floor Level

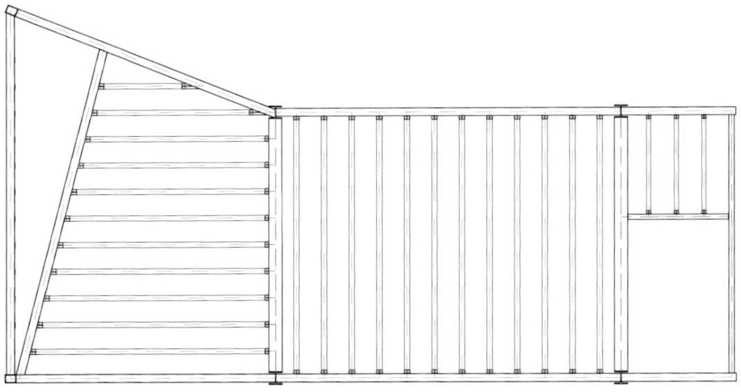

Steel Frame. Level +2,50 m

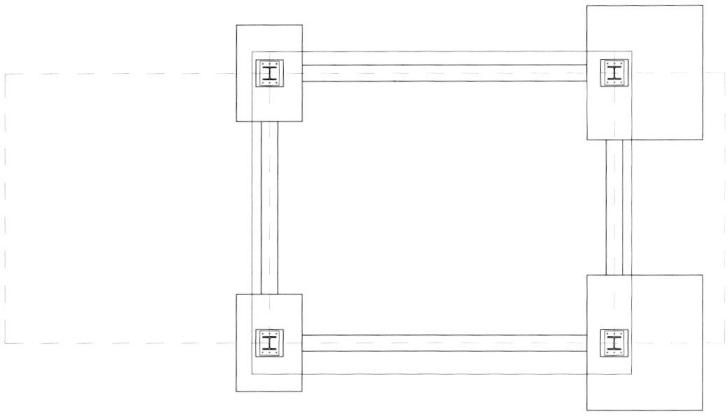

Steel Frame. Level +0,10 m

1:150

STEEL AND WOOD HOUSE
Ecosistemaurbano

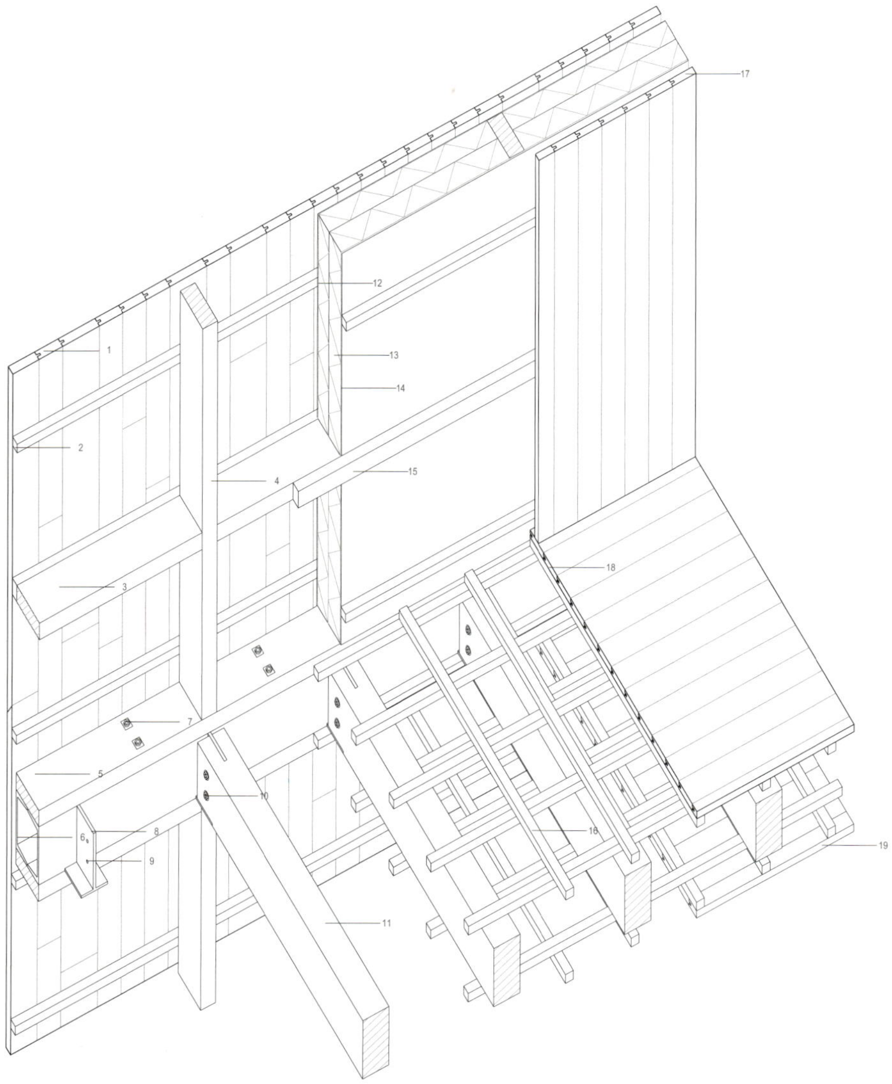

1. Exterior finish with dovetailed board, thickness 35mm, weatherproof treatment. Random combination of two species [North pine, Douglas pine] with two widths[90mm,140mm] and two lengths [2150mm, 3300mm]
2. Secondary batten of North pine 30x30mm
3. North pine plank 150x60mm. secondary structure
4. North pine plank 150x60mm. post of secondary structure
5. North pine plank 150x60mm. Tie fixed to primary metal structure with screws
6. Primary structure. Laminated steel profiles 2UPN200 paired forming caisson. Epoxi primer of 60μm; intermediate layer of epoxi 80μm; finishing layer 40μm.
7. Metal screws welded to primary structure for the fixing of wooden tie.
8. Support for floor slab joists formed by metal sheets welded to the primary structure Vertical sheet [#10.192.100mm]. Horizontal sheet [#8x100x100/75mm]
9. Drill holes for 2T12Ø13
10. Anchor of floor slab joists to primary structure. 2T12 Ø 13
11. Floor slab joists. North pine. Square 200x100mm each500mm
12. Windbreak sheet
13. Double rockwool insulation
14. Vapor Barrier
15. Primary batten north pine 30x60mm
16. Double batten framework. North pine 30x30mm
17. Interior partition with dovetailed board. North pine. 22x90x2150mm
18. Wooden pavement made by dovetailed boards along its entire perimeter, nailed to the batten framework. North pine 22x90x2150mm
19. Interior ceiling finish of dovetailed board 22x90x2150mm

Enclosure and Slab Detail

1. Main structure. Laminated steel profiles 2UPN200 paired forming caisson. Epoxi primer of 60μm; intermediate layer of epoxi 80μm; finishing layer 40μm.
2. Wooden tie 50x200mm north pine. Weatherproofing treatment, fixed to the principal metal structure with screws.
3. Wood lattice 30x50mm separation30mm screwed to wooden tie

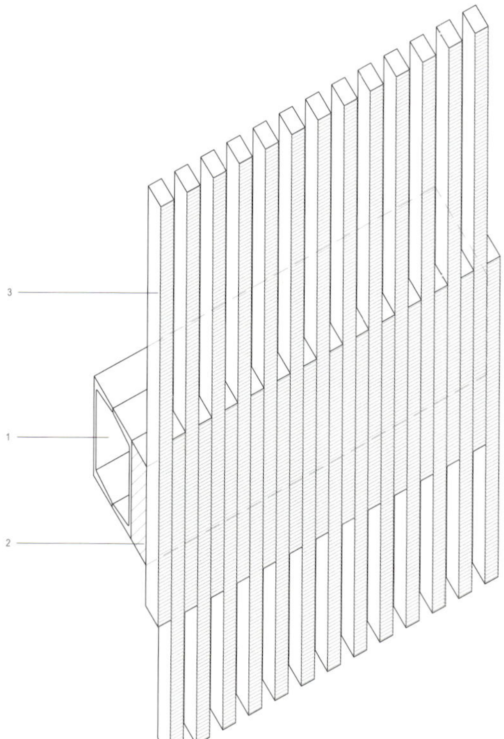

Detail of Lattice Enclosure

1. UPN 200 x2
2. UPN 160 x2
3. HEB 240
4. Untreated concrete

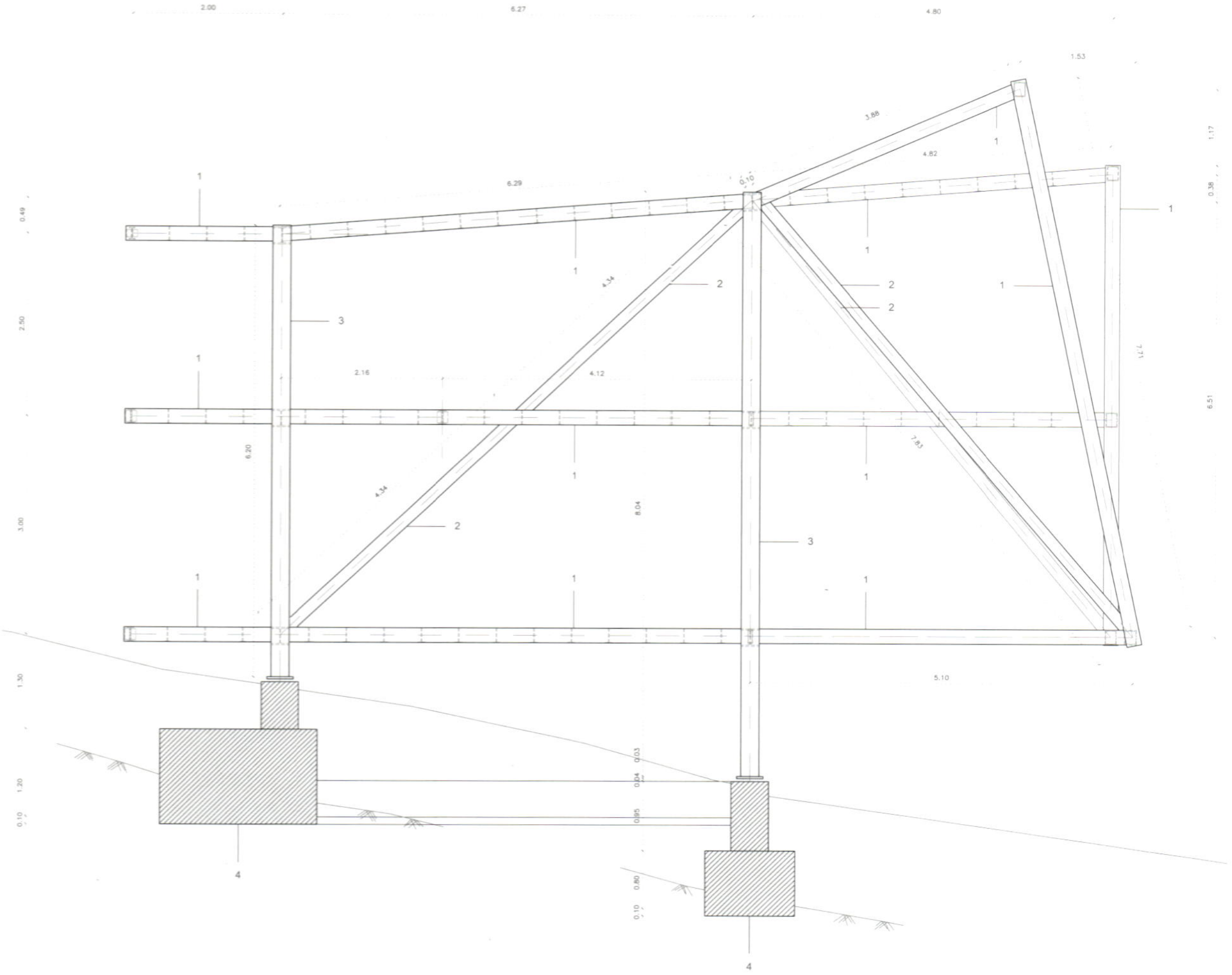

Steel Frame

0 1 2 3 4m

1:100

Formaldehyde: A gas used widely in production of adhesives, plastics, preservatives, and fabric treatments and commonly emitted by indoor materials that are made with its compounds. It is highly irritating if inhaled and is now listed as a probable human carcinogen.

Glare: The effect produced by luminance within one's field of vision that is sufficiently greater than the luminance to which one's eyes are adapted; it can cause annoyance, discomfort, or loss in visual performance and visibility.

Greenhouse effect: The Greenhouse Effect is a natural warming process of the earth. When the sun's energy reaches the earth some of it is reflected back to space and the rest is absorbed. The absorbed energy warms the earth's surface which then emits heat energy back toward space as longwave radiation. This outgoing longwave radiation is partially trapped by greenhouse gases such as carbon dioxide, methane and water vapour which then radiate the energy in all directions, warming the earth's surface and atmosphere. Without these greenhouse gases the earth's average surface temperature would be about 33 degrees Celsius cooler.

Greywater: Greywater (or Graywater) is defined as any wastewater, except in the toilet, produced from baths and showers, clothes washers, and lavatories in a home.

Ground light: Visible radiation from the sun and sky, reflected by exterior surfaces below the plane of the horizon.

High-efficiency particulate air (HEPA) filter: A designation for very fine air filters (usually exceeding 98 percent atmospheric efficiency) typically used only in surgeries, clean rooms, or other specialized applications.

Illuminance: The density of the luminous flux incident on a surface, expressed in footcandles or lux. This term should not be confused with illumination (i.e., the act of illuminating or state og being illuminated).

Impact isolation class (IIC): A single-number rating system designed to provide a comparison between different floor/ceiling constructions for structure-borne impact transmission between vertically adjoining spaces. The IIC is calibrated so that comparable ratings for sound transmission class (STC) give equivalent degrees of protection. The IIC is measured with a standardized tapping machine to generate impact noise, measuring it in the space below at the one-third octave bands between 100 and 3150 hertz. The iiC is calculated using the ASTM E989-84 "Standard Classification for Determination of impact isolation Class."

Indoor air quality (IAQ): According to the U.S. Environmental Protection Agency and National Institute of Occupational Safety and Health, the definition of good indoor air quality includes (1) introduction and distribution of adequate ventilation air; (2)control of airborne contaminants; and (3) maintenance of acceptable temperature and relative humidity. According to ASHRAE Standard 62-1989, indoor air quality is defined as "air in which there are no known contaminants at harmful concentrations as determined by cognizant authorities and with which a substantial majority (80 percent or more) of the people exposed do not express dissatisfaction."

Infiltration: In stormwater management, entry of runoff into the soil.

LEED: Leaders in Energy and Environmental Design is a building environmental certification program developed and operated by the U.S. Green Building Council.

Level spreaders: A stormwater management device installed parallel to a slope that changes concentrated flow to sheet flow.

Life-cycle: The consecutive, interlinked stages of a product, beginning with raw materials acquisition and manufacture and continuing with its fabrication, manufacture, construction, and use, and concluding with any of a variety of recovery, recycling, or waste management options.

Life-cycle analysis (LCA): Life-Cycle-Analysis or Assessment (or LCA) is the study of the environmental impacts of a product or service over its entire life cycle, from the extraction of raw materials, through to the consumption and final disposal of the product. It is a concept and a method to evaluate the environmental effects of a product or activity holistically, by analyzing the entire life cycle of a particular product, process, or activity.

Light shelf: A horizontal device positioned (usually above eye level) to reflect daylight onto the ceiling and to shield direct sunlight from the area immediately adjacent to the window. The light shelf may project into the room, beyond the exterior wall plane, or both. The upper surface of the shelf may be specular or nonspecular but should be highly reflective (that is, having 80 percent or greater reflectance).

Louver: A series of baffles used to shield a light source from view at certain angles or to absorb unwanted light. The baffles are usually arranged in a geometric pattern.

Lumen (lm): The luminous flux emitted (within a unit solid angle or one steradian) by a point source having a uniform luminous intensity of one candela.

Luminance: Luminous intensity of a surface in a given direction.

Luminous flux: The rate of flow of light, analogous to the rate of flow of a fluid.

Material safety data sheets (MSDSs): OSHA-required documents supplied by manufacturers of potentially hazardous products. MSDSs contain information regarding potentially significant airborne contaminants, precautions, steps for inspection, health effects, odor description, volatility, expected contaminants from combustion, reactivity, and procedures for cleanup.

Mineral fibers: Very fine insulation fibers made from glassy minerals that have been melted and spu and are hazardous to inhale .

Mixed air: The mixture of outdoor air and return air in an HVAC system. When filtered and conditioned, mixed air becomes supply air.

Native vegetation: A plant whose presence and survival in a specific region is not due to human intervention. Certain experts argue that plants imported to a region by prehistoric peoples should be considered native. The term for plants that are imported and then adapt to survive without human cultivation is natu ralized.

Natural cooling: Use of environmental phenomena to cool buildings, e.g., natural ventilation, evaporative cooling, and radiative cooling.

Noise reduction (NR): The simple loss of sound level that occurs in passing through a medium. Most often noise reduction refers to a single octave or one-third octave-band noise.

Noise reduction coefficient (NRC): Average of the sound absorption coefficient of the four octave bands 250, 500, 1,000, and 2,000 Hertz rounded to the nearest 0.05.

Non-point-source pollution: Runoff contamination from an overall site or land use and not discharged from a single pipe, such as sediment from construction sites, oils from parking lots, or fertilizers and pesticides washed from farm fields.

Offgas/outgas: A process of evaporation or chemical decomposition through which vapors are released from materials.

Open-web wood joists: Wood joists built as flat trusses, using small-dimension lumber for web pieces. These are also available with stamped steel webs.

Orientation: The relation of a building and its associated fenestration and interior surfaces to compass direction and, therefore, to the location of the sun.

Oriented strand board (OSB): A manufactured wood sheet product made from large flakes of wood pressed together with glue, usually a dry phenolic type. OSB is used for structural sheathing and subfloors.

Passive solar design: Designing a building's architectural elements to collect, store, and distribute solar resources for heating, cooling, and daylighting.

Phenolic laminate: A high-pressure laminated sheet made from paper and phenol formaldehyde resin, commonly used for furniture and kitchen cabinet surfaces.

Photocells: Light-sensing cells used to activate controllers at dawn or dusk.

Photometer: An instrument for measuring photometric quantities, such as luminance, luminous intensity, luminous flux, and illuminance .

Photovoltaic: Generation of electricity from the energy of sunlight, using photocells.

Polymers: Any molecule chain made up from repeated elements, for example, plastics and adhesives.

Post-consumer recycled content: Post Consumer Recycled Content refers to material that has been used by consumers, such as used newspaper, and has been diverted or separated from waste management systems for recycling. To "close the recycling loop" we want to support products that make use of the highest post-consumer content. See post industrial recycled content.

Post-industrial recycled content: Post Industrial Recycled Content is waste that is produced during the manufacturing process that is recycled back into the industrial process. In many cases, industry was already recycling this material back into the process and thus post industrial recycled content is not as significant as post consumer. See post consumer recycled content.

Powder coating: A durable finishing method for metals using a dry, powdered plastic that is heat-fused onto the surface. No solvent is required and practically no waste produced.

Pre-consumer recycled material: A material that is removed from source gathering or production processes (such as scrap, breakage, or returned inventory) and returned to the original manufacturing process or an alternative process. Pre-consumer recycled materials have not yet reached a consumer for the intended use.

Primary output: The thing, item, or article that represents the intended goal of the process. For a specific life cycle analysis, the "Primary outputs" of each process in the life cycle sequence need to be clearly defined in terms of what, when, and where.(J.A. Tshudy, Part IV, Section C)

Radiant energy (radiation): Energy traveling in the form of electromagnetic waves, measured in units of energy such as joules, ergs, or kilowatthours.

Rainscreen: A method of constructing walls in which the cladding is separated from a membrane by an airspace that allows pressure equalization to prevent rain from being forced in. Often used for high-rise buildings or for buildings in windy locations.

Recycled material: Material that would otherwise be destined for disposal but is diverted or separated from the waste stream, reintroduced as material feed-stock, and processed into marketed end-products.

Reflectance: The ratio of reflected light flux to incident light flux.

Reflection: The process by which incident light flux leaves a surface, or medium, from the incident side, without a change in frequency.

Renewable energy: Renewable energy is an energy resource that is replaced rapidly by natural processes. Some examples of renewable energy resources are sunlight, wind, geothermal, micro scale hydropower, and wood. When you use some sunlight to warm your building, more is made almost immediately available. Water flowing in the river or creek is continually replaced by rainfall. If you chop down a tree and burn its wood in your campfire, it takes awhile for the forest to grow enough to replace that wood, but it will happen within your lifetime.

Renewable energy technologies: Active, passive, and photovoltaic strategies integrated into building design. return air. Air that has circulated through a building as supply air and has been returned to the HVAC system for additional conditioning or release from the building.

Reverberation time (RT): The amount of time it takes for sound to decay 60 decibels in a given space. It is a function of room volume and amount of sound absorption provided by surface finishes in the room. Optimum levels are determined based on room volume and space usage.

Sediment basin: A depression in the soil that is placed to retain sediment and debris on-site.

Shallow trench system: A type of drain field used in conjunction with a graywater system that allows for shallow placement of distribution pipes and use of the greywater for irrigation.

Sick building syndrome (SBS): According to the EPA and NIOSH, Sick Building Syndrome is defined as "situations in which building occupants experience acute health and/or comfort effects that appear to be linked to time spent in a particular building, but where no specific illness or cause can be identified. The complaints may be localized in a particular room or zone, or may be spread throughout the building." Occupants experience relief of symptoms shortly after leaving the building.

Solar altitude: In solar analysis, the vertical angular distance of a point in the sky above the horizon. Altitude is measured positively from the horizon to the zenith, from 0 to 90 degrees.

Solar azimuth: In solar analysis, the horizontal angular distance between the vertical plane containing a point in the sky (usually the sun) and true south.

Solar radiation: The full spectrum of electromagnetic energy including visible light from the sun. When solar radiation strikes a solid surface or a transparent medium such as air or glass, some of the energy is absorbed and converted into heat energy, some is reflected, and some is transmitted. All three of these effects are important for effective passive solar design.

Sound transmission class (STC): A single-number rating designed to provide a comparison between the noise losses of different structures for building-design purposes. The STC is calculated from the noise reduction at the 16 one-third octave bands between 125 and 4,000 Hertz. The American Society for Testing and Materials has published a standard, ASTM E413-73, "Standard Classification for Determination of Sound Transmission Class."

Stressed skin: A structural panel with the sheathing permanently bonded to the frame or core to increase its strength.

Sun-bearing angle: The solar azimuth angle relative to the horizontal direction a building surface is facing. Often referred to as the "relative solar azimuth."

Superabsorbent materials: Various artificial materials capable of holding several times their own weight in water. Used in granular form, these are mixed with earth to increase the amount of water held in the soil, the length of time it is held before drying, and its availability to plants. Humus serves this purpose.

Superplasticizers: Chemical additives for concrete that increase the fluidity of the mix without excess water.

Sustainable: The condition of being able to meet the needs of present generations without compromising those needs for future generations. Achieving a balance among extraction and renewal and environmental inputs and outputs, as to cause no overall net environmental burden or deficit. To be truly sustainable, a human community must not decrease biodiversity, must not consume resources faster than they are renewed, must recycle and reuse virtually all materials, and must rely primarily on resources of its own region.

Tight buildings: Buildings that are designed to let in minimal infiltration air in order to reduce heating and cooling energy costs. In actuality, buildings typically exhibit leakage that is on the same order as required ventilation; however, this leakage is not well distributed and cannot serve as a substitute for proper ventilation .

Transmission: The process by which incident flux leaves a surface, or medium, on a side other than the incident side, without change in frequency.

Transmission loss (TL): Noise reduction corrected for wall area and room absorption.

Transmittance: The ratio of transmitted flux to incident flux; measured by a transmissometer.

Trombe wall: A south-facing masonry wall that is covered with glass spaced a few inches away. Sunlight passing through the glass is transformed into heat at the wall's surface, which either migrates into the building interior or is thermosyphoned to interior spaces through vents.

Ultraviolet radiation (UV): Any radiant energy within the wavelength range of 0.001 to 0.38 micron; high-energy components of light capable of damaging materials and increasing skin cancer risk.

Variable-air-volume (VAV): A method of modulating the amount of heating or cooling effect that is delivered to a building by the HVAC system. The flow of air is modulated rather than the temperature. VAV systems typically consist of VAV boxes that throttle supply airflow to individual zones, some mechanism to control supply-fan flow to match box demand, and the interconnecting ductwork and components.

Veiling luminance: Luminance superimposed on the retinal image that reduces its contrast.

Volatile organic compound (VOC): Chemical compounds based on carbon and hydrogen structures that are vaporized at room temperatures. VOCs are one type of indoor air contaminant. Although thousands have been identified in indoor air, only a few are well understood and regulated.

Water budget: The estimated water use within a facility. Flow rates of fixtures and appliances, occupancy, and landscape needs are calculated.

Water harvesting: Collection of both runoff and rainwater for various purposes, such as irrigation or fountains.

Wetland: In stormwater management, a shallow, vegetated, ponded area that serves to improve water quality and provide wildlife habitat .

Source: Green Building Encyclopedia - Glossary of Green Building Terms http://www.whygreenbuildings.com/glossary.php

May 2007